PORTRAIT OF
DELMORE

PORTRAIT OF

DELMORE

JOURNALS AND NOTES

OF DELMORE SCHWARTZ

1939–1959

Edited and introduced by

ELIZABETH POLLET

Farrar · Straus · Giroux

New York

Selections from the previously unpublished papers
of Delmore Schwartz copyright © 1986 by Kenneth Schwartz
for the Estate of Delmore Schwartz
Introduction and notes copyright © 1986 by Elizabeth Pollet
First printing, 1986
Printed in the United States of America
Published simultaneously in Canada
by Collins Publishers, Toronto
Designed by Cynthia Krupat
Library of Congress Cataloging-in-Publication Data
Schwartz, Delmore, 1913–1966.
Portrait of Delmore.
1. Schwartz, Delmore, 1913–1966—Diaries.
2. Schwartz, Delmore, 1913–1966—Notebooks,
sketchbooks, etc. 3. Poets, American—20th century—
Biography. I. Pollet, Elizabeth.
II. Title.
PS3537.C79Z475 1986 818'.5203 [B] 86-12023

Introduction

ELIZABETH POLLET

[1]

Brusson, July 23, 1984

It was here, in the Italian Alps, where my great-grandfather lived, that I first received the news that Delmore had died. That was eighteen years ago—in July 1966. My friend Josephine Herbst wrote me and, thank God, her letter arrived before my father received the clipping of the story in *The New York Times* from his brother. Though I had not seen Delmore for nine years, I was stricken with grief. After a few days of my lying about and weeping, my father became angry. Antoinette, my friend next door, a peasant woman dressed always in black, came in to comfort me, held my hand, told me, despite my lack of Italian, of various tragedies she knew about. The one I remember is of a family that had to wait out a blizzard and then go into the mountains to bring down—in pieces on their backs—the frozen bodies of not one but two dead sons. She also gave me to understand that it was not allowed to grieve as I was doing, with fits of weeping that left me gasping for breath. Life was hard and full of tragedy, and such excess was unbecoming to God.

Let the living resurrect the dead. The sentence appears in my head. It is Delmore whom I have been living with for several years now in the effort to transcribe 2,100 sheets of journal entries and notes, very little of it readily legible. Impossible, of course, to escape ultrapersonal reactions. My life, too, resurges in memory. The truth is somewhere else.

Let Delmore's words speak for themselves. I am struck—perhaps because last week I finished editing the last years of the journal—with what is not present. When I began this project, with some trepidation and reluctance, I said that it would be a portrait by Delmore of himself, and indeed my immediate title for the book was *Portrait of Delmore*. But now I am struck by the lopsidedness of the entries and the impossibilities, finally, of language to render life.

Delmore was extraordinary, and certainly some of the range and variety of feelings and ideas, the magic of atmosphere, the fireworks of metaphor and juxtaposition are present in these journals. But there is also a preoccupation with the process of disintegration—how many sleeping tablets, Dexedrine or Dexamyl tablets, what quantity of alcohol. It is almost as if writing these things down was like the magic of saying spells to control or avoid consequences. It seems incredible now that I did not think of alcohol as Delmore's major problem, nor of him as a sick man, whose addictions were causes rather than consequences of what was happening to him. But alcoholism never occurred to me, and we were all much less aware then of drugs, of the properties of barbiturates, amphetamines, and of the new tranquillizers coming on the market in the mid-fifties. The drugs were prescribed; the pharmacist was willing to sell them to Delmore, an old customer, by the hundred; he took them at will.

True, the last year before I left Delmore I tried to get something accomplished medically through the doctors. Up until then, I had put my faith in Dr. Gruenthal's beneficent surveillance of our lives. A German refugee and an M.D., Max Gruenthal was Delmore's New York psychiatrist, and shortly after our marriage in June 1949 he took me on as a patient, too. Though I often felt his advice was weighted in Delmore's interest, this did not matter, as I considered Delmore's interest mine. Only when I had determined to leave did I question his judgment.

The doctor had me playing games. I left twice, the first time in November 1955, when I stayed away seven months; the second, final time in July 1957. The first time Dr. Gruenthal suggested I wait for one of Delmore's nighttime rages so that he would feel he had driven me out. I did. The second time the game was to be more complicated and the last act so mad (in my opinion), my part so inhuman and immoral, that I refused to play. Delmore had accepted a teaching Fulbright for Berlin for the fall of 1957. Dr. Gruenthal thought he ought to go. I had doubts, was certain I would not go with him, and wanted to tell him so. Dr. Gruenthal told me to wait and I did. He told me to make the preparations for departure, to get Delmore on the boat, and then to "disappear" before the boat sailed. That I could not do.

It is not easy now to know the truth of what happened almost thirty years ago. I have always hated the story of the patient Griselda —hated Griselda for her inhuman passivity, her willingness to suffer. I could no longer live in the chaos and emotional violence Delmore created; I was no longer willing to have my life totally absorbed in his; and I was losing the naïveté and optimism that had kept me semiblind to the worsening reality of the situation, losing the belief that once objective problems were solved—the main one money—our life together would be fine.

It was Dr. Gruenthal who persuaded me to return after my first departure. I thought the situation hopeless. He said Delmore was pulling himself together and that my return was the reward and the motive. I hadn't been back three days before Delmore was again going over the list of my crimes; or a month before he took my typewriter away on the grounds that his work was more important than mine and that he needed it. His behavior was compulsive and obsessive. Any attempts at physical violence had ceased, though; there had never been many, and he knew I would not tolerate them.

I had known Delmore for over twelve years, I did not think he could change, and I knew I could not live anymore as we were. I was exhausted, torn between fears of him and fears for him. Language was no longer communication between us. He was afraid for his health and at times thought he was going crazy. He asked me to stay near him at parties in case the trains in his head started jumping their tracks. I consoled myself, even then, with the thought that living inside the terrors of his state of mind was not the same as imagining it from outside; he was used to much of it, only now it was worse.

That last winter, I tried to get Delmore into the hospital for a medical checkup. He was afraid of what was happening to him. I took him to a local doctor and urged the doctor to recommend hospitalization for tests and asked him also, if his preliminary examination showed anything seriously wrong, not to tell Delmore because of the state he was in. After several weeks of my maneuvering, the local doctor agreed, recommended hospitalization, and Delmore agreed to go (whether at the last minute he would have, I don't know). But after a phone call from Dr. Gruenthal, who had asked Delmore for the number, the local doctor reversed himself, mumbled something to me about insurance, and would not look me in the eye. I think Dr. Gruenthal must have told him there might be a drug-withdrawal problem with which the local hospital was not equipped to cope. I don't know.

My choice at the time seemed to me to be to leave or to try to have Delmore committed. The last I was unwilling to do. Dr. Gruenthal advised against it, said "involuntary commitment might send him off the deep end indefinitely." I did not seriously consider it out of both love and cowardice, and also there was no money. Delmore did know how much I loved him; I also knew that he loved me. But committing him (or trying to) would have been a violation of that love, and after such a betrayal I would have been afraid of him. His rage was desperation, internal earthquakes, and was not as such directed at me. I did not believe Dr. Gruenthal, who said that once I left Delmore might try to kill me, though I believed him enough to stay out of New York for a year. I left in mid-July, and at the beginning of September the police took Delmore to Bellevue.

I left Delmore on the way back from Yaddo, where he had cut our visit short, partly because of suspicions aroused by my talking to other men. We registered for the night at the Hotel St. George in Brooklyn Heights. My mother's apartment, empty at the time, was six or eight blocks away. I took the belongings I had with me and wrote Delmore a note, saying that I would not go to Germany with him and that I would not see him again unless he went to a hospital. I felt dishonest about the last, because I knew he would not do it. Several weeks later, I flew to California and then went to Reno, where the court granted me a divorce in November. In Reno came the news that Delmore had been taken to Bellevue, and at one point had been tied into a straitjacket. He did not stay long in hospitals.

I do not know much about Delmore's life after I left. We never met again. The emotional chaos continued; the drinking and use of drugs continued. I had met Delmore at twenty-two, married him at twenty-six, and was thirty-five when I left. The last years I think in some way I was holding him together. I had said to Dr. Gruenthal about my leaving: "I'm not helping Delmore. I can't. And he's destroying me." I found Dr. Gruenthal's reply astonishingly callous: "Not if you feel that way, you can't."

Delmore's "madness" became more public in the last years. The psychic wounds could not be bandaged by me or by anyone else. His genius went on a mad rampage as he was less and less able to focus his Demiurge.

Tragedy. An expense of spirit in a waste of shame. Negative megalomania. Self-destructive addiction. Hatred, too, a form of love— or so Delmore writes in his journal.

I was asked to look at the box of books and notebooks that Dwight Macdonald took from Delmore's last hotel room. Two lines are seared in my memory:

> *The poisonous world flows into my mouth*
> *Like water into a drowning man's*

These lines from the mouth of a beloved are horrible, well-nigh intolerable. Yet written so close to the end, their very existence is proof of Delmore's lifelong commitment to and joy in his greatest love, Poesia, and of that divine spark never extinguished in life that illuminated Delmore's being.

[2]

New York, January–February 1985

I have been working for four years now with the Delmore Schwartz journals and notebooks, and in some ways it is like being with Delmore again. The transcription is what has taken most of the time. Twenty-four hundred odd sheets became a 1,400-page typescript, which, edited, became 900 pages. The original material could not be "read"—if reading implies a certain pace. Most of the material is handwritten; much of it requires a magnifying glass and patience to decipher; many sheets are so chaotic that in transcribing them I noted: top, bottom, left, right, center.

Once I began to edit, the excitement set in. There was the Delmore I loved, the Delmore who fascinated me, to be with whom meant breathing not only with one's lungs but with one's mind. Above all, there was the poet, the Orpheus, transcending this world to make music out of things he alone had penetrated to and heard. There also was Delmore the man, Delmore the wounded genius, the heavy bear of his poems, the naïf scheming to be practical in impractical ways. There was the Delmore who had no ballast in his relations with people, who was awkward in his physical relation to the world, more at home in the empyrean—language, creation, thought, contemplation —than in the everyday world of ordinary living.

The journals begin in 1939, the year after he published his first book, *In Dreams Begin Responsibilities,* and immediately became a star in the literary firmament. He begins the journal conscious of it as a literary form and therefore conscious of a potential audience. But the focus and coherence this implies is not sustained. He gives various reasons at different times for writing it. I think the most important is that it became part of the process of writing. I can see him now in his habitual large wooden chair, one arm of which had a drop leaf, with a pile or two of books on the floor at his feet and a stack of paper on the chair arm. He is positioned for work, and the so-called journal is a continuous process of note making whenever the author is not focused and at the typewriter. The journal shows many beginnings. It has the spontaneity and wit of the brilliant conversationalist Delmore was. It is, above all, the mind of a poet at work.

Editing was a complex process. My first decision was not to make any editorial decisions beforehand, that is, to try to transcribe everything. Much of the material is fragmented. When I first looked at it I said: But this isn't a journal at all—having in mind more or less sequential notations of happenings. Here, there may be ten pages for one day and then nothing for months or even a year.

Two things surprised me as the transcript lengthened: one was the amount of poetry it contained; the second was how poorly documented major personal events and crises were. One can speculate that Delmore destroyed pages or that at times he was too taken up with events to make notes, or that there were things he did not want put into writing at all, even in notes made for himself. But under the fragmented surface—jewels of wit, perception, epigram—there are the dynamics of Delmore's career and his personal life.

Delmore was obsessed with his past, both in a personal and in a more universal sense. His emotional preoccupation with the past was ultimately destructive, but his capacity to universalize and use that past presented him with his major themes.

He was born in New York, "the last European capital," as he would later call it, both his parents immigrant Jews from Rumania. Delmore mythologizes the world his parents came from and dramatizes the world he was born into. The newcomer's tendency to social paranoia was disastrously reinforced in Delmore's case by the war between his parents that devastated his childhood. His father, who died when Delmore was sixteen, was a real-estate tycoon; his mother, according to her oldest son, drove her husband out of New York with her scenes.

The immigrant experience is dynamic in American life, with psychological consequences that persist past the first generation. It breeds precariousness, fear, aggression, and anger; but also excitement, adventure, the self-confidence and exaltation of success. Evident in Delmore and in the stories he tells of his parents are both chutzpah and social malaise. Foreign-born parents and American-born children bring the two-culture conflict into the heart of the family, a conflict likely to be complicated by class attitudes if the children are upwardly mobile. One of Delmore's favorite stories was of a friend's father saying to his son: "Why should I send you to college? Every course you take makes you more of a stranger."

Delmore's ambitions were not at all those of his father. The continent to be subdued was not material but cultural, demanding intellectual and imaginative powers. The Washington Heights schoolboy was a precocious reader, and as Delmore remarks in his journals, he and his friends as young men assumed their own genius. The remarkable history of the New York Jewish intellectuals of the forties and fifties—and especially those centered around *Partisan Review*— has yet to be written, though Irving Howe touches on it in *World of Our Fathers.**

Delmore's early work has the dramatic vitality he found in the lives of the people among whom he was born. He makes his immediate ancestry emblematic of intellectual and historical currents. Delmore "possessed a tireless, mythologizing imagination, a genius for eliciting

---

* *"The New York writers, and most notably* Partisan Review, *helped complete the process of internationalizing American culture, somewhat as the immigrant Jewish painters helped bring the styles of the Paris school to American art." (Simon and Schuster: New York, 1976), p. 602.*

general laws from the particular scenes of his life," writes his biographer, James Atlas.* In the journal for 1952 Delmore complains that
he is unable to use his later experiences in the same way: "Why does
almost everything since 1937 not show itself as previous years did as
themes: some of it does, more than I usually think: the professor of
literature is in the way, my relations with the people; it is still not
lived out, nor far away, it is not subliminal, sufficiently (as childhood
naturally is)—but?" I would say that Delmore did not achieve the
emotional depths in his later fiction that he did in his earlier because
he was writing about people with whom he was involved at less
elemental levels. But because of his awareness of emotional difficulty
and distortion, he meditated profoundly on the nature of love and on
the nature of man's being-in-the-world.

The philosophical bent of his mind was clear from the start.
From the start, too, he was preoccupied with judgments of good and
evil. He always said he believed in God. The structure of many of
his later poems is determined by metaphysical intensities.

Beginning in 1938, Delmore's critical and creative work appeared
frequently in the literary journals, including *Partisan Review* (where
he became poetry editor in 1943), *Southern Review, Poetry, The
Nation,* and *The New Republic.* His books were published by New
Directions, whose publisher and founder was his friend James Laughlin.
In Dreams Begin Responsibilities appeared in 1938; *Shenandoah,* a
verse play, in 1941; *Genesis, Book One* in 1943; *The World Is a Wedding* in 1948; *Vaudeville for a Princess* in 1950. In 1959 Doubleday
published *Summer Knowledge: New and Selected Poems 1938–1958;*
New Directions reprinted this as a paperback in 1967. In 1961 Corinth
Press, owned by the Wilentz brothers, Ted and Eli, of the Eighth Street
Bookshop, published *Successful Love and Other Stories.* His *Selected
Essays,* edited by Donald Dike and David Zucker, was published by
the University of Chicago Press in 1970, with paperback editions in
1975, 1985. And Robert Phillips, who succeeded Dwight Macdonald as
literary executor of the Schwartz estate, has edited *Last and Lost
Poems* (1979), *Letters of Delmore Schwartz* (1984), and *The Ego Is
Always at the Wheel: Bagatelles* (1986).

Delmore starts his journal on his twenty-sixth birthday, December
8, 1939. He and his wife of a year, Gertrude Buckman, whose family,
like Delmore's, lived on Washington Heights, are staying at Yaddo,
the writers' colony at Saratoga Springs. After Christmas they will drive
with James Laughlin to Pittsburgh and go on to New Orleans for the
Modern Language Association conference, where Delmore is to give

* Delmore Schwartz: The Life of an American Poet *(Farrar, Straus, Giroux: New
York, 1977), p. 3.*

a paper entitled "The Isolation of Modern Poetry." Among the literary people he sees there are Cleanth Brooks, John Crowe Ransom, Katherine Anne Porter, Robert Penn Warren, and, on the way back to New York, Allen Tate and Caroline Gordon.

Delmore is in need of a job. Early in 1940 the Schwartzes will move to Cambridge, where Delmore will spend seven years teaching English composition at Harvard. He is a Jew in a Gentile stronghold. The exacerbated sensibility of being an ill-at-ease and overly self-conscious young man, as well as a brilliant and ambitious one, is evident in the journal. Anxiety mounts. One can see causes: there is an ambivalent quality in his relations with his academic superiors; teaching is often a psychic ordeal; he is always watching the barometer of his literary career and comparing his successes and failures to those of his peers. His marriage does not go well. In March 1943 Gertrude returns to New York and the following year they are divorced.

Delmore's relations with women were full of guilt and insecurity. I remember his telling me of his psychiatrist's saying: "You don't have to marry every girl you go out with, you know." The Oedipal trauma of Delmore's early childhood is movingly presented in his work. He said he hated his mother. I saw him torn by pity and fear as well as anger. When he took me to visit her after our marriage, I was astonished by his voice to her—the high, uncertain voice of a child. When she plugged in a toaster, a fuse blew; she sent Delmore to the basement to find the superintendent, remarking that of course he wouldn't know how to fix anything; she then began to tell me what a terrible character he had always had.

I began to love Delmore in 1944. The course of true love did not run smoothly. After several years I became frightened by the uncertainties, and at the end of 1947 got reinvolved with someone from my past and married him. A year later I was back with Delmore, and in June 1949 we were married.

The first two and a half years we lived at 75 Charles Street in Greenwich Village. Delmore talked a great deal about the problems of earning a living. We were always poor. Part-time teaching, editorial stipends, advances, publication fees, and royalties: Delmore earned enough for us to get by, but it was hand-to-mouth, with no sense of freedom in expenditure. My part-time jobs contributed. The summers of 1950 and 1951 we went to the Midwest, where Delmore taught at the School of Letters: the first summer at Kenyon in Gambier, Ohio, and the second in Bloomington, Indiana. The second summer, too, we bought an old farmhouse near Baptistown, New Jersey, county seat Flemington, taking over a GI mortgage. This was thirty miles from Princeton, where Delmore had a job for the academic year 1952–53.

In December, with a new landlord on Charles Street trying to evict us, we accepted his offer of moving expenses and landed among not very prosperous farmers in New Jersey. As Delmore remarked, the property was about the size of Washington Square Park. There was a two-story frame house with cellar and attic, two pear trees, an apple tree, and several outbuildings, including a barn, which collapsed in a hurricane.

Delmore's conflicts with himself and the world began to have an increasingly ominous quality. His sufferings intensified. Desperation erupted in drunken rages. I think of 1953 as a crucial year. Delmore had about five jobs, was working his head off, and was increasingly out of touch with reality, although I don't think I would have said this then. His plan to secure a tenured position at Princeton depended on the Ford Foundation putting up the money for a chair. Delmore, concentrating on his acceptance by Princeton, told them, although he himself had no assurances, that the money would be forthcoming. Robert M. Hutchins was associate director of the Ford Foundation; James Laughlin, a close friend of Delmore, was also a friend of Hutchins; Laughlin was directing *Perspectives USA*, which the Ford Foundation was subsidizing and for which Delmore was working. Even I, doubting, said to Delmore, But . . . but . . . but. And I remember Saul Bellow[*] arriving as an emissary from Princeton to convey the message that if there was anything questionable, now was the time to stop. Delmore let his appointment go to a vote; the money was not forthcoming; the scheme collapsed. One of two public scenes at Princeton, when Delmore and I were together, was set off by a cruel remark referring to this. At a cocktail party, the Princeton host and professor, referring to Gogol's impostor, said to Delmore as we entered: "Here comes the Inspector General!" Later that night, wanting to make it clear to Delmore that he was too drunk and must let me drive, I got out of the car in the middle of winter in the middle of nowhere; Delmore, to my surprise, sped off—tried to come back, got lost, and ended up in jail for drunken driving.

Delmore was having more and more trouble functioning. Book reviews that used to take him two or three days were now taking two or three weeks. He was trapped in a self-enclosed system of drugs. His "narcissistic supplies," as he called them, had become dangerous necessities. He was on a treadmill of alcohol to reduce anxiety and increase the pleasures of ego expansion, of barbiturates and alcohol to reduce insomnia, of amphetamines and the new

[*] *In Saul Bellow's wonderful novel* Humboldt's Gift *(Viking: New York, 1975), Humboldt is based on Delmore, and the author recreates the intensity and literary magic that Delmore had.*

tranquillizers to enable him to function during the day. He was a sick man, and more and more a frightened one.

In 1955, when I left, I spent the winter in New York, employed by a friend to live with her and take care of her young daughter. I spent Saturday nights with Delmore at the Village hotel where he was living. In June I moved back to Baptistown with him. I felt during these last years with Delmore that I was living on the side of a volcano. He wanted me with him, but he could not stop doing the things that were driving me away. The tension was extreme. I have already spoken of my final departure in July 1957. My main feeling on the plane that bore me to the West Coast was the strangeness of peace. I had forgotten the ordinariness of it.

Of Delmore's last nine years I have no firsthand knowledge. His increasing paranoia, loss of control, episodes of hospitalization, as well as the devotion he inspired in several young women, are portrayed in James Atlas's biography. In 1959, *Summer Knowledge*, a volume of selected poems, was published, and the following year Delmore received the Bollingen Prize in Poetry for that and other work. In 1962 he began teaching at Syracuse University, where they kept him on despite his condition. In January 1966 he left suddenly and returned to New York. Six months later, he died of a heart attack suffered in a hotel corridor, where he lay unattended for some time, in the early-morning hours of July 11.

I have various deep images of Delmore. In one, his large head has a physically precarious quality, as if it were too weighty to be poised where it is. In another, coming partly from a snapshot I saw of him as a five- or six-year-old child sitting on a table with a magazine, which he claimed proudly was *The Nation*, he has an expression that persisted with him, a kind of gleeful cunning, with eyes slightly narrowed, a self-delight in knowing how to deal with the world. This partly interior focus is overwhelmed by the way I see him most: his look open, dazed, star-struck by the intensity of his perceptual world involvement—or perhaps, in the words of one of his late poems, he is existing in a state where "Consciousness has become only and purely listening."

[3]

Some further remarks are necessary about textual matters. The attempt to imitate the graphics of the original in its often chaotic state has been judged impractical. My notes added to the text are bracketed or in italics. The addition of missing words is indicated by brackets. The correction of spelling errors and changes (mostly additions) of punctuation are unmarked. One or two undated pages located in a context of dated pages have been headed "Undated" and left where found. A whole group of undated pages, however, has been placed at the end of the year to which they seemed to belong, prefaced by a note.

The poetry in the journals has presented specific problems. Many of the poems are drafts which Delmore would not have published in their present form. (Some did appear in different versions.) Often there are alternate words or lines. There is also the fact that Delmore tended to break up into lines of poetry what another author would have left as prose.

A volume of poems would have to exclude some of the work I have included. But the interest is not solely in the poem *qua* poem; it is also in the process of generation, and in the poem in the context of other elements in the journal.

My general precept was inclusion of the whole poem or none of it. I did not want to interfere by omission. Where there were alternates I chose the word, phrase, or line I preferred. For the most part these guidelines worked well, but especially toward the end of the journals, where Delmore was working on long poems or different poems grouped under the same title, this would have meant leaving out too much. In such cases, my omissions are noted by bracketed dots.

Some names and initials have been changed to protect the privacy of the individuals concerned.

In editing, my main principle was *readability*, with emphasis on any underlying dramatic themes. I also tried to keep some balance among the different elements of the original: the personal in its various aspects, the poetic, the intellectual. The one major exception is the omission of Delmore's copying of other writers, particularly of James Joyce in both *Ulysses* and *Finnegans Wake*. Much that was cut was either illegible or so fragmentary or chaotic that it would have choked any movement.

These journals end in 1959. There are later notebooks, but the scale of their indecipherability and my judgment of their contents from scanning some of them are such that I did not want to proceed.

Finally, there are various persons I wish to thank: the former and present Curators of American Literature at the Beinecke Rare Book and Manuscript Library, Yale University, where the Schwartz papers are stored, Donald Gallup and David E. Schoonover; Delmore's brother Kenneth Schwartz; James Laughlin of New Directions, Delmore's first and main publisher; the late Dwight Macdonald, an old friend of Delmore's and his literary executor, and Robert Hivnor, also an old friend, for their interest and encouragement, especially at the initiation of this project; Daphne Cox, whose hospitality enabled me to frequent New Haven; Alice Morris, Helen Duberstein, Victor Lipton, and Virginia Admiral, friends in a writing group whose critical reading and aid have been essential; Robert Giroux, for whom I once worked, whose editorial help has been invaluable; and Lynn Warshow, the copy editor. I am indebted, too, to James Atlas, both for access to his files and for his biography *Delmore Schwartz: The Life of an American Poet*; to the late Donald Dike and David Zucker, editors of *Selected Essays of Delmore Schwartz*; and to Robert Phillips, a friend, the present literary executor of the Schwartz estate, and the editor of three Schwartz volumes, *Last and Lost Poems, Letters of Delmore Schwartz*, and *The Ego Is Always at the Wheel: Bagatelles*.

Chronology

December 8, 1913	Born in Brooklyn.
1921	Family moved to Washington Heights, Manhattan. Harry Schwartz was in the process of separating from his wife. In 1923 he moved to Chicago, where he died in June 1930.
1931–32	Freshman at the University of Wisconsin.
1933–35	New York University. Delmore received a B.A. in Philosophy in June 1935.
1935–37	Graduate studies at Harvard University. Bowdoin Prize in the Humanities, 1936, for essay "Poetry as Imitation."
June 14, 1938	Married Gertrude Buckman.
December 1938	*In Dreams Begin Responsibilities*, published by James Laughlin, New Directions.
1939	Translation of Rimbaud's *Une Saison en Enfer*. A revised version appeared in 1940.
Spring 1939	Poetry Editor of *Partisan Review*.
Fall 1939	Journal begun at Yaddo, Saratoga Springs, New York.
February 1940	The Schwartzes moved to Cambridge, Massachusetts.
March 1940	Delmore awarded a Guggenheim Fellowship.
Fall 1940	Briggs-Copeland Instructor of English Composition at Harvard, where he taught until 1947.
November 1941	*Shenandoah*, a verse play.
Spring 1943	*Genesis: Book I*. Editor, *Partisan Review*.
March 1943	Delmore and Gertrude separated. They were divorced in 1944.
1945	Delmore spent the year in New York on sabbatical leave from Harvard.

March 1946	Promoted to Briggs-Copeland Assistant Professor at Harvard.
Spring 1947	Return to New York.
Summer 1948	*The World Is a Wedding.*
Spring 1949	Lecturer at the New School.
June 10, 1949	Married Elizabeth Pollet. The Schwartzes lived at 75 Charles Street in Greenwich Village until 1952.
1949–50	Series of lectures on T. S. Eliot at Christian Gauss Seminars in Literary Criticism, Princeton University.
Summer 1950	Taught at Kenyon School of Letters, Gambier, Ohio.
1950	*Vaudeville for a Princess.* The Guarantors Prize from *Poetry.*
Summer 1951	Indiana School of Letters at Bloomington.
December 1951	The Schwartzes moved to rural New Jersey at Baptistown, where they lived until 1957.
1952–53	During the academic year Delmore was chairman pro tem of the Program in Creative Arts, Princeton University. Teaching with him was Saul Bellow. Delmore was also on the advisory board of *Perspectives USA,* for which he wrote summaries of important articles, and a literary consultant for *Diogenes.* He read manuscripts for New Directions.
Spring 1953	National Institute of Arts and Letters Award.
March–June 1954	Taught at the University of Chicago.
1955	Poetry editor and regular film critic for *The New Republic* (until 1957).
1956	In January, separated from Elizabeth, Delmore moved to the Hotel Marlton in Greenwich Village. In June they returned to Baptistown together.
1957	Awarded Fulbright Fellowship to teach at the Free University of Berlin for the academic year 1957–58. Delmore later canceled it.
July 1957	Yaddo, Saratoga Springs. Elizabeth, on their return to New York, left Delmore.
September 1957	Hospitalization at Bellevue.
November 5, 1957	Elizabeth obtained a Reno divorce.
February 1958	Lecture at the Library of Congress: "The Present State of Modern Poetry."
1959	*Summer Knowledge: New and Selected Poems, 1938–1958. Poetry* magazine prize.

1960	Bollingen Prize in Poetry for 1959. Shelley Memorial Prize from the Poetry Society of America.
1961	*Successful Love and Other Stories.*
Summer 1961	Taught at University of California, L.A.
1962–65	Visiting Professor at Syracuse University.
1964	*Syracuse Poems 1964.*
January 1966	Returned to New York City, where he lived in various midtown hotels.
July 11, 1966	Suffered a heart attack in the early-morning hours. Died in the ambulance on his way to Roosevelt Hospital.
1970	*Selected Essays*, edited by Donald Dike and David Zucker.
1976	*What Is To Be Given: Selected Poems*, edited by Douglas Dunn.
1977	*Delmore Schwartz: The Life of an American Poet*, by James Atlas.
1978	*In Dreams Begin Responsibilities: Eight Stories* (new, revised edition), edited by James Atlas.
1979	*Last and Lost Poems*, edited by Robert Phillips.
1984	*Letters*, edited by Robert Phillips.
1986	*The Ego Is Always at the Wheel: Bagatelles*, edited by Robert Phillips.

1939–1940

December 8, 1939

The Aid to Memory

In this, which is Gertrude's [his wife, Gertrude Buckman] old unfinished notebook, I begin the effort to keep a journal, choosing my twenty-sixth birthday as the neat occasion for the commencement (I have always looked for such schedules and occasions, perhaps because of a feeling for form). My birthday has brought me the usual sentiments of time wasted and work which is not good enough, because I hurry, am impatient, turn to too many interests.

Consulting the expectation tables of the life insurance companies was again a consolation for the disappearance of one more year. I will never be twenty-five years of age again; but thirty-eight years more of life! So reason (or at least mathematics) promises; but not to me as an individual, not to my immortal soul; only to one unit of the class of citizens who are twenty-six years of age.

This morning I finished my essay for the New Orleans meeting of the Modern Language Association, and then I wrote with sickening excitement the stipulated page and one-third of my synopsis or argument. The anger about what had been said about my criticism kept going, with the usual tendency to retaliation by means of the word. There were letters from Will [Barrett, close friend; later, professor of philosophy, New York University] and my mother this morning, Will's letter pleasing me by a brief sentence of praise and comparison.

If I make these entries too long, it will be difficult to continue them when my present fluency vanishes once more, when tiredness comes where nervous excitement was. A sentence should be enough sometimes. The long conversation of the soul with itself ought now, by the help of this exercise, to turn more frequently to objective observation. Self-analysis is easy and has been accomplished often enough. There will also be room here for the observations, metaphors, and projects which I do not like to write otherwise, in their incompleteness as notes.

The wind heaved all afternoon. I grew more and more excited and very nervous when I played the first four movements of Beethoven's Quartet Opus 130. The best way to avoid self-consciousness, which might be a hindrance or lead me to stop, would be not to read what I have written for a long period. This book is intended to help me toward certain habits of mind; but above all, it is intended for the pleasure and insight of an old man. After writing this in script, my own handwriting's disorder offended (again the desire for form), and I decided to change to typescript; then of course, in copying what I had written, it became necessary to make changes and interpolate new sentences, for the critic is never satisfied.

[*The Schwartzes were staying at Yaddo, the arts colony at Saratoga Springs, New York.*]

Yaddo: the pines, the snow; Schubert quartet, "Death and the Maiden."

December 9

In the evening I went to the movie, as I knew I would. I went by myself, Gertrude's mood suddenly changing because I had mentioned our not-to-be-born child. At the movie, I suffered from the sense of guilt and shame which often comes at that entertainment. Back in the East House (having admired from the open fields the immense winter sky, too crowded with the stars in constellations, but desiring all the while to get to the *World-Telegram* and read of the winter baseball news), I was very nervous, full of unrest. I read two pages of Julian Green and some of Hardy's lyrics before falling asleep with the aid of a tablet. In the morning, I wrote the requisite page and a half, and then energy faded, perhaps because the subject seemed so difficult for poetry. There was a letter from John Berryman with a profession of great gratitude because of what I had said of his poems. This perception arrived, that in every economy the aging man is every man, and every man tries to keep time from disappearing wholly, but it is later when you think. This was suggested by the old unfinished poem in which a man runs on the racetrack, looking backward, in order to bring forward the past, and finally finds it necessary to become an acrobat, turn somersaults, in order to conduct his life in this complicated way. I bathed and shaved, and while I was shaving, Gertrude called to me and I did not immediately answer. This suggested a story in which a young man is in the bathroom, and when he is called, he does not answer, permits them to think something has happened to him, until the whole family is greatly disturbed, the door is broken down by the police or the janitor, young man and family mutually denounce each other. This would be somewhat like the story in which a young man does not want to go to the funeral of a friend of his deceased father because of his feeling about death and because he is too comfortable to permit new feelings to disturb him; he is pleased at some success or other. It is a question of how the divinities would help such stories as these. Each of them could be written in a week of reasonable application in which I did not hurry, nor permit excitement to make me write too much in one day.

December 11

Yesterday we went to see the Fergussons, that is, Francis Fergusson [drama critic and professor] in Bennington. It was the completest gray winter's day; after speeding, the car became overheated and would hardly go; when we arrived in Bennington, we were too concerned about the car to gaze with sentiment and memory at the old sites, our white house of the summer of 1938 [Delmore and Gertrude were married in June 1938] and the small factory town in the country. I talked too much, had the feeling that I was betraying myself, made too many remarks of deliberate malice. The two Fergusson children behaved barbarously, especially the boy, who told his father that he was going to hit him. Fergusson resisted the argument at the end about the economic causes of the new war and resisted generally what I was saying now and then, until I felt the old feeling of being unsure of my auditor's frame of mind. We left early; the car had broken down and had to be fixed in a Bennington garage and then we had to drive it home the fifty miles through the thickest waves of white fog, being able to see the road only a few yards at a time. I had been excited all day long because I had been writing so well, but this emotion wore down, partly because of Fergusson's resistance, partly tiredness, and the aftermath of the highballs. This morning and afternoon I finished the story "America! America!" [published in *The World Is a Wedding*, 1948], and suffered from my usual hurry (B.'s [?] spontaneity) to get it where it was going; I corrected an ironic remark to D. [?] about my criticism, which was perhaps more self-control. But then I was angry and ugly with Gertrude when she asked me to come to lunch just before I had finished the story, which I sent away in the afternoon.

I think this must be more than enough to help me remember the day; the test will come only in a year or two. I would not be in such a hurry, I would be a little patient and reasoning if I did not know from the sad past that such periods as these pass and do not come for some time, leaving numbness for weeks, sometimes months. But perhaps the rush is needed for pressure, intensity. But then I have been deceived by this precisely, have mistaken the intensity with which I was writing for the intensity and pressure which should have been in the work itself. Sometimes this period of energy immense seems insane. Great wits to madness are near allied: this is an echo of Dryden and Plato, but also of Lombroso and Nordau. I remarked to F.F. that the Tarzan books which his child was reading were one of the products of Darwinian theory.

December 12

After an excited morning, I walked to town to see the movie *La Kermesse Héroique* (the first time was in Cambridge with Arthur in 1936); the morning mail contained a very friendly letter from Cleanth Brooks, a card from Fergusson, and then later a three-page poem addressed to me by John Berryman and a request for a poem from Paul Engle, of all people. The Brooks and the Engle letters may well have been suggested by the December issue of *Poetry*, in which Engle and I appear and Brooks is reviewed very favorably by William Empson.

At the movie, I saw the possibility of a poem about all the forms of the dance; this came from the imitation in the picture of the pictures of Flemish dancing in Brueghel the Elder. The story suggested itself of a woman of thirty coming not to be ashamed of her body because of her lover's attentions to it. And then also the subjects of man as a stranger amid star, snow, stone, and water; of a father seeing his daughter embraced in the living room; of the need to construct discourses about the nature of life. The stranger draws his face in the star, stone, snow, and water.

In the evening the exaltation of the past few days stopped, faded; I answered some letters and was annoyed by the inadequacy of one of my old stories; perhaps it was this that began the fading or perhaps dinner. I played Beethoven's Opus 18, No. 3 in the middle of the evening.

December 14

Yesterday we went to the movie and then came out and went into another movie. This was after we had walked through the sweetness of the snowy air to town. I wrote a short story in the afternoon and sent it away to George Davis [editor of *Harper's Bazaar*]; it was really a rewriting, but fluency faded into nervous strain, which made the piece shorter perhaps than it would otherwise have been. The arrival of a book by [William Carlos] Williams with an introduction by Horace Gregory made me sick and angry for the usual reasons, more so because it was before dinner. The applejack adjusted me and so did dinner itself. There is the waste of spirit in attention to the literary present, with all the sense of competition which goes with it. Until one is à Kempis, it might be well to avoid or try to avoid this kind of attention. I have fed on it for more than ten years, always personally involved, but more so since my own writing began to appear and this for an obvious reason. I read Gertrude Stein's "The Good Anna" before going to bed, but not with the proper attention. It occurred to me that I ought to set down the conditions of such excitement and energy as I enjoy now, perhaps thus to be able to control it, bring it back, use it with care. Reason can use excitement. The will has to operate always under a definite and difficult set of conditions of one kind or another.

Today I continued writing the present synopsis, which is the third or fourth since September, each one being progress, or so it now seems. I rewrote a poem I had written on Monday, but without much improvement, except that I had taken hold of my blank-verse rhythm again. At noon, feeling nervous and unclean, I bathed and gazed for a moment at the reflection of sunlight shining through icicles upon the bathroom wall. One reflection had the shape of the armless Venus and another one was crossed by the shadow that dropped from an icicle. Gertrude was very pleased during the afternoon, but then very much angered because I spoke about her politeness and unpoliteness. In the evening, Jay's [James Laughlin, publisher of New Directions] letter made me decide to start for New York tomorrow morning; always the emotion of excitement which goes with any decision to travel, for all imperfect things must move. At the same time, the arrival of bookstore's catalogue made me angry as yesterday; not angry, disturbed, my sense of position, status, praise, criticism confronted with stupidity, praise for the inadequate, laurels contesting my laurels.

December 15

Resumé: Trip to New York, the car's battery dead. Argument with Dwight [Macdonald] in his house. C.W.L. James, the Negro, present [an author from the West Indies and a noted Trotskyite]. His views of poetry. Slept on Dwight's sofa.

December 16

Visit with William [Phillips, close friend and an editor of *Partisan Review*]. [Robert] Hivnor [playwright] came to see me at Dwight's and Clement Greenberg [art critic] was there. Meeting with Berryman at midnight. He came to William's house, Gertrude stayed at her mother's house.

December 17

Sunday. Fred [F. W. Dupee, literary critic] came to see me at William's. Dinner at the Buckmans' [Gertrude's parents]. Met Hivnor; his message that Auden wanted to see me. Hivnor in the evening; his story.

December 18

Hivnor called, and I met him for lunch with Auden. Then to Auden's apartment, where we talked until three about America. Then, two hours late, to the Picasso show to meet Berryman and Gertrude. Berryman fainted or staged a faint when I told him about Auden, right in front of a picture. Dinner with William and Edna [Phillips] while John and Gertrude had dinner elsewhere. I met them later and we went to the Jumble Shop, where I delighted J.B. by analyzing Muriel Rukeyser. All this time long conversations with William and Edna. On Saturday night, we had dinner with W. and E., then Philip [Rahv, critic and an editor of *Partisan Review*] and Natalie [Rahv] came, then Hivnor, who stayed too long while we argued about race and I told stories of [Nathan] Asch [novelist]. I received a ticket for parking all night. Berryman on [Allen] Tate's rank.

December 20

Will [Barrett] came and I read my MLA [Modern Language Association] paper to him; then we had lunch in an Italian restaurant and Gertrude was waiting for us outside William's Seventeenth St. apt. There was a letter from Jay that he might come the next day. I was still looking for a garage. We walked long, had dinner in another Italian restaurant; there was another minor brush with Gertrude; we drove uptown to the Buckmans', left Gertrude there, came downtown in the car, talked of Roslyn [Brogue], and then I said goodbye to Will.

December 21

No sign of Jay, but I typed out and corrected my paper all afternoon, had dinner with William and Edna; they went to pay a visit, we discussed a movie, but stayed, and W. and E. returned and we talked about the CP [Communist Party] when W. belonged and was put in jail with P. R[ahv]. Dwight said that one dollar more a page would be paid for my story. "I wish I [had] never heard of Marxism."

December 22

Jay called from Mt. Vernon. Hivnor came to see him. We left after noon in Jay's new car, had lunch by the Newark airport, stopped to see the Tates [Allen Tate and Caroline Gordon] in Princeton, who begged us to stay (I told A.T. of T.S.E.'s [T. S. Eliot] letter and he evinced much interest) and then we drove with Jay all night through Pennsylvania so Jay could get to a Pittsburgh bank in the morning. We stayed in a Pittsburgh hotel, slept until noon. Why J.'s aunt would not have us at Norfolk. J. and Benét, Kenneth Patchen.

December 24

We had lunch amid the whole Laughlin tribe, met Jay's mother, aunts, uncle, brother, sister-in-law, who were very well-mannered. Ingrid's questions, the signing of the book for Mrs. Laughlin and the signing of the other books. Our start alone in the car for Nashville. Gertrude was carsick when we reached Ohio. We stayed in Washington, Ohio. It was Christmas Eve on the radio and a man made a speech for the Ford Co.

December 25

Driving all day through Cincinnati, Louisville (covered with snow), until we reached Nashville at 11. Loss of temper near Tennessee, lunch in Kentucky.

December 27

In a bookstore in Birmingham talking to a bookseller named Gottleib. Drove all day until we reached New Orleans at ten. Met the Mizeners [Arthur and Rosemary] in the hotel bar, stayed at Mme Dufour's.

December 28

Met [Albert] Erskine and [Morton Dauwen] Zabel; went to a dinner with Mizener, Erskine, Jay, and the girls, then spent the evening in [Norman Holmes] Pearson's hotel room, meeting Pearson, [Robert Penn] Warren, going later to a gambling hell where Erskine and Pearson lost. Zabel had gone home.

December 29

G. and I sick at breakfast; rehearsing in Erskine's room while he drank; my speech after the others', the delays, the impatience. The congratulations. Dinner with [John Crowe] Ransom and the Mizeners. Ransom asked to publish my paper. ["The Isolation of Modern Poetry" appeared in *Kenyon Review* 3, Spring 1941.] In the Mizeners' room arguing long about Marxism, while Blum was the young man and Ransom left early, having purchased the liquor, and Jay disappeared to go to sleep. The Blums took us to have coffee *au lait* in the French market, then we went to a Hawaiian nightclub, then the Blums took us home, made a date for the next day.

December 30

We left for Baton Rouge. The Blums had overslept. Jay was almost tender, as vs. his previous lack of interest, turning on of the radio.
Katherine Anne Porter, the Brooks sisters (Eleanor Blanchard), Jay's
departure with one, our men's visit to the Bryans' with the men from
Texas. We were staying with the Erskines [Albert and Katherine
Anne], so-called. Katherine Anne [Porter] and I exchanged the most
eloquent compliments.

December 31

New Year's Eve dinner with Katherine Anne and all; Ransom had
left. Brooks talked long and flattered Albert and myself. When the
rest left, Katherine and Albert and I stayed up until 4, for Albert said
he was a traditionalist in such things. Jay had left.

January 1–7, 1940

Mon. We walked in Baton Rouge, saw the Mississippi for the
first time, spent the evening with the Brookses, went to bed early.
Effort to be adequate to the Mississippi.

Tues. Left Baton Rouge with the Mizeners. Saw the Gulf of
Mexico. Drove to Montgomery, Ala. Went to the movie at night.

Wed. Drove to Greenville, S.C. And I went to the movie alone.
Tension with Rosemary [Mizener]. (*Snows of Kilimanjaro*)

Thurs. Drove to Charlottesville, Va. Went to the movies, argued
some more.

Fri. Drove to Princeton, N.J., and burst in on the Tates; spent the
evening with them and stayed with them.

Sat. Stayed with Tates for lunch, left, came to New York, visited
Dwight, took out the car with much trouble, stayed on the Heights at
Buckmans' and Baba's [Delmore's grandmother], went to the movie.

Sun. Drove to Saratoga, the car cold and colder all the way. The
garage man again infuriating about where the car ought to be left. The
pain of freezing feet, the return, the tiredness, the anger at Jay before
sleep.

January 8

Wrote letters, strove toward order, argued long with my anger
vs. Jay and Dwight and my mother, did not send the angry letters,
resumed the synopsis, and made this resumé, which should make me
able to remember this grand tour when the proper time comes, when
the subject demands the form, the greatest form which is truth (truth

is form, not a thing). The flatteries of Jay and Katherine Anne, Jay on my characteristic remark when I said that this was the last year of the decade, and K.A.'s saying she was envious of so much and that what they said of me was true; but especially the story.

Fading of manic phase in quarrels and irritation.

[In February 1940 the Schwartzes moved to Cambridge, where Delmore had obtained an appointment at Harvard as a Briggs-Copeland instructor in English.]

March 1–10

Sun., 10. I tried to write a purple lyric and then I made an outline of the whole life which is supposed to be the subject of the story. Emily Sweetser [who worked for New Directions in Cambridge] came with a friend of hers to ask us to supper and we talked about Jay and the Harvard undergraduates. They drove us to where [Harry] Wolfson [Harvard professor] lives and we found him at home and he was delighted to see us. We went to [Philip] Horton's [literary critic and friend] tea and I talked with [R. P.] Blackmur [later close friend] while [Harry] Levin looked to see, from time to time, perhaps in demonic pride. I talked to his wife, wishing him to see that; they had been visited by Wohlstetter [political scientist] and his wife, and I told Elena Levin why I disliked W.—and that he had reported with glee and gusto what Levin had said of me. I talked some more with Blackmur—about meter, about the different range of reference in his prose and poetry, about the need to break down a constriction of association by shifting to a new meter. Then I talked with Elena about my feeling about Russia and my grandfather. The party became more disorganized. We left, as they were trying to start a game, to go to see a movie. We stopped to ask Oscar and Mary [Oscar Handlin, later professor of history at Harvard, and his wife, Mary, close friends of Delmore], who were in a state of being irritated with one another because of Oscar's thesis. The picture was no good; the first one, about adolescent youth, depressed me because it viewed adolescence from a comic perspective. On a train a young woman was kind about the directions and at home Gertrude became irritable about our having to go out; it was her tiredness. I was very depressed about all that concerns me, but in [Werner] Jaeger I read an interpretation of the Greek divinities which seemed just like mine.

Sat. At [John] Wheelwright's [poet] party, we met the son of William James. I heard that [Conrad] Aiken was writing about my poetry and that [Howard] Blake [poet, also teaching in the English A program at Harvard] thought it "prosie." He invited us to dinner.

Fri. We heard and saw Stravinsky conducting his string music, standing with [Philip] Horton in Sanders Theatre.

Thurs. At Wheelwright's with Blackmur and Horton until three o'clock, talking of poetry, religion, politics. We had visited the Levins at ten and had dinner with the Handlins.

Wed. This is the morning that Jay left. He said, Don't take anything to heart, before going away.

Tues. Last night with Jay. Lunch with [Theodore] Spencer [Harvard professor of English and Delmore's superior in the English A program], E. Drew, H. Pickman.

Mon. Visited by a young painter, Ossario, whom Jay brought. [Mary] Colum's review [in *Book Forum*, March 4, 1960] of Rimbaud with [W. C.] William's letter about it came today. [Delmore's translation of *A Season in Hell* was published by New Directions in 1939. There were obvious errors and the critical reception was mixed. A revised edition was published in 1940.]

Sat. We saw the Handlins, went to the Wursthaus, where I forgot my rubbers and heard of Oscar's childhood, which made us laugh a great deal. (A genius in general—dirty pictures.)

Fri. Dinner with [F. O.] Matthiessen [Harvard professor] and the Hortons [Philip and Tessa]. Matthiessen mentioned the reviews of Rimbaud with a smile. We talked of [James] Agee, [Allen] Tate.

July 10

Is this verse "just running down the road"?
As Pound once said of "*vers libre*"
        discussing the sonnet the canzone
          and Cavalcanti
Will it look like the verse I wrote at Yaddo
          six weeks after?
It is important to keep calm, not to get excited
By the mere fact of thoughts and observations;
To work slowly; to compose from line to line
Not only the single line; the paragraph as in Milton

July 14

Fishes' blood changed to suit the temperature
But man's not so;
        he catches cold,
Shivers, shudders and shakes
          What purpose then
In calling a man a poor fish?
See the fish gasping on air
So man's soul gasps in the physical world

August 21

Trotsky

Ah, they found out at last
How to stop his angry voice
Hit him in the head, gentlemen,
That's where he lives and is strong—
Hit him in the intellect
That's where his anger is . . .

[I found no journal entries for 1941 among the Schwartz papers. Delmore and Gertrude lived in Cambridge where, the previous fall, he had begun teaching at Harvard. In November New Directions published his verse play *Shenandoah*.]

1942

January 3

My classes. Keeping your eyes open is one of the requirements of the course.

The child is father to the man. William Sigmund Wordsworth Freud.

> O mortal I
> Immortal I
> You often die
> Because you try
> To fight the sky.
> (Hemingway shoehorn)

Hell-bent for Hell in a hack.

A little honesty is the best police.

Never send an angry letter at night—only in the morning.

Parents have children simply for their own entertainment [or] to prove they are neither impotent nor homosexual.

Psychoanalysis is still in its infancy.

N[athanael] West, 1933–1940, killed in a car—*Miss Lonelyhearts*.

Empsonian or Diction Poems.

Teachers like actors must drug themselves—to be at their best / breast / topnotch.

Fighting as in March 1938, Sept. 1941. Scared by planes which fly fly low.

Fascism for the only security?

Nobility often inspired by egotism—why not?

You have a chance. Baudelaire *de nos jours*—R. P. B[lackmur], May 1940.

Loss of reason in sleep. *Genesis* [the book Delmore was working on, published by New Directions in 1943]—all eggs—one basket.

Evolution
Each egg in its development
Climbs its ancestral tree

Letter to W. H. Auden, tetrameter poem.

People don't realize that (1) I will do anything for my friends /
against my enemies / except what will make me lose my friends.

G.: Sex is a focal point / and that is a pun.

Men marry to have time for something besides screwing—

Lend me your sex organs, chum / Lend me your wife and I'll lend
you mine.

How is Winkie? How is he? / I will never call him Harry / Not
Harry—Who Would Stop at Nothing—[Winkie was the nickname of
Delmore's nephew Harry, who was named for his grandfather, Del-
more's father.]

Hemophilia started in
With that Queen, Victoria—(some sin?)
At any rate, it was a famous visitation
Not subject to much imitation

Each city has a Swing
Chicago's Boogie-Woogie's
New Orleans's Barrel-house

Variations must be consistent—

Ballet makes fans so does Swing
But they use the whole of Being
(Shake that thing, O shake that thing)

Now Time is burning like a Christmas tree
Two weeks after the holidays!
So much excitement has stopped in me
The keeping of a record of the days—

It swarmed all over me, like sex!

Thank God I "love" my father, or
I might have been a fairy, or
Too weak to bear my life and wife—

Thank God my father left his wife
When I was six, before we could have fought
For so I would have when I came to thought
And knew from good his evil and his wrong
—The subject of my new deathless song—

Psychoanalysis like a mirror: look at a book and there y'are.

The world is now a unity
A unity in guilt and shame!

Poor Schwartz rapt in his thoughts
Rapped by his thoughts, wrapped in's thoughts
Heavy & gray as his overcoat

Today I made some peace, I did,
I made some handsome wholesome gestures

The genes which make the genius spark

I want to live long enough to find out if R. P. B. lives to ninety.

Marianne Moore in libraries
Learned to cross poetic *t*'s
So that the reader saw the word
As something beautiful and heard

Picturesque Williams / straw Eliot.
I feel as if they took my pants / When others steal my own best
points (critical).
The Great Schapiro / is M. / Is a master and a hero [Meyer
Schapiro].

What fine ideas are generated
When the mind has been elated
Thus a poem can be created

Be systematic in this meter.
His mother is the ice cream queen / ice queen / Mrs. Laughlin /
Jay / drunken father / Laughlin poor lucky boy / He will be his father's
broken toy.
Alfred Kazin: literary criticism now based on R[andall] Jarrell's
incessant sense of humor.
One vice drives out another vice / But only good life can cure
it all.

Versicles
A lot of this is too excited
And soon will seem benighted!

I have been ill—too many vitamins.

January 6

The sexual zones take pictures of events.
In conversation, one pulls up what actualities?
Offered a drink, he said, No, I will coast a while.
Freshen your drink? asked F. O. M[atthiessen].

Fame and Glory, that was all
Literary fame was all
That attracted my sick will—

O Albion must soon go down
Or all the West will break
like glass
Now it no longer serves a need
They are the old men who succeeded

Moved by this extreme excitement
Wrenchéd meters seem all right—
But upon a later ride
Fixed on meter, I'll rewrite
Half blank verse and half in this
"The doggerel beneath the skin."

Sonny's [Harold Shapero, composer] a genius; I know.
Try for one thing—something else comes in the back door.
Rubber ball against a mountain.
[Aaron] Copland, Sonny; Paul G[oodman] jackass.
Use the blackboard, John advised / And from then on, well, it
worked! [advice about teaching from Berryman].
Blow up the picture of your parents / Upon that saddened
autumn day.

Let it cool off, Sherry said
When my essay was just done
Irritated by success
And by my rush, so middle-class
Because her genius merely talked
While some folk went to work

Trilling now hands out the crumbs
For the *Kenyon* from N'York
My suspiciousness distorts
Simple words to horrid torts

All the boys upon careers
Are subject to what deadly fears!
Well and wait with deadly fears!

Was Alice James the Dove with Wings
Who died in James's greatest book?
She knew that she would die like Milly
(Which news they had to hide from Willy).

The moon looked like a pretty girl's
Bare buttock as she slipped from bed

Helen Dickson is much better
Than Larry Smith or Adolf Hitler

Anti-Semitism ever
Sharpens Jews to be more clever

Hope Houser in m'class today
Showed me in her diary,
A page on which she and two chums
Discussed if they would ever choose
To marry Negroes, Chinese, or Jews.
Chinese! declared the other two
Although admitting that the Jew
Might make a child who looked like Ma
And Jews were charming, they were bright
Nevertheless
They started hatred everywhere
Grasping, avid, ravenous
They always seem to make some hate them!

Blowing your own horn, Jew and goy! The party hat, the party
horns, O cheapskate heart! O patent-leather Sunday!
Mmmmmm, the chocolate, Sweets declared / Tastes like childhood.
And on this day a rabbi's son, / Gave me books about the Jews—

Every kind of gift attracts
Followers of every sex
Ugly snub-nosed Socrates
Was chaste by Alcibiades

Sidney Hook,* shoe salesman pure
Put some coeds into heat
It was his mind and not his looks
(Is that why some men study books?)

If you are to be a sot, go South, there it is done by all the best families—David Newton.
Williams never read my verse (Aug. 1938).

Men stand at bars because the sot
If he sits down, gets much too fat
If you drink rum stretched in bed,
Cramps will strike your stomach bad—

Just you tell a poet once that he
Is bad, he is an enemy
Tell him then that he is good
He kisses you in gratitude!
Then then! in many circles, he
Praises your authority!

Thomas Wolfe, middle-brow author.

Richard Blackmur now depends
On my support when he's attacked
Most of all, he likes his friends!
He likes to talk the whole night long!

Helter-skelter in a welter
Schwartz in Poetry took shelter

Long have I lived from hand to mouth
Morally from year to year
When will I be free of fear
And find virtue absolute

Split-second decisions and revisions—
Eliot feared he'd be Prufrock'd

The ices of light upon a riverbank
Europe! Europe! cried the newsboys—

* *Sidney Hook, professor of philosophy at New York University.*

January 9

Only a policy of limited objectives can save us from procrastination and then hopelessness.

Gertrude's movements are not always related to other objects.

Our dinner party was a flop and yet a test of character—*in vino veritas* . . .

January 10

Are you wise?—[Matthew] Josephson. Oh, I don't know anything —G.B.S. [Gertrude].

I love my wife but O Euclid! (the mathematician sang!).

Nexus of snow: sleigh-riding with Father, 1916, meeting Julia Saloman. (Father's feelings? Sled as sex—Lakewood picture, too.)

Chu-chu train, Christmas breakdown, 1920–1922, ill at birthday party. [Delmore's birthday was December 13.]

Ride to Connecticut—Father's only anger.

Drugstore as center of modern life—more kinds of things than nature.

A sensuality that can be violated by any idea, opposite of James— a whore / Swinburne, Blake, James— From empiricism to imperialism.

January 20

Hope springs eternal in the human crotch
for a new debauch

Between the pretension and the motive
Between the abstraction and the actual
Between the . . .
(There is a good deal of fog)

January 31

Two drunkards trying to support each other: Blackmur and Schwartz in the mall.

You can always find something good to say about anything; you can always find something bad to say about anyone, even God.

Aren't you being banal? Goodness is banal.

I am sorry. You have no talent.

I don't like you because your head is too big.

They are just flies buzzing; mosquitoes; ants.

Everything penetrates everything.

Radio voices go through the walls!

The snow outside is trying to get into the Brueghel.

Act inconsistently; then the others will be wrong in the great chess of power (a game invented by soldiers; by a disappointed courtier).

He thought he rose because he attacked others; yet thought others rose because they did not. H.L. [Harry Levin].

If you don't like it here, why don't you go back where you came from? A Fugue.

Despair is my shield: I don't care! Humility is the abyss which will save me!

You really write as if you understood Marx. Shows you're smarter than Auden.

Why are you so loving? I did not say I preferred it. Yes, you do. All the way for a kiss. It is not so far.

Every time I see another egotist, I learn of my own horror.

One vice drives out another vice.

I will leave some snow for you!

Since there's no help, come let us kiss and part. Psychologizing and Drayton.

Wyatt's: "Dear Love, how like you this?"

Where or whence this stamina? never to quit, poem, marriage, teaching; but almost quitting, as in 1941.

An epigram is a form of speed; but poetry is not in a hurry, like an automobile. There is plenty of time. Criticism is not in a hurry either.

Marriage was once like buying some freshly; now like buying phonograph records. John's [Berryman] view of trade names.

Nobody fools anybody much of the time.

I have been walking on the bottom of the river for six months. H. T. Moore [Harry T. Moore, author and critic]. The universe is biting me. Oscar Williams [poet and anthologist].

Complete lack of reticence and discretion. Harry [Levin] looked around when I said that James was anti-Semitic. Thus I learn; no attack from which a retreat is impossible; or reconciliation.

When insulted, I always must insult back: guide yourself by this. If you fight with me, you will fight with all, end with no friends, because never was anyone more desirous of not fighting; with you.

If we stand here much longer, the whole past will rise up! Hi Fane, Arthur Berger. Next thing, you will tell me Marx was a Jew.

I just don't care! Teach me to care and not to care. Ethics of concluding passage of *The Waste Land*: Give, sympathize, control; base one's whole life on this. Imagine *TWL* sans notes. What memories return.

Biographies written of you. It is different with everyone; with the great poet. *Not* moral.

May I tell you something you don't know? I don't like you.

All great men are insane. They retreated farther and farther from criticism, becoming more and more insecure.

There was a genius in heat.

The subway faces were all painted by Brueghel. Now that we have a Brueghel in the house, I enjoy my subway rides. A new meter will come of this deliberate flatness.

The Negro at seventy spoke of his three daughters. First one doing pretty well, married eight years, has seven; the other two don't do nothing. I don't like you, you don't do nothing! Ah'm seventy, almost seventy-one, but Ah plan to do something!

Everyone laughed. Pat Wanning was pretty in her ski cap playing tennis with the doctors at Johns Hopkins.

I do not have enough time for study and remorse.

I cultivate my colds. I have gone too far.

The agenbite of remorse bit me.

The lightning scar upon my face, the fresh new quarry of the snow, the knowledge now of what to do and how many misunderstandings are frequent, the immense pressure of the defeated or held-down libido: all of this in December and January, more than ever before, and the illusion that it will stay, the inevitable illusion.

To think that since you see some mistakes, you see them all.

I have written the greatest poem in the English language!

That is the way I used to speak when I was eighteen.

Paranoia is homosexual, Freud says, and narcissism brings about indifference.

We must all die and be born again! The Bible is our mind.

February 23

The wine tocked as it came from the bottle. The pigeons rose with a sound like a deck of cards being shuffled.

At the horizon, a purple-blue mountain range of cloud, low-lying and extensive; and farther off, a cloud with lines like the human body in William Blake.

It says in the big book, If you take cells of the old body, they do not die, as the body does. Thus death is something which happens to the whole body, not to any of its parts. And there is no natural necessity that the body should grow old.

He walked across the river when it froze over, in triumph over the fear in his gaze.

This prospect is full of posts, the natural trees; the shaven discolored tree of the telephone company, from which pencil lines run, bearing voices; the iron trees of light.

And now the purple-black cloud-range is like a great wing, for it curves in lines which are wing-lines.

In the sky now are various peninsulas, where, during the afternoon, were white continents.

All of the above written on the strength of wine, at sunset.

Who did not know a sonnet from a sonata? M. Moore. Words by words begotten, not by experience in the first intention.

Two extremes of my labor at *Genesis*: to make all of it prose; to make the narrative blank verse. A middle ground was the excitement of December when it seemed right as it was.

The new possibility—to be tried out, anyway, and perhaps abandoned in one day—is to use the biblical style for the dead, and shift the narrative into blank verse (for it now seems possible to concentrate on an eloquent-rhetorical blank verse).

"He, Eliot, convinced me that we were absolutely out in the cold, and there I have remained ever since. While he has crawled into saviour nests"—[Conrad] Aiken.

Last night I read *Enfants Terribles* [Cocteau] and heard Roosevelt's speech, sober and coughing.

In this novel there is immense drama at the end, in which the childhood event as a cause explodes like dynamite. But it is too easy, too much depends on the very thinness; also upon arbitrary coincidence.

Cocteau deifies the organized cruelty and amorality of childhood and youth; he sings it, he is its laureate. Possible causes: homosexuality, a wartime youth, the opposition of the artist and the middle class.

March 3

[Many of the lines in the entries between March 3 and March 17, 1942, occur in Genesis: Book One *(New Directions, 1943) in the same or a variant form.]*

> From darkness to darkness, proceed; depth has decrees
> No one has dreamed! As one (as one! I mean
> A living soul afraid, trembling from fear,
> Escaped from seas on which the ocean liner
> Sank, reaches the shore, dragging the last furs
> Of death dripping from goosechilled legs
> That shook a moment since)—as he
> Might halt, stand on the sand, look back
> (feeling perhaps he has died once, he now
> Begins a second life!), gaze at the rocking carriage
> Of utter softness, grasping his being thus:
> So I await the next of views, so I,
> Narrator, look back on this naughted night
> (Oh, every day is once! never returns!)
> (These are the glowing airs with which Time burns)

... But now I do not contemplate the single line
And view the possibilities and freedom there,
Freedom of strength and freedom of revision,
—I wish to flow with intuition's power!
This is my utmost pleasure! always was!
Where is that growth, where is the character
I thought I gained through drinking down the wine?
I do not look around and soar above
And thrust beneath the line itself
And take it up and throw it from the room
And bring it, broken, back! make it anew!
Alliterated, punned, and incanted ...

Sharpen the long knives of perception
Perception is half creative, half *Anagke*

March 11

O wine-stained, wine-awakened mind!

Avoid such meter words as *now, and, there*, unless dramatized by
the wine. Seek for the flat five-foot statement which is full of energy
and drama: "Blows of the new world struck his mind and heart!" And
seek irony, the ironic-colloquial, and the ecstatic-exclamatory! And if
naught else avails, sensuous description, remorseful-anecdotal-memoirs.

The crew waits, rests on its oars, begins!
Stroke after stroke draws back the shoulder blades,
Draws back the blades of oars, and forward draws
In such a spasm, the long lean shell which holds.

Fatal rotundity, on which we turn,
And where the plants are dry or fresh and where
Many a one has tried to get a statue
And many a one has wished, at times, to die ...

The liner moved like happiness itself
Climbing in grandeur, forward, cutting waters

Seldom in Sodom had they the stamina
To thrust a toothpick through the crevices
Where lodged some poor chick's remnant, like a thread,
Until, at last, this move became a pleasure,
—Everyone liked to pick their rotten teeth.

Let every line contain an observation,
As every street has, at both ends, a light;
And let emotion flow into the movement
Between the words, from word to word, from thought
To daring generality and trope!

The shell shoots forward—slows . . . shoots forward, slows . . .
Under the human will, concerted there!
And by such artifice contriving strain
Not to be bored—whose phenomenology
Makes God regard the tiger as a trope
Insipid, even though striped and murderous—

What! from this nebulae came forth man's mind?
It is not true, it is a stupid lie!

Kites which I flew from empty lots in boyhood.
So I would do again, and touch some angels—
                              in aspiration!

                                                      March 12

    The swift December dusk came tumbling down
    After the full day, midwinter's lapse . . .

    A ring of porter froth upon the table,
    Soldiers on guard upon the torn *Playbill* . . .

    Thrilling and mysterious is the future,
    But most of all to those who wish to marry . . .

    And now the sun is shining full and bright,
    Which was, before, faint, almost pearl-light . . .

    No mail at three; I listened for a time
    —My hope had risen when the postman came,
    Seen down the block and moving to the house—
    And then forgot to listen for the steps
    Upon the stair which meant some mail for me,
    Forgot (since silence brought the news) the sum
    Of disappointment, which is six months old—

    —A band was playing on the deck above them
    When the lean steamship moved from the great harbor,
    Calm and magnificent was the onward motion,
    And happiness itself seemed vivid there,
    The band was playing what a mighty music,
    And O two worlds rang out over the shifting water . . .

    —Leah was shocked and Leah was ashamed
    And yet excited by her husband's daring,
    Nothing like that before, never before
    Had his emotions foreshadow[ed] such a *coup*—

On the sixth day a storm. All things tossed,
Knocked, slid, jugged, knocked and jugged,
No one permitted on the deck for hours,
And then the sky cleared and was blue again—

March 14

O let me put my tongue into your mouth
This simple statement will shock all concerned . . .
I clamber on the heights of Venusberg
A clambering of sensuality
(Coherence is unconscious as the womb's
Exactest shapeliness of limb and arm
Trimness of breast, five-fingered hand and foot)

Now what has this to do with poor Jack Green
Who flies in pain with pride to Montreal
Because he has said *Debutante* as if
A German aunt were named with some affection
                                    (and laughter breaks
Against his face as if he had been stoned)—
Do not, my dears, suppose that it is simple
To see that each hand has exactly five
Not four, nor six! it takes deliberate care—

Turning the bird flys off, snatching the air,
His wings hung high upon his vibrant moves—

When toothache comes who does not think, How did
I manage to forget my happiness
Before this pain?

Be then the active reader, active knower
Even in parts—Bend down the page you want—

"We come to celebrate, to criticize
To praise and deny praise: in praise withdrawn
That gold seen going down in such a blaze
Is Praise itself known best, and celebration . . ."

". . . In evening's still soft darkening air we come,
Yet bring a sense—strong, clanking, black and loud
Of the great domed stations where the self goes
To find departure, dressed efficiently
In uniforms of porter, gate and domed
And dirty skylight, holding most sounds."

To express new aspects, new objects (Eliot-Swinburne): one purpose of expression.

To apply old ideas to fresh instances, actualities—words to old maxims (*carpe diem*).

To apply fresh instances to old ideas.

To renew, refresh, and make concrete in the time ever-new, the traditional wisdom.

Harvard College freshman might be my Rodin; there, too, were hurt feelings; in the end; pride everywhere, springs in identity, springs in being-in-the-world.

An idiom is an idiot.

March 15

The duty of prose is to be a window.
The effort of poetry is to be a stained-glass window.

How blue the street is, just before the sun rises,
Blue-gray, I mean,
Shop windows are like cubic boxes

Suddenly the hot sun covers me, I see gold

Children like a cloud of grasshoppers—

I want to live, I want to travel, *I do not want to become a fountain pen*—

Sand-colored lions go stalking in's heart—

Panting and breathing hard, the runner halts—
Garbed in his shorts, he is a fantasy

The sun is the dress, orange through eyelids,
Dark red when closed more tightly—this, this,
This is supreme happiness, lying in the sun,
Breathing the scent of the flowers, having
Nothing to think, nothing to think, but feel—
Lion's grace, lion's ease, lion's pride and strength . . .

—Dear Pa, How are you, we are all just fine,
Henry is chopping wood in the back yard now,
Dicky is playing with the cat. The chickens
Are getting fat—

"Don't feel sorry for me: I am happy—"
"Like heavy weight it is, upon his mind."

Now Time and Space are two abstractions which
Are far from the warm breathing experience . . .

Perhaps I ought to make the foreign voice Hershey Green himself [the main character in *Genesis*]. This perhaps would justify the alternation—convinced that he is about to die, because of some great guilt, he begins to explain and confess.

We see in kings the wish for certain flags—
Face is a concept purely truly human—

A set of feelings bunched and bushed like grapes—
Our worldwide glances take in many stores—

The father is the superego, the conscious will is the ego, the instincts are the id, the unconscious is where the instincts are forced when suppressed by the id.

"Skinned, cleaned, and boned, the fish of the earth—"

Filled with fear, surrounded by ten thousand,
Dressed in splendid garments, crowned with a coronal
. . . And then my hair stands on end, my heart
Beats fast—

In 1935, I wrote down single words, and that was diction: discriminate, vice, the millionaire self, wound.
"When a child is born into a bourgeois family, he immediately falls heir to a vast number of contradictions growing out of the social order"; "Still more intense levels, higher plateaus."
To go, all of the evenings, from word to thing, from thing to word.

March 17

I lived by intuitions, like a bird . . .
And that was why—so brilliant and so sudden
Were such quick rays, I scorned all other ways

Being, in the hurly-burly, suddenly panicked

Among his head, where his perceptions sail,
Are like white columns, many highest values
COURAGE, JUSTICE, KINDNESS, PATIENCE, LOVE
FORGIVENESS, and FORBEARANCE
And though like titles on the pediments
Of great museums, also like captured lions
Noble in zoos and pacing nervously . . .

Among his head, these noble values shine
And shine upon each thing he looks upon . . .

Now let us criticize this boy's account
With all the well-known terms (Reversal here
And Recognition and some ideas' force
Lighting up many kinds of experience
Which might be looked at very differently—)

—A surface tension ripples on his face
Epiphenomena of the head's great force
And pressures submarine

The Charles lay like a quiet window—
And in the Dutch light I could see the dish
And see the green-black background porcelain-clear
A hard and harsh blue marble sky—

Leaves of light shine in the water's
Current, passing and pressing to an end
Octopus, Jack-in-the-Box, Polyp luminous
—Romantic effervescence there,
Sunlight and sea shine effervescence there—

March 18

The pain goes ringing through me like alarms!

All of this desperate vile aspiration
Can never have an end, Babel once more!

The cruelty of childhood! how they fly
At throats, how they would knock each other down
Just as a game! I can see ten of them
Sprawled over each other in mimic wire laced!
—And the girls try to imitate the boys!

More will than gift! yet will is itself a gift,
And learns so much, merely by fighting on
That, in the end, perhaps it has enough
To rise beyond the merely gifted boys!

March 19

She burned with an extravagant vitality
Exacting and delightful—a log fell from the fire
She went from the couch to put it back
Returned as if from a six months' absence—

April 1941, Hopkinson Award—lethal—deadly expanding bullet
into the brain—"Not entirely awake"—"storms of weeping"—

We who grew up *"entre deux guerres"*
First a great prosperity, and then
A great depression—have learned

The bland Horatian life of friendship
and wine
A Roman vigor—*la douceur Angevin*

A world of pure Extension—like an Aqueous Habitat.

March 21

The visiting fireman and in my book,
And I am not at all surprised and, never mind,
No matter, I don't care, *je m'en fiche*,
Long live musicians, teachers, poets, all
Who have no institutional stake in war—

If anyone says, Why? the answer is,
Why not?! thus to all ontologists—

We are the visiting firemen; from out of town,
From out of life—
And social needs are most,
And many things occur only because
There is a social need for them
(anti-Semitism,
Bathtubs, and singing lessons!)
Then too, is this,
The rich man's son is indolent and lax
Because his father's rich . . .
semenza
Consider your nature and your origin,
You were not born to live like the beast
But to seek out virtue,
virtue and knowledge—

(to Hershey at the very start)

Brothers, he said, who through a hundred thousand
Terrors have reached this ultimate West,
Do not deny to the brief vigil remaining

To your senses and to your quick-moving heart,
Experience of the peoples beyond the Sun,

Consider Mohammed, who preached a simple religion,
And did not make preposterous demands
Upon the mind's belief—tell this to W.
Who ruled his life by the creature-comfort
                    prinzeps—

March 23

"Adolescence, like a stained tablecloth . . ."

I type and standing see the letters leap
On the canary-yellow, becoming words—

Everything happens in the mind of God
. . . This news is thrilling and I hope it true!
It is like looking at the sky's round blue,
Blue within blue within blue and endlessly—

Brother . . . Doctor . . . titles have irony

The autos move with goggle-eyes dead white
And in the glasses of the wet streets draw
Pillar-like rays, slanting, which move with them,
The while the rain on tarpaulin makes cracks
Of sounds . . . Sounds of the grand city—

And Orpheus . . .
Alcestis, Lazarus, Eurydice
Returning from the dead
Acted in strange ways, not the strangeness
                    from
Such an event . . .
Water—crevic'd like an elephant hide

March 30

The brown fog of the three-day snow
The brown-white light of the Boston morning,
The sepia or tan above the blank bright snow
As in the photographs of 1916—

The leaping porpoises, serenely somersaulting,
The leaping fish, the tarpon struggling,
                  fighting like Samson
                  in the foreign air
Against the fisherman, gyrating, leaping,
Jumping and pulling, tortured and torn

. . . And now the tapping of the rain,
Last night, the velvet-black of the Charles,
Under the track of the ghastly rippled towers
Of the light fanned across the flows;
And chains of lights or lights chained to banks,

Repetition, reputation / flows and flaws
And flares and fleas of character,
(See, character begets an endless struggle,
Goodness is difficult, and at its peak,
Almost unbearable, it is hard to breathe:
See how morality is an endless struggle—)

The diddling dolls that Marcel Proust called up,
Aut Caesar, aut nullus, aut Charlus
(There, but for God's grace, I might be sprawled)
—Thesis / antithesis often compels
(Though knock-kneed Hegel was mechanical,
And William James laughed at the Hegelizers)
Because men are against some other men,
                because
The peak begets the plain, the seesaw's Up
Begets by strict necessity the Down—

Dives / Lazarus / hebetude, stupidity, /
Chthonic and Orphic / Fresh Flowers
And trusted doctors on the silver screen . . .
(To live *inside* some of the plays of Love).

Shoulders have irony; with shrugs perform!
Hobby is his survival. Metaphor is my salvation.

        A cool million or silver lining
        A royalty in person, in himself
        A genius bona fide every minute
        Born, Barnum: pure American
                King versus the Duke

March 31

Off and on, now and then, here and there: Alas!
Frays of the heart, phrase of the heart
Profound—
        the day gray as the thought
Of Eternity to young girls. The heart
Hanged like a stocking—

And now I have learned how to take my time, and how easy it is
to compose, as soon as one does not hurry and look to the end; character is this constant struggle; order and discipline I have now learned,
no longer wishing other occupations—
    I first tried to make notes of sayings seeming significant in Oct.–
Nov. 1931—the beautiful American word *Sure*—
    And first wrote in the morning a certain length in Bennington,
June 1938; with more regularity in Sept. 1939.

He had beside his bed a radio / rodeo / hi-de-ho /
And from distant cities danced and sang
And this, in part, began this monstrous night,
After he wrote the letter to the *Times*—
        Don't you know / Jericho /
Fog-colored dusk is on the famous river . . .
Skull-like creases or grooves (brain-like conformations)
What prowess now performs the aching pleasure
(Such as is sexual intercourse) of debut?

April 1

The sun breaks through the cloud like revelation
In long resistless parallels of strokes
Of whiteness and of curling areas
And the wind howls like a chained beast in pain,
And now I think of Coleridge, the friend
Whom I must most delight in, among the dead,
He knew the perils of philosophy—

And now, once more, I come upon an end,
Which might be, yet is not, full happiness

And S.T.C. knew that God was, he knew
How powerful the word, and the delights
Of endless conversation, and the cool
Autumnal beauties of abstraction pure
—He knew how drug seals up the self in sleep,
Sleep in which all is goodness, waking deep!

And all the crewmen seek activity,
But best of all the active mind finds all,
By making humble observations clear,
By following the self in all the fugues,
The joyous days when every line seems good,
The grayness in which Shakespeare, too, is poor—
The boredom of the plane was overhead,
And one red light was flying on the wing—

The sun shone like significance itself,
A dazzling glory on the threaded Charles—
A glorying incandescence in the air,
A whiteshot splendor which cannot be viewed—
And now the river seems a crater's mouth,
Such lava flows are dizzying in it—

The salt sensuality of maudlin tears,
Looking up at the depthless sky for God!
—The light is pure as flame or candlelight
Where the sun is near, but orange down,
Near the horizon where the crew is striving . . .

. . . In me forsaken possibilities
Like corpses on a brand-new battleground—
The bird was arrow, feather, arrow then,
A cinder blown by the wind
                                    curving—
Light. Light. Unspeakable light is blazing

The gray grows silver in the dusk. Solid
Against the twilight-lake sky, solid-black
Become the houses . . . River, flowing carpet,
Children, star skaters; silver screen, magnet—

Where lightning bolts like carrots grew . . .
And obelisks and eyes, upon the bridge—

Ambition and remorse: between these two
Who falls in time? and looking back and forth—

Without crying or striving—supreme over self,
Becoming as a little child, all humility—

The taillight goes away—a moving poppy,
Still on the bridge, is the still red button—

The Kingdom of Heaven is within you,
It is gained by taking in, transforming—

Disjecta membra / clabber milk
And in the Milky Way, ontologies . . .

*[Lew Ayres, portrayer of a young German soldier in the pacifist
film* All Quiet on the Western Front *(1930), became famous later
as the young Dr. Kildare in a series of nine films. He was a conscientious objector in World War II.]*

Lew Ayres, let me explain and also cry
An Admiration: if all were but like you
Even the Nazis . . . Yet in the nation's mind
You have portrayed the young and able doctor
(A man of action and a man of science,
A doctor, sacred priest in our society)
—This is why this will cut to the quick
The national mind. And from Hollywood,
That you could thus reject such fame and fortune,
Because of a belief deny the world,
Affirm goodness as a necessity!
You are like Lindbergh now, a fallen hero;
But you shall rise again, the phoenix-mind
In passionate histories which I will write—

April 2
"Opening the beer will always be an adventure, won't it?" said
Gertrude to me.
Use Charles as Hudson—then use all river images of past month;
crew as Columbia crew—students, activity; Hudson as nature, pre-
carious as water or Zeppelins; [Harvard] Business School as G.W.H.S.
[George Washington High School]—Georgian red brick, white trim.

Goodness is difficult
And, at its peak, almost unbearable!
The air is hard to breathe, the climb almost
A cliff, and looking down brings vertigo
Also disgust and hatred—

—With what variety man goes to hell!

O Sun of Nature! source of all the forces,
All fleurs, all snakes, and Botticelli's views
Of both of these and Venus—

"With cheerful optimism our little Columbus descended into the vast uncharted waste—then stopped, stepped, slipped, and slid."

Give it two more minutes, viz. *The Gold Rush*: the Little Fellow, later two overcoats, bantam tramp, with battered derby hat, flapping shoes, jaunty bamboo cane, absurd small mustache, jaunts along the rim of a ledge unknowingly trailed by a big black bear, as in *The Circus*.

Innocent waddle, peculiar childlike kick, and desperate elegance. Ends up as a magnate with two fur coats, wears one on top of the other. The noble type, and Georgia! Big Jim, a notable heavy.

Many sentences worth renewing and using—in the journal for December, January, and February.

I carried and opened this attitude like an umbrella. I climbed the stairs on hands and knees, and looked down and saw the pearls of a necklace at the bottom (must go down again) and the remains of a gay party: many more like that, and should be introduced.

An image is necessary to bring the seizure; and different ones all the time: apply this to poetry.

> The harsh crowing of the triumphant cock!
> Rich vain intolerable Great Britain,
> —And all the latest Marys, mongering
> Here is a souvenir of Life, a stone—
> Plane like a box kite flew, and looked like sticks—

The subject matter of ballet is walking or, in general, bodily movements and all that they may portend—

April 3

> I turned the corner; there I saw two girls
> Wearing their parents' hand-me-down looks—
>
> And on the scenic railway, have I not seen
> Delirium and romance sought out as hours
> —And going down they screamed at the abyss,
> And going up they laughed in their relief,
> Gathering strength of emotion for the next—
>
> What solo flights great egotism knows
> A boredom of a plane is overhead:
> To these superiorities, man has arisen—
>
> And let your Jack-self fix the broken lamp
> (Absorption makes you suck at your underlip—)

And let your girl-self come with witty sayings
And foremost gaiety, as wild as birds—

The Gothic railroad bridge / the Victorian mansion,
And in the mansard roof the dormer windows—

And now a school of birds, in V-flight flying
And now the new self—prose-verse self found deep,
By working all day long, and not by pages:
This mastery, profession, and a life—

But hold the anger and resentment down,
It is from the body come, and from an end,
A relaxation: but not to be controlled . . .
And now the test, to type all afternoon—
Less easy than to fly through isolated
And not bound-up and tied perceptions . . .

April 4

    I pace up and down a room, just as my father did. This could be
the same kind of body and nervous system—

The moment
The lights go on at the surprise party
—The Armistice when all burst out
                  suddenly singing
—All the voices, quick on the
                  trigger
Quick on the uptake
              quick as a bird-
Man like a shadow on the grass—

I sun myself upon some complex hopes
(Playing experiments on the nerves' harps)
—Who knows how long one can try on this way,
Wine and the simple straight act of attention—

My faculties with each other striving
Help to draw the grand piano up
Up to the fifty-fifth floor—How I will play from there
A rhetoric of memory and forgiveness—

Navy wives: occupational marriages
And all the industry of daily life—

The first green shoots come up like small knives
Pale green, fresh, and young green
                    (all else gray and wooden)
[. . .]
The poor Negro at whom balls are thrown
Upon the boardwalk (what an accuracy—)
The dog racing throws his forelegs back,
His backlegs forward, his forelegs forward then
It looks like dancing sticks from start to finish

Pell-mell and helter-skelter, the wind blowing
The leaves in autumn,
                    like a bad conscience,
Let out the night air, like an old love,
—Freshen the bedroom . . .

    The rhythm of the paragraph I know; the rhythm of the sentence
I know, too; one is a stanza, the other is a line.
    Diction: In any particular use of a word, there is a predication of
the usual meanings with the particular unique state of affairs or
experience. This makes originality and discovery often possible—

        I will grow beans, I will also grow grapes
        —Never mind Fame; but observation is
        The human life divine. The Stagirite
        Said this and said it well long long ago—

April 5

    O Life is wonderful, beyond belief!
    —And when I think of it I have to laugh!
    Earth! Air! Water! and through all them, Fire!
    Memory and Remorse, Ambition and Desire!

    —The waters' muscles rippling, the Sunday look
    Of all the strolling peoples—

The high cheekbones of Wendy Hiller,
The fat man (Morley), his belly far ahead of him,
Or in his walk too much equilibrium—
The lean accordion cleverness of Harrison,
And Bernard Shaw, ever outsmarting himself—
(*Major Barbara*)

The railroad bridge, the Sunday park, the dusk
Of early spring, the Bullfinch fronts,
The limestone mansions and the red-brick mansions
Of Beacon Street, fallen on shabby days—
Life, Look, Click, Spark, and other shines,
Part of the technique which has carried off
Private life to the suburbs—

April 7

A slight inversion of the word order, the phrasing, or the sentence structure can express, or turn to (as on an n-side polygon) another side of the subject, experience, attitude, or actuality.

The dawn came. Came the dawn. I am putting in the mail N.P.'s novel; N.P.'s novel . . .

And still more true, much more true and rich in diction.

The poplars stood like tall guards, attentive / at attention / holding rifles up.

Junior Orestes, as I said before!

Children by Papa and by Mama / In all the senses.

Double consonants always make different syllables which get one strong accent: rock, type, flock, as against buy, no (cp. with know), striking, taking. Fire, power, hour, and desire are other special cases.

A cool colding freshness, like that of coming to the seashore, moves in through late afternoon in this provincial capital, where once America arose, in Emerson, Thoreau, Hawthorne, and Melville (Whitman was elsewhere and Emily Dickinson was later), and the brothers James and Adams were after the war, with Ryder, Winslow Homer, and Eakins.

And he disseminated far and wide; and knew as much as others of that age group. And with their bare thighs they sought for fame / help from their hips / their bosoms as coin o' the realm.

Oraison: Lincoln, by this word I show my own doubt of his words.

Her lips were a broken pear, her bust, open,
A secret Princess long at a convent school withdrawn—

We live between two infinites, small and big
For neither one need one give any fig—

The fourth month since the twenty-eighth birthday,
And one since I again began to finish—

A winter fireside, candles at four o'clock,
Tea and warm hearth rugs, the shutters closed,
The curtains flowing, the wind and rain in drives
Audible coldly outside—(with such cold sounds)
(Images of the comfort of the creature)
(De Quincey's idea of perfect bliss)

In lucid verse, how an attitude is in the body and in an arrangement of the nervous system ought to be explained; whatever the state of affairs beyond the body, different of such attitudes are possible —Not Dolly, Dali; not girl, girdle.

I have arrived, in style, at a greater degree of concreteness and organization and composition in versification.

This is the question to be asked. Is it in some way composed? Does it present some perception?

Filene's: Built on Value, Growing on Values.

How are values created? By use, by need, by shifts in circumstance.

Consciousness (in this moment of the circle) is seen once more as phenomenal: the two brown chairs seen by Mutt and Jeff, not the third one, of Einstein (of Whitehead, of Eddington, brimming with energy and movement, full of holes). And Time and Space are merely forms of the mind. Are only necessary conditions of experience. Now I must reread my Kant synopses.

Too long I admired excellence of surface and diction. More important is centrality, relevance, penetration. [Marianne] Moore's New York is a librarian eye's view. Dreiser's, or Dos Passos's is not; cp. D.P. with W. C. W[illiams]. The two elements to be unified.

To stop a man, to make him lose his face,
His pride before a girl, not to permit
A chance to laugh it off—is infamy
Infamous are assistants true or false

Committees are a special thing (like all else); and when one starts to speak, he clears his throat, and seeks a new tone, and a more formal one. Then there is group laughter, when something is said by the chairman.

Id est, if he is important. Genevieve Mayer wrote of a blade of grass forcing its way between cobblestones, taking a man back to conquered France (conquered in ten days).

Marcia Zacherer wrote of a prince who took a young man to the mountains to guard a prisoner. The prisoner turned out to be Misery. A soldier came, bringing messages and food; then stopped coming. The prisoner became friendly. War was going on below the timberline. The young man grew up during this time. At last, the prisoner was asked his name.

The stars are still shining, said Bosola to the Duchess after she damned the stars.

How long does it take for a holiday to wear out? How far from the dungeon or treadmill of daily life can it go? Even now I find three days a week almost not enough to make a holiday of the remainder.

But I must free myself of this wrong division, work and holiday. Constant activity and constant observation, constant passage from word to thing, from thing to word, is what is necessary.

I looked down on Cambridge, but hardly saw it: the statue standing upon the statue of Lincoln, the green worn out, the stone benches, the diagonal walks, the young wives with their baby carriages; the traffic of cars and of the orange bus.

By working at night, I gain the critical view of the lapses.

They (Wohlstetter and Ragin) quoted you, said R., with praise and snickers. Did they, I said, last I heard was that we were both irrational, but you were the talented of the two. Ben Nelson's face leaped and broke open in amazed laughter.

"No generalization is wholly true, not even this one"—O. W. Holmes.

Dante's *Paradiso* is white on white on white—like a bowl of white tulips in the spring—Holmes.

Giotto was a usurer, in Florence. Later, Picasso owned a Rolls-Royce or Citroën.

All literature is an effort at the formal character of the epigram. [Thomas] Sturge Moore [English poet] is a sheep in sheep's clothing. [A. E.] Housman had savage epithets prepared in advance, the names still blank.

Picasso: Her father drinks, her mother drinks, and she has a red nose.

Man invented the alarm clock.

I hear the cars go sighing on the Drive.

Harvard, home of "the nervous breakdown."

Various American heroes, Lindbergh, Chaplin, the Prince of Wales, Babe Ruth, have now been known—

April 9

Barnum, another true American (one born every minute).
Cold violet April twilight—

April 10

Robert Fulton and Samuel Morse, both artists first, inventors after.
Signs of the *Zeitgeist* traveling through the heart.

> A fog or smokiness upon the snow
> At dusk . . . the April snow, as in January
> The sunset turns it pink— The pebble sounds
> Of rain against the window, or the roof
> Of the frame house / *aut Caesar, aut Nullus,*
> So the ego cries

These works are not only the only works I "care to preserve," but
what a Philistine, what a stupid fool and pedant is the publisher and
editor who disregards this revision.

April 11

"The power of development made Shakespeare what he was; he
had many imperfections"—Chambers, *EB* [*Encyclopaedia Britannica*].
"I must have the strength of humility to say of myself many
times, This is bad, this is a sin or crime. Only striving and correction
can help, yet not to despair."
"*Blessing and Damnation*: title of a book of poems—"
Bible's fecundity in its long vari-uses.
Kipling had many imitators: nothing has come of this.
Yeats has had good imitators; troubled by Kipling, a younger
man or contemporary.
Gide could not stand [Francis] Jammes's vanity.

> Those afraid to go home, that evening will end—
> Now drunkenness mounts in my hide and now
> My mind dances with all the memories
> And I have gone to get the nourishing
> Thus to prolong the pleasure and activity

> Dickens and Dostoevsky were editors—Balzac—
> Shakespeare a manager, Dante a politician
> (I will be editor and politician
> Before I die . . . but father most of all
> Drinking with my intelligent and handsome sons—)

Sleep was to Tessa [Horton] a sensuality (her bed).

The port, held to the light, is crimson silk—
The oars of crews make wing angles, rowing.

Imagination when the evening comes
Tells and paints glowing ten or more attractions
Diversions, and distractions which bring Joy
—The silver screen, the friend, the game,
(How in my script, two years of Greek live on)
The novel or the bowling alley's clicks
(Shall I go there tonight, not Dickens read
Who is so large, says Wilson, almost Avon's
Great height (desiring this man's gift, and that
Man's scope and hope) who might teach much,
And give much joy (he also had bad taste,
Was maudlin, and, says Wilson, "Pretty bad
Are the short stories shoved in *Pickwick Papers*")

Going up the stairs is slower and more labored, of course, than going down the stairs.

Different sounds and individual sounds, Harry and Elena [Levin].

David was one who sent away a man to be killed in order to know his wife; Baudelaire wrote immature novels as a young man, Eliot wrote "The Rock." Jacob tricked Esau.

Pain and humiliation go away with the succession of many new scenes, whether painful or not.

Although there is nothing like a new pain of the mind to make one forget the old, the principle of digging nails into flesh.

The old pains come back especially during tiredness and lapses; but they are weaker and sooner overcome.

If I could make the mind's notes like this when in company; I would not star, but what I would carry with [me], a constant aria: what is the name of this and that—

To express anything is to free it not only from not being known but from personal experience, personal distortion, the limited point of view of anyone at any moment.

The phrase "barbarous beauty," in *CAHM* [*Coriolanus and His Mother*, a play in verse, was included in Delmore's first book, *In Dreams Begin Responsibilities*] must have come from [Charles] Williams's preface to [Gerard Manley] Hopkins, quoting H.'s "barbarous in beauty"; so, too, the Frost echo, "And left me no recourse, far from my home," especially as repeated; and there, too, the Eliot "Burnt Norton."

Give me poetry and strength of character, give me strength, goodness, and knowledge, give me humility and indifference (freedom
from remorse) from my own sins and from all that is said against me.

April 12

If I can, every year, see my shortcomings of two years back—

A story or novel: modeled on *Measure for Measure* or other
Elizabethan plays.

> The fantasy and horror of the circus,
> The crude coarse cruelty, the grace and roar,
> The lion and the whip of reason, dressed
> In a black top hat, notable and formal
>
> —The girls upon the horses, fat and white
> Lolloping deceived and insensitive,
> And marvelous the walker at the top,
> And like a doll and dead bowing to deals
>
> And deals of long loud loving applause
> Almost hysterical and stripped of all
> Secular attitudes and daily life
> —Neurosis is objective in the ring,
>
> Him in the top hat all perforce admire,
> He, he alone can keep the lions taut:
> They bulge upon the face of child and nurse,
> And the frank smell hangs like August heat—
>
> While cool and dry as autumn light abides
> Depth under depth like many Troys denied—
> A noble temple like some mornings clear,
> Beyond the circus and beyond the Turk . . .
>
> The temple never downed, once truly seen!
> The master of the master of the ring,
> Living forever in the heavy head,
> And making laughter for the tumbling clown,
>
> . . . And giving to the bearded lady, white-
> Armed Hera's capital, and to the acrobats
> Giving of balance such an example
> All others are eccentric! criticized . . .
>
> Let me return now in a simpler mode:
> The circus is the sickness in a tent
> Of the old child and of the modern city,
> Regard and judge and having judged move on!
> Judge and judge quickly or you turn to stone! [Alternate]

Farinata, as if he entertained great scorn of hell, cried out, Who were your relatives? Inferno X.

Is my son dead? asked Cavalcanti.

"The Star-Spangled Banner" impenetrates my childhood and schooldom. Played at Lewisohn Stadium in 1926 and 1927.

Jane Austen's Mr. Bennett: For what do we live but to make sport for our neighbors and to laugh at them in our turn?

Institutions give security, but then tyranny and insecurity.

Streamers between the clouds, lakes of light, capes of cloud, ribbons, curls, flakes, and continents of cloud.

> I am striped with good and evil like a giraffe!
> Still will I eat the flowers of highest trees
> And gain a monstrous neck by aspiration
> And let the laughs, awkward and dignified—
> Accepting
> Run, stop, hop, jump, O agile mind,
> Until the pole vault with the breakneck trial
> And then—midair!—with equanimity,
> Gaze on the new event with a bland smile.

> I was by white-black wintry sunset mixed
> With several kinds of weak light. Yet I rose
> And in the black dusk with electric light
> Denied all nature reading Leibnitz's prose—

Although there is a ceiling of purple cloud almost all over, at the western end of the sky a yellow ragged window abides.

A story: The Man with the Frigid Wife.

> Waltz music bringing easy sentiments
> And pleasant ones, Vienna fabulous,
> Adultery as innocent as cake . . .
> I look at the *EB* and see, depressed,
> How much I will go to the grave and hardly know . . .

> This ride will not last long, as I well know,
> And yet I dissipate this height of faculties . . .
> —Make many notes, find many metaphors,
> But hardly make a poem. And yet I will
> The temporal method brings a patient search—
> (But lose to anger, freedom being denied)
> Negroes and Jews are barred, the paper said—
> Listen to everything and then *decide*—

Bay window and false teeth keep Venus far
And thinning temples (how the light
Swirls lightning-white upon bathwater greens)
(Lines I compose, but not in stanza forms—)

Plato saw structures as the cause of things
Because they were the cause of knowledge. But
The Stagirite, having the pupil's benefit,
Saw natures *vivant* in particulars—
Biology surpassed geometry—
Later, the whole world fell to Alexander
And Caesars more mature, more powerful,
And in this aftermath, the sensitive
Decide to retreat to attitudes
Which would console defeat, deny despair—
(Pagliacci cuckold on the glowing air)
Ja! das ist ganz richtig! said the Duke:
Love and anonymity presided there—

April 13

Far off the locking and unlocking oars
—Who comes? It is not Christ. Go back to sleep—

The quick wires of intelligence—

Low stir of leaves; dip of oars—

One o'clock. A rainy night.
The sea air darkens on the wheelhouse
The binnacle glows (the dashboard glows,
                as the country night flows by)

A hunger for experience—

The moonlight seemed only "to make the coldness
                visible"—

Life is what a man is thinking all the day,
each is his own private theater—

Light & space, one boat and easy seas—

The only armor, the only shield, Humility—

To be good is an activity—

Moonlight, he says, was leaking ice, dripping ice.

O try to see the past as its own present
The very latest thing, and looking forward
Disdainful of the years before—

The concrete details immediately provide a fertile ground for
the significance of the symbol: thus, ending a story with a symbol.
In fiction, broad strokes, the secular sacrament, company, love, fame,
striving, humiliation.

A symbol is one thing which stands for another thing and
explicates it: the Cross. A metaphor is the bringing together of two
or more things, one to explicate the other: an ox sits on my tongue.

The object is to be as brief as possible, not as copious: in the
end, it is one book, *Collected Poems*.

What a remarkable find (what a *trouvaille*)
—The lady seen by Mutt is not in view,
The lady seen by Jeff—
Even a dentist would have found this one
Phlegmatic! —The lady seen by Don Quixote
Is not the lady

April 14

Surge on surge on surge is riding in
. . . I have a point of view, I have a room
With a most various and fluent view
—The river now all crinkled like tinfoil—
There where the light a hundred thousand times
Is fanned, or through a turning fan reflashed—
—River now hilly with wave ripples—

April 15

Behold, the parachutist, floating down,
—Here individuality may gauge itself,
And looking up upon the floating drawers
Amid which, like a stamen, the person waits
Passive as rocks, and feeling rather silly
. . . The moral is too obvious for words—

—After he wrote his letter, three days passed
Deliberately. He made Time be his reason
—And then he sent it off: it was the same,
The heart never suppressed, no matter what—

Good will, at least, is a most pleasant thing
In many times, intoxicating joy
To give another one a gift delighting
The satisfaction was another's face—
To be good will's long player: this is well—

Ode to Henry Ford, Somerset Maugham, Bertrand Russell, Lew
Ayres, Babe Ruth, Carl Hubbell, Marianne Moore—

The trap and racket of the plane flew by
—The dashboard glows, the country night flows by

An impossible fusion, squaring the circle—

And all the students gone, like last week's snow—

Everything is measured by the distance from love.
And good will is a most delightful dance—
Discovered himself as one discovered America,
And lost himself as much as maidenhood—

She was no Christian, but surrealist—

The best thing about teaching is that one learns so much oneself;
especially well the texts, such as Shakespeare.

Supreme belief is a captivity—
Willingly—
Objective and subjective, two sides (or poles)
Of the same coin, Experience—

The nature of things is so interrelated that an agile interpreter
(like Burke) can find anything everywhere and anywhere—Marianne
Moore, profound librarian—

Poetry is unexpected and just predication.
"The Chariot" has in it a transformation of the everyday. Why
does the grain gaze?

Yeats's "A Prayer for My Daughter" has too many personal references, e.g., to Maud Gonne; other poems, too.

"Dover Beach" and "The Concurrence of the Twain" should be compared.

> Poetry, Goodness, Knowledge, Sleep
> O Lord, have mercy—
>
> Behind the scenes, appearance nudged
> Reality—
> And April dark blue skies
> Quick-moving—
>
> My heart like an accordion is pressed,
> Groaning! groaning and straining torn
> And unintelligible emotions—

I've learned more from teaching than I ever did from being taught.

He said (David Levine [caricaturist]), Look at the Bride, and think—

You talk too much, she said, give someone else a chance, and mind your own business.

> All mortal things are subject to decay
> And when Fate summons, southpaws must obey
> One ball game does not make a summer
> . . . A soft feather orange in the Western sky
>
> The poplar stood like a rifle and
> Stickiness was on the curved-tip buds—
>
> I wrote a hundred thousand poems one night
> —Not one of them was good—
>
> I wrote a poem which, read a hundred times,
> Revealed new actualities—
>
> An upraised hand, forking to the sun
> The tree, which does not psychologize—
>
> Who is it who has come to say, All
> That I know, I know
>   by suffering only
> The worst despair—

And all the clouds are abstract, in a sense
Nature may imitate; but it invents
Upon the sky's great canvas constantly,
And this, perhaps, is quite enough to see

—A great and curving wing, long purple-black
Composed upon the sky above the sun
Going down orange, yellow, orange
In a smear . . .

(This kind of flow might be a new variation of blank verse.)

Teaching can be self-indulgence—
The teacher dominates the scene—

I am a bird who can sometimes fly high; this is the only reasonable view.

The jigsaw conformations of the skyline.

She came into my life as if she were to take a book from the mantel and dust it.

"Do not touch! Fresh Paint!"

"Smoking Dogs and Love Prohibited."

Dante looked like a three-week hangover; Jonson fat; Shakespeare short.

April 16

When William Guggenheim died, he left his money to three chorus girls. It then became difficult to decide whether the chorus girls were Guggenheim Fellows or the Guggenheim Fellows were chorus girls.

The Giants are trailing 2–1; I think they are going to win. Hp! Hp! And Ott has just hit a homer!—tying the score.

She came into my life as one might come from a rainy October's day.

Dusted the books on the mantel, removed the dead flowers from the vase.

Verbalizing attention plus temporal attention. I tried a more extended prehension than most, eclectic. Naming is beginning, power flows from it, repetition and combination, freedom from abstractness, yet ease with generality.

In "The Journey," an outline of ten incidents would serve to unify. Prehension cut here and there by ambition, forcing, and inspiration.

An attention which all the time reads and then sings.

The mountain of form, the story in which the experience is mounted and surmounted.

The silent private detective and the separated wife might provide the dramatic movement, even melodrama; this and the death of the boy Stanley. The denouement would be a revelation and breakdown of the different families and the being of the apartment house. They refuse to help the young married woman. The scene and then this dialogue, not to forget Metro-Goldwyn-Mayer. Would it be possible to bring the landlord into the picture at the end?

Necessary to make the analysis grow into a scene; not be entirely [past], but leading to a scene. Perhaps attempt the point of view of a girl for the first time: Jenny. The Kramers, the Rochesters, the Foxes, the Lazlos, with the little girl who has convulsions.

Devices of primitivism and repetition, as [in Gertrude] Stein, also possible as a rhythm and movement: the divorce laws of New York State. These characters are unimportant, except that there are millions of them in the big cities of America.

April 17

From the fifty-fifth story I will cry out loudly,
Say, Pedestrians, what are your thoughts?
Say, Muse, the cause of Love and War

. . . Silence, you are the best I ever heard—
That is, after such shock and thunder—
And sorrow

Anything for texture, and this for long was a criterion—consider, on the other hand, Dryden, plain and clear and quick. Psychology is best of all, however.

Wine in the South, and in the North
Whiskey, and on the Rhine, brown beer—
Rum for the sailor, rye for the farmer boy
—Oh, how conditions are our deities!

The lovers like great scissors lay—
And yet I must forgive, and yet in mind
Bear ever . . . Allen married the great
Author who had had four before he came—

Fame, O relation between work and the Age,
Steinbeck, Dreiser, Dickens—
Enough
Of cowardice, enough revenge, for soon
All will be ripe—and how much luck you had—
—The coxswains' Reason and the rest a body—

H.L. [Harry Levin] There can be no friendship where there is rivalry. And yet, the nature of the magazine . . .

Toynbee surveyed the genesis of twenty-one civilizations, and found no laws?

Is it possible that surplus value could come from nature itself, given the proper arrangements?

> The river like a suite was gray and on,
> —Or brick or stone or frames of wood,
> Materials which grip—and in the midst
> Sun, air, adjoining houses, city life—
>
> And like one with a hoop or bicycle
> He walked—

Is it not all, this glorification of the air, a theme with variations, or a theme next to a theme, or both? Like air blown out, all science.

April 18

> The rain like pitchforks fell, this is a trope
> Vividest, now I turn to think it through:
> Suggests, the rain like nails fell, silver-gray,
> Or spears—
>
> The shaven hairs were like quotation marks,
> Marriage is full of new and special news
> Most educational is suffering,
> But equally, serene indifferent joy
> Through different symbols, different airs,
> Like flames, all souls aspire,
>   blessed or damned—
>
> Music, glorying active charming air
> Air and fire and form—blooming with will
> Pacified

Two motions, extreme concreteness or extreme generality, vivid description or bearing on the nature of things—

> Critics, scavengers, and men in white—
> Not to forget burning intelligence—
>
> Brutality and smugness in him ride—
> (Forgive, you are no better, most of the time)

The poetry of wine will never end,
But as for me, I have—this is, I think,
The source of the successes, if, in fact,
It was not luck!?—a different light
And more important light, psychologizing!
Better than texture! and imagination
Seen in the act of making forms for itself—

What slops of feeling from the wine had come,
—What maudlinness! (Psychology will live
Long as the pyramids)

Well, Love and Fame are themes to win the crowd
And pass across the generations quickly—

—Atomic movement is smaller than discs
On which Caruso peals; yet is it all
The atoms crowding, bunched or scattered,
Crowding to snow or to a rain dispersing—
The fire disperses them, and they fly up
The cold makes them unite and they are ice,
Or earth— Here I rehearse the thoughts
Of all the pre-Socratics—

—O singular disjunction, in all Love:
Forked is each soul, twin-legged and lost
"In the labyrinth of another's being—"
I wrote, Calhoun, as well as Esau: uncle!

April 19

The calculated disarray of the garage region, the railroad yards, and the used-car lots. The painted lines of the bridge, the murals of the fences.

"Our country is now at war . . ." said the announcer over the public-address system. Directions for going away, and hiding under the grandstand or bleachers.

Much feeling against Stengel and Paul Waner. The Giants scored three in the first. Mize hit the wall twice with doubles, thinking the first time that he had hit a homer. Melton argued with the umpire in the first, Witek looked pathetic, Tobin disgusted. Werber had a rooting section loudly against him.

A purple-black curtain of cloud, like a quilt or like a great Assyrian army with chariots, was over the sky. The crowd was pleased that the Red Sox had defeated the Yankees.

A strong wind blowing, much smoke, much soot from the railroad yards, the fragrancy of Pittsburgh. I admired the strength of the locomotive, the instruments (what are the names?), pistons, which drew up and down, and moved the wheels. So, too, a child might be given a toy railroad train, Industrialismus.

At the Manhattan, moral research, one after another; in May, the most fecund month.

The dusk is wondrous gray and will not fade until the night itself is full of black.

Johnny Eager, Robert Taylor, again the wicked gunman discovers the strong appeal of goodness, and with his gun destroys himself for the girl's sake: "What's his angle?"

Quixote: They were amazed at the wisdom and frenzy of the man.

"O austere limestone!" other materials with which
We alter space and inform place, and live—

O may I write a *Walden* of the city life!
Living alone a year in the great city—

O in the cause of it behold the news,
The course and running of the secret change—

April 20

Oh, an indestructible poem—and soul— "He rushes after facts like a novice on skates and a novice moreover who is practicing in a forbidden place—"

"Beneath a veneer of calm"; "Beat the drums of the mind"—

Perhaps one ought to have a time limit plus a page limit, thus to prevent diffusion, bring about concentration.

Faint shifting spirals of the light's towers on the waters of the Charles.

I brush my teeth now several times a day,
Ten years ago and fifteen years ago
This was a task my mind would set my will
And fail, fail utterly, after the first day
—To sleep at ten, to do the schoolwork soon,
To read all Shakespeare and the Bible through
How many times I pledged myself to these
And with relaxed relief postponed, put off,

Promised for the next month or year
—But now my will is like a long pencil,
It must be sharpened, but upon the desk
It waits, I am a son of David now,
And of attention now, and I have found
Nothing better than the "attentive will"

Rhythm and metaphor become my hands,
This is the kind of thing which makes a man—

Romance extends actuality, realism examines it, there is no need
to choose.

World-citizen, attention is diffused,
And you, provincial character, I think
Lack generality and wide horizons,
Your garden is beneath the timberline,
Beneath the level of the sea—

There can be no transformation of reality where there is no
imitation of reality: minute attention.

There are new kinds of feeling. They are wine.
Name them like wines after some places—
I am myself from way back a New Yorkist
And that Tiberius of Washington Heights
Knew how I felt about his younger sister—
She giggled then, this is a natural sound
And Winters does not understand Laforgue
And Eliot, in this, that the self-consciousness
Marks a beginning of morality
—See in the later Eliot the later stages—

April 21
*[There is a dated reference to Delmore's receiving in the mail
photographs of his seven-month-old niece, Sandra Schwartz. But
whether the following poem was written as early as 1942 is uncertain.]*

Poem for Sandy
Hello, Sun and Moon! how is Stars?
Sandy, I saw you twenty-six years ago, and you
were pretty then,

And you were beautiful. I told your father that
fifteen years ago.

Hello, Sandy, how is your father, how is your mother,
how is my niece?

Look in the mirror and see the pretty girl!

I told your father fifteen years ago, Chicken on
the car and the car can't go: that is how you spell Chicago!

How is stars and how is Sandy? I say you first
twenty-six years ago,

And you were beautiful and like a star: I told
your Papa that.

I am 3,000 miles away and as near as your father
and mother,

By thinking I can do that, little girl,

For I am speaking to you, Sandy, this is your old
uncle,

He looks like a lion and a lamb, both at once.

April 22

Laval said yesterday, France has served the intelligence for her
pleasure and her glory; she must now serve it for her salvation.

And to the colonies he said, You will remain French.

[Archibald] MacLeish, speaking on the same day, said nothing of
the kind, joked about being a poet and about newspapermen, was
dignified by being director of the office of facts and figures.

In New Jersey, schoolchildren have been growing hysterical about
name bands, a film star, and General MacArthur.

Shifting factors make possible the renewal of the struggle for
power.

Gatsby and Isabel Archer are to be compared, two noble innocents and two romantics.

Knowledge, to be really known, must engage the whole being:
Hippocrene, fuselage, annealed, echelon, querulous.

Do these words penetrate their subject? Do they add anything
to our knowledge and experience of it?

Do they do more than display a rich sense of language?

"So we beat on, boats against the stream, borne back ceaselessly
into the past."

In G[*enesis*], is there not the return to the epic? And also the
benefits of empiricism in the images and metaphors?

Shame (O Grandeur and Misery of Socialism) that there is [in]
the great city no other physical sign of our hope than Central Park,
where many make love, and dead-end Caesars learn their own cate-
gorical imperative.

I woke at midnight and I saw the world
—The belfry threw the chains of bell sounds out
Wave on wave on wave; the Common's plot
Triangulated by the asphalt walks
Held in the center Lincoln as a man
Standing upon a lesser general
(A hideous Victorian pleonasm)
On which a declaration was inscribed—

The college buildings in their red-brick style
And on them decorative strange *Veritas*
... Not only is Virtue its own reward
It is its own weakness, danger, and loss—

April 23

Sonnet

I try to understand the powers-that-be
And sing them with an inner-outer truth
And sing of them seeing them in my life
This is religious, is it not? Causality
Is fascinating-dark like a new myth
I ask, Who brought me here and wonder why
My forebears brought me forth
The twenties' influence swelled a natural-evil pride
And if Prosperity had longer lasted, or
In the first thirties my father had not died,
Who then would be my wife? what my career?
The inner quality would be the same
I would [be]
By many bored, by many hurt, by some
Moved to these very thoughts: what gods are near?
What forces and laws possess the sum?
When will I understand? when will God come?

Poem

Who is this actress of childhood with whom I have lived?
Like a nursery rhyme she is immortal,
Poor thing! who plays the child with no false note,
Moving between her age and eight years old—

Felix qui potuit rerum cognoscere causas

Of every child the fusing paradigm
Immortal as a nursery rhyme

Not the child, but the child enacted!

This year, *Shenandoah*; next year, *Genesis, Book One*; the year
after that, *Genesis, Books Two and Three*, or the Short Novel, and / or
the Imitation of Life.

—A blonde in a roadster drove up to the building
Her nose was smudged and her hair fake gold
(Like Housman's Heine), and her curly-haired man
Kissed her as she fixed her collar and with white
Silk veil did something, who knows what—

The lotus of temptation

Only connect, only discriminate
—For Life is dual and opposite and, as Yeats says,
Antithetical, and this reminds me
(Nelson Rockefeller looks like that fellow
I saw at F.O.M.'s, M. Abrams)

Too much little, too little much: Lo, here
Behold how life is form, proportion, grace,
Matter by structure mastered, or the chaos
—And in *The N.Y. Times* my picture made
Two girls write letters to me: I forget,
Girls feel the opposite of what boys do,
Hearing of promiscuity, plurality
Too much sunlight, or too little sunlight,
The golden mean is in biology
And in the soul. How wine gives me great ease
In writing on and on! Soon I must try
A story in this light, shining from vines!

The molten and the radiance flow west,
The cars, torpedo forms, also flow west,
It is the evening, sunlight, sunset, dusk
Evening of humanism and free will

The sunlight is the first of warmth, and last
—The gull flaps three times and then a straight line
Holds. Motion for motion's sake, on the Drive
(The pediment, like a three-cornered hat,
Rose from the eighteenth century's Enlightenment,
and Neoclassic Georgian style a while)

Far off, a part of the landscape is Mt. Auburn's
Graves, the grave of James
—Two ducks staccato in the flowing Charles
And near the radiance of the setting sun
A light suitcase and a portable
Will go with me, no matter where I go

I use myself up with smoke and wine,
And the heart does the bumps all by itself
But seen today, whence once a tic arose
Which certainly perplexes some of my boys
—Often through wine faces are vivid-grotesque

All that I do not know stands, a row
—The *EB* on my bookcase as a skyline
That photo too will fade, America's Auden
Quickly faded, under other impressions
This year has seen fame spreading like a stain

—Feats of the will I do, having wine's strength
Gertrude in stocking'd feet romps on the lawn
Then standing in the draft, I caught a sneeze
Herringbone cirrus faintly in the sky,
—Is this the style I learned from Joyce, from whom?

Unable now to concentrate on one work, so long it is since I last wrote lyrics and never stories with regularity.

Wise-in-life Tessa [Horton] said: All you have to do is look and see, when you paint. The buildings are heaped as shapes and as styles.

I am examining the parts and new powers of my sensibility; never so much as now. The rhythm bears the feeling.

The metaphors discover the hidden qualities. The symbol by the expertness of part-for-whole discovers essences, generalities, universals, Hamlets, Anna Kareninas . . .

They expressed agreement by moving uneasily.

Lacy pale-green are the new leaves on the posted trees.

All summer long on short poems; from this matrix drawn, able thus to attend to new rhythm and construction and relevance, letting the metaphor go.

"One of Picasso's great sterile athletes who brood hopelessly on pink sand, staring at veined marble waves."

"If you threw yourself on her, it would be like throwing yourself
from the parapet of a skyscraper; you would scream."

> Wine brings all things seen closer—vivider,
> I see the Harvard houses, neo-Georgian,
> just like a Petersburg's, as Harry said,
> A city of canals, bridges, rivers, gov-
> ernment bldgs, white trim on the red brick
> and neo-Georgian style
> > —The cure is wine
> Wine is my inspiration, exaltation,
> Magic, Pegasus, and peerless peaks and heights

I did this and I know that it is good. *Shen*[*andoah.*]
I think that I am going to be sick.
Said Dorothy: Oh, you have no sense of perspection.

> A kind of *tic*
> Against the Kicks
> —(*Kaka*, as the Greeks said, having
> > a word)

> Brinnin was here before, his glands awry
> Hair falling out, good-natured
> > just the same—

Story of him [John Malcolm Brinnin, poet and biographer],
Auden, and Bessie Breuer [novelist and editor]; Bessie Breuer and
Dudley Fitts [poet].
I woke at 5 again, drank wine . . .
This is the ride's stage where it is too easy, not enough resistance.
Maybe it is not my own experience I need, but some experience
with a history: yes, this is what it must be. Elizabethan U.S. (this is
what the chronicles gave).

> I close my eyes and see a crème de menthe
> (How consciousness thus turns upon itself)

And if people are less fooled than you think? or fooled when you
think them not fooled and the reverse.

> I learn so much from my sins and errors
> Especially when public (thus through shame)

To be conscious of tone and feeling as now of rhythm and metaphor: though they have always been there.

> Abstractions are more real than
> this and that
> Tho' human beings give them their
> reality.

> Patient, my soul—
> Your face is my open secret

April 29

Stupid not to believe my mother did not like housework, and not to know it as tiresome, beneath her face.

Penetrate the surface, penetrate to the mind beneath the face. Since you possess the subject matter, it is merely a matter of being vigilant about the form and conceiving it as a sustained action.

Gogol, Plutarch, Proust, Dickens: much more is to be learned from them.

The mutual admiration society next door, two vanities meshing; make a move to go home, said Elena. Had H. L[evin] passed, on Friday, into that stage of success in which all hatreds and resentments rise up to be struck?

Thomas Mann in *The Atlantic*, vanity more colossal than anywhere ever in expression. (The love affair between Margot Asquith and Margot Asquith will live as one of the prettiest in history.)

And wings were waves when gulls were flying / and the gray-cloth sky of the hot day is much / a sullen gray.

I did not know what egotism was and how it stinks unknown to itself until I met Harry and Elena, and this was an argument in which I was too facile in 1939 and 1940 with W[ill] B[arrett].

"Your genius on a silver platter"—G[ertrude] on the train from New York to Albany, June 14, 1938, almost four years ago.

Last night Sonny [Shapero] was here, we played ping-pong, he told me more about my poetry, commentary not poetry, and stayed late to be corrected about his misuse of words, such as rationalization, conceit, ways and means.

This morning G. impressed me very much and gave me much pleasure. Since Saturday afternoon, blow after blow has knocked my spirit down: only to rise again, only to be knocked down again.

And I thought much of the short novel entitled *The Princes*, and of beginning in August 1939 and ending at K. A. P[orters'] in January 1940. And just now it occurred to me that one might write this novel like Plutarch, and thus eliminate the dramatic form.

But I have not prayed to God since Friday, and I have shirked the work I ought to do with my students; but then it is true that they learn from me as they would not from another.

I explained to Paul Malloy the lines in Robinson and Hopkins. I was attacked by the letter from [Theodore] Morrison [Delmore's immediate superior on the Harvard faculty], "other plans and intentions," but now, speaking with J. B[erryman], find that all have received the same letter.

I was accosted by a small Southern girl: Be a good sport, she said, and wanted to guess my weight. And I drank less coffee yesterday and today, and lunch stopped in me the morning sickness.

April 30

Should I begin tomorrow to write the 150 pages of *The Princes*— the first drawing or draft? Yes, or I will do nothing else at all. *Just* three pages and outline of the next day.

Then I will be able to wait on *Genesis*, and have something else if it is no good at all, if its whole structure must be altered.

This may be the way of defeat—not doing nothing as I knew and feared—but doing the wrong kind of thing.

Is explication the end of creativity? Destruction of symbol as such but filling in? Is there no use for the poetry of interpretation? R. P. B[lackmur] must have gone through this with his novels.

Order and disorder, form and formless must have profound psychological roots, nervous roots.

H. L[evin] makes Life impossible—impossible to stay in the same room.

If I lost it again, I really would look for a tall building.

The Princes, a short novel in episodes, and character sketches. The main thing is to keep going until Sept. 1939; and what the great poet Auden said, I can if I try: three pages a day, no more, no less, the rest for *Genesis*; and Dickensian my sense of character.

In the framework of memory, in this way, more can be put in, inclusiveness is a virtue.

T[heodore] M[orrison]: I enjoy teaching at its best almost as much as writing at its best.

A month without progress, except for here and there revision, and that not systematic nor persistent.

Today from Jay, Hays's letter and moral-immoral thrill; all the old feeling about denunciation; Jay is a fabulous character, as Gertrude says: not ashamed to show me this, this is worst.

And in the back yard, the sly fearful looks of E. L[evin], and Gertrude sprinkling the flowers. I showed one, and told the other, ten years.

The source of all evil is how often the choice between two goods or two rights; and the source of tragedy, the source of drama.

(For N[ew] D[irections].) Literary History teaches, the beginning of a literature is often popular culture, criticism, and many translations.

Gertrude is now typing out "Having Snow," or *Genesis*; shades of 1931, 1932, 1933, and 1934, especially 1936 and 1937, afraid to marry before finishing. [Delmore and Gertrude waited to marry until he had finished his first book.]

Shenandoah [a play by Delmore] is a rite of naturalization in America as well as a defense against a joke by telling the joke oneself, an old habit.

I saw an old title, *The Necessity of Criticism*, which appealed to me, with Dos Passos.

The psychology in *Genesis* is all my own, I am Madame Bovary; and in "America! America!" it is clear I do not need my own life to use this psychology, only a saturation with facts and a form which makes [it] flow.

Preface [to *Genesis*]: so many of the few who have read this work have expressed distaste or indifference to its structure that I think I had better explain why I have tried and perhaps failed . . .

There is a substance which certainly will appear in *The Princes*.

G[enesis] will finish me, instead of my finishing it.

The explication of the implication, as Tessa would say.

Immoral impatience; immoral fecundity of error, like Spinoza's.

Fatal dilemma, critic, philosopher, theologian, moralist.

The form is an agent; all good things are mixtures, save for God himself, so pure.

The entelechy of *The Princes* rises in me; conceive an action, you have the subject, the matrix, the theme, and the forms.

Wait for nine years; ribs of clouds, cloaks of clouds, black cloaks of clouds; and the sad possibility of printing only the narrative; easy if I had not already let be announced the plot, if I did not need to have others to read and know what it was; but does it matter, could it matter?

No such view from McClellan Square, blocked by leaving tree; and the light is in the dark river of the hot spring evening like a dry wine in a decanter.

Wait for nine years, or wait at least for two; every year has marked a further stage of the development. And tonight we saw the new house; and if it were a habit that I carried with me a typewriter, then I might take my marriage and my art to New York.

The sun is on my face as I write; and the sherry in my being; not to forget Newton Arvin [literary critic]; not to forget the wonderful strength of purpose and unity of being which wine gives me.

Perhaps in this way I can finish this short novel this summer, before the arrival of dipsomania, but aiding it.

As we thanked the H[orton]s for the decanter, I remarked, Now I can become a dipsomaniac under the best auspices.

Gertrude does not like my poetry, except for my lyrics.

Electric like a sunbeam, Dickens said, unliked by Wordsworth, as Hawthorne was by Emerson.

How coarse and how vainglorious that prose—H. L[evin].

May 4

I hop with hope
From trip to trope
But deep beneath
My simple face
Tangled like hair
Is long despair
And disbelief
In every good
I wish to have

Christine [Weston, novelist] entitled the gallon jug of Swiss Colony Wine a luxury liner, the name of the cathedral in the Auden of 1937.

The Charles [River] is now a collapsed elephant's gray rippled flesh.

If worst comes to worst, then I can construct *The Princes* as a play; after that, to write in the prose I want.

Strange that in writing a story I turn so much from scenic form?

Robert Frost's insecurity and his willingness to say: This belongs to the universe, this is a part of the universe; "I wouldn't go in if asked, / And I hadn't been." The mark of the dark, the silent and quiet desperation, and the insecurity.

It is clear that the dramatist can no more get away from the need for exposition than the storyteller can get away from some scenic form. In the Frost above, the colloquial is used to sign the actuality.

The project of getting a 5 & 10 novel and rewriting it, getting several of them, Elizabethan in this way, being able thus to attend to style and to psychologizing.

I lack practice with a temporal track of behavior; yet most of this temporal track in most novels is important dialogue. The problem probably is to make the dialogue important, in part by selection.

"The cows munch blue eternities," a line improvised and then interpreted well by Jay.

"When lilacs last in the dooryard bloomed!" When the lilacs bloomed in the dooryard last year, the last time.

May 5

The streetlights are tulips, once one has seen tulips. The many kinds of tulips in the Public Gardens were very moving, full of significance, in rows arrayed.

Form is an endless effort, and not only that, but perhaps the secret of life.

[*Delmore had a contract with Schocken Books for* A Child's Universal History, *but this manuscript was never published. The child he had in mind was Jeremy Dickson, the young son of his friends Rose and Wallace Dickson.*]

"A Child's History of the World" is another poem or story. And now all the blue is out and green leaves against shining-blue river is the view.

Eminent, evident. Is it possible that in the new age all will have the sensibility of the Symbolist poet, leading lives of interior richness? But this would be different from single isolation, in any case? Scandal, vandal.

I am tortured by the endlessness of the particular. In a decade, what was particular becomes a sign of the previous decade; it has now happened to the twenties.

A method makes possible generalization and omission. By using the balanced sentence, simple and straight, as a base, much more can be done with the paragraph and with prose as a surface and a movement.

Insight is a name for the penetration of form by subject; style might be a name for the transformation of subject into form. Insight is beneath the face; style is the arrangement of the books on the shelves.

I need a form entitled generalized fiction, the story of F. W. Dupee, like Plutarch, a Plutarchrat, and thus making possible the religious-lyrical sensibility.

Slowly the poison the whole bloodstream
                                        fills
—It is the waste, the waste returns
                                        and kills—

Rotundity of breast and buttock, does it appeal because of the rotundity of the pregnant woman?

I cannot get back to the epic movement of the text, although perhaps if I keep trying?

If Art is an ordering of an experience, it can obviously fail either as an ordering or in the amount of experience grasped by the ordering.

Society is an escape; Solitude is an escape.

A child drowned in the river Sunday, while we were drinking rum punch. Miss Jones's mother, of Bowdoin Street, superior, blind, cadaverous, and imperative, died this year.

An examination of experience, of language, and of sensibility. But this [is] too easy and an indulgence, although who knows how helpful it may later be.

Teaching is a great education. So is scenic form. Since I can write a play, it is not true that my sensibility abhors scenic form in the story.

In R. [?], all is for the prose surface, everything else dismissed, a basket of lyrical straws. But the fundamental question about a work of art is from how deep a life it has sprung. Hence the virtues of my best two stories.

Formalism and realism will exist as poles of Art all the time because they correspond to the two essential elements of form and subject matter.

Perhaps if I reduced the scale and tried to write just one scene a page, I would make more progress.

May 7

Every old insight must be climbed and achieved
Upon the stair within the turning body

The young adolescent girl in the apartment house was reading Michael Arlen.

The subject of the *Iliad* was hurt pride
And actions of the Gods—

The subject of the *Odyssey* was but
A trip (and thus an action, lo!)

Success would be a symbol like the Cross
Or Joseph's story or "God Save the King"—

Not what is left out but what is put in is what counts for good or bad.

Why did not Bergson know that he was but part of the seesaw, after the mechanism of [Herbert] Spencer?

> Behold, in Antony, Reason and Love
> Have made a battlefield . . . And if you care,
> See Egypt and see Rome in struggle there . . .
> I have a method, step by step: then why
> Am I forgetful of it? It is the style, my soul!

Passes the path of the downing sunlight and is charred, amid burning silver. What entelechies dawning in me? Why do I look to biographies of authors? to read my fortune, or to write *The Princes?* —And O the sugar of light at night and the lilies of light or tulips, and the wondrous senses of wine!

"An Angel Regards Arnold Bennett," a poem, 90 pages.

"Extra Pleasure," "You Don't Say," "Wine Burnt the Cheeks," "At Night Apollo Dies."

May 8

> The individual becomes conscious of himself as being this par-
> ticular individual with particular gifts, tendencies, impulses, and pas-
> sions, under the influence of a particular environment, as a product
> of his milieu.
> He who becomes thus conscious of himself assumes all this as part
> of his own responsibility. At the moment of choice he is thus in com-
> plete isolation, for he withdraws from his surroundings; and yet he is in
> complete continuity, for he chooses himself as product; and this choice
> is a free choice, so that we might even say, when he chooses himself as
> product, that he is producing himself.
> —*Kierkegaard, cited by [Otto] Rank, "Art and the Artist"*

The thing that must be done is to conceive of an action, involving one or more souls, located in a fairly well-known milieu (although this is not actually necessary); and then to work at it with all the new powers of style.

The story of the car might not be enough of an action; and yet imagination might be forced to produce an action through surveying the conditions necessary to do the psychologizing which it turns on like a faucet and the metaphorizing which it does like a dance.

How foolish to think that no one notices what you are doing; everyone notices when the edge of self-interest is near, as in the return of books and the payment of debts.

Every success I knew was from the fecundative power of form. It has always been this that has brought fluency.

At every hurt, go back to guilt and humility, and then there is gratitude and freedom from pain.

May 9

Boredom is any King's— O infinite
—Nothing distinguished, colorful and moving
And sleep holds off, though nothing keeps awake
And even pinching pain might be preferred—

O Life is wonderful, living or dead
And when I think of it, I lose my head

My heart was ticking underneath my coat,
O Charles, on a gray day elephantback

A Notebook for the Years: this might be a way to bring together all these perceptions in their succession.

My temples like to burst, Oh, oh, I said,
Is there a Negro in the woodpile, Colonel Tate?

I am not home to anyone but T. S. Eliot, Immanuel Kant, Mozart, and Jesus Mozart. I want to ask them something?

Seek Pleasure, Avoid Pain, Placard
Posted in every heart, and all the parks

Nausea and Toothache teach us to be damned
O Dante, how could you have left these out?

A slum on the way to the end of the night

It is the middle class which thrusts the heart
Aside
. O Convalescence, full of clarity (the which is false),
Even a dog sees more, even a horse (a false serenity)

My diction says, A faucet is quite good,
A moccasin for footprint, shoe for car
Thermos, vacuum, speeding, timing, toe
—Pain stretches time, and Pleasure hurries it!

O Lord God, what a fool I am when once
I put my mind to it, let myself go—
The economic fear is middle-class

O Life is wonderful no matter what!
If you can keep your memory and hold your wit

O Life is wonderful, in the May light,
What peaks, what flights, what colors in the eye

O I think it is just sweet wine, just wine
I am a critic from the very womb

The Academic is the insecure
And actuality is in some slang

But keep in mind the living room and Party,
Party is hero as in Soviet films (O Liben)
The crowd or group and lyric irony
As the rain turned to snow

No matter what you have heard, will not believe, regarding the vivid smiling charming face.

May 10

Perhaps the vogue of Kierkegaard rises from a need for ideas of individual responsibility, after a decade of Marxism, which, although not of necessity, tends to place praise and blame elsewhere. But the wholeness, if possible, would be in thinking the two together in their right relationship, but without platitude and poverty of statement.

Prisoners by the third degree can be forced to the poverty of statement. Anyone can be forced to say I love you. But really to feel love requires the whole being; this is an example. Instances of miracles of diction of this (and of other like things) are to be found in Shakespeare, in *Antony and Cleopatra*.

Yesterday I went to the pictures to free myself of the feeling of forcing myself; but came out with emptiness and depression instead. Yet all this is a growth, at least in that I can describe more, and I can analyze with more clarity, e.g., the nature of a story, the action as the only necessary thing.

I dreamed last night of a wrong marriage while N. stood by, and I came back to ask for her; all the obscenity was there.

It is the action as seen by a certain kind of sensibility, not the action in itself, marriage, love, and death.

Wholeness of being would also and has also been in writing but one thing at a time and doing no other thing, but playing while the dark went to work.

"If you kill a ladybug (now crawling on the black net screen), it will rain": this is from 1920, when we lived on Ocean Parkway, next to a big meadow, where I looked for the four-leaf clover and loved the full-grown grass, or dandelions and day's eyes, fortune-tellers.

To choose myself now—would that be to begin the story, or to correct my class themes? too nervous to begin one or the other, and to do both would escape unity of being, renew the dividedness and extend it.

False wholeness of being: marking papers on the train to New York, unable to do another thing, but nothing; falseness of relaxation in the dark theater.

"Purity of heart is to will one thing," and conversely, I am thus impure, afraid of limitation, avid.

This is a community which drinks much; but not to smoke is very easy.

Looking at this row from the Drive itself makes each house, which has so much inside, seem small.

The experience of the last ten years shows that society is made up of indivisible factors, a good economic order is not enough without an institutionalized good morality.

The whole problem is the necessary harmony of interests; and this through playing tennis and having friends.

May 11

The Kingdom of Heaven is within you, this was my waking thought, just after I poured myself a glass of wine.

Self-delighting, self-affrighting. In our own nature does all nature live.

The proper subject matter, to use such [a] phrase, of the lyric is the emotions.

> Pride, disdain, and irony, three words
> Marking what self's self-pain
>
> With wine do I forgive my enemies,
> Forget my hatred: is this bestial, then,
> —I am a proper Christian when with wine,
> Where shall we get the virtues which Christ sang?
>
> Man's proper attitude is often praise,
> Praise of the turning world, and yet withal
> Fear and despair because unworthiness
> Is in him as he shifts from foot to foot

His lips pursed whistling and his legs
From the knees kicking in sheer happiness
He walked along the Drive

Get into harness, ringing challenge: both
Outmoded metaphors

Who can deny the distinction of form and subject matter, viewing Plutarch, Shakespeare, and Dryden with one subject matter. The inseparability should be in the reading.

The reason I did not begin to drink sooner was that I became sick; beginning ten years ago this month with Bert, the tall drunkard newspaperman, and Manly.

He is a peculiar boy, my father said to his relatives; sometimes a child, sometimes beyond his years. D'y'see the books he reads, he said to Anna [Delmore's stepmother], about *Elmer Gantry* and / or Shaw, who said, They are all popular.

May 12

Non sub homine, sed deo et lege
Humanitas, Virtus, Pietas, Veritas
The Latin of the hope and honor of man
(Appropriate that Latin be the tongue
Famous and dead—)
            A bird upon the wire,
And birds upon the grass, black against green

We are defeated by our successes
We are made naked by our Sunday dresses—

What bull's-eye vision for the
            dollar mark—

Sunlight, canary at the window,
Yellowness flight
            What desperate harmonies—

May 19

O when I met the son of William James I smiled
With literary pleasure

To do a little good before I die,
—Let this suffice

This Obscene War

Hundreds are rushing to wrap themselves in the flag; Socrates, the critic; perspective of victory; inefficacy of intellectuals save as critics; who will criticize the armed camp after the war?

Who will criticize the peace?

The WPA versus the war effort; the outcome of the Depression. Ignorance and unworthiness, humility . . .

The moral being can make only one choice, goodness, the fallacy of the lesser evil.

The spectacle of Archibald MacLeish spitting himself in the face is not one which gives a former admirer pleasure.

The most important thing in America is Europe, the most powerful thing is the English language.

Why is Edmund Wilson silent? And why does Tate apply for a commission to defend finance capitalism, the order he has so often attacked?

If the intellectuals do not remain critics, who will? The war will not be won by conformity to the will of the intellectuals. Our movies are bad, our plays, our books, our education, and winning the war without criticism will be the victory of Henry Luce.

But perhaps to write a dialogue entitled "Lew Ayres"? The non-conformist conscience needs more examples and exemplars. Christ the best literary critic.

The life of constant ceaseless vivid renewed perception is enacted by conversation.

If coitus at tea, then asparagus for breakfast, a dilemma.

She was frigid, he was rigid: what a marriage.

Sometimes realism, sometimes formalism, it all depends on history.

Ontological heroics, Herman Melville, yes indeed. Broken? Hardly! The fantasies of Horace Gregory! Dunstan Thompson a great poet! This is a bet and not Pascal's. Come bet with me that God exists: life will feel better then; death will feel better then.

I like storytelling, like conversing: it is, O Stagirite, a special pleasure.

Tigers are seldom undecided, it would seem.

To work from nine to five for six months of the year, but not to work in the afternoon or the evening the other six months of the year, but only the first three hours after breakfast.

The waste, the road not taken, the pitch
Not taken, ever unknown in sums of feeling
A metaphor being a concealed smile,
The moon being something to advertise
She had better viz. accept the universe
—I have to live with myself, after all!

Everything which isolates, such as pride, damns; everything which
associates, such as dances, saves.

It is not true, as I thought, that pride is the motor of the will.
Oh no!

Oh, let me eat my cake and have it, too!
This is the wish, the heart being the cake.

May 24

Noble and comely girls, another phase
—And in a drunkenness of company
And His Good Pleasure, and his will, alas!

Speech is significant of actuality.
And it was very chichi all the way—
Sharpness of faces lighted by wine's glowed look,
Maine's stories, Chinatown, pieces of art,
For six days you work and on the seventh day,
You eat waffles: Oh, we live like dogs!

[The first line apostrophizes John Berryman.]

John, let us now dismiss, let us now destroy
In effigy the forms of bourgeois love
Every poet, being poet, speaks from his death,
Let us as foetus and as corpse proclaim
Our hatred of the city which surrounds us!

Tired of sparring and genteel pretense,
Let us now say without a reservation,
We wish that you were dead, O stupid ignorant
Adulterous hearts which made us what we are
So that we are bound & blind in your guilt and gilt—

For this, it is clear, is the worst infamy,
That we are not from the city's wrong free—
But in its cars ride, standing with the crowds
Pressed in the common air amid strong sounds
Of true disorder and endless defeat—

Stunning compulsion like the sun's great blows!
Hatred corrupts, pride corrupts, love, too,
Though shrewdness is dismissed a little while,
Makes the flesh grasp at forks or loll upon
The sofas of the comforts of the creature!

Not that, in any case, pure sanctity
From our weak souls might have come, Oh no,
A simple honest humility proclaims
Our foolish hope, inventive self-deception,
Vanity and slipshod error. But that, in the end,
The game is destroyed: this is the worst of all—

We all from glass houses throw stones: hope no more, but look, listen, and to love be obedient.

Octopus stain of radiance upon the Charles; firehouse brick hospital we passed, straight from the nineties.

Is this a Roman day, and Antonine,
—No morning, anyway, & no fresh start—
But it is heavy in the Western heart
That every present in the past is twined—

Sans unnecessary sentimentality, it may be said that friendship is more important than any particular issue of a literary review. Intellectuals as a class must work through the literary review.

Sunday, marking papers on the lawn. Dinner and evening with Tessa and Nela [Walcott, friend and next-door neighbor], writing poems and drawing pictures.

May 27

Little brown puppy, Susie's child, struck by a car. Susie trots by without a second look, returning from a morning trip. Man with a camera looks on, driver smokes a cigarette, stopping his station wagon, screech of wheels as I looked up—and now thrust against the curb, out of the way, no more depraved games on the lawn.

A de luxe body in a fourth-rate mind
Here and there, swerving, a bird flys out
Studded with plums, purple as spring dusk
—Causeless depression, causeless elation,—Life's
Manic-depressive roller-coaster ride!

When in this May I with my mother spoke
Of Sandy's name* & disapproved of it,
I gave my children beautiful names, she said,
And my heart rose and sank, at this pure view

The hanged men like old coats on hooks
Unpressed / The spear-like black bar fence

Flaubert and Dostoevsky, epileptical
Hawthorne a limping boy—

May 29
    In New York, Philip R[ahv] said, Do you have a lot of friends?
(does this mean that he does not?), and I said, Not a lot, but enough;
feeling then perhaps about New York as he felt about my life in
Cambridge.

Those powers which were in quick conception joined
Live on forever after, a new power,
Man-woman penetrative through the life,
Satyr and nymph, concealed and strong and deep,
The id the modern sang who from Wien
Saw with what illness, what a cold and limp
The private soul advanced to slow defeat—

From rivalry, so harsh, arrives his harsh
Disdain and criticism of his fellows,
And this becomes the myth, his honesty
And his detachment; he hardly fools himself,
And yet he does, forcing the lie in speech.

Merely to look becomes a moral deed
(Heroic couplets soon will fall from me)

Harry Bridges today ordered to go,
While last week Browder was released. This shows
The character of Roosevelt, to eat his cake
And have it, too (blend them, he said to Berle)

When the Depression came two roads were left,
War or socialism: knowing the populace,
Can we be surprised at war's selection?
—Meanwhile grow the antipathies next door.

* *Delmore's brother Kenneth named his daughter Sandy.*

The universe: "an incredibly heavy and hot egg," "a single clump
of tight-packed sub-atomic particles."

> The universe was once a hot blue egg!
> Lemaitre's egg; this egg burst into stars
> & whirling nebulae, and simpler simpler forms
> Expanding cosmos in this way /
> Condemning others most for sins you sin
>
> The letters which we do not send—therein
> What a profound declivity of being
> Betrays itself—ontologists, take note!
>
> An eggstain on an old book: I am struck
> By such a detail most most intimate
>
> The trees are green gloves of leaves against
> The horizontal river gray—
>   Will living here
> Make me somewhat Chinese in idiom?
> Learns not to look a while at what he wrote
> —Dishonest, pedantic, and vain
> Powder yourself, disguise the animal,
> Neo-Shakespearean radical!
>   No matter what
> Intrinsic virtue *Genesis, Book One*
> May have, this is a beautiful fact,
> It made a *real* poet and it gave me
> Two methods which can paint the living world.

"The bourgeois is something infinite for me"—Flaubert.

> The racing sparks, the running silver light
> Upon soft sliding Charles
>   and on the chapel, faint and gray
> The moonlight luminous upon fat pillars,
> —The thick green leaves of early summer, bound
> Like many papers, the sense of a milieu
> The bar, with music as the overall art,
> Forms flowing through the drinks and
>   through the talk,
> And through the smoke the good society

The trouble with the first person is that it cannot perceive itself.

My father on his way to America may well have passed Henry James or Adams or some such light.

Last year's diary, gaucheness and self-consciousness of style, yet evocative and perhaps useful someday.

> O wondrous cape, high in the sky, gold-fringed
> By the late light, gold piping or gold trim
> (Only long inhibition held me back,
> Is this what wine has proved?)
>   and wine dismisses guilt
> —Terror in Czechoslovakia, Heydrich stunned
> And in the sky the stunning bursting sun

Bland, blond, blind; the propinquitous affection and sympathy mistaken for love; the rising conscience or is it fear, perhaps both? Incidence of guilt, causes, the worldwide war. Probably mostly fear.

> Forgiveness
> Snow is forgiveness, snow is newness
> Physical

> The city of my birth, Europe's last capital
> Was much too big to give me images,
> Although in 1936 I named the boroughs
> By different objects

You can't marry for the first time twice; this is not a tautology.

Not that early errors could not have been otherwise fruitful, viz. sans error, but that

> How wonderful if true: *if* true, no dream!

The sin is the True Republic or is it—perhaps best of all, the telling of the story in the letter.

Imagination holds significant details, especially revealing speeches, interpreted motives.

Oscar [Handlin] on Harvard, like a tourist in Germany or Russia in 1937, or on anti-Semitism.

> In crowds losing identity / and with
> The uneducated

The actuality of this experience is to be found nowhere else in the writing of our time?

Goodness is rather banal, don't you know?

The Kharkov offensive frees Browder in Atlanta, and sells more copies of *War and Peace.*

> Part of the base hit is the roar of the crowd!
> —Seem to be alone all day, no one anywhere to be seen
> Dry, hot, and windy—

May 31

> A cultivated flatness was my forte,
> Being gauche, I sang of poise and certainty
> Poet, super-id and super-daemon,
> Byron like Mozart

> I feel the growth of powers day by day,
> Perception, narrative, analysis,
> All in a rhythm like a running boat
> —Soon in an utter tiredness my body will
> Take refuge: I will go down to despair,
> But rise again in August or September

> The great work is a summit to be climbed
> —No other way

Dead day, dead Sunday, nervous and tense legs, morning sickness, emptiness of thought, emptiness of paper, freedom from guilt, save suddenly returning as along the bank stepped. But no desire to go somewhere, no desire to go to the pictures, a remarkable change, especially for Sundays; this is the strength and order won from wine.

June 1

> Every perception rejoices in itself
> Like a fire catching fire through itself

> The Stars & Stripes, like an accordion
> Or like a poster bright

Progress from family life to city or school life almost a change of self, shift of roles, such different structures of behavior, inside and outside, preside.

Meeting a friend after seven years' absence the same self leaps up, the same jocose greeting.

Shifts as a good boy at school, a bad boy at home, under different pressures, different resentments.

If ideas are sometimes aspiration, they need not be dismissed for their untruth. Deism, Romanticism.

A sense of guilt and a desire to be generous is all that I have to show by way of goodness in that line and both easily overcome under the pressure of desire.

Politics as an extension or projection of family feelings.

And now, downstairs, as I look up from a page of John's [Berryman] poems, which do not today work very well on me, although I wish them to be very good, the one I would avoid, "Winter Landscape," to be compared to "Ode on a Grecian Urn."

June 3

The difference between an *EB* article and a biography; more facts, different form, different point of view.

The river in evening like a dirty window; and the propeller-like waves from the passing motor launch.

New York intellectuals think too much, said R. P. B. You don't use up your mind when you use it, said M[eyer] S[chapiro], i.e., it is not a quantity.

Won't you come into my parlor? said the spider to the fly? (H. L[evin], F. O. M[atthiesen], P. R[ahv], betrayal—)

And the light like a bone. And the ice blocks of the reflected lights.

Since you can't sleep, what is your guilty sin?—William Phillips. It is not organic, must be neurosis.

June 5

"Fortune's football." Christ the harshest critic. Hopkins knew Jowett, and followed Newman; wrote to Bridges, became a Jesuit; followed Swinburne and Tennyson; was homosexual.

And then there was irresponsible laughter, all in anarchy and shaking and objective.

Diamond of the dew on the lilac bushes; the rose or roses which brought back a distant occasion I could not remember, roses as a child.

To W[illiam] P[hillips], we live morally from hand to mouth, knife and fork: Christine's sex is just a big sneeze, after all.

"The fine delight that fathers thought" and the flash of it.

Morning is Criticism, the Night is
Infatuated Drunkenness, Up and Down,
The city of my birth, Europe's last capital,
With what a cachinnation alls [sic] my sleep
—Where shall I find here what it is
                              right to say?

A pandemonium of pain to a mere murmur

Goodness is banal, alas, but goodness is
Pleasanter by and large than evil is—

Lost in the forest fifteen days, when she was
Picking flowers

I'll walk around a sentence like a cat
—Don't really believe, does what he wants,
May God have mercy on his soul!
Upon the elephant skin the glitter sparkles,
And in the bran is juice, a fruity beauty

. . . I laughed until I thought I'd die
—Soft sofa, grave, descent,—and this is
Full of innocence and full of pleasure
Man died alone and no one came to claim him,
Cut off, cut and cut down by pride

Diary of Candid Cane, a radical
And yet to tolerate such simple wrongs
Who, worse, adulterate, pressed by pleasure

Tears. Tears of a hopeless guilt,
And unforgiven. Light. Light. Light over the wide world
Wheeled, and whirled—

(In Hopkins sound engenders, not sense, but sounds for their own
sake, Swinburnian.)

               Light on the water like a gold sash

               Let in fresh air, the air is quickly used
               & spoiled
                              Expressive silence, singing,
                                             tingling

In composition one part illuminates another part and it is a new thing.

> The violins were full of variants

> Dog from car window watches motion go
> Do not, O sir, put in one basket all
> Your eggs

Education has roots in American life, radicalism hardly does.

June 8

> The paint is cracked, the mortal substance hards,
> O parfait cream and in the world the wind,
> The rocks, the surf

> Job, Job! Job was a righteous man, he was
> A man—this is a sniveling self-pitying
> Spoiled boy

Man has six senses, the sixth is pride, located in the face, especially the nose (twin role like the private members).

R.P.B. was glorying in his own feathers.

I bought sneakers and put them on myself.

Sic transit gloria mundi! the suit was full of shines: my blue gabardine wedding suit.

> Sun goes down in gold glory
> —Knives of light in the mane of light

June 9

"Forster has everything in Henry James and does not need the hocus-pocus (viz. *A Passage to India*)."

Nela is painting my portrait, after tennis 7–5, 6–2, and lunch at St. Clair's.

Jay's three-part novel, lose war, win war, stalemate, MacLeish as President, Germans, chauffeur.

Taking off polo shirt, post-tennis, like losing body when one dies; laborious.

The novel of the Duke of Windsor in the novel *The Princes*.

Jay's novel, "confused philosophical passages" to show that no one really knows anything.

The satirist surmounts himself: the naked sensuality, beer foam about the mouth.

The first green streaks of outline are on the canvas with oil, then it is rubbed.

There were her feet, a different kind of fish; legs like a baseball bat; eyes squeezed, look squeezed, when drawing on the cigarette.

July 9

Reading in "An International Episode," by H. James; social roots; mixture of narrative and dialogue.

> Love has a different reason, new & old
> —Doors slam, a stillness in the back yard
> leaves
> (These lilac bushes bloomed a month ago)

July 12

The slick and famous river (the double adjectival epithet), the play of knives of flame of candlelight, the perception understood by means of literary forms, or grasped anew by means of them.

The couple attentive to each other at the party, boy touching the girl's fingertips, the ice cream of amusement, the long Sunday afternoon through the drone of the motorboat, the foot caught in the shoe, a simple complicated detail which asks for a long long look.

And who says much that he does not mean to say, just to say something? He was without a subject matter, like a tennis player in the Arctic or a skier in Sahara's sand.

Permission, precision; protection, delection; punk, pink, pang; words are the beginning and the end; what happens to one's identity at night; how much would be seen by a boy of sixteen?

Verdi bent to get his collar button, which had rolled under the bed, and choked to death.

August 14

Govern & steer! the inner hum and hymn—

He saw the city behind the picture. He broke through the canvas to see the great city. M[eyer] S[chapiro].

The tree I see is not the dog's tree; he lifts his hind leg up.

O the veritable *ding an sich.*

Inspiration has undone me many times!

Epicene—common to both sexes—neuter effeminate.

September 10

Hope never has a chance
—The green to yellow burns
—Though Hope has many names
(The breast is one of them,
—Rising and falling, no one
Has ever said just why)
Hope never has been called
Gentlemen, make your bets!
Go running in free fields,
Where Hope diminishes
Where Hope diminishes
Despite the finishes
Of panting heroes in shorts
—I can crib and ad lib with the rest
My heart is a waiting room
Fruits, Flowers, Soda, Candy
Are named on marble walls
(On your mark . . . get set . . .
      Go! bang! crisply)

September 23

L[evin] calculates all the time, so he thinks everyone else does.
On the dollar bill, the eye of God. (Frost, symbol.)
One has to get used to a typewriter and a wife.

I read a paper in New Orleans during Christmas week. When I was done, a German refugee came to the platform and congratulated me on my paper, "The Isolation of Modern Poetry." He asked me if he might give me a copy of his doctoral thesis, and he drew one from his briefcase, and I looked at the title, "The Isolation of Modern Poetry."

A distinguished gray-haired Englishman spoke to me also. "Do you accept Joyce?" he asked, introducing himself as Douglas Ainslie, the only authorized translator of Croce in English. Did I not think that the minstrels had the right method of securing an audience? Then he showed me one of his books of poems. It was published by the Hogarth Press. A brochure expressed the admiration of a number of critics, one of them Virginia Woolf, one of them a Los Angeles columnist. There in Hollywood, he said, they possessed the only true understanding of poetry in America. One of his books, he declared, was absolutely unique among books of poetry, nothing like [it] ever before. He opened it up and showed me the frontispiece. "This is a picture of my mother," he said. "I think poets should think more of their mothers!"

I felt guilty as we walked away from him because he wanted to be with us, knowing that we were going to dinner.

One night I dreamed that Gertrude had called me a fool. I woke up and told her and she cried out, "You fool!" "You make all my dreams come true," I sang in reply.

When P. G. Wodehouse was caught by the Nazis at Nice in May 1940, it was remarked, "Let him try to laugh that off!"

When Russia was attacked by the Nazis, I called to William Barrett on the second floor on Shepherd Street, "Now we will get rid of at least one of two monsters!" I was wrong.

September 24

Fat Halpert, his room full of rotting apples, smiled sheepishly and explained that the war was chiefly a matter of metaphysics. When I suggested that he write his experiences as a tramp and schoolteacher in Wyoming, he replied modestly that he had no literary talent, but all his insights were metaphysical.

Esta began to cry, and when I asked her why, she said, "When you're with your kind of people, you forget that there are others who are superior to you." Ralph Manheim [eminent translator] had said to her that he was surprised she went with such intellectuals. "Do you know why I came back?" she asked. After that, after she said in a hurried whisper, "I get scared because my periods are uncertain," she wanted to have a drink, and she wrote me a letter, which I did not answer, although it asked a question which was supposed to bring an answer. "I decided," she said, "that my virginity was something I had to do something about." She spoke to K[enneth], when he came home at midnight, "I have been trying to get your brother to sleep with me"; this was her bogus sense of sophistication.

When Whitehead delivered the Ingersoll Lecture on Immortality, many old people, ladies and gentlemen, came in such numbers that there had to be a shift from Emerson Hall to Appleton Chapel. They bent forward anxiously, waiting for news on a subject of the utmost moment to them. But he began, "The prehension of diverse elements in a concrescence or occasion is the valuation by certain eternal objects of contingency as such," so it must have moved in their minds. After twenty minutes of this, he said, "For example," and the audience broke from its daze, only to relax again as the example proved to be as abstruse as the abstraction it was intended to illustrate.

Thus, too, Herbert Schwartz taught his classes in music the moral evils inherent in the Romantic movement by playing Beethoven or

Schumann and crying darkly, "Hubris! Hubris!" when the orchestra rose.

Tessa loves to be abstruse, and when she is, she has the same quality as Alfred North Whitehead.

"Victor Hugo seems to have lost his prose style," said Anatole France when he went to a spiritualist séance at which Hugo was evoked.

Flaubert smoked a cigar, wrote a letter, and copulated with a prostitute before his friends and on a bet. When this story was told to the Circle, one of the Freudians remarked, "I bet that what he really enjoyed was the cigar!"

"Why are we both failures?" asked Morley Callaghan of Nathan Asch, upon seeing him for the first time after seven years. This was the cruelest question I ever heard.

"I am not a failure," said Nathan. "I never wanted to be a success, so I am not a failure."

"It has all been very interesting," said Lady Mary Wortley Montague on her deathbed.

I spoke with H. L[evin] of Gide's jealousy of Proust and said that there was a hallucination of rivalry, for were not both of them now classics of the age? He did not agree.

At the Bella Vista, Albert explained that the wife of a German teacher, soon to go away, was the pure type of faculty wife who says, "What is your hobby, Mr. Erskine?" and to whom the only effective reply would be, "Self-abuse!"

Unable to endure [Julian] Breen's [a friend from N.Y.U.] taunts any longer, Zolotow cried out, stammering, "You are just—*mnov!*" (non-being).

May Rosenberg sat and listened, more and more displeased, as her husband and her husband's friends, all devout intellectuals, praised the beauty and intelligence of an absent girl. Unable to endure this any longer, she went to the telephone and spoke with this paragon, her rival.

"Do you urinate?" she asked her.

"No!" replied the other girl sweetly.

"Do you defecate?" "No!" came the answer, once more serene and mild.

"Do you copulate?" May continued.

"No!" was the answer once again.

"Then go fuck yourself!" said May, hanging up, enraged.

Two soldiers looked on as I corrected my themes in English composition. They wanted to know what I was doing. When I explained with examples, one of them drew forth a letter from his girl in Georgia and asked me to correct it.

September 27

An ode to Somerset Maugham, Bertrand Russell, W. H. Auden, and other gifted ones who have been wrong.

Every neurosis is based upon a repression. Stekel.

He who eats must brush his teeth. (Green before making love.)

A man of thirty-nine drunkenly expostulating with his mother, You rode herd on me for thirty-nine years; born in 1902. W[allace] D[ickson].

All a man's strength comes from the struggle with himself. Fichte drank champagne for the first time when his infant son said "I am" for the first time.

They can find flaws in anything, said the boy from the Deep South of English-composition instructors.

The trees, their thick green rags.

The rich get rich, and the poor get—children! The dash of hesitation. You can't eat your cake and have it, too; the strength of maxims, a penny in time saves nine: here it is the rhyme, and the economy, a form of speed.

He stroked the beard of his ego; he stroked the unshaven chin of his indifference. He looked as if he looked up from a menu at a waiter, standing at the side of him.

The booths, boxes, cabinets, containers, and tombs of the great city.

September 28

Wallace Dickson said that he was born with a hangover. He warned his mother that I was one who filed things away.

But when the wind is in the east, Bleak House, and here in Cambridge; yesterday, the equinoctial storms.

Puppy, poppy; poodle, puddle; cow, cover, core; naïve, knave; the winking poppy taillight went away, turning the rounded corners.

Part of my progress is the knowledge that the most important element is not the idea but the actuality; the actuality lighted by the nearby idea. For I thought wrongly that the necessary precondition of virtu was the correct idea. But now I know that even if one had the correct ideas about each existent thing, there would still remain the problem, most difficult of all, of their embodiment or relevance at any moment of time or place.

I should have known long ago, had it not been for egotism plus the cultural conditions of the age.

[The following drafts of three poems, the first two entitled "Idiom," the third, "Ode to Dale Carnegie," though found among the papers of this period, are undated in manuscript.]

Idiom

—I think maybe an artist's faculties
Can function at their best only if caught,
Caught like a forest in a blazing fire,
Only if drawn into the age itself,
Like a witty fellow present at a party
Who cannot be himself, cannot be happy,
Cannot be witty and enthrall the guests
Unless he feels *at home, at ease*, marked out
By sympathy, expectancy, and joy:
Yet by the "Age itself" we do not mean
Participation in its politics,
Its burning issues, and its passing fads;
We mean a sense of happy interest,
Effort to which after a strain success
Arrives, bringing, however, new work to do,
New trunks to carry up the ancient mountains
—Friends who are genuinely interested
—Those patrons of the heart—
                              But all of this
Is most abstract despite the metaphors;
What man knew such a time and happiness?
Did Shakespeare rising with a rising Britain?
And did Tolstoy, praising the landed life
Until he knew the nameless, first despair?
The way society moves is not too clear
Partly because it is a mixed affair,
By conflict mixed and spread out many ways
By places, different peoples, different classes—

At any rate, the Civil War destroyed
The period of Emerson. During the fray
Hawthorne and Thoreau died. When it was done,
Melville and Whitman started to be silent,
Emerson grew dimwitted, no young man rose
To take their places and use what they made—

Idiom

We all grew up with Romance in our heads
The Romance that the secret of success
Was genius, blazing gifts lighting the world,
Genius, the noble individual
Long-haired, peculiar, and long-suffering
A kind of Christ, in fact, or Fisher-King

(Thus how much is an ignorant translation
Of Christ's story, of Christianity!)
And when Marxism rose in many minds,
It seemed offensive to this love of heroes,
Heroes who were the essence of the novel
—And yet when we had given it sufficient time,
This doctrine brought us a correction which
Was virtually theological,
For thus we saw that still our lives were moved
By powers far from us, not known by us,
Greater than us, and not unlike God's will:
Is Grace God's will and is the Holy Ghost
God moving in our hearts, no matter what?
May History have mercy on our souls!

Efforts at the Poetry of Statement.
Genius: basic presupposition of [Maurice] Zolotow and me and
P[aul] G[oodman] and W[illiam] B[arrett].

Ode to Dale Carnegie
O Dale, I do not like you in the least
(I'd rather be disliked!). The boys and girls I teach
The slick and famous river where I live
(Named for a famous king who lost his head)
—Billiard-ball moon of a September sky
(The blackout stillness and the ghostly moon)
Bishop-hat spire of the old stone church—
O Dale, I do not think you know at all
What you discuss! A friend of mine named Wright
(Most often wrong!) convinces me much more—

October 9

Delight had a long look
An aftermath in glow—
I read it in a book
Like melted ice cream lay
—The bud, the burst, the bloom
Precarious—tiptoe!—in time
Which is the only space
Joy popped like rockets—up!—
And after grew a beard
—They liked the candlelight,
They liked the firelight,
They saw it as a prime,

They liked the period thing
Yet liked electric light
Because they knew in sense
How Time is like the blue,
The curve which rules all breath,
—Who has seen the length of hope?
And who has seen the Christ?
And who forgiveness seen?
Nothing wipes out what has been
(The Church reigned in the night)
Memorial Hall, huge, black,
Throned the New England night
And memories of James,
And bearded football games
Came from the eighties quick,
The Gas House, mushroom obese
The industry's dull forms
Beside the railroad track
Bared its fat tour [sic] and waste
And smoked the afternoon
Charging the place with sound
—The arc light's a tulip
The street like an old habit,
And after all is death.

October 18

I heard the juices of the midnight rain
—Just look at yourselves, Oh, Oh, just look
At yourselves! Nobody knows very much
—I saw the dove-gray light of early dawn

. . . Twice in my life Necessity has bared
A face expressionless, asleep, and stone
First the Depression came to strip the heir
Of hopes he had not chosen with his heart
(That he was rich!) and then the Second War
(Born with a postwar soul, I was prepared!)

—Do not look the Medusa straight in the face
Or you will turn to stone! But get a glass
And, represented there, strike evil down
(The good and evil of verse has used my heart
And used my youth: and yet what better waste?)

Well, Jesus Christ! Colloquialism moves
(There are no flies upon the lamb of God!)

One saw when Auden made his big mistake
And left the dirty island which charged his mind
With dark necessities of guilt and need
—Elegant tourist in America,
He saw what tourists see and nothing more—
[. . .]

"Sink or swim." Moses lay in a basket
Found by the Princess Pharaoh's daughter
Found in the bullrushes near shallow water
—*Sauve qui peut!* to think that one girl's slip
May well have made the chosen exiled people
[. . .]

—Most men are fools and yet—is it not true?—
There is in them—if one looks long enough—
The horse which is—once roused freely to run!
Noble and beautiful! Remember that!
O intellectual, contemptuous
Of those who do not love profound ideas—

If there is no trouble, I grasp at it—such is my desire—as if I
feared that I would loll and fall through infinite space, a mere balloon—
A neurosis is a state of mind which causes thoughts which are not
true, but imaginary; fear without objective cause; anxiety without
basis; echelon, cinquefoil, nervosity, scur [sic], bounce—

O my inadequacy! tongue-tied stage fright (poor poor
Students, though arrogant in ignorance)
And then the flight to Boston and to wine,
The silver screen (where fear rears up again)
After the obscene acrobats, and Gilda Gray's
Bare shimmy and bare buttocks sequin-barred
And Aunt Jemima playing Texas Guinan
"Hello, Suckers!"—all this, between nostalgia
For Gershwin and for George M. Cohan
(O blessed Mozart, I heard your mind's light lines
Curving through specious space like light itself)

November 20

I taught my class the causes of a man
—Society, and History, and Luck!
His parents and his friends, geography
—What a grotesque I am before my class!
I draw for them in Explanation's light
And I am physical, explaining *deep*
As digging into earth and finding mines—

Then Venus did the bumps to please the crowd
(I learned more than my students did, each time)
(Go wipe your running nose, you polka clown!)

We poets both by the past and future used

—Felicity from curiosity
Blooming momentarily until the downfall comes

And know how our profession cannot be
Merely a grand tour of the beautiful
But we must earth through toil and suffering
Through ignorance and darkened hope

November 27

The spaniel, black, came dripping by. [Wallace] Stegner looked like a cowboy; the postman sauntered from house to house, paused at the mailbox; chewed gum and looked at his watch as he untied the bundles, adjusted to his work. Mark Schorer looks like Humphrey Bogart.

Go and abuse yourself, another refrain; I hope you come home in your coffin; Go knock your head in the wall.

November 28

Last night or this morning I dreamed that I was called and told that my aunt and my two uncles had died (many dreams of the death of relatives or their resurrection, my father's most often), and I went to the funeral, saw Fay Schwartz at forty and Howard Frisch getting married to Claudette Colbert at some previous period, as if ten years back. I smiled and wept at Fay, along a theater aisle. (She was looking at me at H.S.'s [Delmore's father] funeral, June 1930.) It seemed that all three had died on the same day. Howard was of course James Stewart.

The night, no, the Saturday before we were married, she [Gertrude] said she wished she were dead. The night before was rainy June, we met unexpectedly in my mother's house, in my grandmother's house, 700 W. 180 St., and my mother said, A friend of yours is here, and we walked to the drugstore and she bought me a comb, and I went back to Washington Place [where Delmore and his brother, Kenneth, were living] and could not sleep and put on the light when K. came home and took a third tablet for the first time, Romeo, and slept for the first time well in weeks, the vomiting of my stomach at an end. The next night was at the Hotel Wellington and we did not sleep, because of the American Legion convention. The rabbi was in a great hurry to go to a funeral. My mother wept. Gertrude was very pale. I was drunk on three quick ryes brought by my father-in-law. He tried to talk to me back at his apartment as G. changed. Go slow, he said. Take care of my *tochter*, said Mrs. B[uckman, Gertrude's mother].

Ben [Colle, husband of Delmore's Aunt Clara] said, All of this is superstition, and W[illiam Barrett] and I looked at each other and demurred. K[enneth] gave us a sealed envelope. My aunt kissed me, knowing I did not want her to do that. My father-in-law kissed me at the taxi, his skin sandpaper. We bought a copy of Kafka at Grand Central as we waited. Your genius on a silver platter, said G. on the train in the June sunlight in the Hudson Valley. Now you will sleep, said my Baba and my mother. Will and Kenneth carried my mother upstairs as she wept loudly; then downstairs again. There was a mysterious telegram, which we thought might have come from Red [Robert Penn Warren]; but was from Gene and Ben Nelson [old friend and a medieval historian]. We ate dinner at a restaurant with red leather seats and red and tan decor. I will never forget how you looked today with the black cap on your head to acknowledge the superior powers. Will and K. went away together.

It was five-star Hennessey that we had with us and G.'s lace nightgown. Lionel Abel [playwright and critic] rapped on the door on the hot day when we got the license just ahead of the Wassermann test law.

What would you do, said Mrs. B[uckman], if *you* won the Irish Sweepstakes?

I would sleep, said Mr. B., with quiet irony.

But you sleep ten hours a night now, said his wife in hatred.

It would be a different sleep then, said Mr. B., in quiet triumph and insight.

When, after five years of courtship, G. said that she was getting married, they asked in chorus: To whom?

. . .

Activity is happiness. Renunciation is mastery and freedom, as we see in James and Wharton.

Fire is self-destroying. He was a self-destroying being like fire, his will raving.

Never to act on the inspiration of hurt pride; never to speak, even when one does not wish to strike back.

The world is one and indivisible.

In the upper berth, among the other souls prone in length, I knew this was a version of eternity.

Many a secret is a sensuality.

Thirty-five lyrics: The Small Bourgeois; The Big Bourgeois; The Summer People; The Uncle; The Aunt; The Vice-President; The Manager; The Small Banker; To Dale Carnegie; To Bennett, Maugham, and Russell; One Thousand Jokes; Just for a Laugh; Just a Girl; A Man's Grandfather; A Monkey in Silk (is still a monkey); The Leopard's Spots; The Giraffe's Aspiration; The Lion's Roar; Keep Your Shirt On, Marie.

November 30

My face is an open secret / But in my letters I perform like a true diplomat, cunning & sly.

Animals don't enjoy being drunk, since they have no unhappiness to get rid of.

This is the last day of November.

> The blue of dusk turned to the evening brown
> Gloomed and then dimmed. The glossy night
> Was tipped with lights, cars gusted past
> Pleasure to sleep, and nothingness
>
> The apples in the bowls in the window
> In the heart of the hope of affection
> Life is the salvage of Hope,
> Life is the Future of Hope,
> The Future is the salvage of Hope
>
> The sunny afternoon to ashes turned,
> And yet the Philharmonic bloomed afar
> "Mad dreams of imperial glory"—Churchill,
> "I'll send you a telegram, Premier Stalin!"

December 1

From my window, I can see the green metal mailbox at the end of the street, and the letters quickly thrust into them, communicating love.

At 6:30 I saw the soft fuzz of gray light about the edges of the shades. The hallway began to look like a painting by Ryder.

One of the most embarrassing actions is to tell a joke that fizzles.

To want to make one hundred million dollars is a difficulty easily come by.

Egg sticks to the chin, like theology and death as death. You and who else? Why don't [you] fight a guy your size? If he, Cupid, does it, then all the other fellows will. (Love's Deity.)

And a car conductor lives next door and comes home in his uniform.

December 13

Let Brooks be asked point-blank Trilling's question, What does he make of Shakespeare, that man of negation, questioning, verbalism, and disgust? Will he turn out to be a Primary? Brooks ought to be forced to hand down a definitive ruling on Shakespeare.

Nobody can be sure of anyone's motive, but there are probabilities and resemblances.

Catholic, eclectic; expert, one-sided; candid, brutally frank; learned, pedantic; innocent, naïve. How values are insidious in the choice of words—devout, bigoted, or sanctimonious.

Men who start with denying the existence of God will end by devouring each other.

If you don't believe in God, there is nothing you won't do.

December 20

Alice B. Toklas from Bennington, a case of pure love, echoing [Francis] Fergusson's gestures, like Emily the horsewoman.

Gertrude asked [John Malcolm] Brinnin what he was laughing about, he did not know the subject of the laughter; Breen's trick, the lack of understanding that one laughs to be part of the community or from uneasiness or not to be cut off or to give pleasure. This is for a story, not a poem, it takes too much explanation.

R. [probably R. P. Blackmur]: D. is a great holder-up of his finger to see what the winds of doctrine are; objected to my saying there were no great men just then, though he said so in print three years after.

Socialism might be like the seashore, a word and sentence for the essay on Eliot.

Maybe action and commentary are wrong, but it is to me better than nothing.

Isherwood turns priest, against England. Waugh.

Koussie and his Rhythm Boys, Boy meets Mother, two decades. Mixed metaphors, arch paraphrases, and barriers of jokes.

Flowers of evil, Blooms of New York.

Suspicious of excitement and inspiration.

Poetry, the art of putting things next to each other by means of metaphor.

Brahms all of a winter afternoon, gray and snow-burdened streets.

A carless day in wartime.

When the fat ego lolled in the green pool.

Orion was a diagram, and glittering.

The aspiration of the rising hymns.

The whirlpool like a screw, awl, bore.

The day is not long enough.

> You are implausible like a unicorn,
> And you are four girls when you change your mind.

An epigram is a form of speed, but criticism is not in a hurry.

What is the rush? Posterity can wait.

The dogma beneath the skin.

Roslyn that fat pond—Chiappe.

The letter box is hunched, and the tree is outstretched.

Ulysses, revolution of sensibility.

Don't be so smart, said Lionel, I am not a machine; I said he would then talk behind my back.

> He shut himself into a house. And wept for months.
> And slept or tried to sleep in a lighted room.

The sun as blowtorch, on an August day.

> I fear disaster soon
> From exaltation's brink
>
> I know she did not say
> All that she could see

Jews were a Convenience.

December 21

One thing I want to know, H., were you serious, what did you mean when you said you were not a Marxist but a Machiavellian?

Dwight [Macdonald] said, What intellectuals are not Jews?

W[ill] B[arrett], paranoiac, thought that the war had been started just to get him into the army.

L[ouise] Bogan, a mediocre poet.

Give candy to children and see pleasure on their faces.

He is just a weakling and a 4–F.

Delmore de Ellery (de Cambridge, de Frankly).

Clever fools—intelligent idiots.

The beard achieves his masculinity.

1943

January 1

To R. P. B[lackmur]. How is it that such Narcissi as you and I appear to get along so well?

To decide, This is the most important thing to do, and then to do it; can be done; with belly help.

The idea of actuality helps me forgive myself and forget all those hopes of perfection which tortured and stopped me.

The immense attractiveness of the noble act; when not too difficult or too expensive.

[Norman] Macleod [poet] said that I, like Auden, was flip.

When [Morton Dauwen] Zabel starts to write, he puts on a uniform. His letters are witty.

He writes well, term of damnation.

What happens when people stop talking and start writing?

Pretentious habits take hold and dominion.

At the height of the party, Mark Schorer brought out a copy of his book.

I get scared, I said to Helen Eustis Fisher, I am afraid I am missing something. I do, too.

Immoral is only what hurts somebody else or yourself: actually.

Fitzgerald's story about a man and his worst enemy.

Be assured; no news is good news.

Tais-toi, mon enfant: the silence is preferable to the speech.

Liquor king of poets, Atlantic of poets!

When he told jokes and people laughed, he soon lost control of himself!

I am an exaltation drinker; perhaps a sleep drinker or escape drinker, too.

January 2

Sex and money are the values; fame is making a million dollars in six months.

How often snubbed in the Square.

[Bowden] Broadwater said he was coming to see you. H[arry] L[evin]. Utopia on Memorial Drive.

Wine is one of the proofs of the existence of God.

This gives me ideas, he said, caressing her rondure and moon.

If everyone does it, it is all right. The fairies arrange a community to reassure them.

Never mind the moral effect of twilight sleep, there is enough pain to go around.

January 31

From my window, the hunched letter box, proving news and love.

Rewrite CAHM [Coriolanus and His Mother] for next year's book? second *Fidelio*.

I can see anything, R. P. B.; maintaining strongly that he was without original talent in alternate sentence.

February 1

Getting to know someone is like opening a safe: you have to learn the unique combination of numbers. No, this is not really true.

If he is embarrassed, I feel as if I had no pants or drawers on.

"Like most writers, I don't read much"—Sherwood Anderson.

"Meaning is social."

"People do what they want to do, anyway. She at least admits it" —[Sidney] Hook on M[ary] McCarthy.

I just have not paid enough attention to meter and rhyme.

The birth of certainty or faith in newer powers.

The Sunday paper which destroys Sunday.

Two thespians, Churchill and Roosevelt.

Give, Delmore, give, said Janet Aron [wife of Daniel Aron, a Harvard English professor], New Year's Eve, 1942.

"When someone does not like me, I do not understand it"—E[lena] Levin.

He likes issues [of *Partisan Review*] in which he appears, W[illiam] Phillips of [Harold] Rosenberg.

It always turns out all right with D[elmore]—G[ertrude] to Handlins, but he worries all the time anyway. It turns out all right because I worry.

"I would have to change my whole mode of life"—[Lionel] Abel.

You want everything—summer 1942.

Hubris! Hubris! Herbert Schwartz about Beethoven.

R. P. B. thought [Lionel] Trilling my cousin because he is I. B. Cohen's. This was an insult of six months' standing, from the 15th of September.

"Delmore works all the time"—O. Schaftel. It is not good to work too much, said Paul Goodman.

The Soviet-Nazi Pact was the road to Damascus.

A new period has begun, new habits, patience, many notes, faith, curiosity about the next lapse.

There are men like that in every country. Dwight [Macdonald] on German organizing genius.

The rate of acceleration in drinking.

Economy is a form of speed—

February 10

Last night, the dream of doing something wrong to a student before the assembled class, which left, one by one; perhaps because yesterday I wrote verses on Kittredge's repetitive dream. Two weeks ago I threw chalk at a student.

I woke up from wine-drugged sleep, forced by a heavy pain pressing like a wedge near my heart; I did not take it seriously until it began to grow; then I threw up; then Gertrude was sharp about my use of the sink; then I was angry.

I could not remember much that F.O.M. said about his postwar student years at Yale. [Archibald] MacLeish was 1915, and Phelps Putnam [poet] was his friend. Some of the boys found that they could not study at all, after being soldiers.

Nor remember much of Robert Gorham Davis at the Insane Asylum on Xmas Eve, dancing with the patients. They betrayed only by slight nervous excitement their insanity; nor what part Davis played in the Xmas play; nor Claudia, his stepchild.

> Let Mercy, Pity, Charity
> Inspire our Society,
> Politicos, remember this,
> It is the only happiness!
> It is the only route to peace!
>
> My brother has not answered me,
> He moves but for his family.
>
> The dunes of snow are rotten now,
> They look like sunken swan boats, docked;
> New England winter, gray and dim,
> Slips from pure snows drippingly—

I learn to make my students speak
Of what attracts them, week by week,
I question them successfully
Because I know they are like me!

When Eva Tanguay's *I don't care*
Rose in darkened vaudeville
I did not know this was a shield,
Confected by the wincing will!

February 11

The power of the symbol comes from the nature of perception and thought. The train whistle makes us see the train, the footstep in the hall reminds us of the family relative. The oranges bring back the breakfast room.

The relationship of part and whole is that of symbol and thing signified.

Last night it seemed as if the period of numbness had begun again. I read of E. A. Robinson and was not enthralled, but dismayed; in December, I was enthralled.

For the second morning, sleep is rocky and on the edge of waking for two hours.

To learn more and more how to make the body's knowledge rise.

Undated

Mid-Winter Cambridge
The knotted rotten bony snow
Is like dead hope, beside the curb

To Sinclair Lewis, Who Dared God to Strike Him Dead with a Bolt of Lightning, If, That Is, He Existed.

You! drunken exhibitionist,
Certainly, if God exists,
He will not show His hand like you,
Making vulgar gestures so!

One can get saturated with any subject matter, given the proper incentive and energy. This is what James must have had in mind.

Assurance is born of self-acceptance and of the fact that one is accepted, with all of one's shortcomings. Little is irreparable and *will not be forgiven*, if one is worth forgiving. Is this illusion born of rising success?

Churchill of Eisenhower: One of the finest fellows I ever met!

> *To Snow Which Begins to Fall*
> Begin, your slim mortality—
> O accident and pure beauty—
> Next to the tree which Brueghel made
> More actual in bare-black mode

February 14

[I. A.] Richards and [F. R.] Leavis analogy of *TWL* [*The Waste Land*] with music; but perceptions do not exist sans a perceiver: the protagonist. Who is this protagonist? He is not named. Words are by nature representative; they are nothing without their reference to things—G. Stein.

Yeats will reign supreme, thank God, as a poetic model. Eliot never did the same thing again.

F.O.M.'s Eliot consulted Arnold Bennett—on playwriting—when writing "Sweeney Agonistes." One of the lesser James brothers was an alcoholic, because of the war; William James feared a cadaver he had seen at medical school; what did Henry do with himself, since he had no friends, no intimate friends?

Keep the subject in view at all times. Be physical, the slightly moist handshake, and yet be quick to the idea. Why should the idea and the image be inseparable? This is Art, not Life. Their separate apparition need not be the platitude of statement. And the colloquial as the evocation of the actual.

Gertrude looked at me knowingly when she heard Sonny [Shapero] quote Paul Goodman: Delmore is asinine. He decided to be a great man and read all the great books. While I cultivated my own garden. June's [Cannan]: P[aul] G[oodman] is a dope!

F.O.M. explained that he did not like [Theodore] Spencer's book. The first time one to whom a book is dedicated did not like the book at all. They are just Lowell lectures, he said; the first two chapters are good; after that, the extremely loose terms, Appearance and Reality, are used too much; nothing is made of them.

Perhaps sleeping enough will do it; end the long lapses; the old illusions: but since Sept. 15, I have been on some kind of ride.

March 4

> I have [a] flower in my buttonhole
> I have a flower in my dark deep soul

As soon as there is aspiration we are bound by morality. As soon as there is love—denial; a child—a giving up.

> Bearing the insignia of insomnia
> And the long history of hysteria
> Of course the coarse did not my chorus
> like—
> Fat cat bourgeoisie—we are through!

> Who hit the great Goliath? & who thrashed
> Coarse Caliban? Who knocked the Cyclops down?

[In late March, Delmore and Gertrude separated, Gertrude returning to New York.]

May 24

Poetry, my stern stepmother, perhaps I will depart from your house.

At night, when the hair grows on your face, and your body grows longer, and the dinner is changed to the blood, and your nails grow longer, you ought to remember, however empty your sleep, how much is untouched by the conscious mind.

If the glow of the first hour of the morning lasted, I would give myself utterly to thought and art.

There is a big red-brick house on the corner. Mansard roof and dormer windows are on top, and the right and the left of the house present their windows in Bullfinch *embonpoint*. And in the late light, when the sun goes down, the red-brick front gains a singular glory of solidness; the solidness of red.

The black slates of the mansard roof cover each other like fish scales in front, with the forms of shields; but on the roof, they are straight oblongs and laid in a plane.

The lamp post curves at the top, like a giraffe, and the green mailbox is hunched and squat. A yellow sign says flatly in red capitals, s t o p, and the mailbox at the shoulder's height looks like a big lock.

When the god comes, let you turn to a tapping finger or a fountain pen or a pencil.

Let the dark influences rise and be the only light.

Let the room die and let your body be placed in the closet with the overcoat.

Let your mind not be deceived by joy, nor by freedom and the rush of thought. Do not let his free acting seem to you the beautiful object scrawled on the page. It is not.

If an image is the mystery of joy, and it is, then the poem is the mystery of having and grasping the having.

. . .

Suspicion, looking, slow disclosure, act and confrontation, this is what James uses in the novel grave and beautiful; he hardly troubles with the scene.

"The pale unappeased faces," "across the widening strait," "deprecating denouncing hands," many metaphors of light and distance.

Of the four sides, only one side is seen at any moment.

The stair shows the necessity of regular form.

The game shows the necessity of conventional form.

May 25

It comes to life, the past, like a slow lion—

The longueur and the blankness—before the other end of solitude —the quick unmeant unwanted tears—the outland of four o'clock in the morning—the strange city, newly arrived.

In a dream, an argument over the challah bread, in a store; aunt's comment, she will get it elsewhere; and then digging at two graves, one of them an uncle's—

Charlotte Stant in a gold-barred cage, and with a silken halter on her neck, dragged to America; Charlotte and the Prince seen as two of the collection, after, at Portland Place, the cruelty of Maggie and of Adam Verver.

It must be dragged into the light, I will drag it into the light, I will not leave it there in the middle of my head! O fertile mystery—

The barrel organ was disposing itself on Quincy Street and the officers in a platoon marched in step, but betrayed the presence and the influence of the other rhythm, and I gave the old Italian a nickel because he was profoundly against the war. From the banality of the organ and the men in procession to the gaze and cruelty of Maggie Verver, the whole span of the glory of form—

Always too close to tears, even alone, and after midnight, no one to hear—

The Jew squats on the windowsill, "a scruple almost unprecedented among the children of Israel—"

May 26

Beauty, *in flagrante delicto*
The girl fell down the stairs
The cloud moved away and the stars
Spoke the professional secret

Pilasters lined my cheeks
The pediment of my forehead;
The three-cornered hat bore Hebrew
I never understood

The world profuse with tigers
Darknesses and dark woods
Ran away with my youth, crying:
You do not understand your name

The heart of another
Is a dark forest

Nobody knows anyone much
The heart is too dangerous to touch
    Brink and abyss, heavy in the cache

Of solitude the *langueur*, blankness,
Small things in a new light, speech
To speech, "rapture of observation,"
Sudden & causeless emotion—

May 28

George Palmer's invitation to dinner, the idea of seeing real life, the ease of not making my own supper.

To go to pleasure when the god has come
—This rushes up, forced down, it presses up
Desire powerful (I know it well)
—But now at twenty-nine must know of N O . . .
—The terrifying strength the hero climbs!
The god has come. And pleasure glitters yet
And argues in me, *there perceptions wait*
Amid the conversation, glow and ease

Alas, "statue of uninhibited images."

—So much I do not know, never to know!
Piano, Latin, wall paintings of the East
Eppur si muove! Newton in a new light, humility
"I know not how to others I may seem
I feel myself much the seaside child,
Gathering glittering shells in idle joy—"
He did not see himself, but saw the world
Once came the wondrous light, once the rushing joy
Broke through me . . .
Perhaps the peak is near, perhaps the pure
And open prospect, Jordan, green allure!

Harvard, actual the myth in which I slowly walked
For certain years—

All that I ask, it is brave & rash—
Is merely wall space in the Western mind—

May 30

Despair in him threw foghorns in the air
And desperation like a siren shrieked—

Poetry, O stepmother, I am through!
   I am going away
Can't butter me up no more—

R.P.B.: I hope they paid no attention to it—[when] Nela [Walcott] read to Sage and Susie [Walcott] "Gerontion"—No! "Under the Bamboo Tree": they liked it very much. Susie's: The world is a body—with hands—will bite her; no: the world is where trees grow. (The kids the other day.)

Undated

What kind of a kindergarten is this?—Hook.
Orange Ethics: I won't kill anyone; God, a corner in the mind.
Sonny's [Shapero]—a lamb-chop mind; there are no strangers here (inviting me to dinner); Jews world famous for indigestion—Jewish food; morbid self-consciousness.

Organized society—I am through!
Famous university—I am through!
Sick and sad city—I am through!
O hope, at last I know you through and through
   I have your number
   I will not will

Any cold fish can be my dear
Any old hole will suit my soul
Any old sink any old brink
   And the mind of the fine dark deep
      eternity—

June 1

The people want to feel good, and they drink wine and they drink coffee to feel good, and they sit in the sun to feel good, and when they feel good they forget ambition and the sense of glory.

I in the New York mountains slowly rose,
From fifth-floor windows looked at other floors,
And saw the stars and cars, and peoples saw
Moving in crowds moved by a nameless cause—

This formal beauty
Permits the city
The rage of cars
And the quick taxi

A coarse necessity
Which will not want for love
Who will ever believe
The body's promiscuity
In every pain finds Eve!

June 3

Woman, eighty-three, hangs herself.

June 10

A man in Calcutta has not slept for two years. Well!

The fragrance of the green leaves
blows into this living room—

He went to the public library,
full of looks!

Snow as newness, renewal, freedom, the space in which we walk—

From depths I never understood
Comes new darkness and new good!—
Candide is here, and Scaramouche
Symbols quickening at a touch—

"I gave her sack I gave her sherry
  And we were wondrous merry"
                    Purcell

O Sister Life, you were a whore
You stacked the cards, you locked the door!
The King and Queen of Hearts were young
But mine the Shame, Remorse, and Tears
          Remorse racking the years
          Mesdames! Messieurs!
          Les jeux sont faites!

Love like a crowbar stuck my pants
My guilt was great as General Grant's!

O coarse necessity
Which will not wait for love
O thick stupidity
Depart, I seek for Eve
          No one will believe
          I will not wish to leave

Jung thinks each holds in depths of mind
The signs which shone for all his kind
Freud shows the child darkened and wild
By accidents of joy beguiled
              The shoe of nurse
              Beware a curse
Or parents' pleasure, shocking blows
Or mother as the gist of whores
Or father as the czar of pain
[. . .]
Rank says the pain of being born
Makes future anguish picayune
Racks forever the growing man—
While Adler spots in injury
The genius' long tenacity
          His strangeness and his need,
          Have weakness as their seed!

Jung
A memory as old as ice
Which holds him like the past, a vice!

Whales of the mountain ranges! hippo heights
Protuberance! Excess! become the Fates—

I feel the fearful lapse upon my lips
Imagining what I think of Stafford Cripps

Shameful memories
Grip me like an anchor
Love is either
Crowbar or jelly

Look, look, here come two martinis
Colorless & powerful

The boys who went with Eisenhower
Ate filet mignon at the zero hour

America! America!
Here we see your growing power
Bathtubs to all Africa
And Heinz in 57 kinds
Where Tibet monk askesis finds

To George
Why get married unless you must
Driven by the horses and dragons of lust!

No one but God may be alive
Turned by the self-look into stone!

O may I be merely the fountain pen
To celebrate God's glory once again

Potted look:
The pregnant ladies whom I see
Walking somehow in advance

My schoolboy intuition glowed
I drew a long nose in the history book
Upon the pharaoh and I drew
A long nose longer and I crowed
—So time's reborn—both old and new
Refreshed and splashed
The centuries once more unleashed

Bergson, when France was fallen when
Jews were banished from other men
As doctors, teachers
The Jew—denied as citizen
Refused the exception made for him
Because his light bloomed France's fame—
And went to register his frame
With all his kind, and stood in line
Returning to the old design—

Bogan, Louise, a poetess
Understood no verse unless
It was like hers or so exotic
It did not make her feel neurotic
The tropic distance was narcotic
And nulled and numbed the rivalries
That itched the mind of poor Louise

My deathless work has kinds of claims
—The dazzling light draws back like oars
                Five years! five years!
To teach and reach the children's souls
To rise as prophet on the stairs
[. . .]

Vaudeville for George Washington, John Quincy Adams, Ulysses Grant, Woodrow Wilson, Henry James, and T. S. Eliot.

Tristram Shandy does a jig
In mother's womb when he gets big

Maggie Verver seems quite cruel
She shows the Wop she's not a fool

I saw the girls as groups of grapes
Thick hanging ready to be plucked—

June 12

Kneeled beside the balustrade
Drunken I wondered what new raid
Dark God would make upon my heart
Praying to be less torn apart
From brother, mother, wife, and friend
        Vaudeville to the bitter end
[. . .]

Older because I have slept less—
"May you meet her in a better demimonde!"
"Why don't you speak Russian, Grandfather?"

Gide rejected Marcel Proust
His first impression not seduced
The masterpiece seemed nothing much
To a trained master at first touch
            O critic on the quick review
            Learn from this what not to do
[. . .]

Proust knew a life, the sailors' joys
Not vouchsafed to later boys
[. . .]

The self has no nose for the stench
Of egotism. Dark the trench
            (prime in the womb
            where all is warm)
In which the self looks out to see
The girl, the friend, society
Posturing coxcomb as me
Making speeches all alone
Before the dresser looking glass
Souse gross coarse and crass

Narcissus cannot see himself
Nor Ghibelline perceive the Guelph
Ego and conflict scrawl the view
With blacks and whites cruel and untrue
As one who in the city street
Smiles to himself and causeless seems

When Trotsky fell more fell than when
Two months before the fall of France
He made a consciousness as new
As is electric light's wide glance
—They had to hit him in the head
(There was his power, there his light)
—There there! He loved and was strong and right

June 15

Proust knew life, the salon's joys
Not vouchsafed to the other boys
And influence! Ruskin taught him
In clear analyses to find the poem
Ulysses never at a loss
Knew what John Dewey taught his class
Sodom, Gomorrah, Cities of the Plain,
Now the modern city lives on pain

Has another lapse begun? I did nothing but two forced and weak pages of verse. Visited by John [Berryman] at noon—a bit drawn back after Sunday night's scene—letter about [Richard] Eberhart's review.

The library, idly turning pages, after finding the poem on Genesis by DeVries—diluted Auden—*The Arabian Nights*, Vol. I, indolent and at ease. To my surprise it was then 4:30. I came back to the house in the heat—struck—went to dinner at the Bella Vista, where it was too expensive and the dinner not good, not even with the martini. I thought for a moment of having dinner with George [Palmer]. But it was too hot.

Then the Phillips bookstore—then oranges, bread, and cheese, waiting too long at the Dana Spa—and no after-dinner rise. The night —lassitude—pages in Gide—two rhymes.

I am older than most, older than my age, for I have slept less.

Dream Tuesday night: in love with a beautiful girl. We were both disfigured in a car accident! myself more than she. I stood in front of the car—saw the accident happen to myself and to her. Then I tried to resume the love—we were always with friends, but she turned from me and could not look at my face—though I felt all might be as it had been.

At eight or nine the phone rang a long time, as I was going to go after her . . .

June 16

I began the day wrong by answering [James] Agee's letter. Then a mere trickle of verse, as Mark [Schorer] called off dinner. Letters to June [Cannan]—precious fun—and enclosures to G. It was very hot. I made lunch, went to get a haircut—closed; the weather changed, the wind blew hard, spots of rain, I called Sonny, then George [Palmer]: it was 4. I had no interest to read. The temperature dropped from 90 to 60 as I walked to town and drank a martini at the Athens Olympia —worn-out with George as we ate and discussed Proust, walked on Columbus Avenue in the Vermeer light, lean long lemon light on red-brick houses disused and unclassed—like Brooklyn and like the cool light of autumn.

Diarrhea, the bar, relief, the drunkard who smiled about it all and spoke of making torpedo boats at Fall River. "Where do you come from?" He was incoherent. "Little Dixie." The ease and strength of the band, the empty house, the black girls looking about, the gay and thespian waiter; to the Key Club, girls in pairs; George's Do you want a girl? I will get you one. Too cold-blooded, I said.

Unwilling to go home, the Garden Grill, chicken sandwich, St. Clair's, Wursthaus, tongue sandwich, home, rum, depression, vista of no girls, forgetting Radcliffe; and no happy circles, here in Cambridge.

Dream that Hook said my book he did not like as I tapped Ruth S., scolding her for telling me because I was to review his book. Dream of a visit from L. Smith, who kept backing down the stairwell. Sleep on the edge of waking until 10.

By the way, you don't seem to understand—this is the first of all poems on insomnia.

June 17

Sonnyism: You sound equivocal!

In going to my naked bed
As one that would have slept . . .

The phrase's curve has feather form,
Or struck, it is a broken rock
Like this, Massy-black the night,
Under the trees the darkness broomed!

Here in the twenty-ninth eternity
I write this down, that I am glad!

Skinned alive! by every word
(What else is there to do?)

These *aperçus*
Are not for you!

July 10

That Fantast
Drunken, I see Bruegel in every face
Bruegel, Hogarth, or Bosch
       the gaffe grotesque
Thick jowl by wrinkle, wrinkle near
       swollen nose
The feel of fat collapsed, sodden, saddened,
          and limp

Time: The navy is spending money like a drunken sailor.

July 14

In the evening, pleasure in anthologies, glancing at [Louis] Untermeyer; but not at my poems; and still very hot, a Turkish heat, and still and wet through and through, sitting still.

July 15

Drowsed to school, wet bright heat, wrong in the first class on transitive verbs.

Tired at lunch, rising until two, five pages forward, Radcliffe themes corrected, and characters noted, quickly and with pleasure, done at 5, ease, dinner at Dicksons', Stewart Paine [explorer] on Peru, mestizo, black girls, employer solidarity, the Johnsons. Heat lifted, home early, after oppressed at dinner.

July 16

Pleasure in taking care of myself and in getting my work done: shirts, shorts, socks, marks, maid, checks. Tomorrow to N.Y.

July 21

My first wife bright, black-haired, and beautiful
The days are rushed, blurred,
Hypnotized,
A sleepwalker's dim fatality—
The obscene Blindness & Stupid
Recognition—

"Listen, I want you to marry me—"
"First conversation—then I must
go home"
"I fell in love with you at Dick's
party" "I want to marry you—good
cook, sewing socks—four children—"

Second marriage like a trip to the Moon—
School like the Great Wall of China

They looked at me as if it had been raining forty days.

July 24

Dreams. A clock (gold watch), touched, collapsed (fell) into its parts—

Moths in my $55 suit, in the vest. Missing the train in N.Y., riding with one like J. Walcott or a Harvard fellow.

Four men had a drink in my apartment—wine—not the little rye left—kept me from calling the police.

I spoke with Dwight amiably: You must come here so that I can throw you out [of] the house.

Anti-Semite turned out to be a Jew, who thought me [an] anti-Semite.

July 25

Sunday morning.

First visit to Appleton Chapel, white and with red leather seats. Joy in community, breaking bread, and breaking with solemn joy into song.

Pretty w. auxs. [Women's Army Auxiliary Corps], a small crowd as if for a doubleheader between two second-division teams. Hymn, prayer, the book of the Western mind.

Air conditioning (thoughts of jokes).

[Reinhold] Niebuhr, nasal New York, bald and finger-pointing like, more and more, Sidney Hook. I sat in the bleachers.

Prophetic religion, Jews chosen, anti-Semitism, imperialism; "poor think with their stomachs"; thoughts of 1934; Amos, Jeremiah, chosen —searched weaknesses and iniquities. Chosen, terrible embrace. "We ought not to repent of each other's sins, but together of all our sins."

Political and technical gifts of Anglo-Saxon peoples. Fervid man behind me.

In the morning, pleasure and fault-finding in T.S.E.'s early prose; in James on Howells.

As I write my work of fiction, I laugh myself sick sometimes.

And often enough also I burst into tears.

André Kostelanetz looked just like Dos Passos, bald and a round face and serious and gentle and short-sighted.

July 26

Dwight is coming to see me? Hot dog! Now I can throw him out of the house—

Pound is a traitor. Leslie Howard is dead. Mussolini is fallen. (Indeed, the thirties are over.) (Our youth is over.)

Poor fellow, poor Pound.

What an exit for a major poet.

July 27

Powerful touring car, Pierce Arrow flights!

Poems Written in Exaltation or Unhappiness, Boredom and Despondency.

> Frieda Lawrence, hausfrau, fat & flushed
> In 1936 in Cambridge, of Lorenzo discoursed—
> > not I, but the wind
> > —the earth, the green, the burning sun
> > —and the easy & the thick water
> > the cool stars & empty sleep—

The Waste Land is incoherent; lacks that structural unity which in many works of art delights us, but so too [a] certain kind of sky [is] scattered yet beautiful; and certain temples in their ruin yet have a great beauty.

Kay Boyle's modernist Laurentian sentimentality.

Lace-curtain Irish, or the cut-glass Jew.

Alibi Ike, the Patent Leather Kid, the Arch Shakespearian radical.

> Boyle dances: a can-can minuet, hornpipe waltz
> parrot, peacock
> (It was a merry saraband time)
> Brandy to bring out the best in us—

Miss Freddie Schoenfield: Do you speak with authority? or are you thinking—

Enough jargon in that book to sink a ship.

July 30

From G.B.S. [Gertrude]. Celia Buckman dead [her mother], my flowers on her grave—the only blooms; and G.'s prayer.

I'll die before Sunday. She died just before midnight, ten of twelve. Wants to die, don't make it too strong; the window is open, I'll get pneumonia. Contrarieties.

The hallucination that Dwight has resigned.

Miss Rukeyser on the Pulpit, *N[ew] R[epublic]* this week, patriotism; Yes, yes, Old Glory around her bandwagon riding.

Man who destroyed a city for a Helen who was a lesbian.

The Second Edition of the works of D.S.

Desire teaches, so does pain.

> *Poem*
> *(I brought it water, dead)*
> From the broken clay pot shards
> I lifted the plant and soil
> The dirtied roots and the leaves
> Pale green to the loosened coil
> And then of the Father of Light
> Freedom and forgiveness of sin
> Most quietly I asked
> Lord may it rise again;
> Some say that you raised the dead
> Let the Jacob plant yet bloom
> In the shocking and shaken world
> And the studied living rooms
> A natural miracle,
> Green strong & beautiful!

July 31

How are you vis-à-vis sex?

Wystan Auden & my overcoat.

Delmore, Auden, fairies, Corydon, Gide.

Creativity in the p.m.—I say, Delmore, may I take the dictionary!

I've had a lovers' quarrel with the world. But what an egotistical lover.

Thursday rain, raincoat, cowl, A[lison Q., a graduate student Delmore admired]: Hello, Delmore, in a too loud voice, a good sign. Had she waited? I suppose it is inevitable—so nice to see you again. (A[lbert] Erskine—I thought if I were he I might have a chance.) I don't want to go to the Cape with my parents. Call on Friday evening and come. Call ten minutes after—no, I have nothing I have to do. Fresh white blouse, lipstick'd lips, master'd manner.

Saturday. Hot and bedrowsed, two poor classes—in between them, Alison, a slight bowleggedness in her walk toward Radcliffe, plump calves and small.

Auden delighted by Visit story; and by Announcement story.

Auden liked the shrimps and shish kebab—wanted potatoes.

James's beard meant no fine injury.

Girls to teach him obscene words—

WAVES story—my class went to pieces—entering the Waves.

Frost wonderfully cute—a James Joyce to record it.

Dwight's neurotic energy. Neurosis as a pit.

Auden on return—no one heard—double insomnia.

Who are these people?—Schorer (told him the little I knew); Morrison, "too academic." (Dwight's and his curse word.)

August 1

Chapel with Auden—coffee, morning—Thoreau—Tate rebuked—ancient crackle—deep gaze—Ransom bogus, Brooks foolish.

Each of us trying to talk.

Eliot stories—Mrs. E. pretended something lost: all had to agree. Aiken's jealousy—Aiken's story of E.'s marriage—ascetic not to marry.

Let's go to chapel—might be fun.

Discussion of *Family Reunion.*

T.S.E.'s period of feeling all and going to bars all the time.

Sunday afternoon—Memorial Hall—sense of past—yearning for English countryside.

Look at my books—roast beef and chicken—liked the house.

Wanted the *Symphony of Psalms.*

Auden, worn with conversation, yearned for E. countryside.

Lawrence, Dostoevsky, James.

Departing with a student.

Her belly like a curved goblet.

Shenandoah Fish recites the Condum speech (to Stalinist)—just in from Westminster, where he teaches philology.

Suicide, Poet's Occupational Disease.

Shenandoah resents Berg's statement that he has no talent. (Smith found Swift's ["A Modest] Proposal" mildly amusing.)

I've been out at stud—so to speak—but give up all for—Ruth.

Frost's table talk—malice.

Auden: You can only be a Catholic because of those who are *not* Catholics.

Baba and aunt at Buckmans'. Why I was not there: You know Delmore.

I wrote a poem then, of the two poets writing poems.

Are you an author?

Forgive me if you don't like this question but: Don't people just keep falling in love with you? I, hopelessly, in Sept. 1941—on the lawn by the slick and famous river.

Auden bored by Joseph books, Couperin, and "ancient instruments."

Leonard Bernstein pure ham, Stokowskian.

Auden wanted to take my pills—love of love, curiosity.

The army chaplain on the sense of guilt.

Auden sings "The Star-Spangled Banner."

I spilt M.'s drink, the whitened floor; Stegner's "Come to see us," and the Burnhams; Ruth brushed leg and breast against me in the car; Miss Schneider, when she saw me . . .

Auden. Dostoevsky, Gide, T. S. Eliot (fireworks with crippled Heywood—Christian).

My review of Eliot—not sestina, canzone.

Mary S[chorer]. "Is your wife working this summer?" Who were the gossips?

Mark [Schorer]—A. wanted to know all about you—told him the little I knew—tough and truck driver and pugilist type.

A[uden] had to take all my pills—he thought he was missing something.

Land of a coward, I am home too drunk to speak honestly—

Sagittarius—out of the world—

August 3

Mann; Auden, Silone; Prokosch in Asia—Syria.

In honor of the Maker of heaven and earth.

Seventeen. O Eileen, I love you, beautiful, poor unlucky girl—

Gentlemen prefer blondes.

Gravesend, Times Square.

I had known that life had undone so many.

"Five thousand years are at an end—"

She waited, then she asked me, silent before University Hall, Cocktails Thursday?

"With my body I thee wed—"

"To do the right thing for the wrong reason—"

Seventeen. "This is a girl whom Plato would have praised."

Auden used a toothpick.

Mr. Levin could be a good critic if he did not admire so much his own witticisms—and learned allusions.

August 8

The mind is a Trojan horse.

Bogan, toboggan; slypuss, hero; Laughlin, Duke of Norfolk; Gregory, ward leader.

Garrigue—I've got plenty of Nothing by Heidegger.

Repeal inhibition.

Blackmur Senator, from J.'s Delight.

August 9

A train passed, leaving in the silence scars . . .

White scar, like the least moon phase.

Did you fall, did you hurt yourself, did you cut yourself?

Basil Willey, I love you, at the Columbia Library! The woman in the business suit, the middle-aged man, and I better go downtown.

Insecurity and left-outness also mastered, with the finishing-school manner: "I like to have growing things around me."

She was finished at the finishing school.

> Plain at fourteen? Who will be
> -lieve this is true of the swan—
> Is her hair blond? (Does Auden share?)

Keep open the lines of communication.

All that the poet, insomnia's laureate, wished to do was to look at a daughter of the Swan. It was enough f'him—

August 10

Zolotow: You give me a pain. Where?

Symbolists, Symbolists. It was a white night for them—the old stairs of pain.

Auden [notes on conversation]: Hideous jealousy; mother, good woman in the worst sense; baseball—wicket; embarrassed about Julian—madman, imitations, horrid creature; dinner with an almost schizophrenic Arab.

If we forgive each other, God will forgive us.

Auden on intermarriage.—How do you feel?—Different in each case.

Mother as snob.

Abel: Don't be so smart, I am no machine.

Your minuet Marie Antoinette look; still look; absolute control; eighteenth-century face.

[The following is a version of "My Love, My Love, My Love, Why Have You Left Me Alone" in Vaudeville for a Princess.*]*

Midmost his twenty-ninth eternity
When hope and expectation sank to ash,
He saw the one superb in memory—
And then, being cowardly, I drank the fire
Which brought the coal-eyed Poe, in Baltimore,
The rocking and bitter sea of his desire,
The death he sang, black handsome nevermore—

Poor Poe! And cursed poets everywhere,
Taught by their strict profession how little is
The second best, the famous lesser good,
They cry exactly to the blank-blue air
Love lost and absolute.

Experience is the knowledge of error. I find life superior to anything I could invent.

Wife did not like me enough.

The Anglo-Klaxons.

If you see a belle plump Aryan rich Aryan, who takes shorthand, tell her I am looking f'her—

She knocked her glass to the floor. Splash, crash. He knocked the decanter down. Roar and splinters. Dolley Madison, he said—

Sphincter intensity.

May Rosenberg story: genius in Chicago. Says you're Dante.

You had a pretty view of your lit. position.

We have a genius (nobody or a genius).

Spengler is walking home.

August 24

Though not French, I feel patriotism (or some kind of warmth),
hearing the "Marseillaise."
The early morning always is untrue.
Early-morning emotions are untrue.
The body's sink, distrait (disheveled), and low (defeat) distrust.
But mostly then I say aloud that I love you.
Alone in darkness, thus because I must.

August 25

"I am deep in Delmore Schwartz"—very happy.
The body sinks into a wild distrust.

September 1

Seventeen. So honest, frank, modest.
Her blue and opened morning-glory eyes.
He has a great deal to be honest about.

Orphic Mode

Blue-bottle day in which the small boat rode
Blue sky unblemished and blue buoyant bay
It took old consciousness snap—whisked away
I mounted like a plane, the Orphic mode
Pitched between life and death, as the blue flowed
Like a new country, through my dazzled gaze
And I turned lobster in the August blaze
—Darkling I did not know what this forbode.

And she just called—September begins—
Something to live forward to—

September 9

Sound and Fury story—sex fiend.
I don't like it. Q.E.D., it is no good. I don't like it but it may be
good, reasons. Liver, for example.
Balzac: sleep with a woman, there goes another novel.

September 10

Once for imagery, richness—once for style.

Before the dark arena, Hippodrome
With feathers flourished Eva Tanguay sang
I don't care, although he has gone home
I don't care, rang . . .

(Start sonnets at the end.)
Mussolini—headwaiter in Ethiopia.
Hitler—house painter in Warsaw.

September 11

G[ertrude]—cocktail parties—subjectivity because I had a great good time—five years to understand that—

A[lison]'s beauty—denied by her.

Stupidity at Mark's, seeking out Wallace [Stegner] and speaking loudly.

At the party. Alison: Who freshened your drink? Delmore: You're checking up on me.

Poem. She unbuttoned slowly, carefully, his sense of shame like a shirt—

Why did Dick Ellmann [Joyce scholar and critic] not like her?

September 12

Oscar's [Handlin] hint: job at Brooklyn, told not to take it. Congratulations.

Sylvia Berkman [author and professor at Wellesley]: Don't you mean Alison and not me? Stay to dinner?

Well, we're all back at work again—Morrison.

John's [Berryman] not helping himself, at the Har[vard] Employment Bureau.

> Cold flat mornings, like last year
> Cool glitter lines of the first fall light

Pregnant women, ahead of themselves, potted.

Alcestis.

Emotion is a poem; emotion caused by the poem in the reader. Modernism—trite and banal as any other school.

> Her look comes glittering above a smile
> Thin-lipped it is a second secret smile
> All in the gaze gauze thick white porcelain
> (What does she think about, tending her hair?
> How can she then deny that she is beautiful?)

Enormous energy, sublimation, freedom, assurance, since the last week of May.

Abrams—again the unrecognized Jew story, told joyously except for Gerson [Brodie, friend from graduate student days]. Bible, to be distinguished as fictive fabrication versus the actual event.

R.R.'s [?] effort to impose his fable—tilt and curve of his mind— on his friend.

Basic English is composed of the four-letter words and a sleeping dictionary.

Gertrude angered at breakfast, a twice-told story: My stomach made the great refusal. Too late, I clapped my hand to my mouth. And slapped my face with the outcome.

Romanticism escaped. Realism condemned.

H. L[evin]—lived next door, so that he would be unable to talk behind my back, except out of the side of his mouth.

My honesty and the Englishman's modesty.

Alison embarrassed and snubbed by Murdock, followed by him up the stairs.

Oh, hello, oh, Delmore (wrinkled-up nose), look as of a wink.

Nela stuck out her tongue.

Ruth held my hand and tapped me lightly. "Darling!"

September 13

Mother. Baba lives for days until a compliment. Shy until eighty.

Frost-bitten Bostonians. Octopusian Bostonians.

September 14

To write fiction is to be able to be interested in everything.

Now I see how others learned much.

Lardner, Cocteau, Pasternak, Hemingway, Steinbeck.

Repartee, audience.

Mrs. Massey: I buried my husband at Xmas.

"Mrs. Dickson likes you very much."

I see a glitter in all eyes . . . plumber, student, servant, too.

From Berryman I learned to imitate, to do what works—how to correct papers.

Once is love enough. Don't let it happen again!

The Pleasures of Actuality.

"The gods geometrize."

He was a part of every mind he touched.

September 15

A simple intense wish for love and knowledge.

> The sails the soars the loops
> & dips
> of heightened consciousness
> Snow glare, snow blindness
> cold & sleep

Still rheumatic with my old howlers and gaffes. Baudelaire—melodramatic in *"Au Lecteur"* and *"Bénédiction."*

"N[ew] Year's Eve" [one of the stories included in *The World Is a Wedding*, New Directions, 1948]: Richmond overhears Jefferson arranging another party—silent when R. comes up. Being left out.

Frost, Pound—short stories in verse.

Boston dedicated to drink and copulation—good, this prepares the way f'lyric poetry.

> My sensibility begins to screech
> Like chalk upon the blackboard scrawled

White scar, fetish, foot; "For this relief, much thanks."

Intense, overwhelmingly intense, incandescent desire for love, knowledge, and poetry.

Rogers Peet—revenge and triumph.

Swishing bravura; overintense; two people from out of town; white scar, fourth finger.

September 16

Freud, Stekel, everything has a motive. To buy a German dictionary, and learn German by reading Stekel.

R[ose] S[chwartz]'s perception: Your father would say anything, girl who slept with him in the rooming house, same wild impulse and awful daring.

Liffey is Life, and it is a poem of nature, the male and the female principle, and all memory, hall memory.

September 21

If I get an inch, I take infinity—Auden.

October 18

> An intuition like a lightning bolt
> Made me rear wildly like an untaught colt

Prose, Verse, Criticism. I've been speaking verse, using metaphors all my life?

October 19

Gull, plane / New England wet and gray / a sooty night / a cloth (a woolen) day / late and white flowers / tobacco crumb leaves.

> When yellow leaves or none or few
> My leaves have drifted from me—

A clam cold toad day.

Irreversible rack of discrimination.

Anti-Semitism in Boston, hoodlums, Dorchester.

Neuroticism is lack of belief or false belief.

G.B.S.: Nobody likes me. I am neurotic.

Prose in one room, verse in another. Kitchen, I eat; bedroom, I try to sleep; study, I correct themes.

Strength of not doing what you want to do; strength of doing what [you] don't want to do.

Effort-gratification must be close.

November 13

Sonnet; in the evening at 10, [James] Agee, Mia Fritsch [Agee], Henry Hart, stories, Mozart, *Anna Livia* on the recording machine; Jean's dinner [Jean Garrigue, poet]; nervousness all afternoon; too much to drink.

Agee remembered the remark about navy spelling.

Hart questioned Mia. She had been in Vienna in 1934, next to the city hall, and for three days, no water, light, or heat (it was March) and all the apartment houses locked by the police. "No one could think of anything to do."

Hart felt that I had added something to Joyce; Agee that I had not enough modulation, too elegaic.

Jean said that I had been better in Cambridge; I was too close to the microphone.

November 14

Sleep without aid, three times awakened, nervous in the bitter gray November afternoon; the store with old chromos.

Jean, goodbye; Alison on the train: "These are dangerous days"; safe enough here.

November 17–21

17th. Hangover, walked off, the doctor's. Evening with Clark, Whitmans, Phyllis—very cold, late, taxi. Phyllis crossed her legs and rang her boyfriend.

18th. Morrison reading, clanking of radiators, the Whitmans. Scowcroft and classes. Early wine, sleep.

19th. Morning of Xmas poem; sporting with Miss Cupid; evening with H[oward] Blake. "Thank you for this evening."

21st. Millay review ["The Poetry of Millay," in *The Nation*, December 18, 1943] begun, faded, ill, nervous. Crockett in the morning, Valéry foreword, effort at translation, cold black sky, lighted windows twice. [During his courtship of Alison Q., Delmore frequently went to see if her windows were lighted or dark.] At Handlins', discussion divorce, Murdock, academic politics.

November 22

Quiet empty day, after a brief rise in the morning and one and a half pages of Millay review. Lunch with Matthew Josephson, *Robber Barons*, Groton, pleased with me. Putnam and Bill [Van Keuren, close friend], in the evening, Andy [Wanning], Laurette Murdock. Bourbon, Bella Vista, too much to eat.

Emptiness, Joyce, sickness. Andy stayed much too late, until 2, and I slept thinly after 3.

At 4:30 I tried to get Alison.

Morrison "demanding" one term in four—I think of these things all the time.

November 23

Millay review, and then the lapse, I think—a drink with Scowcroft, the classes. On Monday the new nurses at the doctor's, bump—"officiating."

November 24

The doctor's, libido, it will come back as strongly as ever. This day like the day before hard to remember now (on Thursday)—on Monday Scowcroft's.

Alison will come and listen, she might be bored. Have you asked her? Frost, the New Lecture Hall, bored on the balcony.

Frost, balcony. "Ethan Allen, who believed only in God"; Ezra Pound, bad boy; read Flaubert, 1875, before you were born; "The Gift Outright"; "Short History of U.S. in blank verse"; worn out by difference between blank and free verse; teachers did not tell them. Reads too fast.

T.S.E., on *Finnegans Wake*, in 1926: Can't stand much of that.

December 2

Thursday. Nela, John's death, Nov. 18, died, not killed. [John Walcott was in the army.] Nela for lunch; a new building of the fire.

Dec. 1. F.O.M. at 5, two pages of the prospectus [for the English Department], after weak classes, and the doctor; furnace, water.

Nov. 30. Hangover all day, and wine at 4. V[an] K[euren] phoned; Phyllis, 24-hour grippe.

Nov. 29. Phyllis, late, too much Scotch, Olympia, new records, brandy, taxis, emotional attachments, (Kenneth, Richard). Alison as an apple polisher. Awake at 8:30, too late for eight o'clock class—and two fairly weak classes.

Nov. 28. A day of fading: letter to R.P.B. and the completed Millay review—after statement of accusation from V.K.

Nov. 27. Brief dinner with Alison at Bella Vista (Phyllis as nymphomaniac, since her twelfth year, and knowing where Murdock would be each hour). "Now that the ground has been cleared, may I take you to dinner." "Delmore, what a charming idea."

Nov. 25. Lighted house twice, Handlins' Thanksgiving, Oscar's sister, two other girls, argument about Soviet-Nazi pact.

December 4

At 5, visited by Phyllis; dinner at the Wannings', full of metaphors about the existence of God, Van Lennep and his wife, and Andy's brother-in-law, who teaches at Exeter.

December 5

Alison and Niebuhr, Appleton Chapel, the weak win out over the strong because of righteousness, "a cheap and vulgar idea"; Martin the student, after the sermon, where M. found it difficult to focus attention, as in the summer. [Delmore here and in some of the following pages uses the initial M. to refer to himself.] "Don't suppose that because righteousness will triumph that you are the righteous," said N[iebuhr].

December 6

Poor classes, stage-fright moments, and then to the doctor, dug, and quickened by puncture, "merely a reflex action"—hyperaesthesia and jumps—forced writing of the prospectus, as since the Monday before. Opus 18, Saunders.

December 7

Alison called to ask about Pound and also about Niebuhr, "Christianity was a scandal," quoted; don't forget to let me know next time. M. forced more pages of the prospectus.

Thrice cut at the 5 & 10 by Elena Levin.

Phyllis in the balcony, the coming birthday: "See you on Friday, Bill."

> When thirty years were dead, I heard
> Beethoven say
> The Kingdom of heaven is in you
> but also hell,
> Wait & move on, move on, & look back,
> and play,
> With all your senses wait, and then, one day,
> All shall be well—
>
> Sometimes you must wait at
> the black gate
> With all your senses wait, with
> all your mind &
> heart
> With all your art

December 8

The effort to be adequate to the occasion, difficulty in the E2 and the E3 classes, Socrates vs. Thoreau, the German example given by Martin, the argument of Lewis, too much dialectic, not enough energy.

Consoled after class by the three students who argued about C.O.'s. Then A[lison] as M. passed to Warren House, tipped his hat, went as if not to stop to talk.

"Why weren't we given fair warning?" [The day was Delmore's birthday.]

"What was I to do, send out announcement cards?"

"Come over for a drink this evening."

"I am going to hear the Beethoven Quartets, which seems a fitting thing to do."

Discussion of how a girl has so much more to lose on birthdays.

"It feels very strange; thirty dead years, thirty thousand dead imaginations of what this day was to be."

"You are going out to dinner."

"Unfair to say a thing like that; let us stop deducing each other's actions."

"May I call you at four o'clock?"

"You had better decide right now."

"May I take a rain check?"

"Yes, but you know it is not the same thing."

"It is the intention that counts, and I am touched, thank you very much" (politeness learned from her); we had drawn apart, exchanging false last sentences.

"Please ask me again soon."

I departed, pleased by the specious freedom displayed, and gained by the engagement with Phyllis. On Tuesday night, the drunken ring, what is it? Many such questions. Difficulty with the furnace, the plumber at 4:30, Phyllis, stories, the night before, the ring explained, tweed and flannel praised, the doorbell rang four times, the Quartets before dinner, the phone call, specious Alison, all deliberately summoned up. "I knew it was she," a showpiece, make-believe at Saunders, the Whitman, departure after the first Quartet, *Opus* 59, No 1, only the first movement heard, Bella Vista, home. Questions: Do you expect to marry again? Do you want children? I want six, the marrying kind. "You will be disappointed in me." "You in me"; six brothers and sisters, Watteau and a twin at present in Dublin, I hate America, drunken and then full lips, then no more to drink as M. drank and his face sagged and he asked, Who said I was good-looking? Different at different times, sometimes peculiarly beautiful, sometimes something else. Just then his face was sagged from tiredness and drinking, it was by then midnight. "I am not self-conscious with you," she said. The Square on

foot and then a taxi, "I will call you," kissed on the cheek, as at departure and on Saturday given the cheek again.

On this birthday, too, M. walked about in the same grave, not
different.

It was 2 before sleep and 9:30 before waking.

December 9

First the lucid hour, when M. was able to write; he wrote letters
to John Berryman, Gertrude, and Philip Rahv; more than an hour. But
he avoided the work for school most of all. And he looked for things in
irritation, because from childhood he did not have the habit of putting
back a thing in place after he had used it and was not interested in it.

In the afternoon, M. finished his piece for the *Record* about being
a Jew. ["Under Forty" (part of a symposium) was published in *Contemporary Jewish Record* 7, February 1944.] It was a "might as well,
it is not important finish," a page and a half added to the two pages
already written, which seemed good enough because of the artificial
aftermath light, the rise after drinking.

Black at waking, then the growing ice light, and the lift from putting coal in the furnace.

In the evening, he struggled to get ready for class, corrected a few
themes, put them aside, made notes, satisfied himself with these,
thought of not going to class, went to the Quartets, *Opus 76*, left after
the first one, much too nervous, drank himself to sleep, woke at two,
drank once more, slept until 5:30, rose, tried again to prepare for class.

December 10

Difficulty in the first class about Monday's assignment, resolved
by giving the students their way. Home to find the furnace blowing off
steam, discussion with Mrs. Dickson and the plumber; two classes of
debate, both successful, cheered; Mrs. Dickson on the phone again;
forced pages for the prospectus; letter from Eliot, feared, and dismayed
by the withdrawn politeness, for M. expected too much. Letter to
Philip, walk to the doctor, wait in the chromium waiting room, nervousness, walk back, dialogue with Gertrude because of her telegram;
dinner again at 5:30, without drinking (and now Gertrude has just
called).

December 11

No one can truly see himself because he is not another. No one can
truly see another because he is himself.

We live by snapshots, profiles, glimpses.

Yet nobody fools anybody much.

Eliot speaks of the search for form. The form then is the end, this is the final form; it is overt form, which is the beginning like the circle.

The painter's aim is to see more.

The painting's aim is to show more.

We live by an inner fire; we live in the empty air.

No one is twice the same; yet nothing dies, although each birthday is a funeral.

Joyce says, The artist makes no mistakes. His mistakes are the portals of discovery.

No; wrongly stated for the rhetoric of the paradox. The artist always makes mistakes; his mistakes are the only way in which he can make certain essential discoveries.

[Owen] Barfield [professor of language and literature]: "If we trace the meanings of a great many words (or the elements of which they are composed) about as far back as etymology can take us, we find, we are at once made to realize that they refer, an overwhelming majority if not all, to one of these two things—a solid sensible object, or an animal (probably human) activity."

To compose is to put together; to make a metaphor is to bear across; thus both are a kind of love; and they are the same.

Rilke said, To take the world in and to transform it, that is the way.

> They just don't know,
> (He lay in a puddle of sleep)
> What will we do when the Messiah comes?
> We will make merry when the Messiah comes!
> Who will read the Law to us when the Messiah comes?
> Moses the Rabbi, he will read the law to us!
> Who will dance for us? David the King, he will dance for us!

I went through the day as a train passes through a brief tunnel, back in the sunlight again, the darkness forgotten.

Incident, anecdote, conversation, memory, illumination, photograph, correction—the gulf to language—the reader's feeling (the slant of style), the unique and the common, the passage of time.

To perform an endless act of criticism (which is comparison, analysis, and the illumination of texts).

Gertrude, it never ends.

The sky is the color of ice, low white intense.

December 13

The same postponement of work for school, of preparation; otherwise this might be a time of taking in the books unread during excitement, or wrongly read, or just touched; and the magazines.

G.B.S. came, there was an argument, it was about Nela, the writing of letters, what happened in August, how much she disliked M. then, tears, the books picked up, M. felt the old days, the attitudes of refusal, and then the story of being touched, and what she would have asked M., because a man in New York who was married had touched her and she had liked it. This would be the negative test. Then there was trial, tears, effort, failure, no desire in her, tears, she blamed herself, she spoke of a pillow, "You are not a pillow," and as M. tried he thought of return, and was afraid of it. Van Keuren came, the three sat and two drank, and "Do it quickly," she said, as M. spoke too much for her of not taking a drink.

They drove to Locke Ober's, stopping at the Square. "She had beautiful eyes," said Bill.

"Is this canine?" she asked, old childlike charm. And with dinner and a double martini, M. was fluent again. Her face fell as he said he had written of Edna Millay for *The Nation*. This was the jealousy she had admitted as her dislike's root, when she came in August and saw how M. progressed. The look down like the lightning stroke of convulsion on the faces of Levin and Davis (and on M.'s, too, after he had seen them turn away).

Then the Dicksons, then *Anna Livia*, then a repetition, "Why don't you ask the Dicksons first?" for she saw M. as seeking to dominate the scene, which is the resentment perceived by Barrett in the early summer of 1939.

Saturday night at an end, a Sunday morning of brief phrases, the Dicksons' at three, disregarded by the children, a shining look on Gertrude's face, her unease, the Schorers, our departure, the emotion in the taxi here and at *Opus 97*; as M. tilted his head, she came to stand beside him; he sat beside her, after changing the records. Then he kissed her and did not know what else to do, and she did not say what she felt, and M. said, "It never ends," and he read her some of his new poems. The return to the Dicksons', the hurry, departure in the trolley, as M. stood, looking, until he saw the passengers look at him. Again, a rising energy as M. did not drink, then the Palmers', and discussion of the false accusation and the lie detector in a rape case. Then to dinner at the Bella Vista, home, admiration of the pictures, George disgruntled, "Come and see us," and Rose's effort to get him home.

Instead of anxiety, M. suffered from emptiness and failure to concentrate when Rose or Wallace [Dickson] spoke to him. He was at ease at the Bella Vista, he thought of Alison, he did not go to see if the apartment was lighted; this, too, had stopped.

Gertrude was much amused by the story of M.'s student party. She thought Bill adorable. She took the check and the dinner without demurring, one attitude so frequent in marriage.

Today, bright hard cold Monday morning, the idea of not going to classes germinated; too much to drink; and it seemed to be a good thing as M. struggled to go forward with the prospectus. He told Morrison, who said, "We might get in trouble," "Get a good alarm clock," "Thanks for telling me"; and then the mail arrived with the 2A classification and a card from Fisher. The idea of a social circle, and a full life in Cambridge, had vanished with the summer excitement.

December 15

She [Alison] wanted to know more about Phyllis; did she live up to my expectations?

Yes, I said, her name is metrical.

Her reason was to ask me to come to cocktails: "You were so cryptic the other day about Phyllis"; who had been standoffish and was now a reformed character.

I spoke of the gossip we had exchanged; of how she had said, "I've heard more gossip from you than from anyone else in the past few months."

I explained that I had spoken as an intimate friend; and that I had not spoken as much to anyone else before, at least over an equal length of time.

She said that her words had been ill chosen; and that she had never spoken or taken a course with Owen; and that Murdock had dodged her in the Yard (after he snubbed her on the steps of the library?).

She wanted to know when I was going to New York and she said she was going on the sleeper: both ways, if she could afford it.

Is it Phyllis, or my not calling, or both?

I spoke of what she said about Phyllis, and she heard the reproach in the quotation.

"Phyllis is on your trail," she said.

"Do I bore you?" asked Phyllis.

"What do you consider the age of consent?" I asked her.

"Some never reach it," she said.

"What am I to do, if she is on my trail?"

When I called a second time, I put together that remark and the one about the effect on members of the faculty, not the Murdocks.

"I don't think you arrogant," I said to her. "I do think you rationalize a good deal, at your convenience."

She told [Douglas] Bush [noted English professor] what the quotation was. He did not like her. Spencer had spoken of permanent tutorships at Radcliffe.

I tried to call Phyllis between the two phone calls.

Late in the afternoon, I became very nervous. I went to dinner early.

The Harvard bookstore man was annoying again with his persistent questions about books. The waitress seemed to be impressed because I ordered oysters and steak. She was the one who was difficult and irritable in June, when I sat at a table for four.

I bought a copy of Whitehead's *Introduction to Mathematics*. I tried to prepare for class, but I did not do very well; I read in *F[innegans] Wake* all afternoon, after Bill left, and found my ability to read fading through the afternoon.

I was nervous at the staff meeting on Monday. I turned away from Mark; and I spoke of the lack of progress, the lack of a sense of progress when a student wanted to know, "What is a summary?"

I slipped out quickly, after the staff meeting.

Alison had been told by Spencer ("who keeps coming over here") that Harry Levin felt left out and was upset about his book; I spoke of the easy success and seduction of teaching. I explained that I had begun to teach after I wrote.

Gertrude's visit spoiled two days.

Philip's letter was full of pleasure for me.

December 16

Phyllis wants to fall in love once and for all, she seems to haunt you, the blond detective.

You are humorless. Would you want to be a cat?

Nothing until almost three o'clock and then rashes, after an afternoon reading of the kinds and ends of drunkenness: it does do harm, as Agee said, and especially dangerous is "the normal excessive drinker."

A mute and blank cold, near zero, unable to get a taxi to go to the doctor; waiting patiently and patiently, cold and bedrowsed; "You're a better specimen, whether you like it or not," "We seek the negative reaction," "I am surprised it did not happen before; it will come back better than ever."

"I want a lamb chop, I want some ham and eggs."

Noon, the thin and smoky sunlight, rejuvescence [sic], everything interesting.

> What am I but the stooge and the slob of Love?
>   How can I help but admire
>   The rage and the rush of fire,
> Laugh and lie down, arise and run for Love?

December 17–23

Today is a Friday, and the week has a new form, different from the summer's.

By Friday at noon, there is the release of no school for the afternoon or the next two days.

During the first three years, it was from Sunday night until late Wednesday afternoon; then, as I returned from conferences, the sense of release awakened and stretched out, and there was relaxation.

Yesterday I began to tremble at noon, as I ate lunch; this was the same time as in summer. But today it has happened at a later hour. And I feel the beginning of a new period of spontaneity.

M. saw Mary Handlin in the stacks, and met her and her husband at the Bella Vista, after a great glow or sparkle of interest had begun while looking at books.

Clark came with his friend as I went to the store, after blowing a fuse. I was angry with him coming again, and not calling as I had asked him to do several times. So ever the undergraduate: no imaginative sympathy; so I was in my day.

I am a new man; the new man like the suit which has just been dry-cleaned; someone says, "It looks as good as new." And it does, from a distance; closely examined, the nap has worn off or the texture of the cloth is thin; and it looks stale, not fresh and new.

In New York are old relationships like banked fires.

17th. Phyllis, and on the sofa, after Gustie's Xmas tree, brandy.

18th. Phyllis in the afternoon, Bill, dinner at his house, home, early to bed with rum and a cold.

19th. Alison: "Drifting apart."

D.: Alison, you ought to get married. Then you will have the kind of social life you want. You ought to marry some young man your father approves of.

A.: Delmore (like a bell), you ought to see some of these young men! Mediocrity.

Then she spoke of being left out of parties. What parties? She did not know which ones, only that people she called spoke of parties they were going to.

20th. Three classes and well enough, Dicksons, staff meeting, Morrison annoyed—Phyllis at 6:30. My son's name will be Shenandoah.

22nd. Dinner with Phyllis and Bill at Josef's, and drove B.'s car; all night, until 6; and then hungover, nervous, distracted by disorder.

"Are you happy with me?" "Do I make you happy?"

23rd. Evening. Black and cold outside, cold through shoes; empty and yellow inside—letter from Jean G[arrigue], peeved.

Anxiety all day; the shaking; the fear of all undone and unanswered —mss., letters.

December 24

Xmas Eve, a lively happy active day, causeless happiness.

I wrote p. 30 of the prospectus after lunch with Bill [Van Keuren], who brought the Xmas present of a bottle of sherry; for which I gave him *The Great Gatsby.*

I wrote Philip and sent back poems for *P[artisan] R[eview]*. I was impatient for evening and tried to pass the time with Cocteau and to arrange books.

I ate by myself at Jim's Place, after writing down last Sunday with Alison.

It was dull at Morrison's. I talked with McCreary about John Holmes [poet], and talked with Sylvia Berkman. And did not have enough to drink, and avoided Spencer. Sylvia referred to Alison several times, and spoke of teaching.

Collins, Virginia Proctor, Collins's wife's red gown, Stegner, his wife—then everyone wanted to go home, for it was too dull.

But I went to F.O.M.'s, since Andy asked me; or Pat. And Andy drove recklessly and I said, Let's stop f'a quick one.

I had no one to speak to, at F.O.M.'s; and no one was drinking, and the party was fading—Dick Schlater, *Genesis*, the Soviet Union—the architect Worcester, radiant heat, sun heat.

"Have you finished your book?" I asked F.O.M. He had, yesterday.

Sad and amiable, the Abramses.

(Sunday, you defined the character of it viz. our relationship.)

I go back to Alison, deathless hope: did she sleep with F. this week; or tomorrow?

I felt free of Phyllis: "Maybe I won't come back. There is only Kenneth to come back to; he kissed me." Maybe she wanted you to make a pass at her; kittenish. Looked sweet asleep; peculiarly beautiful. It was 1:30. I had waited all evening, wishing to go to sleep.

Home, records, the girls looked at the pictures, Andy became drunk, spilled water, and we argued about Beethoven. (Pat likes me.)

December 26

I did not bring the eggs or the milk. Because of a taxi? she [Alison] said.

Then she wanted a lemon.

"If you had brought the eggs, we could have had a feast"—after the Wannings departed.

She was the second girl I asked to marry me. She punished me on the tram; but why? This time a hundred years.

"These are dangerous days"—her only crude remark.

I don't think we can get a seat together.

Are you riding home on the subway?

Did she get off at Springfield?

The idea of going to New York comes to me: for what can I do here?

H. W. Eliot and wife on Mass. Ave., walking off an Xmas dinner; a pretty woman in middle age.

To hear Jeremy say, Nurse! (*Les Noces*, Nurse)—felicity itself.

We grin at each other—

In the beginning was the *bon mot* (wisecrack).

> The heart laid bare
> (The beginning, the he and the she)
> New York, O what a charming city—

O snaps to you & schnapps for me & the dreams of the dregs for the drastic—

Behold the gold—

I tried two of the white at four o'clock, and lifted to Joyce, it all brightened, I was not "repelled" by impenetrables; and I read Harry [Levin], shamed at myself, for the essay in *N[ew] D[irections]* shows his ability. And I forgot what he had done not only to myself but to others.

I was sad about thirty, a well-known young man, successful, but not with his art and his life in powerful hands.

I read *Finnegans Wake* all day, as yesterday *Thomas the Imposter*. This was after I wrote to [Henry Allen] Moe [for years the Secretary General of the John Simon Guggenheim Memorial Foundation] and the Chicago Title & Trust. It was a blunted day because I woke at 5:30 or 6.

I looked to see the lights; Alison, Concord.

Bill invited me to dinner.

And I thought of Phyllis's telegram and that she must have been drunk. Moe's letter looked to me as if I would probably again get a Guggenheim.

I was unable to have an appetite for lunch at the Bella Vista. I heard Beethoven's Fifth, the *St. Matthew*, a Schubert cello concerto (in which the orchestra was as in the *Emperor*) and wished again that I knew more about music, that is, to read the score. Next year?

"A cold passionate dawn"—a blue hard shining sky, the morning star big as a buckle.

[Robert] Hillyer: Hello, Delmore, we're early poets, aren't we?

Inanely—"I think it's a good habit," staggered by, jump jump walk of mine.

No crime of which the imagination is not capable.

Alison: The kind of dishonesty girls turn to, while they are making up their minds.

I said, "If it were anyone but you, I would think you were using me against him, to make him jealous."

"A new tone; something has been added: what is the news, Alison?" Impatient and kittenish, as when she wished to know about Phyllis, two weeks or three, before.

"Why didn't you tell me you were having dinner with Gertrude?" ever deductive, troubled by this.

"It was not with Gertrude, she was here on a weekend."

"Do you think you know me?"

"I am essentially misleading."

December 27–29

Wednesday: School again, the second class weak.

I painted the table upstairs; with gray and with pleasure. At the library, I looked for the wrong thing, furtive, and this as yesterday.

Gerson came at 5:30, more Babbitt than ever, and conscious now of having done nothing. His five oil wells were dry. V[an] K[euren] was here for a time with Florette. Gerson, "mighty pleased," told me of his new messianic idea, to get rich, and to find out the meaning of life. Bored, at 9 rang Alison, and spoke briefly of being bored. She rang back.

Tuesday: Sleep until 11:30, a letter to Gertrude, an idle afternoon, the hangover jumps, though mildly, and a nervous disheartened effort to prepare for class. I drank too much rum or felt I was drinking too much. But I woke with freshness. I enjoyed setting things in their right order. It was very cold in the street at dusk. Today and the day before I expected Phyllis to ring me and she did not and I did not want to see her—enough to ring her. Full of thoughts of A.

Monday: I did little but write an examination question for M., and read about *Finnegans Wake*. At night I drank beer, rum, and then wine at 5:30. But the fascination with Joyce continued against the perplexity.

Undated

Alison, sibling rivalry; playpen, penis envy; pre-Oedipal attachment to mother all important.

"If my mother knew what I was—"

Tuesday, opera—"I'll think about it."

My arm about her. She did not look up.

Yes—think about it—and I left. (Mozart as sophisticated child.)

> She was a Gibson girl & a doll,
> Intelligent as a King's Jew,
> And perfectly beautiful
> Something new

The men with whom she slept.

Talked too much, I did.

Dinner has been very nice.

Her lips were sticked [sic], her white blouse fresh and new, not withered, wan swan, like yesterday.

Alliteration is like ivy, some of it is poison.

Good will is a gold mine.

Jokes on tombstones, jokes on weddings, Tricky Rituals, take it or leave it—

The war will be over before some of my students learn to spell.

An outstanding nose seen.

Versailles will be an Arcady. See, see they are going to make Versailles look like a Quaker meeting.

What next, O Double Agent—take care, make it brief—

> When Armistice arrives
> hostilities cease
> And all the obscenities begin—

John Berryman, Duke of Maryland.

Tate, President of the Confederacy.

> Blue bottle of the sea and sky, the ship
> Some other world
> And far the faint boom shore, the thinnest strip—

Dream. Paul Goodman, broad-faced, discussion of Noh plays in lunchroom.

Poor Berryman, selling *E[ncyclopaedia]* *B[ritannica]*s from house to house.

The girl outside of Liggett's, her glance across the French sailor's pants—the obvious line of her look.

Blanche Katz, Finkel, Fred. Are you anti-Semitic? —I would not know, I was only in Mexico two years.

J.L. on whores in Mexico City—even better than Paris.

1942. Poems about The Choice, New York, The Choir (unfinished attempts). Story: "New Year's Eve." Essays: "Waste Land," "Auden in America."

Jan., Feb. 1943. Reviews: Schapiro, Aiken.

March 1943. Auden essay.

Late March & April 1943. Nothing.

May 1943. Eliot review. "Real Life," two chapters. "Eurydice," outline.

June 1943. Sonnets & Fables.

July 1943. "History of the Boys & Girls." Sonnets & Lyrics. [Yvor] Winters & Hook reviews.

August 1943. Lyrics, sonnets, Wilson review, satire.

September, October 1943. Sonnets, *Times* review, The Kings.

November, December 1943. Sonnets, The Twelve, Millay review, The Jew, Valéry & Proust, Outline of an Anthology.

1944

January 2

My years have rifted from me. One to thirty. How do I know how many more, and where will I be and when will I die and will I be sorry that I am I? Yes? Guess!

Married and parted, published and punished, unfinished, praised and appeased, and envied and hardly understood. So much is over and so much rejected, so much desired and tossed and untouched.

All in the darkness or fizz of shore lights, and flick of far stars.

I slept until twelve, I built the fire, I read some pages of Joyce, I made my breakfast, I shaved and bathed. I touched over the painted table, I thought with aversion of tomorrow's class, I sent a check to my mother, and this was a Sunday, one more Sunday, one more day, one more waste.

It is for a sexual reason, and a dark one, that I wear pajamas.

I marked two classes' papers, entered the marks, reviewed [Louis] Adamic, outlined the two classes, went to a forced supper at Bickford's, prepared work on the sentence, wrote to *The New Republic*, and thought too often of Alison.

It was a mild day for winter.

I did not take a drink until eight o'clock.

I listened to second-rate music.

To do with some success the simple tasks gave me some relief and pleasure of spirit.

The sky woolen or flannel or fog-colored, it was a slowed wet winter afternoon.

Yesterday Alison rang to ask me to go with her to *The Cherry Orchard*. She wants a literary friend, and she wants a social life.

January 4

On Monday, after class, relieved to be done with the three of them, I felt a new beginning. I was full of energy as I went to the doctor. But then I went to the Clearing House bookstore, and nothing looked very interesting. I came back on the subway, reading *The New Republic* and *The Nation.*

Bill [Van Keuren] arrived, I was numb, we had Scotch, too much, and we drove to the Athens Olympia. George and M[arjorie Palmer] were in a booth, I had another drink, and talked with energy and ate with strong appetite and wanted to go somewhere after that. But Bill had to go home; he had quarreled with his wife on New Year's Eve because he had been with Florette in the afternoon and there was perfume on his suit. I went to the house with him, and faded and drank more Scotch and tried hard to talk with Helen. And then we heard Schubert and Sibelius, before I rode home.

Phyllis rang after I fell asleep, and I spoke to her with drunken warmth, and drank too much to get to sleep again, awoke at 7, forced myself to sleep until 9:30, and was hung over, low and slow, all day. I spoke with Mary at the library, Phyllis passed breathless, going to Murdock; returned, asked me to go with her for a cigarette, frowned when I would not, and did not ring at 6, as she had promised.

January 5–6

Dinner with Phyllis and Bill at Gustie's. She talks again of being a ghost. She is intense. She kisses Bill and she rings me and she tells me of kissing Bill; too much to drink.

I think of going to New York and idle at the library. Morrison speaks of lack of discipline in E-1.

January 7

Irritated in E-1 class; Porter breaks the window, says he is learning nothing, and has spoken to the dean. The feeling of appallment (as I walked out with him and questioned him), but then two fairly successful classes.

Train ride, theme-correcting, Pullman car, happy in New York's glittering center, Jean [Garrigue]'s, the taxi, Polly, Philip's, Jai Alai, William, argument about God's existence, Scotch for sleep.

January 8

At the *P[artisan] R[eview]* office, lunch on Thirty-second St., the titillation of words in the new *PR*, the post office, Marlton [Hotel], waiting for Jean, the winter afternoon sky and the towers, Jean.

Quick coup, "You don't care f'me no more." You don't care for me; thirty, Polly, a soldier, Jumble Shop, bottles of brandy, Luigi's, pretty Polly, evening at Jean's, reading poems—Jane Mayhall [fiction writer and poet] and Leslie Katz [critic and publisher of the Eakins Press], outside, as we read aloud; Marlton with Jean, drunkenness, "You're beautiful, my dear," coup, touched, unable to sleep, discomfort.

January 9

Hangover, breakfast at the Griddle, Polly and Bill, unhappy, nervous, wishing to be rid of Jean; William's, *PR* money, Rosenfeld and war posters, Jean, Jumble Shop, impatient, and guilt to go so quickly (after, the day before, too much avowal).

Train ride in the club car, the drunken-sick officer, railroad lawyer, and effort to hold our seats. Bill, pleased by the weekend, concerned with *PR* money.

Alison, as I came into the ice cold house, rang and the conversation was strained or nothing. —"Then I'll expect to hear from you."

January 10

"Will you have dinner with a bore?"

Idle at the library, Alison, invited to dinner; "I must teach you how to set the table." I dried the dishes, I watched her serene as she made dinner; she told me of her thesis, rhetoric and the Puritans, and of more. I brought brandy for her, and I left as the phone rang. —"Hello, Ted." I wrote notes to Jean, Nela, Jay, and Gertrude.

The eight o'clock class wrote papers of satire after twenty weak minutes of exposition.

At ten and eleven I reviewed weakly the papers corrected on the train.

January 11

Empty and idle, I corrected the E-1 themes all afternoon. Dinner with Bill and Helen [Van Keuren], mention of Alison (my innocent gaffe), Helen's gloomy silence, constraint.

January 14

Day of gloom, although only three examinations to sit through; and again after a brief lucid period early in the morning. Forcing myself to my papers, I turned away, I went to see Morrison ("Acceleration of science has been the refuge of labor") and heard that I had to teach two classes next term. Then I went with Bill to Locke Ober's, the Latin Quarter, the Hut, and home, wakened at 11:30 by Phyllis, who spoke again of marriage.

I corrected papers quickly in the early-morning energy and glow (never correct when not alert, said Edna [Phillips]), and went, driven, to see Morrison (driven as when to the condemnatory letter), and he was conciliatory, spoke of leave of absence for reasons of health, and he told me not to be angry nor to become critical of the English Department. I went away with the idea of a term free from teaching, but was distressed or scared at Phillips Brooks House by Kidder, who looked at me suspiciously (perhaps because of last June), rasped, wet-sucked his cigar, spoke harshly while the rosy-cheeked about-to-be-drafted anxious man—of my age, and probably a husband—nodded at me as if in vigorous agreement. Then I went away with the idea of having to teach at least one class, in order not to be drafted. And again consoled myself by drinking a double martini and eating an expensive dinner as if this was the transference or compensation. Crockett and Paul Haldemann came to call as I sat drinking wine, revived by dinner and brimming with phrases.

I almost wept into my Hungarian goulash at the Georgian in the cold blank winter evening, after trying all day to prepare for class. And I went to bed with sherry at nine o'clock. In the afternoon, I put off Phyllis. Anxiety feelings all day about class and about being free next term. Late in the afternoon I called Bill. I read a little about Goethe, as the night before.

Helpless against the eight o'clock class, after waking up at 5:30 and enjoying the fine feelings of the first two hours; and then I struggled through the second and third classes, better at 10 than at 11.

I hesitated, went to the doctor's, had in mind all day an evening with Alison, walked to Commonwealth Avenue to find that the doctor had gone to Florida, returned, bought a black overcoat, a hat, and a new sport jacket at August's instead of Filene's, rang Alison, and then Bill, hurried, did not answer the phone, since it might have been Phyllis, felt that Alison leaned against me in the car, drank a double martini, and a single one at the Viking Restaurant.

Bill said that I looked like a successful young businessman. Perhaps that is what I am.

Morrison was sympathetic when I saw him (an impatience to see him moved me until four o'clock). I spoke to Mark on the stair.

It looks now as if I will get my term off. I will know tomorrow. Fear of being drafted was what made me feel trapped, so that I could not take the term off.

I liked *The Cherry Orchard*, Bill did not. I sat with Alison at her apartment. She spoke of the falsity of six years. She wants something from me; conversation, or is it more, and has there been a change?

Undated

Tremblingness, Brooks's Emerson, no sleep, Alison's snapshots, mind like a gull circling above that sea beach and rocks.

Sleep until 1:30, and a lifting spirit.

Metaphors
We two are jigsaw-puzzle parts
Touching
Are angles & unfinishedness
—But who shall say we
End one puzzle's plot?
—Yet do not say, at least,
That we are not

January 22

In the little morning, in the ashen light
In a few days, it will snow

"One for whom the invisible world exists."
"The celebrity of parties, the dialogue of knowledge and hope."

O my mind,
Empty turned-out pockets in which silver has worn a hole

Undated

O ashen day,
in the small morning
how cold it's all
I never dreamed to pass my aging youth
On this cold shore. I never thought to lose the child
In whom we love to place our hope. I never taught
Desire what death is
winter truths, but superstition grew from hope
A jungle green
the dune sky,
the bare beach of the January day,
the false spring
all the celebrity of the party,
the dialogue of knowledge and belief

For I am city-bred, theaters nearby,
Apartments, parks, Figaro's cries
Gross in the dumbwaiter

Alison came this day at five o'clock—turned out the light—walked to the stair—

"You look like the Cumaean sybil."

Alison, too much brandy, being upset, frightened, proof only in your decision—hurt not false pride; can't postpone everything; only in love once—sorry if only once—convinced rationally; living with you things opening up all the time (contracting elsewhere); no other man; letter written in December; a withdrawal in the kitchen, but twice going to the door.

False problem: Delmore, don't you worry about them, my family. I'll worry about them. A.S. [anti-Semitism]. It's time they got over it.

Sunday. Hangover, Bill, effort to prepare for class, dinner at Gustie's.

Monday. Classes, hangover, dinner with A. and F.O.M. called off, Morrison, Bill.

Friday.

"Did—Gertrude cook for you?"—faint smile.

"What is going to become of me?"

"I wish I knew the answer."

"You can take what you like. But . . . it would be nothing."

"I don't want to take. I want to give—"

"I don't see the necessary immediacies—" (in the mirror).

"It would be worse then."

All day, amid the blizzard, after the three last classes; two of them applauded; the first and the last.

"Don't look at me—"

"Why?"—hand to my head—

"You could make me a great poet."

Saturday. Papers corrected, snow all day.

Sunday. Sleep until noon, hung over again.

Boredom and apathy, unable to sleep, poems on the telephone to Alison at 10. She rang back.

"Sorry I said what I did."

"I can't—imagine being married to anyone but you."

Silence.

"That means, a good chance?"

"Yes."

February 14

Long papers finished. Discussion with Morrison.

Visit of William Barrett. Silent, hardly a thing to say. Then at midnight, Alison, Roslyn; why I did not write; *Finnegans Wake*; Bill's absence.

February 15

W. B[arrett], Bill, Gustie's, cocktails, car to the doctor's, dinner at the Dinner Bell; Julie [Barrett], see you after the war; W.B. almost tearful.

G.B.S. and I as another worldly poetic couple.

February 16

Library in the afternoon, cold furnace, early dinner, the boys of the navy; Porter: "How do you write them poems?" Intangible, heard about you before I came here.

Alison, the white azaleas, what is my favorite flower? Chrysanthemums.

Candy boxes, gross & gala—

February 17

A letter to Gertrude and a letter to Jean.

Then the doctor, sunburnt; nothing to do, try this—

"What's this I hear about your getting married?"

"That's far off."

"Not as before? Then you were overactive."

With Bill, to Locke Ober's, the old Howard, Hotel Imperial. He has just started in with a psychoanalyst. "Freud, the last great genius before . . ."

"Don't feel you have to be with me."

The ceremony of dinner at Locke Ober's.

The sickly miscurved chorus girls, the banging of the disrobers, the comic intervention from the balcony.

February 25 [?]

Friday. Train, New York, counting the time, boredom, concerned about my coat. At the Marlton [Hotel], Philip and Nathalie.

Thursday. Alison: My thoughts go with you. Absolutely faithful.

Dinner with Bill. La Vostre, Chaucer, purely literary.

Saturday. Breakfast with William [Phillips], *PR* office, the Rosenfelds, the Macdonalds, no flash of personality, lunch with G.B.S., hotel, L., her new interest and awareness.

"Do you like living alone?"

"No, do you?"

"No"—nervous, her knees buckled before she came.

"I heard you were going to marry Alison."

She wanted to come back. No: but was sorry she had left me.

My version was untrue—withdrawn because of being unable.

"It must be awful to be in love."

Dinner at Jai Alai.

Phillips, the Grossmans, and Agee. Discussion of Joyce's purple prose.

Undated

She chattered. I was afraid they would ask me to climb a ladder to get some stocks. I told her to read *Daisy Miller* by Henry James.

She leaned on the sofa, her hand almost at my hand. But then, as Jean returned, she consciously, deliberately straightened up.

Then she left, and Jean said, She did not want to go.

Mia and Agee came, quite dressed up, and drank most of the bottle of rum. Agee talked with leaning-forward interest to Jean. ([Robert] Linscott [editor at Random House], the night before, interested in the thrill and not the hill.)

"You are indifferent to me," said Jean, as they left. "You are trying to flatter me about Agee."

Then, and more, rising, as never before, passion, delirium, strictness, and the second time, the same time, outside and helped.

"You are a good girl."

Catharsis, then nervousness, as we ate dinner at ten.

Herald-Tribune review: "Intellectual comic strip capers."

Rum, to sleep 2:30, awake at 7:30.

Saturday. Athens [chophouse], Ninth St.

Thought you would be disturbed.

G.B.S.:

"I have no right to be possessive of you (anymore)."

"Why don't you give A. a chance?"

Sunday. Afternoon with Jean and Polly—she had something to say to me—must build up to it—(on Weds., her poem).

Gertrude's, Mozart. "This is madness," failure, the idea of staying there to save money.

"Peter Taylor [fiction writer] thinks you are the greatest author in America—"

Jean Lowell's, Taylor, anecdotes of Yaddo, Pappas, gaps, departure.

Marlton, Jean, Jumble Shop, L. (two in one day).

February 28

Monday. Hangover, difficulty in shaving, dinner and evening with Philip, discussing Agee, Wilson, Bellow, et al., Goodman, Kazin, G.B.S.

"I never understood why you married her" (though obviously intelligent and sensitive).

"Wants to sleep with Jean [Stafford] Lowell"—

Exalted by the rum after Philip's departure.

"She always attacks me—"

February 29

Tuesday. Nervous in the morning, and then Baba's, Irving, basketball, discussion of G. ("I felt sorry for her"), tall Josephine; Aunt Clara: not enough cousins. [Delmore was paying a visit to his grandmother Hannah Nathanson (Baba), her son Irving, her daughter Clara Colle, and Clara's daughter, Josephine.]

Zolotows [Maurice and Charlotte], G.B.S. "Are you (Class A) sure you want to get divorced?" Twice, our both uneasiness, Luchow's, comedy of correspondence. "I feel very sad." [To facilitate Delmore and Gertrude's divorce, the Zolotows testified in court that they saw a half-dressed woman come out of the bedroom in Delmore's hotel suite and cross to the bathroom. The woman was Gertrude.]

Charlotte's "Let them say goodbye to each other."

Dullness, Z.'s bravuras.

"It must be awful to be in love—"

Predict that A. and you . . .

March 1

Wednesday. G.B.S. "Your intelligence has spoilt other men for me—"

"Sometimes your face is peculiarly beautiful"; lip stuck out—

Pleasure in looking at *Genesis*—its substantiality or solid observation.

Afternoon with Jean [Garrigue]: "That cold and classic relationship, friendship": she felt my withdrawal.

Evening with Philip and William (his indolence)—discussion of Van Keuren—F.O.M.'s ethics.

March 2

Thursday. R. P. Blackmur, John B[erryman], rum, [Mark] Van Doren, after nervous afternoon, Charles's, Eileen [Berryman], "Enough reading matter for a week."

M. V[an] D[oren]: "Sorry, Miss Q. could not come down: she's very beautiful: very pale—"

Thursday evening. Elevated until the reading,* the hour's wait, nervous and poor reading; Rahv's comment.

Ben Nelson, Jean and Polly, David Newton, Biddy Fisher, Marguerite Young.

R.S. [Delmore's mother], kissed, suddenly face very fat, Kenneth in the army.

Phyllis sent her love. R. P. B.

Where are you staying?

Mrs. Barber's "What a wonderful boy you are."

G.B.S. and Sonny—a wonderful poet.

Ben Nelson liked the x poem—which made Van Doren look at R.P.B.—"He is all memory."

Mother—I go to Princeton tomorrow—but—(cruel) even if I did not—

You came to tell me my brother said I was a crackpot.

But—as I brushed past—

Genesis, pp. 3, 4, 5, 6, 7; p. 65; p. 169; "O Love, Sweet Animal"; "That Heavy Bear Who Goes with Me"; "Far Rockaway"; "O City, City."

"We will see you anon," said Jean, left out (major experience of our time).

Guilt about Mother, poor reading.

Train to Princeton, after quick change of mind.

"Lucky you," said Mary, as Eileen sat on my lap. Gertrude, Philip, incestuous—this is incest, we're not yet divorced.

March 3

"You are all a tossed generation."

Two sections of sleep, Helen on the sofa.

Lunch with Richard, Nela, Susie.

Distillery fire from Princeton train.

R.P.B.'s irrational circle, lassitude, then awaking. Argument about doctors.

Description of Russia, body slaves, Lincoln, Adams, King, Russia's army of 30 million.

March 4

Snow, "The White World," Helen [Dickson Blackmur]'s pictures.

Afternoon with Nela, after the Berrymans.

Bath at Nela's, full body in the mirror.

Dinner at La Hiere's—R.P.B.—"One of most distinguished men of our time." My dear friend Delmore.

* *Delmore, R. P. Blackmur, and Mark Van Doren gave a reading at Cooper Union.*

I was toasted. The Shaffees' musical evening. R.P.B.'s Peter Pan mask.

Argument about factory work. J. B[erryman]'s arisen temper.

Nela's, Just come in for a drink. I hate Richard, he is a bad man; stay with me.

After my outburst—I hate this society where the whores triumph.

March 5

Sunday. Conversation until 4, in the day brilliant & glittering.

R.P.B., my teaching—and like Thos. Hardy, whip of intensity left out of *Genesis*.

John disagreed; I was sad; Huebler, one reading, "chipped ear, the Schwartz chip." "Extremely stimulating teacher."

Penn Station, after Princeton ride, wakened sensibility—G.B.S. absent.

Long ride in which I was patient and spelt these notes, thinking, perhaps here I begin again.

Sunday night. After the long train ride, in which I saw nothing, the cold house, and more thoughts of Alison—it was 12:30, or I would have rung her.

March 6

Effort to get Bill and Alison, causeless cheer, broken-out face.

I went to dinner with Bill, disappointed.

Alison's stories. Her visit to the Levins', with Bob James; his four days with her; his presents; his desire to stay on her sofa (nothing could make him happier); and his lie, that he was not rejected.

I spoke of being the rejected suitor—apropos of the report—and she said something like "unnecessary anticipation."

I heard of her bridge-playing days at Brockton with her mother's friends.

She was pleased by my reports of Gertrude. Glad it ended like that. Will she remarry?

I kissed her in the kitchen as she offered me the white azalea plant.

She was pleased when I said, I love you, I love you, I love you, I missed you like crazy.

"Did you really miss me?" she wanted to know.

I wanted to stay and write a poem.

No, Delmore—gently.

Mon. Day of cheer. Alison ate her lamb chop as I told her news, especially Laurette Murdock's question. "Is it true that Delmore is going to marry Alison Q.?"

She said she did not mind the rumor and discussion.

March 7

Tuesday. Hangover from drinking too much brandy, then sherry; and at 6:30, after seeing Bill, to the ballet with her [Alison], after going to the Viking, where I had a double martini and lost my appetite.

The doctor's injections may have picked me up.

The ballet did not awaken me. I was not awkward with the head-waiter. I did not respond to A.'s conversation. I looked for a taxi through the rain. I held her hand. She took off her wet stockings.

At dinner, I said, "I think you will marry me." Smiling, she said nothing at all. "It is my superstition." (But do not feel bound by it.) "I live in hope and possibility." She spoke of believing in time and I said, "No day is lived twice."

At her apartment I was allowed a big drink and then fluency returned. I kissed her on the sofa, after we spoke of trust and distrust, and after my avowals of pleasure.

She said that she saw things she would not otherwise see because of me.

"Suspicion is a form of the imagination; but hope is, too."

I was not as awkward as I might have been at the ballet.

(She played *"Domine Deus."*)

March 8

> The lovers shut their eyes
> Not to be blinded by self-glare
>   (those who look cannot love, cannot surrender)
> Suspicion is a form of imagination
>   but love is, too
>   The kingdom of heaven is within you,
>   also the kingdom of hell—
>
> Freedom from self-dom
>   the torment of self
> Hooded by self
> and seldom safe

One more weak day. I can hardly remember it. I thought of the Guggenheim award.

March 9

Another day difficult to remember.

Dinner at Gustie's with Bill. Effort to review Winters. But my mind—

Thursday night. I stopped to speak with Rose Dickson, and then slept in two sections.

I had slept until 12:30. We tried to get Phyllis four times.

March 10

Friday night. Rahv's letter, obstacles and remorse, inability to write the Winters review, to the library unshaven, where, as I left the stacks, I saw A. at the call desk. I passed her, she looked back, I waited, she said she was bored, and spoke of her unwritten paper.

"Then we can't go out this weekend?"

"No," and she did not think I ought to stay in her kitchen.

"I will be distracted."

"I have a review to write."

"Then we will both be distracted."

After, when I start reading . . .

The day was dead because I woke at about 6.

I spoke with the doctor and he gave me an intravenous injection.

Perhaps it was this which made me fluent at the Palmers' after I began to drink with Bill and stammering John Kelleher [Harvard professor of Irish literature].

But I drank too much and drank to get back to sleep.

March 11

Gordon's after getting sleeping tablets.

(I had drunk a whole bottle of Bill's sherry, sleeping in two sections on Friday night. Cut out the liquor, said the doctor.)

I had dinner alone in the Sea Grill at Central Square and drank one martini.

I walked to Arlington, but it was not the picture I wished to see.

I had "anxiety feelings" at the Harvard, bored by Laurel and Hardy and then thinking of my lies (about marriage) to Rose Dickson, Bill, and, in a way, the nurse (I saw Elizabeth Drew at the doctor's).

I resisted buying liquor until I went home and drinking it until after 12, when the sense of waste and ignorance brimmed over as I read [George] Sampson's *History of English Literature.* Two tablets and a half bottle of wine took me to sleep at last, and I woke at 8:30, hung over with the drug, sensitive enough to write lines of verse and copy out quotations.

March 12

Sunday morning. I had lunch with Bill, who had a hangover and spoke of going to Philadelphia.

Then I sat on the steps bored by the Sunday *Times.*

The boy, aged six—Lawrence Shevlin—played on the sidewalk. I tried without much success to talk to him.

"What are you going to be?"

"A train man, because I draw trains—my grandmother says that I am going to be an artist when I grow up."

At 6, after hesitation for an hour, I rang Alison.

Bored, a bore, how much I have not read. I said to her, "Methinks the lady doth protest too much."

She had been reading [J. B.] Hannay's *Sexual Symbolism in Primitive Religion.*

"How far I've come," she would have said if V. had risen from the grave.

I spoke of trying to imagine what events would excite my insensibility—Mozart arisen from the grave, playing at Memorial Hall.

She did not [want] V. to have arisen from the grave, for then her feelings would be hurt.

"How far I've gone from you." "In relation to V.?" "To her and to many other things."

"I understand things only when they have died and risen again."

"Things?"

"Bird, beast, and flower, and spiritual animals—"

She spoke again of V., Spencer's foolishness—this time about a taxi; and as I rose to go, she asked me to drink some more of the brandy I brought her last week.

She said she disapproved of solitary drinking.

I took off my hat and put it on again. I came home with happiness, feeling some hope, and probably foolishly.

No, this was the beginning of the second time.

She had recalled me. If I can but be patient—

March 13

A hopeless day, after last night's relaxation or composure as I read the diary for the past two months.

After breakfast, which gave me no lift, I read Edith Sitwell's notebook.

Then I struggled with the income tax return, feeling unbearable bewilderment and finding at last the easy way to make it out.

It was a raining-not-raining day.

I rode to the doctor's on the streetcar, avoiding Elizabeth Drew by going one more stop and drinking a malted in a drugstore.

The black-haired nurse winked at me. I sat in the waiting room with Elizabeth Drew. Then I told the doctor that I was worse and worse.

"No inner vigor," he said.

"You're getting good at that."

"We are not worried about that," he said.

Nothing was interesting and I had the trembling feeling all day.

I looked at J. B. Hannay's *Sexual Symbolism in Primitive Religion,* after deciding, at 4:30, to get to five o'clock without drinking by going to the library.

As low as ever before 6; I drank three martinis at the Coach, but they hardly took hold and I lacked the energy to speak distinctly to the waitress. "You have to tell me," she said.

After dinner, I bought a half gallon of sherry and a fifth of rum at the Harvard Provision. Back here, I read Lawrence Durrell's poems, forcing myself to read through and putting off the next drink as long as I was able to; and bathed, to do a useful thing, on the first glass of sherry, and was at ease awhile, and thought of trying two tablets in order to get to sleep without a drink.

I drank a whole bottle of sherry, almost, woke at 5:30, drank rum quickly and slept until 10, and lay in bed for an hour, in dismay.

Nothing was any use, the god did not arise, though I made two efforts.

March 14

I had a lift; the hangover headache disappeared, this morning was better than yesterday, I read in Kierkegaard pages about this renowned malaise.

It is sunny today. I tended the furnace, I shaved. I took myself somewhat in hand. But when will this end? And why does it come?

I have the trembling from drinking so much last night.

On New Year's Eve, 1944 [1943], I had lunch with Alison at the Bella Vista and went with her in the evening to Joseph's.

We said Happy New Year to the cab driver, on Dartmouth Street.

I looked away when they played "Auld Lang Syne," which I had tried to get on the radio. We came upstairs here and I took sets of records for her.

"Then we will have a really private celebration," said Alison at the Bella Vista. I had reported how, disheartened, I had decided not to go to New York.

At the moment of the New Year, I thought of Gertrude, in New York.

I spoke of four girls who would, who wanted to marry me: Phyllis, Jean, Nela, and Barbara.

Afternoon. Pearl Kazin said that I was a wolf, infamous term; I was more interested in girls than in poetry. She was speaking to Roslyn Brogue's friend, Margaret Pettis, who was to read (or was it one whose name begins with an S?) a paper on my poetry.

I met Laura and walked on Irving St. with her. She looked milky —handsome in the shadow of the yard archway. She had failed her generals; I [saw] some astuteness amid the egotism.

After lunch at Hazen's I did not have the trembling which began in the morning.

The bigness began an evil intention.

Of how much I have been guilty since last April: an unconsidered undenied guilt, aided by choice spirits.

And what is it I feel for them [?] if I so quickly turn.

A pre-spring day; Roslyn here in the afternoon.

No choice spirit before dinner.

Hesitation, then the long walk to the Handlins', under the lighted window.

Conversation about the war and the life or death of the great university—

To sleep without wine or rum, but with two tablets, Goethe's Maxims, Adams's letters.

Awake at 5:30, two glasses of rum, sleep until 11:30, then lying indolent in bed.

March 15

A brief hour of sensibility and then despondency again.

Lunch at 3, as a wet snow began outside.

I read—with the emotion of hopelessness—in an anthology of English literature.

I thought again of the Guggenheim Award, a reason for joy.

I returned to thoughts of Alison all the time: what she will choose. What she will say?

In November and December I said to myself, She will yet want me (amid other thoughts).

And now I do not know what to think.

Last month I thought, If I but wait, if I am but patient, inch by inch—

But she is strong to resist what other girls surrender to—

March 16

I dreamed last night of being visited by my father, in Cambridge.

And I dreamed of being on a cliff where unknown children were, and where one of them hung on my neck and almost dragged both of us down, despite the shouting of a woman, a teacher.

And I saw *Hamlet* being performed by Maurice Evans and Judith Anderson; I saw the mole on J.A.'s cheek. Then I was in a hotel or club and John Berryman had drawn out a miniature chess set and a checkerboard made of cloth.

All this was after the first sleep.

In the afternoon, oppressed by emptiness, I stopped at Gordon Cairnie's [owner and manager of the Grolier Bookshop in Cambridge]. Edman was there, buying copies of Spencer's new book, *The Facts of Life*. He spoke of doing propaganda for the book.

Then I walked to Boston and the doctor's through the wet snow-streaked fog-colored March day, and questioned the doctor, and spoke of being in the dark. He was sympathetic and he said that on Tuesday he might change my treatment.

In the evening, after going to dinner without taking a drink, I walked in the stacks at the library, stopped to look, and although I was anxious about A[lison]—it seemed again unreal and incredible and presumptuous—arrived at a causeless serenity, merely by going from book to book.

I heard with a regained sensitivity two symphonies of Haydn on the radio, No. 96, *The Miracle*, and 104, the *London*. I took care of the fire, I bathed, I went to sleep with one tablet and two glasses of rum, and woke at 5:30, but then slept again without drinking.

"There is always something new in whatever is observed," said Flaubert to Maupassant, quoted by Josephson.

Last night with Alison; the Renoir I bought for her had come. I was drunken by the time I arrived, and I elucidated Impressionism according to M[eyer] Schapiro.

It was just at 5:30 that I decided to call her.

She had to come downstairs to open the door. She was a little drunk herself before we went to dinner through the snow. I think she was a little drunk. I kissed her before we went to dinner.

At dinner, at the Continental Grill (where De Voto saw us) we ate steak and talked about aesthetics.

After dinner she read me her paper, "Rhetoric and Dialectic in Plato and Aristotle."

"Tell me frankly," she said.

"Will you help me?" she said, "since you are [the] only one who knows anything about aesthetics in Cambridge."

She spoke about Sherburn's criticism of everyone, and of not wanting Harry as director.

She said that I, too, sometimes made her uncomfortable by criticism. But I could do better than those I criticized, Sherburn could not.

"Maybe," I said.

Sobered by dinner, I was not as inarticulate as I thought I would be.

"Now you must go."

I kissed in the hallway with trench coat and hat on, just as we spoke of music and emotion and Elizabethan sonnets, which she reads in the bathtub where also she sings *"Domine Deus."*

She spoke of Dick Ellmann's party, where for the first time she had noticed the scar on my forehead—like a plume to write a poem. "A poet who laughs," she said to herself then. "Two roads diverged," I said, looking at her.

I felt no desire as I kissed her except to kiss. She held me off after the first time.

"As long as I can get away with it," I said, moving to the door.

Kisses of fondness and affection, the best I could manage.

I did not take a drink to sleep until after 2; I waited for the tablet to help—in the early morning I needed a glass of sherry and this put me out again. I dreamed of the coming into the room of a child who would not speak his name, when asked. And then I dreamed of a letter from Kenneth [Delmore's brother].

At 11 I woke to the ringing of the furniture men.

Outside wet snow, puddles, grayness, black bare tree branches, wet and new white snow.

A cheered weakly lucid hour, as if I were slowly coming back. Thirty years, the idea which made me feel, too late, too late! So much not known, not mastered.

March 18

"I held long conversations with you" [Alison].

"What did I say?"

"You said that I ought not to say such things."

Yesterday, from 11 to 1, not in love, nothing. Then it ended. Good.

More civilization with you than anyone; more worthwhile books; the New York party; the sweetest thing that anyone ever said.

No, Delmore, no.

No what? I am not trying to do anything.

Different with anyone; and arrogant; and I am not sorry to, I wish I had never slept with anyone.

That you did or that I did.

Seven ambiguities; not sorry that she / I had.

Smiling like crazy, the repetition of three times, and I missed you like crazy.

She was the one who rang and did not ring again, yesterday morning. Then did not tell me when I called her.

She was not in love until twenty-two; not in love from nineteen to twenty-two; the Amherst boy with whom she drank beer; her twenty-first birthday; the gifts of V. Two years ago she wanted a child for the first time (and that was when she was here, in the spring of 1941); but perhaps it was that summer, when I was at Cummington. No, the spring of 1942, when she taught and lived alone in New York.

It is not the first one but the last one that counts.

What an extraordinary statement!

Last night, three dreams: my mother said something about Gertrude to Baba.

Before this, I was sailing with bare-legged young girls on a river; and I wanted to touch their legs—perhaps a memory of last summer's Radcliffe girls who wanted me to go swimming with them.

I can't remember the third one; and there were more.

The night before, a young boy came into the room, I asked him his name (it was in a kind of dusk), but he did not answer, he looked out of the window and then went away.

In one dream, my mother said, "I knew they would stay married"; Gertrude and my mother were perhaps identified.

When I woke, the god was arisen; I drank, slept again, a fitful broken sleep—and wore out the hangover headache.

Yesterday, after my early waking, I tried to read Rilke's *Brigge*; I looked at picture books at the library until 3 (radiant for a moment with the volume *Realismus und Impressionismus*), drank a cocktail before eating at Jim's Place, having a dead sensibility by then—and read in *Miss Lonelyhearts* and Edith Wharton, troubled by the picture of Rosedale the Jew, who wants to marry Lily Bart.

I took *Don Juan* and Flaubert's letters from the library, but I was unable to read them.

A sensibility like a piano (the key to which has been lost), says one of the Three Sisters.

10–12. I drank to drunkenness before I slept.

March 19

Gray dusk, smoky white overcast sky, as if a Sunday afternoon not in March but in November, the long winter ahead like an impasse, a resigned marriage, or a failure (in middle age).

Hung over from last night; I stayed in bed until noon, and was awakened for an hour, and read aloud a poem by Yeats.

But then came the tremors and I ate lunch at 3, and I returned to hear the Ninth Symphony, and if I was sensitive—*Freude*, Delmore, *Freude*—it was but for a while. And at 5, Haydn's Symphony 92.

Thoughts of Alison, like a circling gull above a coast.

The card in the book, her writing, "So very much love."

And a sinking depression, and after plucking limply and after reading in Henry Miller without responsiveness, except to obscenity, blackness, pitbound despair, helpless nervousness—lifted up, though slowly, by wine.

March 20

Sleep until 1:00. A blizzard snowfall. A black afternoon, relaxed by reading notebooks, which seemed less awkward, affected than on Sunday.

University Theater, *Destination Tokyo*, after dinner; nothing to drink until 11:30. But then, in an hour, almost a whole bottle of sherry. And at 6 a whole glass of rum.

The same kind of hopelessness and depression—increased by the fact of thirty—and even Alison.

Letter from Jay.

Guggenheim, wrong—external good—all good must be interior, taken in.

March 21

I had a hangover again, sleeping until 12 while Mrs. Massey cleaned in the kitchen and children struck sharp sounds from the 8-inch snow on the sidewalk. I had drunk almost a whole bottle of sherry between 12 and 1.

I took the long walk to the doctor's—after a half hour perhaps of weak attentiveness to *Poetry* for last August.

The doctor gave me the glucose injection after I waited in stupid depression in his office.

He told me not to ask anymore about "the whys and wherefores" —brusque.

Bill came at 6, late, with Gordon Cairnie; after an hour of revival during which I read *Pindaric Odes* in the N[ew] D[irections] translation.

"What are we?" What are [we] not? "We are but the shadow of a dream." "We are things of a day."

"When the gods appoint it, nothing is too strange."

Gordon was drunk and Donald Duck; they drank and I did not.

We ate at Jim's Place after Gordon shouted "Moo-moo" at two passing ladies.

I felt physical irritation at the poor dinner and Gordon's drunken quacking.

Then, after Bill took Gordon away, he returned with consolation and reassurance.

He stayed until 11, drinking what was left of my rum. I took the sleeping tablet—a new white one added—and resisted the desire to ring Alison, whom I had spoken about with Bill (and Phyllis, too, whom he had taken out, without speaking of it after, and asked to sleep with him).

And by 2 (after the ceremonial of pouring the last of the sherry away) I was asleep, but only until a little after 6—I lay in bed until after 8.

March 22

The whole morning spent in an anguished cleaning of the furnace and starting a new fire. The first effort was a failure because I did not have enough wood. I went out and picked up two boxes on Mass. Ave., after trying to phone for wood.

And then the darkness and slowness of the afternoon. I tried first Alison and then Phyllis (after my scruples of last night). I went to the library, after eating a chicken sandwich and drinking coffee at St. Clair's. The book which I returned, [Derrick] Leon's *Proust*, made me anxious about the Dreyfus case. Came back with [Matthew] Josephson's *Zola* and again was awakened by the story; and rang Alison, bedrowsed again, wishing to see her; not wishing to see her in my present state but trying to avoid an empty evening.

She said that she would call back (but now at a quarter of 9, she has not).

Alison at 5; tea with friends.

"Does that (dark, dark, dark) mean that I am not the right woman for you?"

"Perhaps."

"Is that the inevitable conclusion?"

"Not the inevitable one."

"Hideous self-doubt, it makes me feel unworthy of you."

Dinner, called back at 9:30, just for a half hour.

Sit here; lucidity after brandy; education as method, not information.

Withheld lips, after . . .

Freudianism, Kant, all experience is phenomenal (even the self, synthetic unity of apperception, is only a category). The Incarnation untrue, Christ is, however, a mystery.

"May I not see you Sat. night?"

"I don't see why not."

Home exalted, while reading A.'s paper on *Rasselas* and the Psaltery in the *Book of Common Prayer*.

Nothing to drink but A.'s glass of brandy.

March 23

Morning empty again, the doctor's, the slushbound avenue, Miss Phillips ("Why all the enthusiasm?"), bumps, slip, "breaking neck."

Interest or absorption in the account of the Dreyfus case and then in *Tucker's People* by Ira Wolfert—the chorus-girl scene.

Two applejacks before dinner.

March 24

Calm brief morning. Phyllis on Mass. Avenue, St. Clair's, marriage rumor, Hillyer retired, walk by the river, home, records.

"R.P.B. said that he did not really know you."

"Pearl Kazin said that D.S. does not [know] what he is talking about."

Spencer and Walter Pistol, seventeenth-century melancholy, aristocracy affected by the doctrine of works, smug middle class—idleness proper to their class.

Bill at dinner, cigar episode, his Scotch, his guilt about the war.

"Judy Spivak hated you and cut all your classes; Sophie Freud had a crush on you; you were seen at a nightclub by (Shirley Stowe) with a blonde, and also by an English 1 instructor; married, not married, juicy stories"—"You are quite a figurehead."

"Phyllis R. said that she was the mistress of Orson Welles. She signed out in detail, giving the apartment number. You better watch out for her."

"You can't sleep because of some conflict."

March 27

In the afternoon, a cold and spitting rain.

Sleep until 11. Alison at the library. St. Clair's, Santillana (concealed identity), discussion of aesthetics as an act of contemplation, the waitress, Ladies, the blackout phone call, the Fogg Art Museum, the penis on the satyr (the nymph pointed to his condition), dragons, wine jars, rounded squares.

To the doctor's in the growing rain—after, "This has been good, Delmore"—return, an hour's lucidity, a page on aesthetics.

At almost 6, Bill, a drink, Phyllis, Alison at the window as I left the car.

"I was just thinking of you"—she was thinking of whether a vacation was paid for.

"May I?" She moved in with neatness and consent.

At 10½ Appian Way, Phyllis was pacing back and forth. I was half an hour late.

South African records, supine on the floor (drunk on two Scotches and the two sherrys A. gave me). "I was waylaid"; "He may have cracked up" (Phyllis had called Bill). She thought I might have been skulking about in the rain. Screamatorium, a madman (when she first knew me), the Coach, disgruntled waitress, home, Beethoven Concerto No. 4, tears, darkness, nap, effort, failure, "All imp[otence] can be cured"; a drink of water, and then the walk to Appian Way in the freshened night air. "Most people don't like Alison"—shock, shift, and freedom.

> A beautiful woman said something
> in your praise
> Sensational utterance blinding as sun-daze
> Certain emotions vivid in your plays

At three o'clock, P. E. More, *Criterion*, July 1929, on the Catholic Church, another awaking.

The relief and ease after mixing or the effort to mix.

What was in Alison's look as I came up the stair?

March 28

Cold house, after sleep until noon; Bill at 5, and Phyllis, to get her fountain pen; the kitchen, gas radiator, argument about malicious gossip as feminine, Wilson and Mary McCarthy; dinner at the Dinner Bell, Bill's departure; building of the fire with a fruit box, sudden ease and radiance; "Why don't you be a hedonist?"; dungarees, Murdock's lion hunting; adultery after first year of marriage, better, "You are getting much better," "Why not, even if you are not going to marry me?" And then, despite a weak resolve, and after "You ought to get married"; entered, weakly, failed, and then with the obsession.

March 29

The doctor's after visit of Phyllis to borrow $20 to go to New York to her sister's wedding; as the night before, dismay as she departed, after being told how intelligent she had been and how she was growing. She had been intelligent about Murdock, interesting about Wex, and interesting about her family, who believe that the three girls ought to marry men who are older than they, much older, thus duplicating their own marriage. Her sister had lived with John on the farm, yet her mother would not admit to herself that her daughter was not a virgin.

The doctor, test it, proper stimuli, lipstick stain on the collar; then upon Newbury Street and the wholesale bookstore, looking for a gift and thinking of books. In one gift store was a stone or porcelain dog topped by an ashtray.

A[lison] rang as P[hyllis] came in and I was inarticulate on the phone until she asked if anyone was there, and I said yes, and she said that then perhaps she had better hang up. I drank too much applejack before dinner, fell asleep after dinner on the sofa, woke, went to the Square at ten, "ravenous," returned with food, impatient at the Wursthaus. And drank three glasses of sherry and read fifty pages of [Graham] Greene's *The Ministry of Fear*, and went to sleep with three tablets and indigestion, to wake just before 6, when I took a glass of sherry and waited for sleep until 8. But sleep did not come.

March 30

At 4 Alison—come up 9—at 7, after Benzedrine blaze and $10 at Phillips Bookstore—she starts to beg off—the student had stayed very late.

"Building up," I said—"Come over"—I went, and the blaze went out, and A. neatly ate her hamburger.

"Don't be an extravagant young man—" (the present).

Perhaps I should not tell you this—but if I don't marry you, won't marry anyone—

"From fairest creatures we desire increase—"

"One of my favorite sayings—"

Home at 9, too much to drink.

I kissed her, then she, voluntary [sic], immediately kissed me.

April 1

Alison's birthday.

Sleep until 12, after sherry at 6.

Waiting for the visit to A., photograph at 2, impatient.

With Mary Stegner to the square, high on sherry.

A[lison] on the phone (her mother's voice as if a party line): Moms, Dad, a real party, I'll write you the details.

Afternoon: "My dear, you were wonderful."

Her formality on the phone: "A., you must marry me—that was not you."

The rye, make-believe, stopped, fifteen minutes, 8, go, universal rule, "Delmore, time—till the summer."

Angry, angry, I sat up.

Pure happiness (roller coaster—looking at the pure small perfect formal face).

"Why don't you go away?"

Books, you, a letter, pleasantness, a present.

On the sofa: "Incapable of surrendering myself to anyone" (marry you or not marry at all—meaning of).

Don't have to surrender to me, in marriage.

Anger as I returned. No more, Phyllis, silence, rye, stomach pain—soothed by sleep tablets.

April 2

I woke at 8, too early, after sleep at 3. Still a war with A[lison], changed between *No more* and *Tell me what to do.*

Rang, put off until 1, impatient, a blaze at Mozart, A.'s gift.

Sleepy-tired, tense-tired at Rose Dickson's. Sunday school with the children, pulling off their leggin[gs], coats.

Wallace [Dickson]'s story. I was full of high sentence. It was a very gentle Sunday April day.

Alison's—Why were you angry?—not angry, going to be angry.

Thirty years of false interpretation (exegesis) have I lived.

Take what you want—

"You wanted something I was not prepared for—" "not prepared to give—"

Did not say, "Must it be chastely?"; but "Why chastely?"

"Surrender one's being"—never surrender—two people living in one house.

"Children are a part of marriage—so far only one man whose child I wanted to have."

"I might be able later to give myself to you—as I cannot now—"

"Why did you come to tell me that?"

"I told you—Jan. 20—something I thought you should know— thought you were going away—hard to say in a letter."

It was a battle of wills on the sofa—"unpremeditated"—"Take what you want" sentence as justification.

Is it my optimistic distortion—that you want to wait until you fall in love with me?

It is a distortion.

(How I can't remember.)

"I could talk to you twenty-four hours a day if you would let me."

Syllogism: either me or none; probably not none; hence me.

Saturday night—wait until summer—when these pressures (school) are gone.

"You want to force me to a choice."

Want to take care of myself.

Know the likelihood.

Can't say 50/50, can't evaluate that now.

Waiting for an emotional resolution—no doubt about having the good life—but desire to have children (emotional resolution) necessary.

Question of the child as a Jew.

No question in many "mixed marriages" she has known.

"Many?" "Relatively."

"Both of us isolated from our families."

Myself as product of mixed marriages—point of honor—no passing —jobs.

Fondness for me.

Yes, glad you detected it—sorry for and sympathetic.

Question of sleeping with another—did not care.

F. matter of more indifference than I had thought [he] would be (my handwriting betrays my impatience and indolence).

Pay more attention to the women.

As I left, she gave me the camera. I jumped as if she had come to let me kiss her.

Take, what later I hope to give context—kissing her.

Abstract horrors about surrender; why not asked out more often; people don't *need* you.

I dried the dishes, I felt better.

"I want to want to marry you"—i.e., I want to reach that emotional resolution.

I was cheered by her words and by lunch—her thoughts were neat as serving lunch.

Full of high sentence still when Bill arrived.

Phyllis, Mozart, complicated emotional tie. "Even if you are engaged to Alison"; "Don't worry about me, I'll be all right"; obligations —not the right word—before I saw you—her child Cupid face. Coup, failure, effort, her hard-breathing coming, inside softness.

"I like your body very much"—Rufus Wanning.

April 5

Alison—surprise, surprise—at the doctor's office.

How are you? More sleepless nights?

No.

What is wrong? Jack Sweeney—recommended her. "After what you told me—"

I tapped my lips.

What does that gesture mean?

Speculation. Questions? Tapped her.

Did I do something wrong?

(I said he would beat her head in—emotional shock.)

I won't tell you (what the check was for).

The nurses regarded us.

She took *Vogue* in hand.

We spoke in whispers. We spoke of [the] King of England— Penelope Dudley.

Sleepless nights and something else, some obscure things.

"Do you mind waiting for me?"

At the streetcar: "Won't you come?"

"I'll be seeing you"—improvised, annoyed, or distant? or my own attitude as cause?

Suspicion that she did not tell me. But she said that she had been thinking of going.

(Often I thought of A. and Dr. S[ieve]. Now she will know of the punctures.)

What conflict goes on in her? Something wrong with her thyroid?

"Relax" was what I heard before I saw her.

She was annoyed by my concern.

"He asks the same question twice"—police-sergeant trick.

"You ought to give him some of your reproductions."

He would not like them.

Dept.-store type—carnation in's buttonhole.

"Can you wait for me?" thus friendly at first.

Desire—or hurt feelings—to go to New York.

"Always too sensitive."

Said she would try the recipe on me ("oysters and beer," marriage made in heaven).

Shifting back and forth, New York or not New York. Phyllis, punishment, the aspect of the opera—and not to tell her.

The idea of staying with G.B.S., of going to Princeton, of seeing Helen Fisher, Dwight, Agee, Philip, and William.

"I'll be seeing you"—at the opera.

The idea of missing the new beginning, or postponing it.

What is the hurry? You can't do anything at all.

Hurt pride, excessive impatient expectation move me—

To New York, and such interesting things. Able to work there? at what?

Deliberately, or annoyed temperament, nevertheless I am pressed back—

Either unaware of the implications of her actions, or denying them as a policy.

But not to be devious, not to use flight and silence at thirty just as before.

The chill gray afternoon has changed to light gold.

The sun was melted wax—white behind the overcast sky.

She used her charm like a tennis racket.

It was as palpable as burning fish.

It grew from infancy obscurely like lefthandedness—

Cost—blank check.

I speak just as a friend. Why adopt the harsh tone?

How much did you pay? Outlandish trolley duel.

April 6

Train to N.Y., G.B.S. at Penn Station, on the sofa.

April 7

Blaze of sensibility, Topps [restaurant]. Philip and William, Chagall seder; waiting for G.B.S.

April 8

Blazes, notes, *PR* office; Rosenfelds [Isaac and Vasiliki], cafeteria, Biddy Eustis [Helen Eustis Fisher, novelist] after walk on Fourth Avenue, Jai Alai; DeWitt child, the cat wants to kiss you. Anger, hysterical, late at night—sleep on sofa.

April 9

Sleep to 1:30, remorse, guilt, Easter Sunday on Fifth Ave., G.B.S., dinner at Kavanagh's, William's at 9, Shuster, drinking, William's analysis.

Gertrude, Saturday after midnight—domineering, inconsiderate, and did not speak for a long time.

Domineering—William Barrett.

Always the first to say where to go.

"To share the limelight"—this she weighed, in leaving me.

All the women (as Nela) said that you would be hard to live with.

Richard [Blackmur]: I would do anything for you, Gertrude.

April 10

Awake too early, William visited, evening discussed, lunch at Topps, delivery of the summons, tiredness and drowsiness, G.B.S.'s apt., humid day, endured.

Train ride, highballs, waning sensibility, Phyllis, wine, A.'s call: "Called you Sunday and Friday"—tongue-tied.

April 11

Dozing sleep until 11:30. Dead mind again, doctor's, opera-pointed, errands, streetcar, fogbound day, hurried dinner, rain. A.'s aunt, back turned, Benzedrine, wine room, Murdock, F.O.M. passed, *The Magic Flute*, power of instruments, of silence—and soon, boredom—A.'s apt., psychoanalysis again.

April 12

Sleep until 12, hangover, forced excitement; all day with Freud's *New Lectures*—anxiety as key, duplication of pattern.

Bill and Phyllis, curving down—after contract—Dinner Bell; kitchen, sherry to rise again.

Phyllis's pictures and reassurances.

Eloquence at midnight on tablets and sherry.

April 13

Marriage of Figaro.

"What kind of a man do you think I will marry?" Asked twice.

A guess—Not like me—

"There are not many like you."

"I merely meant to give you reassurance." (The Athens, two double martinis, death blow of children.)

"I went to N.Y., seeking to accept a reality, and to fight you off."

Orals as one of three parts of the summer—thesis, garden.

"Marriage requires more than automatic adjustments. What kind of a bride do you think I would make?"

"People married have taken their orals."

At the opera, she held my hand three times, the second when my arm went back as if to seek her hand; the third, she reached for it.

And her leg touched mine twice, I thought—at first unsure, as when we went in January to see a *House in Paris*, after the reconciliation.

I psychoanalyzed her V., mother-substitute, Sherburn dream.

I spoke of her [school's] anti-Semitism.

Older man? pianist, her first love, was Jewish; and first friend at college.

Is it that she is sure of me?

To make concrete, the idea of asking for time: until the orals?

Smith and Radcliffe's support, can't just sit with my hands idle.

"You always invoke a principle which can't be consistently applied."

The purchase of Jaeger—"As if you had not already broken my heart, you would break it again"—by the duplication of books—"This is part of the common hoard."

Could not remember dinner conversation—famous sentence: "If I don't marry you, I'll marry none."

Both classes false, I said.

"Now I must send you home. I must rise at 6 and read Renaissance prose." She did not want a prolonged morbid discussion.

All serene and controlled—the tablet—at the opera, too.

"To revert to the ghost of a possibility—"

April 14

After the release of yesterday's tablet, at 7, I was given half-tablets today by the doctor.

He admitted for the first time that a depressive psychosis was "part of the picture"; "Not that you will go to a mental institution."

Against the bottle more strongly than ever: rules you, not you rule it.

Spoke of how my body would be strong to cope with these periods, perhaps to overcome them.

"You will be able to help yourself."

J[ohn] P[eale] Bishop, fifty-one, died in Hyannis.

A day of difficult striving to begin.

April 17

Phyllis after dinner. The phone rang, and then the second time, Sonny [Shapero]. I was almost asleep when she came. The first ring, I thought, might have been Alison.

During the morning I read the first part of Eliot's essay on Dante, and the earlier essay in *The Sacred Wood*.

Phyllis, twice, not brought off by myself but by her—and she, like a fountain.

Sonny had heard of "a glorious creature, beautiful, society, Radcliffe."

During the afternoon I wasted myself at the library and at lunch and speaking to Bob Daniels, who told me of H. Levin's being congratulated at the Schorers' cocktail party on Saturday about his associate professorship.

I started a letter to G.B.S. which I did [not] finish; it was started by her letter.

Summary: In 1933, after the excitement of winter and spring, came exhaustion at Brighton Beach, not helped by the trip to Woodstock with Gertrude.

The excitement began after at least four exhausted months, May, June, July, August.

Anxiety was lessened perhaps by the absence of school as a reason.

So, too, in 1937, after February and March as exalted—and part of April—(and the beginning of drugs for sleep) came April, May, June, Woodstock, July, and August. In late August came *Partisan Review*—September, October, November, part of December, Washington Place, and exhaustion again.

April 18

I awoke, drank rum, and returned to sleep at 5. Before dinner, half a bottle of sherry.

I woke up again at 10:30, and my depression fixed on the fact that, at thirty years, I did not yet know the story of Elijah.

In my dreams yesterday and today, an obscene dream of Alison and her mother, and one of the Zolotows' copulation in the kitchen.

It was a perfect April day, the first day of the baseball season. I read much of *Lady Chatterley's Lover*, version 1, and saw *The Lodger* at the U[niversity] T[heater] after dinner, pleased by the London fog.

Phyllis, 9, Central Square, rum, once.

I wrote a page in the morning about Eliot's criticism, but it was a day of the worst kind of downness.

April 20

Two weeks ago I went to New York.

That Saturday the Schorers had a big cocktail party, to which I was not invited. To-be-left-out, the worst of experiences. So I felt at 600 W. 174, when we first moved in and when Herman had his party: I was smitten with his sister as a possibility; but soon they moved away.

So my mother felt about "Rose Berkowitz." So Alison often feels about life in Cambridge.

Today, this morning, it was 5:30 when I woke up. A hazy smokiness in the air, but the beginning of the bloom of a warm gold and blue day.

Gertrude felt left out when Jean Lowell was invited to the Rahvs' party and she was not.

Last night, on the sofa with Phyllis, lighted by rum (so that the room seemed brighter than before we began to drink), I "determined" to copy out perceptions, the meanings of words, synopses of poems by Eliot, though able to do nothing else.

At least I can do that: What else is there to do?

Last night, after midnight, Phyllis said, "I love you very much." "No, you don't," I said. I use her: should I, or should I not?

She wanted to know if she looked very pretty, as the Whitmans had told her.

Yesterday I revived during lunch (which I ate without appetite at the Dinner Bell) and returned as if for a beginning. And wrote two pages, seeking a form for the second and third books of *The Singers* [an unfinished work]. (To distinguish between overt (a poor word) form and the form or arrangement arrived at by means of working at the subject matter with overt form. Thus, in the sonnet, the form Milton arrives at—the mastered deliberate strain—by use of the Italian sonnet scheme.)

Yesterday and in the fine weather, I tried to write until 4, finished my letter to Gertrude (later, with misgivings), walked to the doctor's, returned to the barber's, finding both of them closed because it was Patriot's Day, in Massachusetts a holiday.

Even to this fact, some significance can be attached; for my kind of life and awareness so places me in the community that I do not know what is closed on Patriot's Day.

At 8, I was going well enough; now, after but thirty-five minutes, I feel the fading of mind because of too little sleep.

Last year in April at this time, or a month after, how little I imagined the year to come, the heights and the depths, excited classes, poems, Van Keuren, Phyllis, Alison, the reception of *Genesis*, the eight o'clock class, failure before my classes.

What is in the year to come now? Perhaps a new exaltation, even, perhaps, Alison.

It has all been very interesting, although full of passive suffering.

(At last, it is warm enough to sit in the study, where my sensibility almost without choice shows an awareness of the seen I did not know I had.)

What has Alison been thinking for the past seven days? Has she been angry? assured? curious surely.

"What kind of a bride would I make?" she said, "with orals hanging over my head?"

I was delighted by the word.

She kicked Cedric Whitman at Jaeger's seminar, said Phyllis. She did not know whom she had kicked.

Bradley Jones had sent her flowers.

From 9 to 10, I read Eliot's essays on Middleton and Marvell.

By 10 I was empty; by 11, I had decided to go to the doctor, shaved, and massaged my face, finding again in these activities some relief.

My energy revived with the walk, the fresh air, and the sunlight.

I enjoyed a few thoughts as I walked the pavement.

Before this, I resisted the impulse to ask Alison to lunch. The Latin Quarter picture shows that aspect of her which I ought to bear in mind, to free myself from excitement and adoration.

The summer exaltation contained more of it than I have felt for months.

Now she has Bradley Jones to squire her about; and she does not like the pressure I create; it takes her from her studies.

It must be not unlike my unwillingness to travel.

(I've been happy with the access after lunch; now it begins to go.)

The story about the Baumanns ["America! America!"] was first written in November 1938, amid the worst kind of depression just before my first book appeared. Then rewritten a year after, in exaltation, after Yaddo.

This ought to be a lesson. I should have learned this lesson before. To write, however depressed, for the preliminary arrangement of material gives inspiration freer dancing and transcending.

On how many days have I written nothing at all? At least I wrote what Alison said to me and what I said to her.

(Last night I thought, Would not devotion to God—ultimate sublimation—free me from the dead drain of sublimation?)

"They have a game," said Phyllis, "they play that they are manic-depressive and schizophrenic."

"You have the younger generation under your thumb," said Gertrude. "You are almost unique—the quality of intelligence in your poems."

April 21

A cold gray almost rainy day, Cantabrigian April.

After last night's strong revival (strong as last summer) at dinner (after two glasses of wine, a martini, oysters, and a club steak with *Time* magazine), I returned, began a poem, dwindled somewhat, walked to see the unlighted window, thought of the line "We know he looks at us like all the stars," bathed, and tried to go to sleep at 10. English poetry was empty, Milton empty, I had to take a third pill.

Today, Ransom [editor of *Kenyon Review*] accepted the Xmas poem—three years since *Shenandoah*—I made a fresh copy.

I began without spontaneity on Book 2.

At the library: "Your letter received. The answer is No. I love you"; to F.F.V.; made me seek out P[hyllis].

Spencer rang to ask me to the Gregorys' party—in a second I changed my mind to no.

April 22

Yesterday the eighth day since I saw A.

If she minded Scowcroft's absence, will she not mind mine?

She thinks it deliberate; hence, deliberately does nothing; or is preoccupied, as always.

Lightness of lunch with Scowcroft: this, too, displeased her.

Who she wrote *I love you* to, troubled. Yet hardly a romance so quickly, given her preoccupations. And she would not write a note like that idly. (Perhaps the draft of a reply to the old love, F., F.F.M.)

If, as yesterday, I become panicky, does she, too?

In the winter, she waited two months or ten weeks; and then, for more than a week, tried to get me to make the first move.

Perhaps it is at an end; perhaps just as well; a beautiful girl, but ordinary in all other things?

A sunny day. Visited without warning by George Palmer and Margery. To dinner at a Chinese restaurant with them and Phyllis, after a splitting sickening sinus headache.

George compared me to Goethe, Phyllis said I had beautiful eyes and was charming, and I spoke of my educational value.

All afternoon, note making.

An old kind of depression in the evening; childhood's depression.

Too much to drink, of rum, at 5.

Cheered by the Seconal. A brief visit from Jack Crockett, unexpected, too. He told of [Wallace] Stevens's "gorgeous" daughter, her flight from Vassar, her stay in New York, her effort to shake off her inhibitions. Phyllis was silent, and when he left she said he was a pathological liar.

April 24

Monday. Dream of seeing G.B.S.'s suitor and judging against him. George Orwell, Gregory ("I rather like your poetry"). Dream-streaked sleep from 3:30 to 10:30.

Dream of Bill V. K. drunken in New York—Kenneth's arrival.

A day of drenching rain; morning hangover soon vanquished by coffee; visit to Rose Dickson, discussion of psychoanalysis; Florette with Bill's review, drunkenness and morphine; afternoon at the doctor's, patient on the streetcar, negative smear. A. rung at 5, after hesitation; no answer; determined not to make a move? or much interested in the drive to get done; or no longer interested at all, as in my own fading of the charm?

Sunday. Worn in the morning; A. rung; absent—all day—Concord walk, empty afternoon. P[hyllis] at 5, brandy, drunkenness.

Sex & lovemaking worn of old mystery & charm—at least awake after 10.

April 25

Cold dripping-wet day, boredom and languor. A. rung, not home, not at the library (reading [Erwin] Panofsky, as it turned out).

Bill, burnt child, dinner, morphine, alcohol, B-complex.

Dinner at Gustie's (three martinis, four on Wednesday, nothing at all on Monday).

Phyllis, Bill's departure, sherry, glass of rum, sick to my stomach.

After Phyllis left, after 10, in the light blue, gray-striped dressing gown, I read most of Gide's essay on Goethe, finishing it in the morning; and pleased by the reference to myself in the soldier's letter to Ransom.

April 26

Did A. call to find out if I had come straight home? (As you please, she had said, about premarital episodes.)

Was it her birthday party which made her father ask about me?

Before sleep, a little of the Bible, and a little of Saint-Beuve on Mme Récamier.

The gold cigarette case: "Don't need it now—next time," accepting the present dispensation.

F.O.M. "disappointed" in her before the committee.

Sonny said he was serious and he wanted a mate (like Trilling).

Rahv as big rocks; the death of Lenin as big rocks falling into the sea.

Delmore Schwartz. (Did Delmore have a middle name?) Gertrude's story, withheld or forgotten by Sonny.

Your gift—literary, I suppose—of seeing too many complications, making a pattern, "objective."

Alison's father—check for $25, send it back—flinging dollar bills about as tips.

Again, the outlines of A.'s face looked spread-out and fattened—her hair had just been done—she wore ballet slippers. Aiken had been told about her by Spencer—but what? "I've been angered and humiliated by him several times."

Alison and her father—the University Club.

Who is Delmore Schwartz?

Outstanding poet of his generation in America (Gertrude, Maurice).
What else does he do?
He teaches at Harvard.
Draft classification?
Partisan Review?
What active social experience?
On docks, in labor unions.

F.O.M. as passionate reader of *PM*.
"You make me so aware of my confusions."
"Why don't they ask me?" To the Wannings, to the Gregory party?
Not for a positive, just for a negative reason—no immediate interest to be satisfied.
Come sit over here—
And wonderful adventures and working again. Goodbye and good luck at the door.
In the afternoon, Sonny visited me and made me my Sonny-self; post-sex made him unable to compose; G.B.S., myself as oppressive, Tate and Jean [Stafford] Lowell as anti-Semitic.
Doctor in the afternoon: "We will ask you to read something for us"—he was pleased.
I slept until 3:30; and then I slept again. A., when I rang, sounded surprised, also pleased.

April 27

10:30–11, long breakfast.
Again the flickering, until four o'clock. Thoughts of A. and note making. Poems by Rilke, and a flow of words.
Lunch, Wilson on Falstaff, hopefulness until emptiness at 4.
Phyllis at the library, a renewal.
Saw you twice, once walking across the Yard with Alison.
Home, a lucidity from Rilke and Goethe, wine, wish to be alone, sandwiches from the Wursthaus and Lipton's tea.
"Why don't you marry her (A.) since you understand [her] so well?"—Phyllis.
Drowsiness, failure, tea—couch, drowsiness, departure.
(At the library, stack corridor, plumpening Alison, with horn-rimmed amber glasses—her father strode to the garden, tears in his eyes, because mother and daughter laughed at the baby pictures.)
Nervousness and tenseness after P[hyllis] departed—[Matthew Josephson's] *The Robber Barons*—indigestion, depression at living alone.
Pomposity of Thomas Mann in *Past Masters*—Germanic metaphysic mongering.

April 28

Flickering progressive morning—in reading Rilke after Josephson—what a break.

Lunch, to the library, Poetry Room to get more Rilke. Pearl Kazin: "Are you D.S.? My brother would like to meet you." Nervous and excited. Alfred Kazin.

Blake, 3-volume Nonesuch. Spencer: Talked for three hours at lunch and said nothing; Harry [Levin]: Liked him very much; but hypertension.

St. Clair's [with the Kazins]. After discussion of the teaching of composition: "Mark Van Doren likes you very much. What do you think of his new book of poems?"

"Being a Jew—glad what you said in *C[ontemporary]* *Jewish Record* [February 1944]—came late to me—not a success as soon as you"—I spoke of being a Jew in Cambridge, fluent a while.

Paul G[oodman], Arthur Berger, Sholom Aleichem—nervous and eager Pearl Kazin, whom I asked leading questions.

Kazin's journal—"I can't write in it, 'Today I met Delmore Schwartz'—because I am not important enough."

Asked about book on Eliot, what are you writing now, "The Imitation of Life"; spoke of Philip and Isaac Rosenfeld. Left, all cordial, after affectionate note taking of the books his sister wanted.

Home, arisen on Scotch and soda—but nothing.

Dicksons, George, Wm. Smith, daiquiris, Rose stamped her foot, Jeremy ate or sucked limes, Wallace reproved the stamping.

Rose impatient with all the music, intermission, my wrong guesses about Mozart.

Worn and silent, eager to go home—but not until 11:50. Jokes (derby on private parts) at dinner.

Rose made an effort to draw me out, seeing how silent I was.

Stomachache again—perhaps too many daiquiris.

[Edmund] Wilson's essays on Housman and Chapman (I underestimated him) before I fell asleep to dream of F.O.M.'s deprecating or doubting my relationship with A.

"Like an ostrich, curved in on himself—"

Glass-house Hershey, thin-skinned Hershey, impossible Hershey Green [the protagonist of *Genesis*].

"God was tried & found guilty"—Aleichem.

Let's look at pictures, postures, and impostors.

Celine on the Frenchman who tore pages out of the book: a method of criticism.

Daudet—Gide: We can be sure that the sun is shining, if both of them say so at once.

Decay appeared—this was new tiredness in an aging girl.

The thought came like
a thunderstorm
Over the distant mountain. Swiftly darkened
And strangely cool—the lake of summer days
(—How sensuous is memory! who asked
The number of the senses? It is six,
The sixth of them rises to be most
powerful)

(Some sixth sense said—)

It is the tone in Rilke . . . tenderness, a pressing toward the depths, a solemn "open seriousness—as if he knelt before each thing to worship its divinity."

Mann on Wagner (ever similitudes): Melancholy, sleepless, generally tormented, this man is at thirty in such a state that he will often sit down to weep an hour without end. He cannot believe that he will live to see *Tannhauser* completed—

Valéry on Pascal: This darkness which surrounds us lays bare our souls.

Valéry on Proust: By virtue of our consciousness, we are inexhaustible—but we are forced to neglect that quality of immanence which exists in the depths of our nature—we cannot pause a moment without being immediately aware of innumerable thoughts. The Past is a treasure of surpassing value; each man derives from it the man he is; it is composed of all we lose, or think we lose; and of everything we can hope from ourselves. This was entitled by Proust the Past. In his personal depths he sought for the metaphysics without which no society can exist.

Rilke on Valéry—the next step after Mallarmé was silence.

On Massachusetts Avenue—we see their faces, and their clothes as they walk. But we do not see the lives they have lived which still live in them more living than any present moment. Hence, we do not see them. Unless, eliciting this foremost reality with questions—careful, and blind—we raise this foremost reality into the passing light.

The girls lay on the sofa like cast-off silk stockings (silk stockings thrown away); but once, like fallen buildings; and once like a car overturned.

Who wants to be elected to the Jockey Club
[. . .]
To Skull & Bones, the Hasty Pudding Club
The Social Register, the French Academy
Phi Beta Kappa or the Knights of Bath
[. . .]

Our hometown, Death, a famous capital, / For next to it / Paris &
Rome are merely whistle-stops.

The truth is full of chaos like the Milky Way.

> Flee and do not look back
> —Or you will turn to stone
> Two girls, Lot's wife,
> The *belle* Eurydice . . .

It is the loss of freedom I feel, when my powers are gone; and
freedom, too, when they return; a freedom which makes me nervous,
for then I must choose, and the pleasures of society and the pleasures
of the senses draw me.

The war—not to thrust the burden from myself, but nevertheless
—has taken from me energy and hours of two summers, one of them,
the longest inspiration—which ended in mania.

April 29

Note making morning, sunny, Rilke. Lunch, the library—looked on
by pensive A. in the stall as I passed (what was she thinking?). More
volumes of Rilke; then faded by 4 (suddenly); revived on the chapel
steps, waiting and hopeful, note making, remnants of Thursday supper
for supper. Phyllis, discussion, criticism, objectivity, "Make things
harder for yourself than they need be"; G. and A. victimize you.
Drowsy, change of beds, tension in legs, Coconut Grove fire, Sydney
Kenna (blind date), Stanley Baron, tablets and muscatel, success at
second with—

Bigness of staying overnight, much desired and concealed—desire
to be a wife—Gertrude's red pajamas.

I finished Valéry's essay on Proust—this is as a period of equaliza-
tion.

April 30

Sunny and warm, almost too warm, almost a haze.

Breakfast with Phyllis, conversation breakfast, speaking of Harry
Levin; then Rilke.

Too soon to get up, stomachache, too much coffee. But then, at 12,
the walk to Boston, and much to say, the Athens, after the Public
Gardens.

"Do I bore you?"

"You must not say things like that."

She went to the B Minor Mass and I walked home, flickering at
the warm day of spring, the Sunday people outdoors. Note making at
4, U[niversity] T[heater] at 5, a picture about the underground in
Belgium, and then half of a Technicolor, Rita Hayworth, *Cover Girl*,
the pleasure of the popular dancing.

Return, supper in the kitchen again, walk to the unlighted window, mild depression.

Difficult to sleep, *Hugo, Rochester, The Politicos*, Whitman and Emerson, third tablet, Flaubert, sleep just after the tolling midnight bell.

Ready to begin upon the first of May—after the late afternoon's fluency, taking fire at interesting pages.

April 30–May 1

I have not seen A. for four days again. Is it a new young man? Does she know what I try (or half try) and refuse to give in to is?

"Now I must send you home. I must get up at 6 and read Renaissance prose."

What does she think about me, and about my absences? So far, the withdrawal is unfruitful.

But why did she come in January to get me back?

In the time after that, did she feel that she did not want me? Hand held at the opera—or did I imagine that?

There will be others, and younger and more willing.

May 1

Waking before 7 I began to write again Book 2 of *The Singers*.

Then the bath, to the doctor's with wet hair, the library, seeking more sensibility, and full of hope.

Phyllis came and then, after being twice dissuaded, left. I went and did not see the lighted window, and drank a bottle (most) of sherry (the lightning stroke of drunkenness) and began to read *Swann in Love*, much cheered, before I slept.

All day, thoughts of a routine of rushing to an end of Book 2— the same idea of rush as before.

I wrote in the afternoon after lunch—blank verse improvisation.

E.—shallow, astonished, flirtatious, frank, bohemian; squeamish about house guests; four sisters, Nobel Prize winner; Russian salon.

How do you know? G.B.S. over motivation—an old-fashioned girl, relaxed after marriage.

Ex voto—an offering, fulfilling a pledge. Exalt—to lift up—to altitude, to heights.

Zarathustra: Upon the highest mountains, I laugh at the tragic plays.

Why should he not be delighted with the triumph of the universe?

This comic strip of a degraded life / Degraded by emotion near the wet ocean.

A house, a child, a tree— / A wife, a child, a book— / A house in the country, a car to go there. *Ils sont dans le vrai.*

Tone—generalization or generalized laughter, anger, seriousness, somberness.

Rhythm—fast we go to what we like; or it passes quickly; slow we go to what we do not like; *andante*; or to what we brood about.

Aristotle on diction: not too many strange words, not too many common words.

Down, proud heart, down / Caesar, go back.

R.S.: My mother, who drank Postum instead of coffee & gave useful gifts.

H.S. [father], who had a gold cigar clipper attached to his watch chain.

Rilke: Genius is after all the only thing that really grips us & matters to us. To hold our innermost conscience alert—that is the foundation of every artistic experience. Unequivocal destinies . . . have their god.

R[ilke]: Shadowing his sensibility like a detective.

The reason I cannot sleep: I do not want to sleep. That is why the least ease makes me smoke another cigar & read one more essay (by Strachey).

"Poetry the most glorious high mass of the soul"—where the bread & the wine are changed into sacrificed flesh & blood; & into a story.

Late summer, 1939, Yaddo, like a place where Rilke lived.

In this age, is not God the object of our voyages—and the end— and not the beginning? Yet the end kept in mind, and consciously, and examined.

Some part of life is done. First marriage is. (One marries for the first time only once.)

Access of being—like a glass of wine / Came to me as I read the lyric poem.

A charcoal sketch / A falling tower or chimney slipping—

The dark victor whom nothing protects.

"The poem remains, still looking back at reason, its mystery being inexhaustible to rational analysis."

Gertrude on my visit to the Blackmurs & the argument (but she spoke also of herself): "You tell people the truth, and they don't like it; they don't want to be told the truth, and they don't forgive you."

> Send me a million elephants
> And now & then a tiger and a pig

"The Poet, natural medium of unknown powers"—Cocteau.

> "Don't fool yourself, my dear young man."
> Come! don't deceive yourself
> The night has just begun.

"The kisses multiplied themselves, as in early days of loves they do"—Swann & Odette.

"On one level, my mind assents, on another, there is dissent—perhaps I should not tell you this: but I can't imagine marrying anyone but you."

May 2

A poor day after yesterday's beginning—perhaps because almost a bottle of sherry before sleep.

Flickering of sensibility at the library, looking at Faulkner and *Babbitt*.

Phyllis passed me at the library, went off as if different, returned, "Changed your seat." Asked me to come to see her at her stall and when I did not (descending the library steps self-consciously and awkwardly), she called me, Come here, Mrs. Massey left, withness in a rush (laugh and lie down).

Cold and gray May day, Central Sea Grill, dispute about Phyllis as twenty-one, martinis. "I don't think that's necessary"—after, "Do you have to be twenty-one to get French-fried potatoes?" and "Suppose she takes some when I am not looking?" New waitress, return, absolute weariness, P[hyllis]'s departure, to the square for rum, forty pages of Proust, almost sleep—and then, at 11:30, Nela rang to ask me to come to Princeton for the weekend.

May 3

A sickly day, and hot. I prepared to begin.

Phyllis and Bill called. I wrote to Gertrude, read in Proust with much pleasure, engaged in note making, and put off Phyllis after dinner. Visited the doctor between 3 & 4; rang Omega [Alison], having decided as I walked home to call her. And found in the library the truth that she must be away and came back with essays by Mann. It was difficult for me to sleep and I fell to depression, as I read further in Proust.

A moment when Proust made me see my own works to come—not Time, but Cause,

> Two roads diverged in a yellow wood—
> and Choice
> (and Chance)—

Secret studies of the heart / secret stories of the heart.
Dilettante! (yet diligent).
Enthusiasm—to be possessed by the god.
Spleen—not knowing what to do with oneself.

An education of the senses
  An education of the heart
 An education in relations
   Between the near, the clear, the dear—
     the far apart—

A sad splendid profundity.

Excuses of recusant & addicted, vicious men. Impatience—impotence.

Swann in Love: a new study of turning-seven jealousy, fixing itself on objects & interpreting everything.

Memory, mother of the Muses (Apollo, leader).

Paul [Goodman] reminded—in June 1937—of Proust's inability to write for years—because his memory had gone out (consolation).

Can one experience catharsis from music? or painting, or any but the literary arts?

I can't remember any occasion when I did. There is a certain liberation.

In music the emotions (tone, voice, and movement) reach to pure formality becoming flowing pediments (houses, temples, arches, arabesques, domes, spires). But they are never released wholly from the soil of the *lived-through*, however high they soar.

Paris of Proust!—Paris of Henry Miller!

This lifelong sickness which robs me of my self, which takes away my power, which made me a poor student, the author of unfinished works, or works which deceived me very much: at last I know it is a sickness, and that I am hardly to blame, to blame myself—at least that much is understood.

"How's the libido?" "Test it—with the *proper* stimuli." "Haven't made you eighteen again yet; but it's better."

Like a beauty under cold cream, dark-wet-gray, masked. (O creamy soft!)

   My soul is full of preparations
   (The violinist tight[en]ing the string)

May 4

"They told me at the dormitory that someone who was going away had called and from the description it sounded like you. That was why I called you so early."

"No, I am staying right here."

"How are you?"

"Striving, at least striving—"

"I expect you don't want to see me, then?"

"No, Phyllis: I'll call you soon."

"Goodbye"—banging of the telephone.

Where is Omega?—not seen for the eighth day—no answer.

Was this a pretext? and yesterday, "not at the dormitory"—a pretext.

I feel sorry. "Are these ideas right or wrong?"

Omega: (1) she is ill; (2) her family; (3) a journey and union.

What other possibilities?

A day "unseasonably warm." Empty before noon, after reading further in Proust. More ringing, and at 2:30 to look at the mailbox, two letters, returning in the heat and seeing many "familiar faces."

Emptiness to deep depression by 4—waiting for 5—rum, arisen, *Life of Beethoven*—expensive dinner at Clark's, depression returned, after the lifted spirit.

Infirmary called; Phyllis put off at 1.

To the Square for more rum—and resolves against drinking and arisen—a third time—just before sleep—smoking three cigars; awake at 3, rum, to sleep until 10—a rebeginning despite my lack of hope and impetus.

"To be a man of letters is an incurable disease"—Goethe, 1820.

I dreamed that a cat ran into me, running away from another cat who wanted to copulate with her. But uselessly—and despite my aversion, I felt nothing when they began.

I dreamed that Morrison said the same thing about the manic-depressive psychosis as William P[hillips] had.

The same night there was some question of renting a house on Mt. Auburn St.

How does the dream-work choose its contents? The end product is a brand-new event, like a piece of fiction. There are often traces of the previous conscious day.

Jung (as R.P.B.): You will your sleeplessness. The giver of all conditions resides in ourselves—a truth which despite all evidence in the greatest as well as in the smallest things never becomes conscious, though it is only too often necessary, even indispensable, that it should be. (Quoted by Mann.)

I sat there like a potted plant / I stood there like a palm—

"*Je peux mourir ce soir.*"

Proust revised passage on Bergotte's death, the day of his own death, dictating to his housekeeper.

I hurt Phyllis's feelings & expectations. I am sorry. But indifferent—sorry, not wincing sorry at all.

Proust's metaphors are Homeric & psychologizing, analytic & descriptive.

Cause, in place of Time, for me.

In 1933 Roosevelt & Hitler came to power; and, though touched by the New Deal éclat, it was Gertrude, T. S. Eliot, and being at a new school—with Wheelwright, Burnham, and Hook, (& E[da] L[ou] Walton [English professor at N.Y.U.])—that really were in the center of consciousness.

Anything—choice spirits, too—to get a daily quantity done!

At almost 5 I called, almost as if through habit, after two full days of calling, and saying to myself, Monday will be the earliest day.

Surprised! home (Columbia another possibility, or Smith)—the other two probably improbable.

"I was thinking it would be very pleasant if we could have dinner together."

"Hello, Delmore"—pleasure in the tone—pause—"I think it would be pleasant, too" (having decided not to refuse) "if you allow me to explain why it must be brief."

"Oh, I expect that, don't explain."

"I will explain at dinner."

Did not have lunch until 3:30.

Thus will she not explain why she was away, and where?

"Thank you." "For what?"

Dinner with Alison: home, because her mother was ill (bursitis, baseball pitchers)—lame shoulder from too much knitting.

She rose: "Oh, Delmore, I am so glad that it is May—the leaves in bloom, ice on my tongue."

"Another side of your sensibility—"

The drawing of the family: "But Mother is helpless then."

She peeked from the kitchen to see if I was reading the paper she had put out—on Renaissance criticism.

She spoke of herself as simple—but she had put out the paper—deliberate[ly]; one half of you is simple and noble, I said.

At dinner, at the Commander Grill, we ran out of conversation. On the way I spoke of Proust and Babbitt as a parable for her.

She spoke of her brother J., staunch Republican; of R., mother's baby boy, sharing a three-room apartment: F.O.M.'s coolness about her paper—the point: Renaissance platonized Aristotle.

Dispute about Scowcroft saying that he did not see her—did I say it?

Summoned me to take her paper and included another one as I took albums back.

I returned home—tempted to visit the Dicksons—and drank too much rum as I read more Proust, and rose to see for myself a technique (same kind of mind).

[Oliver Wendell] Holmes: War as an organized bore.

At forty, Roosevelt: Why do you read Plato, Mr. Justice?

H.: To improve my mind!

Proust: Brueghel's merry junketing frostbound peasants.
How about that? voices under the window in the darkness.
You expect (or want) Life to be all exaltation, all pleasure & joy:
No boredom, no rote— / And then, what? And again, what?
Rilke: Two strings upon a violin / Bowed by one song—
Something about Omega: nervous, too tidy, too schoolmarmish—
just one side.

What is it childhood tries to reach in us?
It is the willingness that's not yet formed—
that
Like Destiny, the beard grown in one night,
the holy bestial Id—

Goethe. Facetious, obscene old man.
"All great men are a calamity." (An old Chinese maxim.)

Your mother rises up in you
(rotting Jew!)
The family quarrel resumed in you
You use the guilt in every heart—
Why were you shocked
How can you now be just?
You act the same yourself!

Like a long night, Anxiety which holds
Your being stopped, and half your mind cut off
Forced down, hidden or chained
Or in a thousand masks
Permitted to exercise in the open air
On certain sunny days, deceptively—
[...]

Our hometown, Death, a famous Capital
and next to it
Paris and Rome are merely whistle-stops
The Death which is the other side of the moon
Never shown to your view; yet it is there,
And the bright side shows itself, goddess
of girls

Mover of rocking seas,
And fat and glittering
Far off—
Yet it appears

Cocteau: This ten-line poem: is it beautiful or ugly? It is neither beautiful nor ugly; it has other merits—

> He had a rendezvous
> > With the goddess Inspiration
> > > An old courtesan
> > > > Who has ruined many young men—

"I will tell you what it is all about"—the opera, 600 W. 174 St., one-tube earphone radio.

"I know what it is about."

Shocked that his mother had never been to the opera, he did not know that this was not in the least a deprivation.

Humor, 1928: In the morning: "Shall I ring or shall I nudge?" Father reproved by Anna [Delmore's stepmother]—"Harry: the boys!"

Once she sent Hershey for a sandwich; and he brought back none, because they did not have the kind she told him to get. When he came back empty-handed, she was annoyed, there was little time for lunch—and this made Hershey guilty.

Each term higher seemed to him like an exotic foreign country; and like the region under girls' dresses.

> Of all the dragons, the sea is the least stupid
> Dashing a champagne on the rocks—

Hegel: The way of the mind is roundabout. Everything is twofold-opposed-united.

Nothing more ignorant than an air of false knowingness.

A fruity day—a fast girl.

Restaurant tables like solar systems / White tablecloth, the lamp, flowers, and wine.

> —Plato perceived the plot, chained to the Cave
> Deceptively the light flickers on walls
> Charcoal, chiaroscuro, caricature
> Until we take the blacks as ultimate—
> > > real . . .

> The mind beneath the face, the squeezing heart
> Which clutches at the flows of passing
> > > life
> Two billion times—

> A suit or dress which says
> This is my self, the one I dearly love
> Thus do I seek out finery—
> These are my flowers, foliage, greenery

Like a log fire
The Typewriter crackled
From the apartment-house window
in May
Or like a lawn mower riddled and rattled
the slow warm air—

Proust: Confined to the present like heroes & drunkards.
The thought of G.'s age—a reason—the line near her cheek—the
years, thirty-one—older & older.
The dreadful soft that sailors rock upon.

Met[aphors]
The ego swelled up to a gross balloon
The ego is the vicious serpent which
Destroys the garden of new innocence

As sailors feel the dreadful soft beneath
—So Insecurity—

The snow like minutes fell, piece after piece
—Became the white god, new, come to the city
Slowed the smooth cars & hushed all moving
things
Brought to the air the blue-white shine
And the cool freshness snuffed in blowing
winds

Fondly to smile as when some hear they were
Cunning & dimpled in diaper'd infancy—

His senses like sunflowers turned
And then were left with night
(And then what?
Is and is not,
Bouncing the ball
on the roulette wheel—)

A winter's morning—is a part of truth / A summer afternoon—as
slow as pregnancy.
Valéry: Who are you? I am what I am capable of performing.

What do you do?
I stare at the blue!
How do you live?
I try to forgive

The past which rises in me as a war.

Always it is the Past, revived in us, seeking to renew itself & to commit the self-same crimes—which we must strive to make conscious and seek to alter to bring true newness to the future.

At twenty-two, a gross & naïve though self-conscious egoist, yet not without a growing intelligence.

At thirty, overcome by Exhaustion, and recognition, by madness of exaltation & madness of despondency—

Monotony like boxcars, shunted forward— / "Like a runner unable to stop / When the race is over"—

Philip gave Caroline Gordon's novel to Gertrude for review. She was too delighted—kittenish & false.

A Child's Universal History: Theme of Education (What Shall We Teach This Growing Important Boy). Theme of a School for Children. Theme of Capitalismus.

Eudora Welty: From any observation I would conclude that a secret of life had been nearly revealed to me, and from the smallest gesture of a stranger I would wrest what was to me a communication or a presentiment.

[Erwin] Panofsky. Albrecht Durer: Here in Venice I am a gentleman. At home in Germany I am a parasite.

In New York, G.B.S. spoke of how strange it was that in one year no eligible men had appeared. I said, Parties, dances—if you don't go to them, you don't meet eligible young men. (I forgot about the place of work, though G. met Lewis there.)

When Gertrude's mother said, "While you have done so much—" in contrast to G., I thought she spoke foolishly.

O[scar] Williams to H[oward] Moss: Stop imitating Brinnin, who is himself not entirely in the clear. (The face he made.)

May 6–10

Mild hangover, almost hopeless by 11:30, mechanical work, a lift after forced lunch, and new versification, and content at 3.

Visit to Dicksons, not home, library, continuing elevation, Laurette Murdock on the avenue, Phyllis summoned, report of Pearl Kazin and Charles Rockland.

—Not bullet-headed shining egoist, but charming, self-effacing, diffident.

"Any woman in a pinch"—we drank ale, more discussion, with, failure, fetish, Rockland's intimation of close friendship, troubled, discussed "most people think you are away." No sleep until 2—after Goethe and Eckermann—a glass of rum, a mild depression.

7th. Day of weak effort, walk to Boston, the pictures, *Passage to Marseille*, after seeking to spend the evening in reading Marcel Proust.

8th. Weaker effort, the doctor's, six short letters, dinner at 5, a lift,

with Proust, empty, the library—Spencer passed—the god wine, six
o'clock, choice: wine or waking—sleep until 12, hangover.

9th. Hangover, sleep until 12, dream-streaked. No effort to go forward, depressed before dinner, walk by the river (rejecting other ideas
of what to do), Phyllis called, on the steps of the library, and then she
called me, we drank beer, failure with, Proust and sleep after 2.

10th. Token performance with typewriter and a page of verse,
doctor, Morrison's punch, nothing to say. Mrs. Leisher's *"Deux matelots
si loin de la mer."* Daniels, C. P. Lee, no sight of A., Wannings.

Return, after dinner alone, Phyllis, beer, Beethoven, Veldt [rec-
ords], Mozart—best of all, the first movement of Opus 97.

Failure again, "Try too hard, hold your breath," and after 12,
Proust (Elstir's art), nervousness, three t. [tablets], no sleep until 3 &
wine, waking at 12.

May 8–16

An entelechy, like an ambitious man
To a vocation called

An entelechy like an ambition
  —like a child in the womb

Deer stillness, even star stillness; black intensity, immensity, infinity, propinquity.

Today—May 8—I decline again, five months of my thirtieth year
already passed & wasted—unless something grows by this—

Dinner at five o'clock—to lift myself.

"Will you please tell Mrs. Richard Moulton that her sister's husband has passed away—"

Alternatives: New York, wine, A.Q., P.R., the library (even the
Hut), Bill, Dicksons, Palmers, Proust, films—

None of them takes hold of me; yet, had I joy, they would all be in
some way attractive— What is the block?

Directly as the dogs who sniff
    Each other quickly
Glowing as after violent exercise
I seek the phrase, I seek the face

He knows what goodness is, how much
                within
As one falsely made famous by a book
Some other wrote—praised for his
                craftsmanship
His prose style and his charm . . .
A megalomania such as sultans' lives
Might nourish, monarchs absolutes

Joubert: Many men's heads do not have skylights in them.
Buddha—means the Awakened One, not the Sleepless One.
Maria (*mare*)—means of the sea—Venus.
Proust: A flag snapping in the fresh breeze / Like a hollow cough—
D.S.: Life is a long separation—
R.S.: You are a philosopher.

    A Glass of Wine
    Choice spirits of the god, who rules the senses
    Lifting up laughter, and the wish to sing

    Bring me a million elephants
    Mountainous, yet dignified

The half-plundered dish of plums, the profundities of the still-life —Cézanne's discoveries.

Suspicion is inspired by a knowledge of one's own motives.

Trips to New York from Saratoga—Odyssey-style.

Nothing to look forward to—that's it—when energy falls down.

The Handel Violin Concerto & the Bennington meadow (white house, distant green mountain, blue or a great sponge, "prehistoric fish ashore—").

The Schubert "Death & the Maiden" quartet into which has entered for the rest of life the black pines against the snow, weeks old, at Yaddo—

It was a time of slumber, anger, and loneliness. I tried to write some three or five pages each day.

(Outside, all is in leaf—and much is in bloom, and summer is near—)

"Eternity—is now." (Who?)

"Intermissions of the heart—with A.Q.—now & then, now & then —not now, later—later, but not now—"

May 12

Coleridge, reproached (& condemned even by himself) for the habit of using laudanum, was discovered at death to have an abnormal heart, the physical basis for such lack of will—

So with my own indolence, though not without new [?] causes.

Last night I turned off & on in my mind the idea of going to New York: where I would stay, the tedium of the trip, the cost, the troubles of physical adjustment, the likelihood of writing—I weighed these against the delights of conversation.

The deciding feather was the thought of time passing—more days before something is accomplished.

This morning, waking at 8, the idea renews itself—once more denied.

I tried to ring A. from 5 until 9. And looked at W[idener Library] to see if she was in Cam[bridge], unable to make out.

The weak desire to call P[hyllis].

I finished *A l'Ombre des Jeunes Filles en Fleur*, drinking beer.

May 13

Dream: Reconciliation with Levins (invited to dinner), Memorial Dr.—a guilty wish after G.'s departure.

Scene of fetish, grinding at show. Dream: Return of Kenneth, Memorial Dr., Gertrude present (story told to Phyllis?) (a wish?).

Dream: Gertrude admitted—I was again defending myself—that she wanted most to be an author—as if an admitted fault.

"Schapiro like Goodman is so passionate a monologist that he mistakes good listeners for intelligent men—"

May 13–18

Daily amount, Phyllis, South Boston, Old Venice, spring shower.

14th. Half a daily amount, 8 a.m., worn out and empty by noon, Brattle St., boys' baseball on the Common, too much rum, sleep until 10. *Double Man* [W. H. Auden] reread in three days.

15th. Saul Bellow's novel [*Dangling Man*] read to completion. *Jane Eyre*, Orson Welles in the evening—pure loneliness, Gertrude-nostalgia, marriage-nostalgia.

16th. Bellow review [Delmore's review appeared in *Partisan Review* 11 (Summer 1944)], halfhearted, Yard after lunch. A. criss-cross in ballet slippers, A. after dinner, description of Marjorie Nicholson [distinguished scholar and professor of English literature at Columbia University]. "I am going to send you home." "May I finish my drink"— hurt feelings. Sleeper to New York, dream-ridden sleep. A. as not worth getting, fat and pedestrian.

17th. 7 a.m. radiance, heat, Gertrude's, William, Vaselki and Philip, Philip's in the evening, dinner at Billy the Oysterman's—sofa and rotting night.

18th. Sick morning, C[aroline] Gordon's novel, lunch at Chinese restaurant on Twenty-third, Grand Central, wrong train, three o'clock after bank and Bryant Park, suffered journey, Phyllis after 9 and after waking with rum, after a short wire: W H A T S H A L L I D O? William avoided.

May 23

It is a woolen day. The sky is low gray cloth, an ice-colored gray.

And what if, in my thirtieth year, I cannot write a book? The world will not come to an end, nor will I, for that matter, come to an end.

And if the book I wrote were good, the numerical year of life when it was written will have nothing to do with its goodness. And no one will think of the year.

Fecundity, activity, responding applause: these are good things, but if one does not possess them, how wrong it is to think with anguish of their absence. Such thoughts are an illness. The more serious illness is such thinking itself.

Last night I dreamed that Bill was burned; that I visited Helen; and that notes were written on a brown box, a phonograph, in Bill's house or my own.

The false barriers I make myself: this keeps me from my true life, telling stories & fables.

> Our father which art in Heaven, make use of me
> For Knowledge, Love, Love's Truth, and Poetry.

Couplet on Monday night, May 22, after a May day of dripping rain and heavy-hanging darkened leaves; after a sick day, during which only by using rum did I manage to write a page of verse.

> Give me this day my daily bread & wine,
> The poetry which makes each thing a sign.

> *Met[aphors]*
> They move in fragrance
> As the people in an opera
> Moved in music—
>
> Drawings of flowers and of people
> Among orchids & toucans
>
> The cause of their gaiety was the Virgin
>
> Entelechy like an ambition burned
>
> The words, sweet as a reprieve
>
> She was one hundred thousand miles
> removed from him
> (Seated in the other side of the
> living room)
>
> Like an enormous sofa lay the mountain
>
> The fresh & glittering air
> The thickness of green leaves
>
> O let the whole sensorium
> be hushed
> Before the spectacle of the
> troops, throngs, rings, and gangs of stars

P[hyllis] Sunday, Miss Cupid, Mrs. Massey.
"I must look that up in my tree-book"—G.B.S.
Love the dark victor, over the infinite.
Wine is an illusion.
The two of each kind must be in love.

May 17–24

Behold the curve—he slides from love to pain
Self-pitying although he's sitting pretty

The atoms buzz like bees
(The old drinking fountains)

Thirty years old—nothing to do with himself—unable to flee emptiness & despondency (except with choice spirits, and after that remorse in the morning)—and deceived by inspiration and losing hope & hope's lies.

J[ay] L[aughlin] asked William how I was: he said he had not heard from me in months.

In New York, Tuesday afternoon, waiting for Gertrude to return to 225 E. 19th St., I rested on the hard red sofa & helped myself to relax with a cigar & a little sherry; I decided to ask G. if I might not stay there.

"I don't think it would be a good idea," she said, "after what happened last time."

Dream: Nightclub, star, Radcliffe girls, and touched, but briefly—and waking.

"Sleep, that sinister adventure"—Baudelaire.

Faced by an inner conflict, my one resource is to surrender, first to one, then to the other.

Thoughts of G.B.S. & New York—the uneasiness of true freedom, spiritual indetermination.

In one dream, I had Canadian coins—too many—on a streetcar—no one minded: wartime.

In the *Times*: Music used as therapy in hospitals—catharsis.

Executive, sixty-eight—head of Beneficial Management Co.—separated from wife & daughter in Nashville—kills himself in a New York hotel—*taedium vitae*.

H. G. Wells shoots off his mouth: Don't kill Hitler, put him in an insane asylum.

"You're up before breakfast this morning."

It is not what we make up—invent—but what is there—which we discover (for life is always more than has been seen).

The greater the consciousness, the greater the dangers & anxiety (as in climbing mountains).

Uncollar'd or unbuttoned bliss / Disheveled splashing happiness.
Each attitude reveals different possibilities in the object.

> *Punctilio*
> He kneads his kid gloves on his slender hands
> As if he made love to a swan
>   or queen

> Pajamas gay to wear as I go down
> To the unconscious, to the seas from which
> The past arises, tossing & rocking day's
> Neatest arrangements, doorway exchanges—

Gertrude has her own idiom ("her indestructible charm"), charm
infinite: "I must look that up in my tree-book."

> . . . We must endure
> Our journey on the train. We must be bored
> Beside the sparkling water. And be bad
>   and sad
> Even tho' brassy sunlight like a band
> Plays martial marches
>   Blazing the day's amaze—

To seize upon three definite persons (whom I've known) as the
singers—at least three—more would be better perhaps.

Alison showed Pearl Kazin the proofs of Bellow's book. Phyllis
spoke about this. "You don't give me proofs."

The dropping down of Life just now (how slack I was this time
last week—tempted by N.Y. & the party).

> Joy. Joy. Joy indescribable
> Goddess absent too long—
>   disaffection because some fiend
> Possesses me [. . .] at some crack
> Of my mind's form—insatiable
> And slippery as shadows in day's foam—
> (How strong I am, how long I wait to sing)

> And will she come again,
>   The goddess, radiant?
>   Will she not come again?
> To touch & to teach
>   The powers which reach
>   What we live long & unknowingly—
>   (All that we live & do not know)

Sonny: Geographically, there is no future in it. I want everyone to know everything (orange ethics, bald ambition, lamb chop (bread & butter) mind).

Gide, November 1904: "Since 25 Oct. 1901, I have not worked seriously. Three lectures—do not count (the one at Brussels I spoke badly). A sick numbness (torpor) of mind has made me vegetate for three years. (Perhaps I've become like the plants in my garden.) The least phrase costs me much effort—almost as much even to speak." He tries a trip, travel, traversal oppressed by the horror of the sea crossing (a waiting, a pregnancy).

May 20–22

Saturday. A dead day from the start, after Friday's quickening (& dinner at the Palmers & the fragrant May night air on Harvard Street). Phyllis at Widener, as I looked at books about trials. Rum before dinner, withness, touched wish. Phyllis at 10, a quart of ale & Strachey's essays on "Voltaire & Frederick the Great," "The Rousseau Affair."

Sunday. After early weakness, a quickening and pps. of "A Child's U.H.," and before lunch, outlines & hopefulness; then, sinking, with Phyllis to Boston, Sharaf's, the penny ferry, the Esplanade; withness accursed, her departure in anger, a quart of ale, Strachey's essays on "Voltaire & England," "Voltaire's Tragedies," "Shakespeare's Last Period," and then *The Adams Family*—C. G. Adams during the Civil War; 6 a.m., rum, 12 hung over.

Monday. A dead day begun in the afternoon—the doctor's, and a forced page by means of rum. In bed at 10, *Adams Family*, ale and rum, 1 a.m., 8:30 a.m. dreams about V.K. because of postcard from Maine.

[. . .]
Apples, peaches, lemons, limes, cigars
These, Jeremiah, teach the sensuous
Yes, it is time for you to go to school
Blackboards a specialty & screeching chalk
>   There I will teach, there I will touch
>   On matters I have known too much
Poets are voluble & tedious
Yet valuable (if not too serious)—

Theme: One must eat everything himself [sic] / no one can chew / And be the substitute proxy & lieu.

With a hey ho, the wind and the rain / No day ever comes back again.

Begin, then Muse
In medias res,
In the middle of the brawl, begin, O Sister
And goddess and truant, fleeting, deceptive one
Thirty years of madness have I now known
Because you come & go, and when you are gone
I lounge in boredom and causeless despair
Taught to expect too much from the empty air

Mediterranean
Clear air, blue mountains, & the brilliant sun
Evergreen shrubs & grassy plains, blue sea
And rocky forelands
      Between the mountains & the sea
Arose the city-states which came to be
Hellas (the glorious, lucid, and eloquent)
[. . .]

Affected—avoidance of triteness by effort at freshness in diction, phrasing, or sentence structure.

How much one's appearance is observed: A., P[hyllis], the doctor, G.B.S., W.P., Rose D[ickson]—

I am going / riding to Euphoria—

In 1933 they all began to talk about rhythm—Hal Saunders, White, Matthiessen, Spencer, and Winters—"What the rhythm communicates."

Harold Rosenberg took Gertrude to lunch. "I am too glib," he said to her. "I know I am too glib."

"Animation on the face / Like light from an invisible joy"—J[ohn] P[eale] Bishop.

"The disease, myself."

"Job, false comfort"—

Gertrude angry at Jean [Stafford] Lowell because Jean told Kappo Phelan [writer] of the job with Stanley Young [playwright and executive of the Bollingen Foundation], after Gertrude had withdrawn for Jean's sake. Jean tried to blame her friend.

G. wrote her first V letter to Peter Taylor, who had sent her his love—via Jean.

May 23
I forced myself to write one page of verse, after waking at 9. From 3 until 5, I leafed through a New York novel at the library. Then *Brighton Rock* by Graham Greene.

An anxiety attack took me off to the Yard, where Phyllis sang in the front line. I stayed for a moment, leaning against a tree. Then bought two quarts of ale, finished one Greene romance, and took up another. The ale took away the anxiety, and I must have been asleep before 12. I woke near 7.

May 24

The third day—through which I've seen and spoken with no friend. The silence grows in me.

It is a light green evening / Under thick leaves and a milky (gray) sky—

> *Thoreau*
> "Present a face of bronze"
> To expectation. Smile with a curling lip
> At promise, hope & happiness
> (The great things of this world come very dear!
> The good is always true & difficult.)
> At uproars of applause. Fame always melts
> Like ice cream in the dish.

Emerson: The mark of wisdom is to see the miraculous in the common.

> Dolls, drums, horses (a morning knowledge)
> The sun, the moon, the stars, the cantering animals

Dostoevsky's main point, according to Monroe Beardsley, was absolute freedom (that voluntary love might be possible). This is the point made against the Grand Inquisitor, and against rationalism, and against dictatorship.

Upland, lowland, rockland, cleared land, woodland.

"Wherever snow falls, wherever water flows or birds fly, wherever day & night in twilight meet, the world is full of renunciations & apprenticeships."

Emerson knew less and read less well in Plato than Jaeger—but the periphery of his sensibility, and his sense of life . . .

Emerson, Goethe, development & recognition. Emerson a bard, maximalist.

"The gods are to each other not unknown"—Greek verse quoted by Emerson.

> Is it then so? Is it then so?
> So let it be! So let it be!
>
> My mind is by body much abused
> And body is by the mind often refused

Emerson was editor of the *Dial*, visited Wordsworth, dined with Tennyson, lived with Thoreau, inspected Brook Farm, and walked with Hawthorne.

He knew periods of sterility & boredom; and he was much pained by book reviews. For this, his wife scolded him.

> These *aperçus* like apples need a bite
> Gifts to be given as you go away
> You must eat each yourself
> It does no good
> Merely to give you them
> Here we go now to Canterbury
> Death

Armchair Columbus; one touch of Venus.

> My journal—which is a wood
> which is
> Between my God & me, and no one else
> Not even my true love

Rinehart story & Hungarian; Emile & Community.
Beneath the blue / There was a Jew.
Coriolanus Incommunicado (hiding in his small room).

> Always be queasy
> At that which is easy
> The good is always true & difficult—

A cloudy day clearing, I had breakfast at the Merle. The waning and dried-out feeling began to take hold, but went away as I went through my notebooks, and returned from lunch able to manage a page of verse. By then it was 4. I finished the second Greene romance, and departed for the library, but went instead to dinner.

Postcard from Alison; delighted & lifted from a neutral state of mind.

May 25–27

Thursday. A real beginning. Sonny at 4; psychical research, girls, Chinese restaurant—beginning of a cold, shivering.

"Form is an aggregation of energies."

Narcissus invented painting. Noah invented the gong.

Greene: Thumb enclosed in hand—mark of neurosis.

Impasto—thick application of pigment to canvas or panel (heavy downbeat, as in my blank verse).

Lo, the dark victor whom Love cannot break
He looks at expectation with bronze face
With great aplomb, and cool, a nonpareil
[. . .]

The Truth

What are the things a little boy should know?
Truth is a sphinx—a girl & animal
    Knowledge is like the
        dark water
            where the wake subsides

[. . .]
The things a little boy would like to know!
The truth alas! is like wind, rain
Like rising smoke or falling snow

Noah will show you hope through the telescope (or opera glasses).
Description of the house boat (as an ocean liner).
Instructions for Noah. Socialism. Noah (Hitchcockian kingdom of this world). Noah's Selections.
Kafka story. The man who lived on islands / And had big feet. (The normal as formal.)
Coca-Cola for a girl / A girl like a gondola / A girl like a canoe.
Page head: A great while ago the world began.
Invocation psalm—to children.
A banned book for them (since they have their obscene innocence).
Obscene plays all the parts, and mocks identity, and mocks ontology.

    Truth is the kick
    Administered with power
    Unto the hind parts of the burlesque
        Queen Hope

"God, I wish those psychical research fellows would hurry up: I can't wait"—S. Shapero.

    Desire & fear drew cartoons
        in my dreams—
    Hideous caricatures—
      And can shift gears
    Meaningless
      picking up speed, then, roaring through
            my head
    (Timber! Toothpick!)

Love, the dark victor whom no
one evades, escapes
denies, outwits—

The assassin, the sneak thief; the life-raft story. Jeremiah, meet
Noah; Noah, meet Jeremiah. How do you do? How are you? How are
you doing?

Look at the city stoops above the child—
Rude health
Honor, love, obedience, troops of friends

Hast thou a heart
Coming in such
A guise

(*Mozart mirabilus*, how sad
how gay—)

Agee: Like drinking tepid orange pekoe at a rained-out garden
party of some deep local-provincial unit of the English Speaking Union.

Snob dream life, vulpine, don't hit him on the head. Exit. Use your
head, head first, dear bird.

Mixture of imperfection and, too, unfinished virtue. Much praise
causes dislike.

Friday. Renewal, pages & outline, a unity for a poem—the Yard,
Phyllis's mother, Alison departing from the library, Phyllis best with,
longest night ("watchful waiting").

Saturday. Doctor's examination, "your emotions," fever & infection.

Alison, in the Yard; Dickson's garden, Leisher's dinner, game of
Botticelli—worsening cold. Blazing inspiration, but no effort.

The Yard. Did not see me. Saw & did not want to speak to me. Saw
me & wanted me to speak to her. (She half-looked back perhaps.)

How to tell love from mere affection, from concupiscence, from
use, custom, and habituation, from convenience, from acceptance of a
fact, from infatuation—

(This was on the good Saturday, when Hope arose again.)

Reasons for marriage: to get work done; toils of a relationship;
rebound of rejection; love & comfort; lust, love—

May 28–31

Blazing sensibility & cold, Alison's, lunch, her pictures, seated on
the sofa, blushed (Pearl Kazin & the proofs)—her mother's daughter,
the photo—salutary aversion.

Phyllis at 4—cold thick—headache, lying in the dark until 10,
Charnwood's *Lincoln.*

29th. Forced day, unable to write—the third in a row.

30th. A page forced, and then notebooks reread in the afternoon—with some satisfaction.

31st. Heat, 92, sleeping until almost 12. Day of torpor, after a barely forced page. *Goncourt Journals* and three for sleep, and port. Dinner with Bill, glum; and Elizabeth Pollet rang from New York.

May

1942–1943–May 1944.

Complete: *Dead Souls, Four Quartets, The Brothers Karamazov, The Golden Bowl 2, Notes of an Underground Man, Henry IV, 1 and 2, Bleak House, Swann in Love, Dangling Man, Within a Budding Grove, The Double Man.*

Leafed through: *Germinal, Nana, Arabian Nights, Finnegans Wake,* Casanova, E. S. Millay, Adams's letters, Mrs. Adams's letters, Wilson's anthology, eight volumes of Stekel, two volumes of Karen Horney, Lubbock's *The Craft of Fiction, Put Out More Flags, Vile Bodies, A Handful of Dust, Scoop, Politicos,* Zola, Hugo, Dostoevsky, the first *Lady Chatterley's Lover,* Freud's *New Lectures, The Neurotic Personality.*

Plays: *The Cherry Orchard, Othello, The Magic Flute, Marriage of Figaro;* ballet (poor attention throughout).

Brighton Rock, The Confidential Agent, Goethe, *Conversations with Eckermann, Poetry and Truth.*

Max Hoffmann: *War of Lost Opportunities.*

Liddell-Hart: *The Real War.*

June 1

Gloomy hot day: a page in an unexpected rhythm, after reading Hölderlin & not waking until 12.

The library, Phyllis: "Are you still stuck on me? Would you make love to me, if it were not so hot?" She wept on the steps, and loudly, because I did not.

A year ago this week, a new period of inspiration had begun.

[Conrad] Aiken passed as I sat in the Yard on Weds.

Alison called to ask me to take her to the Wannings' on Sat. "Guess what came in the mail this morning."

Brinnin wrote to ask me to read at Vassar.

June 2

I surprised myself by managing to write a page; weakness and sensitivity both, as never before.

Visit to the Dicksons. Mrs. Dickson, as Rose painted the chair, and Elizabeth came downstairs three times with an injured nose.

Return at 9, Tessa, stories of painting, a colored woman, Nela & Richard.

First Phyllis, then Alison rang: "Popular bachelor," said Tessa. I grew sleepy as Tessa grew drunk—on the sherry I had just bought.

At night I dreamed twice that I had asked G.B.S. to return—it was in New York & William P[hillips] had just announced that he was going to have one, too. "Let's have a child," I said to G.

In the morning, after panic-anxiety before sleep, I woke with a sinus head, and there was a letter from Jay & a twenty-year-old poet.

"You have the younger generation under your thumb"—G.B.S.

June 3

Cold cloudy afternoon. With Alison to the Wannings' punch party; admiring ahead, we took the wrong way.

Van Keurens, and many strange faces; Rufus; I was soon high; A.'s kitchen, I hulled strawberries; empty the trash cans; kissed her three times (should I not do that?) to her unmoving lips, and lost the image of aversion.

Home at 9, her pictures, serenity, effort at early sleep, 10–11, three, wine, sleeping until 11 (I dreamed I almost died and went to my own funeral).

June 4

Elizabeth Pollet—comfort, wait for Bill, four rings, "big poet," "handsome," success, excitement, Bill, interruptus, despondency, forced verses, her return, half-success, relief, evening at George P.'s, and at the Athens, Wm. Smith, Tessa.

"I don't want to fall in love with you." —How strange it's all—nervous-making, the interruption—

Anxiety attack after serenity, when I came back.

Undated

Valéry: To be in love is to be stupid together.

"As terrifying as a gas mask on the beloved's face (frogs or owls looking like gms [Germans?]).

> Sirs, in my mind there was
> a kind of lighting
> That would not let me sleep or shut my eyes
> But steep & deep,
> Stared like a canyon at the gazing mind
> And circus freaks waded like owls
> in it

The owl, its gas mask (pop-eye) look, / The gas mask like an owl / And in the skull the look / Of gas mask & of owl.

Synonym, sin with him / gas mask, skull-like, death's-head.

Sunburnt by love, tanned to a look of health.

No need to destroy yourself / Nature will satisfy that wish—at least—

This sun-shot room at six o'clock.

June 5

Remus & Romulus suckled by a she-wolf; Aeneas, then the Caesars, and then the Popes.

Tinsel, tensile; tandem, random.

Roosevelt on the radio, person & power (friendly, persuasive, ingratiating, sensible); patronizing use of the colloquial "the batting average," "tough going"—Monday night.

Personages in the Ark: Each poem of a page, invoking such a one as Noah, Nero, Hölderlin, Mozart, Burr, Udemore, Jeremiah (disheveled aplomb), Beethoven, George Washington, General Grant—

The true, the good, the beautiful.

Goethe, Schiller, Mann, Baudelaire, Mallarmé, unfallen Emerson & Henry James—

The bell for chapel, at 8:45, rings 350 times (learned at the Leishers). From December until February, this bell gladdened & sickened me, as part of an eight o'clock class.

Last night, I heard Symphony No. 9—kettledrum, double fugue, presto, chorus.

"You're too big. You're a genius. Things are complicated enough"; "this poet giant"—

Domineering, like Beethoven (G.B.S.)—the too-much-loved nephew; W.B. in 1939, after the tennis courts: "Hard to get along with"; Jean, "imperious," the chosen restaurant—& at the Palmers'.

"We live upon the past and the past destroys us, making us puppets"—in an old pastiche, making us rickshaw boys on the unimportant avenues.

Goethe: What fiend takes from me the holy energy? What strong anxiety overpowers me?

In April 1936, I forced myself to write an essay for the Bowdoin Prize [which Delmore won for an essay "Poetry as Imitation"]; in February, a story; in May, short poems; in June, a story; in July, a forced story, which was lost on *The Atlantic*, and an essay for the *Southern Review*; and I rewrote some of my poems.

June 6

Today, June 6, 1944, is invasion day—

In the morning, I glanced at *The Dynasts* and I saw the news as in June 1941 & December 7, 1941, the Russian & the Japanese outbreaks—

This time I stood by Felix's newsstand—big black headlines, but no excitement in the streets. Apathy in the streets. And in the cars.

"The news was received by the nation with calm"—

An eyewitness account—on a landing barge—first assault troops— small-boat weather.

The last thing to be made was Roosevelt's prayer—the guns came first.

But at the Dinner Bell: "This is the day," said the headwaitress, looking at my newspaper.

Faint morning, a story by Saul Bellow, "The Mexican General"— an effort to continue typing of previous day's verses, the Square, news of the invasion, lunch, an effort to write, the doctor at 2—the Handlins for dinner, difficulty with conversation, again discussion of anti-Semitism, Norma & her doctor friend, brandy—return, unable to sleep until 2.

Yesterday: A page of verse by means of sherry, at 5, after reading & note making all afternoon in S. K[ierkegaard]. Pages on despair as to be chosen. Dinner at 7, without appetite, beer & Symphony No. 9, mild drunkenness, sleep to 2:30.

June 7

Dead from just after breakfast, at 10:30, two old tablets after lunch, a kind of revival, all of K.'s "Repetition" without understanding it, and note making, Brinnin's telegram, Rose put off, invitation from Mark (Tessa).

June 8

Yesterday I read passages in Rilke's letters about his own dead end —four years long, six, seven; the account of reading his verse in Switzerland.

Yesterday & today, cheered by the telephone—Mark, even—so much resented—today, the telegram from Fred Dupee, and postcard from Margaret Marshall [literary editor of *The Nation*].

To have an objective existence—to be not altogether left out (the idea of the doctor also helps me from the sick image of wife & family).

Half of the thirtieth year ended & wasted—today. And six months from now? I will be thinking forward to New York—I will draw the line there (neither cause nor cure is outside).

I read some of the Greenwich Village plays of E. Wilson, before drunken sleep.

I drank two martinis at dinner; then bought a gallon of Burgundy & a fifth of rum. At 3:30 I woke up, and with two [sleeping pills] & B[urgundy] drove myself back to sleep.

Eleven o'clock, 12—sensitive, sensitized—passages and a weak sonnet. I read some of *Four Quartets* with breakfast. But the trembling of wine returned. Perhaps not wine, since I knew it yesterday, too.

The invasion news: "fragmentary & obscure."

June 9–10

Dream again of quarreling with Mother—aged twenty-two—and making great claims for oneself (derived from letter about separation).

Half-sleep until 11—Van Doren's poems—emptiness by 2.

The typewriter my father gave me—which I broke immediately.

"Only he who is able to love is really a man"—S. K[ierkegaard].

Honor to him who—endures despair.

(Today ends half of my thirtieth year—)

Dec. 8, 1943. Beethoven, Phyllis, Alison, Bella Vista—the stars.

> The minute concessions, the nervous contractions
> And the small surrenders by which we live
>
> The pleasure boat, the wine cup
> —(Beachcomber sensibility
> Upon a sinecure afloat
> On the endlessly improvised sea)
> Seek ever spontaneity,
> Whence variety
> Shuts out the boarded-up despair

Four Quartets & *Double Man,* reread, seem better & better—relaxation or shift of what?

Jacques, Hamlet, Dejection, R[esolution] & Independence—ever the inner problem of emotion—

> The bed becomes disheveled
> To imitate the sea
> Venus rising up from the foam
> Bringing disorder,
> Stripping the clothes from the girls
> Shutting the looking eyes—
>   Until the fountain falls

"To persuade her to take off her clothes"—one more version of the private parts.

[The following lines are variants of lines in "I Wish I Had Great Knowledge or Great Art" in Vaudeville for a Princess.*]*

> I wish I had a pony or a trot
> To read the obscure Latin of her heart
> I wish, blaspheming, I were what I am not,
> I would if that I could play any part
> (After so many years to come to this!)
> —And yet I know, come to this empty pass
> A shift, a mask, a metamorphosis
> Would merely take me to the heart of loss—

Every birthday is a funeral.

> Disappointment—ever deepening
> Deep & deeper, down & downed—
>   To be among the troop
> Of those who are taken away screaming—

>   In the slow car
> Upon thin faces, misshapen like crushed hats
> Little is clear except the apathy
> [...]

Freud: Self-analysis is impossible. (He was unable to free himself from a compulsion neurosis.)

Art as: expression of wishes; unconscious wishes (exhibitionism); defense against unconscious wishes—exhibitionism as a blind for voyeurism.

Poetry as orality—independence (narcissistic) of the mother. What can be done with the trauma of birth?

Fame reduced in value, for the truly rich & powerful wish to hide their lights & bushels.

> *Name*
> And in the manes of light
> And in the dark-blue sky
> The lines of rain
>   In the first morning
> The birds were rinsing little handkerchiefs
> Bubbles & grapes of sound broke in the air
>
> The deer swam back from Australia's shore
> The day's fresh flowers quickly faded
> Withered by noon

The scrolls of the ears, the bread loaf of the head—
Ravid: is it a word?

David Diamond, Yaddo, 1939: I worked all day. Now I am going to be gay.

It is not the finished work but the continuous activity which brings happiness.

The defects of style are the defects of the man.

Even as a child, I suffered from emptiness & boredom: "I have nothing to do."

"Truism in neurology that higher structures are more readily fatigued than those of lower levels—hence cortical structures suffer first—most severely—from any process of fatigue."

Sunday, nimbus gray day, cold in June.

No day without a line. This will be a day with hardly more than a line.

My hand-to-mouth domesticity; my retired life. Now day by day from hand to mouth & hand me down.

Stevens, Berryman, Jarrell—nothing takes me up.

"What shall I do now? What shall I ever do?"

Exalted sentences—snigger or smirk if you will.

Seven Sundays or eight since that Easter Sunday on Fifth Avenue (with G.B.S.).

Essay by Guterman on S. Kierkegaard—freely assertive.

After dinner, the drop back to insensitivity.

Literally nothing else to do, nowhere else draws me. Handlins, A.Q., library, bookstores, N.Y.C., W.V.K., P.R., the Hut. Palmers, Dicksons, Sonny. Films, strolls, Choice Spirits. The S. possibilities.

June 11

Sensitized & spontaneous until lunch—then rereading, to find defects & nothing.

The sky overcast with rain clouds, fragrant rain air—panic despair and then note making, through hopelessness of a mild kind.

Phyllis rejected—as a burden—also W.V.K.

After dinner P[hyllis] summoned—deadness, Handel, withness, Oxford Grill.

Eight, poor morning, reviving as I read Swift—plan, after another part-poem—lunch, fall, weak afternoon, Bridges, Shapiro, Goodman, touching book after book & finding nothing, hopelessness & wine at 5.

Sahara—prospect—U[niversity] T[heater] rejected, sofa—effort (twice in an afternoon)—surrender, Central Sq.—not the right picture, return, two hundred pages of *Cousine Bette*—sometimes shocked by vulgar[ity], sometimes moved by powerful psychology—resisting wine —sleep with three [tablets], after 12—Balzac woke suspicions of A.

Near 5. There is, at any rate, the hope that it will not always be thus / Since it has not always been thus / A hope & not a probability / A possibility / A hope to be beyond these rides & falls, like other human beings / (To concentrate, though idle by the gate)—

Sunday, June 11, 1944, in the midst of deathly languor—

And when he added wine to consciousness / Choice spirits took the place of Hollywood / And drove the habit from his languid blood—

To face his emptiness, devicelessness, and loneliness, after dinner in the sun-shot room— / And to look at his wristwatch in order to estimate the distance to sleep & nothingness—half-sleep, dream-sucked, / (The birds tear favors in the sunset trees.) (At sunset in the trees, bird sounds like tissues torn.)

His error—to identify happiness with active authorship.

The contrast of the literary & the academic.

No reasonable certainty or reward—the insecurity of literature as a revival of neuroticism. Who can be sure?

Dream about visiting F. O. M[atthiessen] with Arthur Berger & some of Oscar's friends—and having to rush back to Cambridge to be host to some of O.'s friends—F.O.M. said that I looked as if I had been drinking too much.

"It is very congenial here," I said.

"It is comfortable," he corrected me.

I got into a bed, while the company was there—to rest. This occasioned the remark about my health & drinking too much. The material derived from Fred's coming visit & the boys at the Coach & the wine I did not drink last night, though sorely tempted. As before, G. & I are still married. The dream work has not caught on, as yet. And G. made sharp remarks (consistency of character in dreams).

I was "painfully sincere." The body's whimper & giggle. "Naked beneath the darkness."

"I hear the snapping of the shears; and hear the whipping of the carpet—car starting, car in full flight sighing; crackle of shoe on brick walk; murmur & stress of radio: city sounds."

The world is coming in to me. My senses are open to it. My mind has words & wishes for it.

"The carriage trade" (the station-wagon trade); "first nights"; Southern-fried Chekhov; "a Venetian blind," "a pound of palm leaves"; "take in a show"; a stretched-out deck chair in the apartment.

Joy as Maestro
"In joy, as in a stone
A thing is magnified
& purified"

Now what does my emotion
overrate
Or underestimate, wishing too
much?
"Do you know this?—that
I hurry once again—"

May God have mercy on your soul!

The problem of finding the proper form for the subject matter once more torments me.

(My notebooks, full of electrical phrases, but uncomposed—)

I jumped, touched by Bob Daniels. You must be in need of sleep, he said.

The Singers, Book II.

"I am trying to finish what is in its very nature unfinishable." "Two irreconcilable parts of my nature, narrative—comment—"

Since childhood
The sky has been
overclouded
By the four horsemen
How they come forward wildly
Storming, lightning
& thunder
Black thunderheads darkening
Our time in the
earth

If I were you, I would
Not talk so much

The newness of anon
The plump white clouds, like love

Taken in this necessity
What more natural
Than self-pity?

When thirty years were used & waste
Light, clarity, and radiance
—Ultimate verbal clarity
An emotional possibility,
An imaginative possibility,
A speechless thing.

The war weaves in again, waves in again, shadow or real?—through the draft board's postal messages.

> *T.S.E.*
> He had no real serenity
> Only an impeccable demeanor

T.S.E.: The deeper unnamed feelings to which we rarely penetrate and which form the substratum of our being—for our lives are mostly a constant evasion of ourselves and an evasion of the visible & sensible world—

Cp. [Compare] with discursive passages in *F[our] Quartets.*

"The sudden lifting of the burden of anxiety & fear which presses upon our daily life so steadily that we are unaware of it."

June 12–13

Monday. Return to *The Singers*—*Cousine Bette* finished in the evening (melodramatic, naïve, sententious—hard to understand its esteem)—too much beer in the evening.

Tuesday. D-day, draft board, 1-A, hangover, anxiety. Morrison, Phillips Brooks: We are not taking anyone over thirty. Library, after wine & dinner, A. departing—newspapers twice—Morrison: You won't be taken at your age & in view of the circumstances—unless [changes] & the war prolonged. (Thoughts of not taking in my freedom before this.)

Lifeboat (Hitchcock), *Man from Down Under* (laughter, Binnie Barnes), four beers against anxiety in a bar at midnight.

June 14

Waking too early—effort to start—but weak—lessened anxiety by far—wine & interest in "so it doesn't whistle," new sentimentality of new generation.

Pages in Eliot, La Fontaine, H. Adams, *Oxford Book of English Prose.*

6/14/44. This day—marriage—six years ago! & six years hence?! [Added later:] *9/25/53:* June 14, 1950: 75 Charles St., E.P.S. [Elizabeth Pollet Schwartz], *W.W.* & *V.F.P.* [*The World Is a Wedding* and *Vaudeville for a Princess*]—*Kenyon.*

The idea of writing G.—sentiment & sentimentality.

"Now don't get sentimental, like last time."

Monolinear, abstracted, instructed, subtracted; blamed—humiliated—embarrassed; pride-pricked-punctured.

Queen Hope, the fatal woman, more than Love.

To be a part-time thing / to be a half-baked thing (potato) / to be a quarter to nine / to be too soon / to be a leftover, to be left out / to be an extra, to be uninvited.

The major experiences (emotions) of our time—to be left out—to make love easy—to try to be an artist of some kind (and to doubt one's gift and to be afraid).

"The Finns are just high-class Eskimos."

We begin to have important experiences some twenty, twenty-five, thirty years before we have any instrument, capacity, ability to understand them. The desire to look at an image of life—indestructible (to hear the account of others). Poetry begins with the beating of a drum (with the effort to walk).

A graduate-student mode of life. Studied & steadied, touched & tipped over, the skull lifted off, the face turned back, the hair removed, the mind perceived.

> Let us look back
> Upon the dimmed track
>   faint in the dusk
> White-railed & cinder silent
> There perhaps to find
> The dark which holds your mind
> The untouched fear
> Which trembles up
> And blocks the skull's cup
>   And the going & the flowing
>   Of being & knowing—

Tusk, husk, musk; the coffee fragrance, the savor of oranges, the scent of the flowers.

I don't care—that's it—the caring too much (the love & shame) which makes this long disease, my life.

Childhood, adolescence: these parts of our life die and (like Adonis) become by their death & resurrection divinities, secret, in their power unrecognized.

For what does all this suffering prepare?

A stranger to the muses / The muses estranged?— / The poet deranged / The silence arranged.

> How & by what breach
> Shall I enter her heart?
> And how shall I reach
> The soft especial pulsing hidden part?

To double his alienation / The state and the soul / The two chief parts—

> Queen Hope whose fictive face
> Deceives more lives
> Than the white thighs of loves
> Splendor surrendered

Disaffected and rejected / immediacy grasped, touched—ineffable loaves.

June 15

Letter to G.B.S.—nervous waiting for Fred [Dupee]—Fred at 11—pleasure in his conversation—Greenberg & Mary—& poet.

Lunch with F.O.M. after conversational morning—easy floating talk—F.O.M. pleased.

Gray & cool June day. Lift of spirits still in the blood—grave of James.

9:00 Weds. evening—E. Pollet's desire to come here—the god arisen at long-distance conversation.

F. W. D[upee]. Much about N.Y. lives—Trilling, Chiappe, William & Philip. Discussion of neuroticism—thirty—"You've done a lot"—"accomplishment," "great talent," "Not all of it first rate, but some of it first rate"—"Nobody will accept the fact that they are second rate."

Pleasure in *The New Yorker* at midnight—letter—"weepy" from G.B.S.

June 16

Goncourt Journals. Love is the exchange of fantasies & the contact of epidermis. (To love is to decide to be stupid together—to love is to find a certain kind of consciousness—with—withness—another being.)

The brushing of palms, the blushing of cheeks.

In the darkened bedroom in the summer twilight, after love and sleep, the man (boy) said to the girl, "Perhaps we have died, and this is our life for eternity, to lie in a summer twilight like this, pacified & empty, while the world outside ever seems more distant & more vague."

"It is too easy," she said.

> Sudden excitement, horses' running
> wild—
> Brass band outbursts, applauses' downpours

"It occurs unexpectedly like benches in a labyrinthine passage"—Kierkegaard.

"As against God, you are always in the wrong."

Farceur, flaneur, boulevardier, beau.

"Which (what) is the way from childhood to perfection?"

"What is it childhood tries to reach in us?" Two poets, Rimbaud & Hölderlin, who broke their minds.

Unteachable goods, unteachable truths, unreachable & untouchable stars.

Hölderlin, in his madness (he lived to seventy-three): Only now I understand human beings, now, since I live far from them & in solitude.

In 1796, Hegel wrote a long poem to Hölderlin. Rilke compared him to moonlight.

In his madness, H. called himself many names, but never his own.

When you listen to a seashell, you hear the roar of your heart—loud & inchoate.

When you look at a photograph, the years stand looking with you, over your shoulder.

The world is a ball of fat / is an elephant / a glass of wine. The world is a wedding day.

"*La génie est une longue* (in the long run) *patience*"—Buffon.

"Time, strength, patience, cash!"

Dream-struck, dream-ridden.

Rilke: Hölderlin [is] a moon which passes, illuminating "the surprised landscape."

Democritus laughed at the bumping falling atoms.

Noah
    The starry sky about you
    With singular & mute intensity
    The mind has reasons which the
           heart
              Alas! can never understand—
                 Among the stars
  Lost, and other likely stories' silences
      Light and its influence
      (May you remain where you are
      As far as this place)

    The architectonics of the sky
    Thunder, lightning,
    The forms of the clouds
    The forms of the constellations
    (Their motions and their relations)
    These are one in the beginning
    With the bread and the wine
    These cohabit in consciousness
    —The energy which drives the stars
    Moves your mind, & drives your heart

Noah

The arks, drums, and horses
Touched by the mind,
The book like a dish of fruit,
The solid and clear shapes
Of chair, table, and bowl
Touched by the mind
The sofa like a mountain
The window like a lake

—The mind and the mind's shadow
Still in the living room

"The gods are no man's property"
They are the world's & they smile
If we but see them
Yet in each one's privacy
Lies, of love, the secret—

(And I, a veteran of these things,
Freely confess this)—

R. P. B[lackmur]: I am having a drink in your honor now, and
remembering you as you were twenty years ago—at seventeen.
Far from this barren shore / Far from this coast.
The self-quietus of ancient song.

The cat, his soft bounce step
Crouch & withdrawal

The cast-iron lion, the mansard roof

The ego blows up like a big balloon
And sails, a zeppelin,
And sinks as limp—

The frogs squatted; shells on the Charles, swan boats on the
lagoon, the island in the Public Gardens, "the bread-stuffed ducks,"
"the sun-struck shallows."
S. K[ierkegaard]: The love of God is repentance. The greater the
freedom, the greater the guilt—this is one of the secrets of blessedness.
"The choice of despair is—myself."

"He wanted to be a great one"—Gertrude Stein. Only a few are very great, and of these very few, only a very few in youth, even in middle youth.

> Of three o'clock in the morning
> Of four o'clock in the morning,
>   and of the early
> Morning light I would be poet laureate,
> And of the midnight supper and the
>   midnight show
> Midnight remorse & Monday knowledge

Birthday knowledge, knowledge of the eve of holidays, Sunday knowledge, knowledge that is gained in pain, in joy, through love, through loss, knowledge of morning exaltation, of the moment of deception.

> I never thought
> To pass my aging youth
>   on this cold shore
> I never thought to look on Hope's
>   (6/9/53: Medusa)
>   blank face

June 17–19

Saturday. 11, let down, emptiness, postponement—wine, dinner at Whelan's—sleep at 11.

No A. summoned—thoughts of putting off Brinnin—Wolfert's *My Wife the Witch, In Our Time*, U.T.—Henreid, Lupino—depressed return to wine—sleep, twice—two in the dark, whiskey at 7—waking at 11.

Dreams of A., fetishismus, uncle, G.B.S.

Fred [Dupee]: Should write it at forty, not at thirty. All in verse.

Weak day of little effort—regret of Provincetown.

Sunday. Effort to use Socratic method with *Singers*—hopeless by 4—wine, shift to versified narrative—pleasure & relief.

Handlins, a dark couple (tutor, Jewish), Charlie & his Jewish wife —nothing to say—Mary on Laski—Oscar as air corps historian.

Doubt in the evening.

Monday. Waking early to the idea of no Vassar—vanished in joyous reading Eliot & Auden—failure in the afternoon at versified narrative—letter to Brinnin written & not sent—emptiness, pink & pink-white.

Shifted to third plan with wine—haircut—revival—too much wine
—essays on Babbitt—waking twice—third method (prose-verse) abandoned—winging back & forth between going & not going to Vassar—
the library—Wannings' for dinner.

The failure & withdrawal—the top of the mind says, "Don't take
these things too seriously: what good does it do if you do?"

The doctor's—he asked about PEP (1920–30 word).

Shift to "The True, the Good, the Beautiful," a poem of eighty
pages.

One week since changed to 1-A— But what? undisturbed because
nothing is accomplished anyway.

> Day of pinpoint rain—
> And it will come again?
> When will it come again
> The joy & the light—
> The thrilling illusion

June 20–21

Tuesday night. Wannings' dinner—Claude, economist—voice like
F.O.M.—Pat read medical journal. Too much to drink—stayed too long
—inarticulateness.

Weds., 2–8:30. One good hour, gradual decline—notebook—trembling. Three-hour walk to Boston, Old Howard, one hour was all; 4—
subway—library—Clark's—trembling.

Essay on solitude in *Walden*, Heiden's *Der Führer*.

Lines after trembling & wine, 10–5:30—effort to sleep—breakfast
at Hazen's—half asleep until 11—waking refreshed.

Letters to Brinnin, Williams & *Atlantic Monthly*.

Bath, Goodman's story, tidying—a calm, but empty—returning to
thoughts of A. repeatedly—two more days & she goes away for six
weeks. Today sunny after two days of chill & rain.

June 22

Telephone, ten o'clock.

"What's this about young men?"

"As you know—withdrawn into my shell—I wish I knew some
young men."

"May not be here when you get back."

"About to take decisive steps?"

"Not I."

"Let me know if you do?"

"Do what?"

"How long will you be at the Cape?"

"I don't know."

"I hope you have a good time—"

Five minutes, rage at coolness & withdrawal—ringing with no answer—suspicion of a visitor.

Five minutes more. Did you ring? Bathtub— No—

Something I forgot—Bellow proof—& something I hoped you would remember—my ring (embarrassed prolongation of the consonant), signature of my identity.

If that's what you want, Delmore, or, whatever you like.

Means of transport; I'll send it to you.

All over—inspired by darkened windows at 8:30.

Reasons: her papers?—change of feeling?—social life she had expected?—or simple indifference, unwillingness to be prompted by my efforts.

The withdrawal since April as a hint, a provocation or a punishment (the papers)? or as—the response to Phyllis—refusal to be moved —annoyed with me?

The dead day perhaps started it all. If P[hyllis] had called— But it was inevitable. I loitered at 3 at the book[store], tempted to buy *Don Juan*. Hurt feelings striking back from her, as in the train & with the gifts.

June 23

Hangover, elevation after coffee, effort to ring A., not home—twice!

In the evening expectancy of Elizabeth, Phyllis rang—she was going away to Vermont.

The True, the Good, the Beautiful. The three prime musicians & magicians. The comely magicians.

> What do I know? what have
> I ever known
> I hardly know my fumbling ignorance
> My knowledge is suspicion
> & desire
> Now hope is boarded up
> (What can I hope to have?)

> 'Tis right that girls should
> Get & give the oranges
> —They are the juice and brightness
> Nature grows—

Being dishonest, he was outraged by the dishonesty of others.

> The top of the mind said No,
> The top of the mind said No!
> But like a volcano
> The desperate Ego . . .

S. F[reud]: We must love or we must be ill.

To transform repetition into recollection. "The conscious thoughts of waking life." "Dragged into the light!"

"I don't like your attitude."

You can't see the back of your head. You can't see your conscious mind.

Cerebellum of symptoms.

June 24–25

Days of rain—impatient—anxiety attack & eagerness to [be] rid of E.

I told Jean I thought you were wonderful. What did she say? She agreed. Nervous dinner at Clark's—evening's tears—failure twice—late sleep—

Sunday-morning revival.

Stories of Joseph Pollet, Aaron Bell & Paul G.—many compliments.

Fell out of the window, retreating from Goodman's advances. Elaine Gottlieb [fiction writer], P[aul] Goodman, C. G. Wallis—bearded A. Bell.

Joseph Pollet. Unhappy?—even if he were, he would not admit it to himself. Should have "brought up one of the girls to attend & wait on him—" (Barbara [E.'s] sister). Sylvester [Pollet], four, crazy about his father—"grew tired of the *Odyssey*." "I'll cut you dead."

Aaron Bell—"You're slow & deep"—stared at her & walked round the chair.

"Jean [Garrigue] has won the *Kenyon Review* short-story contest—"

Betty [Strassberger Pollet]—Montclair—depression, reduced to one chauffeur—"Father dead from neck up, Mother from neck down" —flowers & poems, broke an engagement [to marry Joseph Pollet]. Sylvester: "I know all about God, you don't know anything about God" —Ulysses, roughhousing with his father at four.

[Elizabeth] wept—I don't care what you do, it's what you say. She went from room to room in the darkness.

> "Oh, what a beautiful morning   (girl, house)
> Oh, what a beautiful day"—   (world)

"You're very beautiful"—
"You're a wonderful poet"—
"You're a big beautiful being"—
"Recoil, withdrawal"

Budapest boy took her virginity & disapproved of his action—her willingness.

"Get out & stay out." "May you come home in your coffin"—his mother often said. Rich minds, rich natures. Psychoanalysis is in its infancy.

I slept too late on Sunday morning—[E.] stood in the door looking in—

"Cold—or bored?"

"Both."

(Me, student of the early-morning light.)

June 26–29

Monday. Five pages of a beginning & happiness—letter from G.B.S.—almost sleep with three [s.t.s.]—forgiveness & goodness, dry nervousness (martini before lunch as well as supper). *The Uninvited*, belief in ghosts, U.T., *Tampico*—dead girl & A.Q.

"Summer afternoon"—H. James—most beautiful phrase—two words—in English.

I laughed to G.'s laughter laughing five years back—mackerel sky —tea-colored (amber) sunset—weak-kneed stoic of I don't care—it makes no difference.

"Perhaps the truth is sad."

"He was so amazed that he was not even angry."

"This is an excellent idea."

A drunkard, playing with dice—

As evening darkens among the trees / As darkness thickens among the heavy wind-driven wind-tossed leaves—

"The child born in advance—"

Salmon-pink sunset (on cirrus ranks), foreboding heat— / The dusk breeze rises.

Tues. Lunch, hangover—intense heat—$100—arrival of *Kenyon* with Xmas poem—the doctor's—afternoon & evening crises—thrice to the library—stories in *Cross-Section*.

Weds. 5—mild happiness—intense heat again. Silone & Gustavus Myers—twice to the library—laundry & face duty—Nela's evening ring —thoughts of A.—but gradual abandonment, but 100–1 belief that . . . and still the intellectual knowledge gained from her mother's face.

Thurs. Nela at 10 (told Sage to kiss me after kissing him). Five forced pages to being hopeless—visit of Nela, Sage, and Susie— annoyed by children's racket & dirtied tub.

Do you want to hear a compliment? John B[erryman] said you were "the greatest living author in America."

"Hello, Moon. How are Sun & Stars?"

The torch of touch, the only nearness.

Brooks, Emerson. "But how control his moods? They never believed one another."

[Stanley] Kunitz: The beginning and the end in each other's arms!

Tag end of Commencement, the sweltering Yard—Spencer (dingling-dangling cortesia, thinning blond curly hair).

Were novels written for railroad trains & winter evenings?

Problems of solitude, problems of waiting & passage, questions & choices—

June 30

Love in its fury.

Failure with Bill—return of $1,000.

Another rejection, failure—return of proofs & ring—I am not desolated.

To dominate the senses, the intellect, the heart.

(Don't be a highbrow, now.)

The endless limits of the senses—"complete & solid beings"—plum-cold, not marble-cold—"It reaches out, like hope to the uttermost limits of the senses."

"Be absolute, my dear / And do not compromise."

Berryman, Taylor: Greatest writer in America (unbelievable) ("depressant insanity").

Blackmur: One of the most distinguished men of our time—

The world is a funeral / is a birthday / is an engagement party.

His gift died young / He wasted his powers / He lost his powers / somewhere.

Let us consult our pride like an angered lion (maddened lion), runaway horse, crouched tiger ("lion couchant"—Eliot at Columbia, 1933, April).

Drawn to success / As well as repelled by it—(Dwight, spring 1942).

Now this admired stone / Though it survive the city.

With how much evil I have dealt, / Failure, error, trash—

Last summer as perhaps / A long drunkenness.

"The Japanese navy is cute / And ought to be encouraged."

"I was a call girl in Venice."

Pearl K[azin] thought & sought A. as "one of the inner circle."

> Shake then, my aging boy,
> Your unintended flies—
> The silences of pride
> In emptiness abide—

1942, R.P.B.—Stevens: He writes too much.

A. shows P.K. the proofs—the impression is—not impressed, but showing off—"one of the inner circle."

"Behind my forehead / lies the whole Atlantic—"

> My lady actuality
> With whom I have lived
> > so long
> & my lady poetry
> The strange princess
> > of song—

General Sherman Miles, Commencement, *"Civis Americanus sum"* —the Roman note.

Variants upon my matchbooks, door, grave, gate inscribed: "It is impossible!"

> Cigars for me
> > And plums for you
> And my mind like your
> > Looking glass

Oranges to you / and apples, / and happiness / and knowledge!
O Fountains of the Summer Afternoon.
"The altars of their ideals"—"the heights of their ideals."
Condemned to happiness / (since you rejected suffering).
You'll learn the luxury / Of boredom's ease ("keen torment").

> I wish that I could
> > See beneath her eyes
> Into her darkened hidden
> > mind
> I wish I had a pony
> > or a trot
> To read the obscure
> > Latin of her heart

Emperor, conqueror, master / Drugged & dragged my / Plovers, limbs, lambs, loams—

> And after all,
> Given the doubts I see
> —Irritability, her mother's face,
> Her family's distaste, her
> Self-centeredness, Fisher— And
> All in me that rouses this

Reason: no motive but drive— / Paper pride, withdrawal, pride—
both. Hurt feelings or revived romance. Revulsion. Probably she saw
me twice in the Yard.

The absolute light, the dry light.

> Me, student of the early-morning
> > light
> And sleeplessness and Life's recurrent
> > Deaths
> The Goddess visits (off & on)

Serena [a name Delmore at times uses for Alison] may not be sure
how much was tactic, how much rejection. "If that's what you want—"
She knows she did nothing to stop whichever it was.

Tempus is fidgeting.

Girls are like oranges and should be squeezed like oranges, and
soon squeezed dry.

G.I. Joe on Cherbourg dock: Where is this Normandy beachhead
they talk so much about?

[Ernie] Pyle: You're sitting on it.

G.I. Joe: Oh, this is it? (*Bored.*)

"What shall I do with his absurdity?"—Yeats.

> "Plain & severe my song and like
> > my walk
> Awkward. Where is the sensuality?
> > (Or is the absence the
> > > narcissist's blunt thumb-generality?)"

> "The night is young—"
> "But we're no longer young—"
> "I wonder by my rum (rye)
> What in the world
> I did until I drank—"

> Look, look, the ripe girls
> Lolloping in the pool
> Brimming their bathing suits
> Splashing the spontaneity
> And giggling nudely—

[Note added later] 7/30/55: If creation without toil is poet's
original sin, jumping to generalization over minute particulars is a
cardinal sin.

Wet heat again—note-taking inspiration as I corrected themes—

Morrison echoed & then mentioned my poem. Return to "TGB" poem
—dinner with Nela at Gustie's—annoyed that she did not pay—return
to Warren House—*crise* of despair—comfort in company (Wanning,
Scowcroft, Selz, Morrison), beer at Jim's Place.

July 1

Again inspiration in crumbs of feeling—Nela, car to South Station
—train & bus to Yarmouth & Truro. Richard Wright's "The Man Who
Lived Underground." Fred, Polly Boyden [educator], drunken Fal-
staffian sailor on the bus.

Gibbons, his wife's lost prettiness, Jane & Bootsie, thoughts of
Serena, Jane's kissable belly—cocktail ecstasy—moonlight summer
country evening—easy sleep.

July 2

Lapse again—to the ocean after a long walk over the hills with
Dwight, Nancy, and Mike [the Macdonalds]—the Chiaramontes, Joan
Caulbrooke [painter], rock & shell of the sea—cloudless perfect day,
sunburn.

"I like Delmore," said Nancy. Lunch on the blackberry patch, lapse
at evening—spaghetti dinner—story of Dwight's parents—sleep at 9.
(Argument bet. Dwight & Chiaramonte about socialism, Marx's Stalinism.) Bootsie's knee in the couch, Mike's sudden anger.

Forster's essay on V. Woolf. Efforts at compliments by J. Caulbrooke, Miriam C. and Polly Boyden.

Dream of going to the city & being kissed by Serena.

July 3

Stories of Yaddo at breakfast with Polly & Bootsie (her dumb baby,
bubbling).

Long wait for the bus, walk in Provincetown, meeting with bland
H. R. Asti [?], effort to look at the place, boat, Bob Daniels, effort to
look at the ride & the sea—patient at the pier. Stern supper, mild
depression. New issue of *Politics*, pages in *Persons & Places* (Santayana), essay on Croce by Chiaramonte, difficulty with sleep. Mrs.
Daniels, blue-eyed Bim—kitten, bicycle. Dinner at Hayes-Bickford's—
a little rum, three tablets, a lonely house.

July 4

They must not be defined. For then they are
Caged birds. But must too be defined,
To see if we are not deceived
 Say what they are not
And that no mere emotion lies to us
Like the soft fog.

Socialism was our evergreen park.

He was a poet of the Orphic school
Chiefly of life and death, of life-in-death
And death-in-life he sang
        He sang his effort's anguish
He made his metaphors for they were love,
They were the bonds, though hidden.

I do not mean to justify myself
I only seek to show you what I tried
The little that I found in sense and sound
Then you may judge, and cast first stones at me.

(Stealing candy from a child / falling off a log / like water from a duck.)
A day of fading—preparation for first classes.
U.T.—*Address Unknown, Up in Mabel's Room*—desire to go & use wine (nothing but a little rum since Sunday night)—wine, Beethoven, Opus 73, "Emperor" Concerto—second sleep with tablets until 10.

July 5
Moments of difficulty with the boys—more successful with the girls, after troubled lunch at Clark's—doctor, return, cheered by ease of writing anthology report—Dinner Bell (third night of dinner without drink), walk to the Hut—CIO organizer. *The Stricken Deer* by Lord Cecil, cigars, wine, thunderstorm, waking three times, beer at 6 & three tablets, skimming, half-awakened dreams.
The cheer after dinner, without anxiety—something accomplished.

July 6
He spoke to the ripe silence, saying
"I am an immigrant of consciousness
—At least, I try with all my mind
And all my heart to play the part
I seek out light within the dark of life,
Nothing gives me more pleasure than perception
I am a knight of such perceptions
As come to me, a fisher or a hunter
Of aspects of our lady actuality
From whom we hide as quickly as from fists

"I am a student of the morning light
And of the evil native to the heart;
I am a student of emotion's wrongs
Performed upon the glory of this world
Myself I dedicated long ago
Or prostituted, shall I say? to poetry
The true, the good, the beautiful
All that has been, all that is possible . . ."

[The last verse above, slightly changed, is incorporated in "He Heard the Newsboys Shouting 'Europe! Europe!'" one part of "The True, the Good, and the Beautiful," a long poem published in Vaudeville for a Princess.*]*

Don't look back like Lot's wife. And don't, like Psyche, look at Love's night face.

Verses after dinner after poor afternoon—three tablets at 11:30—wine at 3:30.

July 7–12

Fri. Nervous before classes—morning preparation—fairly successful classes.

P[hyllis]'s cold shoulder at Radcliffe. Return, library for P.—called by Sonny—St. Clair's—P. all evening.

Sat. Fading afternoon, elevation after dinner at Jim's place. Arlington, *Hostages*, Preston Sturges's *Miracle of Morgan's Creek.*

Sunday. Wet heat, sleep until 11:30, P[hyllis] at 5, stroke of failure, walk on the other bank of the Charles.

Monday. 10, classes, Bernard Cohen [mathematician, later professor at Princeton] (recently married) at lunch—better at Radcliffe than at Harvard—Miss Gaffney: "I am amazed at your thinking of it" (roulette). Letter from Van Doren.

Phyllis, stroke, worse failure, dinner at 8, art-book pictures, letters, cigars, sleep—but not until 2—themes corrected.

Tuesday. Unabating heat, in spite of thunderstorm. 10, [John Malcolm] Brinnin, lunch again at Oxford Grill, conference boredom, eleven Radcliffe students, wine drunken too quickly, Dinner Bell, essay on *War & Peace*, faded energy, library, stacks, return at 9—one theme corrected in the evening, three or four in the office—thoughts of Serena.

John Walcott two years ago said that again America would go through a war without suffering.

Weds. Classes—again better at Radcliffe—no class lists. Phyllis, chicken sandwiches—stroke, strained.

July 13–15

Thurs. Elevation, sensitivity—conferences from 3–5, drop, Mc-Bride's, Simenon, cartoon cavalcade, simplicissimus—Wallace D. at 9 —elevation before sleep, music for Wallace.

> I sit on flagpoles, shouting
> I am a flagpole sitter & a flag
> I come to celebrate, I come to praise
> I come to irritate the switches which
> Redeem the mind

> I am a Hudson River poet. From the Heights
> I saw the Palisades, the night boat, and
> the Bridge

Narcissus discovered painting, Noah invented the gong.
Apples to you, Serena, almonds, knowledge, and love.

> Tell Serena
> that I love her
> more than—myself
> and against my self

The V of the Venus mount.
Shark-belly of the belly / the boring sound.
I hate you. Some of my best friends are anti-Semites.
Choice: We never know the road not taken / (You would have changed, said Fred).

> The secret goodness is
> the best of states
> A hidden smile
> Belief & hope
> Decay at dusk
> & the wind rises
> & the black grows

Fri. Awake at 7—deadness at 10—Phyllis in the evening after a nap—wine, stroke, elevation (good manners).

Sat. Dinner at L. Murdock's after elevation all day and excited note making ("TGB"). Putnam "offended the guy." No sleep until after 2 & three N[embutal]s.

Serena thoughts, again & again.

July 17

Come now, celebration & praise / Though in the midst of war.

Dream: Richards & wife—when will the war end? It will go on for a long time. Mrs. R. looked at my curios in the dresser drawer. He couched at the side with P[hyllis]. They were just paying an evening call. Then Gertrude, "look at her glowing pinkness"; Bill Van Keuren "has beautiful eyes." News about love.

I am myself merely (morely) / A student of the early-morning light.

My subconscience; submarine, running nose of guilt—

For many years he suffered from an illness so pervasive, prolonged, and secret that he did not know he was ill; he mistook the disease for a natural thing in life, like tiredness before sleep.

Neuroticism common as the cold.

Lorn. Slow as molasses languished on a sofa. Lethe, forgetfulness.

During sleep, absence of inhibition.

Dream passages:

1. Washington Heights terrace—toasted ham sandwiches at midnight.

2. Visit with Serena, fall of wet plaster—boat trip in the background, arrival of plumber's men.

3. Sleight-of-hand fortune-teller, who robbed. A story in *Life*—her Italian son, a soldier, who drank the wine of *Life*'s reporter—not for pleasure (all as if read in *Life*, not understanding the explanation).

I live on Wash. Hts. again—a clear return—enjoyed the evenings, smoked on a terrace above the Hudson (like Fort Tryon Park). "It is pleasant to walk here," I said to M. [mother?] "unless I'm deceived again by—"

The idea of the book on Eliot returned. It could be forced—September, October—fifteen days of ten pages each—appendixes of book reviews.

Wrong number: no hanging up. Not Phyllis, because too early.

She might have asked Scowcroft. But she doesn't see him.

She may be passing through, on her way to Buzzard's Bay. She may have stopped to get books from the library, or perhaps she has returned for the summer. I tried the number. Wrong the first time, as so many other days. She can't have used her own phone.

The child, the king of kings / Who values his excrement so much.

S. F[reud]: The work of mourning.

Remember & forgive / Not forget & forgive.

"In the city there was no feeling for the earth or the weather, only one, the sense of many strangers moving about, forever moving."

My fear of falling from the window—darkness—death—fear of Oedipus. Anxiety, danger, repression.

Since you sometimes & often recognize your errors, you think you always recognize your errors.
Mémoires d'Europe—Casanova.

> Winning my way from day to day
> By an ill darkness bound
> I understand the famous play
> Where Avon's hurt swan made one say
> Life's but an idiot's furious sound—

"Were I a cripple (strapped to a chair); or marked & marred by the hideous sponge of a goiter; or deaf or blind or unable to speak— then might I well—seek refuge, and ask to be released—"

"The only victory is over oneself. So it has been & must be—"

H.G. [Hershey Green] unable to bear his mother's effort to sell her old hats to a servant girl.

We are always laboring to forget. This uses up a great deal of psychic energy. March 1938, April 1938—compulsion to denounce. Denunciation, anxiety, repression, collapse.

The self-contained Indian face & dance.

Ambivalence is the result of repression. We fear what we want very much—fear turns to hate.

"I am worn out by the obligation to be a genius."

"I want to do it my own way" (become a father).

Pleasure-principle vs. reality-principle triumphs in the inability to complete a set task (e.g., the manual and the need of spontaneity).

Dream: Albert Erskine accusation of inversion because ashamed to undress.

Dream: A child by A., whom I carried but who died when I dropped it in a place like Harlem on the way to Washington Heights. I thought then I would kill myself, but did not. Then, immediately after, resurrection, the living child, a beautiful round girl—A.'s distant smile.

Then, a sexual dream of looking in a theater, at a man who caressed the mons veneris of a bird-woman, and criticizing him to K.S. [Kenneth Schwartz] as two old ladies in the next row protested against the character of my remark.

The first child's character was that of some (now repressed) being —bird vs. egg. I was triumphant at having had the child—both times.

July 19–23

Weds. Hangover & excitement—Eliot book again—two good classes. Phyllis at 12, not 10—Shaftesbury, departure for milk. Duke girl with a hand under slip as I came in.

Tues. Dead day from 7—P[hyllis] in Square—conferences all afternoon—beer all evening, and drunkenness after much effort.

Weds. "You make me sick," said Phyllis.

Thurs. Three efforts to begin Eliot book. Two hours of conference. Anxiety & failure, boredom, unease—wine, Palmers out. Film—no, because of musical. Blake's sister dying. Letters from Stevens, Fred, Fisher, and a friend of Trilling's. Bard College possibility.

Fri. Conferences in the afternoon, hurried through. Failure with Eliot in morning. Anger with P[hyllis]. Anxiety, extreme nervousness.

Hut in evening—return after two drinks. Democratic convention. Sleep with 2 + 1.

Sat. Too early waking—usual result—wine at 11—P[hyllis]—Sonny—Beethoven—at lunch. Evening with Palmers & Schwartzes after $3.00 dinner—nervousness extreme.

Sun. Is it drunkenness, the triumph over twenty-three papers, or the Benzedrine which has brought me back again—just as last summer?

A conquered crisis before lunch—ending with lunch—building up to this all week.

July 24–26

Mon. Nation review, dinner with Moss & Brinnin, return of the god—nothing to drink. Letter from Serena—stop—revival.

Tues. Lapse again, forced conferences, a page of E[liot], anxiety attack.

Weds. Stage fright at Harvard—better with Radcliffe. *To the Victor* & *Sun Valley Serenade.*

July 27

[Arose at] 12 (as for the last few weeks): E., "TGB," abortive visit to the Hut.

> The year of the girls
> The year of silence
> A desperate error
> Succeeded by terror
> Life in a mirror
> & never nearer
>
> We make our own darkness
> We enact our mystery
> Repression is the total king

Insight like entering a house or perception of a motive.

Freud speaks of a hereditary predisposition to psychoneuroticism; in obsessional n[eurosis], of the strain of homosexuality.

Daemon, Double, I gave you all! It's not enough!

12. Forward with all, (eight papers each day) and E. and "TGB." Dinner with [John] Sweeney [Harvard librarian] and [John Malcolm] Brinnin [poet]—refusal to go to Rockport. Boredom with B.

Wide the silence, like a night sky.

"I don't have my husband, but so don't millions of women"—Tessa.

Schapiro now thinks that Dwight is half-baked. Dwight thinks S. is afflicted with a desperate neurotic competitiveness; and his family too, his children & his wife.

Dwight & the strawberries, 1939. Dwight & Philip—"Ego struggle," said Fred. William invokes middle-class values when angered.

My face an open secret was / And when I laughed, a farce.

Amnesia is bound up with repression.

Fear of electric fans, of the dark, castration complex. Fear of graveyard, the dead, and falling (womb fantasy, guilty conscience) (now largely gone). Oedipus complex—or general fear of sex?— nakedness & mole / limb phobia.

Perhaps it's the anger that's at the heart of the neuroticism—it comes as the manic period begins to wear. Anger generates fear, which then generates repression and guilt.

Last week—two days of 90°.

The black barred gates of consciousness.

"The dream is a compromise—"

Oedipus dream—after V. Proctor, in a moving crowd, withdrawn from, in horror—not in horror, in distaste. Excused by, bed. Have you not met V.P.? I asked.

Phallus & Phoenix / Rising & Falling—

Does not the child want approbation much more & much more often than to see Mamma's privacy? One is suppressed, the other is not.

There's an infinity tips our ends / Obscenity lips our sins.

Outwits, pits, sits / evades, shades, raids, charades / wades, forbades, fades.

Wallace shy, hence daring—

No accident that Swann, Naphta, and Bloom should be the heroes of our novelists.

The drooping Ellery laurel wreaths / The Cambridge heights & depths. Film anxiety—darkness.

Dream: Under waters, very deep, just before waking, U.S. fleet, battleship-gray.

A Shakespeare play—with Serena—Fergusson. Baba said, I have no bottom to sit on. I did not like the play. Falstaff was in it.

Real water—though years since I swam—and since I was under water, years more—claustrophobic womb fear.

> By the river walk
> On the road to the industrial suburb
> Near the exhausted dead,
>   under the stone,
> Above the gashes of fires of refuse
> In the soft fuzz of fog
> In the summer chill—

> Then he cracked wise again

> King Joy which rules the world

> Refrain: When the God comes

> Elm shades on the pool
> Salmon under the ripples
> Sunlight, shadow or salmon

She's not the only Helen on the beach.
The argument of the years, 19 to 32, 32 to 45.
From the harbor, the wakening cry of the boats.

> Noah
> Invented the gong & chose the beasts
> Planted a vineyard & discovered wine
> —And drank

Jay wrote W. C. W[illiams] that he had behaved like a mucker towards [Louis] Zukofsky [poet]—did he hear this word from his father?

> When the moon rose
>   like a famous
>   twice-told story

Because you are generous, you forget how you are evil.
Terrifying excitement; excitement which terrifies—with terror.
Dream: Father with Anna—present—quarrel with Mother—Kenneth—I was afraid he might have seen *Genesis*.

Emily (Brontë) Thunder, Sigmund Joy— There is a destiny /
In all these fames—

> Upon my coat of arms was writ:
> Some things are possible.
> Upon my tomb let them write:
> Metaphor was his salvation.

Sherry, like sunlight, canary. The cheer from deciding to ring
Serena—though not home.

The drawing in of evening / The drawing of the shades.

O Music, flowing temple as we walk—

Sat. Forward with E., papers, typing, verse & variety—river round
walk 10–12.

August 3–6

To p. 25 of "TGB" ["The True, the Good, the Beautiful"], 1 p.
T.S.E.

Thurs. Ring before breakfast (Serena). Rung back because no
longer disconnected.

Forward with ease, with perhaps too much ease. Nervousness before dinner. Again, to see the lighted window. Koestler borrowed, unread. The war almost over. Nervous emotion—because of Serena?

To do what I have to do, not to get done but because it is for me
to do—is the joy & the—

To check emotion E.? Hesitation about Elizabeth since letter.

And with mania attack once vs. J. L[aughlin] & V.K. [Van Keuren].

No longer the least idea of Serena's state: (1) indifference; (2)
anger, her unpraised papers; (3) romance revived or begun; (4) waiting to be pursued & sure she will be—(Scowcroft).

Fri. Ring, answer, anger because return without effort to get me
though pretext is available.

Lady Takes a Chance, Somerville.

To p. 30 "TGB" & 1 T.S.E. Exam. Wet heat—papers corrected.

Sat. Twice in the evening, twice the unlighted window—seeking
to be resigned & without hope. But letter to Woodstock [where
Elizabeth was] before this. To p. 35 + 1 T.S.E. 95° heat.

Sun. P. 40, conclusion "TGB," though augmentation and perfecting
yet to come.

Serena. Indifference it is probably (though she may change again)
for what can she gain by any deliberate show of no longer being
interested.

August 7

Long conversation with Serena—physical sympathy & emotional sympathy—possible, impossible, inconceivable. Partly that (tactile sense), partly the old love.

Did not want to be called to account—felt "watchful waiting" in me.

Irresponsible in not making any commitments. "Perhaps will not marry at all," certainly not for next year or two. Promise about the past—not revived—but makes emotional difficulties—having very much wanted to have a child, she wants to want that again.

It was indifference & a desire to be free of commitments.

(*Mon.*, after two good classes, after seeing S. at the library.)

Gambits—self-analysis—what did I do that was wrong—never tried so hard to please—the poems.

"See you some time soon."

Her mother really ill seriously.

I broke my watch from trying too much with it. I took the books, hesitated, asked her about if she had the time I wished to broach a subject. At the end: "Isn't it better to get it all said at once?"

Did she sleep with A.Y.F. on the weekend—first suspicion. My face, Laurette M.'s tactile sense, Phyllis questioning, "It's hard to know about people." Did not deny wanting me to say that—the ring's return.

"May I keep the volumes of Prall?" She wanted the Gielgud.

You can't have everything. Next time, however, have facial massages.

Dinner refused. April's error—slow habituation's chance thrown away. Here is a new shock—what will it cause in the depths?

She looked renewed & new. Begin (naïve?), a fresh start—no road maps marked out. Had not thought about it for 1½ mos. Gets along well with her mother now.

This disappointment is nothing against the creative spirit's return. Still, in spite of all, the desperate (seven o'clock, a gray cool summer day) hope.

Hardly anything against *Rimbaud* [Delmore's faulty translation], which also has been lived through & surmounted.

Shock—anxiety—repression & fatigue.

Resented the pressure put upon her—did not know in Feb. she would react like that.

Difficult sleep—hurt—Love in Weimar—dismissed for dinner— "dishonesty while a girl is making up her mind."

In 5 + 10 years—30, 35, 40.

It was like going to the dentist / (One was glad after, though not before).

Reading of rivals, but then copying them.

Sacked heart.

If in July I had not met Dick Ellmann by accident while eloquent—

With broken glass mind, look & suspect & distort.

Thin-skinned & skinned alive, dear poet.

What raids upon the heart.

> I broke the steel strap of my watch
> I broke the strip of time
> (This is a bitter joke)

> The body's taste, distaste & sympathy
> She was a pig in a poke

The past lies like an Alp / upon the mind.

Eight-month lapse may be turning point ([Dr.] Sieve).

We Jews are smarter than the other ones (this can be proven in the following ways)—wars, Darwinian, the word.

Mistakes—Love—Experiment. Two Roads, Miss A., Miss B. Self-sacrifice, breathing, self-interest.

Nude as a peeled banana (avocado).

Had I (you) a million dollars / What would I do?

Brandy, dandy, candy—Dublin eternals.

Marblehead. The sea, sails like folded papers, standing up. Peach Point. The landing, the motorboat cruise of the harbor—the offshore breeze—the narrow island like an alligator.

"Boston was made great by the Sea"—1857, Bay Colony.

The sky as a great blue glass, gathering in the light. The desperate toil of the fathers becomes the game (sport) of the children.

"The moon broken in the water, interrogating."

Rockport whiskey bottle in the quarry pond.

"I don't swim *good*"—one of the girls.

At 5 or between 5, 6, 7, Kenneth stabbed me with a knitting needle (sad.-maso.).

Soon after, while visiting with Baba in the Bronx, I saw her biting her nails & the vice began—mother offended as grandmother did not.

S. F[reud]: Libido cathexis withdrawn from object turned on self, causing narcissism, megalomania, inability to make love, formation of an ego-ideal which results in inability to find suitable object & impotence.

Oedipus complex brings about through repression love of women beneath—women of own station are mother surrogates.

Poetry must be as new as foam & as old as rock.

We are loved because we fit into an ego's need.

Who reads Shakespeare, whatever his admiration, when despondent, low in mind & energy?

The fact that false general principles (beliefs)—in poetry or philosophy—tend to true propositions—

Emerson, Hegel, Croce.

And neuroticism too—Dostoevsky, Tolstoy, Dante, Shakespeare, Wyatt, Yeats, Joyce.

Let us rid ourselves of this false idea that Love has anything to do with the grandeur of marriage. Love is like fireworks.

Today I was much pleased to see myself quoted on the jacket of [Karl] Shapiro's new book & included in Alex Comfort's anthology in England.

At almost thirty-one to forswear all for poetry—the girls and the senses.

August 8

Soon thirty-one—four months. Ease all day, the Handlins in the evening. "Jews are smarter"—high.

Mary: Poor Gertrude.

August 9

Two good classes after ease with "TBG" & T.S.E.

The doctor: These eight months may have been the turning point. You're no sleeper.

Tiredness toward the end of evening. A flood of ideas—bar, Schubert No. 5, unease, unshakable returning sorrow, special-delivery advent from Elizabeth.

August 10

Rockport, ease with verse & prose—manic rising excitement, free & flowing—and to be suspected—Howard Moss [poet, later poetry editor at *The New Yorker*]: No greater love hath Onan—the sea, Cape Ann, dry salvages.

Nervousness at 6, the white sea, houses & summer people, eloquent about Cocteau & E. Bowen.

Obsessive pain, even hatred, on the train back, as I marked papers & read. The subway, impatient in going to North Station.

Now it is after midnight, after 1—I have taken two tablets, but there is no need to force myself to sleep—and my obsessive hatred is gone. The thalamus or ego is darked out, which is it? Merely the dulling of the pain.

Serena's dishonesty, selfness—impatient & self-willing.

See, in a few years—and how much better with one of nineteen.

I looked at my face with distaste—distaste or indifference? I wished to ask.

Rockport, sexual desire, a girl with her hand between her knees, a little girl swimming in the quarry.

August 11–13

Visit of Elizabeth P. Extreme heat. Depression after reading poem. *Sat.* Marblehead. *Sun. Mrs. Skeffington*, Bette Davis, Claude Rains. Serena—walk to Boston & back.

August 14–20

Mon. Good classes, T.S.E. Ringing, unanswered—resolve easily broken.

Tues. One T.S.E., eight papers. Serena on Mass.—infirmary. Phyllis on a bicycle, head turned away. [To Serena:] Are you going to be in Cam. during the weekend? I will call you. "Sorry I am tied up." Anger, enraged to—wish to go away. Will B[arrett] ring—Rockport.

I managed to get her to question me just as I was about to say goodbye.

Classes called off.—Weds., Thurs., Fri., Sat., Sun.—Rockport, Phillipses, Barretts, [Theodore] Roszak [sculptor]. Flight from refusal. Rock & shore, rock & shell. Thin girl, sculptress, muscle bend, "Hope I can remember it."

August 25–27

Friday. Pleasure in being quoted again—a pleasure not yet exhausted—NR. Daily allotment & Joyce. Effort to lift the evening with beer & music. Purchase of Gide's *Journal*, $10.

Sat. Last moment ring—no—unlikely—"Afraid I have nothing to say" (D.S.), misery, two martinis, meeting with Larry Smith [Lawrence Beall Smith, painter and sculptor].

Sonny, the Agees at 11, giggling on the studio couch.

Sun. 12:30, argument about [Bernard] Haggin [musicologist], Agee's departure, new version of "N[ew] Year's Eve" concluded, evening with Wallace D., beer at M'Bride's.

August 28–31

Tues. Adventures of Mark Twain. Too late for first Rollins class. *Mon.* Stayed home to read Joyce & felt self-righteous.

Weds., Thurs. Blackmurs [Richard and Helen] & Chafee—George [and Margery Palmer's] party—kissed by Helen dancing—touched Miriam—crush on Helen—George was furious.

September 2–5

Sat. No Serena—giving in—visit of Marget—too much success—I can't stand it anymore. Providence phone call & lie. "I'm a rotten lover."

Sun. Dinner with George, Margery, and Wallace in Square—a slow day—Phyllis & her Gorgon—passed by with a flick'd gaze. Motion pictures of Maine—Jeremy. George's story of an admirer in Hawaii. No one could be that good—a student.

Mon. Serena, no; drinking to sleep again.

Tues. Bill, Florette, Latin Q., Napoleon. B'klyn streetcar scene, moonlight. Forward with TSE (each of these days, though forced).

September 6–10

Weds. Bill V.K. in the afternoon—after calling off Radcliffe class. "When you're good, you're great"—of "TGB."

Thurs. Evening with S.—call of Bradley J. [a presumed rival] (frozen with jealousy "and wait to see if I fall in love with you")—revived question—joy as I returned & an unwillingness to sleep. Call after midnight from E.P.

Sept. 8, 9, 10. Visit of Elizabeth, after waking at 12.

Saturday. Anxiety about long papers of Rollins class—moral failure—after waking late as E. slept.

Friday. Monologue to 4 about father & mother—distortion & melodrama as of old.

Sunday. Waking late—disturbed about spilled coffee—Eliot pages & Rollins papers—relieved to rush through them—purchase of Mozart concerto—recurrent thoughts.

Sunday night. Freud's *Autobiography*, unable to sleep, after 3 +.

September 11–15

Monday. Waking at 10, two good classes—on Lat. Criticism—one T.S.E., the doctor's, five papers corrected in the evening. Three to sleep at 10—waking at 4, too much wine.

Tuesday. Missed or dismissed Rollins class, sense of anxiety, hammered out by T.S.E. page, five papers corrected, five pages of "AA" typed.

As yesterday, oranges & milk & the doctor, so today, laundry & tailor, neatness as sedative—thoughts of S. & party, troubling—unwilling-making.

Weds. Harvard class eager for relativism. "Please let me finish," said Erskine. Evening, Serena—after inviting others—L. Murdock, Phyllis answered.

Thurs. Worn through Rollins class—nervous against typing & rewriting of story. Tempted to use printed page. One T.S.E., five papers corrected, nervous & bored. Lifted by wine to write one-page review for Greenberg—(Shapiro). Beer, bourbon, one page more of "AA" in the evening. Hurricane night—unease—I drank in the darkness, arose, looked at my picture, and drank more. No sleep until 2. I wet myself with the water—ten o'clock.

Fri. Nervous to get to barber (10) & bank. *NR*, Harry's & Fred's review, ten pages of "AA"—nervous anxiety, one T.S.E., three papers, dinner at 7, two papers—idleness all evening with beer & thoughts of tomorrow's party.

Undated

[Following are a number of undated poems or drafts for poems found among the 1944 papers and clearly related to other notes and drafts of this period.]

> I teach the boys and girls
>   of kings and queens
> And as I teach, behind my face Love rules
> Rules me, rules all I know,
>   though secretly
> And differently since there are many schools
> —A girl like an ostrich curved in on herself
> Tho' she was often kissed and squeezed like grapes
> Lost her good health because her heart defied
> Love the dark victor whom no
>   one outsmarts
>
> There was a boy of six sleepless
>   all night
> Sometimes he cried aloud, Snake, snake, snake
> His pretty governess undressed at times
> Before his gaze. He lay awake
> After his mother saw him, scotophile
> Shook with anxiety's deep-rooted raid
> Conquered and overcome by only one
> Love the dark victor whom
>   No one evades
>
> (Evades / shades / trades / raids.)
>
> To love is, in the end
> To stand,
> Looking down from a height,
>   From an infinite distance
> Upon the promised land

Shall he not be told from the first
That there are gods among us and that the gods come
Unknowingly with dark missions, some of them named
Some of them nameless, dark as the green world in March
Some of them melting like genie when touched
                        tripped upon or unmasked
Or seized with violence?
                        The god comes to the table
Where the host and his guests truly rejoice, clink glasses
The god comes as the boy bends over the book
At the moment when the sunlight breaks through the poem
Dazzling his years. The god stands in the half-dark
Near the hat rack, or he stands by the window seat
Suddenly, in the winter dusk, at the
                    moment of the streetlights
When the snow begins to fall and the wind drops
In a collaboration of silences. Towering in sleep
Comes the dark god to punish the
                    reined-in mind
And to restore to the flesh dominion and glory.

Don't fool yourself, my daemon said to me
With noble lies, famous and fabulous
Don't be the fool of mind's pure vanity
And facile allegiance to nobility

(Freud—that giant of profanity!)

               A Desperate Story
     I held a seashell to my ear
              and heard
     My heart roar P A N D E M O N I U M
                  which was to say
     Every demon from hell yells
              in your heart
     —Although you thought you heard
             the senseless sea,
     You only heard yourself. Behold in this
     How often you have only seen yourself,
     Although you thought you saw
                 another's crime
     —Behold the guilt within your glittering eye—
     To the impure all things become impure.

If you search any subject sufficiently, you will come upon all the things which are important.

A True Story
A little boy was asked, *What do you want*
A brother or a sister? Silently
He gazed upon his pregnant mother,
     potted
So to speak, looking as if she walked
Ahead of herself; then bluntly he replied
"I want ice cream!" Wisdom and honesty!
Good sense, frankness, and practicality!

We are but rickshaw boys dragging
     our pasts
Out of the pit (like an Alp upon the brain—Marx)

Touch became torch / Arms were dark.
Character is ravine, love is a river, love is a sea.
Stupid, rabid, livid, depraved.
Hershey Green felt his rib cage—wonder if one was Una?

The Eden Party
The heart is dirty, the silence said to me
Dirty the politics played by the heart
Come join the Eden party, old as God
The party of the true, the good, and the
     beautiful
What else is there to do? What better game?
Where shall we find three loves equal to these?
As lunatics go howling at the moon
Shall we not seek this perfect lunacy?
These are the three in dark deep being fresh
There where the heart and mind
    are one at last

"Are one at last?" I asked, incredulous,
"The heart has reasons which the mind
     alas!
Can never understand! And the mind, too,
Has reasons which the heart can never know
The ego straps the id with unseen whips
The id strikes back with rumors
    of old crime."

Existentialism and Psychoanalysis

Heidegger to Freud: No cure or sublimation for anxiety about the real possibility of death. Freud to Heidegger (perhaps): The anxiety is either objective (care of health) or useless (can't do anything about it): not true of neurotic anxiety. Distinguish between objective anxiety (fear) and neurotic anxiety (fear unmotivated by actual external situation but only by the strong superego relation to instinctual drives, e.g., agoraphobia, fear of heights, suicide).

Questions: Suppose neurotic anxiety has in it an existential (metaphysical or ontological) element? (Freud says it does vary with the psychic economy—a strong person can hold down anxiety). Suppose existential anxiety is largely neurotic anxiety?

Neurotic anxiety solved by analysis (bringing conflicts to light from the unconscious), by uninhibited functioning, conscious self-control, and sublimation (though latter is rare among human beings).

Heidegger to Freud: existential being is being-for-itself (in the world *a priori* like choice and freedom).

Suppose existentialism is neurotic anxiety? (Tolstoy).

Suppose neurotic anxiety is really existentialism? (Tolstoy).

Social and historical roots suggest existentialism of Joy, Health, Achievement. (Children helped by psychoanalysis's discoveries and therapies.) "Don't put the funeral hearse before the wedding feast."

Anecdote about Whitehead: Student and troubled about death, but also about criticism of his work and eager to drink his sherry. His Ingersoll Lecture on Immortality—people attended and were existential. His basic experience very complex. All experience is such that we *must* live as well as *must* die—part of being authentic, too. Whitehead illustrates this and so does everyone.

Heidegger's analysis one-sided at best. Anxiety and Care are basic, but so are Desire, Gratification, Ambition, and Accomplishment, all illuminated and made free by psychoanalysis.

Heidegger's overemphasis (socially and historically conditioned) of one key emotion to exclusion of another. If one must die, yet we live (lightning bolt in summer in country as statistical example or going swimming). Difference between two kinds of Angst—but Heidegger's is a more drastic form of Freud's flight from pain and damaging consequences. Pain is a little death.

—"You will do that only under the pain of death."

The war of the lesser evil.

In certain periods in history, there is no choice except between evil and evil.

But what war is just?

And what cause is wholly righteous?

Nonetheless, silence is honorable; and withdrawal; and a non-commitment.

For what is being defended, civil liberties, Hollywood, the mere absence of concentration camps?

Yes, that's it; we're defending the absence of certain evil things. This is the content of the war—

1945

January 24

Library 4–6; whirling snow squall; dinner in kitchen; two quarts of beer—rum at 3:30. Doctor 11:30. Sleep 12–3:30, 5–10:00.

"The Ego and the Id," "The Man Who Would Be King," "H.M.S. *Titanic*."

Exact, exacting, in the throes.

"I am a stranger in a strange land—"

Gay and gala and sauntering, summer-sauntering, somersaulter-ing, open and empty and sunny and singing, swinging.

Discussion of Gertrude, diffusing charm. Wallace: also poison.

Another drink, and two things would have happened: he would have lost his scruples, but also his potency.

As I am kept from giving myself in love and in friendship, so with the reading of books to the end—and teaching and editing and devotion to literary forms.

The Narcissistic Wound, the Narcissistic Barrier.

January 25

Zero cold; pulling up for class 10–12. "Disorder and Early Sorrow" read aloud to class; yawning, yet they did not know that anything was wrong. Martini—Benzedrine before lunch—Radcliffe class a little better, going on despite faltering, "two classes overcome." Mild depression after mild lift as I returned from class and read in Mann; effort to get Bill; rum, dinner at Jim's Place, resentment, A.'s lights, no answer, telephone disconnected. *Frenchman's Creek*, anxiety. 8:30–10:30—*My Children*. Phyllis and fiancé, as I departed from U[niver-sity] T[heater]. No liquor after dinner, three Nembutal, one Seconal; sleep, dreams in which Nela was. Florette called.

Impulse to go to New York; calling of coal company; resentment, anger, door closed on pride; resemblance of Joan Fontaine and A[lison]; an ice-cold girl, unmoved. "What shall I do now?—what shall I ever do?"

[Delmore, having obtained a year's leave of absence from Harvard, moved in January 1945 to 91 Bedford Street in New York City.]

March 4

"Everyone seems to be successful but little Gertrude."

Feckless, aimless, ambitionless.

Smile like Admiration Cigars, full moon.

Dream of A. telling me that she was going to marry another man —then I woke up.

Schapiro review as example of trap of motivation—undercutting, showing off.

The robber barons have gone into unionism.

She thought a course in A[nglo]-Saxon had some connection with A[nglo]-Saxon words.

Faust Bros. Tailors.

Creative working, Goethe's answer to God. But Aristotle: God, activity.

L[iterary] Crit[icism]: In America it is customary to conduct one's education in public and plein air.

March 6

"Take off your sweater, Hershey," said Miss Bousefield. "Everyone has seen it by now." It was brown and thick.

Not everything is a matter of opium—or wine.

A new language for America, candy bars, and baseball players.

Life has too many details.

Everyone likes to know poets; no one pays.

I am both a Platonist and an Aristotelian.

March 7

The recognition and knowledge of error—is this the secret resource?

Bias and assumption for the knowledge of God.

Like free will—like America—like art.

Secular prayerbook: cannot believe—bias—wedding—birth—trial—art—death—conflict between experience and art-experience.

Picked Audience, On the Spot, The Corrected Shades, The Blown Flag, The Squealing Clothesline.

March 10

Irritable and peevish, he made a fuss.

J[ames] L[aughlin] dead in a dream, long legs hanging loose. Speaking before the coffin.

E.W. kissed in a dream—and then reproach. She was in pajamas. It was probably at the Lowells' Connecticut house, where I have never been.

She was a chain-drinker.

Pizza—the full moon—lobster-red wine—the black-haired girl in a fur coat.

Human beings live chiefly for enjoyment.

He suffered from disorder and a lack of habits.

He lived in makeshifts and disorder, in drunkenness and pleasure.

Lyrical, quick, joyous, exalted.

March 19

After a time, we will make friends: we will make fun, we will make believe.

"He had been despondent because of long illness"—

"She bought six explosives before she came"—

A chorus of angels singing hymn of creation (they still do!).

Irresistible advance.

Struck, struck.

How many saw her nakedness, two or three or four?

And saw her in her cups—the last one surely—

Then the investment of silence.

After brupt [sic] braw raw violence.

"I am not very smart"—Rhoda Klonsky [wife of Milton Klonsky, a young writer].

"Don't hurry, don't hurry" —And after that, the discomfort of a lifetime.

May 23

A Testimonial Dinner to God—compliments or God put on trial.

Destiny is the alibi of weaklings.

Every increase in consciousness is an increase in suffering.

Our feelings—such as boredom, nausea, anxiety—reveal the nature of reality. So all go—back to Plato.

Lionel Abel: Lionel Trilling does not exist. He exists too much.

When a man seeks different girls, he affirms his belief in the existence of the external world.

Diligence is not enough / But metaphor is the same as love / —wet tea bags & rare roast beef.

Undated [May–June 1945?]

[Mark] Van Doren testimonial—twenty-five years—F.P.A. [Franklin P. Adams of *The New York Times*]—Clifton Fadiman— his wife, Dorothy Van Doren, Rex Stout, Dwight Macdonald.

Letters from Thomas Merton confusing M.V.D. with God (a Trappist monk).

"Mark was a pretty child (baby)"—childhood favorite of all the boys.

[Joseph Wood] Krutch—interminable conversation.

[Meyer] Schapiro's glances at me—his door-shaking arrival—his big Christ-like eyes.

John [Berryman]'s heresies—"Winter Tryst," and poem about nuts & cake & wine.

Andrew [Chiappe]: I don't know whether I should be annoyed with you or you with me?

The aspiration to love the teacher.

[Lionel] Trilling's discourse on teacher as interested in the subject—the view of the Western world—& flares of anger—but ethos. Charles Wagner. Self-possessed undergraduate. "This fellow always makes me laugh." Though known as melancholy young man.

"I just could not tell you that Roosevelt was dead"—

"I saw that you were very upset"—

Theme of *Iliad* as passion, force—*dunamis*.

Louis Zukofsky—Fadiman: "He writes very good poems"—pale & dark behind eyeglasses.

M.V.D.'s face turned red—champagne & cigars & red wine & two kinds of cheese.

The headwaiter in a dress suit who admired all and understood nothing—a caterer.

Andrew Chiappe, Dr. Johnson, Brahma & Humpty-Dumpty. "I don't want to seem coarse, but I have to go to the can."

Most people are bound to be failures—hence: etc.

Success after success is not as good as failure and then success.

Who is unhappy at having only one mouth? or mourns because he does not have three eyes? Man is a deposed king, his greatness is seen even in his wretchedness!—Pascal.

Millay: The kind of socialist who loves humanity & hates people.

Dwight: Long since you have published anything. I am successful because I am honest (an honest person) & you are a coward.

Dialectically, [Paul] Goodman is the same as you—"your rival."

You've written nothing since *Shen.*—I mean, *Genesis.*

People have told me that this is the best thing I've ever written—(the responsibility of peoples / German carrot farmers who make sugar / "If everyone is guilty, no one is guilty").

I did read a few pages, it was very flat.

[Karl] Shapiro as competitor.

Bess & Frederic Wertham, *vieux Stalinistes.*

Dwight concealed his feelings, ego-bravado—my wrong was to think he would [not?] be hurt.

Gossip about Roosevelt & Ginger Rogers as Mervyn LeRoy's friend.

He accepted the values of our society: hamburger, Coca-cola, and a brand-new Buick.

As for me, I am incapable of love—

This is seen in the work I do as well as in love itself—where I want [to] run away right away.

Last night I watched a soldier & his girl make love on a bed.

This was after too much to drink, and a quarrel with Dwight.

The night before, I dreamed that I was writing a poem. "There was a fishing village by a *boiling* shore"—Agee and his wife, Mia, were there.

I quarreled with Dwight: (1) because he said writing about Eliot was old stuff, without reading the article; (2) because he made fun of my gossip about Roosevelt. I don't care about these things; (3) because of the quarrel in 1943—"Don't be so naïve, Delmore" (*PR* [*Partisan Review*] editorship).

"I know I am intelligent," he said. "I am honest—you're cowardly. You're neurotic—you ought to be psychoanalyzed."

"You too—why not you?"

"Because I am happy and far more successful than you"—

"You like to make these wild charges & get into these quarrels—"

He stalked off—

He attacked me: (1) because I had not come to see him; (2) because of *PR* & being an editor; (3) because of Trotsky, Burnham—idiotic article.

"I agreed with Trotsky"—I know I am intelligent.

Waterloo Undertaking Co.

The meaning without the symbol is dead like the body without the soul—

It is unexpected and of a strangeness that poems should be written.

They are written because of the writing of other poems, and thinking of memories, and the making of comparisons.

He was having a nervous breakdown. He did not take care of his clothes, mail, hopes, notebooks, or friends.

"I've accepted your friends."

Democracy—not actively intolerant.

Philip depressed: You would not write the book, save for the money?

Prose poem: The father who wants the beau to go home, the younger brother who must be paid a quarter, the hated mother-in-law (she, too!). The cigars given out by the freshly made father to other men, the rice thrown after the bride & the groom.

—Everywhere emotions & things (& relatives) used by the insane powers of Love.

Tate: What are you doing now?

I am staring at the typewriter keys.

Did exactly what was expected of him / Then exactly the opposite, producing doubt & ignorance & bewilderment—

Last Sunday I wrote to Maurice, Stephen, spoke with William, visited Morris, and quarreled with Dwight.

"You're so competitive. You're obsessed with competition."

1918, 1919. Washington Heights. The Hippodrome. When Hershey Green was taken to the circus, and his mother forgot the tickets and his father was very angry, he felt sorry for his mother and he was sick to his stomach the next day—from peanuts.

As from ice cream the day before he was married.

Manhattan like a fortress studded by helmets.

Swords & erections stacking strong in the air—phallic & financial America.

Brancusi's bird in flight like a new kind of palm—airplane, propeller.

Memory & guilt—quarrel with Kenneth in Chicago—1929—bathroom—"That's where he belongs."

Stuck by darning needle at five—taking a bath together—taking away his girl—getting K.S. to phone for the girl. (Father: "I'm afraid you're going to be disappointed again.")

[Arthur] Koestler: "In a world where nobody is well, it is our duty not to accept" aggression & guilt in Luce toward authors.

My emotion in regard to this thing / Resembles a broken arm in a sling.

[Hart] Crane lacked a subject to justify his style—a frame of reference.

Complete Consciousness Is Insomnia.

> I am a fustian King
> In a fool's paradise
> Ranting at everything
> And telling many lies
> & playing with the dice
> To whip excitement
> > up
>
> Lips parted, quickened breath
> The populace looks on
> Uneasy élan
> > Sensing the moves of death

July 5

I took Benzedrine at 3:30. St. Louis 7, Giants 5. I rejected ten mss. I took a haircut. I had breakfast with E.; lunch with [Milton] Klonsky [Delmore saw a lot of Klonsky, some of whose work was published in *Partisan Review*]; I dined with *The New Yorker* at the Sevilla. I wrote one painful page. I glanced through Auden's collected poems and was distressed by the titles. "Do Be Careful." Spoke to Edna [Phillips] on the phone.

September 24

Drunkenness is a toxic condition.

Neurosis is a regression most of the time.

Jung and Adler merely reject psychoanalysis.

Relatedness is the form in which the childhood neurosis passes into adult life.

[Niccolo] Chiaramonte [Italian intellectual and writer], [Lionel] Abel, Wm. [Phillips], Will [Barrett], Gertrude, [James] Burnham [professor of philosophy at New York University and author of *The Managerial Revolution*].

"Why don't you write a novel?"

"The dark is really the blue"—Jeremy Dickson.

"I don't fall asleep until I don't know it."

"To love is to wish to be loved"—Sartre.

But transcendence turns each personal reality into an object— transcendence is transcended.

Annals and anecdotes—the depths of the city.

[Gregory] Zilboorg [psychoanalyst and author]—difference between confession and analysis.

Strength of the unconscious sense of guilt—self-consciousness and shyness and fear of the stranger.

"All hell breaks loose"—Eleanor [Goff, a young dancer in New York, with whom Delmore was involved].

"Why did you tell me?" Elizabeth—afraid that she is caught.

September 27

Chiaramonte, Barrett.

"Who is a better writer, Goodman or Schwartz?"

Ch.: "Goodman is talented but repulsive."

Barrett: "Tomorrow I am having lunch with Wilson. I almost stopped in Philadelphia to see Auden." Pleased that William and Philip were friendly with him.

Dinner with Althea [Bradbury, later an art historian, who worked with Elizabeth at the Guggenheim Museum] and Elizabeth [Pollet].

Visit of Wm., episode of the pickup, loud laughter: "He just opens his fly—he thinks he's still in Italy."

Althea like Phyllis, clipped speech, apt questions.

Italian version of Gary Cooper—Dick Johnson—Puccini—pot-bellied little tenor.

Chiaramonte—Italian syphilis—ornate and splendid prose—adjectives never before used with just that substantive.

"A rust-like bloom upon the brown."

Anal erotic oddity—saves carbon copies for years; he walks from the knees, teetering; he lands on his heels. Anal-erotic about the passing of time?

"Don't underestimate Delmore in social situations; he knows what conventional behavior is, when not to stay for dinner, for example."

Boston social success—braggadocio. "You curb your tendency—being highly moral—despite your choice of profession."

Delmore has come to N.Y. to be psychoanalyzed.

"You have a noble head but not a noble walk."

A strong ego—an ego intact—

Almost moved to tears by the sleeping tablets.

He would write a letter instead of committing murder—selective memory—murderers as supreme egotists.

We have these confessional modes as safety valves.

Gertrude on Commerce St.—"a dreamer."

M[argaret] Marshall [literary editor of *The Nation*] knows that some people are shy.

Jay, [Saul] Bellow, Jean, and Bazelon in Ticino's.

"I haven't seen you for years—what are you doing now—so you're one of those people who are holding up Franco."

. . .

You're not quite like anyone I know, neither is Delmore—*sui generis*; both great egotists, ego-dominated; in his walk he pushes ahead; slow like a weight; an acute sense of the external world; the way he disposes of his luggage and secures a rooming house; unorthodox but successful somehow.

Laughlin, Burnham, Murdock—all father-powers.

[Edmund] Wilson to Fred [Dupee] on habits of work: You think that you're going to write well. Self-absorbed as a writer—not try so hard to be different from everyone else.

Elizabeth—Eleanor—Evelyn—

"Who is Evelyn?"

Oppressive about psychoanalysis, about dead youth—an Irish wake.

"Should have been homosexual, it is much easier."

Rejected by Jessica, who would not go out to dinner.

September 28

A book is Good because it gives human beings something they need.

The need is for a long time or a short time or just for a bored evening: to be amused, to be entertained.

Most human beings live lives in which the adjustive of a job or a family helps them to conceal from themselves their desperation or despair, their imprisoned and condemned hopes, their hanged hopes.

The chains and strings of children's voices, coming from school, going to school, wakened him in the morning and divided the day four times.

"You are so much on the defensive," said Will [Barrett].

The objective correlative is the proof of actuality.

The motive of the imitator (Realist) is acquisition or incorporation.

Listen, they are playing *Der Rosenkavalier*.

They read as if they were chewing gum—to quiet the troubled heart.

"He is strong as an ox," said William. "We all felt limp after your visit to Rockport. We all slept late the next morning"—W. B[arrett].

"You have a strong ego," said Eleanor [Goff]. "I bet you could commit murder."

Althea spoke of Joyce and Picasso as Surrealists. She asked about *Axel's Castle*.

He was both good and bad—not a mixture—but full of both kinds of action, generosity and anger.

The opera was inexpensive in Rome.

The Italians were proud of their churches.

A description of the profession of authorship—as Irish Sweepstakes and as satisfactory activity.

"You think you're not neurotic just because you turn out a magazine."

Lateness as the product of conflict and frustration—he is not in possession of his motives.

Undated

Meyer Schapiro's *savoir-faire* about traveling in Europe; and A.Q.'s, on examinations.

"I learned a new trick," said Carvel Collins [Faulkner editor and scholar], arranging the papers with care.

Affectation is the appearance of the effort in the effect.

The consequences are always the effect.

John Berryman is schizoid, withdrawn.

Richard [Blackmur] is a narcissist, withdrawn.

How many false words I have used! how many false attitudes struck, pounding my chest.

And then, at other times, preserving an expressionless or unmoved face.

Or deceptive, saying the opposite of what was expected of me because I knew it was expected.

September 29

"A meeting of great minds," said Philip, "if Sidney Hook were here."

"Lionel Abel knows nothing"—Hannah Arendt.

"Tate is going to marry Elizabeth Hardwick in a year."

There is no reason to believe in God and it serves reactionary purposes.

So does socialism, Stalinism—

"Just like those boys to give you that name"—Wilson to Will— Moses Brown.

Wm.: Delmore would be a nice fellow if he were not neurotic. He is too intelligent to believe in God.

The fellatio of American women.

Anger against Richard and Philip.

(What is my motive?)

Five stories about Rome—[Edmund] Wilson thinks he is Henry James.

Neurotic cleanliness—statistical norm.

The conversation on the stair.

"That's a nice watch. Who gave it to you?"

"No, my birthday's in January." (It was a beautiful watch, light gold.)

"I'm so sleepy."

"Is that your foot? No, that's your shoe."

Bill: You seem to shy away from people. I don't like to introduce you to anyone.

Hannah Arendt: I must tell you how much I like your novel, I mean your story, something original . . .

Elizabeth wept. "I can see you're not an intellectual," said the clipped chap.

"I'm going home to read some more books."

"I prefer your company unadulterated."

In America every year 25,000 human beings kill themselves, end their lives; perhaps twice as many, if the truth were told.

Dwight [Macdonald]: I like Delmore.

The changes in the time of going to bed; in going to the pictures; in making notes; in admitting neurosis; in accepting criticism and disdain and contempt; in reading novels; in brushing one's teeth; in rivalry; in seeing girls.

September 30

Whether I read Thucydides or Proust
I see the abyss of the human heart

The example of the new French movement, atelier, shop; Kaplan / Chaplin.

Chaplin as a great popular artist who ceased to produce work with fecund regularity.

"I am not that interested in sexual intercourse."

Wilson: [Arthur] Mizener is really a good poet, just look carefully at those short pieces.

"Why don't you tell him the real reason?" said Gertrude, when Sonny wanted to tell a dirty joke and I tried to put him off.

"What girl would want you?" said Gertrude (Xmas 1940) in the midst of a quarrel.

"Did she really say that?" asked Wm., Sept. 1945.

"You're one of the most charming people I've ever known," Eleanor [Goff] said.

It's you who are the wonderful one, she said.

When you go back to Cambridge, this will be the end of an episode.

(The rich girl and never to lift a finger ever again—lies, neurosis, desire to change the truth.)

And I rush, my only! into your arms—

I done me best when I was let—

Thanks very much, I said to Hannah Arendt, thanks very much (but she continued).

Thank you very . . .

Sidney Hook—a wheelbarrow—in [Washington] Square [Park].

Sour Elizabeth, gaffe about walking Betty Pollet [Elizabeth's step-mother] to dinner.

Cold and blowing air, autumn at last.

Existenz in the park—a dog defecating, a man with a sleeveless arm, rollicking running children, baby carriages, arguments on the benches among the Italians.

The women at the bar at the Barrow Restaurant—black-haired, wedding ring, crow's-feet.

"The Italians contributed [Washington] Square," said W[ill].

"Elizabeth knows you are going to drop her—"

"Eleanor was about to discuss her difficulty with you."

"I am going back to Italy today."

I mounted the steps of the high chair and recited, pointing my finger: "I done me best when I was let—"

October 1

Odyssey: Ulysses just wanted to go home, and Telemachus wanted to find his father—the motives of the characters. But the author's: to show a man who was never at a loss; meter measure—viability—go-ability—like the even steps of a stair.

As with laughter, no one finds it enough, in general, to laugh by himself; he wants another one, one more at least, to laugh at his story.

Dwight said that the trouble with Goodman's article was that he was not a good journalist. His own vanity's explanation—the energy released by his own lack of critical hesitation. "His *Fortune* skills," said William.

How immediately different the feeling about Hannah Arendt.

"I don't-care-mechanism"—Anna Freud.

Dream of having six very small children delivered to Baba and Aunt Clara. Dream of courting Alison again and put off as always.

Are they boys or girls? I asked.

"Whom certain ancient famous authors misrepresent—"

"The proud Furies—"

"Snyder predicts that there may be eight million unemployed by spring"—radio.

Energy on Sunday—

"I wrote a first line today—"

The play entitled *Adultery*.

Will's resumé of *Les Parents Terribles*: Mother in love with son, son and father in love with European equivalent of bobby-soxer.

"I hated Nature from the earliest years
And turned to works of art—"
"Nature, that strange abstraction"
                    found in parks
                    & glimpsed from trains—

Mozart's Horn Concerto: the horn's fawning forlornness.

October 4

"Delmore believes in God," said Will to Wm. and Philip. "If Hook were here!"

The specks of a school of birds circle around and around the roofs. (It is a dark cold day.)

Their arcs of flight are like lassos.

External considerations and abstractions—the fame of another, or the year of life, e.g., precocity—

More or less curtailed: the habit of drinking sherry at 5 p.m. exactly, the use of liquor to get back to sleep.

Will's hidden instability and quick depression. The lack of talent as an explanation—at one time or another all possibilities must be spoken.

Sleep until twelve o'clock on Fri., Sat., Sun., and Mon.

"Do you think Milton is handsome?" inquired Rhoda [Milton Klonsky's wife] of the Rosenfelds [Isaac, a writer, and Vasiliki].

October 9

Last spring I was visited—most most unexpectedly—by the sister of my only intimate friend at college. She is the daughter of what the newspapers term a tycoon and extremely beautiful. We had met but once before on that graduation day, which seems to be a part of another life (so long ago is it really), and I had almost forgotten how beautiful she was.

It was astonishing to see her when I opened the door of my fourth-floor apartment.

She explained that she was in the city just for the night and had secured my address from the class annual. It was almost 10 and for two hours I had been drinking the inexpensive domestic wine which helps to make my evenings less difficult, less boring.

I tried to make conversation with her and she saw my effort and she said that she was sorry she had broken in on me.

"I am glad you did," I said without conviction.

"But I wanted to see you," she said.

This remark and her look perplexed me. She spoke as if we were old friends.

I played some of my phonograph records for her and showed her some of the books which, as it seemed [to] me, might be interesting to her. The conversation about her brother William fell flat each time I tried to renew it.

"But how are you?" she said.

"All right," I replied, but when she looked questioningly at me, I added, "The truth is, I am not very well."

"You look very different," she said. "You look much more attractive than you did when I first saw you."

Attractive! it was [as] if the cry of Fire! had been hurled in the hallway. I was unable to believe that this was, in fact, an invitation. And yet her glance as I rose to change records would have seemed to me, in any other girl, a sexual examination.

She had begun to drink wine with me, and we drank large glasses as we continued.

What are you doing? said the four blank walls.

Make money, make love, make pleasure, have some fun.

"Another dinner, the Lord be praised"—Mrs. Barrett [Will Barrett's mother].

Also the capitalist disorder, also the world we die in, waking by the clock. The Woolworth Rome, the Heinz hegemony.

(Vivid events have passed me by.)

The right words, not diction, but the right order of the words— right—straight—*recta*.

The plane, high, like a folded umbrella.

He thinks that if he behaves properly he will be able to undo the work and disease of years.

"One cannot—at the moment of composition—undo a lifetime's damage."

October 12

Columbus Day, a holiday.

By heck, said Uncle Sam, smoking his smooth Havana.

What'll I do with that big bomb? be bully? lend-lease?

> The dog stole the bone
> The cat ate the fish

Guadalcanal, Tarawa, the Marianas, Okinawa.

Manahatta, Manhattan, Monongahela.

Pleasures of sound and river.

What poet made the foghorn? Did he sleep? Did he smoke? Did he feel remorse?

Where were they then? Where will they be? With whom? And warm?

No. Old and cold and worn.

October 13

A veteran, decorated, was slain last night in a bar-and-grill.

He was celebrating his thirty-third birthday with his family. A bandit entered and flourished a pistol.

"Why don't you put that thing away?" said the veteran decorated for heroism. He spoke from the point of view of a great war.

The bandit shot him through the heart, fired twice into the ceiling, and ran out to the curb, where a car [was] waiting for him, the motor running.

When I told this story on Saturday at midnight I made more of it. But by interpretation.

(Memory blazes in the first morning hour.)

The veteran was unable to take a petty holdup seriously, having fought against the Wehrmacht in France. For this he returned. Was he not killed by the war? He should have stayed in France.

In observation, eyesore the day.

To observation bring the motive.

Dig the insight. Prove your wrath.

Don't apologize so much. It is another living room. Where you were not wrong, but wrongly chided.

Tessa and Philip, Harry and Elena, Helen and Richard, George, Margery, Phyllis.

The cat licked his neck, lapped his belly, lay down lushly on his paws. Sated, seated.

Bullying—blustering, a mask of humor and merrying play.

(The best cat in greater N.Y., the handsomest cat on the Eastern Seaboard, and on this or the Appalachians—the Mississippi. Hyperbole fails me! Every praise is anticlimactic!)

A sinus headache, a sign of hatless chill.

The two girls took away time to sleep, energy for work—one at midnight, one at noon.

The structure of phrase, even-Stephen. Measure is a treasure and clarifies.

Affect no more dejectedness.

You may smile & smile & smile & be a villain.

October 16

Adultery, a Play

SCENE 1

N.: I think she knows!

R.: Knows what?

N.: About you and me!

R.: How did she find out? And how can you tell?

N.: She said, You're telling me everything but the one thing that would make all the difference to me.

R.: What did you tell her?

N.: I told her about myself, how all that I cared about was drinking and sleeping around. All that I really cared about. I wonder if I really do—I mean, Is it true?

R.: She said to me, too, that as you know N. likes you very much —is very much attracted to you. She said, Don't be flattered, N. feels that way about other husbands of her friends.

Measure: If the steps of the stairs were uneven, they would be harder to climb.

Going down, one might fall.

Paragraph: If there were no turning and no landing, one would sooner be breathless and exhausted.

Composition: The stairs are in a line, one over the other.

Metaphor: The effort is made habitual by the evenness.

If you add detail to detail, as the details mount, the event becomes more and more real.

After the bath, he felt so good, all a-glowing, freshened, neatened.

Had taken care of himself and made an effort and brought it to an end satisfactory.

Washed out the tub, changed his trousers, and thrown the dirty linen back of the box.

Heard *Petrouchka*—blackened marches, and thought some more of all his confession—finding the form, the unfound house.

> Avaunt! Unknown adversary!
> Sirrah!
> Bare your face,
> Let go my forces,
> Let me enter the mystery of joy.

Taken his lunch. Stopped for his shoes. Reviewed an essay. Sought his memory for reality, writing two pages more.

As the architect, brick and stick and stone, so the author, actuality —the motive re-a-lized.

His father was in the realty business.

He, however, in the reality business—

October 18

What did I do? What did I fail or forget or not know enough to do? I was encouraged, no doubt. By the time I was twenty-five, I had written five successful novels. Two of them had been taken by the Book-of-the-Month Club. Still, I knew that something was wrong because it was too easy and because the intellectuals were not impressed with me. As for its easiness, sometimes I took that for genius, whatever genius is, especially since I had been compared to Dickens. I had a sense of character which was racy and rich, the critics said.

Five years have passed since last I published a book and seven since last I wrote one.

What did I do? What is wrong with me?

As a matter of fact, some of the intellectuals were impressed by me, at least at the start.

During this time I have been separated from my wife and I made love to too many women.

I sleep until two o'clock every afternoon and wake in a panic because it is late. I tried to tell myself that I don't care, but I know that that's just an old trick to diminish painful emotions.

I don't try to deceive myself that I would not like the fame, the success, and the money which I daydreamed about as an adolescent. But the fact is that if suddenly, like a cloudburst in an August afternoon, all these things should come to me, it would be too late. I would take them gladly, it goes without saying. But they would not feel right. They would not be part of the fabulous dream by which I lived and for which I forced myself to work very hard, like all good Americans, when I felt like going out and having a good time.

Perhaps I am wrong to think that there is a reasonable explanation for the sterility and withdrawal in which I live. Don't think, as one says, don't think that it has not occurred to me that it may merely be a lack of talent and an unwillingness to accept one's limitations.

> Desires have no names. As music says
> A crowd is waiting. Throats, throats, and throats
> And if there are gods, there is God too
> Destroying the rest of the world ever again
> For the old Noah looked at, laughed at and laughing
> At himself. Part of him mocks himself, parting
> From mantel, table, and sofa. Distances

> Around him enter him, the years
> > and the bays,
> The city inexhaustible and the senseless sea.
> The one who runs from the empty night
> > of his anguish
> Carries it with him. Pluck the harp,
> Touch the key, thicken the air, musician.

It returns, memory returns, joyous emotion burns, leaps and warms the body and cheers the mind, and it seems easy as reaching for the dish of fruit on the living-room table.

As I was walking in the city inexhaustible, I read the names of the tradesmen, delighted that Yanns was an oculist.

The populace did not know the terror of inspiration, which is like the love of life, but speeded up, because the death is nearer.

"It's just the glue that holds the nuts in place," his grandmother said, eating an enormous coffee ring.

"Who is that distinguished-looking gentleman walking with Rabbi Rabinowitz?" asked Mussolini of Victor Emmanuel.

"This is just a shantih in old shantih town," spurred the funferal book.

"Don't think I don't appreciate good music," said the lady who lived downstairs. "How long is this to go on, Chester? For two and a half years I put up with this."

[Meyer] Schapiro Lecture: Seurat

Seurat as scientific (Gauguin, "a little chemist"), not in using scientific theories, but in being imbued by an organizing measuring constructive experimental spirit.

Dots—grains—each unit a sensation as in [Ernst] Mach's theory of experience—uniformity and variety—effort to get both unity and variety.

Method of old painters: pensée or sketch; model drawing, correction of first by second.

Impressionist: dashing down sensations of color, light and air—an intoxication, a mystical experience—the capture of the immediate experience.

Seurat: use of both—large blocked-out design and sketches (for *La Grande Jatte*). Tried to find out where in the large design he could place the new sketched-out impression.

Violations of perspective to gain collective experience.

Composition in terms of straight-line look: a strong glance, a weak glance—each as an undrawn line.

Comparison with Puvis de Chavannes—painter of the calm of the past—married to the last princess of Byzantine dynasty.

Puvis de Chavannes painted what the conservative Frenchman wished to regard as the order of the past.

Wore monk's robes in his studio, studied Fustel de Coulanges, who wrote of Greek city (democracy) as created by the surrender of individual liberties.

After 1876—instructive era in France—belief that defeat was result of German technical superiority—Eiffel Tower as climax—resemblance to Seurat.

Construction and control, yet emphasis on emotion, warm colors [to] cool colors, above, below horizon. Comparison with Zola—applied scientific theories of heredity but was scientific only in rough-and-ready empirical way.

Use of bizarre three-pronged ornament especially in *Circus* picture.

Distortion of perspective to give maximal range to dancers' legs—to show their full power.

(Syllabic units in Rimbaud, Mallarmé—grains, dots.)

Admiration of constructed objects—bridges, dams, warehouses, docks.

Comparison—Impressionists wish to invade and possess their experiences as immediate.

W.B.: You want all these things poured into you—about painting, which you never studied.

The major effort of the artist to make something which is more than itself; which is inexhaustible; which turns into its contrary.

The colored girl kept mixing up the slides.

S[chapiro] misses the slides when he writes prose—lecturing as his medium—oral eroticism.

"A wonderful lecture," I said. "No, no, I am dissatisfied," said Schapiro.

October 20

The world is a wedding, the sages say.
The world is a wedding day.

The world is a divorce
    the beginning of betrayal and adultery
        anger and separation

I am insomnia's poet, Delmore Schwartz
Harms & the child I sing; two parents, torts
America ignores my inmost thoughts

October 22

A sudden shower. Are you sure? The passing of the morning away and the fading of the new work old.

> Is it like this / in death's dream kingdom?
> at the hour when we are / trembling with tenderness
> lips that would kiss
> form prayers to broken stone*

What happened to that dialectic, boy?
The susurrus of the thickening of the rain, regne [sic], ruin.
The cackling old lady who lives next door, her dog, her boyfriend.
"Andromaque, je pense à toi!"

> Her hollow cheeks, her cheekbones sticking out,
> her peering down the stairs,
> her hurry to get the dog indoors
> —a house in which Raskolnikov lived—a tenement—

The round-faced Irish grandmother of megacephalic boy, who shouts with the other boys, though rejected by his mother.

Basement apartments by black rails barred. A white-brick house, high French windows.

Plato was right or Freud was right—no family or a good family—no contradiction—a child, so helpless, needs love—but not to be a pet. Kardiner Davis—superego as good but as activity (hence repeated performances).

Undated

As with an onion, illusion after illusion is peeled off—what remains? nothing at all—

And I am of the super-subtle-fry, he is too, and question your motives, question your heart, I said to myself—but I did not, not enough...

KING PLEASURE AND KING JOY.

"And let there be no meaning at the bar"—recurrent pointless phrases—uncreased, hemless cloth.

The sky gray and cold again. The warm was Indian summer. Why Indian? Must look it up. The mind gassing away to itself is thought, said Plato, hot air, just gab (as of Leopold Bloom).

The children's cries chained in the street.

Noon and sleeping late again.

---

* *Adulterated version of some lines from T. S. Eliot's "The Hollow Men."*

The message of the Gospels is joy.

"Joy is our duty," said the Protestant Frenchman.

(Joy is our necessity.)

To enjoy every brick and inch.

The bookbag to Riker's, as if in Cambridge to teach—habit's mechanisms.

October 25

"In America, politicians are all low characters."

"The Congress is composed of irresponsible country lawyers interested only in pleasing their constituents," said Philip.

(What brouhaha is this? How fey! Sanskrit to me, estranged!)

"You're wonderful," she said. "You're the wonderful one."

"I was wonderful," he said, bemused. "Not now, but once, once upon a time," he added sadly.

It was not true. In many ways he had improved, though painfully, slowly, and in an eccentric way, as one who learns a language not by lessons in grammar and vocabulary but by reading parallel texts of the Bible.

It rains idly, it is the end of October; the weather of nature is slipping down, sliding down, giving up, waiting, enervated, exhausted, dry-leafed, and leafless, bare in the parks, befogged in the early morning.

Anger is death.

Anger is the desire to wipe out what exists.

October 29

Happy birthday, happy birthday, happy birthday, dear Delmore (Hershey), to you. Sinking under the table. The wax of the cake candles smelt fat.

Ambition—tongue-in-cheek. Actor's son. Lloyd S.: Are you a Jew? A joke. Ice-cream parlor. Management, a euphemism. "Let your fur coat express yourself."

Tomorrow: story of Albert, Porter, Hivnor, Psyche, Cupid, her sisters.

"What an operator," said William.

Harry the haberdasher could not run a hat shop successfully. Truman. Dis-ast-er.

Some things I might never have known except for error, weakness, failure, badness—

The teacher's audience.

"The Medusa face, swollen with hate,
twisted, venomous—"

At Wanamaker's: "I am going to get a plaything for Riverrun."

"I am getting jealous of that cat," said Elizabeth [Riverrun was her cat].

"I will get you one, too."

Laughter.

Neurosis, his chimera, on his back, on his head.

"You're out of touch with reality—"

October 31

Dream of bringing two red presents to Meyer Schapiro's children.

Quarrel with the Klonskys, patronizing.

Rhoda [Klonsky]: You're very competitive.

Polly in the bar—course at New School with [William] Troy [literary critic]—tall, big and blond, moon-faced, friendly.

"We've got beyond that stage."

"The most shocking thing I've heard in years."

November 1

Horizon, August 1945. Wilson's last word.

Jean [Stafford Lowell] to Cal [Lowell]: May I tell Delmore?

"She was slow in coming, but when she came, she came like an alarm clock."

Lowells, Frank Parker [artist and schoolmate of Robert Lowell], Leslie his English wife, W.B., Eleanor, Holly Clark (grown-up, Bostonian).

Yeats, Aristotle; taws, marbles, whips; Bradley, corpse.

Leslie's looks: she asked my name at 8:30.

The discipline of going home at midnight.

Variety of social life.

Collaboration with Will.

"In conversation with some, the true self is realized—"

Sartre

The lover desires to possess
The freedom of the person he loves
(He wishes to possess a liberty as liberty)

Loving consists in the desire to make oneself loved.

A desires that B love A—which means B [desires] that A love B. (Proof that love is self-destructive.) Try to transcend the transcendence, ex., sexual desire.

—to possess another's body
not as instrument or thing
but as incarnation of other's consciousness
—impossible—in the act, both bodies
become mere instruments—

November 2

Dialogue of Wilson and Eliot—on chastity.

Sartre told Wilson that Steinbeck was the best American writer. That's why Wilson thought that S. & S. were alike (his own mind and heart deceived him) (his own subjectivity, psychologizing). (Metaphysical smuggling in Steinbeck.)

"I am a democratic narcissist."

"All you have to do is to become a democrat," said Wm.

November 3

A mustache on the cover girl—resentment; a crude cartoon of genitals upon her tossed-up skirt—resentment.

> How memory held close the cigar clip
> His father used precisely—

> The baked potato and the fresh fall'n snow
> Stretched out upon the sled

> The children chant, enjoying repetition
> In the dell

Most people hesitate in the attribution of low motives—they are not sure, it is too convenient—so Alison, her essay on Auden, the questions about M.'s and L.'s books—side-stepped, dodged, frustrated.

In April 1933 in the New School auditorium, T. S. Eliot sat down, scratched his leg at the garter, and looked with querulous gaze at the ceiling's design. It was modernist, composed of ice blocks and dreadnaught rectangles, to the untutored eye.

He was dressed in a dinner suit. He adjusted his tie.

Jefferson Forbes secured a job at the famous university. He then decided to resign from the left-wing literary review of which he was one of the editors. Then one of the few great poets of the century sent the review a poem. Jefferson decided to return as an editor for the issue in which the poem appeared. The other editors said nothing and let him do what he wanted to do.

(Dwight, Nancy [the Macdonalds], Bowdoin St., May–June 1940.) [T. S. Eliot's poem "East Coker" appeared in *Partisan Review*, May–June 1940.]

November 8

Philip has his good qualities, but he never lets them stand in his way.

Riverrun and I are countrymen, landsmen, both from Egypt.

She has had everything, children, chilblains
     a broken leg and a broken heart
        and a dead son

What tides go in and out and in
     and I lie gasping on the sand

I am writing a poem about your wife

Whiskey on beer, have no fear
Death is no anti-Semite, dear

O what a schoolboy once I was!
The while we read of Egypt's ways

I drew a long nose on a Pharaoh's face
And grinned as if I stole the *Mona Lisa*
        The cat's pajamas
          The cat's meow
       I'd climbed Himalayas

Death is no anti-Semite, kid
It takes the Ego and the Id

"Through suffering comes knowledge."
The artist is the one who has overcome neurosis.
Every dream is an illness, and every fantasy—from conflict flows.
The plane like an ant crawled black on the overcast sky.

                       November 9
     Innocence, experience, purification
     Sin and repentance,
           Neurosis overcome
     Sickness endured
         Inoculation
     Pain and relief

                         Undated
*[The following undated pages, which I have separated with as-
terisks, were found among the dated pages of this period.]*

     While otherwise and mostly glances fall,
     As if through windows, or as if on stairs
     Which merely take us where we wish to go
     While the mind leaps to the yet unopened door
     Where party sounds arise from troops of friends
     And all hearts play like ponies cantering—
            ✿

Ophelia

"Let me assure you," said Hamlet, "that you are not in the least involved in any failure of mine to respond to you."

Ophelia felt a wrath like suffocation. She had been told, it seemed to her, that she did not exist.

"Yes, I know," she replied with a dumbed face. It was useless for her to say what she felt, since she was only told again that she had nothing to do with Hamlet.

❀

[John Crowe] Ransom: unpleasant conclusions, harping on funerals, astonishing number of funerals. Not cheering, not optimistic (but neither is life). ["Instructed of Much Mortality: A Note on the Poetry of John Crowe Ransom," Delmore's review of Ransom's *Selected Poems*, appeared in *Sewanee Review* 54 (July 1946).]

❀

He rubbed his nose in
        the dirt
It hurt his mind

A richer cadence
Her gaze blinked

❀

The doodles of unconsciousness
    Wherein formality
Raises a monster face

Walt Whitman was at first Walter Whitman—the diminutive bespeaks an overfriendliness which is characteristic.

❀

It is as easy to get lost in Whitman as in the Sunday edition of *The New York Times* and for somewhat the same [reason].

❀

Since I have never seen the hanging of a man,
Since I do not know the Chinese language,
Nor how to draw nor how to play the
                piano—
I often become sick of the years of my life . . .

❀

"Sisyphus rolled the rock up the hill. All is well, he said"—Albert Camus. [Delmore's review of Camus's *Mythe de Sisyphe* and *Le Malentendu* and *Caligula* entitled "The Meaningfulness of Absurdity" appeared in *Partisan Review* 13 (Spring 1946).]

Pyrrhus and Cineas—Simone de Beauvoir. Why not rest right away, instead of conquering all those countries?

"I love and I must."

G[ertrude]'s departure liberated bound forces in the unconscious.

❋

Economic expenditure of inhibited energy.

Sexual difficulty as the expression of character–situation, instead of vice versa.

❋

Sullivan St.—buzz-buzz—Eleanor [Goff]'s room—a low bookshelf next to the bed.

Venetian blinds, a mantelpiece on which books stand, a fireplace beneath.

A green curtain to hide the stove, icebox, and cupboard.

A low studio couch on which lie pillows of different colors and a red bedspread—red billowy quilt.

White stucco walls, a white plastic radio, a reading lamp curved like a crane, dull nickel-colored.

A bright brown male cat named Put-Put.

A thin nose, bird-like eyes, a gay and flickering joyousness.

Thin lips.

A cultivated grace in walking.

Five ft. 4 in.—but slender and tall in appearance—brown hair, brown eyes—

❋

Klonsky, evasive, invaluable source of information.

Not oral but anal persistence.

First impressions misleading.

December 1934—you looked sickly.

Pasty-faced D[elmore]. D., you thing of dirt. "Delmore is an ass." Sonny and Aaron Copland. June [Cannan, poet] walked away.

Two guinea pigs and a rabbit died to prove that you were a father.

❋

V. Woolf: No more lasting impression than the stroke of a stick upon water.

Bennett—Bloomsbury.

Quotation as a substitute for critical work.

Motives—"To see behind things." "Nobody sees anyone as he is." "What have I done with my life?" "What is Life?"

Eloquent canary—singing, beating wings against the cage.

> From gaffe, from howler, from boner
> > and *faux pas*
> From shyster, ham, and quack—
> A dirty mind and a black heart—

All of the things he did not know are
named
Once, by edge of traffic, bound and passing

❋

Being is Power, Activity is Happiness
Freud: Doctor, and candid, and fearless to say
Love is the sickness, love is the secret
And let the underlying mountains
speak
And let the hidden fountains
flow
Make you remember! the first December

"The powers assembled in sleep"
"Sympathy with the abyss—"

❋

Dream of being operated on [on] the back of my head. "You don't want gas," said the doctor, but I did. I had been cutting a mathematics class at Harvard. My mother was there.

Valéry: a writer of inscriptions.

T.S.E. said Marlowe was synthetic.

Matthiessen said [Alfred] Kazin was synthetic.

❋

Sartre. *Existence de trop*, absurd, out of place, not bursting with desire, nausea—irrational, unlike shoes and chairs.

A fear of life, not fear of death; neurosis, point of view; inspired by a philosophy.

Jaspers broke with Heidegger on Nazism. 1936—Heidegger had a nervous breakdown.

Scheler—*der Teufel*, said Husserl.

Heidegger—an old shoemaker, said Scheler.

Da Sein—concrete reality (the body, too).

Existenz—self-conscious, present-to-itself; being—the leap of self-determination.

Sisyphus triumphs through scorn. He triumphs as he starts downhill for the rock over his Fate.

(Antigone—*une jeune femme.*)

❋

If a man's sister has been seduced, the heart responds with the desire to seduce the sister of the seducer. Or perhaps his wife.

Now justice is to punish the man and not to wrong the innocent sister or wife.

He hurt me. She hurt me. I want to hurt him / her.

1946

[Delmore's leave of absence from Harvard ended and, in January 1946, he returned to Cambridge.]

January 16

Tuesday morning, breakfast at the Dicksons'.

"Where's the young master?" J[eremy] sick, turned to the wall, wanted his cat Simplex-Carrie.

Ignore the lights, see if he has an erection—two successful J. stories.

Questioned by Rose [Dickson] about A.Q.

"The trouble with women is that they take too much time. If I eat a sandwich, do I have to look at it after that and write it letters?"

Soon he succeeded in putting everyone in the wrong, the one art learned from his mother.

Jeremy must be king—presidency lasts only sixteen years.

"Where's the candy?"

"Remember how you used to bring us candy, Delmore?"

"The plane trip boring but very existential"—to quote Lionel Abel.

Sunday afternoon with the Dicksons, Jan. 13.

Sat. night. Airport, Athens—George [Palmer].

Ware St., Bill [Van Keuren] and Florette—"I ought to be spayed."

Marjorie [Palmer]: Delmore is always slipping away and absent.

George: Delmore is reality. That very peculiar evening—

"Reality is very inadequate, reality needs another double rye."

Kissed Rose's cheek. Fatigued, depersonalized. The thick lamb sandwich.

Jeremy (steals) sugar for horses. *He likes horses.*

The story of Odysseus after Pinocchio.

D[elmore]: What is right and wrong? J[eremy]: Good and bad.
What is good and bad? I don't know.
Neither do I, J., but don't think they don't exist.

Story. First person, self-analysis and failure.

Quarrels with Gabels, Dicksons, Morrison; that compromising mind.

No one exists in the real world because no one knows what everyone else has said behind his back (paranoia).

Laughlin—delayed, concealed spite; New Directions—neurotic symptom formation, "because he could not be a writer himself."

Each newborn child / Has a blind date with reality.

January 24

Alas, my broder, so mote it be. Chaucer?

Muss es sein? Muss es sein?

Es muss sein! Es muss sein!

100,000 edition of *War and Peace* during the siege of Leningrad.

Fire, double draft, no coal, quickly, thirty. Yesterday 11:30–10, six shovels, too little heat in afternoon, increasing heat toward evening.

Stephen Daedalus Zolotow, Seldom Rodman, Lionel Thrilling, Philip Slav (psychology of the immigrant).

Fixing the radio and turntable—three wires.

Records—castration complex about.

September 12

Born to great wealth, Robert Randolph had everything outside of himself that a human being might want.

His inner weakness was greater than anything he might want, although he took up the toys and the candies of this life as one might turn the pages of a book.

His father had been a drunkard who was much devoted to his son, who was also devoted to him.

When Robert Randolph went to the university from which his father had failed to graduate thirty years before, his father came to live in the nearby city that he might be able to see his son whenever he wanted.

When his son went to fashionable dances, he was afraid that his father might appear, drunken and irascible.

And when his father died suddenly, Robert Randolph appeared to be unmoved because he was moved so much.

Since his father had been a failure, he was afraid that he, too, would be a failure. And he was afraid to drink. By not drinking, he marked off a line between his own identity and his father's.

When one looks at one's face closely, as to prepare it for strangers, the unending unhappiness is pocked on it: it cannot be removed, it cannot be washed away.

A little boy saw his mother's anguish and growing anger when he would not eat his dinner. He turned over the table, not with his hands, but with a sentence.
"Be happy, Mama!" he wailed, "be happy."

Deep cried to deep, as the wind and the rain cry to the seas and the forests.

A boy of seven, sent to a strange school, the Hungarian Catholic School, when his parents moved to a new suburb, returned later the first day in tears to say: "I want to be a Hungarian!"

A young man, thirty-four years of age, had put away his hopes as if they were old love letters: tied, in order, in the closed drawer, no longer to be regarded. It was then that he said: "I do not wish to go through life without possessing all of Beethoven's Quartets."
This was the musician who said: "He who truly hears my music can never know sorrow again!"
The speech of one who has teetered upon the abyss where hope exists no more.

September 13
When the inner being is stretched tight like the strings of a violin, the strings of a tennis racket, or the bow, there rises from the illimitable depths the images of that which was so desirable that the desire, being unbearable, was forced back to unconsciousness.
To sing to the animals and demons of the underworld, enchanting them. To bring back the beloved dead, making the fixed glance of the bust glow into a smile and the lips move in easy and intimate sentences.
Then there is a hurrying and a rushing because the knowledge is held like suspicion and fear that the freedom will fade like morning.
"It's a wonder you did not end up in a glass jar."
"My brother, he's at Harvard. Has two heads!"
Abraham Lincoln did not know what he wanted. He suffered from the melancholia of the frontier.

"We are all eaten by the same worm, insofar as we attach our wills to created objects and temporal ends."

The moment when the drinks take hold and gaiety sparkles up— the moment when the feast begins—is the dream of continuous excitement, unending joy.

Looking back each autumn, [I find] each past year has a new look and is understood differently. The old interpretations, too, are taken up, laughed [at], and discarded as if they, too, were past years, understood for the first time.

Wine was made for the first time by Noah after the boredom of the Ark. His desire to live had to be freshened. Narcissus, however, invented painting.

September 15

> He is writing the work entitled
> A *History of the Boys and the Girls*
> He is nervous, he is forgetful
> He hardly knows how much he knows
> If he knows what he knows, writing
> A *History of the Boys and the Girls.*

> We are chanting the Book of the Dead
> This life is all red blue and green
> > is green or blue or deathly gray
> > > ashen!

"It's not good business if you have ulcers."
I could make a million dollars but I don't want ulcers.

October 31

How long to get used to and accept and forgive the inescapable dislike and hatred from those who have been offended or driven back?

Will: Life traps us in its rewards.

The Lowells separated; Jean has gone West.

Julie [Barrett]'s choking fit, at dinner—the latest slander about you—Why don't you commit suicide— Will [Barrett] moved away when she leaned her elbow on his knee.

E[lizabeth] disgruntled in the morning—"You make fun of my father and my friends"—mollified by evening.

To Philip: "Certain forms of naïveté seem to resemble honesty"— [Randall] Jarrell.

> The muse is mute
> The flute is silent

November 4

Schapiro: Anglo-Saxon art—two clashing systems, not distortions within one system. The intrusion of the irrational.

Classic art did make use of the frame as a means of setting off the painting.

Realism is abstract because it makes the space between objects important—atmosphere, shadow, etc.

Each judgment endlessly verified and corrigible.

Night Watch was always *Day Watch*.

Will: Trotsky said that when privilege became hereditary, the Soviet Union would no longer be a workers' state.

[Wilhelm] Dilthey: Man has no nature; he only has a history.

Schapiro on Cézanne: An early period of subjective painting; domineering father, bastard until five; repressed, aggressive, destructive.

Color, prime expression of violence, absent from early painting.

Met Pissarro—though but ten years older, he had a white beard, became a substitute father to him. Showed him how to use color, told him to paint in the open air and to paint landscapes.

Painting became a therapy, an act of hygiene, a means of escaping from his aggressiveness (which returns in the pictures of the eighties). Abandoned quarries, ruined forests. (The two motives combined.)

Distortions explained as process by which painting becomes the process of contemplation as well as objectivity contemplated.

Nudes, bound or far off, as if at the wrong end of the telescope (by arabesques contained).

November 5

A single moment of perception yields the object to the memory. "The whisper that Memory will warehouse as a shout."

A squeamish hero as he loses his squeamishness; two years at 430 Hudson St. [Elizabeth Pollet's flat].

The painted screen, the green kitchen table.

Versification creates the four walls of the poetic object—and the floor, the flow, the wallpaper, and the windows.

Elizabeth goes to her Uncle John's as the Russians entered Prague.

P[artisan] R[eview] meeting. The eternal third camp, or, waiting for Lefty. Clem and Koestler.

Orwell: Swift was a Quisling and not a well-bred English gentleman.

Wm.: "Never hit a cat or a dog—they don't understand it—creates an association with the hands." The cat, the lady with toilet paper.

[George] Mayberry: His stupidity is of the kind that is mistaken for honesty (certain forms of naïveté seem to resemble honesty).

Spencer had learned that it was profitable and becoming to speak well of others, and to place upon their actions the most sympathetic interpretation.

November 15

The therapy of food, the therapy of ordinary tasks.

He shaved, he brushed his teeth.

He went to the haberdasher and took his two pairs of slacks. He ate his lunch. He went to the shoemaker and waited for his shoes. They had been fixed but the back had to be stitched.

When all this was done, he felt better than he had before lunch. At lunch he had begun to shake a little. He was surprised to be hungry.

The idea of a flight to New York was put aside.

"I am feeling better," "I am feeling good"—rising from the emotions comes the tone of consciousness all day.

Almost a panic in the late morning, after waking tense and unrested. A dream of Sullivan, Hudson St., and rats.

Sonny talked on the phone for an hour last night about sex and creativity. He has just been reading a book by [Theodore] Reik in which sexuality and the Oedipus complex are rejected. He wanted to apply what he had just learned to me, to my periods of depression. I listened impatiently, but by the time he was done I had gone from drunkenness to clear elevation. Sonny supposed that my fault lay in seeking out sublimation. "I don't know much about your private life, but—" he said. He thought that Cal had not made love to Jean, which Jean must have said to him, expressing her resentment.

In the dream there [were] two rats and a man named Sullivan who was a pugilist who was going to kill them and eat them. Sullivan St. is where Eleanor lives. The dream took place in Elizabeth's house.

Yesterday I walked into Oscar [Handlin] and he sat with me while I had lunch at the Coach. I was full of energy then and for a time after lunch. Dolores Rogers did not come and I did not feel any real disappointment.

"You come like an angel," my grandmother said, peering at me with weak eyes.

The rats may have been cats. They were gray like Totem Tertius [Elizabeth's cat].

In Will's interpretation, the boy who cries Wolf! is really calling the wolf. "But I was really calling the Wolf," he says. Theseus *liked* the labyrinth, he trembled and shivered.

Two causes of conflict, R.S. [his mother] and E.

This week, A.Q. But the fading had started last week.

November 16

Conflicts between self and reality as the only true subject.

Club 100—two reaching manicured hands, an orchid; the object of nightclubs—to be with other people who are fashionable, and yet not to have to justify one's identity, apart from paying the bill.

Dream about E.P.'s insisting on eating eggs in the restaurant instead of making them at Hudson St. We argued, I hit her, and I woke up.

Dream about teaching an advanced composition course of Radcliffe girls—who wanted to meet at a bar—I talked to Claude Simpson at the Faculty Club and found out that he had insisted on taking the Harvard section.

Equinox—Alan Seager shames one about the profession of authorship; a resentment of psychoanalysis—he makes the villain an analyst.

November 17

The story itself—the explicit subject—is never the true subject (which draws forth the author's motives sufficiently to enable him to write). Thus Milton—his twenty-seven plots—before he arrived at *Paradise Lost*—and thus Tolstoy, who studied the Decembrist revolt before coming upon *War and Peace*, the true subject of which is the normal family life—just as the true subject of *Paradise Lost* is not the justification of God to Man but Satan's indomitable will.

What are Shakespeare's themes? Melancholia, despair, distrust, sexual disgust, love versus duty, the mixture of the angel and the beast in man.

In New York, Elizabeth forgot for more than a day about telling me what she thought of *The World Is a Wedding*. I did not know that she had finished it.

All week an illustration of the sublime dictum: It is not good for man to be alone.

Philip R. amazed when I said that I'd rather write than make love.

November 18

Dreams in which Will and Eleanor appeared—and Ted Williams on first base.

Sunday nothing to drink until after eight o'clock, and I started to run down after that.

In conversation, the pleasures of authorship. The oral immediacies with the Dicksons and the Handlins.

By midnight, three quick ones, hurrying to peace.

George praised Gertrude when Rose said that she was irresponsible.

[Allan] Nevins and historical prize-society (Buck's gossip).

"Buck would like you, he would find you refreshing," said Mary [Handlin]. "He would get a kick out of you—salty."

Peasants converted to Jews—vice versa—few disabilities, no tithes.

Writing is—either easy or impossible.

"I am living on a keg of dynamite."

Johnny the placid husband whose untidy wife is going to law school because he is not ambitious enough.

He is an engineer but thinks of teaching but likes to have money to throw around as a Raytheon navy man—he has two children.

When I told Philip of my difficulties in working, he said—almost as if I had touched on a delicate subject—"We all feel like that sometimes."

Oscar [Handlin] also troubled—unwilling to admit it—placidity as a defense. "I don't worry—period." Mary [Handlin] accepts this myth.

Sinclair Lewis became a great man and had to keep on being a great man and did not.

Lardner as profoundly literary, verbal—marred life, world's serious.

Rose [Dickson] sewed the lining of my topcoat. I did not listen as I should have to Wallace [Dickson]—I was surprised by my volubility.

Diary of a Superfluous Man—hopeless love again.

You can't make an omelette without breaking eggs. But human beings are not eggs; and the good society is not an omelette. (They were discussing the Soviet Union.)

Unconscious sense of guilt is incorrect; means "need for punishment," S. F[reud].

Psychosexuality is not the same as physical gratification—"A mental lack of satisfaction *with all its consequences* can exist where there is no lack of normal sexual intercourse"—S.F. (But the waiting is the loss of years.)

Indolence, a story of the love of drunken excitement.

As a child I wanted my father to be at home, or to return.

But I also had the fantasy that my mother was not my real mother.

The superego punishes him after anxiety and sensitivity have led to acts of aggression.

A prosperous period renews his narcissistic and megalomaniac hopes, leading to anxiety.

Sexual overactivity as an effort to compensate for other frustrations of the ego.

The case history as an influence on the next development of fiction.

November 19

Dream—in which it's clear that Pope still remains. The Egypt (Russia?) of the unconscious will not let him go.

Undated

From the deck of the ocean liner they cast overboard their dead hopes. These corpses resemble statues without heads and vases on which the decoration has been blurred or disfigured.

So much mystery, so much splendor.

Joy was a butterfly.

The fear of success is a feeling of guilt.

The fixation on authorship is the desire for the free and spontaneous creativity of the father.

As the child cries, he becomes a poet. His mother goes to him, his lost love returns, and he enters the desperate kingdom of mountain-peak exaltation and the darkness of the pit.

Tired of suffering, tortured, doubtful—as hesitant and full of care as tightrope walkers.

Yes was calculated and no was ecstatic hope.

Julie leaned her elbow on Will's lap as he read *Time*; he opened his legs, parted his lap, and her arm fell awkwardly. She was rejected. He made poor amends by saying that he had done no periodical reading for some time.

"Never mind, we are having fun," said William as the evening grew and we were about to depart. He told stories of the patriarchs among his friends, Roszak and [Arthur] Pincus [publicity man for MGM].

He spoke of Will Olson's praise of Stalin's writings in 1903. Even then could be seen his greatness. But S.'s first writing did not appear until 1911.

Baba had been given an old coat which belonged to the late Mrs. Buckman. She was ashamed, she did not like it, but she wore it. She was afraid that she was losing her memory. What is the name of my son-in-law? she asked. You see, she said.

Allen Tate on Hudson Street—we crossed quickly, and looked. It seemed as if he were about to come after us.

November 26–27

Housekeeping, apron for Xmas, Marcel wave, the mother who kept secret her dyed hair.

Of Turgenev's life we must say, with the poet [Yeats]:

> The intellect of man is forced to choose
> Perfection of the life or of the work

Turgenev like every author chose the [work], if we suppose that choice, not compulsion, governed him.

Agamemnon—Sigmund—toppling pride.

Self-knowledge as a priceless boon.

Bias as illustrated by a biographer of Aaron Burr.

First Love compared with what actually happened.

An egg—"Feels like one of your testicles."

"After all, I come from Switzerland where they eat eggs raw." A Swiss in Great Neck, pinpoint, drank egg; his wife still thought she had twelve eggs.

Wm. and [Robert Gorham] Davis [Columbia professor and critic], review of *[PR] Reader* [for *The Nation*]: Maybe he will attack me, I'm not that much of a masochist.

"Why are you standing up?"

"I am nervous and sensitive."

Lies, Neurosis, and Art—"That's what the psychoneurotic is always trying to do—make other people believe in his lies."

Harvard as part of the superego.

Cain, *Mildred Pierce*—magnetism of identification.

December 9

"Shove off, my dears, there's nothing here, I know!
And let us go away, we've had enough."
The knave and the fool who in his heart were loud
Uttered these sentiments in drawing rooms
On boulevards, to friends and enemies.
But when a stranger said: "You speak thus
Possessed by such feelings, a critic of this life,
Because you want to be loved
            (perhaps) because you want
To hold to the state in which you want to be loved
Because you want your want.
            For you are loved
Though not as love has seemed to you.
            Your love
(Far as the stars & nearer than the lips)
Can never be in others, being in you
Private & hence deprived & hence alone."
He listened and felt the light upon the bone
            And knew the weight of the short stone.

1947

January 15

Old Letters

Written last year or ten years old, and bold
And warm, pretentious as a top hat, and yet
With the ego's pomp, self-conscious as a stammer
Self-conscious as a stammer or a whisper

These pieces of the self are with my friends
They show me as I am, which never ends
The word betrays the heart and mind. And now?
Silence is empty violence, let me bow

Before the looking glass and smile at last
Forgiving myself for the future and the past
Most difficult of all is self-forgiveness
Tied to the Siamese twins, self-witness and withness.

On thirty-third birthday: All he wanted was the joy of joy.

Till death do us part?
O fearful long thought
To the bitter, curved heart!
That all must be sought
Within another's heart

[May ?] 21

"Did I tell you—a man in Calcutta has not slept f' two years."
My blood froze.

Ella Wheeler Wilcox [inspirational American poet, 1855–1919] in
Furs. Sonnets for Sables.

September 10

Best when I don't write what I expected, write, but something else, unexpected.

Talk English. Don't talk Spanish. This is America—dirty rotten Jews.

It's not hard to be stupid.

It's too hot to be serious.

South America does not exist so far as I'm concerned.

Rising from sleep as from ruins; rising from the ruins of sleep.

E.G.K. [Eleanor Goff married Seymour Krim, a young writer]: bar of chocolate so that every moment would be packed with pleasure.

I'm going to love the pants off you, she said, and came rushing across the room at him.

Klonsky, tedious manuscript, locked out.

Are you trying to get me drunk? You're like an international spy.

For a long time he was unable to eat alone without reading a paper or a book; but then his thoughts became so interesting that he preferred them at dinner.

"The British persevered with an unyielding fidelity which could well have been reserved for a better cause."

Twenty-first St. Mrs. W.: *Bist du ein yid?* Come in, let's do business quick. I like to see a Jewish boy get ahead, especially when he's educated. I'll fix it up nice for you. I'm a Jew—I believe in the truth, but quiet. If you're at Harvard, what are y' doing here?"

Better fiction—you know, at my age, you don't care so much for poetry.

(Lucky Schwartz—unorthodox methods.)

W.B.: I overestimated you. When I heard the remarks of others they seemed strange to me.

Philip: You are procrastinating. Let us have no wit. Never mind the pure demagoguery.

The drunken girl: I have more fun than real people.

Street boys call each other by their second names.

Demoted, demented / controlled & contented.

To write new repetition poems & to rewrite HBG as well as using stories from the first draft & to attempt Lardneresque humor.

> In going to my naked bed
> As one that would have slept

A dream of headlines about a suicide.

A dream of being with Baba in a house overlooking the Hudson.

Chickie [Brown, a student of whom Delmore was fond]: How did I know that my mother was an anti-Semite?

How seldom he has tried, for two years, to write poetry—yet
F.W.'s [*Finnegans Wake*] idiom bubbles in him.

"Peter Stopwell thought of England as a sailor thinks of his ship."

"Her beauty was poised like a tightrope walker's over death—it
was her way of thrilling them."

Will said he would go with me, were he not bound by other
matters.

In bed until 12, 1:15, 1:30—three successive days.

September 24

The gray weather.

"A wonderful story—meant to write you a letter to tell you so."
("M. Life" ["The Child Is the Meaning of This Life"])

Will—"a psychological setup"—Julie, "furious—have you seen
him today?" Madness, madness; remorse, guilt, fear.

W.B.: That was when I was still clowning.

"Who said that you have stopped?"

Jitters, haggard—forced himself to Fifty-ninth St. for the sleeping tablets.

Home, home on the range—W.B.—Delmore is home from Cambridge.

A nous la liberté—charade—mislaid by Gordon's.

Who is this guy, Gordon?

Poem, poem for a change.

"Trilling compared himself to Eliot"; "practically identical, practically the same."

Do what you will, this world's
a friction
And is made up of contradiction

September 25

Gray weather, sinus headache.

"If you're drafted, my mother-in-law says to me, I'll lay 8–5 on
Japan."

Mrs. Mulvey: "A girl just called—she said she would call again
or drop by later." Elizabeth? Eileen Berryman? Chickie? Who would
have my address and number?

For the first day in two weeks neither the false exhilaration of the
hangover nor too tired to hold open my eyes an hour after breakfast.

W.B.: Elizabeth would have lived with you in an ashcan.

"If Elizabeth lived there, it would have been an ashcan."

Excitement—who was the girl?

When will he be in the married state—able to eat dinner not alone?

"My stomach thought that my throat was cut."

Will on Sonny's letter: One of the most amazing documents that I have ever read. Utterly dishonest and fatuous.

September 26

"Sh[akespeare] amateurish"—Robert [Maynard] Hutchins [president and then chancellor of the University of Chicago, 1929–51; since 1954 at the Center for the Study of Democratic Institutions] "a boy wonder emeritus."

Clem [Greenberg]: Anne Sterling as unaffected and unassuming at Manny [Farber, film critic]'s. Agee: She's not as bad as she seems.

A sinus headache all day.

Dream about a message from the Italian consulate with an honorary appointment.

Several dreams which reached the point of "it is not true, it is true"—appointment at Columbia (I wanted it, after all)—then thought of not being able to write as much as I want.

Will to J.: "We must take her under our wing"—Shirley.

"Will no longer speaks of you—He used to all the time."

"Isaac [Rosenfeld] is looking always for a piece of mud to dig into."

Will: Here lives the Jewish Franz Kafka.

Editor: Tell him it is because he is a Jew.

"William will die." "But he takes care of his health."

The necessity of returning to Cambridge.

Internalized guilt of homosls. [homosexuals]—arrested development.

October 18

From crackpoet to crackpot
just an *e*
A day like an endless empty sea
Trembling & shaking, gray

Wm.: "When I'm dead, I will keep on talking." "Don't talk to me."

October 23

She wore her morality like long underwear (fur coat, chemise, a rope of pearls).

Mother, verbal, long-winded, self-righteous.

"What do I want"—tears in his eyes.

R[ose] S[chwartz]: Women came after him. Your father liked me to scratch his head.

Englishman to J. Lardner: Whatcha know? Is it true all you boys make plenty of potatoes?

Forced rising, shower, shaving, dressing, visit to office, dictation, visit to Mother—eating.

Homage to the superego.

"We were happiest in the house—competition between brothers —Louis would make himself mean for a couple of dollars."

October 27

"Don't you write poetry anymore?"

Zolotow (gloom, analysis, the D.S. mood). Empty evening with W. & J. B[arrett].

Touching bottom every night & early morning.

> The bottom of despair
> Shaky & trembling every afternoon

Bill: Never saw you drink so much. You're looking very well.
I began to drink at 3, in bed by 9:30.

"If I sound vague, it's because I've been sleepless for four nights."
F.O.M. adores you—quoted you four times.
"You're too famous (for me)."
R. P. Warren did not look like a happy & successful man.
"It's like trying to swallow a horse."
The curse of romantic love, enforced by novels & pictures. Madonna & mother & far off & overestimated—a curse because it blocks the love of daily life & night.

The dinner on Thursday night—release when talking to Wm. but not Will.

Weds. Anne Sterling—Ingrid, tan, orgy of showing off.
"Delmore is selfish—he wants to be loved before he loves anyone."

November 10

I will call you—the brush-off.
Clem's bone to pick with me.
Sat. Deep in the heart of Bklyn., Ocean Parkway.
Sun. Manny, Hal and Barbara White—porcelain skull, strep throat, white gown, thigh exposed.

Nothing succeeds like mediocrity. The triumphal car of mediocrity.

Sun. & Mon. Chickie. Give your mother my love. Ask if 6 million dead Jews are not enough.

Undated

Predictions and Predilections or The Realm of Nonsense
after One Year of Marriage or You Do What You Want To

Fooling oneself is a pleasant occupation if it is not carried on too consistently. To fool oneself, or to put it more blatantly, to refuse to recognize the truth of what one knows about oneself, is to gamble with one's own desires, one's ambitions, and one's intelligence.

The lovely folly, which a slight smattering of self-analytic technique gives to one today, is the belief, first, that one knows all about oneself, and second, that one can really never know oneself. The result, of course, is an individual paradise in which everything can be understood, anything done, and everything explained (after the fact).

This bewildering and fascinating condition, in which the subject feels himself, at least imaginatively, to be capable of anything, supplies much of the material, and dominates the modes of experience and perception, in most "good literature" today.

With science as the jailer of what can be considered external reality, the miraculous has been banished to the interior of each one of us, and personal mythology has been deified.

[I found no journal entries for 1948. Delmore had returned to New York the previous spring. He was active as an editor of *Partisan Review*. In the summer New Directions published *The World Is a Wedding* (stories).]

1949

January 10

John Berryman: You look haggard.
The sour juice and tears of the knotted psyche.
Lenin, the George Washington of Russia.
Kierkegaard: the Danish girls admired him as we admire George Washington.
And the full-fed beast kicks the empty pail.
E.B. 14 [*Encyclopaedia Britannica*]. War guilt, Garvin, Hegel, Sophocles (*Coriolanus*).

> Pontiff Vicar of Christ (Vicar! look here!)
> The dried sweat faint in unaired rooms is holy
> It is the sour juice and tears of the knotted psyche
> Tied in humiliation to the body
> (Like melancholia's thoughts, haggard and heavy
> In houses where life, fallen nervously
> From hands and arms conflicted pointlessly
> Declares there is not time enough to live
> When self-guilt is the guilt you must forgive!)
> [. . .]
> Vicar of Christ, this is our Purgatory
> We tell ourselves our own bad dirty story
> And cannot trot or romp like animals
> Whom presence and activity fulfills!

Antigone (where poem has conflict of two rights), divine law versus civil or communal edict.
Do you have to go to college to make a fool of yourself?

The *Encyclopaedia Britannica*
Published the first time in America
Discusses war guilt from three "points of view!"
The French, the German, and the English who
Preside—or keep the score—when the other two
Accuse each other of beginning war
(As if the first punch were the final score)
And like a judge or like a referee
Garvin the editor judiciously
Weighs the two pleas and quotes *Antigone,*
Or Hegel on the heart of tragedy:
The conflict of two rights, Garvin declares,
Is tragedy, so that if one compares
The French and German charge and defense
Both sides are right!
      Well, maybe I am dense
(I am I know!) But how is it that he
Never thinks both are wrong? and endlessly!
[. . .]
Or as my mother used to say to me:
Must one attend a college just to be
A most judicious most elaborate fool?
Many a dumbbell never went to school.
Thus speaks a man old in experience.
One grants them both a certain innocence!

January 19

    He was seeking to impress himself. He was not seeking to force upon other people his own image of himself.
    His own image of himself which he was trying to impress upon himself was self-originating, and this was the sense in which he was creative and poetic.

[Libby (Elizabeth Pollet), who had married someone else in January 1947, a marriage that lasted less than a year, was again Delmore's girl.]

Wherever she is, love is, like light
Wherever Libby is is Love.

    Having heard all the reports about himself, he decided that he was a lesbian. A lesbian is someone who likes to sleep with girls.
    She was the wife of the party.
    He was engaged in holy deadlock.

You can't win. Time is the sin. Every day you lose a day.

Relativity and nuclear physics predicate a complete distrust of the senses. Einstein is holding the younger men back.

Allen Tate said that Oppenheimer had bad manners because he told him to call him up, not to be bashful, the next time he came to Princeton.

He was able to write when he was depressed, a profound discovery.

Cal [Robert] Lowell had pored over his poetry books. John Berryman was always waiting for his cue. He said, in effect, that he was the greatest genius of all time and told Will to come to Princeton if he was feeling particularly anti-Semitic.

William said that I had become the *PR* librarian. Mary Wickware [advertising and business manager of *Partisan Review*] talked about our seminars. Will was asked why he had chosen to forfeit the psychological privilege of being a Gentile? Alger Hiss charmed everyone because he was so corrupt that he could tell anyone a lie and he could brazen out any lie. No one wants to believe that such a one could be a spy also. It means the corruption of the entire ruling class.

The American idea of love, says a Frenchman, is: "Pucker up, babe, I'm coming in on the beam."

Come on, let's break that Oedipal deadlock.

January 20

There are no Open Sesames. There are. There are plenty of push buttons. There are the eggs in Arizona which will end Western civilization.

There can be at least nineteen more wars. And nineteen categories of megalomaniacs.

If you always do what you want to do, you are bound to do something awful. If you always do what you don't want to do, you acquire enormous strength.

To argue with William [Phillips] is like arguing with Vesuvius.

There is not time enough to live as a human being.

Al Johnson wrote in *Commentary* that no Jew can be admitted to the really ritzy part of the upper class. But he added that it was not worth being among them.

700,000 Jews beat 40 million Arabs: David knocks off Goliath again.

Philip liked the metaphor about being an author: Being an author is like treading water in the middle of the ocean; you can never stop, you can never stop treading water.

He said then that it was the worst way of acquiring status. If you're born a duke, you remain a duke and that's all there is to it.

To do what you really want to do means that you are willing to take the responsibility for what you have done, once it is done.

Electrifying moment when Dr. Gruenthal said that he believed in God: "It may not be a person, maybe it is atomic energy"; he was thinking of an élan vital, a creativity—"whoever it was—God or whatever his name is, who imposed the functions of consciousness upon the lower part of the brain—the cortex—made trouble because of, for example, the necessity of fear."

We still remain with the Cartesian dualism—body, soul, and the mysterious connecting link—not the pineal lobe, but something in the brain—the ductless glands, the endogenous area.

One must be prepared to be bored. Once I stood boredom like a patient man. One must be patient, one must bring back one's habits patiently, step by step, one must coax them back, one must not pull them down the stairs.

Writing is the way in which one solves one's problems. Van Gogh said that painting brought him very close to things. But it would be foolish to expect writing to bring Dostoevsky close to things.

Writing is a way of working off anxiety. Writing is a way of drinking less, smoking less, making love less, and getting rid of one's feelings of guilt. Raw with guilt, said the good doctor, I absolve thee. If I were a Catholic priest, I would now say, I now absolve thee.

You don't have to see your mother. Others have felt about her as you do, as you yourself observed.

Mary [McCarthy] fell asleep on the sofa, rude and friendly.

Bowden [Broadwater] said that such a one (I can't remember who) resembled a baked apple.

January 21

I write the earlier date—1948 [the manuscript has a 9 superimposed on the 8] because I want it to be earlier.

Bad, bad in the sense that you have done some things regardless of the consequences. Bad for yourself or bad for others, or bad for bad, or bad for both.

Sobiloff's party [Hy Sobiloff, a wealthy businessman and poet], Bridget, Cloris Leachman, Julie, Chandler Broussard [novelist], Klonsky, and Rhoda.

"I don't want to be a member of the chosen people. I just want to be a good kid." You are not asked whether you want to be chosen. If you're chosen, you're chosen.

Sobiloff spoke in Scotch, Yiddish, and with an English accent.

"Say hello to gay Paree, give my regards to Tel Aviv."

Malicious, destructive, paranoiac, said Rhoda; You always blame other people, said Julie.

I may never see you again, I said to Klonsky, who wanted to

know if he could change his check for dollars which he could use on the black market in Paris.

"There are many Klonskys in Tel Aviv."

"The Presidency has made a *mensch* out of Truman. He no longer wobbles around the way he used to." "Praise and success have made a *mensch* out of Truman," said Philip. The Alsops said that the man grows in the office.

Sobiloff kept talking about the Czar poem [Delmore's "The Ballad of the Children of the Czar"] and how I was a great man.

Depressed because of days and days of drinking.

January 23

"I like you," said Charlotte [Zolotow], "although sometimes I wonder why." "People like you," said Julie [Barrett], "even though you irritate them." "Jay really likes you, even though you irritate him sometimes," said Margaret [Laughlin]. "He worries about you."

"I hate you," said Rhoda Klonsky, "but I really have a warm feeling for you."

"You worry too much," said Julie and Jay, "you make too much of everything."

"For psychological reasons, it would be best for you to write something new," said Gruenthal.

"What this country needs is a good five-cent psychiatrist."

Maurice [Zolotow] said that I was rude to you.

You were critical, but I deserved it.

> Overreaction is my name
> Metaphor is my nation
> Neurosis is my hiding place
> And thought is my salvation.

The crucial error: to suppose that what is unconscious in people is really conscious. And because it was conscious in me. The paranoid error. And the naïve error: to expect too much of other human beings.

In reading psychoanalysis I don't just say, That's me, I say also, That's A, B, C, and D.

And I look for others with the same fixations that I have. And the same guilt.

Alienated from oneself by success.

"I had an uncritical admiration for you"—M. Z[olotow].

"However much I might regret or resent the fact that I am not a writer."

"Mann is a profoundly humble man-instrument of God," just as Rilke thought of himself as "the interpreter of things, the things of God."

"Meyer Schapiro's name occurs in more analyses than that of any other teacher"—[Anatole] Broyard.

"We are engaged in mutual accusation"; "the mirror of malicious eyes."

[Edmund] Wilson in this week's *New Yorker* is still trying to prove that many great authors—this time it is Swift—were bastards just like himself.

January 27

Too much to drink again, hence it is hard to do anything co-ordinated.

The way to solve one's emotional problems is to sit at the type-writer and solve them. Here they are controllable.

The manic period is waning or ended.

"He who distrusts good motives ends by destroying his own good motives," signed Stephen Daedalus Barrett, collect. But he was afraid that it would not be collected.

Hatred of the lecture. Scott Fitzgerald and the American Dream, which is now moving east and west.

Desire for variety in all things. Impatience with E. Impatience, he said, is one of the modes of your being.

To stop drinking and to start reading and to start looking and to start listening.

If you only did that page a day! Farewell to Klonsky as he left for Europe. We walked down Fifth Avenue to Twelfth St. "I may never see you again," I said, quoting my mother again, "a piece of rusty tin."

People don't want to read about children, they want to read about themselves; not identification but participation.

Elizabeth was joyous about her book [the news that New Directions would publish her novel *A Family Romance*]. Gruenthal did not like the fact that she would not answer the phone nor open the door.

The hero is a physicist or he is a psychiatrist. He suffers from manic-depressive moods.

I am wasting my time, I am wasting the day. I do not know how to live and to play. I have forgotten how to sleep. I have learned about loss. I have tried to dominate my body and my life.

If I'm so smart, why ain't I rich?

If I'm so bright, why do I fight?

Jay's account of Auden at Spencer's funeral: Nothing that Auden likes so much as a good death. He was closeted with the Vicar of Christ Church. Someone had to take the corpse away to be cremated. Harry, who was running the whole show very efficiently, offered to do so, but Auden insisted that he was the one to do it. And he insisted on lifting the coffin lid to take one last look at the rouged cheeks of our departed friend. Meanwhile, Matthiessen's cheeks were streaming with tears. Harry tried to get some John Donne into the service.

January 30

It is snowing; all is slowed.

It is slowed because of snow.

"You must not believe in the people," said Eliot, who much of the time listened to the people with care and with love.

Margaret Marshall goes to [a psychiatrist], who tells her that she has a mother-relationship with Freda Kirchwey (editor of *The Nation*).

William Burford [poet] called up and wanted to talk about the snow. Then Elaine Gottlieb [fiction writer and friend of Elizabeth] called and insisted on talking to Elizabeth.

We spent Sunday afternoon with Bowden, mostly. He made Italian coffee and tea. Later, he wore his bowler hat. He spoke out his likes and dislikes of Pat Blake Nabokov ("her technical efficiency" was reported by her husband), the Hortons and their frumpish friends (Tessa is a Wallaceite and Philip blandly commits himself to nothing), Gertrude's rasping quality, Dwight's rational cuckoldry.

February 1

Bowden reports that Dwight went to Polly Adler's [author of *A House Is Not a House*] with Geoffrey Hellman, but finding that the price was $20, he decided against it, but then Polly Adler took a liking to him and asked him to take her to the movie and he did and he was sore because he had to pay for her ticket. A wicked tongue, a gifted boy.

The large part played in American life by humor.

Last night's visit of the Zolotows. Charlotte is going, too. She builds up Maurice's ego by knocking mine down.

Jane, said Elizabeth, found me "inspiring." It was because she felt very happy. Leslie is "too good to be true"; he speaks of saving enough money to send Jane to Denmark next summer.

Elizabeth irritable because there were no eggs.

Meyer [Schapiro] called up to say how much he liked my lecture. He spoke so fast and had so many ideas that I had a hard time following him.

He corrected me on the great library at Alexandria. The disappearance of the classics was not due to any such burning. It was a canard of tenth-century Christian polemics. Papyrus is a very weak material, parchment is not. The manuscripts were lost through general neglect between the third and fourth centuries. The best plays of Sophocles were those which survived, if quotations of them in the ancient era are to be believed. But perhaps they were not the best judges.

February 4

Gray light, shaking hands, eating nervously without an appetite.

The effort to resist the desire by thinking the thoughts of: "You are destroying yourself"; "You will feel better"; "It's not as bad as you think."

A sweating brow after the first feature, *Larceny*, silky, Tory, and the social ice pick; wild merriment at *You Gotta Stay Happy*, after I had relaxed myself by promising myself that I would after all drink some vermouth when I got home.

I vomited trying to drown down the two new tablets (their purpose is to make me tired). Then, in pure drugged tranquillity, I read with admiration my own essay on Eliot.

I woke up at 5 for the second night in a row. In the morning I read Wm.'s story; in the afternoon I tried through extreme nervousness to read *The New Yorker*, *Time*, and *Commentary*.

> Again the sense of fading powers
> As ever the prick of wasted hours
> Slowly comes the approach of death

"I feel I am being born again—but being born is no great pleasure."

Slowly the slum and tomb of death approaches.

February 6

Significance of the shofar—the blowing of the horn.

A job at Princeton peculiarly offered to me [in a letter from R. P. Blackmur]. Consultation with William and Edna. "Sleep on it." Their sharpness—there is no use in worrying.

Sobiloff arrives and talks for fifteen minutes. "He thinks he can transfer success."

Torah: The Law.

Elizabeth depressed for the third day in a row: "I want some sympathy." "How much?" "You spoke as if I were someone unclean."

The effort since Wednesday night to stop drinking. And still my hands tremble. I cannot dissemble.

Gruenthal's warning: Alcohol is not a useful drug. There is always the chance that the heavy social drinker will become an alcoholic. Alcohol induces pathological reactions and chemical reactions. Since you are still very young, there can still be many pathological reactions. Senile at fifty instead of at sixty.

The big project—to stop drinking and to stop taking sleeping tablets.

Losing and lost, the grip of habits of concentration and attention.

I tried to read John Peale Bishop's prose and verse, and it looked very bad, pretentious, and snobbish and foolish.

February 7

So softly down the haze I made the maze
Mirroring in my lids the waves of wars
    A streaky sleep I slept, as if jerked down
              by jarring levers
              'twixt joining cars

Town Hall, *Brandenburg Concertos 3, 5, 6*—the Blue Ribbon—two poor pictures—Seventh Ave. home—the great temperance campaign—no sleep until 4—one drink—two sl. tbs. [sleeping tablets] (less and less each day except Friday since Weds.).
"This is not a bed—it is a trench."
"We don't talk—you look so sad."

February 9

A changed image—after a year—a changed possession.
Sun., Mon., Tues., (Weds.)—nothing to drink.
Gruenthal, of R. P. B[lackmur]'s letter: He tries to look at it from all sides. E. P[ollet]: Take my point of view.
The Heat of the Day by Elizabeth Bowen, *The Price Is Right* by Jerome Weidman—the uses of plot and morality.
The Lost Weekend by Charles Jackson—the uses of identification and concreteness (passage on the early-morning light). Shaking and sweating and fumbling—and looking in the mirror; being sure that one's thoughts are wonderful. The uses of fiction for the sake of fear.
Counting the dead of these years. Theodore Spencer, Phelps Putnam, John Walcott, Russell Cheney, Sonya Bosworth, John Wheelwright.

February 10

Another day without drinking. Lunch with Philip, Mrs. [Victoria] Ocampo [South American novelist], and [Niccolo] Tucci [Italian intellectual and author]. Hard to say "I love you" in Italian (a theological and juridical language).
Teaching with more confidence from 7 to 10.
Will says he may write a musical comedy in five years.
In the morning I felt as if not drinking had made me feel very good—but by afternoon the feeling was gone.
Mary [McCarthy] liked E.'s novel and she was pleased and went to write another one and a half pages.
E.: new image, new dismay; coldness and hostility from her; too much freedom at thirty-five.
Alcohol was a quick trip to seeming experience. Alcohol was a way of unfurling the self to other people.
"That's not what you wanted," said Wm., "to be a brilliant conversationalist—what do you get if you fuck Mary?" Endless common sense.

February 22

Malraux, during the resistance, is stopped by the Germans while driving in his car from place to place.

Instead of showing them his false card of identity, the customary thing, he gets into a fight with them and lands in jail.

In jail he keeps crying out: I am Malraux. I demand an immediate trial.

The Germans pay no attention to him. They do not know who Malraux is.

Meanwhile, the Resistance radio broadcasts a report that Malraux is dead.

Finally Malraux's hullabaloo gains him a trial. The judge, however, does not know who Malraux is.

An attack on the jail frees all the prisoners and Malraux.

Yesterday I tried to read Gide on Dostoevsky, Fitzgerald, Saroyan, Eliot, Norman Mailer; and an album of American history.

I drank half a bottle of sherry before dinner and more than half a pint of whiskey after dinner. It did very little good until the very end of the evening.

The new depression began in the first week of this month—about the 5th of February. It crept over me slowly.

It was easy to stop drinking. All I had to do was to suffer a little nervousness for an hour and not be upset by not falling asleep.

March 24–31

Thurs. Another empty day, six tablets, trying hard to talk to E. One bottle of sherry, three bottles (quarts) of beer—dream that I was all better—E. cold again.

Weds., 30. Editorial meeting, anguish before classes, one bottle of vermouth, underreaction, successful with E.

Tues. Gruenthal impatient: "You are getting more nervous and that may be a good sign." (Knocking wood, party at Jane's, too much to drink with little effect.)

Mon., 28. E. angry at me: "You don't make me happy—maybe no one would—but maybe not." She went to look in the country for a place. *A Letter to Three Wives.*

Sun. E.: "I don't love you today." *The Snake Pit*—scared.

Sat., 26. John and Toni's [Pollet]—"I love you yes and no—I don't know."

Fri. Baba's—hardly able to talk, after lunch with Philip—again hardly able to talk.

Questioning E. about reasons for marriage—"I love you but I don't love you enough."

Thurs. Visit with Zolotows, breaking through after dinner.

Year before: "Are you going to marry me?" "Probably—(Let's hang up)."

April 1

No more hangovers since when? Anyway less and less. Three bottles of beer instead of two. No lift from almost a bottle of sherry. Shaking hands, something wrong or imagined wrong in walking—"pathological reactions." "To drink almost a fifth of sherry without getting drunk—that's terrible."

April 2

Here I am at six o'clock, watching the clock, my hands shaking, and afraid of what alcohol has done to me.

Last night at Wm.'s—Maurice Merleau-Ponty the visitor.

"If you want to stop shaking, you have got to stop drinking"—no driver's license for you.

Days of darkness, numbness, and boredom.

Losing tolerance—no longer able to get drunk—"brain tolerance and liver tolerance."

The idea of not drinking does not really bother me so much—or does it?

The fundamental PROBLEM IS NOT TO BE DEPRESSED.

Gruenthal: Now, in some ways it may be easier for you to stop drinking when you are depressed; you will use the same argument when you are manic—that you can't stop when you need enough sleep to get some work done.

Evening at Margaret Marshall's—the tremors increase, as predicted—terrifying nervousness and inability to listen to what was said to me by Stephen Spender.

Only two glasses of sherry before dinner and less whiskey.

Spender: Liked your poems very much; school of young poets in England who imitate you.

Mayberry's girl: Is that really Delmore Schwartz?

[Anthony] Tony Bower [art critic]: Liked your stories very much —book makes a unity.

Jack Delaney's.

Brood mare, fillies—studs, geldings, colts—associate moguls—limber up my tongue. W.B.: you've become a clown—you used to use a deadpan expression.

"Raw intelligence is not enough."

"How do you like Kipling?"

"I never drank it."

April 3

I broke a dish and E. was angry. But she said that she was sorry.

"I can't write," she said this morning. "All your shopping, parties, moods." "Does that really stop you?" "No."

"You really are feeling better," she said last night. "Your love-making has improved (immensely? a lot?). Maybe improve is not the right word—more relaxed."

This morning: "Now you've put me in the wrong again" (brief tears)—"You knew that I didn't want to."

Writing straight at 6:45, after two and a half glasses of sherry.

"The tremors may even increase, as you cut down," said Gruenthal. They started to be serious when I was living at 312 W. 12 St.—in Sept. 1947—when I paid for breakfast.

Spender was anxious about Mary [McCarthy]'s story. Auden had reproached him for his portrait of Isherwood. "But Isherwood approved of it." "You shouldn't have published it, anyway," said Auden.

"This is delusion—you know it is delusion—this is not reality"— at Margaret's, because of my difficulty in being interested in the party.

And it will come to an end. And all your powers will be restored.

"The danger is not entirely passed," said Dr. Gruenthal in Feb.

Each morning, a pickup after breakfast, after a feeling that I don't want to get up—but one must try to live.

Shirley Broughton [dancer and choreographer] in the park—she had seen Will the day before, after our editorial meeting.

"It is by hope that man lives and dies."

"Life begins on the other side of despair."

Despair in the evening street and on the bus—relaxation and peace of mind after three tablets, though I did not fall asleep until four o'clock.

Gruenthal: "Then you will have a choice"—as with all creative writers.

Margaret wanted me to write satirical pieces with illustrations by [William] Steig.

"Are you still writing poetry?" Jackson Mathews [critic and translator, editor at the Bollingen Foundation] asked me.

I read the Sunday *Times* with a little more interest than last week. And then a story by D. H. Lawrence: signs of life.

Undated

H. L[evin] must have encouraged F.O.M. to write his book on James because R.P.B. is writing one; thus he encouraged me to write about Wilson and Brooks, Wilson especially, because he thought I would attack him.

Very strange, said the Trillings, you have such dramatic events in Cambridge: Chiappe, Matthiessen.

Diana Trilling: "You look like Eleanor Clark. Have many people told you that?" Last time she wanted to know if I thought I looked like her (1943).

Discussion of [Clifton] Fadiman's praise of [Louis] Zukofsky.

Trilling is honest because he is aware of his motives—like all of us, he talks too much about them.

Party at M. Marshall's. Quarrel between Greenberg and Trilling about anti-Semitism—"You feel guilty."

April 4–9

Yesterday E. read *Dombey and Son* all day long—she felt that she was neglecting me—she said that she was not depressed but in a withdrawn state (after I made love to her).

When I walked to the office I was very nervous, but I improved as I had lunch with Philip. Nervous again while rejecting manuscripts, but less nervous walking home with Philip. Yesterday the beer instead of lifting me left me limp.

5th. Tues. Dwight's extreme nervousness and difficulty in talking —Edouard Roditi [poet]—but as I came back from Gruenthal I was suddenly hungry.

Mon. night. Pappas [restaurant], the movies, nervous and impatient and inattentive at *Day of Wrath.* Two bottles of beer before I went to sleep and one at twenty of 4.

6th. Anguish over the YMHA classes and the lecture on D. H. Lawrence, but it went off well enough. Most of a bottle of vermouth before I went to sleep.

7th. As if the depression were ending—news about Cal—walking with Philip—in the evening at Wm.'s.

8th. Again the feeling of swaying, although only three glasses of sherry and three quarts of beer last night.

Visit to Great Neck [where Elizabeth's parents lived]; depressed about the summer and E.'s indecision, as I have been for two weeks.

Impatient for the hour of meeting. But this last week has been better than the week before, although I still talk unclearly.

9th. Three times to the park in search of something interesting, the third time sitting with the Zolotows. Three glasses of sherry before dinner and three quarts of beer after dinner—and then two big shots (on Friday night, three).

"Maybe I'll want to marry you before Halloween," said Libby, and I fell asleep happy.

In the evening, after dinner, first I was trembling—but I did not attend to it much or let myself be troubled by it. Then for a time I was calm and interested enough to read last winter's issues of *P[artisan] R[eview]*.

April 10–16

Today, Sunday, E. tried to explain to me about her problems of independence, her fear of asserting—which, she says, would be ten times intensified by marriage. She said that I did not understand her feelings.

I felt panicky again at the idea of E.'s not marrying me.

Cocktails with Jane and Leslie and then a sad dinner in Chinatown (after coming too quickly during the afternoon and E.'s discussion of marriage).

"Will you leave me again?" "I doubt it very much."

Mon. The office, editorial meeting, trembling again. Sonnenfeld [M.D.], after walking impatiently in Central Park. E. miserable. We went and saw two poor pictures.

Tues. Looking at a loft—the park in the sun. Gruenthal. E. cheerful and talking about an apartment. "I'll probably be married to you by Sept. I switch about so much."

Weds. Another empty day, waiting at the office, tiredness.

Thurs. Hardly able to read *Time* and *The New Yorker*.

Fri. The office, Philip, walking downtown and then uptown to Sonnenfeld.

Sat. And again an empty day. "You'll just have to wait," said E. when she returned from the doctor's. Pressing myself to do ordinary tasks, two poor pictures from 5–8, and then too much to drink.

April 17–21

Slow, slow—visit to Joe Pollet, drawing him out after dinner; Sid Kline [journalist], wife, and children.

Mon. Caligula by Camus, three times around the park, dull editorial dinner. E. out at Great Neck overnight.

Hook: You don't look so alienated today.

Tues. Editorial meeting. Gr.: "You are better each week." Marriage a symbol to E., and a child even more.

Sonnenfeld: "Don't let it get you down—it may never come back."

Betty Pollet [Elizabeth's stepmother, who had separated from her father] for dinner, E. tipsy.

"I want to get married." "Aren't you being premature?"

At Gruenthal's—as if I were coming back to life.

Will and Wm. announce that they are going to Paris, Will during the summer and Wm. for two months in the fall.

Betty said that she had better not tell me something because E. would be displeased. She said that she was going to get married. E. asked if she got along with Richard [Crane, whom Betty subsequently married] and Betty said they got along very well.

Weds. Impatient for E.—who was tired and depressed—angry at dinner—too much to drink and in bed right after dinner, arguing with E. about getting married.

"Cross Purposes," by Albert Camus. Meyer called about getting the Fitzgerald books while we were in bed. Too much to drink. Hung over in the middle of the night.

Thurs. And in the morning. But the hangover may be a sign that I am coming to life. (In the evening we went to see Sylvester [Elizabeth's nine-year-old half-brother], who was sick. In the afternoon, Giants 2, Brooklyn 15.)

April 26–30

Tues. Gr., alert again for the third time. Two pictures with Libby. Hubbub about Will's essay.

Weds. Lecture on Proust.

Fri. Letter from Cal—dinner with Clem, Lillian Blumberg [psychologist]. Wm. & Edna—the country—Giants 10, Braves 9.

Sat. Long Valley, Mrs. Otis (seventy), Mountain Lake, a cottage for the summer. [As a rental deposit for a summer cottage, Delmore left a check, which was returned in the mail when the renter realized the party was Jewish.] E. angry in the morning because no one listened to her the night before.

May 1–4

A clouded-over Sunday in the country—too much to drink before dinner.

Mon. Nothing, nothing all day long, or I can't remember.

Tues. Visit to Meyer S.

Weds. Lecture on *Hamlet*, after going to Polo Grounds with Clem, Wm., and Eve.

May 8–13

Sun. Sherry resisted. The long walk to the Polo Grounds and then to 110 Street—old neighborhoods.

E.: "We might as well get married"—35½. (E. sorry about.)

Mon. She goes to Woodstock.

Tues. Gruenthal: Coming out of it, psychogenic factors. Dinner with Jane and Leslie.

Weds. Anguish and anxiety over lecture on V. Woolf—when I could hardly read or understand.

Thurs. Dexedrine. Peculiar feeling of well-being after lunch with Joe Pollet, well-being without my mind working. Tertia [Elizabeth's cat] sick.

Fri. Again feeling good without being able to respond to anything printed. John & Toni Pollet came to dinner. Editorial meeting. Dowling, lunch with Philip. Less nervousness, no more trouble with sense of balance when walking. Tidiness and pleasure in errands.

May 30

Notes for Alma Venus

Again—late at the gate and poised
With trembling hands I strike the harp I made
Roughly, shaking with hope in other years
—How many beliefs have passed away like clouds
And left an empty sky. Distant the stars
And doubted. They are empty too. Like the poems
I did not write.

Forced.

June 18

When half of life was lived, he was afraid
He sang no longer, silent for four years

The god of the wood under the grove of trees
The word of the will amid the weird of the world

(Going along the track which is the self)

Patience. Patience in the blue. Patience anew
Waiting watchfully, carefully, and patiently.

Goodbye, O God be with you. Do not die.
"Don't you write poetry anymore?" G.B., R. Warshow, W.P., Jackson Mathews.
Some perceptions involve the sacrifice of other perceptions.

June 19

"Saturated in literature."

When my grave is broken up again:
Some second guest to entertain

Tues. Dead-end call to Gr.

June 25

Yesterday—the first murmur of beginning again—after seven days of not drinking—more and more confidence.

At the movies on Tues. night, no nervousness or anxiety.

Gruenthal: Hypomanics, though happy, are too uncritical of themselves.

Gr.: Three reasons for not drinking: upset system; harder for sleeping pills to work; harder to resist overindulgence in manic period.

[On June 10, 1949 Delmore and Elizabeth married. Later that month they went to Woodstock to stay with her father and young half-brother Sylvester.]

June 28

The old-new love of the country returning, fragrances and lighted forms.

> The richness of being
> The green heavy shoulders of the mountain
> The earth dark beneath us
> The leaves lisping a memory of form (murrmory)

Joyce: style as reconciliation, exorcism.

June 29

The change of habits and of feelings.
No reading in bed, no effort to stay late, no desire *not* to sleep.
No nervousness and eagerness to drink after dinner.
No need to knock myself out.
No sharp conscious sense of rivalry—since late Jan. or Feb., but a return from time to time, as on Monday, when I was angry with E. because she did not want to make love—the old sequence of sulking, a sense of injury, a harking back, accusation, the aggressions of silence.

The old damned Adam not dead but retired comes up quickly, under any pressure—the new "Gestalt" (Gruenthal) falls off like a new hat poised at a perilous angle on the head of one who seldom wore hats. Thus, resentment of Wm. but corrected somewhat.

Some deep change; no longer afraid of what people will say or think; no longer so passionate to impress them; no longer angry at their misunderstandings; no longer hot to have them accept my myth (and statue?).

June 30

> Go away now, pretty girl,
> Flee his (quick) embraces

"It may be implausible (but it is true!) that God discusses with the angels (and with some of the selected dead) the private lives of the living.

"If you but think carefully of it, very many things (and many, even more, events) are implausible. Are improbable. And strange."

A new period is beginning. Has begun. Renunciation—concentration—silence and a new kind of assimilation.

We got married—it was like a dream. *Es war ein Traum.* Greenwich, Jersey City, the Holland Tube—two stations too far.

July 6

Hearken, Lords and Ladies gay,
Time which gives shall take away

Time has frightened every face
Time has darkened every heart

We are used by the depths inside us.

July 16

He tried to write. He tried to be a writer. Thus he might become
the myth he made for himself—in a reverie. He read books and they
excited him, and he tried to make his own kind of excitement.

It was as when, a schoolboy, he returned from a summer long in a
distant city and he tried to speak in a different accent, to show that he
was different than he had been, the ugly duckling become a swan. The
forced effort faded. In a few days, he stopped.

July 18

"And so one might get used to it. If there was something. But there
is nothing."

"Something will come to be done; journalism of some kind."

(This morning this is not believed. Energy and emotion.)

"Before he hardly knew it, he was thirty-five. In-cred-i-ble!"

July 23

E.: Delmore you know that J. is crazy. So you slept with her while
her husband was in the same house!

I went shaking to Smith to lecture on T.S.E., April 1945.

Meeting Wm., in 1939, at *Henry IV*, he confessed that the play
bored him. O'Donnell was there. B., beaten up by sailors, in love with
Timothy S., a submarine chorus girl.

All the times you made one of those hearts weep. But how about
the joys and lights? Which ones? And K. and G. especially and W.B.
also; and also Julie; and Eleanor Goff.

Detective story almost never wholly unites recognition and reversal. Swift's journal more poetic than his poems—how forms shut out or
bring in perceptions.

*[Delmore was worried about the reactions of his aunt Clara Colle
and her husband, Ben, to his book of stories,* The World Is a
Wedding.*]*

E. on Clara: "It depends on how she sees herself." Ben's comment. And hers: "You know—no one likes to see themselves in print—but after a few days I thought, All right, now we'll go down in history." "It's wonderful that Delmore kept coming to see us—if that's what he thought about us"—"That's all he said." C.C.—"smartest one of all," said E.

Gruenthal: "Daumier—whether you succeed or not is another question (Can't understand poetry in English)—but the caricature coexists with (very?) warm feelings."

Stop hurrying and stop jumping.

The leaves *winking* with light.

How I *basked* in wine and whiskey.

Describe the mountain (Overlook)—a great green lion.

E. on making bubbles in the water (a phobia liberated) and on the morning of our marriage while in bed: "Excuse me," "Pardon me."

Feeling that there is not enough lascivious striptease, foreplay, *Vorspiel.*

"Morally precise?"—I don't know what I meant.

How universal 'tis—even angered when Tertia slips through my caresses—helpless and sad, depression. As Philip said, "Why do you have to inject yourself into everything?" I was speaking of how wonderful it would be to be with impunity drunk (inebriated) all the time.

Those two boys—Hershey and Aaron—when they were told how love was made, conferred a long time. Discussed it, analyzed it, thought some about it, checked with previous theories and private observation, entertained it as an hypothesis and a wild rumor, projected it as a possible adventure (Aaron thought of his sister, squatting in the bushes) —and in the end decided it was quite implausible.

Improbable! It was not very likely!

Aaron said: If so, then my parents don't do that very often: not more than once a year.

Then they discussed the scars of appendicitis.

Sunday. Quarrel with E., shouting. Discussion for reconciliation. Manic-depressive excuse—cruel, self-satisfied.

July 26

Riding the Unconscionable Seas.

Sing for your Supper / Breakfast and sleep / Sing for your wife and life.

Loss of Meaning in the Morning.

(Can't remember what I dreamed and dreamed, mixing all the characters.)

He got used to everything, including the outhouse: squeamish. Including the hall toilet at Bedford St.: bashful (body unworthy).

When he had a toothache, he became a brat (teething infant). Or anyway, adolescence showed up again.

> There I was at the New York Public Liberty
> Faced by those fabulous lions—virginity!

La Roche[foucauld]: If there were no novels, no one would fall in love.

Sheffer [Henry Maurice Sheffer, philosopher] banished [from Harvard] to the limits of the continental United States (Seattle) returned by writing *neither-nor*. Use as type of obsessive dedicated mind.

How Richard [Blackmur] got married, the license; "not the way it should be between a man and a woman"; his mother's name his wife's name; just the same visited his mother without taking his wife for seven years every Sunday.

Use double romance (E[lizabeth] & E[leanor]) as horn of plenty, possibility; realm of authors in love: looking 'em over in the park at Atlantic City (Phoenix).

To Will (unsent, May '48): I've crossed the Rubicon—she has yet her Waterloo.

From the window, age eight: "I'm going to have a hundred children when I get married."

Tolstoy: Bias and choice and value at the root.

July 28

Dream: I pulled it up (as if it were a ball) but much embarrassed. Her father, round, drunken-looking, sullen, told me in an affable way that he had done the same thing many a time himself.

News from Eleventh St. oracle: E[lizabeth] Hardwick to marry Cal Lowell. Merrill Moore [Boston psychiatrist] responsible. Reported by Jean [Stafford], whom Cal called. (Why did Cal leave Jean, then? Why didn't E. marry Tate?) Mrs. Lowell, like a Jewish mother, says it's all because Cal didn't stay at home.

Last night Joyce—*F*[*innegans*] *W*[*ake*] imitation—Cyclops scene delightful. Joyce for richness, a return.

Just a week ago—bored and so sleepy I went to town to get *Life*, *Time*, *New Yorker*, and detective stories.

Excited by Jingle Bells moment in Wilder as by birthday in *Our Town*.

Many books brought from N.Y. and office, manic sign, manic relaxation while driving.

I am relaxed, utterly relaxed, I am so relaxed that if I were any more relaxed I would have to be put in a coffin. (Exercise in Joycean expansion.)

Ref. the book of R.H. [Ruth Herschberger, poet and author of *Adam's Rib*, a feminist work], feminist metaphysician. Was not the clitoris, ladies and malefactors, quite as overwhelming a little thing in the modern epoch (I mean, of course, the half-done twentieth century) as Cleopatra's nose? Had it been, one remarked, an inch longer (even 1/4 or 1/16 of an inch) history would have taken a different course. But how much more so in so many lives the unknown little clitoris! (Measures of Ruth Herschberger, 430 Hudson.)

August 3–4

God created the world, like this like that, like throwing a pair of dice. Because he was bored. There was nothing else to do.

And they showed him the redwood trees and he said: "O.K.!"

And he looked at the Grand Canyon and remarked: "Exaggeration!"

And he took a good look at Eve in her birthday suit and exclaimed: "That's snazzy: one could become extremely preoccupied."

He was extremely enthusiastic.

And the newborn gunman looked about at the red white and blue world, spoke candidly, sincerely: "You've quite a stash here, boss! Yes, sir, this is some dump! I don't get it, but I must admit it's quite a joint. And we'll have a marvelous time!"

Tutti: "Yes, we'll have a marvelous time!"

(God as a heckler and a rhapsodist.)

Library trustees' meeting [the Woodstock Library invited Delmore to participate]. Reedy polite genteel Gentile voices. From Strindberg to cookbooks in one sentence. There's a new biography of Strindberg. Their sour-cream section is very good—if anybody cares?

This book is very dry. This book is very cool.

Not the ignorant—but the half-educated.

Problem of an elite within a democracy & a democracy recognizing the need for an elite.

To S[ylvester] P[ollet]: "You go to N.Y. for me and I'll fire your cap pistol for you."

Sunday night, driving to New York after dark.

E.: "I won't speak to you for two days after you come back. Because you are going away."

Afraid of the dark and the lights—hurrying, measuring, watching the line—8:35–12:30—the American experience.

Dream of getting blue tablet to prevent cancer from Cal (cancer = insanity) and E. Hardwick showing what I could have had if I wanted it—necking on the floor.

I was the one who was sick, not he.

In a later dream, J. P[ollet] confessed to an old man (sixty-two).

Dream last night of waiting for the right papers (the right directions) at a hotel with E.—a tall bellboy stared at her, in shorts, and I was angry and thrust him through the door.

Waking with a painful erection which would not go down.

Weds., Aug. 3. Mild deadness. Sleep until 11:30—to the office, sending back poems. Wm. wanted me to come in next week: "Are you going to leave me alone?" and wanted to talk of his story.

Back to Woodstock in less than three hrs., 4:40–7:30—swimming. An evening wasted on Ellery Queen, waiting for E.—and no fun, too quick.

Depressed before sleep—35–36 again—and hungry. But pleased at drunkenness really passed by. A season for hope. Two new things: married and sober.

The Creation. It is tricky. It is touching. And it is a mystery, and inexhaustible, fascinating, irrational.

One nose—easy; one hand—simple; two eyes—maybe (seems a purpose); but five fingers and five toes? Just five! why not four or six? seven or nine? These unexpecteds are delightful.

And then there is the gentle ooze and sticky gush that takes the acid and soothes the valley where love arises, rides, and writhes.

The rule of dears.

G.B.S.: An arch-especial soul like Purcell.

August 5

Hurdy-gurdy / Squeezing of the Heart. (Looking in the Flows for Flowers) (Under the Floors Behind Doors.)

Book of the Black Princes.

George L. made his wife bathe in his own dirtied bathwater: it was his way of life. He asked all of his friends if he should marry her.

Robert's girl was offended when it turned out that he had been prepared to go to bed with her with the proper precautions.

"Woof," said Kitty, "use a rubber. Now you're dirty. Don't like it, even if I'm French. You read too many books. You're too smart."

"So easy with some," said Klonsky, "that you jump at all of them: wrong."

"Women have to be aroused," said Philip.

August 10

Jingling and Enjoying It.

His tongue was in his cheek as he laughed up his sleeve—Mephisto had come again!—(devil out of hell!).

The customer entered the restaurant and seated himself.

The waiter came to the table and asked politely: "Your order, sir?"

The weary way-worn patron, leaning his face on his arm, said wanly: "I'm so hungry, I could eat a horse!"

The waiter departed primly and properly. He returned with a horse, an old nag who looked suspiciously at the customer, who looked suspiciously at him.

Wild laughter. Uproarious excitement.

Confusion. Panic.

Chaos.

Describe the horse's face: naïve? wide-eyed?

The Doggerel That Sings Within
Your face is a farce
Your eyes they are worse
Your body is bad
Your mind it is mad

The crow caw-cawed
The catbird ow'ed
The katydid seesawed
And the cow mooed

"Tell me, pretty maiden,
Are there any more at home like you?"

Philip, New Year's 1938: "You're just a baby."

Do what you will, this world's a friction (For love is friction / or love is just friction).

"Sh! You are Shem! You are mad!"

Philip to E.H.: "You're not that important to me."

Back-yard B'klyn, 1931 (excited): Enjoy yourselves, children, said Mama.

What do you like? she asked. I like to come (evasion).

August 11

Waking-Up Wild Wives and Wines.

As if it would not last. Quarrels and letter to Clara unwritten— not to be written if . . .

Cut off from experience more and more. No clubs, no games. And no close friends. And what do you know about anyone but yourself? And not even your self.

But it's time to die: to be middle-aged and so to die. Though this is called the prime of life. Hope is an incurable invalid and entertains death as a lyric.

Will in 1948 said what Bert Spira [college friend at the University of Wisconsin] said, in 1931 or 1932: "How about considering me?"

Will: "I have a feeling that if I were at my deathbed, you would talk of Elizabeth."

I might have a child age [of] Sylvester [who was ten]. (Toby or not Toby.) Goodbye, my son (Toby to be named). You're almost undone.

And to give up is good, in a way, because then you say: I might as well do my work, working for fun.

"What a human being you turned out to be!" "Cold, indifferent, mean, and nasty—at best you don't [know] what you're doing most of the time."

"What a silly question: I read it (the detective story) because I was bored and it was a way of passing the time."

"It's time I felt lonely and isolated and bored some of the time." No playmate—Jane—no one to talk to. Wanted to show off her new husband.

Hearken to the legions and the lesions of experience.

Wilderness Wanderings.

Balderdash! Tom, my foot. My heart has been dented!

And he thought for years that if only. If a princess. He would sleep and wake fresh and strong.

Is this true? a little—a half—somewhat.

It's getting late and late. What makes you think so?

Rah, rah. Let's break through to reality—rawlity—reeltree.

Bickering over trivials. Recoiling vanities, hurt feelings from words & vanitears.

How are you? they asked him. I don't know, he answered. What do you mean, you don't know? I mean, I am ignorant. And bewildered. And changing from moment to moment.

August 13

Wm. did not want his mother to know that G. and I were divorced. Why? she can go through life without knowing. No explanation. "How is your charming delightful dear dear wife?"

Wilson: Mary [McCarthy] as an OGPU agent. Fred [Dupee] as a cuckolder.

"He's slightly gaga. But don't get into a tizzy. Most people are. They see what is not there. They say what is not true, although they think it is"—e.g., E.P. on G. getting married as my motive; or Will's idea of me shirking work & avoiding him.

Harry Stack Sullivan would say to his interns: "Remember while you work under me, keep one thing in mind: In the present state of society, the patient is right and you are wrong."

Used by [Cyril] Connolly—Beddoes and Swinburne, their declines and decays.

Chekhov (where?): We are guilty merely because we are alive.

The world is in a state of hopelessness, says Connolly (in *Horizon*, June 1949 issue [in his regular "Comment" as editor]).

"Regardless of class distinctions, Death carries off all (like an express train?)," says Cocteau, echoing Horace.

In *Crime & Punishment* Dostoevsky submitted the absolute will of the ego to reality testing.

"The gates of his pride"—J. J[oyce]. In *F[innegans]* *W[ake]* a new kind of development of associations from step to step—not merely the thing-man parallelism.

It is difficult not only to use four-letter words but awkward and self-conscious [*sic*] to use the medical synonyms. Vagina is an ugly word.

Elizabeth (20 Ellery St., May 1944, a Sunday, after Wannings' party) tried to relieve whatever uneasiness she might have made for me: "All you have to say is that I have talent. My friends agree on that."

At 10, she read book after book below the deck as for two weeks the ship passed through the Panama Canal. The deck steward kissed her. She told her mother, who told her not to tell Rolph [Scarlett, Elizabeth's stepfather].

At eighteen she refused to join a sorority. They all had sent her letters which she did not answer.

She never decided to be a writer, she just wrote naturally as an emotional outlet, and writing became gradually the justification for her mode of existence. How most important turns are taken.

Yesterday I did not understand the stories by C[aroline] Gordon or [Dennis] Donahoe, although I responded to some of the images. But Sinclair Lewis novel gripped the mind because of its subject matter. As when I told R.P.B. about Clem's liking his new poems—it's always some common denominator (sympathy) in the subject matter which makes another see what the author is trying to do.

One month more in the country—at most—no more Dexedrine. Chitchat before the holocaust.

How scared he [Delmore] was upon the roller coaster (1929): "I thought this one was going to pass out on me!"

She had been bypassed by the boy [Delmore] who invited her. And she was mad. And she showed it, sullen. And wouldn't sit on his lap. And the colored chauffeur smiled faintly, politely looking ahead as at something else. And he was much offended. He did not understand at all. He was sickly personal in all his understandings.

Nothing coherent comes—no plan is entelechizing—germinating like a geranium in a jar. And yet more responsive after lunch than in the morning, perhaps the aftermath of sleeping tablets.

Breen was ashamed that his mother could not read English. I tried to be friendly with her and show her a newspaper story about a man insane who thought he was God. And ashamed of so much else. Spoke in a curt voice, curt and clipped because shy and self-conscious.

Grace A. was very shy, but eager to cultivate experience. Pretty, small-featured, doll-like beautiful.

Her father was a minister and she wished to be bohemian and to know artists and the intelligentsia and the literati and the liberated. But had to work for the telephone company.

Told Gertrude it was no good to be bohemian. Lent us her apartment.

Told G. one night to sleep with all the young men one could before they were killed in the next world war.

Married a fat gross sympathetic stage designer who looked as if his weight would crush her.

Ethel Merman on television, according to *Time*: "I am George Washington—um—cannot tell a lie—um, I cut down the Cherokee."

"Let us call Pocohontas by her maiden, Indian name, Alka-Seltzer." (Strip-poker Pocohontas.)

Strindberg's wife: Caviar wouldn't melt in her mouth.

New Yorker's view of writing after reading Kenneth Roberts: I thought that perhaps I had been crowding my destiny.

Plato or one of his characters said that philosophy is the study of death.

At Deanie's the girl asked the counterboy if one could put chili sauce on mustard. She was seasoning her hamburger. "You can put anything on anything, if you want to," he explained, if one can call it an explanation.

Able to read novels again. Progress. No lift after dinner. Three weeks since I felt on the edge of being manic again. During pregnancy, manic-depressive women are not depressed (endogenously, i.e.); and they get rid of stomach ulcers. The diminution—almost disappearance —of the chief phobia-feeling.

"I assume that you want this marriage to work as much as I do." "Don't do that. Wait until I'm excited and (then I won't notice it)."

How is Gertrude?

He thought of time, of the passing of time, of the years he had lived—as one might hear the news of an incurable disease.

Time! incurable! inexhaustible damnation!

Conscious villainy is really rare, and this is one of the errors of paranoia, and paranoid systems, such as orthodox Marxism.

August 14

> Here a little child I stand
> Heaving up my either hand.
> Cold as paddocks though they be
> Here I hold them up to thee
> Hoping thy benison will fall
> On our meat and on us all.
> Amen.

J. J[oyce]: poetry as predication: heaving, cold paddocks (what are paddocks?).

The effect on William and on Edna of Philip [Rahv]'s book. He had not mentioned it to her. When I did, he had to explain to her that "Laughlin was putting out a small book of P.'s essays." Then she looked grim: identification. She wanted to be an author when she was a girl.

The same grim look as Mary Handlin, hearing of a new book, after telling me that *WW* [*The World Is a Wedding*] would be appreciated in time to come.

The novel will exist as long as the daydream: or some version of fiction for the sake of vicarious consciousness.

Pisgah: the mountain from which Moses looked at the Promised Land.

August 15

Last night, E.: Big hands and big feet, the peasant; N[ew] E[ngland] conscience; hysterical; schoolgirl novel reader, devout about heroes and heroines. Feminist. Maternal feeling toward sister; psychologist; bashful adolescent eager to speak up in class.

"I don't recognize the description."

"You would not recognize an X-ray of your brain."

(And who, for that matter, would identify the inside of his belly or bowels?)

In this dream our life, dim and unconvincing.

A cool and sunny day, waning summer.

I'll bet my last cent. You can bet your bottom dollar.

He has bats in the belfry (another synonym).

> Like wild bulls in a china shop, Liz dear
> Are my awkward hands of love
> But but
> Where you are, Love is, Liz dear

The Poem of the Creation is the essential sensual plum.

Finnegans Wake was ruining his spelling. "As modern as tomorrow afternoon."

Nothing doing from 10 to 5 spite of the dextrous Dexedrine. Only a flare for twenty pps. of *F. Wake*.

Why yesterday and not today? Was it June, or was it two failures betwixt the withness of her lambs?

Postponing the letter to Clara again.

Last night I dreamed of Gertrude, of a book called D.S.'s miscellany, of Jean G[arrigue], and of having a lesson to learn for a class.

> Like jewel-y drops among the leaves
> The late light glitters, wet white pearls

Standing naked after swimming, naked surface, unclothed flesh gleaming, smooth and glowing.

Sylvester wants [to] know: Are you going swimming? Are you going later?

I tell him to ask E. She comes from the cabin to ask if I asked that —surprised? annoyed? And I get annoyed with him: his friends have just departed and he is intent on new pleasures and companions. E. goes to play cards with him, telling me to tell him when I go swimming. (E. accursed—the explanation of sullenness-ness.)

Story of a man who tries to make sex funny: but really funny! belly-shaking! hilarious! ridiculous! (Tittering, giggling, smiling, grinning, smirking, cackling, haw-haw-ing.)

Dream of . . . a doctor in pajamas in a drugstore; and of marrying the daughter of Wallace Stevens (about whom I talked yesterday morning as an example of the chances talent is touched by). The second day I was remiss, I did not go to the right place at the right time.

Most of the day in the entrancings of *Finnegans Wake*.

Nervous-depressed-excited after dinner coming back from Woodstock (because I had done no beginning, after Sunday's unexpected coming-forth-coming-up).

Undated

"You don't do anything (ever) for me," he said [Sylvester to his father]. "Why should I do anything for you?"

"Doesn't he drive to town to get your friends?" [Delmore] "And doesn't he wash your clothes for you?"

"Him?"

"Yep: I saw it with my own eyes."

"He was only washing his own clothes—not mine," said Sylvester, grinning.

I was angry and did not want to take him and Nancy [Kline, a playmate] to town—meanness— and so with the second ice cream the night before.

Chewing over the cud of between-us all evening.

"I did not know that you get angry when you're upset—and not because you don't like someone."

August 16

S. Daedalus is neither Joyce himself nor Joyce as he saw himself but Joyce as he wished to be regarded, trying to admit what others might or must see.

"Charles Haas (Swann)—shy because he was a Jew." He belonged to that society of witty and useless idlers—a luxury of society of those days—who dined and gossiped at the Jockey Club or the Duchesse de Tremoilles'. "Marcel can never be more than a man-about-town."

Dream in which I said goodbye to Bazelon, going to Bard. And heard arguments and laughter about a Holy Cross in the starry sky.

Jealousy, "the green-eyed lobster," J. J[oyce]—*FW*.

"Adam [Moncure, husband of Elizabeth's sister Barbara] wants to belong to the upper crust" (the cake, the icing). Comes from a Southern family, family military. Thinks his father quit too soon, retired; yet one side of him admires the retirement.

What the Woodstock paper in 1914 said about the man who had just had his hundreth birthday: "He doesn't look a day over eighty."

Ezra Pound, "bundle of unpredictable electricity."

Yeats of Joyce: Never have I encountered so much pretension with so little to show for it.

Joyce of Yeats (1901): It is equally unsafe to say of Yeats that he has or has not genius.

> I am an apricot
> or an orange
> (not a peach)

Joyce's lyric from Jonson:

> I was not wearier where I lay
> By frozen Tithon's side, tonight,
> Than I am willing now to stay
> And be a part of your delight;
> But I am urged by the day,
> Against my will, to bid you come away.

Two wars have exhausted the century, leaving it empty.
Say what you will, you will say what you are.
Character is fate, language confession.

Sylvester is my brother-in-law. Tertia is my cat-in-law. And Libby is a dumbbell some of too much of the time. [I] would not cut the bread at breakfast. Yet wanted me to drive her to her former mother-in-law's doorstep [former stepmother, now remarried, Betty Crane]. Why didn't think of that before? The good-night kiss—always afraid of being disturbed. Fond of the weak and the foolish.

> I wish I had a pony or a trot
> To read the obscure Latin of your heart

ENERGY! PLEASURE! HAPPINESS!
Epithets for magnificence of movements.

August 18

Sour with sorrow, pricken by pride.

A play which begins with a hero who enters a city street, looks about him, and exclaims (at each phase of the city's life he sees performed before him): "*So this is Love.*" So then Canada, Australia, Iceland: "So this is *Love.*"

Ten thousand dollars for a few of your thoughts.

Black spit rots in the wild wet green grass. TNT, TNT—blow up the wicked world.

It was just perfectly priceless, thrilling, tingling.

He hurried like greased lightning! He came in the flash of Pan.

> Sour sorrows, rainy rotten days
> Reading Roman ancient plays
> Seeking for true gods to praise
>
> Until you can parody
> To pure perfection
> You will not abide cheerfully
> Your long election
>
> A demimondaine in a high hotel
> Wanted an apple from William Tell
>
> Freewheeling, free-willing
> Sunning & sinning
> Sitting & spying
> As sneaky as a snake

J. J[oyce]—unable to see easily, he tried best to see clearly—afraid of the thunder, he made it break in his last book.

Anger like a regression, mistreatment. To have a quarrel, cruel and compulsive, repulsive ranting epithets.

August 19

Breen: He was cruel but not a fool. He could not read. He liked comfort. His appetites were strong. He was full of pride.

The story of an institution: The name of this school is Appearance. A. Pierre Ransom and Reality. Dean Brick and President Conundrum, two minor characters.

Holy Wet-Lock, the tenderloin passions *passim.*

"Swimming is my chief abstraction"; "An enigma is an animal"; "A horse divided against itself cannot stand"; "The slightly ugly part of the city"; "It's a nifty setup," said Gloria Rockwood.

Coming in out of the shadow, near the barn, the sun is warming; as if it were autumn, as if summer had by now—so soon—fallen, all full, the green burned out and turned brown—

As the clouds are making abstract white sculptures—blouse and shirt, breast and thigh and shoulder and archipelago—in the bright blue sky.

Nature has no vices but has quakes, snakes, volcanoes, tornadoes, plagues, tigers, and thunderstorms—that kill a man by accident. Who can deny it?

Thus accident—let's not speak of it, it's a dirty word, I mean, a dirty idea (like death, in a way). It's low, it's rude, it's vulgar. It's an ontological insult.

Chance, however, is all right: it is the whiskey of a game.

How evil had to be restored to the world—the talmudic story.

"As Rabbi Akiba says in the Talmud," said Morley, "I have not read the Talmud." (The Berrymans were delighted.)

Connect me with Connecticut, suburb of *The New Republic.*

Delight me down in Delaware, where the Du Ponts bloom.

I told Robert Phelps [novelist and editor], when hard-pressed by his questions, that I was delighted to be able to keep the typewriter going; I had a very hard time writing.

"I'm glad to hear that," he said carelessly, thinking doubtless of himself.

"Everything happens to me," said R.S. (1934?) [Rose Schwartz], hearing that her sister had cancer.

"Everything happens to Delmore," said W. B[arrett].

I feel as stupid (dumb-numb) as a pair of old shoes.

"He knows as much as your foot!"

Stumble Bum, Has Been, Grifter and Grafter and Chiseler and (to be) a Klonsky, do the Great K., Klonskyesque or Klonskyian.

O what an Oedipus.

"I collect dirty pictures like some collect mothers"—W.B.

A plague artist.

Sermon on Mt. Venus, *mons veneris.*

The Art of Denunciation Taught Him by His Mother.

If only to say—I know what I want to do—and I am doing it— and I am as sure (as sure as one can be, in such things) that it is good, but even if it is not, it is what I want to and ought to be doing and that's enough—so said the cyclists in the six-day bike race, and the professional mourners, dental surgeons, elevator boys, morticians and gardeners, regents' examiners, streetcar conductors, and the president of Boy Scout Troop Number Minus Ten.

"Nasturtiums to you, sir. I beg your parsnips!"

W. P[hillips]: Some people like you better when you're slightly depressed.

Edna [Phillips]: Then you disappeared; call us up next time you're in town.

Will: Did you finally get married?

E.'s mother, a good woman, objected to cynicism and to the being critical-clinical (like a doctor of the heart) because it did not work, because a belief in goodness did work. But when it does not work?

Sylvester's plans for me: a caddy at the country club during the summer, a hawker at Madison Square Garden during the year. "You'll make good money—you'll have a lot of fun—you'll be out of doors."

Mrs. Potter's description of the [Depression]—father, uncle: "And then we lived in the country and I liked the country better than the city, so that was nice, too."

A milk-fed painter and a ground-glass playwright.

[Lillian] Hellman: When you buy a new suit, you feel better.

Truman: When you dine well, you enjoy a sense of well-being.

A.Q.: When a girl feels downhearted and depressed, her spirits are revived by the purchase of a new hat.

[Albert] Erskine: The quickest way is to have a quick one.

Death is the dancer-answer forever.

August 20

Skimmed *The Man Who Came to Dinner*—how unspeakably amusing is an unspeakable bounder and egotist. *Green Pastures*—God is cute and folksy. *Ah Wilderness*—youth as nostalgically touching and good for a slow affectionate smile. *Dead End* and *The Little Foxes*—attacks on the status quo as (1) degrading; (2) avaricious and calculating and utterly destructive. *Life with Father*—God and father as comic and ridiculous, the family life as a child's cute pantomime. *Petrified Forest*—helplessness of intellectuals, doom of gangster individualists, and deadly crisis of civilization.

Life with Father, Boy Meets Girl, Our Town (you'd better be satisfied with this life & our town).

[Harry] Levin's Joyce—weak characterization. Stephen more real than Bloom & *Dubliners* better than all of *FW*. *FW*—Sin & Fall & Death & Guilt necessary for Resurrection.

Saroyan, *The Time of Your Life*—life is really wonderful if you try to believe it is. [Arthur] Kober, *Having Wonderful Time*—Jews as quaint and cute, regional hillbillyism. C. B. Luce, *The Women*—woman/wife must protect her man from other women. Ben Hecht, *Front Page*—glamour of being a reporter.

Deep discussion of being a writer and telling a story with Sylvester, who was not very interested. As previous deep discussion of the importance and responsibility of being an uncle—so also not interested.

Eight pages of notes—euphoria from 11 until—at its height—at dinnertime.

Deep discussion of how an artist should be an artist with J.P.

Letter to [Sidney] Hook about job and how I always will suffer from a frustrated desire to be a metaphysician.

Glossy sunlight, cool shininess all over.

Esoteric Pictures, Ltd. Present!

"I may surprise you," said Will, "and write a musical comedy in five years."

The Ghostly Lover, E[lizabeth] Hardwick: Her idea of heaven is to be goosed by one of those tap-tapping chimpanzees.

A man afraid that his pajamas will keep him awake.

One could see thoughts crossing his face like caravans of camels lurching slowly across the seemingly endless Sahara.

Shirley Mae France announces she will swim English Channel without wearing anything. A photograph accompanies the story: her father, coach, and bathing suit.

Give the football a good kick in the behind, Hedda, said Jymes.

Peggy [Erskine, on the *Partisan Review* staff] sat upstairs in the office all day eating thick sandwiches of various kinds. (Can't you lick your own envelopes?)

Banjo: How is the mattress business? She just stop to change girdles and check her oils.

Detective story as religious—evil punished, innocence and goodness redeemed. (Do religious people read detective stories? They don't have to because God will punish the wicked.) The detective as the avenging angel. The conclusion is perfect justice in this life.

But new genre of detective as tough guy? (Christ sits with publicans & sinners & is one.) Police or institutional justice is mistaken, foolish, and fails. Morality motif—need for strong blacks and whites in world of increasing ambiguity, ambivalence, dimness, and uncertainty.

Marxists, too, do not need whodunits because society itself acts as Providence. Detective stories in Russia? Marxist-minded detectives?

First cult of scientist against evil; second cult of intellectual Holmes against evil.

August 21

Suppose a divorced couple—like Klonsky (shoes unwet) and J. P[ollet]—through habit or because one issue has long since been a dead one, they fall into bed, despite that all else is wrong and wronged. The gradual depreciation in one way of sex—and the blowing up of it in other ways.

Love is as slippery as a greased pigskin.

Love is as quick and passing as lightning.

The play is about Love as difficult, hard to deal with, define, recognize, control, understand, preserve, adjust to, relate oneself to, incorporate in one's life.

"Cream-colored shades were drawn in the reception room."

Kober: He has a very fine vocabulary. His sister is a librarian.

H[*erald*]-T[*ribune*] editorial announces that neither prayer nor prohibition helps alcoholism or tuberculosis. Secularity.

Yesterday's letter to Hook—manic inaccuracies.

E. H[ardwick]: A narrow band of moonlight lay / (Like an extra blanket) at the foot of her bed.

E. [Pollet]'s insight, which may be wrong (her *freshness* & sincerity & genuineness often make her sound accurate), that I start quarrels as a way of getting attention.

J.P. surprised that an art critic (M.S.) wanted to talk to me; and surprised that I might write a humorous column. Read E.'s book, not mine, though people (e.g., Sidney Kline) have spoken of it.

Cold-blooded f——: "Don't want to make love—but just f—— for the fun of it." "Have you an erection?" Shift from Saturday's: "Why don't you speak to me? Are you angry at me?"—"I'm not much of anything right now." (After hesitation.) Fri.: "Why don't you get someone else?" "I don't want someone else." —"I'm going to try my best, but we can't go on like this with you bawling me out all the time."

F U N—the real nexus which makes profession, vocation, and dedication. Schapiro loves note making—example of the truly sublimated man.

At 8 or 9, a bully DeVoli (an orphan) hit me when [he] could. I remembered this, but not that a man once got off a Fifth Ave. bus to stop him. It was once, but *not* never, as emotion presumably supposed.

August 22

[*In the following Delmore recalls his first encounter with Barbara Pollet, Elizabeth's sister.*]

"He has a hangover," said E. to B., charming & naïve in her introduction.

She wanted B. to play the piano.

I stood in the cold john—10 above—and I was angry and Barbara was angry because she had been kept waiting [out on the street].

"Oh, you're one of those people who like to analectrilize everything," said B., because she was afraid and angry.

"Barbara!" said Phyllis [Elizabeth], reproachfully correcting her antagonistic tone.

Night before at the Rahvs'—Mary (Peggy Hines) did not want to come for a drink. Philip slapped me on the shoulder as if to console me, also being pleased. "You should have fucked her," said Philip, vindictively destructively in Sept. '48. —"What do you get if you fuck

Mary Peggy?" said Wm. argumentatively-wise. "That's not what you want to be in life—a conversationalist."

By that kind of reasoning, every value could & is in the end undermined. Why try to be a great writer? The trouble is hardly rewarded if in the unlikelihood that you succeed & the stronger, stranger, unlikely improbability that you know & are convinced of it & most of all that everyone else & many more fellows & girls also know . . . Or passing as beautiful as briefly cold & new snow unsullied—THE WHITENESS OF FAME AND CERTAINTY (KNOWLEDGE).

Mary [McCarthy]'s view of me "as the only 'Jewish man' who does not try to make girls by means of his ideas." How did she know? She had observed you, said Will. She was pleased. It was an attack on Philip, Clem especially.

"An irresistible sexual object," said Arthur Koestler. I agree, said Mary, smirking. I wish I was Delmore, said Bowden. "Destruction of perspective" in *WW* (*The World Is a Wedding*)—paranoid—grammatical errors—preachy.

E. was not disturbed, not even when Nathalie [Rahv] spoke of being unconvinced of my account. M. & B. had told E.H., who told Philip—who told Wm. & Clem—who told me.

P[hilip] R[ahv] observed to Wm.: "We're not criticizing you, Delmore," they said as I tried to defend myself—half falsely—that Bowden must have known what occurred. "If a girl does not want a pass made at her, she does not act like that." E. no longer insecure about fidelity, but no dinner—only lunch—with Chickie.

Edna thought E.G. better than E.P. because spunky? (stand up to me) or worldly—well-dressed & poised? Cp. with Wm.'s: Every time Delmore has an affair, he marries the girl—i.e., exists in a state of marriage.

Peggy Phyllis—Twentieth-Century Love and Death opera.

Wm.'s wisdom, Clem's foolishness. Anne Sterling (another member of the comparison chorus) as shallow—as devoted. Gr[uenthal]'s wonder—You're artist, you're confused—why then feel so guilty about your affairs—why afraid to tell Chickie, if she is not in love with you? Because I think others are sensitive exactly in the way that I am.

Will's abstract idea of knowledge as mere encyclopedic inclusiveness—Cologne—a Roman colony (errors about Joyce, Valéry, Rimbaud, E.P. & letter to Woodstock).

The girls reveal what their husbands conceal.

Peggy and other Martyred Modern Gulls & [word?] Barbered Bums.

The girls are told by the boys their best friends' secrets. Will, Roslyn, D.S. & G.B.S., Will & Julie.

The gels tell the boos about the previous bums in bed: "They al-

ways think that this is the last time they are going to sleep with anyone." (Philip's shallow cynicism—as with Kafka book rivals.) It is
really the deep need for intimacy & revelation & shutting others away
in the conversational distance: "Here is my mind, here is my heart"—
"I tell you all & everything, true love" (true-bed-door). As shown in
F.'s Bennington girl—"First, we fuck; then we talk," she insisted. "But I
wanted to go to sleep," said F., "I was very tired. I was worn out. I was
absolutely exhausted." (Rival fell asleep for half an hour.)

Philip & Nathalie got married because they had to go to Chicago
—epigrammatic misstatement.

Will got married to get some work done—wrong again. Julie was
tight-lipped & on the edge (shore) of tears.

William's wisdom: Oedipal feelings; Trilling's primal feelings;
[Paul] Goodman's self-dramatization; Dwight's ego-bravado. (Mortimer Spike?) (Julie's—Will's journals.)

Good example of reality testing: Levin quoting the no. of copies
of book on T.S.E. Harvard Coop could sell. He wanted to see if I were
going to write it.

August 23

A solemn vow not to quarrel—but be devoted.

How my feeling changes and my seeming phobia and face. Coldness no go, as I thought with A.Q.—too sensitive, insecure.

E. at 7, 8 told her sister she must choose between having her and
loving her mother—rivalry. Emily told the weeping younger sister that
she did not have to choose.

Peggy's strong visual malice. Fred as [if] his face made by plastic
surgery. Philip "encrusted in lard." D.S.—exotic—delighted by Nathalie
like a head of lettuce or cabbage & M[ary] Wickware [*Partisan Review* staff] like an owl. Wm. fawning, "not socially acceptable."

[Louis] MacNeice: It is a strange thing to discover that people
love you (are lovable) and strange, too, that they are clever, perceptive, skillful, and gifted in ways one hardly imagined—one generalizes
too quickly on the large areas of stupidity, helplessness, and blindness
—the rest is there under the dress.

Don't you feel the coldness to Jews? Nov. 1935.

Academic-Ruling Class Meeting at the university (Mortimer
Spike's Social Rise).

There is a tacit exchange of rare commodities and it is increasing
(there are dangers, no doubt, but they must be risked). Those who
have studied have knowledge to give (dangerous at the borders, for
the students may pass over), rare delicate flowers of knowledge (por-
traits and other paintings, French and sonatas), and for these posses-
sions (given and yet retained) they are welcomed to the teas and

cocktails of the ruling class. The payment is that they feel good to know such well-mannered people. Mama would be proud were she not in the cold chilly grave. Papa brags to his associates at the garage.

At Groton there are lectures on Marx. And at Vassar Freud is furnished as a recipe for brides (highest divorce rate on Eastern Seaboard).

This August fades in lush and lagging foliage.

Zolotow story. Horror of Charlotte's parents and reconciliation. How she got a library book to tell her about all. His recognition—she is very young. Proud that she can say fuck—M[oss] Hart would not believe it. How her beautiful sister's husband was ruined in Czechoslovakia. How C.Z. simpers, tiptoes, is sweet & defends her husband's sensitivity like a tigress. Afraid of New Year's party—"You like it buck naked, big boy?"

"Must be strong homosexual element in me," said M. Why? (Thou —homo!—says Shaun to Shem.)

Self-centeredness—he wanted to read books when she wanted to be affectionate. She loved the country and he could not bear to be away from Broadway. Now changed. Why? A devoted father.

His mother liked Charlotte at first, thinking she could dominate her.

He took me [Delmore] too uncritically in youth, he told psychiatrist (wrong). Distortion of "We are both successful, you as an avant-garde writer, me as a commercial writer"—neither is true, and if true, neither would be satisfied.

Very funny when at ease, and a seesaw thinker, Dewey v. Stalin, capitalism or Communism, and so in literature, Stein & Joyce as one. Hook told M. we were his favorite students.

Love of theater—not of films—sniffing at his mustache when taking thought. Lean to cadaverous, goggle-eyed behind glasses, now a little puffy.

Barbara lost her virginity on Sat. night; was hysterical when Adam was four hrs. late the next day. He had been drinking (because he felt so extremely guilty)—(& this was true love forever)—(mountain, river, fountain, river).

(Body and soul, rising and falling, in the twentieth century.)

Bohemia. In the provincial capital and sad used city, Jack, whose wife had been raped at a Dartmouth ski & snow festival & who talked with a Tenth Ave. accent after Princeton, declared when drunk as he took off his shirt that he was sorry he had not been a woman so that he could have married Philip.

R.P.B. was disgusted.

I don't like that, said Tessa [Horton], as the man at the dance slowly reached his hand higher & higher up her leg in back.

I don't like you, she cried, as Philip [Horton] drove drunken recklessly up Beacon Hill.

Let's see a map, said Tessa to the waiter.

Tessa & her sister watched from the window as a man from the Mass. General Hospital took away their father's overgrown heart in a little black bag.

Mrs. Gilbert [Tessa's mother] put Kotex in the girls' lunchboxes. Leapt into husband's grave. Guzzled at the pictures. Denounced Brown & Eliot as one & the same: Catholics.

In this bed, said Wallace, I slept with my wife [Rose] for the first time. Rose rebounded from a drunkard & took it out on him, said R.P.B. N O T rectal, anal, she corrected him, when he was on tear. (Dostoevsky quarrel between John B[erryman] & him about [whether] Raskolnikov was an intellectual. Wallace did not want him to be.)

Why Mary Handlin told me Wallace did not like me. It was after I had taken the S[aturday] E[vening] P[ost] ad & showed E.'s picture and said that that was the girl he said was a horse—"an overgrown horse of a girl?"

He used psychoanalysis as a means of insulting people—undressing them—blowing up the living room with *je m'en fichism* sex. "You've been riding herd on me for years," he told his mother. "You made me wear a Russian blouse." His two beautiful sisters & his need for neatness obsessed him almost as much as his desire to be an author.

August 24

Dream in which Eliot lectured in Washington (some official place) & read a poem I had written about him (ending with the rhyme P I E). (My book about him—my poems?) I expected no comment, but he gave me back papers, saying: "You ought to read my correspondence with Witter Bynner [American poet] published by the Gotham Book Mart." I took this as a reproof or judgment (for what I had said about him) but E.—in N.Y.—found passages to show that it was not. I was pleased & relieved. But this dream woke me up.

Then a dream in which [William] Empson lectured on Tate's poetry, as T. & C[aroline Gordon Tate] listened & I was annoyed & Empson found profundities but said he hesitated to interpret it like *F[innegans] W[ake]*. He had also found a passage in *Romeo & Juliet* to prove (as he tries to for *Measure for Measure*) that some character is really Jewish (by the way he talks). This made me think or remember that he was Jewish—a memory doubtless of how Cal's father had asked if he were a Jew because he talked so much.

Soon after I was seated at a Faculty Club with someone I feel guilty about avoiding—Bernard De Voto (yesterday I wondered about *ex voto*)—and another plump academic man who had read the *Time* review of WW [*The World Is a Wedding*], bought the book and found it unreadable—obscure. I told him I tried to be as direct & simple as possible. I was disturbed. There were girls all over, in Cambridge—and an English girl.

Reading *F*[*innegans*] *W*[*ake*] must satisfy some deep need—beyond love of language in rhythm—since I go on, month after month, hour by hour.

Less drawn to E. yesterday—less fluent—but again, inspiration in the late afternoon (wasted in town)—[. . .] phobia by the tent by the quarry—it pulses there, too!—it is nothing right after—conditioned by obsessions in the mother-grandmother half of the family life.

Beginning to learn to listen—as to ask questions & to proffer favors —Sylvester's resentment.

August 25

Wm. on Solow [a writer for *Fortune* magazine] (unique as one who slept with both E. & M., too)—hearing about marriage customs in primitive tribes, how at the wedding the tribal medicine man deflowers the bride (so that she will not all life long resent her husband as her castrater): "So primitive tribes also have their Herbert Solows."

J[ean] G[arrigue]: "How sensual you are" (& Elena, looking at Nela's portrait: "How sensual she is").

In July 1935 on a Sunday afternoon, on Seventh Avenue, a girl goosed the man with her as they walked along—it was as if they had been in bed before coming on the street. He brushed her off.

And two men goosing a girl in July 1935 on Horatio St. And one girl goosing another on Hudson St., coming from Jai Alai [restaurant] at noon. And one girl goosing another on the steps outside Washington Square College. And the drunken girl who goosed the cab driver outside the Latin Quarter.

The officer who goosed his girl on Mass. Ave. "I hate that," said Marge of Scandinavia. Are you a Greek? said Bob & the girl at the Swing Club. Oh, a rear admiral! said the girls in the Latin Quarter chorus. And Gloria Rockwood in the de Musset play; and the servant girl in *The Cherry Orchard*; Ruth Hussey in *The Philadelphia Story* ("I think I've been pinched"); "Who put the sand in my Vaseline?" at the Latin Quarter bar; Ina Claire's "That's the base of my spine to all but my most intimate friends"; Jean Campbell & Tessa Gilbert, Rhoda Klonsky (always tense), (Isaac—why did you?), and Julie Antioch; the couple in the back yard on Seventeenth St. in Oct. 1931; Nathalie in Italy; "I think it's disgusting," said Jean Harlow. E. did not know what the word meant, when we dined with Theodore Roethke, nor did Joan H.; Nela was surprised; "Something happened to him," said Helen, "when we stood in line at the pictures & he leaned against me." "Then he buggered her," said Andy Dupee to Ellen Adler or Ellen to Andy. "Two guys & one girl," said William, speaking of a sandwich, "and the girl yelled holy murder. Illness of Wm., Mary Wickware, Fred (three months before end of his analysis). "Never that as yet," Toschka [Rosetta Reitz, owner with her husband of the Four Seasons Bookshop]; "I don't believe it," said Chickie. And the English girl who said that she did not care for rape. And Charlotte, the Radcliffe French girl, who giggled at the idea; "Don't vulgarize me," said the lady novelist; normal except for fixation, said Phyllis Roehm; the answer to everything, said Joyce & what he said to Budgen: "You are sitting on your answer" (moon pictures).

Wisps of the libido, filtering up into consciousness.

Mary [McCarthy]: That's the part of my anatomy I take the least pride in.

August 26

The put-put purring of the pleased cat (Miss Tertia P. Schwartz —no feminist, she; no Lucy Stoner, she!), seated in E.'s lap after being fully well fed.

Ever the sense of power at the wheel of the car, beginning to drive. And the egoist in the eyeball looks (though no one is near) for admiring faces to be turned toward him, as if driving were an extraordinary feat.

"I'll sneak up some night & slit your throat," Sylvester announced to his father.

"You'll just be cutting off your allowance," I told him judiciously.

All laughed. Except Sylvester.

"You're a card," said E.

"I do my best," I replied. (King of Hearts, Jack of Clubs.) Thinking: A deck of cards? a card factory. That's not funny. But maybe it might be used as a remark which tried to be funny?

"Have you thought any more of your duties as an uncle, Sylvester?" I inquired.

But this morning I told him to jump in the lake, angry because he wanted us to go upstairs before we had finished breakfast.

"Have you digested your coffee yet?" he kept asking, taking over my phrase.

The story of our marriage (Stamford & Jersey City, the late judge) —it was a dream, truly a dream. Not at all like the storybooks & Hollywood say. (Detail by detail makes the reality.) Ruth H[erschberger]: "Eat your string beans, Delmore."

How easily everything flows today, despite delay & a trip to Saugerties & the distractions of powers awakened. After a quickly patched quarrel. And all relaxed.

Two efforts to call P[*artisan*] R[*eview*]—uneasiness about the conflict between staying here and working or going away to N.Y. to see that no real changes are made without me. E. says that then they will be able to say I was away & that Philip's letter was a complaint. Putting off the writing of a letter to him & to William—staying here during trouble is bound to cause resentment? is bound to?—clichés flow naturally.

My Associates & I. My New Brother-in-law (aged ten) and I. (He thinks I am a high-school principal in hiding.)

Manic again—talking too much & interrupting at dinner—J.P. surprised & a little irritated because I spoke of Buddhism & then of the age at which Sophocles wrote *Oedipus Rex* (ninety). He came back with the old age of Rembrandt, Ruysdael (& Vermeer)?—"Ruysdael the greatest landscape painter that ever lived."

He was irritated, thought I, because Sylvester had gone to dinner with his mother. She drove him back, and drove away.

What people really like is not to be dazzled by conversation (this after a time only makes them voluble, too) but to be made to feel important—to feel that you are really interested in them very much. (Use for effect of Peggy on women.) The point, like most points, can be exaggerated: Wilde, Trotsky, Kafka—other examples of personal magnetism, and actors, teachers: but the ever danger of prima-donna-ism.

Literal acceptance of J.'s affirmation: WAKE O Yes Yes! Joyce, compare with Swift on view of man, on eating (Bloom).

Span of Life increases (*Time*) two more years—another paragraph for endless (in principle) Almanac story.

E. has made me a novelist by making me think not only of her "point of view," but of the effect of what I say on her & how difficult it is to deceive, even when I am deceiving myself. E. says I over-motivate the cat's behavior. She sleeps all night in the next [room], comes at dawn to sleep at my left calf so that she will know when I have gotten up for breakfast. How invariably she distinguishes between the farmhouse & the pig house [guest house], between J., S., E., and myself. How she climbed to my knee & beckoned gently with her paw (when I was eating) to get herself some meat.

Manic again—toward nightfall (five Dexedrine, 3 + 2)—almost incoherent at Riley's tonight, as at the liquor store last night.

"Teach me to stare and not to stare." To give, to sympathize, to control, to sit still.

Now that I am manic I ought to reread *The New Yorkers* I found dull in June & July & even three weeks ago. And read books to which I am usually deaf. In Feb. [Isaac] Babel ("Benja Krik the Gangster") was meaningless. Last October he was unbearably exciting, and two weeks ago he was interesting & delightful.

Self-subjected to F[*innegans*] W[*ake*], as, in 1942–3, to Cocteau.
And before then to Auden, Winters, Eliot, Yeats. (Dos Passos, Chekhov,
and Faulkner & Mann in short spurts—& short stories.) How different
if Joyce & not Eliot from 1930 on! or not different? or impossible?

"A new gestalt is forming," said Gruenthal, during my last manic
phase.

How clever & wise for him to say that to see my mother would
not only hurt me (for then the same old vicious circle would operate
emotionally) *but also would hurt her*: the touchstone to motives. But
perhaps I ought to go with E. to see—for the sake of avoiding future
remorse.

> *[Delmore and I did go that fall to visit his mother, for though I
> had met the rest of the family on Washington Heights, I had not
> met her.]*

Now, and at last, and after twenty-nine years, learning (as this
page shows compared with the last one) how helpful it is, in a small
way, to keep one's pencils sharpened (Pound's line in "Homage to
Sextus Propertius").

This is better than conversation with another—at least some of the
time—and it is made possible by not drinking. Firmness of handwriting
now as compared with May, April (when I felt troubled about my
balance while walking), Nov. (in Princeton, where R.P.B. told me that
alcohol adheres to the cells of the brain & my hand shook so much
when I wrote a check at the liquor store).

Next reform: to smoke only pipes, no milk & sugar in coffee, and
to get up at eight o'clock. And to join a gym. And to take vitamins, buy
new clothes, answer mail, and work better at *PR* with W.B.

To try to write direct parodies & paraphrases of lyrics for the sake
of getting back to the medium of verse.

W[ill] B[arrett] said last fall: You think I've been seeing a lot of
William.

Simple scientific demonstration of cause & effect relationship: when
I stopped drinking too much milk with my coffee (and then sticking
my pipe in my mouth), I stopped feeling like throwing up. When I
wore my hat in the wet, I stopped having sinus headaches.

But drinking is more complicated; and in addition to whatever are
the psy[chological] causes, the country air, swimming, and the rest of
being here may have been very effective.

No wonder that T.S.E. can never bear to reread his own prose (by
implication the same is not true of his poetry & this may mean I ought
to be able to make something of it).

Sophisticated simplicity—P[hilip] R[ahv]: "Maybe we ought to
give Malraux the prize just because we admire him": astonishment.
[The *Partisan Review* award was given to George Orwell.]

August 27

Breakfast. E. did not want me to open the jam because I did not know how. Annoyed that I brought a spoon & fork as well as a knife. Did not want me to eat the jam.

"Angry at me?" "No, but you're rude, and once you were polite." Not interested in the Aristotle–postage stamps story.

Two detective stories all evening waiting for Jane & Leslie, and then nothing to say before going to sleep—tired & sick?—meanwhile, I grew stultified & frustrated on pp. 173 et seq. of *F[innegans] W[ake]* after much ease & excitement. And went to bed very nervous & depressed (Dex. too late?—4:30) & could not sleep until 3—awake at 9:30, erect.

Gruenthal expected [to be] the victim of my rage (Will had told him that I tear people to pieces) & was surprised not to be & to be tendered authority.

Peggy—distinguish between the kinds & forms (disguises, masks, and mechanisms) of love as identification.

It was a very silk & saraband time.

A story about people who are composing a dictionary, and one about people who are composing an encyclopedia.

August 29

Hegel: "The tree of life is greener than the tree of thought." (All theory is gray?)

Calligraphy is destiny?—Susie Greene.

The act of writing is an act of guilt. (Dreams about T.S.E. (*HCE*).)

How Wm. must have been offended by Mary [McCarthy]'s story (& hidden it), for it aims at his most vulnerable point—his self-consciousness in certain social circles. He is described as an usher.

"Gold Morning" is mine!—not J.J.'s, though suggested by *FW* "*gudn modning.*"

> Gold morning, dear Libby, let us go
> To the moon pictures to light & to delight us
> with the shades—
> And to forget, forgive & our scissor selves
> cutting all shows
> Toby (or isn't Toby?)—waits in the wings

August 31

The Darkness & Demon Pictures Hanging in Him.

Dream of Kenneth dead suddenly of pneumonia (coming down from Cambridge, I found out about it—he had been in California with his wife). Josephine [first cousin of Delmore] was somewhere on the scene—later she was my sister—I kept waking to tell myself that my dream was untrue—then I was at an earlier moment of time with Kenneth & Josephine my sister, knowing he was soon to die & undressing myself to bathe (saying that I had never been undressed before them before). I was afraid. I talked to R.S., who was present most of the time. In the background were his wife & children. In the second, later scene, K. was young, small, and resentful. I did not want to use something he had used (a typewriter) though I thought my fear foolish.

Dream of reading Cal Lowell's first book, a library copy, with a title I had never heard.

J.P. [Joseph Pollet] used anchor, not roots, speaking repeatedly of stability. His becoming an artist (husband, father, advertising): "I started drawing a man washing his hands instead of writing ad copy. My teacher—impressive man with simple ideas—told me to draw an arm so that it would be real on paper." Rubens makes a body sparkle, Hopper does not. ("Fifty aspects—pick 1-2-3 and make them do something to each other.") Rubens is like a party at which one falls in love.

The Motive Is the Truth (Honesty Is Often Dishonest)

E.—cantaloupe morning & then, asked about her writing, brushed me off with a return question ("a painful subject") and was angry about the stove fire at night. When I questioned her, she first denied being irritated & then said she had only been "slightly irritated"— realized it was different conditioning (she was trying as she always does to be rational & forebearing). She said had been drawn in on herself all day. Asked about what? she repeated what she had said. And when I said she had become more explicitly irritable, she cited the use of one clean glass after another in N.Y., "which irritates me very much"; I told her of Philip & Nathalie [Rahv], the glasses often and "You don't love me." Nathalie is right, I said, to which E. replied by telling me how I was irritated with the way she threw her clothes about in N.Y. ("I used to irritate my mother & sister in the same way"). "I don't want to discuss it now. I'm tired & I want to go to sleep—it's a painful subject." "Still your throat?" Shifting between resentment & appeasement. "We'll notice these things less as time passes."

At 5:30 the door shut, I went to look, she was in the back room & she seemed to pull her dress down (perhaps only because she thought I might become amorous before dinner). Suspicion & resentment & self-inculpation as an effort at resolution.

Dreiser, *An American Tragedy*; *Abbess of Castro* & other stories by Stendhal; & then *FW*—after "Ivy Day in the Committee Room" & leafing thru *Dubliners* & *Awake & Sing* by Odets.

Style as an obstacle to identification & as unnecessary (to judge by Dreiser).

E. as systematically confused about her feelings—"You don't understand" that "I don't know what my feelings are."

E. so often denies what to me seem her emotions, as, when Toni & John [Pollet] were here, her attentions: "I'll make you some coffee" & bringing up Coca-cola (though we had quarreled the day before).

E. kind—Don't get wet in the rain—your cold—moved by maternity—gurgling delighted as in June 1946? and during visit of uncle & aunt.

Tertia has four kittens (at breakfast time will not begin until E. comes to pig house with her). Sylvester keeps score, comes running over from pig house across the meadow to announce each new kitten. I announce that I ought to be handing out cigars. E. peeks into closet with the flash to see what color is each new kitten. Tertia is pleased and proud indeed.

Various versions of vestal virgins—the virginity of the last half inch.

Description of a tight ball game & then a tennis match as part of new poetic (like a battle—back & forth).

A five-year-old identifies the pleasures of defecation & having a child.

September 1

Lady Libby! Hark to me
When that I would talk to thee
How foreign words half mispronounced
Concealed the joy which in me
                    bounced

(Pounced, flounced, bounced, announced, counts, founts, sounds.)
My tendency is tenderness, I'm naturally affectionate.

Gold morning, Libby. Tonight shall we go
To the moon pictures to delight in the
                    beautiful creamy shades
         Forget, and forget—to live—the scissor self
—We must because Toby and Emily
                    brother & sister
                    wait in the wings

[In discussions about naming a child, the Schwartzes favored Toby and Emily.]

September 2

I am a snapper-up of unconsidered trifles—a maker of mountains from molehills—and A Modest Megalomaniac.

Sylvester bet me that he would catch a fish. He did. But he threw it back.

"You owe me a penny," he demanded.

"You owe Tertia a fish"—D.S.

September 3

Costume party. (I did not feel like going.)

A fat lady showed me her poems. Asks me why she has not seen me if I've been here all summer. Delius: "Why is Karl Shapiro not here?"

An art dealer wanted to know if I was an abstract painter. He said he was looking for abstract painters. Delius wanted to know if I felt more Russian, Jewish, or American?

A man came as a nun & so did a woman. They were man & wife.

Heywood Broun, Jr., auctioned off paintings—struggled with his father, the ghost & great man of the twenties.

"Love Is Hate," "War Is Piece"—two signs; "I don't know what it means—it's just something I thought of."

A cave man, a forest nymph.

"No masks—not like Europe—more primitive than Berlin, Paris, Vienna," said Delius.

Someone wanted to give me a party hat. I refused—after three drinks, I will know what kind of a hat I want.

"Why are you not in costume?"

"I am impersonating myself. Some of these people want to hide from their selves, but I want to find myself."

J. P[ollet] introduced me to pretty girls—tongue-tied, I could not talk.

"Mrs. Bruce is very nice," says Delius. "She has a little girl, or two, and used to work for *Reader's Digest*."

People stared from behind a chicken-wire fence; a middle-aged balding Italian clung to a very pretty blond girl.

One girl had two painted hands clutching her buttocks, and two girls had red hearts curving over them. A girl dressed as a devil jiggled her tail, as if the tail were thrust into her as love or joy.

But little sex [?], little frenetic drinking, no rebellion (accepted) or desperation or fighting. One girl was very drunk: she resented girls who were not.

September 8

He rose up in the gold morning
Looking for a smattering of life
And found by the windowlight . . .

"It is neck or nothing" (no alternative), German proverb.

In the dictionaries, ancient & modern, how many columns are devoted to the synonyms of guilt?

If I speak, she is not interested. She is reading. But she does not try to speak about what she is reading. "You don't try to fit my mood."

Pirandello: "Truth is all right—up to a certain point." Lived with his wife, insane for seventeen years, because too poor to keep her in a private sanitarium & unwilling to commit her to a state institution.

J.P. said that I was not yet housebroken. E. told me. I said I think too [much]. Her remark came when I did not turn off the faucet. You don't think too much. It's automatic, like flushing the toilet (pulling the chain). But it is not automatic.

E. is now critical, more & more—as last night, when she was irritated because I had not told her it was getting later & later. While I for my part waited for her to finish her book as I had had to wait most of the other summer nights.

September 26

"Freude! Freude!"
Crying aloud the German *joy*
Summoning from the dark earth
   fertile with the dead
The Master of Joy, the Doctor of Light

Oft-told Tales from the Vienna Woods.

The Family Elopement and Romance.

The question which the children ask: "Is God an anti-Semite?" (visitors to Dachau).

Moses was not a Jew. He was an Egyptian bastard.

Wit is a Broadway hit.

Dostoevsky's father was the Czar. Leonardo's mama was Mona.

My father and my mother made me stubborn.

Consciousness is preferable (or the draining of the Zuider Zee).

Venus and genius.

The hangovers all over Athens / After the first performance / Of *Oedipus Rex.*

The body is a sofa / the first of sofas / a famous sofa.

   The monarch of the flesh
   Lounged in its sofa
   Tired & fallen
   The rivers of the blood
     and the heart
   Slowed and drifting
   [. . .]

He was a king
of emotion
He sailed that famous
ocean!

October 20

Nelly belly Botticelli.

October 27

Gide speaks on the radio (and Jean Cocteau), rewrites *Phèdre* as a ballet for blond Greta Garbo.

Ode to Princess Elizabeth
How is Philip? how is he?
Do all the swains adore him?

December 16

Idea of a story, short novel, about a literary review; part of academic novel?

Parties of Fred & Margaret [Marshall]. Trilling & Will present.

Philip on Mary [Wickware] as stupid—ex[ample]: the distributor she did not see as no good; he would have, he said.

Will's flutter in Mary's presence—he gave her the cigarette he had taken from Philip.

Will & official acceptance by the Rockefeller—"More than you," he said, "you're getting the best girl of all."

Philip & Will talking at the window & seeming to stop when I came in. Philip's habit of speaking to Will rather than to me when the three of us are in our offices.

Will's kindness about Aristotle's *Metaphysics*: "I never expected to get it back"—too many books at once—but he wanted the inscribed page.

Philip as fundamentally unscrupulous. Last summer: "Where is Delmore?" To Wm.: There is nothing for you to do. I am not stopping anyone from writing articles. Philip's pipeline—a girl, who is his friend & Rice's [Philip Blair Rice, professor, author, and associate editor of the *Kenyon Review*]. Will's piece rejected. His attitude to Elizabeth Hardwick.

Sherry at Hudson St. with Ruth, Jane, and Leslie.

Pleasaunce with E.

Skimming selections of Santayana & Faulkner.

A day or evening each week to see other people, as editors always have. T.S.E.?

Anthology Fees
1. Rodman "100 Poems"   7.50
2. U of Hawaii mimeo-   1.25
   graphed syllabus

   _____

   8.75

December 18

Maurice called Elizabeth *Gertrude.*
"He lies like an eyewitness."
Joyce to Gogarty: It's a miracle to believe in anything.
Gogarty: Yeats hated hatred—loved love?
Yeats: "The pouncing & surprising word—" to G.

December 19–20

Dream that in Cambridge Philip invited Levin to the house and I did not like it and I was ashamed of being in bed. (Transfer of shame about office-going? Levin's student Nellhaus has just sent a piece about Schlovsky, the Russian formalist critic.)

Philip is at bottom intuitive—i.e., he has no real education, being habitually autodidactic.

Why do people like Dwight, dislike Will, though he is much more intelligent, witty, sensible, etc.? Is it because in the writing of one they face a scorn & contempt, & showing-off coxcomb, but in Dwight a real friendliness & curiosity about people & good-heartedness? Though both are very egotistical, Will is less self-assertive, at least in these groupings.

Philip is always watching and imitating—he violates the intuitions out of which he ought to write.

Dr[eam] of something about a fun house (as in current *PR* story, "The Peeler" [by Flannery O'Connor, *December* 1949]) visited with F. O. Matthiessen and Theodore Spencer. They went to a peep show, I did not & there was a girl with the three of us who was a student. Meanwhile, the difference of our visits had been reported by the student—the student, now I remember, was Katy Carver! [important member of the *Partisan Review* staff with the title of editorial assistant]. And [there were] manuscripts, or something of the sort, returned from T. S. Eliot. And it was as if the peep show was involved in the rejection of the manuscripts—peep show, peeping Tom, and gossip in book on T.S.E.—hence rejection and guilt. Katy identified with Phyllis?

Last night—E. napping and then drooping all evening. The doctor told her that she was afraid to have a child.

Find common denominator if there is any (my own indifference & lack of initiative) in Margaret's, Fred's, and Clem's no invitations (the Zolotows call up all the time—I was a significant other in his self-system). The Nabokovs are different, for I acted as if I did want to back out.

"Anxiety—it is somewhat like a blow on the head."

Maurras: *Ontologie serait peut-être le vrai nom car la Poesie porte surtout vers les racines de la connaissance de l'Être.*

Alcoholism & inadequate emotional security during childhood.

December 30

How Sigmund Koch [N.Y.U. College friend and brother of the poet Adrienne Koch] like Philip marveled at my misty-eyed absent-mindedness & devious maneuvers.

The Ancient Congress: all the, or many, myths appear: Oedipus, Theseus, Orpheus, Daedalus, Jason, Perseus.

A Book of Private Combinations: Confucius, *Bhagavad Gita*, Koran; Psalms, NT, Isaiah, à Kempis, Hebrew prayer book, Talmud, *Book of Common Prayer.*

Auerbach: Biblical story reaches to history; Homer to myth.

Rubenesque—I'd rather sleep with a horse—a pig.

> Young ladies of the lower classes
> Often have more responsive masses
> But the social relation
> Of a deb's excitation
> Is a thrill which little surpasses

Undated

Parody—For Polly
Libby had an errand boy
   His name was Delmore Schwartz
And everywhere that Libby went
   He followed her in shorts

M. Wickware as an owl, or as a head of lettuce; J.B. as old stony face; Wm. as a little rabbi.

Luciano said that he was in New Jersey, shooting peasants.

Klonsky's "personal Jew" scapegoat.

Dream of Faulkner as red-headed and living in the Village.

"It was not the nurse's fault" (coming too early).

[Martin Ellery—like M.—is a name Delmore sometimes used for characters based on himself. One recalls that he lived on Ellery Street in Cambridge.]

After dinner, Martin Ellery paced about his study in a state of nervous excitement, sometimes sad, however, that he had lived so long without knowing this obvious truth and sad, too, that it should amaze him.

It seemed to Ellery that if he were more interested in a child's comments than in his own experience of storytelling, then he must be more interested in other human beings than in himself. This remarkable discovery, which most people are fortunate enough to learn in infancy, made Ellery happy and afraid, afraid of the other obvious truths he might not know and which also might delight him.

"To think that I have lived so long so stupidly," he said to himself.

"Are you talking to yourself again?" asked Ruth Ellery, his wife, as she entered from the kitchen, where she had been annoying herself by washing the dishes.

"Yes," he replied. "I am getting to be afraid to talk to my friends. They know too much. They see through me."

"Your face is an open secret, anyway," said Ruth. "It's no use dissembling or pretending. You can't fool anyone."

"At least I can fool myself," said Martin speculatively and hopefully.

"You can't do that either," his wife insisted with stubbornness, "not anymore, anyway. You know yourself too well."

"No, I don't," Martin declared, "I have just made a very strange discovery, strange at least to me, which suggests that I am still very much in the dark about myself. And although I may make more strange discoveries, then again I may not."

1950

January 1

Party horns and party hats and drunken (rowdy-bawdy) cries. The essences in New Year's revelries, hilarities.

Italian husband killed by wife he had given a $5,000 mink coat to.

Happy half century. The next fifty years can't be any worse than the last fifty years.

Meyer's story of Australian tribes: children at puberty taken out, told there is no God, and warned that if they tell the women & the children, their heads will be chopped off!

January 2

[The following entries are drafts of poems under the general title "Dear Pope."]

DP: Love As Misrepresented

Father, how love is feared and difficult
Because we suffer from a sense of guilt!
Because it is accursed at first, misunderstood
Or made a squeamish thing like maidenhood
To think of making love is—shameful and no good
And love is made a point of ought or should,
Should not, ought not—vulgar, obscene, a sin
Hidden, forbidden.
      This is where I come in
—Not that the freedom of the animal
Is possible or is desirable
And that ceaseless promiscuity,
Does not destroy love's possibility.
[. . .]

DP

O Spiritual Father, holy Pope
I speak of matters not within my scope
As if I spoke of mothers or the hope
Of an eternal life beyond the grave
But certainly you know, when poets rave
It is because the law of averages
Becomes their frenzied hope, the marriages
Which are their poems, their notes. Their metaphors
Are pearls & swine, or four-leaf clovers
One in a hundred thousand genuine
Far less than gamblers can we hope to win
The deathless unforgettable epigram
The bard, alas! must often play the ham!
(Yeats was a ham so much so long he was
At last a ham no more, but in the stars
Like the Greek heroes risen and redeemed
His poses pushed where ambition seemed
Ridiculous as monkeys reading books
He took more chances than most heroes take)
[...]
He played the roulette wheel, he played the stars
He made himself all that he never was!
His peers more gifted maybe (like a wife
Adorable at twenty, but in middle life
Heavy and gray) destroyed themselves because
They sought to take Olympus by main force
Dowson & Wilde! Johnson—all the rest
Beings as marvelous as a new child
Lacked the one gift of Yeats—which was the best
The stamina merely to live, to survive
Whatever shame, rejection, or love denied
To make life's dream become unbearable
He faced his foolishness. This made him powerful!
[...]

DP: Freud

Father, let us consider stubborn Sigmund Freud
Mistake me not! and do not be annoyed
By the great name & fame his doctrines won
Truly his lights have freshened everyone
And his denials must be understood

As narrow efforts to increase the good
If he denied that God existed, he
For the mere sake of vain consistency
Denied that Shakespeare wrote the famous play
In which the Danish Prince was brought to bay.
[. . .]

DP: Freud
He suffered the little child to come to him
He succored those made nervous, dull, and dim
By fear, by guilt, by foolish prohibition
Or a disgusted mother's inhibition!
Master of Joy! Doctor of Love! though stern
And stiff, yet warm enough to burn
The early-morning fire in the house
Where blue-faced winter brings no Santa Claus!

Master of Arts! Doctor of Hearts! and true
To what James named the country of the blue!

January 6

A Reading List for the Pontiff.

An Index Unexpurgatorious (?).

The Karamazov Bros. (father & four sons) by Fyodor Dostoevsky (already mentioned, once or twice).

How to Win Friends & Influence People by Dale Carnegie. (Not that you don't know how!) Sold sensational no. of copies (vicious, depraved, insincere, and, in a sense, an ontological insult).

King Lear by W. Shakespeare (sometimes thought of as King Shakespeare), full of sexual & emotional disgust & distrust (*contemptus mundi*).

The Great Gatsby by F. Scott Fitzgerald (already mentioned, *passim*). (Latest views of the affair of Faust & Helen. The eternal feminine. The Virgin or the Lady as Eternal Object of Admiration, Aspiration, and Adoration (hopeless) on Long Island in 1922.)

World Almanac (cite different & strange facts and facts of injustice).

Encyclopaedia Britannica. Essays on War Guilt (both wrong), Ireland, Parnell (?)—ontological richnesses & difficulties.

Lives of the Caesars—Suetonius. (What happens when anyone has absolute power—Nero, Caligula.)

Book of Common Prayer (differences in attitude from—).

Education of Henry Adams (suicide of his wife). Special American list? James's *The Golden Bowl, The Ambassadors. Moby Dick.*

Duchess of Malfi.
Anna Karenina.
Pennant Race of 1936 (description of a baseball game).

Which is a bigger liar? Broyard or Klonsky?

> I am the boy
> What can enjoy
> Invisibility
>
> Dexedrine, you have undone
> Certain poets, including Auden.
> > No matter
> > He's a great showman,
> > > said the GIs
>
> Vicar of Christ, are you vicarious
> A good mixer, blond and gregarious?
> Forgive the question (and I do not grin)
> But may I know if you ever drank gin?

(Hilarious, carious, various, nefarious; guests, ghosts, gusts, geese.)
Story of Philip, Abel, myself. He ought to go with Gentile girl
(echoing Marge's The best thing is to be fucked by a Jew). Rather
write a poem than make love.

> There was a young lady named Frances
> Who engaged in amazing romances
> > She stood on the bed
> > Like a horse on a sled
> And the bedsprings rattled in Kansas

The startling or extreme metaphor.

January 7

> DP: *Vicariousness,*
> *a Major Industry in North America*
> [...]
> Pleasures and plums! luxury, laughter, various
> Revenges, anger, power, gunmen, actions
> The ego fears and loves, gets gratification—
> When Cagney squeezed a grapefruit in the face
> Of the blonde who merely tried to embrace
> Or touch him warmly at the breakfast table,
> After all night's affections! How the fable
> Made all the menfolk roar! and ladies, too!

—The instances are many, old and new
Ingenious as magicians and as various
As a Cook's Tour! And to provide vicarious
Epics is now a major industry,
A well-paid up-to-date necessity
A habit like tobacco advertised
[. . .]

[. . .]
There are no substitutes for anything
Though each thing substitutes for everything
And every fancy parodies each actual thing
The bird cannot devour the painted fruit
The bird cannot be mimicked by the flute
The picture cannot hang on painted nails
Imagination's mimic always fails!
Nothing but genuine reality
Can give a soupçon of satiety!
This is, I think, an endless principle
For metaphysics! and the nervous will!

Vicariousness proves Reality. A.: What have you against vicarious experience? Only what is wrong with masturbation.

January 8

"Jesus died for you," said the mother of the boy.
"I never asked him," the boy pointed out petulantly.
Meet *Moby Dick*. Meet Walter Whitman. Meet Henry James.

DP

Meet Gatsby, Pope, or have you met him, striving
Like Faust, in some ambitious and conniving
Young man who strives upon the rising stairs
Glittering like ice in January's airs
[. . .]

An international cocktail bitch. Carmen, Delilah, Mary McCarthy.

Pacelli Meet Moby Dick

Flower and fauna are quite various
Vivid and tricky, warm and precarious
The seas are soft, the bushes thick, nature's scene
Is sloppy, sprawling, awkward, and obscene.
Thus Moby Dick is very dangerous
To him who pins his hopes on consciousness
Being is full of mountains like the Alps . . .

In Switzerland the landscape is declamatory.
Every day is Sunday. And authors have no holidays.

> Oh, Pope, I am a friendly fellow, you
> —How could it be otherwise—are friendly, too!
> My attitudes have been misunderstood
> If seen as aught but a wish for what is good
> [...]
>
> *Domine Deus!* Everything is on fire
> Leaping and falling in the flames of desire!

January 9

Track race of American capitalism.
Suburbs haunted by desperation and sorrow.
Agee: The world well lost for loving description & bohemian Xtiase [?] piety. Agee: New Jersey—one of the most incredible mileages of the world.
Hair-raising. Thinginess: a toad touched in the dark garden.

> *Dear Pope*
> The yachts, the yachts! says slanging Doctor Bill
> And shows how pleasure boats are beautiful
> It is much like that Thomist argument
> Evil is necessary, evil is meant
> To be the cobblestones for carriages
> [...]
> —The yachts, he says, "brilliance of cloudless days,
> And groomed and sleek upon green water ways,"
> And if their beauty is paid for by the poor
> Their whiteness bright as light, chic and allure
> And neatness like white poplars rising svelte
> Their sacrifice is loved, its good is felt
> In daydreams, reveries, and images
> Like poor boy–rich girl Cinderella marriages
> Which give a luxury to consciousness.

W.C.W. [William Carlos Williams]: marginal short biography & comment. He is troubled (to J. [Laughlin]) because he has had no imitators.

> Americans are tourists and voyeurs
> And peeping Toms in love with fire alarms

"I love the rich," Claude Vermont declared with vim & verve. "They have perceptions which the poor cannot possess."

But Terry S. replied to him: "The poor have perceptions which riches would make impossible."

January 18

NT: It is easier for a camel to pass through a needle's eye than for a rich man to enter the Kingdom of Heaven.

DP

The rich are in the Church—and honored there!
To cite the needle's eye is—not quite fair!
                    (is wrong, at best)—
Some Catholic students once explained to me
A camel entered a needle easily
The Needle's Eye was but a hole well known
Somewhere in Palestine, a breach in stone
                    —which made me nervous
Facing once more the mind's ability
To justify all things with swift agility
With cleverness, disingenuity,
Talmudic, Jesuitical, casuistical sophistry!

January 29

Cocktail party & pursuit by Stephen Scott. I love you, but Stephen can do so much for me.

Wedding night—GPU.

Lost nights & Spencer. Provincetown, Providence, and New York. Accusation of Fred: he always suspected the wrong person. Mary at Bard and Fred. The visit to Cambridge.

Out all night, accusation & counter-accusation. "Only a Jew would think of something like that."

Wilson looked at me suspiciously.

Mary as a complete adventuress—proves her freedom from W. by committing adultery.

Is it you, Delmore? asked Fred (comedy of suspected disingenuity).

The difficulty in writing about sophisticated people—that they are hardly significant of anything but a certain destructiveness to which the intelligence lends itself, lacking other strong motives. Also, they draw up hostility & contempt, such as they themselves embody. On the other hand, they are heroic insofar as they are committed to the dangers of consciousness.

Mary's cleverness about Will: "Who has said anything against him?"; and about publishers: "Any objection, however favorable, is bound to have an unfavorable effect."

May 24

E.P.S. first met me in an anthology by Oscar Williams—liked Thomas better—but liked my poetry more. (We both got fat.) Harold Rosenberg [art critic] tried to be pleasant to me. How appearance victimizes reality!

May I ask you a psychosomatic question? *Voulez-vous coucher avec moi?*

Play or story: New York Jews—rejected by nationalistic Israeli.

December 26

H.'s "about time that my daughter came out of her cellophane wrappings."

The cellophane wrappings were removed.

Her father was punctilious—his picture on the wall.

What would you do if I died?—hypothetical question. Answer: Beat it the hell out of here.

The maid, although not ordinarily thought of as such, is the first of the erogenous zones.

In petting there is no Mason-Dixon line.

Abomination of squeamishness—see him, her in the morning—don't deserve to make love.

Topics & Subjects: Love, Sex, Success & Failure, Friendship & Hatred, Authorship, Editing, Teaching, Being a Jew, Psychiatry, Family Life, Pornography & Literature.

The innovation compelled by the subject matter & the way in which the mind possesses it.

He was as honest as the night is long.

It was as feeble as a joke which has to be explained.

Klonsky's way of keeping himself from coming too soon—thinking of his mother's face.

E.P.S.: People are afraid of you. People don't like to be afraid.

1951

I know what love is! cried Chickie, jubilant and joyous.

What is it? What is love?

A girl in school told me—you're in love when you don't mind at all using the same toothbrush as the man you're in love with!

This was, he reflected, a corruption or perhaps a creative extension of an ironic remark of Freud's: "Is, then, your own toothbrush any cleaner than another person's?"

But the feeling, he reminded himself, was genuine & widespread or universal. No one minds his own stink or, if he or she does, minds it less than that of others.

"I am my body," Barbara might have exclaimed, asking her husband & not her sister to leave the room when she went to the toilet. She knew that the gurgling sound of urinating would be clearly heard by him since the acoustics were good . . .

In the country, at Adam's family's house, they were ashamed to make love because the bedsprings would be heard. In the end, after two weeks, the desperate young wife took her husband into the nearby meadow with her.

Stories by O'Hara & Spender's *Autobiography*.

The mountain rose to a snowy peak, as to say, *Pourquoi?* Pointing at empty blue and the glaring senseless sun.

Unmentionable practices: which seemed revelations of their deepest natures.

He was not afraid of life.

She had a sense of catastrophe.

She loved us and she wanted us to be happy.

Yeats said to S.: All poetry should [have] a simple underlying lilt, like Byron's: "So we'll go no more a-roving / So late into the night."

Methods as precise as those by which a watchmaker screws jewels into a watch. Time—is an art to the Swiss.

The great O of pure invocation.

Eliot to Spender: The important thing is whether or not you believe in Original Sin.

"For Lawrence . . . meeting is a dark mystery, a kind of godliness . . . even in the sexual act, the separateness of man & woman remain."

When I see dogs, I first think, drugs.

February 23–24

Thurs. By 4:30, when I went out for a walk, I was very tired. *Quel coincidence*, said Meyer [Schapiro], passing the stoop as I left the house. The wind blew hard as he told me of his lecture at NYU about how countermodernism always fails. In an early picture by de Chirico, the frame & the palette are real & the external world [is] not—this is a witty perception, said Meyer. But in a later picture, in which he says that all he cares for is "the metaphysic of the thing," he is dull—no metaphysical thought is present. I can't remember what he said about Picasso except that he was neoclassic in two respects—and aware that he was *not* classic but *neo*. M. also said something about Severini & pyramidal forms—that the pyramid is not a genuine unifier —there is a clown's hat on top and something—an ace of spades?—at the base.

One girl asked a question which Meyer could not answer: What did he think of the notion of hierarchy in the new critics? I did not recognize the reference.

I departed, having heard about half of what he said, and he apologized for keeping me so long when I told him E. was sick. "I hope it's nothing serious," he called back, blown by the wind, a few seconds after we had parted.

Hyman's was closed—G.W.'s birthday—I thought of buying a roasted chicken on Eighth St.; I felt an intense tiredness, the wind bothered my eyes. I stopped at a butcher's on Bleecker—there were too many people waiting. At the OK Meat Market the old Italian sold me 1¼ [pounds] of filet mignon for $1.75, adding fat & two Italian sausages, treating me like a bridegroom—or a new customer—and speaking of the meat as a great bargain. "After you eat it, you come right back again." I did not like the dark reddish look of the meat & the bloodied smell of the shop was faintly disgusting.

All morning I went forward very rapidly, writing about the day before, Moravia's novel, reading De Mott's story, and writing to him &

to Jay [Laughlin]. After lunch at 12, I looked through these notebooks and found them full of interesting or poetic phrases, almost entirely free of false notes, which made me think—with more conviction than at any other time since Dec.—Here I go again.

I bought and ate a frankfurter just before I walked across the park, and I did not buy the chicken at the rotisserie because I did not feel like crossing Eighth St. & Sixth again to get to a phone book. I was getting more & more tired, and when I went out a second time for the sherry: "It's a close-out, but it does not say how many cases are being closed out," I said to the small gray man with glasses with a real liveliness. "It's a close-out, all right," he said. But as I left I saw a case with the letters C U V I L L O stacked high on top of other cases near the long window.

I bought butter, frozen string beans, and three qts. of beer at the W. 4th St. grocery & started drinking more sherry than for several days, at least—five or six glasses—to pull myself out of tiredness. I was looking at *New Yorkers* & *Times* I had saved from last spring & marked, bending down the corner of the page, but unable to remember, as I looked at the bent-down pages, what I had found exciting—so with *Tomorrow*, an art magazine, and a new little magazine. Just before dinner, I looked at descriptive passages in *The Bostonians* (thinking of J.L.) and read the very delightful and amusing beginning of "An International Episode," in addition to an essay on James in the theater. Shaw is quoted as saying that no verse playwright can write with half as much beauty as James.

After dinner, I forced myself to read *The Aspern Papers*—my first attempt was in 1942 or 1943—and was bored from beginning to end—perhaps too much sherry.

A middle-aged spinster & a very old lady, aunt & niece, have letters by a famous poet, long since dead, to the aunt. They live, poverty-stricken & secluded, in a Venetian palace & an American (man of letters?) visits them, hoping to get the letters, which have been refused to a friend of his. He conceals his identity & purpose, and finds out that the very old lady also has an ulterior purpose—to get the American to marry her niece, Miss Tina, for the sake of possessing the papers. The aunt dies, Miss Tina offers herself—but this is part of the bargain—and when she is refused by the appalled American, she burns all the papers. E. liked it very much, and Philip [Rahv] did too, and this is the story about which Wilson asked V. Nabokov. I was really too tired—drunk as I read it, for now the pathos of the niece, the intense purposiveness of the aunt, and the American's unscrupulousness (he is scrupulous, except in literary matters) come up clearly. As I read I kept looking to see how far I had to go.

With only twenty to thirty pages unread, I went out for the

H[*erald*] *T*[*ribune*], eggs, tea, and bread—returned & read the Alsops with low delight. They still sound conspiratorial & in the know, inside the latest top secrets, but now they think that the Chinese have suffered a very great defeat in Korea—they have lost over 400,000 men—and they write as if they had not said there would probably be war by spring—an utter rout had occurred—and the like in Dec. On Weds. they expressed a new optimism about a long armed truce brought about by the arithmetical increase of American aerial superiority every three months. David Lawrence said there was an immense slackening of tension in official Washington.

During the afternoon, I was a little suspicious of my unclouded pleasure in notebook entries (which included last summer at Kenyon —pages which had distressed me when I looked at them before).

If I had kept this kind of a record in 1935 & 1940, how much more material (and habitual observation) I would have at hand. False pride prevented me, each time I tried—and under it, the intense ambition & doubt.

I felt cheered to think, as I have before, of how easy it would be to work up backgrounds by using other books—in *The Bostonians* I found recognizable Cantabrigian weather.

Last night I dreamed I had just read a new important preface by T.S.E. & praise of H. Levin by E. Wilson, praise of his ability to quote relevantly when they went to a Boston restaurant & H.L. trotted out a sentence from the New Testament. From the first dream may have come the impulse, during the morning's lucidity (the enjoyment of the ease of synopsizing Moravia's novel), to write the book on T.S.E. right now. Impulse to write an editorial about Gide for *PR*.

Before dinner, I was too tired—really exhausted—to call Aiken. During the afternoon, I tried, telling myself not to be self-indulgent.

I pushed through a story about shipboard cruises & first-class & tourist snobbery by Emily Hahn in this week's *New Yorker*.

"If we invite Jackson Pollock, we might as well invite Sugar Ray Robinson—" (or a truck driver).

Photos of Madison, Wisconsin, in this week's *Life*—the capitol dome, Lake Mendota, sailboats on the lake, the boathouse, the Union, and the lawn going down to the lake (a panorama photograph, but looks bigger than in the smallness of memory).

J. P[ollet]'s voice—quavering a little on the phone—uncertain of his reception.

Barbara G[reenfeld, advertising and business manager of *Partisan Review*]: "I like your hair that way—it's so boyish." "You always like it when I need a haircut."

Katy [Carver], who has had the flu, wanted to know if J. Berryman was coming to the party & was ravished to know the gossip I thought

Si [Seymour Krim] had mentioned to her—quick reports—not grape-
vine, but wires (or wives?)—in the Village.

Now, at 4, full of intellectual energy—but without objects—I really
am very fond of descriptions & of writing descriptions. Yet I could not
describe Twelfth St. between Fifth & Sixth very well because I don't
know the names for the façade decorations—cornice-floral designs,
imaginary animal figures, scrollwork & hornwork—stoops—areaways,
glass door entrances, dormer windows, white floorways—the small red-
brick house with the dormer window opposite the office, canopies, the
zigzag ironwork, fire escapes, railways, fire hydrants, pumps (like
mushrooms), street lamps & streetlights, French windows, awnings,
linen curtains, shades and blinds. "Chocolate-colored houses," says
James, instead of saying "brownstones." Fifth Ave. buses squat (poised
lightly? as if precariously?), grillework porches of the houses sit back
on Eleventh between Sixth & Seventh—cream- or tan-colored apartment houses.

The cold late-afternoon winter light as sharply defined by the
green (empty) shadows as in Edward Hopper's paintings—it is the
emotion of emptiness or endless and lonely striving which makes me
like his pictures so much.

An International Affair—title of a short novel (F.O.M.'s suicide?)
Czechoslovakia.

Another manic sign—loss of temper at cat in the paper bags—"You
don't hit her: you just push her away"—and appetite at lunchtime.

Kafka's Poseidon in *Parables* does not have any time for himself
(hardly has a chance to see the sea)—he is so involved in "endless
work—since he took the job, he would in the end go over all the figures
& calculations himself"—he was irritated that he was said to be "always
riding about through the tides with his trident while all the while he
sat here in the depths, doing figures uninterruptedly"—i.e., even a god
has no time to enjoy himself, no freedom from his post or station.

> Poseidon became bored with the sea
> He let fall his trident
> Silently he sat on the rocky coast
> And a gull, dazed by his presence—
> Described wavering circles around
> His troubled head

Philip Rahv thinks that in *The Trial* it is the death itself which is
the justice—unfathomable or irrational—which has come for Joseph K.

"The Silence of the Sirens"—silence is a greater weapon: "Someone might conceivably have escaped from their singing, from their
silence, never."

Against the feeling of having triumphed over them by one's own strength
> & the consequent exaltation that bears down everything before it
> no earthly powers could have remained intact.
> (Name for book of poems: *The Causes of Exaltation.*)

> Odysseus was thinking only of his wax & his chains
> he did not hear their silence
>> he alone did not hear them
> Save for a fleeting moment,
>>> their throats rising & falling
>>> their breasts lifting
>> their eyes filled with tears, their lips
>>>> half-parted
> (thought this was just part of the music)
> They lost all desire to allure
>>> —wanted only to hold, as long as they could
> The radiance that fell from O.'s great eyes

They did not possess consciousness.

Proof that inadequate, even childish measures, serve to rescue one from peril.

Embryo of a plot. Barbara G[reenfeld] spoke of a man who was having an affair with his wife's sister (this was in Oct. or Nov.). The wife knew about it—could do nothing because she had four children. (The sister . . . looked prettier because she went to work—a natural process.) They lived in the country, in New Hampshire. The two sisters are very different, the wife weak & passive, the sister energetic & self-assertive.

I protested that something else must have been involved. "But they live in the country," said B.—propinquity & opportunity & the seduction of continual presence and awareness. (Sister had had an affair with "the guy I'm going with now.")

Opportunity knocks just once, they say: Let us observe that opportunism knocks all the time.

Kafka: Daily life is the only life we have.

Kafka. Bucephalus, Alexander's horse, has decided to become a lawyer—since India is unattainable, it's best "to bury oneself in the law books—far from the fray"; under a quiet lamp, "he turns the pages of our old books" (as if to find out the reasons for India's distance, for all the failures).

Rhoda [Klonsky] to Isaac R[osenfeld]: "Do you think Milton is handsome?" Isaac—Feb. or March 1945—his hidden & overwhelming hostility—and his hatred of Katy.

Clem's farewell party at Jean R.'s. (Jan., Feb. 1943? or 1942?—

probably '43—Clem was drafted just before I.) [Delmore was rejected by the draft board for reasons of health.]

"Tell Lionel [Abel] I think he is a fake," I said to Margie Mason [Irish girl, raconteur].

"Tell Delmore he is just trying to be friendly," said Lionel—a witty and self-possessed reply indeed.

"I sleep in two sections, since I began to knock myself out each night. And I can't decide if I have doubled the amount of sleep or reduced it in half."

"Why don't you try love?" said George Barker [English poet].

"He'd sleep with a horse," said Clem.

The girl I was paying attention to kept tickling him and he was annoyed with her. We danced & she told me to stop. Why, I said. Because it is not decent.

Agee told Dwight I had a greater degree of consciousness than he did. Dwight blinked. (We were discussing the existence of God.) H[arold] J. Kaplan [in 1945 contributed Paris Letters to *Partisan Review*; worked for O.W.I., and later for the State Department] said I was applying the wrong categories.

In 1940 Hivnor went to sleep soon after he arrived at 41 Bowdoin St.—it was late morning.

"That's why I do it—because it looks good." P[aul] G[oodman] on his use of numbers, in 1934.

How memories begin to pour back—as mind wakes up.

1942? Kit G. was with Agee, who ate before going out to dinner so that he would be able to drink still more before dinner & after dinner. They were going to a play—Odets & Tallulah Bankhead—having decided they really must go to a show. After the last act Agee said, "Now I want to be a designer of stage sets"—same re-con-struction of reality as in *Let Us Now Praise Famous Men*. They rushed out for drinks between the acts. After that, went to the Silver Dollar on 42nd & Times Sq. It was just after Pearl Harbor & we talked about the war.

Pearl Harbor compared to visiting team scoring six runs in first inning.

Story about a baseball game (major league)—intense struggle, home team is losing—pitcher's weakening—pinch hitter eager. (In the first person?)

West Indian figures playing cricket—leisurely, patiently, solemnly, hardly or not at all aware of the roars of the crowd—as if they were in another century (a streetcar passes, an elevated train passes—as if the passengers inhabited separable & incommunicable worlds).

Short short story of being hit repeatedly—is it a dream or not: WHAT DIFFERENCE DOES IT MAKE IF IT IS A DREAM OR NOT (that's what the doctor says to him?).

F. H. Bradley: "all our perceptions"—each in his prison. E.g., R.S. [Delmore's mother], hearing that her sister had cancer: "Everything happens to me"!

Lyrical prose. The Polo Grounds were gala and sunny and green and sparkling with activity. The Giants were playing the Dodgers.

The flags on the grandstand snapped in the breeze. The sky was an unmarred and brilliant blue. The crowd was very excited.

The gates had been closed two hours before the game started. Two fights between fans of the two teams broke out during batting practice.

Flies soared far into the outfield. Outfielders threw the ball home to nab an imaginary runner, as the crowd noted, waited, marveled, and applauded.

[Edmund] Wilson told Jane [Mayhall] (at Yaddo last winter) that Schwartz "has great personal charm." How did he know? (Berryman? pieces in *PR*?) He had asked Will & Julie about me. "He was curious about you," said Julie. Will had said nothing at all.

Maupassant started by writing anecdotes which continually became longer—until they were stories.

Turgenev & Tolstoy marveled at M[aupassant]'s ability to get an erection merely by taking thought—by an act of will. (Tolstoy had previously been unimpressed by M.'s stories.)

A half-conscious purposiveness (an entelechy, like an ambition) shows in the way I keep at works of fiction instead of poetry or criticism—and there is something which looks new & different in the difficulty of attention I have with trivial periodical reading at the same time as I have a good deal of ease with first-rate writing—I don't try to skip & skim.

February 24

Two (or Five) Years Before the Abyss / The Cultivation (or the Knowledge) of the Abyss.

When Bertram Harris first started to drink every night, he was a charm drinker. He was charmed by the way everything began to sparkle and everyone became very interesting and he himself seemed to himself very witty. Certainly he became gay and spontaneous.

He did not drink until five o'clock, thinking that this rule would keep him from becoming a drunkard. He drank mostly sherry at first, buying himself a gallon jug of Italian Swiss Colony sherry. The gallon seemed endless, a well of inexhaustible emotion. He decided to call the jug a luxury liner, for there was a luxuriance of experience in drinking sherry and looking at it.

Each afternoon at five he sat in the armchair near the bay window and began to drink. Soon as he looked from the window down to the street, everything was sharpened, the shapes of everything were underlined and very interesting and very pretty: an impression intensified by winter sunset and winter dusk. The boards of a back-yard fence were magnified and clarified. As the sun went down, a cold and clear pinkness touched the red-brick house on the other side of the street, and scarlet reflections of the sunset blazed on the windows. The air was like a bell on the verge of ringing out. Where there was no redness of the winter sunset, there was a blackness of shadow & outline.

After a year of drinking he did not want to eat dinner until he felt drunk. He wanted to keep the drunkenness going as long as possible. It was really highness, not drunkenness—so intense was sensation and consciousness. He drank after dinner, too, and it was not long before he hastened to drink soon after dinner because the food had sobered him and taken away his exultation. He listened to music on the radio and read as he drank in the evening. The drinking intensified the music and the reading to a point of joyousness & delightfulness he had never known before.

He went to sleep quickly, full of wine, after having since childhood had to wait an hour or hours to fall asleep. Being full of wine, he jumped as from a height into the warm depths and seas of sleep.

Then he began to wake up at three or four o'clock, and he began to drink wine and get drunk again, lying in bed in the darkness and enjoying a growing softness of serenity and a slow mounting peace. Sometimes he fell asleep before finishing a drink and the glass on the floor was half full in the morning.

(I am not getting anywhere—I don't have the feeling that this will lead me to some point to which I want to get.)

Last night I did not understand Kafka's "The Hunter Gracchus"—

> Two boys were playing dice
>   a man was reading a newspaper,
> (on the steps of the monument, resting in the shadow
> of a hero who flourished his sword on high)
> A girl was filling her bucket at the fountain
> A fruitseller was lying by his scales
>   staring out to sea
> Two men in the back of a café were drinking wine
> (The proprietor was sitting at the table, dozing)

Ended, descended, splendid / simple, ruble, steeple, people, feeble.

The drop has begun—1:30. 10:15–12:45 = 2½ hrs., a little more than the recent average.

Margie called: E.'s aesthetic sense must be more developed than yours.

Klonsky called: I want the air—feel a bit logy. Will you be home all afternoon?

How glittering and liquid and bright the colors—especially the blue—become in the Rouault when the sunlight is on it.

I would not be surprised to find a lot of usable material in the mss. I put together for Princeton seminars.

Temptation again to write a piece of criticism—about Gide—simply to get something done—for *PR* (to justify being on it) or for *The Nation*.

The ease of writing synopses is something new—now, if the habit of observation & description would only grow stronger—synopsis as a way of assimilation & possession—like memorizing or writing out or reading aloud but better because less mechanical.

How Louis Kronenberger [critic and novelist] in Aug. 1939 did not want to take the money he won playing poker with Nathan Asch [novelist], Arthur Arent [playwright, novelist], Eugene Joffe [fiction writer], and me. It was a day of all-day rain. It's a good day for two things, said A.A.

How I tried to get Margaret M[arshall] to give me Louis, the Siamese cat, last spring. After an hour of pleading that I needed Louis, I reversed the appeal, arguing that Louis needed me, would miss literary cocktail parties & be bored by all the middle-class respectability he would have to live with [in] the suburbs.

"The Pupil" by Henry James. Is about the history of a precocious young boy who is exploited. His [tutor's] salary is not paid him by the boy's parents, who are pretentious snobs & bluffs, and (unsuccessful) social climbers. At first the tutor (who tells the story) tries to protect the boy from seeing what his parents are. But the boy already knows. The tutor's devotion to the boy is used by the parents to keep him without paying him. He breaks away at last (to take on "an opulent student")—is recalled when the boy supposedly suffers a heart attack (his heart has always been weak), but this turns out to be a pretext: the family is finally bankrupt & resourceless—the parents want to give the boy to the tutor, a project the two have fondly discussed in the past. But the boy's shame and shock at the parents' shamelessness & dishonesty are too much & he dies of heart failure.

The theme is the fate of superior beings in worldly life, this world, the fashionable world—for both the tutor & the boy are utterly used & ruined. It's close to "The Author of 'Beltraffio'"—and not at all like *The Aspern Papers*, where the point—which now gets clearer after a day—is that the schemer is himself the victim of scheming—in that he suffers from being confronted by Miss Tina's pathetic proposal & does not get what he wants—the papers.

"Ten Indians," [by] Hemingway. Is hardly more than an anecdote.

A boy finds out that the Indian girl with whom he has been sleeping has slept with another boy. He thinks his heart is broken, but the next morning "it is a long time" before he remembers that his heart is supposed to be broken: the quickly passing emotions of adolescence.

In another story, an American soldier in Italy suffers from insomnia, and his Italian friend tells him marriage will solve everything. So does the waiter in "A Clean Well-Lighted Place." It is a recurrent note, like prayers, Catholicism, religious belief, and the priest—and like courage (Francis Macomber), skill, self-possession, the stiff upper lip or frozen-faced containment of emotions, the lady as destructive (Lady Brett), and the lady as infatuated recumbency (*Bell Tolls*).

Hemingway asserts traditional moral values often by an action which seems an inversion or violation of them—e.g., the desertion in *A Farewell to Arms*—& Jake's introducing Lady Brett to the bullfighter.

"A *Son* Also Rises"—Peter Arno's comic character, Hemingway, as a resentment of H.'s overasserted masculinity.

Kafka's narrative movement as the examination of impossibility— or hopelessness—or unattainability.

Dr. Bucephalus—you can see he was once a horse by the way he lifts his legs going upstairs. I did not notice this piece of humor when I read it yesterday—it was Clem's paraphrase or conversation—the same with John B.'s account of Isaac R.'s story & Clem on Poseidon—it must be the translation or my way of reading or Kafka's method.

February 26

Go down, Moses
　　Go down, Milton
　　　　(This is the winter of his discontent)

"What is there to do except go to the movies or go to Louis's?" said Anatole [Broyard].

At 10:30, though I was in my pajamas, I did not think I could get to sleep; I thought of beer, and thought of how it would wake me up— dressed, walked down W. Fourth, up Sixth Ave., and home again. The fresh air made me feel much less tense, and I went to bed in the little room, looking at Tauber's book on Kafka & Farrell's short stories—two extremes—and responding to both. Three s.t.s [sleeping tablets] & one s.a. [sodium Amytal]. I was drowsy in an hour but the drowsiness faded, I came back to the bedroom—one s.a.—slept until 6—one s.a. (six all told)—& woke at 10, after dreams about having a tortoiseshell cat, a house in the country, and reading a story in which the style tasted like fruit leaves (whatever that taste is)—or like greens.

Four days of not drinking in one week—Sun. (pictures)—Tues. (———?)—Thurs.—Sun. No real craving, no expectation of a transformation of emotions (since sometimes it does not work very well), and no real attempt to check or reduce nervousness—perhaps because the nervousness (& anxiety) are much reduced—the habit is broken, for the time being at least.

I mistook habit for necessity.

Especially last night's abstinence—since it was after an evening of hard drinking—now if I could carry morning sentiments about reading into the evening (how easy it seems each morning!).

The chain of consequences: snowball, snow fight—a broken window, the cats go out, OK the kitten is lost, returns in ten days, weak & scrawny, dies of distemper; his mother is infected but much more slowly, does not get well, is put out of her misery by the vet.

("Are you writing a story about it?"—Rosalind—the sense of a pattern.)

Anatole: You're looking very well—you're looking like that photograph of you in the Gotham Book Mart. "Suffering has given a new dignity to my countenance."

Undated

George Mayberry in the store on W. Fourth & Perry at 6—I turned away. I did not want to talk to him or greet him, though I did not want to walk two more blocks to the Tenth St. store. The same with someone across the street, as I came out, who I thought might be Leslie [Katz]. Neurosis of avoidance of unexpected meeting.

Dream about drinking too much—almost a full bottle of whiskey—because Sylvester was present. There was a girl who drank a lot also and took a sleeping tablet from a drawer quickly. A long dream, R. Scarlett [Elizabeth's stepfather] wanted to buy another bottle of liquor.

Quarrel at breakfast, 10:30.

"I'm in a bad humor, but not you."

"What you want is practically *impossible*."

The fried egg with the white having a marble consistency: irritation, shouting, anger, and tears.

I woke before 8 and fell asleep again without taking a sleeping tablet—relaxed enough & not nervous. So—I did not care if I fell asleep or not, and since I did not care, I did.

System of Routine (last night, after midnight): one poem & analysis or paraphrase—Blake or Baudelaire or Stevens or Yeats. Elizabethan or Donne or Dickinson, Emerson, or Smart, Pope, Byron, or Wordsworth. One page of *F[innegans] W[ake]* and analysis of rhetorical & syntactical forms. One page of narrative fiction or dramatic poetry (Stendhal, Racine, H.J., Shakes.).

If part of this, at least part, could be the occupation of evenings! & the late afternoon, too.

How J. Joyce in *FW* bears contrary witness to Ortega's thesis about mass man. How T.S.E.'s criticism of poetry must be transcended by a reading in which a historical consciousness is more active.

E. felt dizzy again, thought it might be pregnancy, came back from the doctor disappointed & irritated because deprived of her pleasures, smoking, drinking, eating—10 lbs. too much.

The effect of A.Q. was certainly to revive & intensify ancient fears & rejections & to plunge me into a chaos of personal relations. The defenseless ones are always the most eager to put all their eggs in one basket. (Defenseless is an exaggeration.)

When we reproach some for egotism, we ought to remember how hard it is to depart from one's body—the closest, most frequent object of attention & source of sensation.

Wm.'s old love of literature, suspended so long, may be reviving—to judge by his comments on Joyce, *The Immoralist*, and how he found more in them now than when he read them in the thirties.

When I told Gr. [Dr. Gruenthal] I felt some guilt in [the] pleasure which I took in conversation with E.'s mother—I should take the same pleasure in conversation with my own mother—he asked me if she was an intelligent woman & he told me these outmoded notions ought not to move me any longer.

The Negro Anatole pointed out in the Circle on Sunday—a really evil face, said Anatole. He had curly black hair which glittered as if it were wet, a smile which curled his lips, and his eyes were narrowed & thin—like acute angles.

The face ought not to be as hard to describe as I feel it is—two eyes, one nose, cheek & cheekbones, forehead, hair, shape of head, mouth & lips, chin, neck, carriage of head: ten to fifteen aspects at the most. What is needed is an epitome & a use of the common denominator of impression. And the same must be true, in general, of most visual impressions. James turns immediately to the impression of the object—its impact, impinge, on sensibility—he does not try to take it up as an object independent of any particular impression.

One function of criticism: The instant resuscitation & excitement of interest.

To write with a more conscious sense of the *experience* which the reader will have as he reads.

The lists of reading look more impressive than they are—since at least half is not really possessed & remembered. But each time I go back to *FW*, it becomes more familiar & clearer—as just now, though the reading began to run down, wane.

Not enough of the trying and the enjoyment of trying & arriving, not enough of getting up & walking around the sentence & looking elsewhere for the words.

February 27

Moon Pictures [for moving pictures].

Beau Friend. He was her beau friend.

Ad: An orange drink, plump with juice, awaits your pleasure.

Ad: Beware the ice of March.

It's not the humidity—it's the stupidity.

The oppression of sleep. The prisoners of the dark heart.

"She feels strolling so refreshing, after sitting so long, that she smooths her hips down with the palms of her hands."

"No fixed abode," he says & laughs. "Unavoidably detained, Officer! Official business."

[Delmore's first cousin Josephine had a breakdown. Upon hearing the news, Delmore sat on the edge of the bed, his head in his hands, and wept. The tragedy, especially for his aunt Clara Colle, seemed to him unbearable.]

West Vale (Rest House Sanitarium) looked like a small & distant summer resort.

Cottages of different sizes, neat and of differing wood & design, were scattered about the hilly uneven ground. At the bottom of a little hill was a day-tennis court and there patients sat idly with orderlies & nurses. They looked limp & round-shouldered. They might have been seated in Washington Square Park.

Elsewhere on the soggy ground were wooden beach chairs painted a very bright red and green.

On the staircase of Josephine's house—"the garden house"—stood an old woman who had a fixed look—fixed on nothing—and grasped my arm with a hand tightly (as if she were trying to hold to something which might be slipping away very quickly).

The air was faintly gray & faintly sunny—in halfhearted alternation—late winter on the edge of spring.

Once, in "the therapy" we heard a long moaning—groaning—howling rising and falling and going on as if patiently.

Josephine looked relaxed & rational & a little indifferent.

"Are there men here, too?" said her mother.

"What, did you think only women go crazy?" she said & laughed.

Later, not long before we left, she became irritated with her mother for not bringing her hair shampoo. She told Clara that she did not miss her.

"That's good," said the anxious, devoted mother—for long the rag (the soldier) of the family.

"I sometimes miss you a little," she said humbly.

A middle-aged woman sat down nearby. Clara thanked her for the ride home her husband had given her on Sunday.

"My husband is such a nice man—sooo good. My sons are very nice, too. I'm the only one who is no good. All I do is make trouble for them."

She was bothered by vibrations—electrical vibrations in her head —and could not sleep. She had had shock seven years before & it had cured her. Now she was back & she was impatient. They could not give her the full treatment until she lost more weight.

Apartment houses were cropping up all over the northernmost half-empty regions of the city.

We waited a long time for the bus in a small business center (Isham Hill). Bar & grill, bank, delicatessen (Frank's Famous Sandwiches), lunchroom (the old elevated passed by). Clara had waited for us in the last car. She was dressed in her best. In the subway, patient faces looked & waited—others, looking at papers, were slowly feeding. (Ulysses-Daedalus in the Paris library.)

Two old women had decided to live the rest of their lives at the rest home. They talked all night, disturbing Josephine.

Clara did not think I looked well—she asked E. if I had been sleeping enough. I was edgy, nervous, and irritable, and apperceptive.

"No wonder you can't sleep—taking five Dexedrine." When this irritated me, E. said, "Don't be so touchy."

The fresh & chilly air made me feel cold and hungry. I had had no lunch. We stopped on 231st St. & ate soup, sandwiches, and coffee, bent over, voracious & hurrying.

The length of the city and the regions and the areas (the neighborhoods) came back. As we rode downtown I could not get interested in either of the afternoon papers—Dyckman, 181, 168, 157, 137, 125, 117, Cathedral Heights, 96.

E. was sick, and bent over the sofa. I glanced at Tauber's Kafka, and sentences sprang out of the page, vivid & dramatic & mysterious.

The bus driver was impatient about my absentminded, uncoordinated payment of fares & request for a transfer.

"Find out what you want, bud. And then we'll go to the same school."

E. pushed me away as we walked on the path. "You were pushing me into your aunt." I stepped in the rain drain. In the bus coming she said, "You know you can't smoke"—smelt smoke—it turned out that the bus driver himself was smoking. At Sheridan Square I asked her if I had to have a haircut & she answered, "I don't know about such things!" But wanted me to tell her which dress to wear.

The unconscious pushing against me—the unrelatedness to physical objects which comes on when she is disturbed or ill—kept on as we walked crosstown. When I stopped and said how I was annoyed, she said: "Don't control your temper—just tell me."

Margaret Marshall kissed E. as we came in & when we left. She had to get up on tiptoe and it was an effort and she was trying to say something.

She talked of Judy [her daughter] as she opened the whiskey & we talked of how pleasant the sanitarium was.

"You sound wistful, Delmore," she said. Gaps of silence until Val[borg] Anderson [professor and author] came in, chatty, friendly, lively, hungry—told E. she could not wait to read her novel—which a friend in Boston could not get. We discussed television as superior to radio.

The Trillings arrived, very friendly and very mannered. Diana immediately took off her health shoes & came into the kitchen.

"I have not read your review of *F.*," said L.T., "but let me congratulate you on it." [Delmore reviewed *The Far Side of Paradise* by Arthur Mizener in *The Nation*, February 24, 1951, under the title "The Dark Night of F. Scott Fitzgerald."] (After dinner he read it, pronounced it very good—announced that one seldom took a chance on reading something in the presence of the author. "It is very good, isn't it?" said Margaret.)

Talk about Jim—Jimmy—Lord Jim—his chanted catalogue of all the people who love him: "M. loves Jimmy, P. loves Jimmy, Velma loves Jimmy . . ."

Jackson Pollock's signature seemed, to L.T., to be, if not like, his: autistic thinking.

Trilling had been in Cambridge & reported that [Professor George Wiley] Sherburn had spoken tenderly of me—to his surprise, I explained incompletely about my comparisons of cynicism. Soon after, L.T. declared that he liked Cam. so much—none of the undertone of cynicism one found at Columbia. Diana asked if I had not disliked Cam. I said I was no longer sure.

"They really believe in teaching, in education there," said L.T. He would like to give a graduate course in composition, and treasures his training in high school, at De Witt Clinton.

"John Kraft is one of the few boys who have really benefited by having money," said Lionel of some boy who wanted to write reviews of fiction for Margaret. Margaret wanted to know what to do about G[erald] Sykes's [novelist and critic] novel. L.T. found it disgusting. Val spoke of copulation in the water & always copulation standing up. "Ernest Jones has refused to touch it," said M.M.

Lionel declared that he hated literature—felt great hostility to books. Val was shocked. He explained that it was because he was meant to write books, not to read them. (Where is the conflict?)

I said, "In the name of what do you hate literature!"

"In the name of self, of course," L. & D. replied in chorus. D.T. is appalled & disgusted that Tocqueville wrote a masterpiece at twenty-five. She knocked over the stool on which were the ashtray & my drink.

The T.s find Gesell deplorable. He is statistical & middle-class about the norm for each age (that's inexact—something about what the American mother requires of her child). "The three-year-old is the adolescent of the preschool age."

I was a little nervous after dinner—but not so that I just had to have a drink.

L.T. expressed a mannered irritation with Wilson's crack about Trilling-thrilling—and at Kazin's piece on Richard Chase [literary critic]—it was jealous and personal—what he minded, however, were the apologies.

"Lionel is wonderful," said D[iana]. "He knows just what he is going to find in a book before he opens it." This also disturbed Val.

We walked a block, after refusing to let the T.s drop us. I resisted the whiskey I had thought of; we took a cab, went straight to bed. Two Sec[onal] & three s.a.—no sleep until about 3 when I drank two glasses (+ three s.a.) of the beer, stoppered up, left over from the day before.

E. was annoyed by Val—as I was not—but found the T.s friendly & interesting, as she had not in the past, "when I felt as you do."

T.s' mannerisms may bother me as much as they do precisely because they are directed to others—insofar as they are other—each unique and special to himself.

"The self is a unique combination of experiences."

"The undeveloped heart." The possession of joy, the mystery of joy. "At once so appealing & so appalling." "Unbearably loaded with meaning."

February 28

List of reading (like counting or adding up bank accounts):

Billy Budd, The Counterfeiters, The Miraculous Barber, The Woman of Rome.

Still unassimilated: *What Maisie Knew, Bostonians, Ambassadors, The Awkward Age, Spoils of Poynton.* Dickens, Dostoevsky, Dos Passos, Lawrence, Céline, Green, Kafka, Compton-Burnett, Kierkegaard.

Last summer: *A Tree Grows in Brooklyn*; Wharton, *The Reef, The Age of Innocence*; O'Hara; *Fathers and Sons*, Chekhov, Tolstoy, *The Dead*, Eudora Welty. "Fifty Grand," "A Rose for Emily," "A Simple Heart." Kleist, Poe, F. K[afka]: "A Country Doctor"; *The Gambler*, "The Nun & the Radio." W. F[aulkner]: "Justice," "Red Leaves," "Carcassonne," "The Odor of Verbena," "Spotted Horses," "That Evening Sun Go Down," "Story from Dr. Martino." F. S. F[itzgerald]: "Crazy Sunday." "The Summer Within the Mind," De Mott. All of *Dubliners*: "Ivy Day in the Committee Room," "Araby," "Counterparts," "Grace," "A Painful Case," "A Mother," "Evelyn." [T. Mann]: "Disorder and Early Sorrow." Proust.

Daisy Miller, "An International Episode," "The Siege of London," "The Author of 'Beltraffio,' " "The Pupil," *The Aspern Papers*, "Lady Barberina." Agee, *The Morning Watch*. Aymé, *Crossing Paris*. *Alcestis*. *Ash Wednesday*. Two chapters of *Pickwick Papers*.

E.H.: "Fifty Grand," "Ten Indians," *The Sun Also Rises*.

Moravia: *Back to the Sea*. Borges. Angus Wilson: *Life and Letters*.

Kafka: *Parables*: "The Hunter Gracchus," "The Silence of the Sirens," "The New Lawyer," "On Parables," "An Imperial Message," "Prometheus," "Poseidon," "The Truth about Sancho Panza," "Robinson Crusoe," "The Tower of Babel," "Aphorisms."

Skipped & skimmed: *Look Homeward, Angel, Too Early to Tell, Brave New World, The Old Man, Sanctuary*. Farrell's short stories, *Tender Is the Night, The Crack-Up, They Shall Inherit the Earth*. Santayana: *The Middle Span; Revolt of the Masses*, Gide's *Journal*, Giraudoux: *Chaillot*. Mizener—*Fitzgerald*; *Kafka*—Tauber; Dupee—*James*; Handlin—*Boston's Immigrants*.

Missing books: *The Hamlet*, W. F[aulkner]. *Robber Barons, The Politicos, Fenichel*, Alice B. Toklas. Proust, Vol I. Hardy's Poems, *Daisy Miller*, and "An International Episode."

"She had expected her heart to tell her what to do."

Tues. Fred's [Dupee] book on James, *Daisy Miller*, "An International Episode." [Edmund] Wilson's essay on James—no dice. Two or three glasses of sherry before dinner, one quart of beer after dinner. Two chapters of *Pickwick Papers* (no dice) and a faint beginning of anxiety (since on Sat. & Sun., the changing seemed to be underway in earnest). Wm. came for two books, nervous & diffident.

In the late afternoon, after I came back from a walk about the Square, James's prose was sparkling and shining, the nervous energy of the strong effort at expression in the description of New York Harbor (in *The American Scene*).

How there is the same femininity of tone—"so tenderly, so pleadingly"—in Rilke's & James's prose—in their letters especially.

Fred [Dupee] does not let himself go in his book—tries to maintain a style—hardly lets his own passions come to the surface (though he does call James "the great feminine novelist" & writes: "American writers & their families!")!

The conventions which *Daisy Miller* violates do seem old-fashioned now & they did not when I first read it fifteen years ago. Hence, the lack of shock spoils the effect. Perhaps the change in morality (as well as in my own experience) is a matter of these past fifteen years as much as anything.

Failure in writing stories to take the initiative of invention. When invention comes, I take it. But I don't go looking for it.

March 1

You're a fast goer, said Nathalie [Rahv]. I left with a kind of quick swoop for my coat, on the bookcase near the door.

Philip [Rahv] was feeling very friendly—probably because he had separated himself from William [Phillips]—had expressed his independence of any need to be a part of the association between Wm., Clem, & Sidney Phillips. He was free—he felt freed—of the need of being near William & free of resentment of the close friendship between Wm. & Clem (the sun in the Admiration Cigar advertisement).

I had a hard time saying anything to Philip & Edna (I mean Nathalie—the slip is like Nathalie's saying, when I phoned, Do you want to speak to Wm.?!) and did not get started until, after my review of Arthur's book had been praised, I found in it a means of discussing the Trillings.

"They want to be bourgeois," said Philip. "They don't want you to be unhappy because it reflects on their unhappiness (they can't help, he said, identifying their success with the world's—or they can't separate their success from the world's).

I remarked on how hard it was for me to take the Trillings—it was the lack of genuineness, of sincerity.

"You cut under it," said Philip.

"But how can you?" said Nathalie.

[Philip's] foot hurt him, he limped home, Nathalie was tender in tone and in facial expression, as sympathy.

"How is Elizabeth?" asked Nath[alie].

"Dwight is suffering a writer's block," said Philip. "He's had an affair & sex has upset him." (A girl had told him that Dwight was pretty good, which would certainly mean, from anyone else, that Philip had had an affair with the same girl. But Philip's relentless questioning —cajoling & amiable—makes it possibly just his curiosity.)

I put out the absence of a magazine's bolstering of self-esteem as an explanation of Dwight's block & Nathalie thought this more likely.

At the editorial meeting, Nabokov's book came up again. And the party invitations, the symposium, and, after that, the international situation. Philip is against containment, which means declaring to Stalin: "We are not going to surprise you, do anything unexpected, anything but defend ourselves." Question of why Europe will not be unified— petty interests in nationalism, and the undermining of Stalinism— Europeans still think in orthodox Marxist terms. Borkenau—a general who thinks of the whole thing as a chess game—says the Germans will fight (Hannah Arendt insists that they won't) because—why do people fight? they fight because they're in the army.

Philip & Wm. were a quarter of an hour late (they may have been having lunch with Sidney Phillips [owner and editor of Criterion Books]).

I left home at 2 (fourth & last Dex.), ate a second lunch, turkey sandwich & coffee, and felt as if I were manic again, looking at contributions, writing to Vernon Watkins [Welsh poet], talking to Barbara about shock therapy, and skimming two new novels, *Shield's Island* (Dial) & *Where Town Begins* (Greenberg)—attention was crackling (like logs taking fire?) (like firecrackers going off?).

On the way to the office I thought again of rewriting my essays & reviews & quickly put it aside again.

Press relations or advertising man as literate hero (to justify his literacy) & revival of Orpheus-lawyer theme (West Vale Rest Home).

I thought: Why can't I just move characters about from island to mansion, to any place I have not been?

And why can't I just write in straight dialogue (there was a new novel by Compton-Burnett in the office), beginning with Elena, Harry, Mark, Ruth S., George Mayberry and Rita, and Philip & Tessa Horton. (I can't even read that kind of novel & it is just a seemingly easy way of doing things & getting started—no more easy, really, than a play.) The primary problem is: What am I interested in enough?

Barbara was against people being stopped from committing suicide—when I demurred, she said: Some of these people who just go on like that, year after year.

When I came home at 6:30, after one drink at P[hilip]'s, Jane & Leslie were there. I was pleased to see them, but again without anything to say after I had asked them to stay for dinner.

E. & Jane were drunk—E. floundered about, spilt wine, could not go to dinner because she had drunk too much sherry to have a martini, spilt wine on chair arm, and on the floor, insisted that J. & L. stay & have a sandwich.

"You've spoiled dinner for four people," I said. I wanted to keep her from drinking more sherry. "It will make you unhappy." "More unhappy?" she said, which I took—wrongly—to mean that she had been very unhappy all day.

Tension & glaring—Leslie was disturbed—the hidden denunciatory storm of rage came up as if latent. But I said nothing I had thought of saying when the Katzes left (pacified by what I did eat) & lay down after dinner, first in the bedroom, then in the little room. Went out for beer (as E. kept throwing her head back on the sofa) without saying anything—returned with two qts. of beer & two papers (manic excitement was all gone), thought of drinking just one & going straight to bed.

"I know you're very angry at me, but tell me why," said E.

"It's useless to say anything—you just transform it with a kind of systematic stupidity."

"I won't say anything: just tell me."

I let myself go—the smoking in the bus on Mon. as a classic example, social life & the whole burden being on me, the virtual impossibility of the fried egg, the wrong doctor, how I complain too much, how everything keeps getting worse all the time, her literalness & insensitivity about getting up at 8, on Saturday night systematic stupidity.

She answered very little, almost nothing.

Philip said that Wm.'s quixoticism (which he mispronounced), unlike most, was directed to practicality, practical channels, such as Sidney Phillips's publishing house: "Seven years of analysis have done him no good at all—I can't see any good—I spent the whole day in Washington with him—he must have gone to the john about nineteen times." As for Will: "Perhaps he is too much of a philosopher to be a literary man, and too much of a literary man to be a philosopher"—a mechanical antithesis.

Philip, at home, denounced Wm.'s idea of psychoanalysis as a panacea. He said again how Katy was incredibly efficient.

At midnight—delights of translating a Greek play into verse or Racine, as I glanced at Burkhardt. By morning *Phèdre* had become a short novel.

Last night, too much sherry, too little dinner—four s.t.s and then, at 6, two more s.t.s. I woke up at 12 with a mild hangover anyway, still feeling angry—did not want E., penitent, to help me with breakfast, tried to write about Gide, with little luck (as if I were depressed). During the afternoon *F[innegans] W[ake]* kept lighting up, as it has not for a long time, except for two times when I was drunk—once after John Ashbery's party & once in, I think, January.

I told P[hilip] & N. that I had written my review of Arthur's [Mizener] book when I was drunk—an untrue version (or only half-true, for I did take seven Dexedrine tablets) and the consequence, probably, of the desire to be interesting.

"I'll have to read it again," said N.

"I can't do anything when I drink," said Philip. "All I want then is to have fun."

During the afternoon, I was possessing myself of books as if manic. (Perhaps I've not been eating enough, I thought, after eating a second lunch.)

From 4 to 6—*FW*, losing melody, vividness, and rough shadow of outline: not at first, but after sixty pages.

Closed up again: the difference between yesterday & today. Yet not like in September & October. Not nervous, but pressing. Without knowing toward what. Fewer pages than any other free day for weeks. Hot forehead—almost sweat, a little wet.

April 27

A play: The Noble Rounder / Scoundrel / Bounder.

Will is out on Beyle.

Klonsky is hiding his light under a Bush.

Odets: Do horses have plans? This is like living in the subway.

Conscientious objector to life.

What's the difference between scatalogical & eschatological? E.: You are my orchard. You are my fertilizer. You're getting scatalogical this morning.

May 6–7

E.P.S.: No one ever said such awful things to me—some have done worse things (just what [Gertrude] said). If true, all right—if false, all right. Wrong. The point is that you should say such things, "that anger."

May 11–12

Journal-American: Story of three girls who raped twenty-one-year-old handsome construction worker in the back of his car. Scores of women called him—his mother won't let [him] speak to them. Does not have to appear in court & face them—no more of early charges of indecent & lascivious behavior—but three are now booked as delinquents.

Why did he tell his mother or anyone?

Phila. 6, Giants 5, bases loaded, none out in ninth.

E. was sullen when she came home—asked time, asked me if I was coming to bed. "You're a sophist," I said stupidly. No sign of Klonsky! $5. Krim's borrowed book.

Fri. PR office—Philip & Trillingism—Will's flirtation with Barbara (slapping her on the back)—Saul Bellow—Dowling & Sandra Wool's poem & E. Hardwick's story & his failure to see the Robert Lowells & his long stay in Vienna.

Committee on Cultural Freedom—Wm., Edna. Fred & Andy [the Dupees] in interpretation. Looked like a call house, 37 W. 56 St.

Riverdale. Burnham's formal hello—stories of India, low standard of living. Müller (Nobel Prize, ex-Stalinist).

Norman Jacobs [classmate of Delmore's at New York University]:

Do you keep [up] with developments in philosophy?

I don't keep up with any.

Not even baseball?

That's different.

Logical positivists are in a panic—they're no longer sure about the difference between analytic & synthetic propositions.

May 14

Clara—Josephine. She comes out of coma: asks for "Joseph," Catholic accountant; she met his mother; she never liked him; go out only in the daytime.

She's getting worse. R.S. [Rose, Clara's sister and Delmore's mother]: lost her appetite, she has to be fed & dressed, she's not safe, afraid to be alone.

What Faulkner or Anderson said about being a writer—morning, evening, and night.

Philip: [Yvor] Winters is a mad rationalist.

June 4

The longer
    you live
The more often
    you die

The heart-shaped apple fattens
    on the harp-shaped
        tree
[. . .]

Phoenix Lyric
When I go down to sleep
        To sleep
I am wood I am
        Stone I am a slow
River, hardly flowing
& all is warm & all is animal
—I am stone, I am river
I am wood—a wood but not
        A leaf . . .
    [. . .]

November 11–12

Mon., Nov. 12. Anxiety after E. went to Leslie. I asked her to come back—long & tired discussion—until 5—impatient for five min.—too much.

Klonsky called. Larry Rivers [painter] came by with the wrong hat. Wm. & Meyer Schapiro (I was drunk) called, then came in, uneasy.

Sexual frustration again—You do blame me—anger & maybe you're right. Why don't you eat?

Phone call from Wm.—hostility after—glass of milk.

Sun., Nov. 11. Letter to [Louis] Kronenberger—nervousness—three hrs. for three pps.—the circle—photograph & scandal.

Nervousness & tiredness—uptown to [Conrad] Aiken's—calm of gin & renewed discussion of gossip & T.S.E.—quarrel with E. ("Why did you have to pay for Kenneth & Aiken?") Phone call to Joe—chiseler, insulting & anti-Semite—my mother at 3; the priest at 10 said the Jews put Christ on the Cross.

Gruenthal: hysterical versus personal courage—leave, beat it, can't do anything.

November 15–19

Mon., 19. Quarreling again? Lunch with Jay at Joe's [restaurant].

Sun. Kenneth all day—"crackpot"—still would say so [Delmore's brother and his earlier epithet].

Fri. The Charles for dinner—$18—Philip's—Bert[ram D.] Wolfe [Lovestonite and author of *Three Who Made a Revolution*]—Eve Gassler [*Partisan Review* staff member] ("unrelated to physical objects"). Stomachache—St. Vincent's at 3:30—woman who had attempted suicide by cutting her wrists—no sleep until 6. —1½ [hours] without attention.

Hook smug & told E. not to let me put her to work.

Deans as those who know nothing. Anne Hook aggressive about my silence once, not now.

Weds. E. went to see her father to tell him I had "legitimate grievances."

I tried to write *Commentary* piece & gave up after 1½ pp. At editorial meeting Wm. kept saying, "Delmore is right."

November 20–22

Thurs., 22. Thanksgiving—Fred called—Dwight invited us to dinner. Argument about Bellow ("consumed with envy"). Churchill & Dardanelles campaign & Italy & C.'s prose style & what would have happened if Germans had taken Paris in 1914. D[wight]'s gyrations of attitude.

Rage about Joe again when we came home at 2—E. paid no attention.

"What a memory"—Nancy [Macdonald] attacked Dwight as an egotist.

Weds. Ed[itorial] meeting—[Allan] Dowling [who helped finance *Partisan Review*]—no award. Philip had gone to the country—Wm.'s invitation refused after being accepted—loan refused by bank.

Quarrel about Joe again—and about 1½ [hours] before E. would call Wm. to tell him her sister was coming, and about "That's not what you said." (Letter to [Princess] M[arguerite] Caetani [publisher of *Botteghe Oscure*].)

Tues. [Chandler] Broussard in the afternoon—Jay & Gertrude Huston—"I thought you would be mad at me"—applejack—Jay not as doubtful or unwilling as E. thought he would be about making me managing editor.

November 23

[Barbara Moncure, Elizabeth's sister, is visiting. Her husband, killed in an automobile accident, had left her with two small boys and a daughter, born two weeks later.]

Barbara—one-man girl—wants to go pick up men in bar or at USO, and to do it on her own.

"My poor dear Adam"—killed at intersection—would not look at him.

She does not [know how she will manage with] the baby.

Albert—not home. Louis—Barbara fascinated by Bridget (her eyes began to shine)—Cedar Bar & home.

"I'm beginning to feel more like a brother than a brother-in-law."

"Maybe we ought to take the baby?"—E. called [Dr.] Gr., who thought it was rather a good idea—preview (practice) if I was willing. E. thinks it's a good idea because she is so afraid of having a baby— "It would revolutionize our whole life."

November 24

Will [Barrett] invited E. for a cup of coffee after ed. meeting two wks. ago. Last week he wished I would attack him so that he can dissociate himself from *PR*—"That's because you identify me with Wm. & P[hilip]," I said & he said nothing. He was defending Wm. again.

Wm. called three times—once about Guggenheim & not thrashing everything out—then to tell me about committee of three.

Hook told Philip (Sat., Nov. 17) he was afraid Wm. would not do a good job—but was on the spot since Wm. had quit two teaching jobs.

Fred asked about Tauber book on Kafka & was halfhearted about our getting together.

Barbara: I'm basically a very considerate girl—I'll do my share— you haven't gotten in touch with Albert yet, have you?

To Rhoda: You're counting your chickens before you've got your cock.

December 8

Barbara Moncure & Philip: "Nathalie has gone to Florida again." "That's the way it is when you talk to Delmore, he jumps from one thing to another."

Nervousness all day—too much to drink the night before—walking to Macy's on 33rd St., between 5 & 6 to get liquor for the party after forcing myself to invite Kimber Smith (kissed by B. as a reward)— simple after complications.

Hivnors, Dupees (Andy's steak-eating visit to Texas), Albert Erskine, Kimber Smith [painter]—(He is trying to impress you. He's not tall enough for me, said Barbara)—Anatole Broyard & eighteen-year-old Nathalie Rogers, Leslie & Jane.

Breaking thru after 10 and after having nothing to say.

B. on couch next to Albert, drinking in every word & looking like a pretty cat.

Make a list of all the things you don't want me to say.

E.: Stop interrupting Delmore.

Albert & Kimber stayed until 3:30—Albert wanted to take B. home. Fred was bored because there were not enough boys to talk to—for a while he seemed interested in Leslie. Delighted by what seemed to be the erotic situation at 3:00. Barbara looked in after we were in bed to say that Albert should be told she was coming down on the twenty-second.

December 9–11

Sun. Hangover, nervousness, the pictures—*Anna Karenina* & *The Captive Heart* (about PWs & mistaken identity). Depressed, more depressed, in the Irving Place Bar & Grill—almost one half pint of brandy before dinner, three qts. of beer after.

Mon. Lunch at 12 with Wm. about new Symposium. Whole bottle of sherry before dinner, three qts. or more after dinner. Dwight in the evening at 8—the Trillings, *Catholic Worker*.

"Poor Delmore"—after making love.

Tues. Awake at 4, asleep from 8 until 2—E. went to Princeton with Jane [Mayhall] & to Flemington—forced chores—dishes, shaving, shower, newspapers.

Extreme nervousness & numbness at cocktail party for Isherwood (44th St. & Sixth, near Algonquin): Will Barrett, Hollis Alpert [movie critic and fiction writer], Djuna Barnes, Auden, Eddie Tisman, Gertrude Huston, Dave McDowell & his Italian wife, Malcolm Cowley and his wife, Oscar Williams, Jay, Kathleen Paine, Jackie Clark, [Robert] MacGregor (ND), Barbara Ash, Kimber Smith, Kimon Friar [poet and translator].

Misunderstanding about when E. would be home.

Quarrel with E. about her reading a book—a mystery—the day before (while Dwight was here & while waiting to make love). "Have you been feeling like this all day?"

Undated

[One can be sure from internal evidence that most of the following undated pages belong to late 1951 or early 1952, and they were found among the papers of that period. To indicate separate entries, rather than repeat undated, *I have used asterisks.]*

Philosophical comedies, romances, tragedies (The Nihilist?)

The hero is a metaphysician who examines & compiles all contemporary views, beliefs, and values—talking to his wife & his daughter —finds himself cut off from them in the end—as he has been cut off from everyone else.

I.e.: It is necessary to believe in something.

It is better to believe in what may be false than to believe in nothing (but doubt)—as better to have loved and lost than never to have loved at all.

He makes a dialectic of proverbs & maxims.

❈

[Theodore] Roethke [is] underestimated. The reader who supposes that Roethke is really a primitive lyric poet loses or misses a great deal. Perhaps the best way to define what is under the surface is to quote Valéry's remark that the nervous system is the greatest of all poems.

❈

The Pajamas Opera. The Man's Pajamas—a story, dialogue, comedy.

William, Marguerite, Eleanor Rockwell, Albert-Peggy (bought pajamas).

Is pregnancy a social convention?

Statistics of life and death, of men & women.

Conclusion: Each couple putting on pajamas self-consciously before going to bed (in anger or quarreling).

Philip as theorist who shifts back & forth. Gertrude (beginning of the story—first my wife, then my mother): is it tactful to ask her the size? Jean buys me a pair of pajamas for $5. Cal objects to the price & the act. Peggy regards it all as pure theater. Brief discussion of the cat's pajamas (who buys the tomcat's pajamas?).

Marguerite—choice of man versus career. Pathetic answer.

Capitalism—anxiety.

Relation of sexes.

❀

Flaubert: the right word (& phrase)
    Is always the musical one—
The scent, the smile
        But no more than these

But hey, presto, the mirror is
      Breathed on
& the young knight-errant recedes

"Have you got that kind
Of memory? that retentive memory?
Murmuring, under his
    breath,
          moving with aplomb
Behind the simple mask of his
           face
Adorned with vine branches—
Under gold spices & cords
The other face of our dreams
    sailed

The source whence the magicians
Draw their strength, their
Strangeness, and their sorcery

❀

Afraid of joy
Living in fear
In terror of life
  & love

❀

"Our Poor Dead King," an Essay on the Critics of Joyce—Life,
Guilt, Zurich. Wilson—groundwork. Levin, Fadiman, Eliot, Winters,
Gorman, Bogan, Troy (an old myth (egg) will do as well).
    Poor Fish! too witty to be understood. He must be wiped out.

❀

Freud, thirty years of shameless behavior.
Tell them I am Aryan—W. Phillips.
Honesty is the best Machiavellianism—
People have this desperate need to be honest—sometimes.

❀

I am one who has been taken
Advantage of—all of his
Life—

    By his mother
      By his brother
    By his wife—the second
Far more—though it would
Have seemed inconceivable
—Than the first

Frowned upon by his father as
          peculiar
The pet of the teachers, shunned
By the pupils, the students, the campers
The boys on the block

❀

Lecture Themes

1. Tourist, student, paid admission (and the world of the future), "Far Rockaway"

2. National & international causes of private experience

3. Childhood as symbol of life used by uncontrollable & ignorant powers

4. Time & history as essences—Fugue & "Lincoln"

5. Prose & verse reasons for (our literary experience & psychology of reading—intensity & history of the novel)

6. Commentary—reasons for—interpretation—*Coriolanus* at Corioli

7. Poetic of everyday experience (twofold motion of poetry). Effort to see all as a sign—effect on the imagery & meter

8. Choice & freedom as most important aspects of human behavior (marriage in *Genesis*)

9. Values & ideals as transformation of life (Xmas poem)

10. Reasons why poetry is misunderstood—irreversible track of discrimination.

❀

I play only
For my own pleasure
I write slowly,
At Death's leisure
And the true measure
Which guides me wholly

(Wholly, treasure, leisure, posterity, roly-poly, holy.)

❁

I drank just a little beer—hardly half a glass—before starting to eat dinner, and there was not much dinner, which is a help too, under certain conditions.

When I woke up at 6, I was very nervous, as another drinkless night—perhaps the absence of liquor makes for this first reaction (as when, going to sleep without s.t.'s, I felt jolts, too), like railroad couplings & uncouplings in a sleeper after midnight.

It's as if anxiety exhausts itself, uses itself up—and then I am free for a time—the only anxiety I felt yesterday was about not going to see [mother]. I reminded myself that [Dr.] Gr. had said it was not good for her, but the thought kept coming back.

"You were wonderful—just by being," said M. K[lonsky] of my hospitality. But Margaret is not for him, he says; she gives him neither excitement nor comfort.

"*Arma virumque cano, qui Troiae qui primus* [Virgil, *Aeneidos* I 1]" he recited in the park.

"I'm not a beer drinker," said Roslyn (or Rosalind).

"No one is born a beer drinker," said M.K.

How much my behavior depends on how I feel about myself!— yesterday as an excellent illustration.

❁

Of the dark powers, the threat—

"To think one's way into the night."

"You'll go home, you'll get a job, you'll go to work—you'll be just as important as anyone else."

Unrelated glances, unfocused eyes.

"Sometimes I even miss Delmore." "Sometimes I miss myself."

"You're not strong enough to be sick."

His doom in the river
Is the revenge of things

"The world as a stage play to the glory of God."

❁

Train back from Washington, confident little girl, married. "You guys ought to be in Hollywood." "Whenever they want anyone to fight they send the Marines—they're expendable." Green seersucker uniform, perky nose. "My boyfriend says he won't marry me unless I'm a nice girl in the daytime & never a nice girl at night."

Draft story told to Aiken: kidney station, psychiatric & orthopedic station. A wonderful story, said Aiken.

Argument about [General Douglas] MacArthur, "politically backward."

Sinclair Lewis, after drinking for thirty years, stopped drinking for three weeks and died as a consequence.

"You see," said Milton, "first he tells you about his drinking. Then he drags in a literary figure."

"Let's go to the Griddle Shop."

"Goody, I'll have a chocolate frosted."

"Who cares what you are going to have?" (Why are you always talking about yourself?)

Mrs. V. [the landlady at 75 Charles, where the Schwartzes were living]: Don't yell at me, I'm not your mother. (She kept coming in without knocking.) Don't worry, let horses worry: they have big heads.

Stalin at Yalta: How shall I explain it to the Russian people?

"He came out of his cave," said Milton.

"He's come out from under his rock," said Anatole.

"He's going right back again."

(In that salt mine where I toiled with my mind, my heart.)

"The purpose of life is to grow fat & old," said Anatole.

✿

$$ *In Hoc Signo Vincit.*

Notes for $20 [the story "The Fabulous Twenty-Dollar Bill" was published in *Kenyon Review*, Summer 1952]. Why Tate reported Eberhart's questioning. Manuel Risk (a foreigner, & wife?), Spanish or Italian, sent over by the Rockefeller Foundation. Authors instead of painters?

Humidor, liquor cabinet, description of living room, of committee meetings.

Bill is lost or stolen. Letter is written about book given him by Professor Robbins. Complete misunderstanding & misinterpretation on both sides. Robbins snub.

(Ross Young's aggressive play, stolen base, fans cheered Ashburn's catch. Irvin has just stolen home, tying up game—first time in years Giants have done that when it meant a ball game.)

Complete misinterpretation of the letter written by Manuel or his wife on book given him by Robbins—discussion of letter by Robbins & his wife (no mention of $20 bill—how could they?).

1952

[*At the end of the summer of 1951, the Schwartzes bought an old farmhouse in Baptistown, New Jersey, and in December they moved to the country. Delmore had a job for the following academic year in the creative-writing program at Princeton (thirty-three miles distant), and Elizabeth obtained an immediate though temporary job at the Princeton Art Museum.*]

Undated

W. Jersey . . . I've been told by irritated friends that this is (a) a retreat [?] (b) Thoreauesque (c) a desire to be Wordsworthian (d) death.

In all truth, as this letter shows, I like to live here best because I can discuss myself with myself freely & interminably & without encouraging others to do the same (except for Elizabeth & our profound cat A[nna] P[lurabelle] Schwartz).

February 21

Anti-Semitism is humanity's self-hatred.

(E. loves human beings, hence is not at all anti-Semitic.)

"From a certain point on there is no turning back: that is the point that must be reached"—F. K[afka].

But it often seems that one can always turn back, or what is freedom?

Death is point from which there is no turning back (unless the Christians are true).

March 11

Arrival of state police—fear for Libby (right after typing *wife*).

May 3

Wm. called this morning to ask us to dinner.

The Aikens called to find out the way.

Emily expressed her impatience & resentment of Rolph [Elizabeth's mother and stepfather], how he had directed her driving at each turn when [they] drove home—"He's a jerky soul—very high-strung—very intense, an alarmist." (Donald Duck, Andy Gump, the man in the straw hat, the man across the aisle in the club car.)

"I'm getting a later ride." Condensation of phrasing as creative.

F.O.M. was amused—87 Pinckney St., Xmas 1942. Duncan [?] had just been killed in North Africa. Harry Levin said this was too just. I was in a state of intellectual & verbal heat. Mark Schorer asked me, half-conscious of what he was doing, to get him a drink. I talked about Emily Brontë & her brother (Harry tried to be friendly), also [about] Freud, Edmund Wilson, and Poe. F.O.M. paused at the doorbell to hear, since derivation was in question—Poe as "spiteful, ——, ——." I was elevated so much in good will [as] to say to Elena I was sorry I had not been able to talk to her & she spoke of how glad she would be if we visited her & I drew back (contracted—convulsed—spontaneously).

Almost ten years ago! The working of memory, returning in unexpected fullness & concreteness.

When we went down Mass. Ave. I saw in the Phillips Bookstore a copy of Kreymborg's *Poetic Drama*—from Aeschylus to D.S. [*Shenandoah* was the last play in the anthology]—and congratulated myself, feeling that I was on a summit & satisfied.

E.: "You always think that someone is putting something over on you." (Jay, Fodi [local garageman], power lawn mower, Ditschman [local car dealer], Joe Pollet.)

Fall when we moved to 20 Ellery [Cambridge]—walls were scraped but poorly so that the paint ran. G.B.S. [Gertrude] was the fine girl who said that sex was disgusting. I finished a last revision of *Genesis*. Morrison told me I would get a 5-year appointment. I was drinking seriously with pleasure, reading & writing as I drank, and thinking that alcohol was going to free me of depressions.

It was the fall of the Coconut Grove fire, invasion of N. Africa, Stalingrad—June Cannan's visit to Cambridge when G[ertrude] was in New York ("She always comes when I'm away"). [June] was very flattered when I said she should have married me.

Fall before going to see [Dr.] Sieve—violent quarrels in middle of night with G.B.S.—pumping up from much drinking (of rum & sherry) & going to class drunk without knowing it.

John B[erryman] married Eileen—avoided me for a time—had heard something (Giroux) [Robert Giroux, friend of John Berryman and his editor, now a partner at Farrar, Straus & Giroux]. I tried to cultivate "younger set" as social circle: R. G. Davis, Hope, Mark & Ruth Schorer, but it did not work very well.

F. O. M[atthiesen] came to dinner with the Schorers. We were an hour early for the Davises' big cocktail party—I talked too much and monologized. And when G. admitted I had, I had self-pitying that no one really liked me, and she tried to explain that in close intimate groups my monologues were fine.

Angry with Mark about Kazin & going or not going home—vented my hatred of Harry [Levin] to Davis & Schorer. Davises tried to get us to stay. "We'll just sit here staring at each other." "First to come, last to leave," I replied.

May 27

Black excrement—second day as if had been drinking wine.

Reading Robert Frost in the country, in the city (in winter, after snow, at twilight, just before dusk). Essay: Nature in Wordsworth, Hardy? Tennyson, Shakespeare; Whitman, Blake; *Walden*—*not* Robinson? (Not what they said of nature, but the specimens they culled.)

> Come, my soul, I said, let us
> Collect the jewels of perception

(Add: descriptions, witticisms, epigrams, formulations.)

Is it not likely enough that a new harvest of fruit grows, however slowly, in this underground of days and nights? It is likely not certain.

Calm at 12 after two Dexs., more sleep, but very nervous—too frantic & noise irritable at 7:30–8:00.

> I am a true American
> I own a car
> & like
> Coca-Cola
> Very much

> When asked what I do, I say:
> Write
> And am told that my interlocutor
> Reads *Reader's Digest*
> regularly

Poems about Flemington, Frenchtown (1880, Ringoes), New Jersey.

> This is my house
>   *"   "   "* land
>   *"   "   "* wife
> This is my life!

I regain the habit, the mind-pose, mind-lounge, of novel reading.

New book of lyrics, 50 pp. enough.

Desire to travel by car this summer to the Cape & Maine.

How many years have I shortened my life / By barbiturates & by alcohol?

Rosh Hashanah to Yom Kippur. Days of Awe. No roots, no religion.

R. J[arrell] on J. B[erryman]: A darting style.

Giants 4, B'klyn [9?]—in the car—under the stars in the cool of the evening.

Convinced last night at 12 that I will make much & much more if not the most out of the next manic phase—as once I did ten years ago.

So alienated that they do not know they are alienated—as the deaf don't know about music & their distance from it.

The pleasant idea of: *Collected Poems*—after gone / before gone.

Poem: The smut & smog of my native city.

High Society: A Short Novel. (Letting the imagination run not wild, amok.)

An American Comedy; A Little Comedy.

> Crystal ball sky—aloft
> Pure crystalline
>   A single puff of cloud
>   So still, it seems as if
>   It had been painted there!

Slowing down—3:00.

Outside, in the meadow, one dyspeptic cow.

Poetry: to name E. the Hudson St. Ophelia.

Manhattan means in Indian the place where we all got very drunk (last Sun.'s *Times*).

Dope means unaware / more aware: as: inside dope. Etymology of slangs—too difficult?

Synonyms of money: spinach, moola, grand; leaves, dough; clinkers, folding stuff.

Cocteau: I look at the sea which always astounds us. Women, of an insolent beauty—

> Take more trouble, take more time
> To make the chinkling tinkling rhyme

Smut, glut, slut, mutt, rut, cut, nut. Squiggling, jiggling, giggling.

Who has driven nails thru my heart?
Who, being touched,
was broken glass?

A single silly cloud
Hung up—irrelevant—
(Blue, blue arched over all & all)
But this was our essence, is
The truth of accident
The fate of all intent
Of destiny, the signs
The psyche's yearly scores
The pathos, the chaos
The hopes, the tricks, the lies

Take any theme & blow it up!
This noon, after breakfast, *Springboard* by Louis MacNeice. A little of Cocteau—just a line here & there—unconcentered, unfocused.
Took off the jackets of books—compulsively irritated by the cat Ethel—one bookcase almost fell down—felt mild pleasure, slightly euphoric as if coming closer, slowly to m.p. [manic phase] ("the ride").
Choric, Doric, Nordic. Wicket, thicket.
A bush! A thrush! A meadow! A shadow!
Small townspeople—scared by the idea of living in the city.
Sour grapes—make a fine dry wine—

Mallarmé was
playing
Strip solitaire

May 31

Yesterday, superficially—Rilke's Sixth Elegy.
"I'll loaf & invite my soul!" said Walter Rip Van Winkle.
"Anchors away!" said Emily Dorothy (Dilly) Madison Post.

Doggerel or Nothing
Outside the house the cows
Indulge in idle moos
It is the last of May
The spring has passed away

Notebook—Giants doubleheader—second radio breaks down—listening in the car, pleased by the vernal scene (framed in the small back mirror) & the existential prospect (swinging over?).

The Aikens at Josie's [Josephine Herbst]—too many Orange Blossoms. Rolph yakking away—home with E.—drunk & hysterical—no dinner—bed. "There's no grass in the bedroom," E. wailed, and "You don't like me" (twice hit—same irrational sudden temper as with the cat) & went out on the slanting roof to be sick.

Emily told me how beautiful E. was & how "we always wondered what man would get her and now you've got her." I told her how much E. liked the house; having no comment to make: "You like it too, don't you?"

Emily came to the bedroom door to ask us to eat—"Can I see her, say good night to Elizabeth." "If you can find her." (She was out on the roof.)

Reconciled at 5:45 when E. woke & ate half a veal chop & lima beans, conversing downstairs with Emily.

Fall, winter, 1942.

Mark [Schorer] tried to get G[ertrude] to sit on his lap.

Hope Davis would not sit on my lap in the amorous phase of the Arons' New Year's party.

Give, Delmore, give, said Aron's wife as we enacted charades.

Ruth announced that she would sit on my lap on our taxi drive to a Boston seafood restaurant. G. did not like this at all—frowned, said nothing, saw to it that she would be sitting on my lap on the way back. (E.'s formula: "Possessive without being responsive.")

"Delmore is going to turn out to be homosexual," said Hope Davis when I spoke of the masks the war was lifting.

"I know someone who talks just like that," said Aron, much taken.

Eileen [Berryman] called M. Schorer "the intellectual Humphrey Bogart." We visited with the S.'s & John said the conversation was "brilliant! brilliant!"

Mark marveled at my R[ogers] Peet pinstripe. "All I need is a bottle of Calvert's," I said.

Harry [Levin] winced, jerked, overhearing my mention of anti-Semitism in Cambridge.

Gaffe about *CAHM* [Delmore's *Coriolanus and His Mother*] & Morrison ("He always speaks well of you"—responding prolixly to Davis's polite remark).

Nela stopped by in the fall, on her way to Washington to see John, who was then in an officers' training camp. John visited us, and I looked in guilt at him—he had found an unsent letter to me in a book of Nela's.

"Delmore is ardent," he said to his father, president of the Cambridge Draft Board.

Told G[ertrude] to get out—in middle of night—feeling more & more sorry for myself.

G. called Sieve—he was away (after outburst: "Why don't you go?").

Warned me that we would see Schorers if I attacked him about play. G. a year after: "They like you but they're terribly afraid of you."

Advocate party—"Were you goosed?" asked R. G. Davis. Mark, asked about dinner, wanted to know our relations with Levins—"I see that Ruth is talking to Elena now." Aron & Davis told me of Mark's review of Hillyer's novel—Davis said he had had to speak to Mark about it: about Mark had gone too far.

As G. & I left a Frost reading, we walked into F.O.M. & I said: "Did you see the handsome things that Kazin said about your book?"

He decided to come to the *Advocate* party for Frost—since we would be there—and afterward came to dinner with us at the Oxford Grill.

G. thought it was very nice of me to speak (spontaneously & freshly) in that way as a greeting—as, after, when I said "I knew about that," answering F.O.M.'s announcement that *PR* had asked him to review G[*enesis*]—Spencer looked impressed & annoyed to see success of calculation & cahoots.

G. disgusted by calculations about Gregory & *Accent* (I would say I was going to review his book).

"You know you're devious," said G.—about what, though, that time? Gregory?

She was working up the strength to go (one of her doubts: not to share the limelight).

Visited by Roslyn Brogue—John & Sonny S[hapero] were there—maddened by Roslyn, who ran down Will & told of his comments on Rimbaud.

Corrected John [Berryman]'s poem on Brueghel—he drew himself up to his haughtiest frigidest in arrogance.

"Don't act like a horse's ass," said Roslyn.

"What language some people use," said Sonny, shocked & titillated.

Sonny remarked on John [Berryman]'s sharp eye for detail—three birds in Brueghel's *Winter Scene*.

Roslyn, overconfident, was sickened by sherry, threw up.

George Palmer & Phyllis visited us in midst of a quarrel (car driving—"You're not a good driver").

Sonny did, too—on another evening—*Gatsby* & *Portrait of a Lady* expounded—photos—G.'s—she did not want it shown—vanity!—"You're the vainest person I know," said G., infuriated. So that's the way it is, said Sonny, delighted by the drama of an unhappy marriage.

John insulted Wallace [Dickson] (was that the night after Wallace stayed too long when F.O.M. visited us?) about Raskolnikov—as not an intellectual. "I don't like you."

Rose left in a cab, also furious at Wallace.

Wallace's country place in Sept. Rose still in Maine.

"Now I am going to devote myself to my wife (& life)." G.: I don't believe it!

G.'s jealousy of June: enormous tension—house agent with whom I quarreled said she was like Joan Fontaine.

Just 28–29 years of age! and I did not know the beautiful possibility of the reality!

Dickens's *Bleak House*; Dost. *The Possessed*—biographies—manic phase for almost six months—from Sept. until (Oct. Nov. Dec. Jan. Feb.) end of Feb.—with ups & downs.

"What will you say in five years?" said G. about my drinking rum in bed at night.

"That anger," said G., reading G[*enesis*], annoyed by my impatient questioning.

Reviews for *Nation* & *NR*—attempt to attack Bogan—Jarrell in review of Aiken—Kazin then literary editor of *NR*—I was overmotivating situations. (First draft of "New Year's Eve"—only completed piece of six manic months!)

"Brilliant diseased mind"—"like A. Huxley," Catholic student said to Anthony Clark [Harvard faculty member in art history].

Very pretty, said G. of blond Irish girl who died in C[oconut] Grove fire. I won't stand it if you sleep with Radcliffe girls (they were in a special category). Milly Jones came to house with her paper. "Who are you?" she said to G. insultingly.

Theory: full memory restored by sobriety? But I drank more last night than on many nights.

Growing annoyance with J., leading to blow-up in ("They're going to get you")—began to read books about alcoholism.

G. called from N.Y. after Grove fire: "You know I would not go to a nightclub." "I thought the Schorers might have taken you." Tears of girls in Rad. class—dead girl's friend: "You were just tops with her—wanted to write about theme of one of your poems (love & hate together)."

Visited Agee in N.Y. & Wm., Dwight, and Philip (reunion began in spring of '42 at Agee's, after Wilson piece).

I tended furnace, made coffee—rationing had first effect—which did not last long—on coffee supply.

Began sinking-ship poem—walked past Cambridge cemetery after finishing "To the Reader" of G[*enesis*]—read Rank, a little, as G. read Horney, went to a psychoanalyst, much conflicted about staying or going away—maddened sexual deprivation more & more exacerbated.

Went to Jean Rogers's party in N.Y. (Barker, girl, Lionel Abel,

Wm.—Clem about to be drafted—or was that the spring before?
No—).

I had spent the night with June at a hotel.

"There will be biographies of you"—when I went to get back my
pipe at hotel.

I did not want anyone to know I had been at a hotel, though
staying with Dwight.

No answer when I called Cambridge, tried to get G. to come to
N.Y.—I claimed that G. was not answering phone.

Fred [Dupee] spoke of *N[ew] D[irections]* description of
G[enesis]—"Sounds wonderful"—Feb.? Jan. 1943? or when?

No lack of episodes—infidelity between two cities.

Question of transposition—not really insuperable—or even difficult.

June 1

"The House." Images in Agee (*New Letters*)—urban description,
exact, minute, hypervisual. Two views of a middle-sized provincial
city (Knoxville), one residential, one downtown.

The slick surface of a photograph—America's essential feature!

Ferry, Eleanor Clark [woman of letters, fiction and non-fiction]:
the ferries landed—with a snarl of churned-up water—rumble of prows
against pier.

See *Manhattan Transfer* (lost copy?).

Giants lose in ninth—disappointment after working listening
pleasure looking at the cloud-ridden sky.

Rain dripping day, chuggling spouts & guggling roof—the sky
clearing in the west (a deep old image—smoky lines of clouds lifting
in front of a lighter cloud background).

The Poet's Way of Life (In the Trough).

Hopkins: descriptions of clouds. Blake: studies of Greek & Latin.

Like the blown smoke of burning coal, diagonal to the cloud background, at angle, slanting.

Book of Tobit, story of Tobias; cadence & phrasing; and they went
forth, and the young man's dog went with them.

Patience—patient nobility of the trees on the lawns.

Confessions of a Child of a Century.

A dark summer afternoon
a clarity of air under the trees
the leaves hanging wet & limp
but sharply defined
now—as June begins—near
the full summer

Greek revival, post-bellum—smoked brick & geegaws—Hudson River bracketed.

Distressed—knew the name of the *wicker* chairs—but not the kitchen chairs we took from Charles St.—wooden? curved backs, four rods.

The Yogurt & the Commissar—The Commissar's Yogurt.

Friendship of Rilke & Valéry.

Rilke: First Elegy—T.S.E. Rilke wrote as if he were already dead—or wished to be—much modern poetry produced by old men—Yeats ("Byzantium")—Valéry—halfway beyond the circus—the early dead—the lovers—the children—the angels—great works of art.

Apollinaire: "at the frontiers of consciousness."

Kafka—hallucination, prehistory. Mann—middle-class life. Joyce—world of sleep & cauchemar & unconscious.

For ten years—fled, as much as possible, from the reality of pain & suffering—the vigil of suffering, the truth of rejection, the experience of emptiness, the lesson of boredom.

New Letters—Eugene Joffee (1936)—pathetic middle-aged trumpeter—can't get work—genuine but conclusion-less.

Eugene's fears? prophetic, a depression story. Louis Guilloux. Little sketch about mother torturing child verbally in train—that she will throw him out of the train when it goes through the tunnel or passes the river.

The Promotion; The Divorce (as comedy?).

Ten pages of notes, a sudden overflowing—about 1942 in Cambridge.

The Scarletts, Aikens, Helen D. B. [Dickson Blackmur] to dinner. Rolph like a dictator's radio consuming all attention—Orange Blossoms—gin & bitters—too hot & then sudden late-afternoon chill on the lawn.

Feeling of contentment & of health. E.: "You're looking very well." She felt exhausted, making too much of an effort as on most visits & became angry, arguing with her stepfather about democracy & Communism, an inevitable topic.

"Your voice has such an ugly ring," said Emily tactfully!

Gin & vermouth to help one s.t. (supply down to three) get me to sleep—which it did! no specific addiction.

Rolph insisted on going to town with me for the laundry—wanted to come back when it turned out that we had forgotten the old wash—Emily toiled with the flowers zealously, absorbedly.

Bodenheim another dead duck (Zukofsky—O'Neill).

[Dr.] Gr.: There are always threatening situations.

No intensity of desire—little desire—but enough for *mildness* (viz. sleeping & s.t.s, liquor, appetite).

Goodbye. God be with you.

Critic, at least, no doubt about that! voracious reader again (*The Promising Young Men* by George Sklar, *Murder at Arroways* (can be used for Yaddo background) by Helen Reilly & *The Other Elizabeth* by James Gregg—800 pp. between 5:30 & 1:30 a.m.).

Leading themes in Am. Lit.? Adultery & Fornication: *Gatsby, Scarlet Letter, Golden Bowl, Age of Innocence, An Am. Trag., Jenny Gerhardt, Ethan Frome, T.W.L.* (?copulation), "Prufrock."

The Discovery (recognition, attack, flight, or rejection) of Experience: *Moby Dick, Leaves of Grass, Walden, Life on the Mississippi, Let Us Now Praise Famous Men, Education of Henry Adams.*

As beginning of chapter in academic story or novel: a professor's lecture.

Rolph—big frog in small puddle—Caesar in Spain, a doormat in Rome.

Has the recording angel recently / Learned shorthand or another rapid code?

A saint—timid & brave. Fifth Ave. bus. A Yankee Buddha. Grandson & distances between Chi., S. Fran., and N.Y.

Death of John Dewey.

Groton Fellows read of Branch Rickey (to admit Negro student), Jackie Robinson was pioneer.

Does not tyro partake of the connotation of tyrant?

For the lawn—an iron Negro jockey—a marble-topped table—a beach umbrella—privet hedges.

> Why are you so nervous
> Because I drink too much
> And why do you drink so much
> Because I am nervous

Special glitter, aura, mystique of symbol—because it shines with the visible darkness of the unconscious / unknown—powerful—important (A adultery Hester Prynne).

> Whiskey and beer, brandy and rum
> Aspirin, Seconal
> Drawn from the dark earth's rising plants
> Sucked from the secrets of vitality
> To pacify the anguished gaze of old mortality

(Serenify, restorify.)

Was Jesus illegitimate? Think of it, hypocrite.

Working at night will be sign of a real reformation.

E. sick, returned at 3, loaded with penicillin.

Aymé: In sex propinquity.

June 3

My ceremonial sentiments about third wedding anniversary, E.'s thirtieth birthday.

Dreams in which Van Wyck Brooks & Zolotow appeared, made an engagement with me. *Shenandoah* was produced, found to be ridiculous. I turned away from the reviews, and "Delmore, what a pretty name." It should not be spoken with a Jewish accent, that's what [is] wrong, I told someone sympathetic. A student & admirer had just said the play was very poor.

On Attic steles, did not the circumspection of human gesture amaze you? (Rilke, Elegy 2).

Shakespeare: sophistry (the caricature of logic & reason) as wit, persiflage.

Novel or short novel? about author who marries with young girl— who will support him & literary review & a literary social life (wealth & art & classes, as they come together—as wealth seeks out art).

June 4

"You hurt me," Frost's Job says to God.

Three moves improves in past six months: sobriety (+ s.t.s), money, living room.

Now at almost 4, working mood & mood of contentment spoiled because Cubs scored 5 against Giants in seventh to end 6–2.

Dispersed interests & loves—what has baseball to do with the rest of my life & mind? A little—as American & of the people.

Sense again last night of how I let relationships decay—depression-hindered—Meyer S., e.g.

Irving Howe's new book on Faulkner looks as if it had been turned out by the yard, but I just glanced at it.

Pleasure—the dancing of the body & the mind. Speech in a play: If there were enough pleasure, would ambition trouble anyone? (Many must have thought of this.)

The Laws of Pleasure—title of poem (Book of).

The day dilapidates—urge to [go to] N.Y. tonight—but for what?

Any move a sign of change—hope says: better—probably better than this discontent.

Play (or story) about colony devoted wholly to sexual happiness & to rearing children for it (too late for the adult)—how it breaks down—sex as overestimated & disruptive.

Montherlant, *Queen after Death*: "Being alone with good people always makes me awkward." She repeats forever the same cry—like the malmus[?] bird, at the fall of the evening above the melancholy of the lakes.

Play or story about author (portrait of) who whips up—against reproach—the publicity machine of legend-myth-greatness.

Queen after Death: the extreme ambiguity of meaning of passions & of motives.

King cries out, at the end: O my God—cut this appalling knot of contradictions that at least for one instant before ceasing to be, I may at last know what I am.

Too linear? Racinian?

France 1940 (P. R[ahv]): All right—so now we'll be Boches.

God has had a bad press!

God exists if anything exists. (Attraction of any true religion: how much devotion & spiritual nobility it brings forth & forward.)

Helena by Evelyn Waugh, clever & worldly propagation of the Faith.

Did not listen to ball game, unwilling to suffer.

Stupidities of the intelligence: regularity, symmetry, type-etry, consistent intelligence or foolishness. E.g., someone is intelligent—to expect them always or for the most part to be—to act & to think intelligently.

Julie—perceptive about my noticing things when I seem not to, about Wm.'s obsession—but surprised that I minded. Bedford St., Fall? 1946.

To Wm.: "You talk all the time anyway"—somewhat mixed up with her tone of voice—not severe, but off-key—she tried to sound like one of the boys. "Camaraderie," said Wm., "is all right between ourselves."

The clever (cats with sharp claws) (like Wm. & R.S.), like the hare, get way ahead & become overconfident—then the humble or the lacking in confidence, like Clara, move ahead of them at some point—what point?—where the daily collecting & weeding of perception & observation become more important than the flashes & dashes & razzle-dazzle of intuition.

Last night so poor & weak & energy-less or lassitude-full—soon after returning from Flemington, at 6.

But pleasure in the house, outdoors, and E.

Waugh, *Helena*. Delicate touches: Helena asks for her tutor's freedom—meets him years after—asks if he ever got to Alexandria.

Rubens: Camel peeking in, bemused, perplexed (in [Arnold] Hauser's *The Social History of Art*).

Like me,
    You were late in coming
    The shepherds had arrived long before
            Even the cattle
    They had joined the chorus of the angels
        Before you began your march

For you,
> The primordial discipline of heavens
>> Was relaxed
> A new defiant light blazed amid the
>> Disconcerted stars

Especial patrons:
  Patrons of latecomers
  Of all who have a tedious journay to make to the truth
  Of all who are confused with truth & speculation
  Of all who through politeness make themselves partners in guilt
  Of all who stand in danger by reason of their talents

June 5–6

Trip to N.Y.

Fri. Sleep until 3:30, quarrel with E.—leave me alone here with nothing to eat—about going to pictures—dishes. More & more pocketbook drugs—three last night: *The Wheel Is Fixed*, James M. Fox; *Hunt with Hounds*, Mignon Eberhart.

Dwight [Macdonald] called today, surprised not to hear from me: I did not know that I should have called him—ignorance of social & interpersonal reality.

Ernest Van den Haag [political scientist] in the park—thickly worldly, mannered and friendly.

Decay, day after day—

Most people are fools—interesting fools (& everyone is a fool in most things).

Dangerous knowledge: dangerous in occupying the mind, although unspoken. For it is bound to emerge—however sideways through implication & connotation.

Wm. invited here, wanted to know of my relations with Clem (doubting his with me—and asked if I was asleep when he called).

Will, trying (lonely, nervous, waiting for a call from Mary Wickware) to bum a cigarette from Barbara, was refused—"My last one— I'll give you a quarter, however."

Philip bored by country, by social life, by *PR*—"a mausoleum." His only subject was himself—quite undisguised.

Fortune: physique & metabolism—as a destiny.

This is what I've been doing in one or another way since taking up with coffee jags in 1940—after Hivnor told me at Xmas 1939–40 that that was Auden's way of working—explanation of defective meters.

Louise Bogan & Ciardi other judges on Michigan Poetry contests & my choice won!

Teased for several weeks by notion that if I were in N.Y. there

would be pictures to see. But I did not go to them at like times in N.Y.
—the few times I did, there was no large choice—but I was drinking
then.

What I did once I can do again—I can return to—thus it's not a
question of not accepting one's limitations.

6:02—E.'s return—and I don't want her back now, as I did during
winter.

Fake jobs—living off a reputation declining for years. Absence of
passion, obsession, pleasure.

Helen [Dickson Blackmur] came to say goodbye for summer (she
was animated)—when I thought of & did not buy liquor.

I've already been depressed longer than I was manic.

At St. Vincent's, clerk willing to hand out s.t.s without prescription
—"You're an old customer, Mr. Schwartz." True sign of deepening depression—very slight effect of Dexedrine.

Barbara [Greenfeld] looked me over: You need a haircut (I'd just
had one) & I do, too.

One of the early images of marriage: drinking to drunkenness,
listening to music, and talking.

Wm.: "We need another editor like we need a hole in the head."

"But when you have a hole in the head, what do you need?"

Will did not eat lunch & departed portentously—ignored. "I have
to go to lunch, boys," he said—twice? Said same goodbye twice.

Since 3:30, brushing through Malraux book about art—new feeling for what I think is composition—for Caravaggio, whom I had
really never heard of.

Animus against poor E., whose sins are mostly defects & omissions.

What to do this evening? Question on the agenda of consciousness
since 3:30—now it is 5:55—but writing notes does [give] me a little
minor pleasure.

A lot of eating on Thurs.

Notations of inner waste & decline—it is now close to three months.
Existence in a smaller & smaller circle (letters, friends), like the
whorls of a seashell.

Yet I have been trying—to some extent, half-extent—all week—
notes (three novels, *The Scarlet Letter, Helena, Queen after Death*
& Rilke).

June 7

[*The*] *Ego & the Centaur* [title of Jean Garrigue's book of poems]
—Jean Garrigue's ego obsessed with Jay (N[ew] D[irections] em-
blem), vivacious, contagious.

System—forced five pages are not nothing, after all—only during
last week has amount of note pages pleased me—why don't I truly

try her & others?—even T.S.E.—culling of other books' phrases & sentences. Habit, inertia, vice of spontaneity—why can't I free myself as once I did—in the spring and summer of 1938—at 73 Washington Place & at Bennington & in Cambridge.

One depression lasted eight months—Cam., Dec 1943–July 1944, and one six months, Feb. 1949–Aug. 1949: these were the longest ones I can remember. Manic periods were as short as a month (or a day) & as long, with breaks, as six months.

Why does almost everything since 1937 not show itself as previous years did as themes: some of it does, more than I usually think: the professor of literature is in the way, my relations with the people; it is still not lived out, nor far away; it is not subliminal, sufficiently (as childhood naturally is)—but?

Diarist element in modern lit.: Kafka, Gide, T.S.E. in [*The Waste Land*]—Kafka's agonizing—

Yesterday: pleasure in reproductions of John Sloan—as well as Malraux—nostalgic element (adults dressed as in my childhood)—but this can't be the whole explanation, since all photographs have that effect, e.g., Brady, but perhaps the medium of the photograph is itself enough to provide the pleasure of nostalgia.

Stupidity of letter to Brooks, written at height of mania [?] when anxiety was intense.

Cruel to E.—but set off by her—she is lying down now—by her answer when I asked if she minded my going to dinner & the pictures in Flemington.

38½ [Delmore's age].

Dig Me a Grave by John Spain; *The Best Go First* by Frank O'Malley.

What is lacking in detective stories now is characterization such that the reader's interest in the true criminal is governed by his growing knowledge of the characters?—that is, logical connection between characterization & ultimate discovery.

In any case, the puzzle has been reduced for the sake of fast action which titillates & shocks.

Murder: Is there a mystery-detective story without murder, the primal sin?

Yesterday, Friday, a drowned day—3:30–6:00.

E.: "You certainly look miserable—are you depressed or mad?" "Mostly depressed."

Rilke, Third Elegy.

Low of entire depressed period, nine blues & then, after waiting for ½ or 1 hour, two s.t.s—waked by E. talking to cat. "I'm trying to sleep while you conduct that conversation."

Gin before dinner, no effect, no lift.

Moonlight like a lotion, salve, powder (eau de Cologne).

Last Saturday this time: a spout of memory about 1942.

At least I am not now—2:10—deaf & dumb but eager & agitated & nervous after two Dex. (two the first time I woke up), two cups of coffee, the rest of breakfast, an outburst at E., who was trying to be friendly. "All I wanted was for you to help me when I was sick." "Life rotting away day after day, month after month, and I have to bicker about dishes."

Announcement of marriage of Meyer Schapiro's daughter Lillian —a nudge & hint?

E. bought this morning a lawn mower—with which she is very pleased, I think. Eager to show it to me, as if it were a secret surprise present.

Arbitrariness of most marriages—since so little of possibility is examined—but what Barbara said, not just one man or woman is suitable. Still, there is a possible most suitable, which may & perhaps mostly is missed. Story of a doting father oppressed by sense of this as his daughter becomes nubile.

Today, unlike most other recent days, the Dexedrine has some positive effect (not the negative one of getting me back to sleep at 8 or the evening one of pulling me up out of the hangovers of s.t.s & too [much] smoking).

I write down anything I can think of—thus: E. has just gone to bathroom—glanced in the study as she went—returned & slammed the bedroom door.

Manic—depressed shift—though I've not reread it, I felt an aversion toward "Illustrated Classics" which is supposed to appear in the next issue of *PR* ["Masterpieces as Cartoons" was published in *Partisan Review* 19, July 1952]. It might be said: you have some memory of it. But hardly a reliable one.

Repelled by thick neck & popeyed profile after haircut on Friday. At picture last night I looked to see if same profile perspective was part of most faces.

Example of unconscious: pushing off blanket when it gets too warm, tossing in sleep, and waking early when alarm is set.

E.: You'll never give up (last fall?). You're bound to break through (at beginning of this depression).

Maybe no positive effect of Dex. but hangover of too much barbiturate.

Theme of (for poem) two world wars—one of the subjects in which I have a natural interest.

4:30—sunny, the wind blowing.

It is true that no one else is doing what I would like to be doing (J. B[erryman]?—but I know too well how unhappy he is)—except for those who are writing? But who is?

It's easy now not to drink because I know that it will not make me feel any better—this may be a virtue of depression—anesthesia to alcohol.

(Narration as possibility on principle of Better than Nothing.)

Letter to Will S. rejecting his manuscript in what I thought was a way very friendly; Katy [Carver] said she tried very hard to make him when she was in Cambridge. Lily, ignored & very pretty, thought he wanted a divorce because his brother had a divorce & the family was imitative. I touched her. ("You're a bastard," she said, then quoted Florette on all men.)

Five o'clock—up since 12:30 or 1—all of my small store of intellectual energy used up.

The Promotion

The Dean was in general of the opinion that the proposal, whatever the motives (and he was very much aware of the likely motives), merited acceptance. Seated at his desk in the elegant colonial room which was his office & which overlooked the elm-guarded campus, he looked again at the memorandum of the proposal, holding it lightly at an angle and smiling. Academic politics was a game to him, a delightful game, the most delightful chess of all. He had once been a pawn—but pawn was not truly the right word, since pawns did not hang by their thumbs. Now that he was a power, a prime mover himself, he played his part with perfect propriety. But he remembered well enough what the underlings' experience was.

It was proposed in the memorandum that new promotions to five-year instructorships be matters to be decided by a committee of five. This had been the customary procedure at the university for fifty years, but during the last ten each new instructorship for a term of five years was the choice of the professor in whose field the new instructor was to teach: and thus it had become naked patronage: each new instructor owed his appointment solely to one professor. Nothing would have disturbed this procedure had not the area of new appointments tended very much to occur in such a way that some professors had many more new appointments than others: which constituted patronage, although nothing in the memorandum which the Dean held in his hand suggested anything so crude and coarse.

A rotten borough, English A. Theme is merely that academicians are fools.

June 8

The Scarlet Letter all day & all evening—from 1 until 12 with interruptions.

Mildly interested & not very responsive (as I've been at other times) to the style—more pleased to be reading it at last—America's first masterpiece—than pleased by it.

It is passionate, operatic, eloquent, but naïve and thin—as James himself says.

But Hester's proposal of flight—after Dimmesdale & she have faced their desperate situation (here is the thinness, that the evil of Chillingworth is hardly more than a baleful attitude of reproach)—is perfect "by the most rigorous standards of fiction"—and so, after the description of the procession before the holiday, is the climax of confession.

Pearl is thin, too (after the children of Dostoevsky & Gide & James).

James's critical characterization is wonderfully exact: distance & frozenness—all the passion is before the novel begins, the characters exist for, only, and as part of the situation.

The prologue is moving as lyric poetry—lyric essayistic personal poetry & makes a frame the appropriateness of which does not immediately appear.

The lovable sad warm brooding passionate human being—as he comes through in the tone and the moods of the style—is probably what keeps Hawthorne esteemed & read—as much as he is read—in the absence of the really-reals of fiction: character, story, situation, and theme.

(Do I adopt a pompous professorial tone? Very well then, I do: pomposity better than nothing!)

T.S.E.—line from Emerson, Thoreau, Melville, Hawthorne, James. New England divines without portfolio.

Greatness—Eisenhower, Taft—status, prestige, fame, reputation.

Dream of seismograph & Roman emperor—knows of earthquakes, predicts them, gains power.

Most people are merely trying to continue to exist—as individuals, fathers, mothers, officials.

Once some certainty of existence is clear, they are trying to improve the quality of their existence.

They are seeking states of existence in which there will be more pleasure, comfort, excitement, gratification.

(Vanity or the sense of glory is epi-survival, epi-existential.)

T.S.E. revised conditional judgment of *F[our] Q[uartets]* as part of his whole work.

The politics of pleasure, the politics of existence.

Jesting Pilate was an Ur-Hegelian.

Pilate and the poets as philosophers. Poets et al. are philosophers of a certain kind, but their work is valuable not for its truth but for its relationship to its experience.

Two hundred thousand million human beings inhabit the globe. God regards them all.

How green & normal life is (most of the time).

Only when the formations of the family and of the city have established themselves does the pursuit of glory become an important motive of consciousness.

So, now, after being scared by depression & war so long—the dried-up springs of thought & art all over Europe & America. And the clutching at Catholicism for stability, to prevent new vertigos.

Rilke: Fourth Elegy: ". . . here where nothing is what it really is . . ." / ". . . *alles ist nicht es selbst.*"

Weak effort to begin to write story, one page quickly without real feeling.

Yesterday: *Malatesta* by Montherlant—really, failure, compared even [to] *Queen after Death*—too linear again. Malatesta as the image of the hero obsessed with greatness & self-will. The indulgence of all that the self conceives—rape, sodomy, carnage, murder.

E. angry after Handlins called—"Help me instead of reading." Pretext—"What do you want me to do!" "I don't really know what I want you to do except to be aware of how I feel."

I went to Frenchtown, bought ham, sweet potatoes, lettuce, olives, Coca-Cola.

Finished *Malatesta*—abided E.'s outburst—mowed part (exactness since Rimbaud, "It may be good for you"—G.B.S. & W.B.) of the lawn & with the new lawn mower, acquired a blister.

The Handlins were unsure of the directions when they reached Flemington. I went to get them, passed them on the street (tarred?) which goes from the country road to the macadam highway.

Handlins appeared to be very cheerful & content. Mary was very eager for a drink. Good reference to Oscar's Pulitzer—"I bet Mary was more excited than Oscar"—"What in God's name is Oscar's face doing in the newspaper?" Oscar deprecated the prize—went into the living room—asked where all my books were (visitors often excited by my books).

Will [Barrett] visited Handlins, stayed overnight (still using and going after whatever was mine, sibling as ever? or just at a loss?), mentioned Julie ambiguously.

I cut the pie correctly, leading to an anecdote about a Handlin dinner party—colored maid's stupidity. Will told Handlins I was running *Perspectives USA* all by myself.

I drank before & after dinner—& I was drunk before dinner & fell asleep easily but woke too early, drank a glass of water, took two Dex. and slept until 1, when Wm. [Phillips] called.

E. answered, asked to speak to Edna: "Wm. hems and haws so much you never know what's what." (Hems & haws are the human condition.)

Now—as I've written so many times before during the past eight weeks—I should be thinking of what I will try to write tomorrow—Cummington v. Chicago.

Really, apart from a few months in 1949, I have not been a practicing poet—practicing as I used to—since 1944—or have I been in a different way? (& a few weeks—two?—in 1946 & 1947—and now and again whenever manic—and in the way I take hold of language, quick to pick up rhymes & metaphors).

Woman gets divorce because husband tried to trade her for a new car (today's *Times*).

Oscar likes you very much (Dec. 1951) & J[osephine] Herbst (March 1951) & the Schapiros (spring 1951) & Annie Rogers (Nov. 1946)—E.

German proverb: "The Heaviest Baggage Is an Empty Purse."

June 9

A picture-book Sunday afternoon (*House & Garden*)? Irving [Howe] is scared—scared as a literary critic about where he is going. Unfavorable reviews & being turned down by the Guggenheims & Rockefellers? Speed of success makes the hard going harder.

I drank too much, was really drunk after dinner, quarreled with E. about the dishwashing, introduced denunciatory generalities into my tirade.

It was really a pointless visit. Thalia [Mrs. Howe] was mostly bored, talked to E. whenever she had a chance, turning away from the conversation between Irving & myself.

Irving has a crush on George Eliot. When I asked him about *The Scarlet Letter* he said, "The forest scenes are marvelous!"

This is the first day I've gotten up in the morning (apart from trip to New York) in perhaps months. The two Dex. did not put me to sleep after I woke dreaming of the summer issue of the *Kenyon*, my story in it—very complicated—poems by Auden & MacNeice, a very thick number. I looked at the cover, distressed that my name was not in big type. There was an essay by [Yvor] Winters on "Complexity & Complication," or something like that, and I woke as I read the first sentence: something like: "If the writing is clear, the definition of moral intent cannot be given."

Today is very hot—a thick clear heat.

Celebrated his 38½ birthday by losing his temper foolishly.

The lines with which I woke up (in a chant) (in a charm, spoken).

> It is enchanting, it is a part
> of music
> > it soars
> > > like kites, like birds

"I sought a theme"—(W. B. Y[eats]) I sought for weeks in vain.
Will mistakes his insolent fantasies (about the future) for patience.

Tiredness—from last night's too much drinking, using up of energy
—a brightness & jag at breakfast yesterday with the coffee as I looked
at the Sunday *Times*.

"You're looking marvelous," said Irving.

Nap or doze—11:30–12:30—a hot thought-streaked nap, not even
desire for solipsism [?].

A passional relationship—who? a few, a very few—Adam &
Barbara had it & lost it; George not; Knox, Tessa's friends in Cambridge,
reported by Tessa to have it; the different degrees of unsatisfiedness;
Helen [Blackmur] said, "The way it should be between a man & a
woman is not the way it is between Richard & me."

Lawrence's image as destructive, since it pretends that an ideal is
a perversely rejected or ignored actuality—it exists, among the Indians
& the Negroes perhaps—the vitiating image of the excitement of courtship or seduction—which, when it is possible, as with the roving boys,
still does not keep them from being dissatisfied, though here, too, there
may be a few who make the most of it & are truly gratified—and successful marriages, like the Hortons' & the Handlins', are not successful
because of sex—while on the other hand, Will & Julie & Joe Pollet &
Betty were not sufficiently supported by successful sex— The Trillings?
I don't know enough about them.

The ego has roots beneath the surface of consciousness—like
teeth, and it's under the surface that the unhappiness is generated—
relation to career, society, status—the ego's relation to its image of itself
(to its ego-ideal).

Today's *Daily News* inquiry on whether one is normal—maybe
Wm. is right & people are fools.

I've never seen a play of my own performed—but I might have—
and I have written very many.

Auden likes you—I could tell—and Oscar Williams, said Will.
Norman Jacobs, Wohlstetter, Alison Q., Sonny, Jane, W.V.K.—"staunch
admirers." (Laughlin, acc. to O. Wms., and Morrison, according to
O'Donnell.)

E.: "Berryman has a crush on you"—"Richard is very fond of you."
Zolotow & Kenneth.

It was Alison Q. who first told me that I did not appreciate myself,
though not with E.'s clarity & directness.

"Your mother regards you as an enemy to be placated."

Not uncomfortable, not bored (not agonized by outside point-
lessness & meaningless [sic])—able to read (e.g., Rilke & Montherlant), to listen to music—but some new minor level of depression—
it was clear enough when I tried to tell the Handlins about our ad-

ventures with the State Police—which does suggest a psychogenic explanation (& yesterday the Ukraine fable to Irving).

There is a secret, ill-kept but not bruited about or publicized very much. Why are most human beings living? Because they're alive & have not yet died. (No better proposition, [no] more attractive alternative has appeared.)

Solipsism's pictures.

$434.80 in the mail from J[ames Laughlin] "for work on first issue of *Perspectives USA*"—four items—immediate lift—can economic anxiety really be one of the troubles? Conscience & guilt money, since J. did not have to give me anything of what he got for the first issue itself—he worked out a formula for not giving me what he was supposed to—but giving me something—it's still $800 less than I should have gotten.

E. said that since Dec. [when the Schwartzes had moved to the country] we've spent $700 more than we've made—$300 for the car, moving?, $100 for space heater, $50 to $100 for repairing old car.

I feel like calling E. but sixty cents wasteful—she'll be just as delighted at 6.

A thunderstorm in the distance—it is cooler now.

June 10

Impulse, adventure, age, falsehood—the ancient famous place, 1920, like Coney. Monday empty—gray wool sea—no impatience driving—hardly 1½, if that, from 4 until 12—pleased to have gone with impunity & no gratification—a long clear drive both ways—detached from connections.

June 25

The Intellectual as Self-Hidden—Crippled / W[illiam] B[arrett].

After such knowledge, what forgiveness / After such forgiveness, what knowledge.

Will. Did Will's opinion of me improve (he said he had been continually surprised) when he read "AA" [the story "America! America!"] in July 1946? Or was he thinking in terms of self-comparison? Probably the first.

Will not like Stendhal but like a Stendhal hero. A sheep in wolf's clothing. To G.B.S.: Do you think any girl would ever love me? Amazed & annoyed to find Katy Carver at publisher's parties where he vaunted himself [on] being. As he spoke, in 1945, of how little his brother Nicholas understood how he, Will, traveled in the most elevated circles—the State Department, the embassy in Rome. He showed me Shirley's declaration that she was taken with him; told me Eleanor Goff's friend was in love with him; showed Julie [Barrett] his new review in Rockport, and mention of his pamphlet in an English journal—"One of my agents, Delmore, brought it for me."

Changes ideas every three months—excellent for a leading character.

Hero: 1935: Reis [Lincoln Reis, married to Will's sister Mary]—he thinks he's a mastermind.

(Dostoevskian motif.) As a murderer? Julie—Providence—discovers after Julie's death his life is the same, i.e., he knows Julie, suicidal, may find out: he does not make sufficient effort to prevent the possibility.

Lord Chesterfield of the Gluttons. "She's up—she's down." "Either me or the gin." Libby's roast beef.

Slow downfall, politics in hell, heaven. Cop (as ashamed of), mother as servant (as ashamed of), potatoes—poor father's anger, death.

Resentment of Hook, Wm.

Girls on horseback—ruling class—fuck them—Will was very pleased.

Klonsky—patronized seeming (possessiveness). Parkers—Europe —& *PR* as stimulating (after telling me not to be limited to small circle).

Use Will & Jay together—upper-class Scotch-Irish; lower-class shanty Irish.

Ex. of Playboy of Ideas: T.S.E.: "I was looking for the point"—he kept looking under table, under carpet, under sofa—very comical.

But I explained patiently: "E.—all men equal before God" but not before *men* (Ethiopians & Italians).

Will overconfident: "I knew I'd get a copy." Competitive—Respectability & Conventional Recognition—Rockefeller offer. I answered: But Harvard better, because not a false front like Rock.

Background of only yesterday, etc.

June 1945, July 1940—"I expect to be on that magazine," he said, hearing of Jay's projected magazine.

1936—lost his voice—McKeon (1945–9: you were right.)

1946—Hudson St.—*Nation*—Jarrell—[Isaac] Rosenfeld (Jewish F. Kafka). D.S.: "He expects justice." W.: "This is an extremely pleasant household to visit."

1947—Sends Julie for a sandwich (she was going down, anyway—coming to tell me Will had returned)—Julie's distortion, too.

1951—Not an intellectual—Bergsonian—Lawrence better than Proust—libido & conversation (tells women).

Competitive—visits mother (who won't discuss past at first). "Your mother was, in a way, a better preparation for the world than mine."

Use Wm.[-like] figure instead of attachment to me.

Xmas visit of Roslyn—argument about homosexuality (with Chiappe)—overmoralistic accusation.

Klonsky as mirror character for contrast.

1941. Intellect—intellectual—no question of the truth of immortality.

[Randall] Jarrell—Xmas 1946—book reviews—"penalized for being intelligent." Will showed him passage he had misunderstood.

State Dept. quiz.

Could have been a truly classical man. Lied about friendship with Jaeger—affair with Italian girl. Klonsky on Will in Paris. (Look up eating & marriage stories.)

Use *Green Huntsman*—Santeuil[?]: "a most extraordinary jackass"; "not exactly devoid of ideas, but so vain & conceited that one itched to toss him out of the window."

Digression—Mann's obsession with homosexuality—Mario—death; Kinsey; disease-decadence.

1946—Will's sympathy for & articulation of Catherine Sloper in *Washington Square*.

1941—Valéry—stubbornness (unconscious plagiarism, sermon on *mons veneris*).

1945—Discovery that Klonsky is not stupid. Argument with Berryman about Irish, Ireland; shame of Irishness in Boston subway. Stendhal ("too sincere"—cynicism—how can you be too sincere—yes! like too conscientious). Episode of coal stove & kerosene (fall 1945) & fixed electric wiring ("He sometimes fools you"). Berryman as counter-character?

D.S. 1937—Kant—"But man *is* a rational being."

Julie's return from Italy. Hotel Penn comedy (sneaking in)—bourgeois agitation about cold-water flat.

1940—"The work is the only thing that matters."

1937—Visit to Woodstock—no violence. (Nicholas, razor blade—at pictures).

Will—Julien Sorel—"His suicide is a rejection of civilized society."

Kindness—thirty-six—money, 103rd St.—1946–47, coaching, typing lecture. 1947—uncashed Harvard checks. 1947–48—dressing up to kill to see G[ruenthal]. (*Finnegans Wake*—St. Patrick's Day parade.)

Nov. 1945—"You don't know the Irish"—O'Dwyer telling Irish not to vote against a Jew as a Jew (as double talk & direction).

Bourgeois Freedom (a short novel of wife & husband, born too late [1934]). Use *Pajamas Opera*. Use Hemingwayesque for parties—vacations (academic younger set).

Frederick the Great & cavalryman & horse: Abominable! Demote him to the infantry; and Krafft-Ebing, cf. woman's nostril.

Up to the neck (eyes, scalp) in reality.

Methodological & activating principle: One Novelist Can't Do Everything. Stendhal's light opera, serious & gay.

Ed Wynn's "I could eat a horse" (not as in the discipline of cats [?]).

The unmistakable amoral pleasure-aggression of killing flies.

To imagine oneself inside a character (not composite: possible), a joy mistaken for a fearful chore.

Nightwood—the real (underlying) motive is Nora's love of Robin, the lost girl.

Not everything—Stendhal lacks Faulkner's vividness & intensity (lacks Dost.'s search of the depths); but F. lacks S.'s light, penetration, command of intelligent human beings, social compass.

(Camera, chimera / mortadella, umbrella.)

Alcibiades: The Classical Playboy, The Playboy of the Ancient World (use Socrates—Plato).

June 29

Dedicated poet & novelist: if I could be that two-thirds of the time: could I? by discipline?

R.P.B.: "obvious narrative gift."

G.B.S.: most wonderful stories in world.

E. & J. Herbst: such a wonderful way of telling stories.

Cummington girl: every word exact (read proof on "AA").

Dwight: narrative, humor, and analysis.

Caroline Gordon: fascinating (Wilson-Mary story, fall 1939).

Norman Jacobs: stories not novels & Wohlstetter (good ear).

Mary Handlin: someday it (*WW*) will be appreciated; (Joanna) ("If even Delmore can't find words for it").

Mary W.—does want a baby—came to get Scotch—hated family —saw withdrawal—would not touch. Howard Moss bitten by dog as we walked in Vassar woods. I had hangover & guilt—detested Moss— dog tore his sweater suddenly.

Mary M[cCarthy]'s story about Dewey—and Will—who's attacking him—swollen with power & with wine.

Stendhal—"the eternal novelist of the postwar world" (review of *Lamiel*).

Will: "Married couples tend to be grasping" (wedding presents). The White Whale Reelity—Reeling Reality ("the turning world"). Mary resented the theorist—of the double bed in the country.

"Millions of spiritual creatures walk the earth."

Last night—TV, last part of Shaw's *Pygmalion*—Wendy Hiller still overwhelming.

Gide said Simenon was best French *novelist* (my italics—interpretation).

Another book I can't find: Milton's Poems, Madison, 1931.

Irritated by Sylvester's [on June 28 Elizabeth's brother was thirteen] gourmandise of pleasure—packing & stacking—Coca-Cola, watermelon (anxious that it might get soft)—poor manners greeting Leslie, inspecting pleasure objects in house.

> What bird sings the scissors-clipping call—
> in our trees in our woods

Joe [Pollet]—in patriarchal frenzy—wanted to fix carriage-house roof, buy something for house—pleased by farmland—wheat fields. (What kind of a painter am I, anyway?) Something of the bone and the blood?

The pull of the wind on the kite—thrilling—as if in touch with fountains of nature's powers. Leslie & Sylvester were playing with kites.

Evidence, necessitous images, dream plots—not enough of the unconscious.

Thurber "has never been able to get thru *Pickwick Papers*," thinks Fitzgerald was strangled by lack of humor—best estimate of his work by T. S. Eliot.

He took / did not take overweening pride in mastery.

He was unable to distinguish between relaxation & rigor mortis.

Sylvester—a quintessential (constitutional) denigrator, his mind is full of suspicion & melodrama. (Woodsman.) End of good manners of Betty [Sylvester's mother].

Writing. As if it were whaling—pursuit of the Rawality. Pierce Realty.

Philip [Rahv], a mordant observer of human nature, errs in his wish to find the worst.

Clara Bow & Astor actress—"That's the small of my back to everyone except an intimate friend"—and Ann Sheridan—"The boss is always tying my apron behind my back—when I'm not wearing any"—and Veronica Lake in early picture.

Catherine Morrison's You're a gentleman—you said you're sorry (how she misunderstood about).

Certainly it is not a universal taste—slapping? (discovery of murderess in G. H. Coxe mystery)—aversion as intense as desire—a symbol of form of humiliation, of intimacy—a target of slapstick and topic of dress designers—important in reducing, active in dancing, the center of the rumba, the limelight of the can-can, basic to the bumps, the striptease, the real McCoy.

Phenomenology of the Erotic.

Days wasted by visitors—Joe & Sylvester & Kenneth [Schwartz]—almost half the year dissipated.

Sandy [Delmore's niece] would eat a deck of cards if you gave her one.

All Sylvester needs is an oxygen tent (this is decadence—sprawled on cot, reading book, eyeing TV, licking candy, and sucking soda pop).

> Roses are red
> Violets are blue
> Dogs have fleas
> And so have you

Duress, express, undress, unless, success / elections, rejections, erections, subjections / devious, lascivious.

Prosperity is just around the coroner.

The cat's pajamas (special, rare, *recherché*).

"Hot as the business end of a pistol."

Drugstore cowboys cracking wise: "After love most men are sad." "That way we'll always know where we stand."

"If God had wanted people to be naked," says a small-town uncle, "he would have given them a lot of hair (like bears and the other animals)."

Baba, Flatbush: Dozing woman, seventy-eight, loses $8,000 in subway theft (took it out to buy a house).

Suicide of man whose babysitter stole from him.

Dallas—after fourteen divorces: Somewhere in the world is the girl who is just right for me.

Berserk, Armageddon / coma, aroma, La Paloma / shag, rag, brag, sag.

"The perfume of profound melancholy." Tuning up like orchestras.

> This is the danger
> of sincerity
> music
> and great forests.

"He was disappointed that Paris had no mountains."

"What the pride of the rich calls society."

"Don Quixote made him laugh the first time since his mother's death."

Malraux—Bunyan, Defoe, Dostoevsky. Cervantes—jailed, pilloried, exiled. Returned to write the book of Solitude.

> Happiness is subject to
> The wiles of chambermaids
> Happiness flits from branch to twig
> to branch
> Like a hummingbird quick as a sparkle
> The enthusiasm the ebullience
> The brio
> The cold mountain air of joy

12:20–2:00, *Voice of Asia*—Michener during Giants' twilight doubleheader.

A brandy-tense night tight as anger.

"Screaming with joy." "In dread of the clock which ticks."

Counterpoint of Zolotow's virginity? Girls ahead of the boys?

Gossip—of girl made pregnant by elevator boy in apartment house.

Philip—the girls want just what the men do.

Clem says to himself: Now I am in a house with a butler.

Lincoln: You don't know what it is to have no one.

Mary—is a complete adventuress—lost nights—Providence—Spencer (married to millionaire Wilson)—glittering look when I invited Nancy to elope to Poughkeepsie. Dwight: Those who talk are not to be feared: they do nothing.

D.S.: No! it is like Hitler & *Mein Kampf* & Hitler's attack on Czechoslovakia, announced in advance.

Marriage without children is just an affair. Unemployed intellectuals (heroes) subsidize their indecision. Girls tell all, thinking, This is the last man I am going to bed with.

Waking tired & sinus headache—as yesterday I ran down, felt drowsy by 3—after morning alertness conversing with Joe over coffee.

Feeling some wakeful strength after 9 at night as on Sunday night & reading *Voice of Asia* (or Stendhal's *The Telegram*) instead of pocketbook mystery.

Rising from inertness & depression over midday breakfast, conversing with E. on the lawn.

August 10

(Elicited last night by Josie's [Herbst] query about [Ralph] Ellison's book.)

"The Hartford Innocents." (Chickie Brown, Leslie B., sister [beauty] Anne Margaret, Christopher B. [the genius].)

Use Shirley Jackson's [fiction writer] book for details.

1. Finding of Baby (A baby is left at Easter—or during winter recess on the doorstep next to the milk bottles. Crying, it is thought to be a cat or kitten. Note? Please take care of the child.)

2. The 5/6 decision by evening—decide to adopt baby. "One more," says Papa, nice to have an infant in the house, like growing things, like something (a piano) to make music with. I've become used to this concert and (solemn music). Pride in illuminated views, Liberal, Christian, generous motives articulated.

3. Discovery that child is colored. Crisis—father explains, or tries to, the impossibility of keeping child (unfair to child) to Vicky (when it is older, self-conscious, aware of diff., worst victim of race prejudices). Vicky (model & nurse & mother's surrogate) runs off with child to Fairfield—progressive school.

4. Crisis at Fairfield (Bennington). President & faculty convene. No precedent—no situation remotely. But it's not my baby—I did not *have* the baby (promises to support it—in Village). The baby is very pretty & has a very "good disposition."

5. The child is no longer an infant.

[After many revisions, "The Hartford Innocents" was published in Successful Love and Other Stories, *Corinth Books, New York, 1961; reissued by Persea Books, New York, 1985.]*

August 18

Images of Innocence & Experience / The Little (Black) Baby / Holy Infant / The Advent of an Orphan Child.

The finding of an infant two weeks old, on the brick doorstep, next to the daily allotment of four bottles of milk, was the cause of unmixed joy in the entire Russell household.

Susan went running upstairs to tell Mother, who came running downstairs with her oldest child to see the little baby. Father, in his study, hearing the commotion and, fearing a new crisis, hastened from his study & arrived in the living room to find three of his children & his wife in a cooing huddle about the unexpected small stranger and visitor.

Professor Russell [was] relieved, for he had feared that the police might have come again, as they had four times in the past five months; after his children had stolen (lawn mowers), broken store windows, and turned in false fire alarms.

"Perhaps the police ought to be informed," said Professor Russell, causing his children to groan a vehement no, like baseball fans who object to an umpire's decision.

Part of his reason for suggesting the police was his desire that the men of the law be summoned to witness that in this house and in this family ideas occupied more space than sofas, chandeliers, and the Electrolux frigidaire.

(Begin by describing house? morning? Professor Manning? Lawyer: Civil rights? rich & disinterested.)

December 27

Katy [Carver]—proof call. $1.10 + tax.

I hope I will not seem too naïve or farfetched when I close by saying that whether or not one believes in God, one can hardly help but believe in Posterity, and certainly it is obvious that the latter will be concerned with you. Yes! This is so naïve a remark that it must seem laughable. And I allow it to stand merely because it is part of the point of view from which this letter is written.

1953

January 3

Story about getting rid of infatuation by writing a story about the girl as middle-aged, after visiting her mother. (Theme of control of the emotions—their inculcation & extirpation, as last September, after second game of Giant–B'klyn doubleheader.)

Story of Uncle Sam's daughter, with astute man, captain of industry, courtship.

Story or novel of poet who has failed after early success. Writers? Crane, Fitzgerald.

Kinsey interviewer story.

January 8–9

Nothing doing / nothing done / Save to read *Ulysses* / & to get angry since Thurs. night or Friday morning.

Six Dex. yesterday—easier to sleep—even though I drank. (First pocket-book absorption since last Sunday.)

Drowsy enough to sleep after dinner (after six or seven drinks of bourbon, which wakened me up to pps. of the Shakespeare chapter in *U[lysses]*).

Dream of being reviewed unfavorably in *S[aturday] R[eview]* & *Kenyon Review* as, night before, of going to be a student (at twenty-two) at CCNY.

Call from the office (after I'd decided not to go to N.Y.): no meeting.

To write criticism at night (as I did on Thurs.) and run down road at night, too.

January 23

Invention is the Mother of Necessity. Invention is the Mamma of Industrial Problems.

Sermon against Adultery.

> *The Kings of Emotion*
> He who learns from his mistakes
> Will triumph over snares and snakes
>
> Will rise at last and clearly see
> His joy and belle and victory

If you want a thing well done, get someone else to do [it], an expert, and pay him well.

Time-saving devices / Make work for the devil's henchmen.

May 17

As I came into the Pierre, Jay [Laughlin] and [Robert] Fitzgerald were leaving. Jay did not see me—I touched his sleeve. Bob said: see you soon.

Slowdown. *Sun., May 17.* Letter to Emily, two films, lawn-mowing, and love. *Sat.* Letters to Carlos Lynes, Dexter Perkins, and a card to Martin Greenberg, Princeton English Dept. picnic, beer. *Fri.* Princeton, *Anna* with Silvana Mangano. *Mon. 11.* Ruth, Jane, Leslie, the dog, no New York, sherry, wine, and beer. *Sun. 10.* Ruth (Ford Found.). *Fri.* Prince[ton]. *Thurs.* Prince[ton] seminar—Borges—new story. *Weds.* Carlos—Saul [Bellow] (stood up)—Irving. *Mon. May 4.* N.Y. Dwight [Macdonald]—story of Hutchins & Hoffman & Ford—gin—beer.

June 21–22

A curve up & then down & then up—lassitude—extreme torpor after breakfast—factitious rising intensity, and responsiveness toward 4–5.

Waking up two or three mornings in a fighting nervousness after fighting dreams (one attack on Philip R.).

Nothing to drink Sun. 14, Mon. 15, Tues. 16. Sherry before dinner Weds. 17. Nothing to drink Thurs. 18. Gin before dinner, nothing after dinner Fri. 19, Sat. 20, Sun. 21.

Reality passes by—like ships at night—like a veiled Mohammedan woman—like a distant train.

Look at the downpour now (at which you do not look).

This morning—claustrophobic dream—trapped in a low cellar of the subway—shouting up, Help! Vainly—nothing to do but wake up?

An Art of Patient and Grave Attention (ex.: how Klonsky & Broyard compose their essays).

I knocked on the door but could not enter.

Trollope—I. Compton-Burnett.

1926 crack at H. James. He achieved reality through the accomplishment of an uninterrupted tedium.

June 25

Jackie [Wilentz] thought I looked well & gay—"Are you leaving us?"—showed me what a French review said of Barzun's remark about pragmatism: "*Sottement*"—and how he must have been five or six when he saw a sculptured horse in Paris (mentioned in his editorial).

"Are you leaving us?" stood or moved close to my shoulder. I told the story of Freud's Hans & the (?) brewery horses. Neither Jackie nor Eli [Wilentz, co-owner with his brother Ted of the Eighth Street Bookstore] wanted to hear anything Freudian.

PR—Will & Barbara—*PR* tax exempt—kidding of pronunciation HARASSED INVOLVEMENTS—

Arabella Porter [editor at the New American Library and of *New World Writing*] call, forced, dutiful.

Madison & midtown impinged(!) as worthy of the benediction of prose—still the middle class buying & possessing (lunch in a cafeteria).

Barbara's legs were on the desk as I came in the office—she pulled them down & Will [Barrett] moved to sit down farther away from her.

B. thought I ought to give $10,000 to *PR* "because you're so successful."

Letter from Kitty Morgan [wife of Frederick Morgan, editor of *The Hudson Review*] praising story and from Pat Hartle [wife of Robert Hartle of the Princeton faculty].

Wonderful idea—about married homosexual episode in TBU [unidentified title of work] (the dream of boys)—drives boy to retreat [?]—fails and seems to betray himself by making pass at the older brother. (Eloquence of his argument. Buddhist monks, Greece, Kinsey, Wescott.)

July 4

Two Mil[town] at 6:30, two Dex. at 9:30.

From Times Square forth 3,000 miles / To the Golden Gate—or Sunset Boulevard.

Boulevard, canard, bard.

"In Miss Moore's poems, morality is simplified into self-abnegation & Gauguin is always content to stay home with his . . ."

> Times Square crowds, flowing or choked
> Don't let yourself be duped or hoaxed
> There are no substitutes for flesh and blood

(That's good, choked and hoaxed as rhymes.)

Success (!) is the road to wisdom
(The wisdom of the ashes of desire)

"Poets who looked at the Past
As Blücher looked at London
!What a city to sack!"

The cracking of the gravel
As a car passes

Undated

Marianne—the emerald's grass-lamp glow.
Laforgue on Corbière:

"His poems are as strident and tireless
as the cry of gulls"
As the crying and the soaring of gulls
Over a bare shore of rocks where the waves
break—

"We others are all *poetic*—
he is of a different mettle
an unseizable smoke-dried Corsair
bold in his raids"

Corbière: "Rocks like boiled potatoes"; "Surprise is my profession."

I drove twelve miles behind a truck—
In which—by some ingenious luck
Two horses stood, gazing, solemn and mild
Upon the countryside

Malapropisms: "They sparkle in the Northern Lights of her continual irony."

Tamarisk
He meditated on the rump of things
The buttocks of experience the bold bad backside
Swinging and shifting with a kind of
knowledge
Known instantly before the world began

Clearly! Clearly! Birds in the branches
whistle
Clearly—wetly!

Blake?: You never know what is enough / Unless you know what is more than enough.

Danish proverb: If you eat cherries with your superiors / You get pits in your eyes.

Tennis and music, archery and hawking.

She dealt (wrote) not as if she were walking on eggs, but on the eggs of a swan.

July 5

Sunday. N. Y. Times. "A charlatan with plenty of cheek and a small conscience."

"She had a kind of leggy elegance as if she might become a tree, and not a woman."

"The velvet growling of the pigeons."

Fri.—drunk and as if manic again, after Phila. & after midnight. Yesterday, 9:30, Jarrell's book all morning.

> How close are you to that great city
> Experience?
> We are not close
> (but not too far)
> We have commuters' tickets, or on Sundays
> Stroll in the park and listen to the band's
> Fireworks and false romances

We want both Pegasus and a Cadillac.

To Ethel [a Schwartz cat]: Quiet please / We're studying!

Early & late morning / responsiveness if declining to drowsiness —blankness-anxiety.

Dickens—or Joyce. The wrong assumption that one must be interested. Bored is good enough—something comes through, makes its impress on the mind.

August 1

"The American soldier has just one fault: he has too much to live for."

"I don't want to be a hero, I just want to be alive."

"Like an elephant on a skating rink—"

Greene—"a slight suggestion of Al Capone."

Jarrell's anecdote: Why are you fighting? Because I was drafted!

"The eloquence and the appetite for life that are the trademarks of the great novelists—"

"Life does not respect bankrolls—is not intimidated by the folding green."

Byron, a 110-proof lush and sexsmith, sex-cessful.

Einstein: "I cannot believe that God plays dice with the cosmos" (when nothing seems very important).

> The Moon as Bald as Billiard Ball
> Arose in the Early Afternoon
> A Wallflower,
> > An Epigone
> > Withdrawn in the Light's Ontology

To memorize a poem is my desire. Dear God—a story—or a poem / Would make me feel myself at home.

Subjects and attitudes / statues / the city / ceremonies, rituals, prayers / time, nature, death / orientation / self-confrontation.

Manic / 1953—four months / 1952—three months / 1950—three months / 1949—four months / 1948 / 1947—four to five and a half months.

"I get up so early that I have five o'clock shadow at two o'clock."

1946—five to seven months / (psychogenic depression in October & Nov.) / 1945—Oct. Nov. Dec. / 1944.

The Dexedrine—after I had reached ten—between 2 and 3—focussed consciousness on the primary anxiety—being manic or depressed. And I made a list of these periods and their relationship to getting work done.

Good work finished but mostly criticism when depressed—review of *Four Quartets.*

Poor work (exceptions—first draft of "AA"—*CAHM* interlude), this judged when manic—Paris & Helen, argument in 1934—Faulkner —versions of *Genesis.*

Isn't it mostly a question of concentration and sensible choice and effort (& continuity, which I have not maintained very much [as much as once] since 1947). Even T. S. E[liot] as Lit[erary] Dic[tator] was hardly revised—poorly proofread.

September 9

TBU. Must begin to type five pages, write five new? + Heine— after Heine: poems—Orville—and stories.

Rear entrance, dead end, back entrance, back way, backstage, back up, stuck up (girl), pin-up.

Touched—bottom! Mrs., Mr. Ramsbottom. We'll all have a ball. *Blitzkrieg. Sitzplatz.*

September 17–19

Thurs. night. Saul [Bellow]'s party. Hivnors, Will [Barrett]. Like a wedding the bride was an American life. Kimber's. Pat Blake kissed! My friends, I am not happy. Gaby emaciated. Milton Babbitt's knowingness. Manheim, Sparks, Stone.

Fri. Lunch with [John] Tibby [senior editor of *Time* magazine], [Bernard] Friwell [contributing editor of *Time*]. After sixteen years! His wink! "*Time* has always been very kind to me." It should be.

"Fairly hopeful of being able to offer you a regular reviewing job." [Max] Gissen [associate editor of *Time*]—book conference—no one but Gissen spoke. G. very glad to meet you (stiffly).

Too much to drink.

Sat. Saul's visit—reviews—"two great writers" (after reading [Harvey] Swados's [novelist and social critic] review in *Post*—ecstatic & driving 70 miles an hour.

In the afternoon, after a walk, we dictated notes & an introduction for a textbook to Sandra (who no longer resists Saul or holds herself stiffly on guard). Too much to drink.

September 24

Many a Boy and Girdle Romance (concludes, consummates)—wet pants.

[Budd] Schulberg: Fifteen thousand dollars later—

"You have a million-dollar personality," said delicatessen store man to me.

"I'll trade it for a million dollars," I said.

September 25

Sept. '53–'54

NDs	600
Bank	1700
Sept. 30	550
Jan. *Ps*	275
	3,125
Wellesley	100
	3,225

(Certain except for *N[ew] D[irections]*)

Likely but not certain:

Time	100	3,225
PR	50 + 100	3,425
Saul	750	4,175
Poetry permissions	75	4,250

E.

| Overtime | 100 | | 4,350 |
| France | 200 | | 4,550 |

Possible Chicago   1,200

Richard—Princeton, Rutgers, Brandeis, Chicago
P[erspectives]
editor	2,000
Bank	1,700
House	5,000
	8,700

Debts: Gruenthal   ?500
        Emily   1,000
Advances: 1,500   Schocken
            2,500   Holt
            1,800+ Jay [*New Directions*]

Backlog for next year ('54–'55):
Perspectives ed.	2,000
House	5,000+
Bank	1,700+
	8,700

Possibilities for next year:
Princeton   4,000 or 4,500
Rutgers
Brandeis
N.Y.U. ?
Columbia
New School
???*New Yorker*
New Republic   60–90
?*Saturday Review*

Possibilities for this year:
Chicago (Blair)	1,200
Joyce or other essay	150
for *Kenyon*	
3 *Times*—reviews	150
Poetry—essay	50
?*Commentary*	35

September 26

Revised budget Sept. '53–'54

Certain or almost certain:

Bank	1,700	
ND	600	
P Sept.	550	
P story	275	
Wellesley	100	
	3,225	

Possibly or likely:

Saul textbook	750	$3,975
Anthology permissions	75	
PR Reader	50	
PR review	50	
Times review	50	
	225	$4,200

Libby—B.O.	100.	
France	200.	

[At *Time* magazine] Friwell: Do you still like eggs? You were almost right about my not being married—lived for a year together before marrying—*Life* girl—Lee—much in demand—not interested in Gerson H. Brodie—has been writing a novel—dissatisfied with the end —but Scribner's is keeping it.

I have had two children, boys—his eyes bulged and his head thrust forward (his old habit of winking to indicate friendship, rapport) (twice last week).

Gissen first praised Saul [Bellow]'s book [*Augie March*] very much—then when campaign began said, Doesn't have much to say, and, when Friwell did not like first 100 pp., told him: *We* don't have to praise it. After his review was written, said: You were too kind. Had told him Saul's Einhorn story was the perfect short story.

He tried to tell me (at least twice) that I was better off at F[ord] F[oundation] (You can make that last eight years) & that it was impossible to do one's own writing while writing for *Time* (you have to take on someone else's personality).

Friwell: You married that girl you were so mad about (a light on 1935, 1936, 1937)—you were too young.

Why did you drink so much?

I am not patient anymore (concealed ambition in 1936).

Last week I was set up because I thought I was getting the *Time* job. Tibby had said: "I am fairly hopeful (of being able) to give a regular reviewing job—" Yesterday: "I have nothing very encouraging to report—will scrabble around and try to find another book for you— did show your review around." (I thought he said at the meeting, but Friwell thought this could not be so—he did not & it would have been most unusual.) "I am glad you called—will call you on Monday (?if I find something)." (Friwell said on phone at 5:30 that this was not a good sign—not to count on it—would write me if he got "the pitch"— to be sure to call him in any case (meaning? it was out).

I should have tried second version of review on F[riwell]—did not because of what E. said, which I took to be the wrong kind of pressure, but which she explained as based on my saying I did not trust Friwell.

Anthony West's *New Yorker* review of Saul as "pretentious—all forced symbolism" for New Critics—a schizoid novel (connected with my inability to write for *Time* reader).

Very nervous going in—as to hear the results—the final score. Distressed at Miss Heck's greeting—and when Tibby did not greet me in the elevator going down (he was with Roy Alexander, the managing editor).

Episode about going to "briefing"—Friwell thought I was going, backtracked and forward-tracked about my going. (Tibby, when I got him after nervous-panicky phoning, said: "I don't think there is anything particularly encouraging to report.")

Impatience: I called Tibby—two Sats. ago he said situation was "fluid"—last Fri. "very hopeful"—yesterday "nothing very encouraging —will show book review at meeting."

This morning I wrote to Tibby, enclosing last fall's fiction chronicle —on the assumption that I was on the one-yard line, i.e., almost rejected—though it is "just barely" possible that he is looking for another book, has not found one (Kronenberger's "tentative basis")—impatient to get things.

[Malcolm] Lowry, verbose Anthony West, Irving [Howe], Wm. [Phillips], Harvey Breit, Howard Moss. Friwell said all kinds of people from well-known characters to kids had tried & failed—and that there was "an outside job"—and that they were hard-pressed.

Gloomy and blocked coming back on train—as after [Ronald] Freelander [associate publisher of *Perspectives USA*] in August. E. sympathetic last night, irritable this morning.

[Last] Weds., 9/23. Poems in morning in bed (Cupid, Ethel, two epigrams) and one really serious poem (about being beyond success) —& I almost wrote a Variety—feeling I was on verge of being manic. (I thought of how much better my poems & stories might be if I

worked as hard & slowly on them—and with as much painstaking research—as on the *Time* review.)

Thurs. Letdown except that I did read with delighted sense the
notebooks I kept during depressed period in 1951 (and in 1949) and
also unfinished or forced poems between 1937 & 1940—if I had worked
harder on them, instead of going on to new poems, been less neuroti-
cally insecure & hence able to reread them without drawing conclusions
about my destiny, I would have made much more progress—if I had
struggled—

> Poem: Look Now the Foaming Flora.
>
> Poem (about what? who?).
>
> He always was
>   Drawing conclusions about his destiny
>   (which the cosmos had not yet compounded)
> He lived at a slight distance from reality
> In a nearby suburb, one might say
> He commuted
>   From fantasy to reality every day
> He was prepared to argue that his version was true
> Certainly no one could cogently deny
> That his fantasy was not superior to reality

"Drinking spoils your sense of rhythm" (says a professional dancer
to a call girl in a pocket book).

"Talking to [Allan D.] Dowling [member of the *Partisan Review*
advisory board] is like trying to have an erection."

Barbiturates lead to a disease of lack of white blood corpuscles
(*H[erald] T[ribune]*—Dr. Alvares, Mayo consultant).

Kazin proves that Captain Ahab was after gefilte fish—Ellison.

Klonsky pleased: A rush of hubris to the head.

Chekhov: Ballet girls (in the wings) stink like horses.

N. Nabokov: Spring like a ballet girl in the wings.

So sexy. Let's tuggle. Let me have my explosion. Oh, you want
me out of the underbrush.

Today: letter to Hutchins as well as Tibby. E. against it.

March or April 1952. The pastor came to call on Sunday. Episode
of visit of minister of Assembly of God.

Institutional religion argument about God's infinite wisdom & a
small nation. Hebrew Americans (Auden's Jewish Americans). You
can't get to first base without Jesus.

He is just like Robin Hood: he steals from the poor to help the rich.

Underdog eat underdog.

[Delmore, maneuvering for a job at Princeton, asked the Department of English if they would agree to appoint him to a chair if the Ford Foundation subsidized it. They agreed. When Delmore's expectations from the Ford Foundation were not realized, he cast about for other possibilities.]

On Fri. [9/25]—in late afternoon, glow after returning from Flemington—I thought of R[oger] Straus [president of Farrar, Straus & Giroux] & W.V.K. [Van Keuren] & [Gideon] Schocken [publisher of Schocken Books] as possibly helping me at Princeton. E. was dubious of first—"Why not just give you the money to write poetry?" —but not of the second.

I thought of writing Roger & began to compose the letter in my head.

E.'s epigram: You are demanding the job because you are a Jew.

E.'s fine phrases: "Your sense of yourself" (you were happy last winter but I thought not because of money but because of your sense of yourself). "Feel my way into the situation" (in writing fiction). Unable to write because of difficulties with herself. Her acute perceptions of [Arthur] Mizener, Albert Erskine, Burgerhoff [Princeton faculty member].

Will [Barrett]'s resentment & fourteen years of wasted friendship (that means it's over) and of Zolotow & who? Kenneth—having a special need of my approval—good opinion.

Day after Pearl Harbor: The other team scores six runs before we come to bat (inaccurate & it was better).

Homeric metaphors (which pleased Broyard so much).

He (Sonny Shapero) is distorting what happened (the truth) as Stalin distorted the truth about Trotsky role in the Russian Revolution.

"What will I do when you write *The Divine Comedy*?"—Lincoln Reis to me, 1936.

Turgenev & Pauline García Viardot were having a big long platonic fuck through the years.

Milwaukee, Bellow pleased. It's as if Malenkov, Churchill, and Eisenhower all suffered a paralytic stroke at the same time or on the same day (during the same period).

Philip [Rahv]'s style—like a limousine being backed into a very small parking place.

On arising greater intensity at climax (despite less fun building up).

Tomorrow: Klonsky (first choice), or Mary, or Levin (the Masters of English), or poems, or Chickie.

Friwell spoke too often about being honest. Did not seem really dismayed about "not a good sign" when I called him at 5. Said I had overinterpreted Tibby's attitude at the end of last week's conference. "That's because of living in Cambridge—where no one says what he means"—inter. within interpret. within interpret.—like H. James (and Chickie Brown).

Today Sat. [9/26] two Dex., three (two Dex., one Mil.), 2 Dex., 2 Mil. = 9!

> How Ethel is now an enameled black
> Her fur, a black gloss, shining & thick

> How the leaves are turning, green
> To yellow, yellow to
> red and
> brown

Just now (4:10–4:40) half hr.'s lawn-mowing—a sweat—a stitch.

A half-darkened day, a slight haze in the sunlight, quiet and almost windless and the sky looks very distant, very still, very empty.

I've worked morning & afternoon every day except Friday, yesterday, this week. But apart from the review—not concertedly & in concentration (e.g., Weds., jumping from poem to poem).

Trailing off now—near 5—and probably a letdown tomorrow.

The vice of spontaneity resembles drunkenness.

September 27

Rameau at Walden [a projected story]. Brooklyn—Rameau— Klonsky—Romantic. Nature. Draft board. Outbreak of war (as Yaddo) & no personal courage. Graveyard. Blowing his nose in American flag. Trying to make Margaret. Letter from Rhoda—mistaken inter[pretation] of melancholy.

> Under the rain and reign and white pepper of the sky
> salted thickly with stars
> The colorless peppering
> aimless aim of the rain
> A sense of power, a sense of being
> The experience of power is the grasp of being

> *Cocteau*
> Je ne savais pas ces trésors de coeur . . .
> Ne fouille pas trop le coeur, George
> Il est mauvais de fouiller trop le coeur
> Il y a de tout dans le coeur
> Ne fouille pas trop dans mon coeur, ni
> dans le tien.

Joyce
Aye aye she was lithe and pleasable
Every old skin in the leather world
Was it a high white night now?
Whitest night mortal ever saw!

The delicate cold pleasure of a winter morning.

Cream-colored mongooses
Putty-nosed monkeys
Brush-tailed porcupines
Pythons, panthers, pangolins
Gigantic water shrews

All Gall is divided into three parts: arrogance, insensitivity, self-dramatization.

Sat. Yesterday. Resilience, quick recovery from Friday's disappointment about *Time* & Tibby. (*Time* & Tibby wait for no man.)

Hurrying—letter to Tibby—notes about the week (about 10 pp.). Trailing down after lunch—"unsuccessful love"—"but it was fun."

Mowing with pleasure (but hurrying too much) 4:10–4:40. Back to desk. Dinner outside—nothing to drink.

Two jarfuls of gin at midnight, one s.t., after Thoreau & F.O.M. on Thoreau—perhaps I could have managed without both, certainly with only one—waking with a stomach pain & tense.

My Injuries & Negligences: E., Helen, Berryman?, Barrett, Trilling, Kazin, and Klonsky, Joe Pollet, A.Q.?

My Good Deeds: E.—fiction chronicle, Jane & Leslie, Saul, Tom, Clara—Kenneth & children, Irving.

Tally of Injuries: Jay. Princeton, Sept. '52, cheated him of $400. Berryman: You can't trust Delmore. Rahv—letter from Ramsey—H. Breit's poem ("He no longer works for the *Times*"—a trick). Barrett.

[At New Directions] MacGregor told Irene to count my visits. My salary was cut in half.

[Hayden] Carruth [poet and editorial consultant for *Perspectives USA*] sent back mss. I should have seen. Did not pass on Jay's instructions (from Paris).

(I did the injuries first!)

Slight: [Tom] Riggs: Someone without money will cut your throat. M[onroe] Engel: Bulling your way through.

Tally of Benefits & Good Will.

Saul: You look better. Riggs, Jay—*ND*—Feb. 1952. Monroe—dinner. Carlos [Baker] and Princeton job. Kronenberger, Helen, Hartles, Jane, and Leslie.

Eight script pages easily about Rameau—Klonsky—too quickly. I went too quickly to do well—five before, three after lunch—if every sentence is to count, the writing can't flow out like that. The real trouble is probably that the subject does not mean *enough to me*.

I felt as if I were manic for a while.

Joyce, too, was alive as it [sic] has not been for months—and the *Times*, too, at breakfast.

Must try chronicle method—or Mary—or Chickie or Levin tomorrow.

September 29

Men who hunted, riding
But those who followed the muses
Seated, indoors, in solitude
bent

It is beginning to snow slowly.
Time staggers (lurches) on.
He was a member of Alcoholics Unanimous.
1941—"I have run out of consciousness."
The doctor said, My intuition fees are—
I would not trust him with Whistler's mother.
Corinthians: Love hopeth all things.
1945—"I was halfway up the mountain / When I broke my legs—"

October 4–5

Possible Themes for Philosophical Romances & Comedies: Cupid & Psyche. Plutarch—Idealistic Spartan. Suetonius?

Measure for Measure—reenacted in a Balkan kingdom.

American airman by accident lands in perfect Thebetan society— it is feared he will corrupt populace—description of wonders of society (implicit critique of all Western societies). In the end he escapes— though pledged not to—his motives & emotions being entirely ambiguous.

October 7

The Antagonist (letters in passionate prose denouncing the lies, confusions, and deceptions of poetry).

Corn Shucks (Life, the Shenandoah in autumn).

October 13

In bed until 11–12. Tired after breakfast. Moholy-Nagy, Whitman. No progress until seven, eight Dex. + Mil.—nine. Pepped up but with no content & direction. Hölderlin (second) did not get very far.

After 3 straightening out room, tidying up, changing desk's position to face toward barn, shed, woods.

Pleased with some of *KC* [*Kilroy's Carnival*]—on which I don't concentrate (and H[eine] & Baudelaire).

E. restless. Love more successful than recently—high & smooth.

3–4. Running up toward R. Ethel [the cat] following (Death on Birds).

Pocket-book addiction—*Noon* (Spillane type). Unable to read L. Bromfield.

Two sherry on two bourbon before dinner (three after)—tired-tired—depressed after dinner. Three s.t.s, almost sleep at 11:15, awake at 11:45.

October 25

Oh, the heyday halcyon red-letter days. Heyday Sunday.

Tossing Body plashed by tumults of waves of sensation.

The balances of sentences: extravagant praises, petulant rebukes.

> R.G. One more such kiss
>   And I am ready to be roasted
>   Upon a slow fire like any chicken
>   Or duckling
>   (Turning

November 7

The way I copy. Hurrying. Trying to dominate. Don't talk to me like a bully. You have no right to, now that we're not married. Gertrude in August. Auden—best poet of our generation here in this house. Seems to be very nice, she said, hearing of the party—how he offered to explain to all (*The Portrait*, too).

Mrs. Stegner: Does your wife work in a defense plant? No. Bang—we're separated. Oh, I did not know that!

But a beautiful voice, Rhoda Klonsky and Margaret Laughlin said to Gertrude, who told me.

Joyce loved his country—as [Van Wyck] Brooks would have the writer in America love America. Mencken, Brooks, Wilson, Babbitt. Attack Empson & R. P. B[lackmur] & New Criticism for ignoring *F[innegans] W[ake]*. Was she mushy mushy?

"You were tops—a crackerjack, but you always look uncomfortable"—Millie Jones, Rockport.

November 9

Mon. Breakfast at 11—dizzied by first, very strong, coffee (two Dex. & first cigarette).

E.: He gets up because he gets hungry.

Much more response today, reading quotes of I. C.-Burnett in *Commonweal* review.

Sunlight of winter—pale white sunlight—icelight in the ambience of the sun—cold bare brown fields—ragged stalks & sky cold—faint white far clouds.

Whatever happened to the schedule?

Annoyed by Trilling & Philip in the new *PR*.

And now what? A N D N O W W H A T? Not Joyce (how much fun he must have had, how he must have enjoyed the hard work, the research, the looking up, the rewriting of sentences).

Drive to town, to Flemington—papers, pocket books—the drugs of consciousness—the "narcissistic supplies"—novelty & distraction.

(Just before eating a small lunch, five, six, seven, eight Dex.) I looked at memo books of 1935—no great difference—always looking for words & descriptions & ideas which will explain experience.

November 11

Five s.t.s (second time in past two or three weeks), jarful of whiskey at 10, two glasses of Zinfandel.

Yesterday unrest/dissatisfaction/resentment/anger, in several directions before sleep.

But two runs—almost two miles (that may be what is wrong).

Dizzied by coffee, Dex., and cig. Very sleepy right after breakfast—quickened a while, in bed.

2:00 dropping, reflections again (and again & again) as what I do wrong, how I can improve.

Quickened at 9:30 by coffee—I. Compton-Burnett, copying.

A page (which I have tried again repeatedly, but never when manic) on H. L[evin] (as if in I. C.-B. idiom) quickly, and quickly arriving nowhere.

Looking at Faulkner's stories & *Sound & Fury* & *As I Lay Dying* —looking for story (it turned out to be "The Leg") and the nostalgic paragraph which started me off eighteen years ago, that July afternoon in 1935 at 8[13] Greenwich St.—"IDBR" [perhaps Delmore's most famous story, "In Dreams Begin Responsibilities].

At 6:15 began to drink—trying to track down last year's turn after blocked fall.

Nov. 28—after much quarreling—after getting nowhere with story (which I did in the first week of February)—to N.Y.—coming back (driving too fast) at 4 or 5.

Between then, Fri., Nov. 28, and Dec. 7th, I wrote piece about Trilling ["The Duchess' Red Shoes," *Partisan Review* 20 (January 1953)]. Hardly a trace of what happened is in my mind or in notes (too interested in what I was doing).

I remember driving to Clinton Point after a new addition—arriving in N.Y. on a Friday with mss.—party at Wm.'s—Pat Blake, Sonya Orwell, Mrs. Silone, and Katy [Carver]. Sandra retyped the mss., which I went back to *PR* office to get.

Instructions from E. on making love during that time.

I had recently finished first version of periodical listing [précis of interesting articles for *Perspectives USA*, edited by James Laughlin for the Ford Foundation]—felt mounting in me, with the Dexedrine—as I worked in the Princeton office—the manic surge. "You've really broken through," said Saul.

As I drank, last night, I could not put together Sept. & Oct. very well, looking at appointment book—did not know, remember, before or after of visit to Wm., visit of Saul. *Time* episode also a little displaced save for dating of Saul's party.

(My hand is not really shaky as it was yesterday.)

Copying as minimum (since it is mechanically possible), I said to myself—promised—forgot about it.

Yeats before bed, in bed—unadmiring (a positive thing); his affectations of the poet's role—of simplicity.

No desire for a pocket book.

Run up the road the second time—after dark—more nervous than before.

"Stop playing games with me," said E. when I said I would eat when she did.

Today, 11–12 waking, slightly hung over (the wine?)—still angry.

12. Breakfast brought up by E. Mrs. W. in kitchen.

Quickened (after expecting a dead day—after looking at *Nation* —while reading Levin on Joyce to write page—then pages—2 + 2 isolated ones—on Am[erican] criticism—fading again (not what I really wanted to do).

How often (as last night) tracking down past is interesting when so little else is—or leads to organized & sustained activity.

This is the heart (or something important) of my mind: the fascination with what the past was—the perceptions, looking back, the variety of the kinds of connections, the pathos of "Had I but known."

Back to last year. Dec. 12 letter from Lionel [Trilling] written, arrived on Mon., 14? E. told me about it on phone. When I did write to Lionel—after showing piece to Philip & Wm.—Dec. 5th, probably, or Dec. 6th—or Dec. 8th (!). Judging by first typed copy, I began on the very day after I came back, at 4, from N.Y.

Breakthroughs last Nov., Dec.

Almost 5 p.m. How did I waste so much energy during last m.p. [manic period] Dec.–Apr.

Teaching—two days a week & one evening, Thursday nights.

Going to New York—two days a week, beginning in Jan. or Feb.

Socializing. Macdonalds, Pat Hoey & Arnold, Jay & what was her name?, Katy, Klonsky, Anatole, Phil & Tessa, Howe, Lewis, Riggs. Wm.'s party, Meyer Schapiro's (April 19th—toward end). Gruenthal's party; English Dept. dinner. Mizener, Margaret Marshall. Nov. ed [itorial] meeting where Philip was jealous & insulting. Van Keuren, Jane and Leslie. Students (successes in classes).

Trying to get a job at Princeton.

Fighting with [Robert] MacGregor, Jay [Laughlin].

Seeing Ober, Straus, Breit, Hutchins.

Mentions & prize & salary & *Diogenes*.

Drinking, overconfidence, optimism, enjoyment.

E.: You seemed very happy but I thought it was "your sense of yourself—"

Letter writing all around.

November 14

Lyricism seeking an object (or running up & down the hills and dirt roads of sensibility).

Theme: A Geographical Tour of Emotion, Joyous in Jersey

Ousted (outlasted) in Austria

Deflowered in Florence

Begotten in Bologna

Poked & pushed in Pisa

Penetrated in Paris

Licked (all over) in St. Louis

Seduced, sucked off, sodomized in Cincinnati

A cherry in Chicago

Frisked in Frisco

Shamed in Chicago

Charmed on the Chesapeake

Raped in Rome

Hotted up / Hot pants / Heated on the Hudson

Seated in / Sated in Siam

Hung over in Hong Kong

Kicked in Kalamazoo

Caned at Grand Canyon

Invaded in New York

Passed out in Pittsburgh

Delinquent / Delayed on the Delaware

Done in / Dallied in Dallas

A pass in El Paso
Nude—in New Orleans
Jerked in New Jersey
Goosed in Greece (Gary)
Gorgeous in Georgia
Fucked in Philadelphia
Pinched in the Parthenon
Violated in the Vatican

November 25

Brief effort to write about Saul's book ["Adventures in America," a review of *The Adventures of Augie March*, appeared in *Partisan Review* 21 (January–February 1954)].

Drive to Easton, 3:30–4:30, anxiety, return. (Smoked 4 + 10.) (Too much to drink, ten shots before dinner—three beers, one jarful, and three shots of whiskey to sleep.)

Really depressed? or blocked? Unable to concentrate while reading. Unable to read pocket books. Since when?

November 26

Eliot's interview in the book section of the *Times*. [John] Lehmann [English publisher and critic]: Did Editor Eliot think there had been any outstanding development of literary talent recently, say since World War II?

"I must confess," he replied thoughtfully, "I don't see much—in poetry, at any rate. In fact, I sometimes lean toward the view which has been propounded to me, that creative advance in our age has been in prose fiction—the novels of Henry Green, for instance." Between 1940 & 1943, it's true some striking new English talent in poetry had appeared.

December 11

Either it is true and I am not good—not first-rate or I am unread (repellent) because (1) of having turned to the theme of the Jew after my first book (but essays?) or as intellectualizing poet or read and not liked because the fashion has been different—or / and / having alienated the poet critics—Tate, Winters?, Blackmur?, Auden? and alienated Jay and been identified with *PR* and abused by Philip Rahv —or have left too much time between books? But how about [Dylan] Thomas—even before his readings—years between books (and Frost . . .) (Malraux: thirteen yrs.; Silone ten—Hemingway—Faulkner—).

One version: very promising in his first book—lost his lyrical quality after that—

An agreement that my first story was best—among all—even Pulitzer: "no music"—R.P.B. "flatness"—

But reviews of *WW* [*The World Is a Wedding*]. *Time* & *Harvard Advocate* & *Jewish Studies*.

Jay & Tate & decline in activity & *Genesis*. Even those most admiring—Hannah Arendt—had reservations on the form. War: 1943 (as *The Great Gatsby* [depression]).

Friendly (in spite of resentment) or newly friendly, C. Aiken, K. Shapiro (Washington), R[obert] Richman [literary editor of *The New Republic*], J. C. Ransom, S. Bellow, and favorable, *Time, Commentary*.

S. Hook: Before you've become successful—famous.

You're a star. Even Karl [Shapiro] & John [Berryman] ready to be reconciled. Kazin: respectful. Even Philip Rahv—well-known writer (important writer). Oscar [Handlin]: You didn't get where you are by being well-mannered.

December 18

Thurs., yesterday, slept until 1, another quarrel—unable to use this room—something always going wrong—attitude toward literature —sexual difficulty—E. angry, tearful, frightened, "a quick one—just for you—this is just for you—a really quick one." "Neurotic—psychological block—cannot make love (?) respond spontaneously."

"If you're convinced that sexual difficulty is the cause that you are blocked, why don't you get rid of me?" "You yourself suggested that." Days before: "I know you don't mean it. But I get scared anyway."

Unable to eat—shouting after dark—and it would have been far worse had we been drinking—

We were drinking Coca-Colas, sucking & puffing at.

S.t. Attempt at making up —Yes: let's try something— No. O.K.— two more s.t.s—one sandwich & milk.

12:30—out to get beer—Baptistown—Frenchtown—all bars closed—very cold—back at 1:30—still awake at 3—awake just after 7 after tense-up wrestling racked and tremor tic'd sleep.

Dream of being killed (the relief of waking) in a truck—being guarded after an attempted suicide—very ashamed of attempt—unclear, but Friwell and girls were involved.

Suspected quarrel to come—promised I would avoid it—forced also by being dead again after being manic at 9 after making love (on Weds. night). ("This is for you" after waiting "until I finish my tea.")

Mon. or Tues. of this week—beginning to write an essay on neurosis and art (for *Times* or *PR*)—no copying. Mann's pompous unbearably egotistical lecture on Freud: unable to keep away from the *Joseph* books. Tues., Freud's foolish paper on paranoiac girl. Effort at going ahead with crit[ical] article.

Coming back from Flem. and Frenchtown, where I bought comic books.

Mon., Clinton House—three martinis—sudden drop at dinner— lovemaking after beer—too much beer—"Rather wait until after dinner." Food tasteless.

Neurotic fear (that I had not time enough) and neurotic self- doubt (that I was utterly unable to describe anything) kept me from looking very long at anything (turned in by fear and lust, more fear than lust, the fear of shame, and of death and having been shameful) like the blowing winter sky outside the window now—

A bird is rising in it, lifting, lofting, balancing on the air. Names of the clouds and the names of their shapes and the words for the colors—I do not know, possess not the patience to look for, and find.

I see a cloud which is a dragon's shape. Rain dark and rain gray toward the horizon. A white cream cloud behind it. Blue (sky blue— which blue?) in between. The blue screened by the clouds. More birds, black parentheses waving, and double commas.

The weathered planks of the carriage house—red rust stains running down from the top—the rusting of the tin roof (crenelated?) —its fadedness glows in the sunlight, shows under sun special bright graynesses. The door is like a mouth where teeth missing: black.

Here the school bus comes, heaving, shaking, and squeaking to a stop. Children's voices emerge, and scatter, calling as they go away.

Today the dirt road is bone-white. Brown woods, black woods. Bushiness of the winter fields.

December 20

Five pp. of *U[lysses]*, Flemington, *Time*, [V. S.] Pritchett's review of *PR Reader*. Walk at dusk. Clinton Point, old timbers, one drink, two drinks, dinner, guilt & misery, extreme nervousness, three drinks, ten to eleven cigarettes, home at 8. Two s.t.s, three pocket books— sleep from 3 to 12.

December 21

12–6, 16 pp. of *U*—at 5 Flem. & back, no liquor, no cigarettes & bubbling of ideas.

U, 16 pp. copied. No lunch but lemon yogurt. Little appetite for dinner, after soup. No sport. Two pocket books scanned. Bath. 8:30– 11:00. One more p. of *Butterfield 8* copied out (new record for one day: seventeen pp.). Two s.t.s took hold—did not go to sleep on them—faded.

Three s.t.s. Hagedorn's biography of Robinson, Winters on Robin- son.

Eating: bread & butter, hamburger, nuts.

3, 4, 5—two Dex. Light sleep broken by school bus, by dream in which I argued about a girl as heroine.

You become the music. You are the poem.

It is your consciousness, its rhythm modeling your nervous system—

But who wishes to become ill-tempered, a sadist, a neurotic—more than he or she is?

So the poem & the music must be more than these things if they are to be desirable.

But if they are unrelated to the evil of the self and of experience— then how can we join with it—identify ourselves in it?

Who would wish to become more stupid, more unintelligent, more ugly, awkward, more a victim of passion?

A Philosophy of Fiction (& other essays).

The spirit—and the spirited.

First one up has a guilty conscience—

December 23

Yesterday's 12–2:30 spurt. Three pp. of *U*. Four poor pp. of criticism. Whole bottle of sherry between us. Argument about Auden's *Times* piece. Beer & TV.

Awake at 8:30–9:00—hung over—but not too bad—two Dex., two pp. of *U*—nap from 11:30–12:15. Robinson & Winters on R.—woke between 2 and 3—fifteen Dex. & 2 Dexamyl—another *U* page (unfelt mostly), letter to K. on Dexamyl demiurge (blocked about check to postman and going out to see if there is any mail—any Xmas cards)— hardly any effort at criticism piece (except for idea of purpose).

Call to E.—Jane—Aiken (not home).

Excited & exhausted 9–12, reading & drinking beer. Tolstoy's biography. Smollett. My own story at 1:20, my own poems (as if manic again).

December 24–26

Xmas Eve. Depressed at nightfall, after trying to write a piece about Auden's piece on the *Times*, sleep at 8, awake at 12—sleep again from 4 until 12—to bed after getting irritated about Aiken, Ransom, E.'s wish that I give the prize to Conrad. [The National Book Award for poetry in 1954 was awarded to Conrad Aiken. The judges, in addition to Delmore, were Norman Holmes Pearson, John Crowe Ransom, and Richard Wilbur.]

25th. 12–4—after a poor night in which I dreamt of Tom Riggs— of A. MacLeish asking me if I was teaching at Princeton (I said yes, knowing it was not true) and of Eleanor Goff (and Alison Q., too)— very low: date put off: six pp. of *U* before Jane & Leslie arrived at 4:30—too many martinis—bed & one s.t.—up at 10:30—talk about the assumption of immortality in all serious ambition.

26th. 11/12–5—letter to Ransom—ten pp. of *Ulysses*—rising mood as Saul and Sandra arrived—very happy & looking very well—Saul looked much younger, not heavy & drawn.

$1,000 each from Viking for textbook.

Tom Riggs [a friend whose death in a diving accident raised the question of intent]—discrepant stories.

Monroe [Engel] has next year's Princeton job. Philip is moving to Riverside Drive. Drinking beer mostly until 2 (and talking about Hivnor too and getting tired & tight—annoyed with E. about being unamorous before sleep).

Dylan Thomas: wet brain.

December 27

Up at 10—somewhat hung over—letters to *College Forum* and Oberlin (asking for $250). Flemington—papers & Dexedrine—another pack of cigarettes (one yesterday), making list waiting for E. to be ready—2–3. No take in looking at the *Times*.

4–6—seven pp. of *Ulysses*, which takes me away from everything else.

December 28

N[ew] D[irections]. Jay glum & long-faced—"rather quiet," said Mr. & Mrs. Freelander. "Aren't you glad I could come," said Bob MacGregor.

(Two Dexedrine at 2:30, one at 3:30, one Dexamyl at 10:30, one D. & one M. at 1:30 = 7 all told.)

Nat[ional] Book Award

N[orman] H[olmes] Pearson talking about himself—how he never writes book reviews anymore (as in 1939, how anthologies kept one from one's own work)—said he used to see me frequently?! Twice—New Orleans & Choate—did not remember last May. R[ichard] Wilbur timid, shy, poetry-centered (Aiken as Jacobean), dwindling interest in Cambridge because can only write when teaching not interesting but uninteresting courses. Ransom's letter: 45 to W[arren], 35 to A[iken], but much more praise for A[iken].

How eloquent I grew with arguments—A. leading on first ballot —against Roethke—*Collected Poems* of Warren, C[ollected] P[oems] of A[iken].

Wilbur explained that he had sent nothing to *PR* because he thought a certain kind of poem was expected—after first saying he had written so little—been warned about first refusal by Stevens (but only $100), asked by Katy [Carver, the editorial assistant of *Partisan Review*] for a poem.

Pearson was certainly not backing Warren very much.

Statement: To C. A[iken] for his C[ollected] P[oems].

He has shown that a poet can be both traditional & modern, lyrical and philosophical. In fashion or out, he has continued to deal with the great themes of love and death. His work is important as a testament of modern man and as an expression of a pure devotion to the vocation of poetry for forty years.

Undated

A Jayne quote: The press always likes me. I don't know why.

> It is true that the Jersey Turnpike
> Is a monument to the song of
> the Open Road
> A memorial & an invention to
> Delight the heart of the
> Poet
> Whatever his misgivings

Dante—placed his enemies in hell—but it was something else— he found he had to put some of his friends there, too.

K[ilroy's] C[arnival]: "Sure my shirts are clean—they ought to be —they're up over my head so often." "I know how to be naïve about sex."

> They are silent—in the silence (which becomes them)
> Dear worlds I never knew nor ever will
> But surely would have found most lovable
> Supple various & most beautiful

Elia Kazan, *East of Eden* (Steinbeck)—hopped-up, stampede, hysteria.

James Dean is a new type, a shy ham.

Raymond Massey—eminent & pure representative.

December 30–31

Tues. night. Return from N.Y.—collapse of pseudo-manic.

Weds. Sylvester [Pollet, Elizabeth's brother, now fourteen] here, very shy—very tall. Bottle of sherry quickly consumed. Forced effort to write one *Times* piece—Yeats—five pp. or six of *U* copied—drive to lobster dinner in Easton—no lobster—Sylvester sick, unable to eat, vomited when we left restaurant. Beginning—though I did not [see] it of quarrel about Sylvester—wrong turn coming back—edgy tempers—disappointment because no sport but beer.

Thurs. Yeats again (?), beginning of pocket-book piece? Sylvester's departure at 5—E. back at 7—sport—disappointed again—pint of whiskey for N.Y. E. quarrel about Sy. & J. P[ollet].

Ho! Ho! Ho!
Now any man is an emperor
His dollar is his might

Hero of all fiction (friction).
The New York world.
Auerbach—Joyce—Racine.
History is a nightmare: during which I am trying to get a good night's sleep, which gives me insomnia.

1954

January 1

Asleep at 9—awake at 2, unable to sleep again despite two more s.t.s, breakfast in Flem[ington] at 8.

Pocket-book piece (?)—E. did not like it—liked Yeats. E. still angry—sport not postponed "because that seems too mean but I'm still very angry at you." Not too much sherry before dinner—too much beer after work all day on Yeats piece.

[*The two pieces appeared in* The New York Times Book Review *under the title "Speaking of Books," the pocket-book or paperback piece on January 17, 1954; the Yeats piece on June 13, 1954.*]

Sport postponed. New sentences on other piece at midnight. Ten Dex. Sat.; Sun., eleven Dex.

Undated

The act of reading is a solitary one. In a physical sense, at least, it separates one from other human beings, and if one reads books which others do not, the separation is more than physical. As long as the student is in school, he can talk about the books he has been reading in the classroom and to other students, and talking about books is apparently a necessary part of reading. Outside of school there is always the risk that one will be talking about something which others know nothing about. Although this, of course, is not the whole story. And in another context it would be worth considering at length the lack of imagination which keeps the literary critic from understanding that anyone who has worked from nine to five is in no condition to read Shakespeare and Henry James in the evening.

The important point about the pocket books is the proof that many more human beings like to read than has commonly [been] assumed. This assumption has long been reinforced not only by the facts & unquestionable experience of publishers but also supposedly by *Middletown*, the Lynds' 1929 sociological study [with a follow-up in 1937] of a representative Midwestern town where anyone who read many books was regarded as extremely peculiar. (No one wants to be thought peculiar, unless some special incentive is present, just as no one really wants to be disliked.)

It may seem unreasonable, but the fact is that when hundreds of thousands of people do the same thing, it ceases to be peculiar. It is true that most pocket-book readers do not discriminate between Faulkner and James M. Cain. Being perforce a literary critic and also, I am afraid, a highbrow, I cannot feel that this is the perfect state of affairs.

But the lack of discrimination works in two ways. The pocketbook reader may not discern the difference between Faulkner and Cain, but he reads both authors. I cannot believe that undiscriminating reading is not more desirable than no reading at all.

January 3

Sun. 5:30–2—finished pocket-book piece & Yeats—both "wonderful" to E.—still angry—typed & sent off to Brown. Ten Dex. Euphoria. Made date by mail with Harvey [Breit]—beer (case used up in two days)—amicable discussion of Tues.

Again—or when each review is finished—some kind of euphoria (which is not going on now).

Three and a half s.t.s.

January 10–12

Sun. Guilty and hung over after quarrel the night before (I wish I were dead, on & on) and too much beer. Forced myself to finish *NR* piece on criticism, almost amazed that it was done. Drove to town with it after dark, as it was slowly snowing, sweeps of white currents on the road. Nervous.

Two beers before dinner—two after (easy sleep)—E. forgiving and kind: "You're just a suffering human being."

Mon. Sudden breakthrough (as if manic) at 11—15½ pp. of Dostoevsky (only six Dex. or ?eight & Mil.)—but too much on theory of art, too little on *The Brothers K.*

Baptistown—stuck—Fodi [garageman] sucking his upper lip and his ulcer: "Many thanks."

Night: sherry, beer, happiness, and music.

Tues. 6:30—too soon—hung over—nervous—decided not to go to N.Y. with E. Flem.—lunch at 11:30—return—pocket book—more & more Dex. & Mil. (ten?)—drowsy but still manic—Freud on Dostoevsky. *U* copying.

Car stuck in ditch—snow—minister. "Are you from South?" Princeton—creative writing. "Do you attend a church?" Steve's Atlantic garage—one martini.

"The Jewish Jews" (fire—oy oy, the poor chickens).

Four beers—*Last Days of Hitler* on TV—*Nemesis of Power* until late. Three s.t.s.

January 13–14

Late heavy sleep, 10—forced two & then six pp. on Dost. & nineteenth-century Russia, using piece on Turgenev—not really connected (but can be) with Mon.'s 15½ pp. (Ideas in fiction.)

Excited after 2 by letter from Jay (reviews—job). Distracted by Meyers—plumbing broken down.

E. returns from N.Y. at 6—long & swollen face—gloomy. 7:30 trip to French[town] for cigarettes. Clinton House, two martinis. E. cleaning dishes, irritability, anger—better go to sleep, I'm in a grim mood. Reading *Times* pieces, about eight cans (7½) of beer, two s.t.s.

Thurs. Beer hangover & shakiness. Nine pp. all day, copying *Ulysses* with Dexedrine pleasure all morning. Page of beginning of essay on "Nature of Art"—then Jay, Ellie [Eleanor] Peters [on the staff of *Perspectives USA*], R. Richman—from 2 on—having a hard time & being careless or discoordinated—disoriented about figures, ending in jokes. 4—taking Mrs. White [cleaning lady] home as snow began to fall. 5:30–6—waiting for E.—waiting another hour as she expressed her depression, disappointment, and resentment. Two or three beers— three, four, five shots—drunk—difficult sport—dinner at 9 (!)— nothing to drink after dinner. Two skimmed pocket books & *Nemesis of Power*—sleep after or about 1—after 2 + 2½ + ½ s.t.s after resisting temptation of beer downstairs.

January 21

Tired waking after coming home at 2 and getting stuck in the ditch. Telling E. about N.Y. at breakfast until 11—ten pp. of *U*—five before postman came, five after he helped me out of the ditch.

Drowsy & relaxed by Dex. and Mil. (only six)—after lunch (when I was very hungry). Pocket-book sex, a murder trial: *The Girl in Poison Cottage*, sodomy performed upon a young girl.

At 4:30 stuck in the ditch again, going for mag. & cigarettes. Angry & exhausted as E. put off [going to] get Vlesta [the neighbor].

(E. wanted to make love, we did—passionate but passive as ever —left in the lurch again—)

Pocket book skimmed before & after dinner. First sleep from 8:10 to 9:30, then Trevelyan & pocket book about Gandhi—another deadened wasted resentful day.

February 12

Pan

Come let us chant once more
In high astounding terms
All men were created eagles!
America! America! O land of liberty & of luxury [?]
—All who have been reborn
                    Land of the stranger
Full of the sound of the fury of hope
Persistent as pioneers
                    In the dark forests of fears

[. . .]

March 13

Five pp. of new story. Six pp. new essay on T.S.E. for *Poetry*
["T. S. Eliot's Voice and His Voices," *Poetry* 85, December–January,
1954–1955]. Eleven pp. of *U* copied—to pp. 666 (+ 3 in four months).
Letter to Sobiloff, notes, roadwork at 5:30, two pocket books at midnight.

March 14

In Euphoria, America
    In the United States and Transports
                    of Humorica
All men were created eagles!
("The pen was his tiger and his sword")
("Nor cream cheese nor soapsuds would melt
                    in her mout")
(Here lives the patent-leather kid,
        in a duplex apartment)
(—Here Venus does the bumps and grinds—)
(Here little Lord Fauntleroy examines his sister
        In a dark closet when no one is home
He calls it playing doctor: she is the patient)

There was a young man from Caracas
Who simply adored Ritz crackers

March 17

There was a buoyant young heiress
Who loved to abash and embarrass
        She grabbed for a prick
        Like a hockey stick
And shoved it right up her bare ass

March 18

VW [*Vienna Woods*] (*Hope and Suspicion*)

It had been a slow evening at the Vienna Woods, it was the dead middle of the week, and it was raining slowly outside, so slowly that some of the time it was not rain but a drifting pinpoint mist which gathered about the streetlights like strange false grotesque costumes for a masquerade.

So it appeared to Tobias Simon. Perhaps it was his mood.

[. . .]

Tobias had not visited the Vienna Woods for several weeks and he had come tonight only because he did [not] feel, tonight, like drinking alone. He was too full of himself, surfeited: and it was too late to visit a friend. But he felt like drinking: it was not only tiredness but the desire to conceal himself from himself: he felt himself an undesirable stranger.

Gabriel, the bartender, was not at the bar when he came in; it was with Gabriel that he conversed. He went to a table near the jukebox brazen and blazoned though silent. A waitress had been hired since his last visit: she was small, pretty, but she directed a grim look at the outside world.

"What do you want?" she said, bored and mechanical.

"I wish I knew," said Tobias, feeling that her bored tired brusqueness permitted this kind of answer. She glared at him, a hand on her hip. "I wish I knew what I want," he added, explaining, and in a less meditative tone.

"Never mind the horsing around," said the waitress. "I'm not in the mood for it tonight. What do you want to drink?" her teeth clicking emphasis.

"Scotch-on-the-rocks," said Tobias. "Where's Gabriel?"

"Who wants him?" said the waitress, careful. Probably Gabriel's wife was after him again.

"A friend of his: me," said Tobias, trying to suggest that he felt friendly to her, too. "He knows me. You must be new here? I'm an old customer."

March 22

And then, turning a little, he stood at a different angle and saw, in the tall French windows of one of the backs of houses, a girl naked and barefoot dancing back and forth—appearing in one of the tall French windows, in the other and back again: she was practicing ballet steps, lifting one leg up onto the ballet bar—swinging a leg out, pivoting, pirouetting—from the distance (as D. Bradley's voice droned on) she appeared utterly unselfconscious—and to make for his true amazement, he now saw a fully dressed young lady on the studio couch against the wall conversing with a fully dressed young man—they were paying only a little attention to the naked and dancing girl.

Having resigned his effort to win the friendship, Martin was struck by the way in which Cornelius loitered on the grass near his window, casting glances toward him, tossing his ball in the air, casting glances toward him again. Martin resisted these overtures, if they were to be interpreted thus, continued to drink coffee and look at the daily news—which succeeded in being both astounding and banal—until he recalled, turning a page, what Isabel had said last night—that Tessa had gone to Washington for her brother's marriage and had taken Marian along with her. Marian, two years older than Cornelius, was destined to be a flower girl at the wedding. That was the reason for his new attitude; he had [been] left with the maid, which was a veritable vacuum.

As these thoughts occurred to Martin, a stone struck the window. He looked up—looked out: Cornelius had grown impatient, decided to forgo all protocol, stand on no ceremony.

Yielding, rising to go out and to greet Cornelius, it occurred to Martin that this was the city in which the citizens cast the first stone: but this was but the stone of loneliness.

Standing upon the back porch, he called to Cornelius.

"Are you lonely?" Martin inquired tactlessly, raising his hand against the blaze of the May sunlight upon his gaze.

"No," said Cornelius in a commanding voice. "Tell me a story."

"What kind of a story, glad or sad?" Martin asked, descending to the back yard.

"Tell me an *old* story," said Cornelius, looking down at the grass, for he was shy and disliked being forced to cultivate this stranger, who was stupid enough to ask him if he was lonesome.

"There was a young man named Rinehart," said Martin, "and when he went to the famous university, he did not have many friends and he felt left out—"

"What's left out?" inquired Cornelius.

"Left out is like not being invited to the party some of the other boys and girls at kindergarten or in the neighborhood are having." Regarding the boy's face, Ellery saw that his explanation was unsatisfactory, probably because Cornelius was quite popular, invited all over by the small shots.

"When you are left out, you feel the way you feel when it is raining all day and you have to stay indoors; or it is like being sent to bed when it is still daylight because your mother and father think you have done something wrong while all the time you are sure that you did not do anything wrong," said Martin Ellery. Cornelius sucked in his upper lip. He must have understood, for his look required the story to be continued.

"Anyway," Ellery continued, "Rinehart felt left out and he did not know how to make friends. He came from a small town where everyone knew everyone else, so no one ever had to make friends. Here at school, he was distant from his family & friends; no one tried very hard to speak to him, or be a friend of his, not even the boys who lived on the same floor as he did in the dormitory. During the first month at school, when Rinehart saw the other boys going to town on Saturday nights, whooping and yelling on the back platform of the streetcar, he felt rotten. When they came home early in the morning, singing and shouting, he felt worse than ever.

"This is an old story," said Ellery to Cornelius, seeking to hold his attention and perceiving that the child was getting bored. "It is also a love story. But all stories are love stories. Rinehart felt that no one loved him or liked him. So when spring came (and when the desire to be loved is sharp as a toothache), when after six months he still had no friends, Rinehart decided he would show the others that he was just as popular as anyone. Early one Saturday night, he stood outside the window of the dormitory room in which he lived, on the second floor, and he kept shouting his own name up at his own window. He kept doing this at intervals of two minutes until one of the other boys looked out the window and saw that it was Rinehart shouting his own name. He thought that Rinehart had lost his mind, and called the other boys, telling them that Rinehart had gone insane because he was shouting his own name up at his own window as if he were someone else calling himself. They dragged a hose to the window and turned it on Rinehart, drenching him until he was soaked and making him feel worse than ever. But when the other boys found out what had really occurred, they thought that Rinehart must be a very interesting fellow and he soon had more than enough close friends."

"Rinehart! Rinehart!" shouted Cornelius at the top of his voice. "Is that the end of the story?"

"Yes, and I suppose when your mother comes back home with your sister," said Martin, "you won't want to talk to me anymore."

"I don't like that story," said Cornelius, "it has no ending." He did not wish to discuss his future social relationships with Ellery in the open and explicit manner which Ellery seemed to think desirable. He was unwilling to commit himself to a new friendship at this abnormal time.

The middle-aged servant called out: "Cornelius! Cornelius!" from the adjoining kitchen. By summoning Cornelius to lunch, she resolved the impasse in which they were. Martin Ellery had been on the verge of asking Cornelius if he wanted to hear another story, since he had not liked the one about Rinehart.

Martin turned and went back into his own house, climbed the

stairs to his study, took up the volume about famous trials which had fascinated and distressed him the night before.

(Elaborate: make M.'s surprise felt—hooked on to reading.)

But just as his wife came in, he put the book down on the armrest; he was an image of sadness—limp in frame, languid in posture, his eyes unfocused.

"I see that you're blue and depressed," said Isabel, kindly though impatient.

"Yes," said Martin, peeved at any and everything, "although it's pointless to answer, since you see through me."

"Yes, your face is an open secret," said Isabel, but with fondness. "You can't dissemble or pretend: you can't fool anyone."

"At least I can fool myself," said Martin hopefully. He had become interested in this new topic.

"You can't do that either," Isabel insisted, "because you're also critical and suspicious of yourself! What has upset you now, your conversation with Cornelius? I listened as you told him that story. It is a beautiful story and you told it very well."

"I suppose," said Martin, withdrawn.

"It was a fine story," said Isabel. "Your trouble is that you don't appreciate yourself!" ("You appreciate yourself so little that you need the child's enthusiasm!")

April 3

The Vines of Vigor. The Virgins of Venus.

Bonfires of Hallelujah. Baskets of Elan. Bonnets of Jubilee.

Eve favored us with the poem about the serpent in Eden, cf. Paul Valéry.

> (I was in the Womb
> Unable to believe the world is as it is)
>
> Each shall be
> In the first great morning of ever
> A bridegroom or a bride
> & a newborn child

The Students of Joy.

White Towels of Touch. Towers of Excitement.

Disguised Blessings Are the Best Prizes and Surprises.

Beethoven: Joy: He who truly hears my music / Can never know sorrow again.

Happy Ending in the Gold West.

Pure Occasions. (Lincoln, Burr, Jefferson, H. Adams, C. G. Adams.)

Leaves of Grace.

April 4

America as the Native Land of Poetry. History of America.

> Which country is the country of the Blue?
> And was—was ever!—and must be!
> Because it was and is the land
> > Forever new!

> Let the beaked eagle soar in hope or anger
> > Fanning the wings
> The eagle and the dove / the eagle and the mole
> > The mole and the flagpole
> > The state capital
> Where there is a poet in residence at the university
> And at the zoo a resident hippopotamus
> And Minnesota—the land of 1,000 lakes
> And Niagara Falls—which left Oscar Wilde
> > > unimpressed
> And the handsome Hudson, a flowing dragon-god
> > Beneath the bronze palisades
> The Schuykill, the Susquehanna, the Shenandoah
> The immense Mississippi, Mark Twain's home & poem
> [. . .]

"Moral" idea is versify passages in H. Adams, Jefferson, Madison. [*History of the United States of America* during the administrations of Jefferson and Madison by Henry Adams.]

Duel between Burr & Hamilton. Weehawken.

[Lord] Charnwood's *Lincoln*. Theme of life lived basically by century [?]: The planter aristocracy—the blacks—the soldiers.

> Kentuckians had bulk & bone
> Craft and science favored Virginians
> The one looked for victory from power
> The other expected knowledge would
> > Bring him triumph—

> In America in 1800
> > The principal amusements of the populace
> are visiting and dancing,
> > listening to music, conversing,
> walking, riding, sailing, shooting,
> > playing checkers, playing chess, playing cards,
> and going to plays—

H. Adams: A society often coarse, sometimes brutal yet, drunkenness apart, entirely moral.

> Fishing and hunting,
> journeys for pleasure,
> For the boys football, quoits, and cricket
> A fondness for skating in the winter
> And sleigh-riding, too, favored, popular—

The president of Harvard regarded whist as an unhappy dissipation, the theater [as] depraved and immoral.

In 1792 the importation of the famous stallion Messenger. A source of endless interest to future generations. In Virginia, above all, race-courses, pure-blooded English running horses. The racing of horses the chief popular entertainment.

Freud—and David & Hitler—use and describe through psycho-analytic techniques.

David the Psalmist, first poet. Uniqueness & miracle of each, immortal & fathomless.

> *Joy, the God Joy*
> Joy is better than Love and a cause of Love
> Love is often bitter and dark and unforgiving
> But Joy is forgiving
> Joy is triumphant
> [...]
> The last knowledge of Joy requires the long &
> desperate experience of suffering
> This is the meaning of heaven's joy in the sinner who
> has returned, penitent
> [...]
>
> How when a boy I walked in the meadow
> in late winter
> And broke the ice that glassed the
> brooks
> Waiting, impatient, for spring's green resurrection—
> How I feared the dead, and the graves of the dead,
> Unable to understand the apartment houses
> overlooking the great cemetery
> —The terror of the dead is the love of joy and being

The private parts of sweetheart are tender wincing intimate intense (full of the juice of the joy of love).

"The fool is happy, for he knows no more—"
He who is entirely smart is half a fool.
"The virtuous life consists in abstention / from the tensions"—
murder, theft, fornication, falsehood, slander, insult, gossip, envy,
hatred, dogmatic error.

*[K.J. possibly stands for Kilroy: Jackson narrative, one section of a
projected work with the general title* Kilroy's Carnival; *or possibly
for "Kings of Joy," a poem to which there is a later reference.
Jackson is a persona of Delmore's.]*

K.J.: Spengler episode

[. . .]
In the autumn of the city
There can be no more a Keats, a Mozart
    neither a Pericles nor an Alcibiades
    nor a Marlowe, a Plato, Sophocles
    only Octavius followed by Nero . . .
        the eagles of the Emperors only
        but not the eagles of the Muses
Jackson is troubled and made anxious by Spengler's
                      description
       and by his philosophy of history
              doom & destiny

Only the courage, and innocence
(in the carnival of time and the city)
[. . .]
The daring of the dream which
        the half-wakened
           enact, advancing
Frees us from the body and burden
       of this death, this life
Jackson at thirteen is a captain like
                Perseus
(As he will be at thirty the latest
        son of Sisyphus)
And as when he comes to the ever new
        ever undiscovered
        country of love
Whence no mortal adventurer returns
He will participate in the terrifying
        alienation of Orpheus
And as in the end—knowing

And possessing the knowledge which
    Is behind knowledge and after
        consciousness
After consciousness is known to be a part of passage—
      to be overcome & surpassed
He will chant anonymous among the illustrious
        nameless multitudes
    The saints who have survived the fire of all desire
        rising and chanting
In the choir which praises forever
      The blaze and beauty of Being

April 8

K. J.: A. Burr

Aaron Burr was as much a child of America
        as honest Abe
           (honest enough to be afraid)
He was a confidence man (among the first of them)
      He was an Iago, a Cassius
        a Machiavelli
      (he loved his daughter too much
        as if she were himself
        and another man's daughter)
He preceded Barnum in bold contempt
        and in arrogance outranked—
He sold the Brooklyn Bridge to all the country boys
        or the Louisiana Territory
He came close to cheating his way to the White House
        as President
[...]
Jolly, he married a widow (merry, pretty, and monied)
(Favoring her with the praise of his hands upon her
      and the witty flattery of his admiring mind)
Jolly—in Jersey—on his deathbed—after eighty
    He was asked to recant
      his mind's freedom
Ask[ed] to affirm that he accepted and with devoutness
    God, Immortality, the Incarnation
      and Resurrection
To which jolly Aaron answered—aware that he was dying
    unable to deny the joy of his mind
      and the will of his wit—
"Sir, on that subject I am coy."
    These were the last words of a student of joy.
[...]

K.J.: EP: A Princess' Progress (first draft: very weak)

Although it is ungracious to praise one's own wife (it is thought to be unmannerly as if a peacock—but what peacock praises his wife?), I must once more praise my wife, Elizabeth—she who converts impatience into anticipation, which is an act of majestic moral poetry comparable to the transformation of fat green grapes into wine.

Libby at twelve. Passing through the Panama Canal in the twelfth year of her age & beauty, she refused to come up on deck because she was reading *Old Mortality*, a novel by Sir Walter Scott. She felt it was far more interesting than any Taj Mahal of engineering, however marvelous.

In the fourteenth year of her age and beauty, she climbed so high up in a tree on her father's farm, she was no longer [able] to come down again. (In Woodstock, an art colony in the Hudson River Valley and the foothills of the Catskills.) The fire department was finally summoned to restore her to terra firma.

The Latter Day Lives of the Gods: Venus, Juno.

Everyone a lover America
      is devoted
   unknowingly and spontaneously
   to the making of little poems
      as fresh as the first morning of Eden

Lear Dresses, Faust Tailors, Juvenal Detergent, Hawthorne Apartment, Medea Dresses.

Puritan America (what is the idiom?). Notes of other usable incidents.

Mrs. Chatterton Smythe has bestowed on her husband
                               six children
A girl and a boy and a girl and a boy and a boy
The youngest boy is a genius
Mrs. Chatterton Smythe celebrates each of the six birthdays
   with all of her six children
      with a levee in her boudoir
Which begins when she draws from under the conjugal bed
Winsome and winning ever, a tree of R E D bananas
Giving to each of her six children one of six red bananas!
   This is the end
   Of the story
   It is

*[Some of the following lines are in "A Dream of Whitman Para-
phrased, Recognized, and Made More Vivid by Renoir" included
in* Last and Lost Poems.*]*

*A Dream of Whitman
Dreamed by Renoir*
Twenty-eight young women bathe
        by the shore
The bank of a woodland lake
Twenty-eight girls, and all of them comely
In the wonderful unconsciousness
        of their youth and beauty
In the full summer and spontaneity of the
        flesh's self-awareness
Heightened, intensified by the soft and
        the silk and
Blooded by the sexhood which nakedness fires

A young man of twenty-eight regards them,
He owns the house on the farther bank
He is rich, handsome, and richly drest
        Standing behind the soft
        linen curtains

Which girl does he think most desirable
        and most beautiful
They are all beautiful, and desirable
[...]
Where is he going? he is going to be among them
        To splash and to laugh with them
They did not see him, but he is
        there with them
        His gaze possesses them

Nature: A Pastoral Ontology
To the chief musician (witnesses of being)
The birds in the first light chant
        mellifluous
        gratuitous,
        and for nothing
Save to augment their sense of being
[...]

Poetry

The object of philosophy is the mastery of emotion
The object of poetry is the ascent to joy
It is not the glory of the bronze equestrian statue
It is not the limelight nor admiring glances
It is not the triumph of the hero returning after forced marches
To the pomp of parades & the passionate applause of the populace
It is not the charm of the magnetic personality
It is not the desire to be a poet—
  The poet's desire
Is to be consumed in his poem as fuel
    is consumed in fire
 As the sunlight vanishes in the apple
[...]

The Power and Glory of Poetry
(The Stations and Privations of the Poets)

The novice poet questions me at a cocktail party
He wishes to know my methods of work—at night, in the morning
Do I read my poem aloud or shout it?
   Do I read other poets?
Do I wait for inspiration, seek it in intoxication,
   find it in emulation
Tired by his questions, unable to answer them, I say to him:
"[?] Do you [know], it is often very difficult for me to write
        at all!"
"Oh, I am glad to hear that!" he says with pleasure.

The truth was that I was unable to answer him,
Being in the same state of spirit which stops me from writing
The truth which I did not make clear or understood
Is that the writing of poems is for me either easy or impossible
The whole truth is that we are the natives of a dark wood
Groping in the dark of the heart for the miracle

In vain, the labors of ambition and will
In vain, the study of ancient famous works—
Unless the agony of love or infatuation
Bringing the nearness of obsession to possession

In 1949 Sylvester Pollet remarked to me: My teacher could write far better poetry! He has five children. He knows all the words.

"Anyone can have children."
Malice leads to insight.

    Once my brother-in-law aged ten remarked to me
    My teacher if he wanted could write far better poetry
                      than you
    He has five children. He knows all the words you do.
    Is there not insight & profundity in this youthful view?

    The poet must be one acquainted with the night
            By the Pacific
    He must know that in the real dark night of the soul
            It is always three o'clock
            It is always Calvary
                And Armageddon
    But know also, near him, like sleep
            The everlasting Eden
    And know the eternal Arcadia or
              deathless child
    Which cannot be annihilated, blinded,
                or defiled

    For love is a dark horse and a white elephant
    For love is a birth and a death
        an ecstasy and an agony
        There is no poetry where no love is,
        No love without the assent and
                intent of poetry

April 14

Jackson narratives. (Hook—egg sandwich—student intellectual.)
Johnson Jackson at nineteen years
      espoused the doctrines of St. Thomas
The gospel according to Aristotle, Alexander's tutor,
             Plato's student
He taunts the other students turned to Marxism
"If the true cause of works of art is the class struggle
If art is the product of the structure of society
Then in the classless society, there will be no art!
      (Since there will be no classes)
    Gleefully: 'That's what you said!' "
They call him an aesthete as they call him a Sophist
Johnson Jackson, undisturbed by them, is troubled by Marxism
(As once, years before, by Spengler's philosophy of history)

His sense of selfhood, his intense conception of authorship
Made uneasy by the thought that the author
                          and his masterpiece
Are formed in the womb of historical powers
Nurtured by the nature of society, drawn forth by the
                          need of the age
He argues—with himself as with others—
                    The great ones and the lesser
Lived in the same years, enjoyed or suffered the same
                          historical powers
Supported or inspired in the same society: but the great ones
Made the masterworks—the mediocrities were—mediocre.
          Autonomous, free, self-creative—the crackpot inventor—
This is the sense of selfhood
Nurtured often in America—it is the pioneer, it is entirely
                          native!

April 15

Chicago trip[s]: July 1928, July 1929, 1931 Sept.–Oct., 1932 May,
1935 Sept.

Death and morning: the Blue: the silent Snow. Fugitive from the
tyrant & demon of hurt feelings. (How I almost destroyed the poet of
death & morning, blue & snow.)

*[The following draft of a poem about Delmore's trips to Chicago,
first as a boy to visit his father and then later to see about his
father's estate, is extremely rough. I have taken excessive liberties
in combining and omitting lines and phrases. My reason for including this material is that some of it bears on the complexity and
depth of the poet's attitude, central in his published work, toward
snow, the morning, and the blue.*

*Jackson, a persona of Delmore's, is journeying to Chicago but
has remembered an earlier train trip to a summer camp in the
Adirondacks on which Jackson had persuaded his younger brother
Martin to keep "a sacred vigil" looking out the window from their
Pullman berths.]*

What would the boys of nine & seven discover
                          what hope?
What waiting: Jackson was lost—he entertained
          the child's hypothesis
The tantalizing theorem
          that he who waited watchful
                    all night [. . .]

Won his way to a new height of perception & being [. . .]
Knew a hiddenness, entered a secret, sustained an access
              in the power of perception
The morning was a secret at the instant of passage, it was
                    a show
Sustained by the inner secret of passage [. . .]
When after two stations of vigil, Martin, moved
              only by his brother's wish [. . .]
        Slept the exhausted sleep of an excited boy
Then Jackson tired, too, for the passing night outside the
                   window
        was empty or black.
[. . .]
When the first morning was done, he woke
He looked from the window, perceiving the
           purity and the silence
                the newness and strangeness [. . .]
Marveling amazed—the morning
Was truly the trophy of supreme meaning
          which he had supposed it
Only his failure to watch in vigil deprived him of
    The lights and rights of a knight of the morning
So before, beginning in infancy,
        returning each winter
          continuing and to continue surely and truly ever
He had seen the snow's advent as the descent
        of the victory and the divinity [. . .]

The trip to Chicago is a trip from what is to
        what may be (but elsewhere
              and distant)
He brings with him his sense and assent to snow
        and his hope in the first morning
As he looks at the lake which is a sea where it arches
            with the blue [. . .]
He looks with eyes and mind and heart
        taught by the love and lore of snow
          [. . .] the quest & question of morning

(Chicago 1935)
Jackson journeys to Chicago once more in his
            twenty-first year
Jackson seeks the funds of his inheritance to
        "pursue his higher studies"

He is poor, he is almost penniless, he stays at
              the YMCA
He visits attorneys—and amuses them by saying
          how he is interested
            in studying philosophy
          his chief interest is—Ethics
On State Street idle and bored on an early evening
A furtive nondescript calls to him from the
            shadow of a doorway between two stores
          How about some company, Cap?
          Want to meet some pretty girls? [. . .]
Told to choose, not to be bashful, by a dark knowing girl
He chooses the youngest girl among them.
She is pretty. She is kind. She is flattered that he has
               chosen her [. . .]
It is seven in the evening; the night has not yet begun.
He tells her, as she takes off her gown (under which still
        is the freshness of girlhood) [. . .]
How he would like to know how to awaken a girl
            making love
How his true love, whom he is going to marry, is patient
        but thinks that "sex is disgusting."

    Virtue in verse: less need of detail & narrative context. Defect: thin & pedestrian unless pumped up & jacked up—and if p. & j. then risking forced feeling, false rhetoric.

                                        Undated

Jumping Jehosophat.
"A giant problem / a dwarf solution."
Love—drunkenness—brandy. Insults 69! 96!
    Oh, mouth (frequently:) in mouth-genital contact! (A nation of women who are cocksuckers.)
    To be continued Poetry! till Death do us part—
    Particulars—vivid & unique. Alligator with big warts. Black bear floundering and groping for roots & honey. Scalloped cumulus.

            Trip-hammers of pulse
                of the heart
            Heard in the ear
           Bearing stigmata of neurosis

The great stars and flowers of truths
                    Take new forms
Which are strange, repugnant, and difficult
                    to recognize
Thus, the striving of Odysseus must be reviewed:
He was not seeking to return to his native city
                              or his wife
He was seeking himself, seeking to return
                              to himself
He sought Ithaca and Penelope because they
                         were part of him
Lost parts of the self. The new version of
                         the ancient story
Was implicit before, but . . .

English poet as goat—women. Thomas, *Bazaar.*

Think of the famous English lyric poet Friendly
Consider his statements in an interview when
                    it was learned
He had been living for weeks with a goat
                    in a New York hotel room
"This goat is more sincere than most American women"
[. . .]
He does not attempt to disguise the truth of nature
He does not pretend to be what he is not
He is candid. He concedes that he is a goat
He will neither deny nor affirm that he is also the
                                    god Pan

[. . .]

            H.'s Elephant & Reality | Avoirdupois
Hegel's elephant dances as lightly as all the—
He dances the waltz, the polka,
                    the alla tedesca [?]
The cavatina—the schottische—the samba—the mamba
                         the Charleston—the "Blue Danube"
         The day and the night and the year
                    and the galactic drift
                         toward Arcturus

He pauses patient and the Blind Men grasp him
One touches his tusk—says he is a piano
One his hide—says he is tree
One, groping, grasps his testicles
                    Declares him stud of nature
One holds his leg—claims he is a column
One finds his rump—calls him a continent
One fails to touch him—says he is superstition
[. . .]
One [. . .] asserts he is nothing that he seems [. . .]
                Appearances are not the underlying reality
One puts his hand in his mouth—is bitten
                Cries in pain that he is evil
Several, humble, suggest that consensus will yield the truth
Two suggest that there is no truth
One says in a friendly way: Let us compromise

When I was a student: and in a class in metaphysics taught
            By one of Hegel's grandsons
                    And a nephew of Marx
I waved my hand after six weeks to ask
        "When does the class begin?
            When do we begin
                The study of metaphysics?"
Professor Hegel Junior joked and was jolly
[. . .]
He made the class laugh whipping a repartee of epigrams
        I said: "There are inherent forms and norms in nature
                Objective reality is full of determinate beings
                A living thing has an entelechy like an ambition
                Only an egg can become a chicken
                It is not any of many things [. . .] depending upon
                    Each one's vision, condition
                        need or interpretation—"
        "Only an egg can become a chicken."
        "What of it?" quipped Professor Hegel Junior—
        "Only an egg can become an egg sandwich!"
(And the class roared merry, and I blushed, shamed.)

April 27

Hem[ingway]: Three Day Blow
As the rain stopped: there was the orchard
The fruit had been picked
    The fall blew through the bare trees
The road after the orchard went to a hilltop
    There was a cottage:
        The porch bare
            Smoke coming from the chimney
    In back:
            A garage, a chicken coop
    The timber like a hedge of the woods behind

The big trees swayed far over
    in the wind as he watched
—He crossed the open field above the orchard
    He stood on the porch, looking out—
They stood together, looking out across the country
    Over the orchard, beyond the road,
        Across the lower fields
Beyond and across
        The woods of the point to the lake
They could see the surf of the waves
        At the point—

Undated

"Father Knickerbocker's Slaughter House." *New Yorker*, Feb. Story by Roald Dahl in which husband kills stray cat thought by wife to be reincarnation of Liszt.

Feb. [27] Wife kills selfish husband who keeps her from being on time for trip to Paris to see daughter & grandchildren. ["The Way Up to Heaven," Roald Dahl.]

April. [10] John Cheever ["The Five-Forty-eight"]—Girl threatens to kill junior executive who had affair with her, then had her fired. Compromises by pushing his face in mud at suburban junction.

May 5

Episodes (Incidents, Advents)
in the Balkan Kingdom of the Emotions
At the bar the drunkards were singing:
    Ding-dong, the witch is dead
On the beach the children were chanting:
    Pain! Pain! Go away
    Stay away and let us play
    Mama, Papa; doctor, nurse; and
        doctor, patient

You show me yours, yes
    And I'll show
        You moan mine
The sun shone upon the just and the unjust
Guilt sickened the innocent,
        And the generations
From the small womb moved in pain,
Moving to the small room of the tomb

Leaping to touch the melon of love
    Between the first and last
      Advent of claustral claustrophobia
      Confirmation
Leaping between the kinds of sleeps
    And deeps to touch the
      Sunlight of euphoria
[. . .]
This life may be a play: or perhaps a story
Told by a schizophrenic
    To an exiled Viennese doctor
Who is under the impression that God does
        not exist
Who is certain that the doctor is an
        hallucination
  (and also his true enemy's impersonation)
And convinced that he himself
      does not exist
Being merely—and clearly!—a figment
    of his own imagination
[. . .]

For as marriage is the chief cause of divorce, Life is chief reason of death.
    The drunkards are singing again, arias from the operas:
    The Island of Selfhood
    The Land (Capri) of Luxury
    The Sovereign State, Sensuality
    The Bourbon Kingdom, Gluttony
    The United States of Euphoria
    The Lido of the Libido

The Lives of the Poets
"But how can you be a poet?"
                said to the poet [by his] mother
                        in the seventeenth year of his age
"Was your father a poet? Were either of your grandfathers
Poets? Am I a poet?"
        "Shakespeare was the son of a butcher,"
                        he answered absentmindedly.
"So you think you are a Shakespeare!" she said
        (She had never liked him. He was her first child.)
        She felt that he had defiled her: he and not
                        her husband, his father
        He was the living the dirty demanding infant
                the final rottenness of the degradation of sex

Thus before then, she had become furious
When he bought a new book of poems
For which he paid three dollars.
"It is such a small book," she said
"And besides you could have taken it for nothing
                        from the public library."

(Quote Baudelaire; the poet's mother's curse. Cal Lowell and his
mother. Criticism of Berryman.)

Thus—but not wholly thus—but kindly, in sympathy
When he sent his brother a copy of his first book of poetry
His brother wrote to thank him:
        "I like it very much, except that I don't like poetry
        I have shown it to my friends and they like
                        it very much
        And they would buy a copy except that
                they can't afford the $2.50."

                Whitehead
        "There are no whole truths
                there are only half-truths
        It is by taking the half-truth as the whole truth
                that we make the truth a kind of falsehood—"

[Freud]

Freud was the great genius—of courage—as well as intellect.
After he had been told—again and again for thirty years—
That his view of the writing of *Hamlet*
Was incorrect in regard to one fact
That Shakespeare's father's death took place the year before
      Hamlet was written
A fact hardly necessary—at all—to the Freudian
      interpretation
Of the neurosis of the Oedipus complex as the cause
     of Prince Hamlet's madness
And the emotions of the poet and playwright
      the sexual disgust
      the fear of betrayal
      pathological suspicion and
      pathological jealousy
After the passage of thirty years, Freud in his last work
     acknowledged the error
Admitting an error had been made, but
Asserting that the plays of Shakespeare were "probably
      the work of another,
     the Earl of Oxford!"
  a young man who had suffered the loss of his father
  the year before the first performance of *Hamlet*!!!

            May 13

  Tuning Up and Tuning In: America! America!
. . . Here where morning is spoken in more than
       seventeen languages . . .
Here where morning is the native language [. . .]
Here Experience remains fearful and unknown ever
   As love to the never-loved or not-yet-loved
For here experience and the future are inseparable [. . .]
    What has been and what is
Under the arching immensity of the future, as under
    the blue dome and cave of the sky—
[. . .]
So all minds and hearts, being infinitely hopeful are
    infinitely brittle
    and quickly broken
    and frequent[ly] caught in lunacy
       and suicide
Return, O Tocqueville, and you will have arrived
     for the first time

As Dickens, Wilde, and Matthew Arnold were never here
So you were not: but read in the Baedeker of yourself
    and reached—which is something to say—part
        of the upland of your self
[. . .]

    AA—The Fate & Faiths of the Saints of
The witnesses dedicated to the light and the lights—
    and the country of the blue, of Apollo
Wake in the world of morning to the terror of Experience in America
Waking, they seek to take it all in, all of it, the
    enormity in its enormousness [. . .]
This is the mode and will of Whitman—to be
    omnivorous, to consume America.
[. . .]

  (Light's peculiar grace. Polaris, the morning star. Stendhal, the
Winchell of the romantic ego.)

    America's Witnesses: The Saints of Light: The Angels of
    Insideness

[There follow some chaotic lines I have omitted about Whitman,
James, Melville, and their ominous separation and isolation.]

    [Melville]
Lives thirty years in the prison house of solitude, in the midst
    of the millions of New York City
And lives in silence . . . and Ryder . . . and Winslow Homer
As before them, Poe & Irving—
        For Solitude or Isolation or Separation
        Are like America and are America
        Hence America was known to all, long before
[. . .]

See then how they go down into themselves the cells
    and the labyrinthine interiors
Emily Dickinson in her bedroom in Amherst, the
    window being Eternity, the window curtains Love
Looking out upon the white race track, the pale horse, the
                pale rider [. . .]
Parkman half blind & surrounded by roses
Hart Crane having jumped from the bridge of love
    Must needs cast himself into the Caribbean [. . .]

Woodrow Wilson innocent as Daisy Miller at
       Versailles among the King's Medusa mirrors
       (Henry Miller more innocent than Daisy Miller)
As Lincoln in the isolation of melancholy or the
       exhilaration of momentary exaltation telling jokes [. . .]
               from his private heights
As Grant in the separation and confinement of
                       solitary drunkenness
       (deprived of his horses and his children in California)
As Emerson following the guidance of self-reliance to
                    second childhood [. . .]

May 16

   The Laws of the Emotions (are studied in the texts & memoirs of hope).

May 18

   [. . .]
Here where we are, we must pause because
Dionysus seeks to wrestle with Apollo and
Apollo, with charming gaze, to hypnotize Dionysus
And we, too, in chorus, given to incantation
Call Behemoth—merely burly—
Cast jokes at the juggernaut
And seek to lull Leviathan with levity
Little Davids terrified by Goliathans
Persuaded, deceived of the powers of pebbles and Psalms
And wipe our hands across the (years of tears)
Numbed by the nemesis of the pride of self-possession
       When will the kings of joy come to us
           Triumphant, glowing glorious?
       When will we find them within us
       As Bach moving upon the mountains of
           consciousness?
       And in the underworld under the thunder,
       After the splits of lightning! and
       The following all over darkness

   (Tuning in and forcing. Forcing & fading in the day as on the phone.)

We may say with assurance that
Joyce used language with greater consciousness
Than any other author in the
              history of English literature—
He knew how [. . .] language and abstraction
Often distort and hide actuality and truth
—If he moved constantly from the word to the thing
He moved as continually from thing to word,
Devouring the energy in the life of the street and the city
Moving all over and everywhere by means
          Of the energy and the light contained within words.

("At once a great stylist and a great realist.")

            Most readers are for Whitman or against him
            As if he were a candidate for public office
            His book is regarded as a sacred text
                  or as the shouting and the braggadocio
                        of an overwrought barker
                              a manic salesman
                              or a radio announcer
            This is partly because he writes in the modes
                        of the doctrinal and the declarative

    Whitman was in love with experience to the point of morbid
infatuation. He tried to force his genuine experience to be a kind of
witness and a proof of his idea of experience. (In his prose, however,
doctrine can be seen apart from observation—the observation of the
degradation & greed of postbellum America.)

        In reading again, carelessly, the
                books of Virginia Woolf
        How one hears—how one cannot help but hear
        A voice like that of a marvelous soprano
        Singing from the darkness of old phonograph records
        Singing passionately and pathetically
        That life is beautiful, noble, and tragic
                        that no [one] knows anyone
                        that we are all forever
                              lost and
                                    alone—

Huxley. What if many writers have said the same thing about many important questions? Agreement is not proof, it is not illuminating, it is often deceptive. (Mere age, repetition, and popularity require little attention—the doctrine itself requires as much attention as the mind can realize.)

> Mr. Huxley's perennial philosophy
> Is at once brand-new, old hat, and a hodge-podge!

[*These comments refer to* The Perennial Philosophy *by Aldous Huxley.*]

Tuning in on the intensity and underlying poetry of book reviews.

Here after apt and relevant remarks
> such as
> "I feel drunk all the time"
Are queries which would tax the talents—the intellects
> of Immanuel Kant and Sherlock Holmes

How literary and how bookish he is
When he is trying most of all
> to be one of the boys in the back room [. . .]
He says: You don't have a "look-in"
Just as an Englishman might say: Let's be full of "pep," honey.

He is not truly full of humility
Before the mystery and richness of existence
But like tourists before Niagara Falls
He enjoy[s] the emotion of being impressed

(They like most of all eloquent language, profound in sound.)

> *Apollinaire*
He is innocent and sophisticated:
When he writes about the moon as a frying egg
Or compares the bridges of the Seine to sheep
He [is] inspired as a child is: surprised & delighted
> By what others take for granted or see
> in terms of utility, or ulterior purpose
> in terms of conventional ways of thinking [. . .]
But he is sophisticated—being neither a child nor a savage
Knowing that this kind of innocence
> cannot be simulated
> cannot be taken for granted
> nor compelled [. . .]
It must be discovered continually

(And it can be only if habitual attitudes and feelings are rejected [put aside] like tuxedos [dress suits, uniforms, costumes].)

[*Gertrude Stein*]
Tender Buttons were her aim—and amorous success
Toasted Susie was her ice cream
     (The world was her ice cream or her lollipop or,
          in any case, chiefly delightful)
Her common sense, her complacency,
        her fascination with herself
Are one with her prose rhythm and her affections
[. . .]
She does not understand war—or peace
But who does? She is vain enough to be sure
That it is true that she is read
     To the children in the public schools in America
But her vanity is necessary, charming—and creative
As when the GIs take her for a ride in a jeep
As when they tell her she is read in grammar schools
         in America!

Randall Jarrell
It was as if he saw his objects
         through opera glasses
Or saw the dim and ghostly negative
Not the developed photograph
    Full of daylight and defined objects
—Here the event is grasped by intuition & premonition
    Not as the event and the aftermath
Controlled by a passion to be aware, awake—alive
        avid, ravenous to know
        to take in what really exists
. . . Here are the emotions of hopelessness, helplessness
        animal terror, animal tenderness
        shrieking perplexity at senseless death
        or silent despair that men kill each other
(The dead soldier says: Why did I die? Why?)
[. . .]

May 20

Project after *F[innegans] W[ake]*—summary of each page & reading aloud instead of just copying (or with some copying).

Dost.—Jackson MacLow [poet and playwright and a college friend of Elizabeth's]—beard—shyness—father—hotel.

> The debt of parents to their children
>   is immense
> The children give the parents
>   dignity, authority, belief
> Give a new meaning
>   and a new dimension
> To the parents' lives

Essay, Leavis: provinciality. Bridges, Hopkins. Arnold as Kidglove, Cocksure. Joyce, Hardy, Milton. *The Secret Agent, Fathers & Sons, The Possessed.* Literature as guide to life. *The Great Tradition.*

Play: Hiss, Chambers—cynicism, self-interest. Man never lives by bread [alone] but only by (love of) belief in something taken to be all-important—family, nation, God. (Collective myth.)

> If we cannot love ourselves (so near, dear, and inescapable),
>   how can we love another?

It is an endless circle—which must not be ended?
1. Seeking to love ourselves
2. Striving to love others
3. Desiring to be loved by others
4. Trying to be loved by ourselves—that part
    of the self which judges whether any and
    all are worthy of admiration and love

Job—whirlwind. Confrontation of Joy Singers of Eden (use of *Mein Kampf*, etc.).

May 25

[. . .]
Narcissus now as before continually as time's self turning
Looks and beholds himself and plunges in
                          the nausea of self-disgust
(Unable to love his own image and thus
                          barred forever from love)

Plunged to drown himself in the flowing of
                waters which became [?] [...]
The flowering of the abyss of nothingness,
         the gorge of absolute abandon!
[...]
As once more on Parnassus Pegasus prances
      An untamed favorite—wearing the colors of Venus—
        (Cheered by all the harpers and songsters)
This is the Epiphany Purse, the Ecstasy Handicap
The Beatific Derby [...]

All of the cosmos is open to the beholding
               of consciousness
This is a pure and perfect and everlasting
                 possession
[...]

(The rondure is a pleasure—and all is!)

May 28

Conrad A[iken]: A honey of patience place.

The poet once lived in a perfect realm [...]
Where each found in the other love like color
Where beauty had an unheard utter grace

The sheen of Dexedrine
        Made wings sprout in my head
[...]

A strange brightness
Triumphant and radiant like the moon
        A marvelous radiance
Of intrinsic vitality—
        At the heart at the center of all
The incandescent quivering of the moon
A white body of fire writhing and striving
Drawing itself together, asserting and reasserting itself

"It is only in the experience of poetry that we are fully awake."
    After the deluge, the delusion. De luxe, à la king. The wandering
you, ewe, yew.
    Dialectic: No work: no holiday!

Carnivals—festivals—
Cartoons, balloons, and party hats!
Rockets and Roman candles—after the soaring
        of champagne's cork [. . .]
On the dizzy heights our daring hearts
Tiptoed and danced—with jingles of bells
Aces and trumps! Banners & minds aloft!
Playhousing as Players, Mummer[s], and Lovers
Finding the festival which each discovers.

Who is the king of the feasts?
Who is the queen of all dances?
. . . Now, new in May, who can summon
The memory of winter, dead white December,
And watercolored dusk . . .
       . . . For now the birds are on the bough
          Bush blooms, branches flower
          Toward the sun of summer

      Chickens wuck wuck wucking
      Jerk staccato at their picking
        The foliage thickens
     —Birds nests in barn corners
     —Piercing the whistle of the red-hatted cardinal
     —Raw the cawing of starling and crow

May [?]

    Method & Versification. An essay on the tradition as it grows. To combine Joyce, Pound, Whitman. To use St. Leger, Eliot choruses of *Rock* and of *MC* [*Murder in the Cathedral*], *F*[*our*] *Q*[*uartets*], W. C. Williams, Marianne Moore.

    Coleridge, Hopkins, Bridges, Sandburg, Imagists, Claudel (Valéry's free verse).

    Shakespeare's versification of Plutarch et alia.

June 1

    Joyce, *F*[*innegan's*] *W*[*ake*] copied.

    Halfhearted page of a new beginning on [Elder] Olsen—[Dylan] Thomas.

    The Gentle People (usable sentences), Maupassant (*Bel-Ami* & skimming), John Evelyn (descriptive & visual), Johnson, *Life of Savage*. Unable to get past p. 1 of *Emma*—Austen. Twenty pp. of M. Eberhart. Unresponsive to Leavis's quotations (as I had not been two or three weeks ago).

Asleep (three s.t.s) 11:30 or 12—awake at 2—no sleep until 6–6:30—then two Dexamyls—troubled sleep until 12:30, very nervous. A slow slackening & slowing (in copying & reading as well as in writing) since the first week in May despite spasms of activity & lucidity.

June 3

F[*innegans*] W[*ake*] triple take, quadruple take, n[th] take.
From erection to resurrection.
The charmed or tied (freed) self.
A full-fledged member of the upper crass (crasst).
Stroke & strophe & catastrophe.
On a Cook's tour-de-force.
What consort of a thing is that to say, Queen (Princess)?

Huxley. (Tibetan *Book of the Dead.* "O nobly born, do not permit your mind to be distracted.") This is the problem—to remain not distracted—by the memory of (1) past sins; (2) imaginary pleasure; (3) the aftermath of old wrongs & humiliations; (4) by all kinds of fears.

Latest desire which ordinarily eclipses the liquor.

June 29

You don't appreciate yourself. I am not the only one—by far.

How much I must miss—as G.B.S. [Gertrude] told me in 1933 or '4—of social world (reminded by society pp.—dentist marriages).

Red Barber: "We're really going with the ringer on this one." (The ringer, wringer.)

Koran, Confucius, *Bhagavad-Gita*—Lao-tse—NT—Homer—Aristotle—Plato—Aquinas—Ovid—a nodding (skimming) acquaintance with them.

Mary: "That's the part of my anatomy of which I am least proud" —toilet & pinching obsession—sexual parts disgusting (Freud says so, too—father—primordial like dinosaur).

Not only paralyzed during important years, 1943–1951, but kept from full development when it was most possible.

July 5–11

Thursday, July 8. I called Jay—Carruth. No sleeping & one Dexedrine at 6 a.m.

Fri. No sleeping & two Dexamyl at 2:30–3 a.m.

Sat. A highball, glass of wine, and two s.t.s (five Dex. & one M.). F[*innegans*] W[*ake*], 300–314. Giants doubleheader (losing second game)—distressed by nightfall.

Sun. Wine, one half or three-eighths of a half gallon—half of it before two s.t.s. Four s.t.s.! and only two Dexedrine, one before, one after breakfast.

Weds. All day alone & wildly manic—all.

Tues. Walk to Frenchtown on the back road with Leslie [Katz].

Mon. Leslie came at end of Giant doubleheader.

July 17

10:30–11:30. Some change through forcing & eight Dexedrines.

Faulkner, "Notes on a Horse Thief."

Giants vs. St. L. & copying *FW*—almost no change.

Tidying room, making bed. Mowing the lawn as resentments rose.

Two glasses of wine—only half of second, watching and losing interest in *Paris 1900* on TV with dinner.

8–9 Flemington—cheered by finding two pocket books.

Undated

It is better than nothing in this sense: on the one hand it is now often necessary, because of the New Criticism, to insist that *Moby Dick* is about a white whale whatever else it may be about; on the other hand, *Moby Dick* was left unread for seventy years after it was published. In a like way, the poems [of] Emily Dickinson were not published during her lifetime, while for twenty years Edwin Arlington Robinson & Robert Frost suffered the lack of understanding which E. Dickinson would have experienced if she had been published.

The consolations of a historical perspective can be overestimated. Yet one has only to read H. L. Mencken on the art of poetry as a pack of lies, [the] avant-garde as a pack of poseurs, the "puerility" of Thorstein Veblen and John Dewey, the nobility of war to see how the supposed glory of the first postwar period is chiefly a nostalgia for exuberance. And if one goes back fifty years to the time of William Dean Howells, George Woodberry, Henry Van Dyke, and Barrett Wendell, the literary scene is a desert (an appalling gentlemen's club) inhabited by a host of mediocrities.

July 24

Fraternity House, Jelke-Laughlin, third attempt.

Chapter One

It all began, I suppose, on a dreary day, dreary as only a fraternity house can be on Monday after a pretty big weekend. Most of the fellows were nursing hangovers. They were too hung over to let anyone turn on the radio or the phonograph. There were a few postmortems but it was supposed to be in poor taste to talk about your dates at Fair-field—because of several incidents the year before which I will come to soon, and besides, we were all beat, all except Gordon Dearborn.

Gordon was the richest man in our class—which is saying a good deal but not describing just how rich he was. He was so rich that not even Gordon or anyone else knew just how much money he had and was going to have. But one of the boys said that he was so rich that he would probably get married in an absolutely disgusting way to some-one like Barbara Hutton or Doris Duke.

Anyway, as we sprawled around the leather chairs of the den and moaned a little now and then because of our hangovers, you could see two of the buildings and the stadium which Gordon's grandfather had given Fairfield before the income tax came along to make gifts like that customary.

Gordon never had a hangover and he was just wasting his time with the rest of us so as not to be lonely. In fact, Gordon hardly drank at all; the reason he gave was that drinking made [him] more silent and more silent, just as [it] makes most people more and more talka-tive. I would have known that this was just a coverup except that I never [cared] much for the stuff myself. I suppose I was usually excited enough without it. But Gordon was afraid of it. It seems that his father was quite a serious drunkard and off the beam also, that drinking brought all the insanity to the surface. Gordon was afraid that he would turn out to be like his father, though I never saw any sign of his being cracked in any way, but then they say that you can't always tell even if you're one of those experts that testify in murder trials.

But if Gordon was not in the least crazy, he was certainly one gloomy guy that day as much as any. And he was off on the song-and-dance which most of the other fellows had told him to kindly omit—how awful it was to be very rich.

". . . it cuts one off from the rest of the population," Gordon was saying when I came back from the john. I knew what the line was because I had heard it before.

"Oh, sure, it does," Ralph Huggins said. "It cuts you off from chorus girls, yachts, trips to Europe, skiing in the winter, and many other sufferings. I wish I were cut off from the rest of the population."

July 27

F[innegans] W[ake]

. . . a happy and instructive lesson which ought to become part of the history of the work. For [Edmund] Wilson began quite reasonably —like many another admirer of U[lysses]—with the feeling that the enormous power to record experience which *U* demonstrated was being, although not unused, not sufficiently used: his general point until 1944 was that Joyce had given himself to an overelaboration which was the self-indulgence of his lyrical gifts for language itself, all to the unnecessary perplexity of and obfuscation of the most laborious reader. His most recent comment in the revised essay in *Classics and Commercials* on *FW* is a beautiful and generous and exact statement: "The demands that Joyce makes upon the reader are considerable, but the rewards are astounding!"

July 30

> We are the lyres of the gods
> & we are the drums
> > & the gongs
> > & the fifes
> Of Apollo & of Dionysus
> > &&
> We are the inventions of
> > dream
> > & hope
> > & desire

August 7

After breakfast each morning Bertram installed himself, with the deliberateness of a large animal, in a chair near the cabin [. . .], which had once been a pighouse, and tried with the patience which seemed to him like erosion to write. Here he remained all day, rising only when the mail arrived or when he went to get the sandwich his wife had made for him and left upon the kitchen table in the house. Nearby was the old barn which had [begun] to fall from the top and the sides over the abandoned 1933 Ford and the even more abandoned paintings of his father-in-law's early period, the period which had [made] him for a time famous and now made him furious, since they were not only praised, but praised in a way which seemed to the artist an insufferable condemnation of his mature canvases.

This subject was the staple of the breakfast conversation between Bertram and his father-in-law. Bertram sympathized with John Murray's attitude to an insensitive world. But he knew very little about the art of painting—knew so little that he liked both periods of the painter's work, and knew enough to conceal the fact from his father-in-law—and knew at least enough to suppose that to like both styles was probably foolish, whether John Murray or present-day fashions were correct.

October 3

These Runners
Each one must run to be first
Anyone who looks back
Freezes to the staring ghost
Of the triumph he might have
                              won
As, minute by minute, all over
More and more races begin:
Jack & Jill on the judges' stand
Diddle the dominoes & paper dolls

October 11

Nevertheless! you were right and when wrong
You were right, too—until you do not see
The heartbreak risk & cost of liberty
How the infinite of hope
            Hope's whole brings with it hope's
                              infinite tragedy!
Sometimes a sense and a suspicion rose in you
Sometimes you were disgusted or dismayed
Sometimes you sang you "would
            like to live with the animals
They are so placid & self-contained."

But you did not go to live with the horses
Nor did Thoreau live at Lake Walden more
                              than a year
And Swift who felt all life
            with the worst intensity
What you feared at times
Found himself forced to live & to love
            a few human beings—

Yahoos!
Give me Libby or give me death.

October 22

She was a Pullman, she was a Club Car.
Poor Arbuckle, who made us chuckle.

            A winner in vineyards
                  Grasping the grapes
            With the ease of leaves
                  Assimilating sunlight

Be careful
    Drive slowly
        The wife you save
            May be your own

The polite audience
More concerned with an act of spiritual mercy
    Than with having a good time
Is an exclusively twentieth-century phenomenon

October 28

For Blake has done the self-same thing
    That all the ancients did
Has shown that every living thing
    Is miracle & prodigy
        Improbable or impossible

October 29

He could not tell the difference
    Between a nude girl
        a white egg
           a bowl of fruit
Say it so—and you do not know
    The power and the glory of his story
As:
He could not tell the difference
    Between a white egg and a nude girl
        And an apple
        Red upon the worn brown table
Or better & still more & more exact
    Each was to him an object
        Natural & valuable & beautiful
"Giving rise to endless reflections"
        (Shadows & shades of light
          degrees, intensities
          of brightness
    Snow & glare & cream & soft
        & hard & ice)

The modern painter as a Monarch of Joy. After looking for the second day at Jarrell's "At the End of the Rainbow."

Truly many in America disregard poetry
Although it is one of the mind's great powers
Although it is used frequently and joyously,
　　　　Freshly and spontaneously.
Would poetry be studied, desired, and loved
Like cars, planes, games, and campaigns
　　　　Flowers and medals
　　　　Publicity and loving cups
Desired like money, sought like success,
　　Hunted like love
Studied, loved, desired, cared for
　　　　Attended and truly admired
(Not honored and disregarded like Latin and humility)
If it were well known that poetry shines and is beautiful
As a new Buick, a lake, and a chorus girl?

[The following poems contain some of the same or variant lines finally used in "The Kingdom of Poetry," in Selected Poems.*]*

　　Poetry is certainly
More interesting, more valuable
　　And certainly more charming
Than everything contained in the zoos, parks, or poppy
　　　　　palaces in Hollywood
It is far more interesting as it is far more
　　　　Coherent & organized
Than the Atlantic Ocean, Niagara Falls,
And other overwhelming phenomena.
It is as useful as light & as beautiful
It discovers and renews the original freshness of reality
Again and again and forever, like the sun and the morning
It is necessary, it is preposterous, it is unpredictable
Precisely, for it is as implausible and true
　　　　As the kangaroo.
It naturally imitates, illuminates, celebrates, and improves
　　　Upon the raw glory
Of reality's festival & circus.
For as it [is] fecund & beautiful, it is very powerful
For only the faithful, straining
To be adequate to the edge and extreme of dream
　　　Can lift, carry, or move mountains
Succeeding only as wrestlers, in an overwhelming labor
　　　　Triumphant but exhausted.

It is true that poetry begins in the chaos of pandemonium
[. . .]
Since poetry like nature succeeds through profusion
[. . .]
[. . .] and poetry must be ubiquitous
If it is to be gay, exact, and serious
As it is when it says: a sunset resembles a bull fight,
   The dew upon the grass resembles cuff links,
These are acts of invention & love,
    Uniting experience & heightening consciousness.
Hence poetry makes the past rise from the
   Sepulcher, like Lazarus
It makes a lion into a sphinx and a girl,
As it gives to a girl the splendor of Latin
For poetry invented the unicorn, the centaur, the
    Phoenix, the sonnet, and the limerick
As the sonnet augmented the nature of praise
So the limerick discovered new structures &
    Somersaults of laughter.

Hence it is true that poetry is an
    Everlasting ark
An omnibus of all the mind's animals.
It is the supreme sunlight of consciousness
Making love eloquent, giving tongue to forgiveness.
Hence a short [history] of poetry would be a
    Short history of love
(It would also be a text, a testament, and an epitome of joy)
For love requires the diminutives & the pet names
Which only poetry provides with fullness, with richness
   Spontaneous & original
    Adequate to the advent
     Of the event of uniqueness
And joy requires the soaring choirs of poetry
    Rising as the flames of
     The bonfires of jubilee & hallelujah!
For poetry is like light, and it is light
It shines over all like the blue sky, with the
    Same blue justice.
Since it is the sunlight of consciousness
It is also the soil of the fruits of knowledge
    In the orchards of being.
It is also the fire which burns the black coals
    Of desire
Poetry is quick as tigers, clever as cats, vivid as oranges

Nevertheless it is deathless: after the Pharaohs & Caesars
                         Have fallen
It shines and endures more than diamonds
The praise of poetry is like the
                         Clarity of mountains
The heights of poetry are like the
                         Exaltation of mountains
It is the consummation of the stars
                         Of consciousness in the
                                   Country of the morning

November 12

This is the time to praise poetry clearly
                         and loudly
For now poets are regarded as having
                              the limited significance
Of flagpole sitters, deep-sea divers, or marathon
                                   dancers
They receive the same care as xylophones &
                                   equestrian statues
& now they are honored and ignored like
                         famous dead Presidents
Supported like holidays & given less attention
Than a circus, a musical comedy, or a catastrophe.
Hence it is proper to declare the power & the
                              glory of poetry
         It shows us the pleasures of the city
         It lights the structures of reality
         It is a cause of knowledge & laughter
         It sharpens the whistles of the witty
         It is like morning (the flutes of morning)
                  It is the first morning forever
This truth must be proved anew unendingly
                         like the truth of love
I will write a poem about the kings of emotion
     The monarchs of the heart & of English
The lords of the joy after the suffering
                  without hope
The children of the new birth after the
                  death of the heart
The type of Orpheus & Lazarus, and of Jacob victorious,
         and Joseph triumphant.

Hence it will be a joyous, jubilant, mercurial poem
It will be full of triumphant repetition
It will be full of stories of light and
                              international romances
[. . .]
It will assert that America is the
                              new world & new Eden
The promise of the freedom to begin again
                    forever at the frontier of hope
It will seek the festival of exaltation
          After the tree of the knowledge
                    of good & evil
Has been struck by the ego's lightning
It will declare that that tree grows
          And is green again in the May of
                    forgiveness & hope
Because America is adventure, as it was
                    in the beginning
Because freedom is existence & persists only
                    as the freedom of hope
& of beginning again after the blessing of forgiveness

The Polo Grounds. The Golem will be photographed with an A-bomb. Astronomers, physicists—atomic ping-pong.

November 13

Bing-bong, Moscowitz, junk man.

> This is poetry as America:
> Moscowitz many times a millionaire
> Fifty years after arriving at Ellis Island
> Goes down to look over
> The used ships discarded by the merchant marine
> And finds the ship which fifty years before
> Carried him to America in steerage
> And buys the boat and brings the captain's bell
> Home to his dining room—and there
>   He rings it!
> [. . .]

November 14

Plays. A Confidential Report (colored baby). Rational Love (wife-swapping). Fathers & Sons (dramatized). A Historical Play (using Plutarch or Suetonius). Alcestis (version—as Cocteau's *Orpheus*).

Malraux. The modern man goes to the museum as once to a church.

> So—these are the tidings of joy overwhelming
> that I bring to you
> That after twenty-five years of dismay and suffering
> After twenty-five years of seeking for what I did not know
> But knew it existed and I had need of it
> Despite periods of rapture
> Despite days of self-domination
> (good works & the applause of others)
> I have come at last [. . .]
> To the knowledge with all my heart
> That to write poetry—is enough
> To be creative is enough—and more than enough
> To be the poem when writing or to be the
> poem of another, reading—
> is enough—is supreme plenitude
> & the waking clarity of spring plenty
> & the horn of the richness of autumn
> & the jewel & light of the whiteness of winter
> & the green glow & glory of the successes of summer

(It is enough—like dancing / It is more than enough—like the sunlight (glanced at, looked at directly) / For as those who are in love write poetry / Those who write poetry are in love—love more than & including—romantic love.)

November 25

Richmond Rinehart (pictures, look up, describe).
Twins in the Womb (in a Joycean *FW* idiom).

> Her voice sounded like a mountain brook
> Like a music box & a distant bell

A girl's best hope is her chest.
The Marauder (back to Oranges [Delmore's Cambridge cat]).

> Oh, the lemon sun of early December
> The light day—clear—sharp—pale

"We'll be God's spies."
Analyze: since Nov. 1953 manual sedation of copying (when eye will not stay fixed on page).

> Did Paris say to Venus (as the other girls listened)
> May I say that you are slightly terrific?

KJ: the real theme, as arms & the man, as that world traveler going home, as the m[an] who ventured down to hell: Is temper! Temper! *Temper fugit!* (And thank God it does.) (The rust is silent.) (The rest are silent, silenced.)

"All absolute sensation is religious"—Novalis.

Cat, not purring, but prprpr-ing.

In-spur-ation
A lust or greed
    for inspiration, ecstasy
A ruinous riotous gluttony
Sparking most ordinary joys
       —And in the end
        So great the
             cost
A sin against the
        Holy Ghost!
(Asking for
     fire or for
       death
The blaze or the
      cessation
         of breath)

Sensational as sunset or as deep & dumb as sleep.
Comic history of World / U.S.A.?

In the prisons of love
He served (serfed) his time

The Marauder—to add to other cat stories.
Ballerina, delicate as frost work.
Now—at 1:10 p.m. I am happy—serene—happy & active, working happy (tho' perhaps intoxicated)—copying *FW* & letting it suggest the beauty & the future of language & of poetry to me—& after five pp. rewritten unexpectedly yesterday (Jackson—Spengler confuted).

November 26
Versification—keep in mind, reread—versification of T.S.E.'s prose by Henry Reed.
Poems on poems, old Amer. ballads (Melville) (Flying Trapeze: O Nirvana / Won't you wait for me?).
Today. Make schedule while copying *FW*.
Go over, reading & aloud & then typing, Spengler, A Second

Morning + New Passage or Lyrics Rewritten. Should choose passage the night before. More about Jackson, Richmond Rinehart.

Last night Dexedrine—exalted—I thought of a long narrative poem or series of narratives.

Teeth & Hungarian. Use yesterday's letter?

Attitudes: cow, steak, corpse, sirloin, filet mignon.

Undated

Gentlemen prefer bonds—I need hardly say again (but I will say it again!) what has been so often said: "Money talks." You will understand, then, my conviction—nay, certitude, that my name—Cash Howells—possesses & resounds with the brutality of truth.

At midnight, in midwinter of my thirtieth year, I heard the ghost of Horace Greeley: "Go rest, young man, go rest," as Lucrezia Borgia laughingly asserted to A. J. Volstead: "Let him who is without sin go out & get stoned!" while Salome sauntered & insisted on her point of . . . : head or tail?!

November 27

The farce of the face.

> O Nirvana
> Won't you wait for me?
> I'm riding Pollyanna
> I'm eating a banana
> With gourmet luxury
> And gourmand ecstasy

Ghetto, mulatto.

November 29

[A quite different version of the following poem, "The Foggy, Foggy Blue," is in Selected Poems.*]*

A Ditty of Diogenes

When I was a young man
I talked to myself
And I called a spade a spade
And the only thing that made me sing
Was lifting the masks at the masquerade
I took them from my own face
I took them from others, too
And the one romance in my song & dance
Was the view that I knew
What was true!

But tonight I'm going to the ball once more
>> To try a different cue
It occurred to me like a discovery!
That the masks are more true than the faces
And all the falsehoods are true!
The only only thing is to believe—in everything!

"Days of dry coldness / Nights of wet wind whistling."
He was "aslimed of himself."
A very farce of a face.
You son of a psychiatrist.
"The use of the body is the mind."
"Certain hopes I would not have surrendered for fortune, power, or years of pleasure"—Socrates.

>> It requires little perception
>> To recognize that frivolity,
>> Knavery, debauchery
>> Indifference or—idleness
>> Do not make for well-being

December 1

Distinguish between rape & assassination—elation & deviation— seduction & arson.
>> G. Stein: What is the answer?
>> Profound: What is the question?

>> The modern man I sing
>> The modern in America
>> Immense in passion sets new records
>>> now
>> For drunkenness, divorce, suicide, and insanity!

Undated

Primal joy: Oh, I see what it was I sought to escape.

>> Said I to myself
>>> The cold dirge of the baffled
>>> Sullen hymns of defeat

Piercing & pealing. Flush'd & reckless. Motley, particolored.
The sperm whale sports with his flukes. The leaden-eyed shark.
"A vast similitude / Interlocks—all."

Behold Carol Foster cavorts with a camel
        in the London Zoo
Kissing his nose, dressed in a tight bathing suit
Leaning & looking like a pretty piece of fruit
A peeled banana ripe pear & double cantaloupe

Behold the footlights—whence my name first came
        Barrymore Delmore

Miss Buttons does a striptease. [Buttons was a Schwartz cat.]

December 9

The dice of God are always loaded
[. . .]
What a remark—it must have been
        Bismarck!
[. . .]
& *U*—Was this the book which launched
        A thousand censorships?

When Emily—at last met Thomas Higginson
When she had seemed (& knew she had) peculiar
        Fey, too strange
When she perceived that this powerful critic
        & editor
Was hardly wholly entranced—enchanted
        by her
Then she wrote to him:
    "Birnam Wood has come to Dunsinane—"
Which puzzled him, perplexed the
        Critics after him—
Clearly it is no mystery—that Emily
Should think ambition quite in point . . . Macbeth
        & Lady Macbeth
And feel ambition as a guilt . . . writing the news
        & views she wrote!

What did angelic Rilke say at last—
        Who speaks of victory—to endure is all?
          (Hölderlin)

December 20

The monks said
    Of the frescoes
        On their walls
They are the realities
    —We are the shadows

December 24

KJ Lyric or Chorale
Interlude—for Mask & Voice

To the minstrels blackface frozenface
    Buck & wing, jigging & japing
Pray you, gentry men, be sated: I'll give
        your ears
Arrest: a mossy silence, pretty please, my
          peers
My peering gaping peeping Toms of peers
You too, and mirror mirabelles prancing the lances
Of sheathed legs & melons of bosoms, looping
          the cantaloupes
Of romping rumps
    Rumping nether lands in the newest
      Salacious saraband sequel of
        The can-can

Is there a Tenderfoot—a maidenhead—a virgin unbiased mind among us? Are you of a kid-glove kidney?

Forgive yourself first!
    if others you would forgive
        & be forgiven
Love yourself—if
    you would love any or
        all—
      or some

Diogenes was [in] his tub because
    Like all the cynics he—hated himself and hated
      His body & thought it dirty
[. . .]
Innately, essentially filthy—dirty as his
        mind's light
Glowing at best in lurid intervals like his
        lantern

Narcissus equally stared long & long
Looking upon the looking glass
    of the river's laving [?]
And looking—looking not in love but in hope
Some breeze upon the flow might show—in a new light
   [. . .] a version of his face
   Not suggesting Nausea
     And plunged—

Shampoo ye well & comb & brush, my peers and pretty dears. Self-love begins.

               December 30

Voices & Faces. Persons & Masks.

Running down. Bleeding—infected at both sides. Infected tooth since Tues. week.

Jane, cut it out—I don't know what's gotten into you tonight. Jane & Leslie—so funny—universal—Saul—all points of view.

Saturnalian—Xmas—end of year—winter solstice.

Studies of Joy, The Study of Joy, Judges of (I'll jump for joy!).

Private & secular devotions.

New Year's Birthday, Rites of Autumn, Rights of Spring.

    "To peek aboo
    Durk the
     Thicket
    Of slumbwhere"
      (*FW*, p. 580)

                Undated

List of Dead and how—where—when. Elegy. Lament.

John Walcott, killed by a car: in Italy in World War II: in the pride & prime of his manhood.

Celia Buckman, 1943, of cancer—in a New Jersey sanitarium—middle-aged, hopeless.

John Wheelwright, 1940—struck by a car as he walked across Commonwealth Ave., drunken after midnight—against the light, ignoring the red light (the last time—one time too many—of the thousands of times he had crossed that street).

Adam Moncure, 1951—in Kansas, driving, a collision at the crossroads. Dead in young manhood—hurrying home to his pregnant wife, Barbara, and his children, Peter and Stephen.

1951. F. O. Matthiessen—death by suicide—on the first of April—jumping from a window on the thirteenth floor of Hotel Statler.

Anne Nathanson—in her eighty-eighth year—in a home for the aged—lost, hopeless, unable to remember where she was, what had happened.

Theodore Spencer—failure of heart—in a taxi—going to a cocktail party.

Dylan Thomas—brain insulted, after a stroke—at the Hotel Chelsea and St. Vincent's Hospital—far from the Wales whence his voice first sang—and too much drinking.

Jean Rogers—in France: of a cerebral hemorrhage.

Victoria Schrager—at Northhampton, Smith College, in a tub, bathing—of a cerebral hemorrhage—age twenty-four.

❀

Find minute particulars, atoms of observation (through pocket books' Time & Place).

Musicalized as in *FW*'s modes, Plump Grass Eulogy, The Structures of Reality, The Ballrooms of Joy.

What are the structures of Reality: Knowledge & Sleep, Dream and Becoming.

Phenomenological Analysis of: Fiction, Poems, Plays, and other Artworks. Irreversible track of Arthood, of Selfhood. Lists & Catalogues fugalized as by: sensational juxtaposition, etc.

❀

The nun waited—looked up—at her black suitcase.

Rinehart reached up and lifted her black suitcase down.

"I was saying a prayer for that," said the nun. She smiled and looked younger.

Rinehart tipped the brim of his self-conforming hat. He forced the shadow of a smile, unable to answer in kind.

And in a moment the undertow of her utterance sucked the seas of consciousness.

(Rinehart was en route to the Plaza—T. Capote—Hotel Pierre. It was 12:10, a Tuesday in the third week of April—a dim damp sticky morning.)

❀

Kilroy

Are you insane?
Probably no more than most humans
I had periodical nervous
Breakdowns between my thirtieth & thirty-seventh year

Where were you—in June 1928
I had been drafted into
      The army & navy
         of Hope

Are you a buffoon?
I am a disciple of
Various comic masters
The most recent among them
Is Ringhold Lardner, Jr.

*

A native gift is certainly necessary. But the writing of poetry is also an art, a collection of skills which can be acquired with greater mastery and rapidity when they are cultivated as a matter of conscious practice. Some good poets in the past have acquired these skills partly by reading a great deal of poetry, by a kind of saturation of the mind. But it is significant that most great poets have written a great deal of bad poetry: the writing of bad poetry was a necessary stage, very often, to the writing of good poetry.

This should make clear the value of cultivating poetry as a collection of conscious skills. The writing of bad poems has been a way of consciously practicing the art of poetry.

First and perhaps most important of all is practice in the various forms of versification.

*

1931 House Players

As they stood, waiting, and the elevator lifted them to the sixth floor of the apartment house, Gerald saw how tense Jerome was.

"Relax," he said, poking Jerome lightly in the belly (but it hurt, he was so tense & tight). "And don't [let] them hurry you: don't forget we're putting [out] good money."

Jerome forced a grin which was almost a frown: forcing, he felt his cheeks as if they were fat, and wondered that Gerald was so casual. You would think, if you did not know, that he was about to have an ice-cream soda or play ping-pong.

Ping-pong! The doorbell of the girls' apartment sounded . . .

"Greetings, Sherry," said Gerald gaily, and like a real man of the world, and brushed Sherry's cheeks in a light deft kiss and slapped her buttocks lightly. They might have been close friends, younger brother & older sister . . . "Meet my chum Jerome," said Gerald with casual largesse. "Looks shy, but you know, Sherry, those shy boys"—he winked & leered—"dynamite."

"Hello, Jerome," said Sherry. "Not a big bull like you with hands like two octopuses."

Octopi? thought Jerome: as they moved forward to the pleasant living room where the other girl was seated upon a long luxurious sofa playing solitaire—the cards upon a coffee table. Before looking up she moved a card tentatively, drew it back, then decided and placed it. She was also dressed lightly in what seemed a housedress—for it was midsummer & very hot & she was pretty but quite plump: she looked like a well-heeled satisfied *Hausfrau*, not like a—he tried to avoid the unfavorable words even in thought—like a courtesan: he was pleased when he settled for the most glamorous synonym. It was as if he were reading a romantic novel.

Gerald had bent over to whisper something in Gladys's ear.

"Oh, go on: you're getting to be a real fruit [?], Gerald." She pushed [him]. "Stop tickling my ears." She winked at Jerome, who blushed & paled.

"You loved it last time when I tickled your ears."

"That boy will have us hanging from chandeliers just to be sure that he's not missing out on something."

"I'm just an all-around all-American boy," Gerald simpered, sitting down on the chaise longue & lighting up. "Anyone want some of my nicotine?"

"What's your name & sit here," said Gladys. She brushed the cards together & shuffled them.

"How were you making out?" asked Jerome, unable to think of anything else. "It was solitaire you were playing, wasn't it?"

"Yep, solitaire. I was cheating myself," said Gladys. "I was doing so badly. God, it's hot." She raised herself & pulled at her gingham dress.

"Lucky in cards—lucky in love," said Jerome, surprised & pleased with himself. He had spoken a little self-consciously but at least like a man of the world, however unexpected to himself & the others.

"We shall see," grunted Gladys & rose. "Sherry, I guess this beau of mine wants to start playing house right now." She took him by the hand: it made Jerome think of the seashore last summer when Sybil Older—so beautiful, sexy, the post-debutante—had taken his hand as they went to swim out to the float.

❋

> In Princeton, New Jersey
>   The astronomers and the physicists
> Are playing atomic tennis
>   And H-bomb ping-pong
>
> And in the vast offices of the directorate
>   of heaven
> The recording angel has recently acquired
> An electrical typewriter—has recently invented
> A new kind of shorthand which resembles
>   Seismography—auscultation
> And registers motives, earthquakes, infatuations,
>   And the lyrics of idle glances
>   In the forest of morning.

Baudelaire has conferred with Whitman on *Leaves of Evil,*
   Flowers of Grass . . .
Baudelaire and Pindar have decided to write choral odes
  In praise of the testicles of Pegasus
Poe has suggested to Shakespeare a new nuance in
   Ophelia's pallor
[. . .]
Samson and Keats discuss Fanny Brawne & Delilah
   (golddiggers & bobby-soxers)
Marlowe talks shop with Rimbaud, Galileo
  Chats on the telephone with Alexander Graham Bell
It is a party line—Herodotus, Pepys, and Proust
    eavesdrop
St. Augustine converses with Longinus
   On the teaching of composition
St. Francis, Aesop, and La Fontaine talk about animals

     ❀

   Pedagogical Sketch—Freud
   Unless ye become all
   As little children
   What was unconscious
    Shall be conscious
     Id-ridden
    Shall be
    Ego-mastered
   It is reclamation work
   Like the draining of the
     Zuyder

Four of Aristotle letters extant: Did anyone save the stamps?
"Our sponsor presents: the mills of the millennium."

     ❀

   Poem?
  I am *Sturm.* I am *Drang*
  I am *aus Rom*
  Je suis
   Aussi fin de siècle
  I am Renaissance—Greek Revival
  A Primitive—a Decadent Survival

     ❀

Dante, the Florentine politico / Was only a disc jockey on the
period's radio.

    .   .   .

Here is a slice of reality. Shot [of] honeymooners [at] Niagara Falls:

> I wonder where all that water
> > comes from?
> I am unimpressed
> Experience, as such, is clearly
> > formless
> Experience is a distraction
> Maybe this is what was missing
> > every time

Shame! Shame! Hear! Hear! Can't they speak English? He thinks he's Dante. No wonder they kicked him out.

A. Lincoln, Oscar Wilde, Atlantis, Henry James, Thomas Manville, the Goddess of the Falls.

✱

Poor Paraphrase of H. Allen Smith
A Brief Message to One & All

Here is a message composed by a man named Smith:
"Life in the United States of America
　Should never be dull
　　And yet
I have the sensation sometimes
That I am living
　　In a vast industrial establishment
Devoted to the manufacture
　　Of putty knives

"Although I live all summer
　Throbbing with amusement
　& gaiety: the hurrahs of holiday: the shine of
Delight & the foam of
　　　The screeching of girls
　　　On the roller coaster or
　　　The hush of girls in the
　　　Tunnel of Love
Yet I feel at times that [. . .]"

(Know everything but what is important; all information but the truth. Boarded up. Filing—accountant of sales taxes.)

✱

Jerome Weidman: hero, I can get [it] for you wholesale.

Lady Chatterley as heroine, Kate Croy, Millie Theale, Daisy Miller, Isabel Archer, Jennie Gerhardt, Mary Pickford—the Americans' sweetheart, Iris March (suicide) (back street).

The heroine discards her widow's weeds when the campfires are ashes: and when her faithful servant reproaches her—It is too soon, she says, after husband's death, Kathie replies: "It is never too soon to live —or too late"—only an addled egghead would feel that there is some connection between this utterance & the moment in Henry James's *The Ambassadors* where the hero says: "Love, live" (quote). But there is a connection, however distant, just as there is a connection between Henry James, Daisy Miller, Jesse James, and Henry Miller: they are all Americans in far more than a nominal or legal sense—or thus it seems under the hypnotic spell of the films.

✿

KJ

Rameau, morose, sits with Bayard (Broyard) who is high
          And who is cool—
    To be in fashion at all times
    Is a mode of his being
And Jacob Jameson Jackson (despondent)
Upon a bench in Washington Square Park
Late August—long dusk, it is almost dark—
As they wait
They are silent, these cats are sick of
          digging each other
When a drunkard appears swaying and correcting
          himself
Accosts Rameau
      (who looks like a jockey
        who has prune eyes
        who made a circumdecision
       in Iowa City)
     And accuses him of being under the delusion
That he is Johnny Weissmuller the Olympic athlete
Oh, remarkable undaunted ever-responding Rameau
Springs up from the pit of his sadness, from the bench
         and from the walk
Climbs the tree within the railing and calls down to
        the other cats
Tarzan's ape inchoate gurgle and howl

✿

KJ

Readers: historians of the heart & of
   the mind in unknown generations
Come let me tell you what there
   is in me for you
I was one who wished to be a poet
   And thought that once he was a poet
Everyone would love him, want to be
   him and be his friend
I had been a child who supposed
   That all adults (save in his own family)
Loved literature, the history of thought,
   The analysis of experience,
   The excitement of intellectual
     conversation
Clearly I had an inevitable
   Appointment with disappointment
[...]

    ❖

The ringing of bells,
   The surging and swelling of bells
    Supra Urbem: above the whole city
     Swaying
   A hundred voices:
     A Babylonian confusion
    Blaring, booming
Clanging clappers: excited and dinning
   Echo resounds: *in te domini speravi*
Covered by echo: *Beati tecta* [?] *sunt*
     peccavi

    ❖

He felt the wood-secrecy
   He knew the June softness
    The crackling warmth as it surrounded him
He glimpsed the shadowy light on last year's dried
     brittle leaves
   His groin was fever-moist

    ❖

Moby Dick, Mount Everest! "The Figure in the Carpet"! Gold mines—gold rushes. Captain Ahab–Captain Ahab. Jenny Lind—Lindbergh.

The Fig on the summer boardwalk hardly hidden by a bathing suit (bikini).

The virginity of Mother's Day!
Poked at Pocahontas, named Miss America in Atlantic City.

Screw, gash, violence of sexual or related words. W. C. Fields—
depth bombs women.

See now—Pocahontas is named Miss America in Atlantic City. She
says to turning cameras, to the mike, to the press, to—Americans:
"Come up and see me some time, unless you guys are cigar-store
Indians."

✿

That's no Gentile, that's Delmore.

✿

She loved him so much
She would have given him
The shirt off her back
Her right arm

(My wife does not understand herself!)

1955

Poem based on the way a visual image—and sexual—is the beginning of physiological changes (in loins & palms) (Rilke—Apollo).

Moon—almond—whiteness.

Dusk—stilly lucidity—milky serenity / lucid stillness—and motionless light.

Sonnet

The country winter dusk wholly possessed
By milky serenity, still lucidity
As if a tableau frozen for eternity
Or posed by Poussin—perfected in arrest
Only—along the horizon in the west
A ridge of salmon pinkness faintly glows

(It is not true—nothing at all is still.)

. . . In [Dostoevsky's] later work there is a clear and consistent line of ideas (as is not true of Dostoevsky's early work before his exile and imprisonment in Siberia), a line which leads straight from *Notes from Underground* (1864) to the great masterpieces which he wrote in middle age at the height of his powers, *Crime and Punishment, The Idiot, The Possessed,* and finally, in 1879, *The Brothers Karamazov.* He had had the themes of this last great work consciously in mind during all those fifteen years, as his letters show. And in a certain important sense, he had had them in mind, unconsciously or half-consciously, most of his life. For Dostoevsky's father, an army doctor, was a cruel drunkard who mistreated his serfs for so long a time and so violently that finally he was murdered by some of them.

[. . .]

The father Karamazov and his murder as the central incident in the novel is clearly connected with the diagnosis by pathologists and psychiatrists of epilepsy as a form of "father-murder," to use the customary technical phrase. There can be no question that patricide was one of Dostoevsky's obsessions—perhaps his greatest obsession—to judge by the recurrence of the act of murdering of a worthless evil human being by one who is clearly superior which takes place in *Crime and Punishment*, disguised to the extent that the victim is an old woman, not a man and not a parent, and also, with similar disguise and variations, in *The Idiot* and *The Possessed*. And we can hardly help but think significant the fact that it was only in his last work, at the end of his life, that the great novelist was able to give himself to a direct confrontation of the theme of patricide. Indeed, the fact that this theme is so clearly linked to the dread disease which caused Dostoevsky so much pain testifies to the overwhelming honesty and courage we could expect of a great novelist, but it is not an expectation invariably fulfilled.

[. . .]

Dostoevsky's reversal of attitude . . . culminated in a passionate though unconventional dedication to Czarism and Russian Orthodoxy, after the years of his youth in which, like most young men of his kind and generation, he had been a moderate liberal. The Czar was, it is clear, a father symbol—as he was, in fact, called in colloquial the little father of all Russians. Dostoevsky's extreme reversal of attitude, which was intensified by his years in Siberian prison and exile, and further heightened by the only reading he was permitted during the first four of those years, the Bible, has naturally been interpreted as reflecting an overwhelming sense of guilt—even though it may have been only a guilt of intention. He did not feel that the Czar's punishment—which was precisely like Dmitri's, too—was unjust, because he felt guilty of the desire to murder the father and all paternal authority. And in the depths of this guilt . . . as the discussion in *T[he] B[rothers] K[aramazov]* during the trial of Dmitri Karamazov clearly reveals, Dostoevsky found himself forced to believe that only Russian Christianity & Czarism could prevent human beings from being animals & even murderers. "If God does not exist," says Ivan Karamazov, "then all is permitted," which is to say, everything is lawful. This fear that atheism would lead to absolute immorality was Dostoevsky's starting point or primary basis of conclusions about morality & what a good and just social order ought to be . . .

Now the order of Dostoevsky's [works] is quite important in relation to my final point, the most arguable and extreme one, and one which has not been made before, to my knowledge—though *TBK* is one of the most studied & criticized of books the world over. This is all the more suspicious, since so many of those [who] have studied Dostoevsky have been theologically minded critics—in Russia, most of all—who would be naturally inclined to the view I am about to propose . . .

The underlying & astonishing & most important meaning of *TBK* is the discovery by the leading characters, who begin in atheism & agnosticism or unbelief, that whether or not God exists, God does exist. This is an attempt neither at paradox nor at wit. What I mean, and what Ivan & Dmitri in particular discover as the book moves forward, is that God exists in the sense that human relationships, social relationships, the legal code, the code of mankind have for so long been based upon the belief in God's existence that all human experience is bound (particularly any action which harms another human being) to cause emotional reverberations which can be understood only in these terms: whether or not God exists we feel & live as if he does, in fact, exist; the quality of human emotion, and the connections of human experience, exist within a structure [of] which God's existence is the primary basis. Hence Ivan feels & is able to argue that if God does not exist, everything is lawful—which is to say, there is no law, no wrong or right, and guilt is an irrational aberration. But when one does commit an [evil] action . . . however much provoked (or seemingly justified) by a wicked vicious human being, then one experiences an unbearable guilt. This occurs to Raskolnikov in *Crime & Punishment* just as it does to Ivan & Dmitri Karamazov—and that unbelievable guilt (which none of the three expected, none of them believing in God or in morality before that time) cannot be understood except as having this basis in God's existence . . .

For I must emphasize my point again. I do not say that the experience portrayed by Dostoevsky in *TBK* proves that God exists . . . What I have maintained is that the nature & quality of the experience to which guilt dooms the leading character is of such a kind that they feel *as if* God existed—or to repeat my first formulation, which may seem less paradoxical or contradictory: their inescapable experience is such that they discover how God exists, whether or not He exists. Hence it was possible for such [a] convinced atheist as . . . Gide to be overwhelmed by a novel devoted to the question of God's existence— to think it, in fact, the greatest of all novels.

February [?]

The views of how literature is related to life resemble theories about government in one important way. There is always a great deal of argument, yet no one fails to assume that one form of government is preferable to another—however often he changes his mind.

February 19

The relationship of literature to life troubled Plato and the critics of Euripides as profoundly as it disturbs those who suppose that comic books are one of the primary causes of juvenile delinquency. The power of literature to influence life has been the subject of such genuine and disastrous tributes as the burning of great libraries & of the books of great authors. Perhaps it is an exaggeration to say that the disputed interpretations of biblical texts have set religious wars in motion. But when the Puritans shut down the Jacobean theater, a blow from which playwriting in English has never entirely recovered, or when a great author like Racine stopped writing plays, partly because of the religious view that the stage was immoral, the power that the pen has was acknowledged by the sword.

Undated

Time pays alimony to
                    Eternity   (Maternity)

The hospitality
    of Eternity
        Is unimaginable
            immemorial
            & immutable

[Many film reviews by Delmore appeared in The New Republic *in 1955 and 1956. Animal Farm was reviewed January 17, 1955.]*

Orwell

It is troubling to have to say that the cartoon film of *Animal Farm* is at best a valuable experiment or beginning. For the intentions, the skills, and the hard work—to say almost nothing of the money which went into the making—are clearly of a superior kind. And the medium of the animated film is largely a terra incognita in which a great many wonderful possibilities remain to be discovered: possibilities which are moreover actual . . . The film version of *Animal Farm* actually suggests how much might be done with *Gulliver's Travels*, some of Kafka's best stories, certain of the most spectacular passages in *Finnegans Wake*— to say nothing apart from mentioning Aesop, Ovid's *Metamorphoses*, etc.

Considered in itself, apart from satirical parable, *Animal Farm* as a cartoon lacks the enchanting brio which Disney sustained most of all in his Silly Symphonies—before the overwhelming sentimentality, which coincided with success, gained the upper hand. Perhaps what is most wanting in the film is that stylization of structure, design, and action which appears to be rooted in the musical framework . . .

[A review of East of Eden *was published in* The New Republic, *April 25, 1955.]*

Anyone who goes to see *East of Eden* because he read the book would do better to read John Steinbeck's novel again, or better yet would be to read some other novel which is really a more genuine study of good & evil.

["Mary Pickford: The Little Girl in Curls," a review of Sunshine and Shadow *by Mary Pickford, appeared in* The New Republic, *June 6, 1955.* The Seven-Year Itch *(Marilyn Monroe) appeared August 8, 1955.]*

The relevance of Miss Pickford's conception of herself to Hollywood films today—and to what is a star system—a star imperialism need only be named: the star's conception of herself can become the most powerful influence of all in determining the quality of films. It intervenes in the writing & the choice of the scripts, the direction, the other parts, and the acting. As Miss Pickford came in the end to play America's sweetheart, so Greta Garbo came to play one part, in every film, of an imaginary being named Greta Garbo. And we may confidently expect Marilyn Monroe to play herself forever . . .

Of such is the Kingdom of Hollywood . . .

One perceives that this is [a] region beyond ordinary criticism: since the Little Tramp is as great [a] creation as Leopold Bloom, yet required the same process, which did not permit [Charlie Chaplin] to become Hitler in *The Great Dictator*. And through the years, as biography became a source of scripts, [the] actor Muni became Pasteur and Zola so powerfully that even for one who is literary to a fault Zola's name suggests Muni's face after fifteen years.

What seemed a theoretical limit occurred in *The Jolson Story*, where the real Jolson meets the screen Jolson, and Gloria Swanson played a fading star of the silent pictures. It's easy to say that a real actress by vocation surrenders personal identity for the satisfactions of imaginative projection. And it is commonly assumed that the vanity of the actor is the reason that this occurs. But really, it is the voice & the heart [of the] people which demand gods and goddesses—as every popular film magazine demonstrates.

(Hollywood / Cagney, Tracy / gods & goddesses / adventures / Cocteau, Hugo) . . .

The happiest years of [her] screen life Mary Pickford says in SS [*Sunshine and Shadow*], her autobiography, were those which she enjoyed with Adolph Zukor & Famous Players. She became one of Mr. Zukor's three children during those four and a half years and "to the end of our association he was a devoted and loving father" as watchfully concerned as Miss Pickford's beloved with everything in her private & public life. Once, when she traveled to Boston with Mr. Zukor, she wanted to go to the club car because Pearl White was there, an empress in a black velvet picture hat lifting a highball to her lips. "Mary, are you out of your mind?" Mr. Zukor said. "The answer is no, Mary honey. Now be a good good girl," and thereupon departed for the club car himself—to drink & to regard Pearl White "with unabashed rapture." It was during this time that Miss Pickford's attorney persuaded [her] never to lend her name to commercial uses, the advertisement of evening gowns, cosmetics, and perhaps less alluring products of business. A wise decision . . .

Miss Pickford's *Sunshine & Shadow* is not a triumph of self-knowledge, nor would anyone want it to be. Mary is concerned with those things which delighted her more than with any other aspect of her life . . .

Miss Pickford's last film was made in 1933. And her popularity began to decline eleven years before with the appearance of Clara Bow. The rapid and radical shift of the public from America's sweetheart to the IT girl left Miss P. bewildered; and it resulted in unfortunate attempts on her part to gain a new screen identity & to establish a direct connection with that ID which was the source of Miss Bow's IT. This crisis—like most of those which Miss P. reports in her [autobiography]—involved the nature & doom of Hollywood stardom: "If reincarnation should prove to be true," Miss P. says at one point, "and I had to come back to earth [in] one of my roles, I suppose some avenging fate would return [me] to earth as Pollyanna, 'the glad girl.'" Yet Miss P. does not really feel that fate is vengeful in casting her; whether as Pollyanna, the poor little rich girl, or Little Mary, she was & she remains America's sweetheart . . .

[John Wayne's] great predecessor [was] William S. Hart, the strong silent man of the silent screen who seldom spoke but when he opened his mouth uttered deathless sentences: "I got along fine with most Eastern boys but they did not understand our ways."

March 24

Claude [a fictionalized conversation between Delmore and Sylvester, Elizabeth's young brother].

Do you think that I have a kind face?

You look like that mangy old lion in the pictures.

What lion? what picture?

Oh, you know: that old lion that roars before the picture starts.

Oh, you mean the Metro-Goldwyn-Mayer lion. He's not mangy: he's as sleek as that comb [?].

Job / Just a few lions to show the strength of my affection.

Rejected.

May 16

Of this remarkable period in his life how little he understood. At least not yet. A great event, and slow and quiet [?], as many great changes are.

One evening he stopped drinking, after seven years almost. He played on the lawn with his new brother-in-law. And after dinner, he was not nervous, and at night he fell asleep sober.

Was it that he was newly married, or in the country, or both?

He was not very nervous after dinner, as he had so often been— nervous, anxious, shaking with anxiety, as so often before for years.

After a week he was very pleased with himself & after ten days he drank before dinner, but he was not nervous after. And he did not wake up, as so often before, in the middle of the night . . . [or] have to knock himself out again.

And yet during much of the time, he was depressed and sad about himself & sometimes angry or resentful of his wife. And sad about his life.

He had been warned several times. "You will kill yourself," said one friend.

"I never saw it do any author any good," said a second friend. "X paralyzes his mind every night."

"You have a good liver now," said a doctor, "but you won't keep on having one. Give it up. I've seen it ruin other men just as ambitious as you."

"You have got to stop drinking so much," said the last doctor.

I. C.-Bur. [Ivy Compton-Burnett]: Edmund still looks as if he were at a solemn musicale.

The years do not give back (return) what they have taken.

Torn things may mend
and more
& be whole
But the inner wound is open in the ultimate
reaches of the soul

June 5

Consider how short the duration
Of hope—how merciful—for
Disappointment is proportionate

June 20

*[Many poems, jokes, wisecracks of this period are grouped under
the general title* Kilroy's Carnival. *Orville—one of Delmore's
personae—a radio impresario, is at times the speaker.]*

SOS?, news analyst has predicted: Hallucination, a Nightmare,
will win the Kentucky Derby. A cold war all summer. Physicists &
astronomers will play atomic ping-pong.

June 25

—Sometimes I must admit he is inclined
To say things, in a way, a
Bit risqué: I hardly know what
To say about "A woman runs a
Terrible asterisk!"
—Yes and what about: "Hermes
Was admired for his cannon balls"
—And "Civilization has decreed that it is the destiny of
Cows to become shoes—pigs to
Become footballs, trees to be-
come paperback novels.

—One thing must be admitted—he's
Always interesting: but the same
Might be said of a crime wave
—He's probably a Jew—cerebral, deracinated
Unscrupulous—Don't misunderstand me—
Some of my best customers . . .

Negative comments on Orville:
Just a regression to Chautauqua.
Milton Berle is much better.
Send him back to Russia.
He is intelligent & sincere.
Just a tempest in a crackpot.
Those guys used to have to stand on soapboxes, answer hecklers,
kid the kibitzers: now no one can interrupt them.
Likes the sound of his own voice. Has fallen in love with it.
Dippy, or punch-drunk: belongs in the loony bin.
Illustrates the dangers of universal education.

Negative & Mixed Comments:
I sort of like the guy: but I don't know why.
Has a peculiar sense of humor.
One of those N.Y. big-city intellectuals.
One of those human beings who thinks too much.

Underlying all his pronouncements is the provincialism of the hill-billy & the hick: his popularity is probably backwoods, the last flare of populism.

Orville: Reality is stronger than any imagination. Nothing in reality is more likely than the implausible.

The Creation / K[ilroy's] C[arnival]
Orville's wise & foolish versions

The creation occurs again every morning and all day long. The world is a fire, a great big bonfire: it must be sustained by continuous fuel. So it is with all the species: begetting is a first priority.

Many were the comments, then as now: some angels snickered, others were suspicious, still others conservatives.

During the first day and in the fading faint light of the first evening, here are some of the cheers and sneers which the angels made carefully or carelessly, sincerely or in surprise:

A throne said: Wow!

Sambo exclaimed: Holy Smoke!

A Domination declared: This is pure virtuosity.

One angel remarked: It seems remarkable. And one angel added: What's the big idea? And one: Too early to tell. And one other: No comment!

And among the others, these were some of the expressions of impressions:

Well, blow my horn.

Personally I see no reason for this production.

This is the beginning of the end.

All aboard for Armageddon. Here we come: I[t']s going to be overcrowded.

Let us be fair—reserve judgment, wait and see.

Gratuitous: self-indulgent: Jehovah's Folly.

More trouble than it is worth . . . more impulse than good judgment.

What does he have in mind?—what next? what now? Now anything can happen and sooner or later everything will happen.

Mark my words, we will be accused of being responsible.

All aboard for Armageddon.

Undated

Disillusion defined as against
PAIN
The world can & will hurt you and take away . . .
Despair: There is nothing to win or lose: there is nothing—
(Impotent, potent, skills)

June 27

Definitions &&&
Erogenous zones, Atlantic, Luna Park.
The multitude of the stars is the measure of the Poems not yet written.

June 28

Orville: now our question & answer period: What is your opinion of nudism? Let the nude & the prude lie down together: This will be a sign of [the] kingdom of heaven & earth!

Where do you come from originally? Bohemia! I was born during a false dawn in the fourteenth year of the most terrifying & perilous of centuries, save the night of Calvary, the hour when the ark cast anchor & the moment when the gates of Eden shut on our first parents.

Orville / Birth / Twins.
Oedipus: winner of the first quiz program.
Narcissus: founder of photography & portrait painting.
Again (as twenty yrs. ago): to let doctrine & didactic mode weaken or drive out character, drama, and narrative. The framework and suspense of the contest is not used here.

How many languages do you speak? Only one: metaphor, but I have a smattering enough of others for practical purposes.

Why don't you get yourself a sleeping dictionary? Maybe you would be less nervous if you had someone to listen to your intimate disclosures. And also use big words with less frequency.

Thank you for the suggestion. I have reservations for an upper berth in the super-limited headed for eternity.

As to who wrote Shakespeare's plays, the answer is Albion—John Bull—Merry England.

June 29

The self
Patient at the Travel Bureau
Waits for a passage
To Euphoria
[. . .]

Narcissus
The words for what is in my heart
Do not exist

Whether death comes
         as a hyena
     or riding a bicyle
          hack or taxi . . .
[. . .]

Little Satire
All these loitering people
Are merely prudent
They ask for a guidebook
    To the absolute
They desire a visa to the Delphic
        And inquire if the Noumenon
States have a legation. If!
The U.S.A. has established a legation
If! As Kipling remarked: If you can find a consul
Standing upon that elevated exaltation
        At right angles to a cliff [?]
Drinking ginger beer, reciting Shakespeare
To music without self-consciousness
        Or fear
Then you are likely next to find
The celestial Baedeker you have in mind!
    —To Kismet
       Nirvana
       Maya

    Come & come forth & come up
        from the cup of
    Your silence, stunned & numb
    The statue you found and believed
    Thinking this is waking but deceived
       Come to the summer's sum
       Come and see on that height
       Seedtime, reaptime
       [. . .]
    How the ball of the body
       is only a drum

Summoning the soul
To rise from the catacomb
To the blaze and the death of
     summer
Rising in the forms of the
    flames of fires
     of candles, torches
       pyres

   Lyric
It is light!
 & faint
  & raining
In little chips of sounds
  chips and buttons
   splinters: light gravel
Not the pebbles, stones
    & nails
 of the pouring-down rain

  Little Lyric
If all who are arisen
To the height of the light
Had not once fallen
Or found beginning
  first and root
Where the fallen find the end
  of descent (a full
    night)
How can [sic] any ever have risen
   To height's
   might
   and
    light?

 (Pit to tree / tree & bird / Root to fruit / Root to flute / By word
of bird!)

              July 2
 Rameau found himself stiff with fury—seated, toe of his shoes
pointing up, wiggling the nervousness of his impatience.
 Yet Marcel, dapper, hepcat, and *flaneur*, equally a citizen of
Bohemia and fashionable society (with a capital $) was a mere fifteen
minutes late. And the reason had nothing to do with his attitude to
Rameau—nor, in all truth, with any of his characteristic attitudes to-
ward existence. He had been delayed at the charm school he attended

—this was his rubric for the Freudian doctor—because the maimed human being—a young lady in the hour prior to his own—had become hysterical, first giggling, then vomiting. The doctor's methodological apology at the delay had pleased Marcel so much—it was the doctor's first kind word in four months—that M. was in a particularly good humor. But [if] Joel was wrong, he was also right. For Marcel might have delayed his arrival for a dozen trivial reasons which would show that his attitude toward his friend was one of contempt as well as indifference.

Marcel was also pleased because he had no date with a young lady tonight: thinking of his pleasure, which surprised and perplexed him, he wondered if the possibility of a chance encounter lent the evening the bloom of novelty & the unpredictable.

Rameau. A Met[ropolitan] Gauntlet. Miss Farmington's School.

Fire Island—we went on a picnic but S. refused to bare her behind—which has an ineffable beauty—to my camera so that it might be made immortal, lifted above the cruelty & destruction of time.

Bohemia resembles the kingdom of heaven.

As children, playing doctor & nurse, or doctor & patient, etc.— approach & caricature the actuality of Love, a Hospital, a Medieval Theater.

Self-indulgence may not be true freedom—it may lead to the bondage of addicted & wasting practices, or worse. But it is not yet bondage and it is not a dungeon: the penitents are blessed by some self-energy.

Joel Rameau sat upon the park bench in the cool of the evening in Wash. Sq. It was the worst of August, the death of summer. The bench upon which he had seated himself was under a tall tree, near the drinking fountain and the chess players immobilized and fixed in an intensity of study, a tense concentration comparable to the painting called *The Card Players* by Paul Cézanne.

Rameau was intense & tense, too, as he awaited his intimate friend Marcel Binaud. The two were very close: yet although neither had ever fenced, their friendship might have been based upon being fencing partners! As friends: they were duelists . . .

Marcel was late: he was cavalier & insensitive once again—so indifferent to Rameau that Rameau, thinking of it, [became] more convinced of it . . .

Cast of Orville's Gag Time Band, traveling, touring play company.

Orville is most purely American phenomenon since Buffalo Bill, W. J. Bryan, Chautauqua.

Clubs: Bk. of Month, Canadian Club, Club Soda, Club Scouts.

A box of Chautauquas: better for your teeth than chocolates.

Pleasure is a soda: it fizzes and hisses, fades and fizzles out.

Chinese girl—her name is the epitome of her personality: Chow Ming!

Orville hires, later quarrels with, a pitchman, an ape Sultan, barker, Madison Ave. high pressure.

July 3

Rinehart &

For verily I say unto you
    Kilroy was here means this:
That every day is the 4th of July
That Christmas comes the whole year long
That Christ returns each morning
        (Dies each night!)
The kingdom of heaven
      pulses within us

This is positive affirmative optimistic. Thus spake Kilroy Rinehart.

Look: the tiger lily
    Has strange wings
The swift rises on black petals
    These true things
And infinitely more: more
Are only known to the kings / monarchs
    Of metaphor

M. Monroe to Marie Antoinette: Let them eat cheesecake.

July 6

Orville's *Kilroy's Carnival* is all a . . . fantasy or dream—showing he does not wholly believe his own visions of America's culture.

Use the Snake Pit. Humor, that is, has been "institutionalized." Butts—cigarettes. Jokes like the stems of cocktail glasses. Kinds of association.

July heat like tailor shop. Wrongness of jumbo Coca-C. bottles—king-size. Like beer in Lily Cups. Smoking in the dark.

She's fly fast.

July 11

Cinéaste, post-urbanist Narcissus.

Ferris wheel. Ding-dong, bell clapper, snare drum, bull drum.

Black Pool of Narcissus, Dens of identity. Jars, bottles, cells of the self. In the prison or penitentiary of identity.

How do you like that Mister (Miss) mystery?

Bubbles of words slip to the surface, "with tumblerous legs," Eiffel Tower, Empire State, Joss & Chaff. Icarus, Aetna, Cupid, Psyche, Oedipus.

Little Lyric, heather, ravine, ridge, Oh, the Leaves and the Lives, the Days of the Dark of the Green & the Praise.

Juvenile metaphysics of sauces, garnishes. Heart, harp, hope, might of night, majesty of light.

Velocipede, bicycle—bisexual, Cumberland Comes.

As I burst into flames. A latent heterosexual.

July 12

Times today: More parakeets than planes / Were discovered / Upon the / British aircraft carrier.

Movie of Total Recall / on: off / God-quest as my [?] life.

Ferris wheel: classroom, paid admissions, spectators of building construction: old women looking from apartment windows. Lumpen-Olympians!

Movement, motive, target, desire-desired.

Ahab, Huck Finn, Walden, Thoreau, Emerson, Whitman.

Henry VIII (lust) / N.Y.'s sale (swindle) / cherry tree / Columbus / Errors of Love (effort) (concentration, patience).

Poe, Dickinson, H. James, Howells / Cabot, Ponce de Leon, Balboa, Cortez, gold? / Washington, Lincoln, J. Adams, Jefferson, Burr, S. Q. Adams.

Wonder drugs, monkey glands / paid advice.

See Behold Virginie! East Indies Co.

Religion. Mayflower—settlement; Virginia—tobacco.

New Yorker: as otherness, as appearance, as judgment & conflict of two masters.

July 14

Morning
    is a lake
        —then the river of a capital
But evening
      & sunset
        an
           ocean
      over which the tides of
        light . . .
  [. . .]

July 17

... husband normal but undemanding instead of being exposed to a continual crisis of deprivation and extraordinary courtship, demand, awareness, and experience: nevertheless, surely the Aristotelian view [instructs] properly: her potentiality was prior to her marriage's weird & helpful tutelage: and in a trial marriage with the right consort it would have been realized perhaps less quickly & with less frantic energy: (she might have even been more interested in the ordinary forms of romantic induction) but surely the loss would have been regained many times after in serene and serenely periodical enactment which did not suffer the pressures of what was nothing less than starvation: To think that Holly's training was best was exactly comparable to supposing that a man who has almost starved to death can judge best of the sensation & the experience of eating a dry crust of bread.

He was relieved a little of the acuteness of desire as he followed this problem and river to the sea of his own answer: the affirmation of the normal pleased him, relieved him (to say it again: made him feel himself less drawn to the periphery of human nature where poor Holly lived), convinced him in itself, and by convincing him restored to him the faith in his own mind which had been disturbed—disturbed very much—in a way akin to David's ...

July 24

Here on this farm the secrets of summer & light all day ever changing & changing all else.

> This tower of a tree
> walking among
> trees who
> live in their own
> fixed astonishment
> of the Green
> Dream
> & the Green
> Glory

September 9

After two days in New York: lunch with [Pat] Covici [editor at the Viking Press] & [Malcolm] Cowley [noted critic and editor] (friendly for the first time since 1938!)—wanted to know about his piece on the first poems, first versions, in *Leaves of Grass*. "I think you do a wonderful job." Spoke of French—Smith—*Gone with the Wind*—Germany.

Troubled when I spoke of Jay (Wheelwright's friends putting up the kitty).

[Gilbert A.] Harrison divides up *NR* with [Michael] Straight! [Harrison was the publisher and Straight the editor of *The New Republic*.]

Could not stick to point—"Hello, Malcolm"—cocky & confident as hardly ever before, not in 1943 or '42—was it the martini which made me lose control?

Saul [Bellow] did not take [me] to Covici's when Sandra suggested it since I had had enough of him.

Reported: "C. thinks you're terrific, wonderful—wants you on his team but thinks you are overcommitted—told me to calm you down."

Told story of unwritten novel—accepted.

Nothing from *Times*—augurs what?

Probably would write me soon—Brown took two weeks to turn down Saul—new novelette—retreat to Illinois—flight from Anita—father's estate.

Discussion of Insanity after—

1. Warshow's death [Robert Warshow, 1917–1955, critic and editor of *Commentary*]—first electrocardiograph showed nothing—wife in asylum.

2. Sy Krim has "flipped"—Klonsky committed him—God—Waldorf-Astoria—furniture thrown from window—

Ellison's [Ralph Ellison, novelist] cagey politesse—Rome, Albert.

[Weldor] Kees—suicide? died same week as *TLS* favorable review.

L[ouis] Simpson—new wife—had had a breakdown—

Praise in *Playboy*.

Schwartz, Delmore—U.S. poet (1913-   )—in *EB*—&&&&& Bertholde Schwartz—very low when I spoke to her.

Dexedrine—pleased at 42nd [St.] Library.

Heine—felt I could write 15,000 [word] introduction there & then.

Riverside Drive & Panzer Bros. & the years & the hopes & all—

Laughter about—G.B.S. & mosquitoes—Kazin & Future.

Simpson fascinated by my explanation of artist & thematic opposite: change the world—deny the world—

Tried, unable to get underway.

Name recognized by salesman in store who had worked for Jay.

Did not go to N. Directions.

Two trips to N.Y.

Changed mind, feelings about Heine several times.

Diarrhea urine attack in bookstore—which passed over.

Calm of not smoking, in Reading Room 42nd St.—New York and memories of Breen at the turn in marble stair—simplicissimus—did nothing at.

Slept very little—calmed by party—did not drink too much (more getting back to [sleep]).

Next day's light—use as analogy for point of view, standpoint, point of vantage, perspective, purview.

Elliott Cohen [editor of *Commentary*] remorseful about Warshow: illness—

Pearl [Kazin]: "Delmore, just because you live in the country, don't think you're Gogol!" No one had read Alfred [Kazin]'s piece.

Memories of meetings with Saul: (1) hung over, Hudson St. (2) Gertrude Samuels? (3)—

September 10

Letters to Ransom, Jay, Hoffman, Evett, Harrison.

Dostoevsky—*K*[*enyon*] *R.—Hudson Review*—suicide, *The Listener*, London, *Playboy, Botteghe Oscure* story, *Poetry* N.Y., *Poetry* Chi.

Budget: Bank (1) $1,700; (2) $1,500. *Perspectives*, $1,000. *NR*, ND, $1,800, $1,800.

Editing: Viking (1) $1,000. (2) $500. Beacon, $500. Hemley, $1,000.

Anthologies: *Playboy* $50 (?), Williams $155, Kreymborg $20, Austin $20.

Times (1) $50; (2) (?) $250 *Kenyon* (1) $150. (2)? *Encounter* $100, *Times*, Washington, Chicago, (Beloit), YMHA.

Viking Portable of Un-anthologized Poetry of Wordsworth. Dostoevsky—*The Philosophical Novel*. Camus, Rahv, Hopkins, Hardy, Rimbaud.

+ Book of Essays: Hemingway, Faulkner (2 + 1), Dos Passos. Disputations, Gide, Grapes of Crisis, Trilling, Brockberger, Fitzgerald (expanded), Turgenev, Dostoevsky, Tolstoy—*War & Peace, Anna Karenina*—narrative method, type of the great author & human being.

T. S. Eliot, as critic, as poet (rewritten reviews), as International Hero, as editor, as moralist & as social . . . W. H. Auden (1) (2) (3). W. Stevens (rewritten), E. Pound (rewritten), A. Tate, R. Jeffers, Yeats (1) (2) (3). Y. Winters (1) (2). V. W. Brooks (1) (2).

Undated

Book of Essays: Popular Culture: *New Yorker*, Masterpieces as Cartoons, Marilyn Monroe, W. C. Fields, Mary Pickford.

Henry V 1, *Animal Farm* 2, *Country Girl* 3, *Bridges at Toko-Ri* 4, *Underwater/Blackboard Jungle* 5, *East of Eden* 6, *Dream World of Davy Crockett* 7, Films on TV 8, Hitchcock: Grace Kelly 9.

Book of stories: The Almanac Story, A Confidential Report, A Remarkable Summer, The Fabulous $20 Bill, Tales from the Vienna Woods: An Inside Story, Successful Love.

Hugo Carmichael, Virgil Gibson.

TVW ["Tales from the Vienna Woods" was to be the title of a book of stories]: Hope & Suspicion, Memory & Hope, The Children's Question, The Gift, The Heights of Joy.

What Difference Does It Make?, A Family Farce, Jasper Hart's Crisis, A Fairy Tale in America, A Dish of Ice Cream, The Fur Coat, An Author's Brother-in-Law, A Metropolitan Gauntlet.

A Colossal Fortune, A Country Weekend, A Testimonial Dinner to God, A Strange Discovery, The Idea of a Party, Four Children, Two Pets.

New Lyrics: Baudelaire 1, Hölderlin 1, The Children's Innocence & Windows 1, The Children's Innocent & Infinite Appetite 1, Yorick 2, All of the Fruits Had Fallen, The First Morning of the Second World 4, The Kingdom of Poetry.

Dream of Kings in America.

Use Father Zosima as interpreter & Dr. Adams.

Saul—Moravia—Pat Blake & Moravia, Anita Maximilian Philips.

God's long affair with Possibility / Promiscuity.

> His / her
> knot of identity
> like shoelaces
> carelessly tied & retied

> Clarity is charity
> A vicious & delicious circle

Anchor, encore, anchorite.

Delmore de la Mort.

Solitude, eminence, mountain.

> The instrument which I discovered
> on the monument
> (where patience sits upon a pyramid—)

> Perfected—irresistible
> circuits of earth, water, fire, air

A rare name / A rare disease.

One by one they fall / They cave in, crack.

August 1935: Thomas, Mann, Wallace Stevens / Warshow, Agee, Kees, Krim / Guilt, exhaustion, suicide, fear.

Dylan Thomas, G. Wallis, Jeanie Rogers.

Dear Pope, T Singers, *Genesis* II, III.

Principles of Joy. The American Dream. Orville's Circus, *Kilroy's Carnival*. The million dollar?—Does God Exist?

Hegel's White Elephant, Zola's Camera.

September 11

Two letters—Jay (unsent), Ransom (angry). Whole bottle of vermouth 11–3. Three letters—[Robert] Evett [book editor, *The New Republic*], Ransom, Hoffman.

"National phen.: Eisenhower," J. Reston's column in S. *Times*.

Magnified contemplation—Sat. & Sun. Libido Drawn & Frustrated. Reasons for long depressions. Also. Never so much concentration except perhaps? ball games & films.

September 15

Still no word: *Times*, Viking, Hemley.

Lorelei—M. Monroe. Heine's Vaudeville.

De la Mors + De la Mere, war, mare, Mars, Del mors, I Del mented.

His attitude is piscine, canine, avuncular, meteorological.

Undated

Panzer—Genghis Cohn
Short: A History of Love / Poem, Lucretius

The Lady Stripped for Action
There she was
Displaying her Glasses
& Making a Rumpus

"The vicissitudes of solitude are inexhaustible."

The Eumenides
The demons innumerable
Rising from Hell
In a storm of tides

Narcissus (?)
Compare magnification's thrall
Beyond moving, untouched by denial
Behold the first withering [?] streak
—It is the scent of relation

September 21

K[*ilroy's*] C[*arnival*]
What is your religious affiliation?

You mean Belief?—Am I Semitic, anti- or philo-Semitic? I believe in Belief, Hope, and Love (and I believe that everything exists in the mind of God)—

Nothing written in all September save the first (and several drafted) film piece. Letter at last to [Gilbert A.] Harrison [publisher of *The New Republic*], Handlin, Marshall today. William, Cowley, Covici, Gruenthal—and seeing more people than for several months.

October 2
Delmore Schwartz, Sunday, October 2nd, 1955, after being visited by the Hartles [Robert, on the faculty at Princeton, and Pat], their children Shirley, Johnny, and their dog Missy. At six o'clock—after depressive gaps and lacunae at dinner—lunch.

> The stone on which my hope was set
> After the apples & the eagles
> Helped me—for a while—
>   for a time to forget
>
> The coats of pride
>   were summer thin
> Beneath them voice & ghost
>
> "She became all
> O became belly—"
> Buttock cheek & white heels
>   Flying?
>
>   *Sartre*
> "The fixed &
>   unchangeable
> Face
> Which he
>   Called Being"

October 4
Story of German masquerading as Jew (doctor—"disbarred," thinks it will be easy).
F[*innegans*] W[*ake*]: 562: "Ah plikplak wed my Biddles." "In the dancer years."

October 5
Thirteen Dex.—hangover—11 a.m. Robert Hazel, *The Farmer's Bride.*
TLS—"As prudery destroys love / so false reverence criticism."

> Lust thou art
> To lust returning

October 6

Not Milton E. for President but for chief of staff.
Sing-Sing & Alcatraz farther from New York City than Canada.
More distant than love lost?
Ten years since 1945 shorter than the ten, in 1945, since 1935.

October 7

Yesterday Joyce copying too & trying to write to Covici & it was raining—and it is gray & cold—& *Mask of Glass* by Holly Roth & depressed at forty-two years + three Seconals & two beers.

["The Man Who Read Kant in the Bathtub," a review of Further Speculations *by T. E. Hulme, edited and with an introduction by Samuel Hynes, appeared in* The New Republic, *May 21, 1956.]*

This kind of biographical information combined with some of the selections published here for the first time reveal Hulme's powerful personality far more than the *Speculations* volume published in 1924, which contained little to justify the immense intellectual debt to Hulme professed by ———— ———— ————. Thus Hulme was a student & disciple of Bergson, "a great influence (though with growing reservations) & a great excitement"—while most of Hulme's supposed debtors either ignored Bergson or actively opposed him in their mature views. Hulme's personality, his authority as a gifted young thinker, set an example of independence and courage of mind which helped his friends to find their own directions, which had nothing in common with his, apart from a general antagonism to the leading ideas of the nineteenth century.

The same strength of mind shows itself in more extended examples—in Hulme's dispute with Russell . . . and in his advocacy of Bergson at a time when the French philosopher was anathema in fashionable intellectual circles. This may well [be] the clue to Hulme's influence . . . He set an example of intellectual courage, and indifference to being fashionable, or appearing an eccentric. This strength of mind combined with a wholesale antagonism to the leading ideas of the nineteenth century . . .

[Professor] Hynes speaks of Hulme's habit of making startling remarks in conversation, saying that they are to be taken seriously or literally, as further evidence that Hulme was a proto-fascist, an impression rooted in the fact that his intellectual debtors were certainly conservative or reactionary. One such remark is Hulme's assertion that the finest pleasure in life for him was that of reading Kant's *Critique of Pure Reason* in a tub of hot water. Surely this kind of remark must be taken seriously—whether true or not, and it was probably true: for the significant thing about so innocent an assertion is that Hulme said it . . .

Another day in trying to write a review of 500 words & trying ever more to keep writing the review, to keep trying.

Slept again from 4:30 until 2 & many streaky streaky dreams again—and some nervous-making efforts to deal with mss. & write to Covici.

November 11
[This entry might be a reference to my departure. I left Delmore, for the first time, some time that fall, went to Woodstock until Christmas, and then spent the rest of the winter in New York City.]

Big quarrel // Go Go Go //
Detached in Silence / Distant / Removed b. thru inertia

December 22

River
   River
When buttock bumped
     like a
       wave
        and
         yet
Was butter-smooth & thigh

Conclusion
  Beauty
  Beast
Love is the Reality
  Echo
    knew
      true Love
& true Reality
   River
    River

Undated

[A review of the movie The Country Girl *appeared in* The New Republic, *April 4, 1955.]*

Glutton for Punishment

It's been said that the film of *The Country Girl* improved Clifford Odets's play, but I doubt that this can mean anything more than that the director of the film and the actors had the benefit of the Broadway production. Only a few sentences have the poetic quality which made Odets eloquent from the start and which Eric Bentley described exactly when he reviewed Odets's most recent play.

Odets—with his reformer's message, his sad & seedy poetry.

"—finally mastering his impulse & returning triumphantly to the stage" / confidence / all the flair & eloquence which are notoriously the actor's equipment.

Given Odets's dark picture of the theater, can one care about anyone's success or failure in it?

"Carefully sustained dismay."

An imagination for people inhabiting a special milieu with a language and a logic of th[eir] own.

The backstage world of the theater.

In his forced retreat from the Communist eluctable he has simply found the equivalent of it in the dance.

✲

. . . It is this overwhelming development which, as it seems to me, R. P. Blackmur has entirely overlooked in his essay on "Lord Tennyson's Scissors." Despite my admiration for what Mr. Blackmur has to say in his other essays on poetry, I cannot but think that here Mr. Blackmur is the victim of what he himself wholly condemns: the received idea—in this instance about versification. Lord Tennyson's Sc[issors] are good for one thing only: they make it possible for any living poet to cut his own vocal cords.

✲

> The water coins
> Spangled
> Striped
>
> > The checkerwork of
> > Scales
> > overlapping
> > (Fish scales)
> > Lapping
> > Barnacles

Hushed
Hushed
Waters
Woolen & wanderful
Wool
Woolen
Willing & having no
Will

Look at the Delaware and Anna's Liffey—
A Paper Tiger: Chinese & proverb.

❀

Kilroy: He suffers from Bright's Disease.
Orville: He is too bright. He would rather be bright than President.
Everyone wants in on the act: Amateur Night!

❀

Show it to New Directions—L[eslie] Katz's book [*Invitation to the Voyage*, published by Harcourt, Brace].
I must tell Dr. Gruenthal that you said I would marry J.L.
Fulbright's Disease.
The Artificial Jewery Store.

❀

Captains, Officers, Enfants Terribles / Ezekiel, Marcel & Joel.
The two boys were the infant terrors of the entire class structure of society: they entered the mansions of the upper class like firemen and like bandits—they sauntered among the lumpen bohemians downtown like commissars in the Soviet Union appointed to guard & watch & examine "the political orientation" of all the officer cadres: thus they were also inquisitors and their pronouncement of anathema was certainly not ineffectual—
Rhoda [Klonsky] & Auden (that foreigner!): I am a democratic narcissist.
Psychic & Auden.
How did I know I would feel like this?
"I now practice the genre of silence"—Anatole [Broyard] on getting paunchy & middle-aged.

❀

A message from the White House: You have served the commonweal. Distinguished Service Cross.
Armageddon, Kingdom of Heaven, Death, Messiah.
1. Statement of Universe—God.
2. You are chosen (among all these).

3. Long Island RR is one of God's public utilities / holding companies.

4. Invisible Church.

5. Efficacy of prayer, of her prayer, of her mission as of her vocation.

Aquinas & intellectual sympathy, honor of Being, the mystery.

> These sentences are enough
> To make one silent forever
> —Silent and in solitude
> Removed
> If Heaven and Earth may suddenly appear
> A stranger's
> ✿

> Let's hope
> There will [be]
> No more
> Of these sad bad
> Passages
> Of dreary weary
> Time
> Untolled

[The following note in a printed scrawl was found among the journal papers.]

> 5 a.m.
> Had a hard time getting to sleep. If the *Times*
> calls while I'm asleep please tell them that
> I've gone to the library or Princeton—
> Love to the breadwinners,
> De la Mort

1956

Reality is Love as Hatred is Death.

Theme
Love is reality, as it was
In the beginning
The kiss which moved the world
Began the self
Begot the city
& sowed the future's
flowers

Theme
Serene & submarine
The river's whale
& fish
Narcissus' wish
To be a fish

[Delmore was translating Heine for an anthology of his poems, for which he had a contract with Viking.]

Heine's reputation in the middle of the twentieth century, a hundred years after his death, has a peculiar character: he suffers from the obscurity of fame. Thus he has never been more famous nor less read. He is perhaps more famous than at any time since his first book of poems appeared and he has fewer readers than at any time since 1827, when *Das Buch der Lieder* was published.

The immortality of which great lyric poets have boasted (almost as often as they fell in love) is usually not [at] all identical with possessing or attracting the devoted attention of many readers generation after generation. It is, most often, the fame of being a text for schoolboys, the source of quotations, the subject of biographical speculation, and a constant, consistent presence in anthologies . . .

(Shakespeare, Goethe, Burns, Catullus.)

Heine's writing . . . was the cause of passionate admiration & detestation in Germany—and perhaps even more—in France & England. For during the latter half of his life & during the second half of the nineteenth century, any list of his friends, admirers, translators, and enemies would consist of the most gifted human beings of the nineteenth century. In Germany the list includes Goethe, Bismarck, several Kaisers, Karl Marx, Friedrich Nietzsche, Lessing, Schelling; in France, Gautier, Jules Laforgue, Sand, De Nerval, Baudelaire, Cocteau; and what is more, in England, Heine was the most translated of all foreign poets—among his translators were E. B. Browning, George Meredith, Thomas Hardy, Havelock Ellis, Olive Schreiner, James Thomson, Arthur Symons . . .

The effort to translate the poems of a great lyric poet is usually not so much of an effort as a labor of unrequited love. The result, at best, is not a genuine equivalent of the original poem but a new poem in the new language inspired by the original. And often enough the inspiration leads to errors. The greatest of translations, the King James Bible, is full of errors—and Baudelaire's translation of Poe's poems [is] not only based on a systematic misunderstanding of the quality of most of Poe's verse but there are howlers—"He made a beeline," literally translated, should suffice as an example.

January 13

Narcissus says: He is the starting point
 Each being exists as such the
 First time when he says:
   I am myself—I am Narcissus
   Therefore I exist
    Or when he recognizes
Himself in the looking glass   (cats don't)

  I am Narcissus: I am
     conscious
  I am Narcissus: I am
     consciousness

Narcissus, his analysis of each part of the body as mirrored in the river (change & the infinite).

Venus, Cupid (Eros), Sisyphus, Dionysus / Apollo, Dionysus, Venus, Poseidon, Athena, Diana, Jupiter.

Narcissus on the Judgment of Paris.

Undated

Cupid (*Breaking the silence*):
... It would be wrong
... It would be knowledge
Knowledge is more and less [than] love
Knowledge is far more than the god of love
Can bear without becoming powerless

[Psyche]
Why is love dark? Will you not tell me?
Will you not bare your face to me?
To touch it, it is so beautiful, to hold
Its [word?] warmth—
                    Is almost as beautiful
As your voice is, and as your voice was
When I for the first time heard
Suddenly from the woodland your first word
Thinking: It must be some miraculous bird
Neither the phoenix nor the nightingale
But one unknown, unheard before

"O Cupid, Dan
        Dearest of hearts
  Why is love dark?"
        So, by the radiance
& afterglow of making love restored
From need & immediacy to curiosity
Psyche questioned her true love hidden
In night's black mane
            "Will you not tell me, bare
            Your face to me but once? A glimpse like
                a flare
Would be to me as the overwhelming glare
Of sunlight's blond buffalo rush"

March [?]

To do: train, bath, shave; tickets, book, gin; Rules & Regulations; druggist's, tailor, books, gin.

[Delmore, as part of his campaign for my return, wrote out for our signatures a list of house rules and regulations. Most of these were in answer to my complaints with, tacked on at the end, one or two of his. I didn't take this with any seriousness, though I do recall how much I disliked so often eating dinner alone, which I did because of his erratic hours. I had left in November and I returned at the beginning of June.]

["Ring Lardner: Highbrow in Hiding,"* appeared in* The Reporter, *August 9, 1956.]*

June 14

Donald Elder's biography of Ring Lardner, the first full-length study, is excellent in a variety of ways. It makes one want to read Lardner all over again, even though Mr. Elder quotes almost too copiously [and] repeatedly provides synopses of L.'s most familiar stories. But perhaps this is justified, since Lardner's writing has been admired since his death in 1933—as it was during his lifetime—"in one or another one-sided way." Some admire him as a humorist & read his stories only as [the] product of a professional funnyman . . . [Among other] admirers, the general impression is that [he] was a sportswriter & columnist who wrote [about] ballplayers. This is, in fact, what someone who should have known [better] Mr. S[cott] Fitzgerald, his close friend & drinking companion, thought at the time of his death.

Yet a good deal of his best work is not about baseball . . .

When the stories which express [Lardner's] grim vision of life appeared in *The Sat. Eve. Post* & like periodicals, they were [seen] as merely amusing—Lardner hardly would have continued to be a very popular writer for so [long] a time otherwise. Any particular story in isolation certainly seems no more than droll & diverting, particularly when the author is [a] humorist & uses his comic devices in his fiction. But when *Round Up*, the omnibus of all Lardner's short stories, appeared in 1929, it was impossible to miss the fact that L.'s work comprehended American life at every level and was inspired by a consistent point of view . . .

This attitude, characteristically American, of the disappointed idealist is, in fact, the source of everything which makes Lardner a great writer of fiction & one of the greatest—perhaps the greatest—of American humorists. Lardner's idealism & his disappointment is purely American & Midwestern in both his humor & his fiction. But the two ought not to be separated: his work is of a piece, more than that of most writers; his stories are often funny & his humorous pieces are often unmistakably instances of how a humorous piece, when it makes use of anecdotes, begins [to] turn into fiction. It is only when we read his work as a whole that its character as, among other things, a social criticism of American life becomes entirely clear. It is far superior, Lardner is much the better of [many of] the writers of [his] generation who seemed far more serious as social critics—particularly Sinclair Lewis, Sherwood Anderson, Dos Passos, who satirized the same kind of human beings.

June [?1956]

Harder to fix [Heine] than any other of greater German poets.

Buch der Lieder struck a new lyric note, not only for Germany but all Europe.

Daring use of nature symbolism.

Poetry of the sea.

Self-consciousness, wit, cynicism in & out of season.

Concrete expression to spiritual . . . [?word] of intangible undefinable spirituality which the German people regard as indispensable element in their national lyric poetry.

But he did exercise a fascination over his generation. And the writing of his French period—marks a new era in German prose.

Exiled journalist / very great as wit & satirist.

June 24

Narcissus + (Baby, Summer).

> He who awaking gazes
> > Upon the world
> Has already
> > Committed adultery

(Venus, Eros / In-out of the wind & the snow.)

You can't afford to work any longer on your Lardner piece. Afford! Taken out of context.

Variety, freely offered? Wednesday.

Does she want a strong weakling or a weak and strong or a weak man of strength?

—Make my life wonderful . . . all of them says.

I must stay here and say nothing . . . never to move until the odds are in one's favor and one's fedls [sic] in possession of the freedom of alternative: through money, situation, a job, a literary moment or year of advantage: and the [days] and the months to get used to and to get over and to stop think[ing] of possessiveness.

June 25

Angry that I was absent & that . . .

July 11

> I have been putting off sustained
> Effort—to get to the end
> > More & more
> > Increased depressions
> > > dead
> > > paralyzed
> The drinking & s.t.s
> Stupefied me each time when
> I was free to begin to create a new life
> > Heightened all neurosis & fear
> > > Brought it all
> > > > to the
> > Surface
> > > More & more
> [. . .]

July 12

Are the emotions a clue, key, guide / To the nature of reality—the structures of existence?

Unamuno: Life is [an] agonie, a struggle with God.

Drive to Frenchtown. Interest (desire) as opera glasses (spotlight).

July 22

Beginning of Lyrics

Cherchez la femme
> *La fille de joie*
La fille de joie de vivre

Bind the mind in laurel's story
After the summer's lush green glory

Under the overcast, indeed midsummer heat
Softly shines the faint gold of the rising wheat

When sympathy like sweat
> Runs down
> The windows
How we admire the beast and flower
> > And power
> > > Of nature's natural
> > > > Creatures

Undated

Biomorphic—unlike the geometry of truth and the human mind.
Rear-en-tranced. Shush-picious. "Sass pish us."

> He begged her to bare her ace. Basking
> She said: It's yours for the asking.
> She bent revealing
> The ultimate plumpness & sofa's softness
> [. . .]
> An absolute for feeling
>
> And the fluted orifice
> > at the center
> > So difficult to enter
> So intimate and dark—
> > It was great [?] secret & pure ark
> A moon & white—& basking
> > An answer to all asking—

August [?]

Now the *trompe l'oeil* has become (*déja vu*) *M'sieu l'ambassadeur*.
A fascination & an obsession—more than anything but courtship
has ever been—surely than poetry or sex for any sustained time.

August 6

> The riverly papyrus &
> > the scrolls
> Of the waters
> > Books
> > Flowing pages
> The Kingdom of Ongoingness

The Jews said: I don't raise my boy to be [a] soldier.
Asia Minor, 1926, Egyptians, Assyrians, Persians, Macedonians,
Greeks of Alexandria / Philistines, Samaritans (Sumeria?).

> Hath not the river's flow
> The structure of music, ever
> The brim in motion of the present
> As it turns to future.
> > O wave, O light, O flags
> > > of waves of . . .
>
> Drawing its energy
> > From
> > The riverbeds
> > > of the past
> It just has past

Nature is (1) dappled (2) curving (3) full of entrances, doors, rings & swings.

Sources of metaphor: geometry, biology.

> Look now—
> > Early morning—an overcast
> > > Plum dark / pearl gray
> > Having the fragrance of rain
> > > —Though the rain has not yet fallen

The chill fresh odor of the rain clouds & clouded-over day.

Undated

> Do not look—[word?] will what
> > You have to have found
> > > Losses
> Wait for what comes
> But do not look, hunting
> > Narrowed
> > Gaze & focus

August 14

Pictures: and so late it was easier to begin Tuesday than to try to go to sleep.

Jackson Pollock killed driving a car with a girl.

When I was doing what? trying to be a poet conscious of literature.

August 17

[Adlai] Stevenson rallies his party & America to the tasks which are ahead. Does not intend to make political capital of the President's illness, "reverence for life," "if you would make honest citizens of your hearts."

A new America, New Deal, Fair Deal.

Another day of almost no work except for collecting & finding papers.

August 25

Stability is just as (or more) pervasive a need of human beings (e.g., as children & human parents) as is variety—Gruenthal.

As for me: variety terrifies me . . .

August 26

Poems 1953–1954. (The important thing is that I like these poems, some of them very much.)

Hölderlin, Baudelaire, The Fulfillment, The Children's Innocent and Infinite Windows, The Innocence of Children and Childhood— Hungarian, Jeremiah; Yorick, All of the Fruits Are Fallen, The First Morning of the Second World.

Unfinished or too imperfect, 100–150 pp.: The Kingdom of Poetry, The Dirty Light of a Winter Day, Rinehart's Travels, To Walt Whitman in Heaven, Hegel's Elephant.

(1) Ethel [cat] (2) Buttons [cat] (3) My nephew Winkie Schwartz / Absalom, Narcissus.

August 28

                    Delmore Schwartz
                    On the 28th day
                    Of August
                              1956
                    After a night
                         of purchased
                         & a morning
                         of unpurchased
                              sleep
                    Spend [sic] the afternoon
                    Gazing into, idling
                              & frustrated
                              the depth
                              pictures

Chaste, chiseled (Valéry). Just now remembered how yesterday I came upon a sonnet by Valéry I did not remember that I had translated.

Undated

               The café's smoky atmosphere
                    Its mirrors on all sides
               Reflecting & expanding
                    The scene of lights
                    And animated faces
                         To infinity

               Reality is a cheap romance
                    In the form of an infinite serial
                         Syndicated to every whistle-stop
                                   all-night bar
                         In the Milky Way

September 1

The change in climate—profoundly emotional change—said the suddenly world-famous biologist—shows itself:

> In every quartet
> in the atoms of the physicists
> in the stars of Hollywood
> But perhaps most of all
>> in the jokes of the time
>> which
>> like the common cold
>> tend to be
>> ubiquitous . . .

September 5

Poem

Now I have all my power
Now I must truly
Begin
To draw in
The birds the stars
& the flowers
& lead all the animals within

September 11

Noah's Ark: a brand-new serious.
How do you feel? Zest wonderful.

Limerick

You need a gimmick
Just to be a mimic
And to write a limerick

Anyone who writes a limerick
Depends upon a well-known gimmick

The milky way: a built-in joke. The milked way.

Upon the lips
Of the apocalypse

(Hips, pips, slips, slaps—slopes.)

September 12

Narcissus, Psyche. Swedish exorcisms.

> What magic & what ingenuity
> Serve hidden & forbidden Cupid's will
> How Psyche swings from the chandeliers
>   assaults
>   & somersaults
> "You promised me you'd show me how to be
>   A pail, a pole, a swinging door,"
> She whimpers to the dark god childishly

How Dexedrine breaks down—bad habits of coordination and blocked patterns of nervous response. (Up to a point.) Verbal? copying? In handwriting. Backhand in tennis. In the depth pictures. Intuitive following of the pattern instead of forcing to what is looked for.

September 13

> Elizabeth made a racket
> All over the study—this room,
> —This morning—while
> I slept in the dining room

[The dining room was directly under the study.]

September 20

Play. Private Parks or Nakedness.

Film star & husband quarrel. Has gone far too far. How: turns out to be something (?what)—private—neurotic—thigh—armpit—navel? pubic hair—not commonly agreed by community.

How we, E. & I, live directly as pagans & the fact of no community. Extravagantly another first page.

Among the various ways of introducing a volume of Heine's, several are extravagant. Since Heine's friends, admirers, and translators were the greatest names of the nineteenth century (in England and America as well as in Germany & France), one might very well make a catalogue. Such a catalogue would clearly suggest a moral like a command: to read Heine's work since these remarkable human beings of one or another kind of genius were enchanted by his poetry, his prose, or his personality . . .

There are several extravagant ways of recommending Heine's writings to the modern [reader]. List of admirers, translators / insults & accusations / list of epithets / German Apollo / list of comparisons / Nazis.

September 21

[The following paragraphs come from a very scattered page and most of the remarks refer to Elizabeth Pollet.]

Luxury of indecision—seven months. The first freedom—the Freedom of Emotional Blackmail.

Spite—quarry. Would not give you the satisfaction. Something in me: Yes!

Jane's remark about training husbands. Takes time to train them: person who picks up. Filing cabinet. [Delmore was very proud of his practicality in hanging his trousers by the cuffs in his filing cabinet drawer to keep them pressed.]

Here I go again. Limitation on friends. Silent—not jolly with them. Talk—if not to you, to whom? Contributions—expectations.

Talk, spite: The death of the novel. My novel.

Interest (money unconscious). California, Fulbright.

Lack of connection: Schorer's book.

Thurs. morning. Smoking & you smoke. Talking & slowness. You don't talk unless drawn out under very special conditions.

September 26

LL   *Little Lyric*
Joy is the light: joy alone
Though the sun shine, nevertheless
If blackness or torpor
   Hold consciousness
All things become or are
   Nothing but stone
 ([Alternate] No more than stone.)

Desire/Fear
Movement to   (to is always from &
Movement from   from is always to)
Movement with
Movement toward

LL
Alone is unreal—& is [?fantasy]
Together is with, is real: it is reality!

September 28

We die by pieces, fragments
As the teeth rot & decay—
   ragged chips

(She was a blue chippie / lidded / one of Hardy's favorite favored words.)

September 29

Heine's Work

It is best to read Heine's writing, paying as little attention as possible to whether it is written in verse [or] prose. The distinction between the two is very important, of course: it is more important in Heine than in a good many other great poets . . . because Heine is a complete master of versification, and in his lyrics he often depends upon the emphasis of alliteration, meter, the frames of stanza, line, and structure, and the bells of rhyme to get precisely the right tone, mood, and voice. But these depend upon the German language to such an extent that . . .

September [?]

Poems—first draft—Aug.–Sept.

Who is the powerful ghost
Surprising & Guide [of] my mind
Deciding foe & friend
And making me, at most
A servant of his choice
A subterfuge, the host
Of his unpredictable voice?

The scenes of sleep are ruled by him
The waking moods or moons
                    which follow
And yet I know no more
                    of him
Than of a random fugitive swallow

October 6

Heine & Nietzsche.
Heine's prophecy of Hitlerism.
An attitude toward Spinoza as toward lovers of Poetry.
Poetry of mixed feelings.
[Walter Arnold] Kaufmann [*Nietzsche: Philosopher, Psychologist, Antichrist*]—N: Convictions are prisons.
N.'s debt to H. & Goethe emphasized.
"Goethe's heart opened up at the phenomenon of Napoleon—or, as Hegel had called him, the world soul (the absolute) on horseback."
(This event made him rethink his Faust. G. admired what Nap. had made of himself.)

December 28

All night, resentment / Growing & moving from one to another resented one / E.P.S. [Elizabeth], Saul.

After beginning a letter to Bill & beginning & ending a letter to Wm.—after midnight.

The refusal to admit to a reality beyond desire or beyond pleasure.

The unwillingness to chance rejection & failure.

Nothing to fear but fear itself is fear of everything.

The fog is like a white animal.

"At the sign of the Recording Angel."

"It isn't everyone who can afford to go to Corinth."

December 30

The Dying Novel. Ghost Stories. Hallucinations. Fish Stories.

Some manifestation of fiction prevails & is habitual to human beings.

Nevertheless, those critics who assert that the novel has again suffered its last & fatal disease can refer with some justification to the fact that storytelling is not the same thing as the complex literary form which we call the novel and which is, as a matter of lit. history, the latest born of all the literary forms. If the novel is thought of as an extended narrative in prose & the prose narration of imaginary events, then the novel did not exist until the seventeenth century. Books like the *Arabian Nights*, the *Decameron*, the *Morte d'Arthur* are short-story collections. But this definition of the novel becomes arbitrary & inaccurate once we remember that, long before the official appearance of the novel, the pleasures of prolonged narrative fiction occurred in verse. This is the reason that T. E. Lawrence called the *Odyssey* the first novel (when he made a prose translation of Homer's epic poem) and it is for precisely the same reason that Fielding called [*Joseph Andrews* a comic epic in prose].

Undated

You can't sue, have juries on courtship. Courtships have little to do with marine architecture or / and case law: witnesses are undesirable.

Cocteau & Resonances.

"The mystery—of what comes next!"

"I follow you blindly."

"It is one of God's latest things."

Poem / Lyric
Let us seek to make mountains
Into molehills. This
May be a triumph more memorable
     on occasion
Than faith moving mountains
—Faith is far better occupied
In projects less akin to real-estate engineering
Faith has its works and its own mountains
Surely the perilous mountains of
     human emotions
The emotions of others and most of all the self's
     emotions
[. . .]

     ✿

   Rhys Davies:
"The great street lamps like arrogant
     kings
   Shine in the sullen rain"

     Lyric
Your eyes are tender
   & small animals
They are shy
     they are quick
(Then)
Moving without [?word]
   Reveal
     Neither thought
Nor feeling unless at times
They are as an evening, reverend
     & delicate
Awaiting the first stars
Beyond all wrongs & wars
     ✿

  E.P. She was so intent upon the perception of the emotions of
others that she often overlooked the presence of her own emotions—
as dusk, darkness, and night obscuring the others—and the gift of
seeing in the dark became another obstruction.

1957

January 7

T.S.E., 1949, Dec., Nobel Prize. *From Poe to Mallarmé.*

1940s—war poets Shapiro, R. Jarrell.

American Dream (Europe, Sanctuary of Culture).

In each generation of the present century (except the present one —& the first decade—until 1914) some varying relationship to the A[merican] D[ream] has moved the most important & the most representative poets.

R. Jeffers, C. Sandburg, V. Lindsay, H.D., J. G. Fletcher, E. L. Masters.

H. Crane, W. C. Williams, Imagism, Free Verse (Experimentalism).

Boom America, Agrarianism, Regionalism, New Humanism (self-mastery through writing & study), Proletarianism.

A. Tate: Invocation to the Social Muse.

How some poets—Frost, MacLeish—were forced to be concerned with different matters in the course of the alternation of national prosperity, national crisis, and depression—international crisis & world war.

Industrialism (the machine), Puritanism, Internationalism, Bohemianism / Freedom, Europeanism, Democracy, Class Consciousness & Marxism.

Americanism, Nationalism, Whitmanism, Social Credit, Fascism, Populism.

Colloquialism vs. conversation & artifice.

Undated

Pound / T.S.E. The revolution of T A S T E has been consummated: it is now taken for granted by the new poets under forty.

Reviews: South, N. England, Chicago, California, London, Paris, Rapallo. Moscow. TLS, American Literature 1955, English Lit.

There is no longer an independent entity called English Literature or American Literature. All literary work—all reading & all writing
—is (revolution of taste) now in a literal sense concerned with com-
parative literature.

(Define as: International & Historical sense.)

Frost: "Once by the Pacific." T.S.E.: "The Hollow Men." "Richard
Cory."

Brahmanism, the poetry for Mandarins. Objectivists. Rexroths, the
Howlers of San Francisco & New York.

Rebels in search of a revelation—since nonconformism is accepted,
countenanced, and made comfortable.

Automation, 55 million cars (books of poetry). Paperbacks, TV,
and mass culture. Typewriter and printing costs. Internal combustion
machine and rhythms of poet.

W. Wordsworth—to T.S.E.

The present as a period between two epochs. A transitional period,
standstill.

(Russia—Armageddon.)

Mass culture—criticism of American life—illusion of prosperity
& hallucination of the Apocalypse—the Last Judgment.

The Lost Generation & the Last Generation.

American Dream—out of this world, Cats, Squares, Hipsters.

Gone—illusion of great prosperity & great insecurity.

Cool Generation, rock 'n' roll. Silent / Beat Generation. Security-
Conscious Generation.

Frost:
I choose to be just a
New England farmer
With an income, in cash, of say
a thousand
From say a publisher in N.Y.

1912–1916. Worked in factory / newspaper / schoolteacher.

R. Hovey, Bliss Carmen. Stedman. Twilight Interval. Children of
the Night. Armageddon.

Whistler, Pound—Renaissance. Imagism. Revolt against Puri-
tanism vs. New Conformism. Invocation to the Social Muse. Lost
Generation—Hem[ingway], Dos P[assos], Cummings / Hart Crane,
Jeffers, Winters, MacLeish.

It is a strange thing to be an American.

January 8

Lyric: Rinehart's Summer

Rinehart is
The king of flutes
Rinehart's kiss
Wakes March's roots
Rinehart reaches
All colors and all curves
Apples, peaches
Eye hand nerve
A tutor of Cupid
Of work as fun
In the dark of the sun
   He says:
The clever are the stupid
& the stupid discover
That sleep & love are one

Rinehart is
A student of leaves
A scholar of Eros
A student of consciousness
Of sleep's wine-dark seas
Of the heights of birds
& the depths of words
[. . .]

Schedule Jan. 8–Jan. 31. Finish Heine—entirely by Jan. 24—one week for intro.—one week for mss. Type out "The Hartford Innocents."

January 20

Make a list of Heine's poems in terms of subject matter and chronological extension of subject matter.

The sky's mid-afternoon midwinter sun—a blob of tin gray, a leaden shine, a chromium and intensest blur.

Brooks beyond discussion according to Harvey Breit.

A N.J. license is like getting married after having children.

The ten-year period of preparation between *Das B[uch der Lieder]* and *New Poems* probably was crucial for [Heine] as the Abbey Theatre for Yeats—less so, since he could hardly have turned outside by then.

February 4

> History is the excuse
> of weaklings, the oratory
> of demagogues
> Ambition is the tyranny
> Of the imagination, selfhood's suicide
> Or disgust
> & Eros too
> For all the excitement, all the obsession
> Making so much that sparks[?], blazes
> Or breaks the heart—you too
> Collaborate with Death and not
> with Nature's
> gushing rushing pleasure

No sleep—enormous amount of Dexedrine—not much to eat.

February 14

"A Colossal Fortune"—where should the cuts come? (to get it down to 40 pp.).

"The New Kinsey Method," a story—window backyard—fence, red brick house. A girl nude, dancing, a young man fully dressed eating in an armchair conversing with a young lady fully dressed.

What are the relationships of the three to each other? A party discussion?

February 26

> *The Country Bronze of the Green & Gold*
> O what a ragged richness is in bloom
> The sunlight celebrates itself in the gold
> of death
> Exalts itself in the oak leaves fire-ripe
> & burns upon the field of browning rye
> The meadow flecked with daisies & with
> golden rod

February [?]

June 10, 11, 1956—E.'s return—three days & nights of no medication. Piece on Lardner's biography.

July, Aug., Sept.—Heine—Fulbright.

Oct., Nov., Dec., 1956—*Kenyon, New Yorker,* Viking, *Hudson Review.*

Hotel Times Square. "Are you all right, Delmore?"

Jan., Feb. 1957—Fulbright, phone calls. [Delmore was awarded a Fulbright Fellowship to teach at the Free University of Berlin the following academic year.]

Feb., Mon. 25, Frenchtown; 18, Josie's visit [Josephine Herbst, writer, friend, and neighbor]. Sun. 24, quarrel, 18 pp. of Joyce, M. Monroe; 17, Helen's visit [Helen Dickson Blackmur], young painter with her. Fri. 22, *Playboy*, mailed at last. Tues. 12, phone call from Covici.

The DP's, Compulsive Obsessive Devouring Day & Night.

March 8

Perhaps I ought to cut down Dex.—and see if it is calm—the calm of the freedom from the dark god will help me get to work & really get to work.

March 10

Lyric

The question which they
cannot ask is
Whether the questions which they ask
[are]
Likely to lead to any answers
Which will fulfill the task
—Nor do they ask
whether the task is
Exactly what they think
it is

Lord Russell was a solipsist, a pacifist, a stoic, tried out D. H. Lawrence.

Wittgenstein.

Logician, magician.

About Positivism
Grub worm & butterfly
Duckling & swan
Attempt to testify
To the likelihood
They trip upon

March 21

Kilroy's La Scala on West Twelfth St.

Orville. This is an opera which has been revised by Kilroy and translated into the American language. These are operas which [have] been revised by Orville and his accompanists for the American people who until recently regarded grand opera as only for women, children, bricklayers, housepainters, and foreigners.

March 23

Whitman

To Walt Whitman upon this
Midsummer, mid-century day
What, indeed, do we have to say
   —to explain—to elucidate
If you go to the Walt Whitman Hotel
In Camden, New Jersey,
You will not find that the
Daughters of the American Revolution
Have placed a copy of *Leaves of Grass*
   In every bedroom
[. . .]

March 29

The mind is like the sky
   An infinite accommodation
Wherein through ingenuity
   Reality becomes imagination

April 8

To get! week of April 8–15. Typing paper, folders, boxes.
Umbrella stored—but parachute [in action].
No, D.S., she is really saying.
More people go to analysts than ever before. [Sylvia] goes to an
astrologist. "My approach," she states, "is scientific."

April 15

How the ads show us what the others (the ones who do not &
cannot know us) want us to want.
Each soul unique & in perpetual prehending is ontology.
An editor who is an anthologist. An ontologist who is a metaphysician.

April 22

See Rilke, Berryman, [Frank] O'Hara [poet] too & [James]
Schevill [poet].

Brueghel's: The Road to Calvary
Where are we come?
Further than any horse can bear us
   We shall soon see:
Further & farther than
     consciousness

Rode before now into the heart
of reality
& the reality of the heart
(They do not look as if they were going
to discover, in the end,
the Xmas tree)

(Poems are made by chaps like me
But mankind made the Xmas tree.)

April 27

Lyrics (unterminated)
Alas that I should know
Much more
Of words than flowers
And of that
Dark long ripened flower
My body
Much more of words
Than of bird and of
Those quick birds
My eyes

May 10

When I was a child, the family my brother & I liked to visit most of all was that of the Gunns. If we had been asked what family we would choose to be born into (& we understood the question), we would surely have said one of the Gunns [sic].

1949, Mrs. G.: You look just like your father. But I did not.

Is that why Mr. Gunn told (squealed), because he knew that his wife was in love with the adulterous man? He had seen him in a down-town N.Y. hotel when he was supposed to be in Pittsburgh or Scranton.

Undated

When Tobias was fourteen years old, his mother agreed, at last, to give his father a divorce. The divorce agreement provided [that] Tobias & his younger brother, Martin, were to live with his [sic] father every summer, after school ended.

May 16

An Author's Brother-in-Law (second attempt today)

Claude regarded his new brother-in-law from a careful distance. There he was, seated in a beach chair, his head bent over the pages he had placed on his drawing board, ten books stacked on one another in the grass beside him; sometimes he was motionless for hours.

"You can't read all those books in one day. I know you can't," Claude had said to Raymond the day before. Claude had never known anyone who seemed to him so peculiar, strange, and difficult to understand.

"I don't always find myself able to decide which book I want to read," Raymond had said then. The look on Raymond's face made Claude feel that he was being teased. It was like the beginning of a game except that R. was not a gaming kind of guy.

"Can't you go back to the pig house?"

The pig house was the name of the cabin in which Raymond lived with Barbara.

(The words he used a form of barbarism. N.Y., bully, city slicker. You're just one-third as old as me.)

"Say, why don't you get a job as caddy at the country club," said Claude.

May 26

> The dream is knowledge &
> Knowledge is a dream
> The self is a story
> > Ever unconcluded
> If Time takes away the evil
> Time takes away the good
> > But it is not the same
> > The wounds of time are
> > > healed by
> > > > Time
> [. . .]
> Time heals all wounds B U T
> Time opens new wounds
> Time is not a river
> > Time is a fire

Extreme masque. Time is. It transfigures whatever it touches, as it annuls & annihilates.

Of eternity space is the double *O*.

Undated

> Time is the dream &
> Time is the meaning &
> Time is the meaning of the dream
> In time & in time only
> The only reality of time is

The future: the present is only
The beginning of the future
                    The past is only
The soil from which the
                    Beginning rises
(By series of deceptions, moving
                    Like pictures)
This is the future which is time truly

K[ilroy's] C[arnival]

Orville: We will now hear an inside tip from the pure American; the words will be accompanied by the military Band of Hope.

I bring to you the gospel of Kilroy, that each is a profound mystery to himself, first of all, and to others even more; that each being of mankind is secret, concealed from himself and from his fellows, yet alive in every inch, every atom, in the curl of his handwriting, in the shaping of glove & shoe.

H. I. / She opened doors / entered / wakened the sleepers (to the joy of the newborn).

The first to write / Before he moved on / Kilroy was here.

June 8

43½
[Delmore's birthday was in December.]

        August, a country house
           A dry bright day
        Summer already waning

        Birds—shears & the trimming of hedgerows
        A recurrent splash
        Above which
        Whistlers   warblers   trillers

Both extreme patience & extreme impatience are forms of genius.

        All men are siblings (a s. fraternity)
        (& all sisters are Judy-graded)
        All sisters are a sibling
           sorority
        The siblinghood of man—
        The grandstand, tier on tier [. . .]

June 13

Published or prepared for publication. Princeton—through June 1953–June 1957.

Recent criticism: Aiken, Lardner, Stevens 1, Stevens 2, Auerbach, Hemingway, Faulkner, W. B. Yeats, Lawrence, "Pocket Book Revolution," Bellow, Thomas, Hulme, "Life as an Interpreter of Literature," M. Pickford, Compton-Burnett.

"Successful Love"; "First Morning of the Second World."

R. P. Warren, M. Schapiro, last *Periodical Review.*

Animal Farm, Bridges at Toko-Ri, Steinbeck (*East of Eden*), M. Monroe, Films & TV, D. Crockett, M. Pickford, Nelson Algren (*M[an] with Golden Arm*), Father Bruckburger, *The Big Knife*, Danny Kaye, Leigh-Loren-Brando (*Guys & Dolls*), Dwight Macdonald, "National Phenomena," Randall Jarrell.

Unpublished: McKeon, "Poetry & Religion," Cash Howells, Dore Schary, *Poetry Omnibus.*

Indiana, Chicago, lectures, readings.

All of the Fruits Had Fallen, The Innocent & Infinite Windows of Childhood, The Fulfillment.

Hölderlin, Baudelaire, T. S. Eliot (17 pp.?).

Rejected: Kings of Joy, A Colossal Fortune.

Unfinished: Hegel's White Elephant, The World's Dream, Kilroy's Carnival.

The question of the guest room: "You can put a few boxes in there." "I have to have room to move around in."

June 18

[Another version of this poem appears in Last and Lost Poems.*]*

Lyric for the Summer
Resorts of the Dead

Under the yellow sea
Who comes & loves with me
The daughters of music? or the morning's waters?
Both have sauntered in these
        unending waters
Where the sunlight turns to tea
& all things are equally
Reduced to nonentity or comedy
By the ocean's immense intense
Sensuous insistence instability
      & triviality

[A slightly different version of the following poem, "In the Green Morning, Now, Once More," is in Selected Poems.*]*

In the green morning, before
Childhood was destiny
The Sun was King
& God was famous

The merry, the jolly
The magical, the musical
The carnival, the feast
Of feasts, the festival
Suddenly ended
As the sky descended
Yet there was only the feeling
In the rain falling
In all the freshness & all the fragrance
Of birth, and beginning

Fame was destiny / Time was infamy.
Milton Klein / Delmore Schwartz.

*A Prominent Clubman He Belongs
to Several Clubs*
He plays the cellophane
He scrubs the rag & he
Buttons & belts the bonds
Quakes the—
In Alexander's Ragtime
Band

Cold light on the sea
Cold light on the sea
Celebration
Likeness
& light
Stars & seeds & steeds

*[The crisis of our marriage came in July–August 1957. As far as I
can reconstruct the dates, Delmore and I went to Yaddo July 1 and,
at Delmore's demand, left abruptly July 21. We spent that night
at Saul Bellow's in Tivoli, and on July 22 we registered at the Hotel
St. George in Brooklyn Heights, where I made a preplanned escape,
going to my mother's empty apartment nearby. Within a few weeks
I had flown to San Francisco and gone on to Reno, obtaining a*

*divorce on November 5, 1957, after a ten-week residency. Del-
more's increasingly threatening behavior finally got so out of hand
that the police were contacted. Over the Labor Day weekend (I
was already in Reno) he was taken to Bellevue. Saul Bellow and
other friends came to his rescue, raised money, got him trans-
ferred, first to Mt. Sinai Hospital and then to the Payne Whitney
Clinic. He was not hospitalized for long.*

*There are many references in the following pages to imagined
lovers who conspired with me against him, to lawyers he went to
see, legal steps he wanted to take.]*

August

Yaddo and absence at Yaddo as possibly deliberate deceptions
rather than authentic: or perhaps both.

Eleanor Kunitz's departure for California.

June 1957. The Picasso show & visit to [Dr.] Gruenthal. As, during some previous month bet. Jan. & June—her return with a martini
hangover (and also, in the same way, after going to Woodstock).

*[During the winter of 1956–57 I went to New York once a month
to preview gallery shows, and the reviews I wrote appeared in the
magazine Arts.]*

Aug., Sept. 1956–June 1957—E. often went out to get the mail—
as if expected a letter (and she never [had] done [so] at any prior
time).

Nov. or Dec. 1955 as probable beginning [of my hypothetical
affair].

J.L.'s marriage announcement. When?

September 8

*[References below are to Leonard Wolf, a poet at Yaddo whom
Delmore suspected; Gordon Potter, a friend of my father and my
lawyer; Vincent Stanzioni, a private detective whom Delmore
hired in August; James Jones, novelist, who aided Delmore
financially.]*

The pattern has not been broken—neither for E. nor for me.

What will happen, however, is not what anyone expects right
now—other patterns, entering into the hurly-burly, are bound to make
the new something other than a repetition (rhyme: reputation) of
the old.

Leonard, Potter, Stanzioni, Jim Jones (famous in hospitals, among
the nurses—Miss Pettigross, Miss Mier).

Poem: Ishmael?

Call me Mishmash
Mélange adultère de tout
Call me Rinehart
Call me Uncle Tom,
Nigger, yid, bluenose or fat cat,
Gentile or jig,
But anyway call me / and
Never stop calling me
Just call & call on the hour
Like the whippoorwill in dark June, like
The telephone ringing & ringing unanswered
In a dark apartment of the housebroken
    Heartbroken
    Musician Crèvecoeur

We will never arrive
  At the future in
Which we exist, or know
The present in which we
  Breathe and living die
(Unless . . .)

Call me.

Week of Oct. 1—Gruenthal.
Hivnor & lecture. [Robert] Coles [executive at] Book-of-the-Month. Isabella Gardner [poet], Oscar Williams [poet and anthologist], Joseph Bennett [editor of *The Hudson Review*], M. Marshall, S. Phillips, R. Straus, G. Potter.

E.: You had given up before I met you.
First-person song.
King of the Beach.

Delmore Schwartz
October 28, 1957
Alone, in a hotel room,
almost penniless—in the 44th
year of his age—his second
wife have [sic] taken flight
after eight years of
troubled and quarrel-
racked marriage

November 11–13

Bloodshot eyes after dinner—a sudden drop after lunch uptown with Dwight [Macdonald] after packing & moving from W. Twenty-third to W. Twelfth. There was a phone call asking for me from Potter [Elizabeth's lawyer]. [P.] said that I was to be one of her dinner guests —Potter then said he wanted me to call him between 6:30 & 7, at home—not to "bother" to call him at his office.

Mon. Lunch with Dwight. Potter called while I was out.

Tues. Hanlons—Arlene, Bob, and Kathie came to dinner. A man committed suicide at 203 W. 14th on Sunday.

Wed. I was awake long before it was light and tried to use Dexedrine to get back to sleep. But I smoked & I was too restless, too obsessed—and when it was light, I made myself a small breakfast & wrote the same long lecture for what must be at least the tenth time.

R. Chandler: She looked like nine million dollars.

November 15

Again & as before, the compulsion returns and takes the place of obsession with the injury of abandonment & rejection. This occurs during the afternoon, during the early afternoon, after the first or second tide of artificial energy has arisen and fallen.

Today I woke up too early again—at 7:30—after waking for the first time in the middle of the night, taking two more s.t.s, the fourth & the fifth, and getting back to sleep after drinking the last can of beer—I drank too much late in the afternoon—when I became very nervous after jacking myself up all day with Dexedrine.

Delmore Schwartz—Friday, November 15, 1957.
"The privileges of beauty are enormous."
"The licorice which looks like shoelaces."
"The whole dream through which he was living lifted him into a zone of ecstasy"—

November 17

Saturday night, Nov. 16. Goody's Bar when I became very very depressed. Hanlons [Bob, Greenwich Village writer and his wife Arlene]. Detective: in your mind—I did not.

The lies of a psychopath. In the fall of 1952, about J. P[ollet]: true, or if not true, E. said, sufficiently characteristic. As with the story after coming back—"an (extreme) nervous disorder." Final decree in mail & bill from parking lot. Manuscripts & clothes & exaggeration of money. Is it this which makes so much trouble? Others get away with the same kind of thing, when they do, because they "function" less erratically or rather are productive at a more reliable & constant rate as E., G., Wilson, Faulkner, Hemingway. Jay alienated because M., W.B. because of J., E. because of attacks on herself & her friends & the sense of being regarded critically a great deal of time. MD [manic-depressive] disorder & sex & liquor & s.t.s & Dexedrine are causes, at least in part, of "extreme nervous disorder"—Dexedrine, Dexamyl: [John] Tibby [senior editor at] *Time*, & Francis Brown of *N.Y. Times*—

E.G. & "criminal, absolute criminal." Probably [Donald] Dike noticed something at Syracuse, just as Carlos Baker certainly did, not only at Princeton but at Yaddo. Wm. did in April 1956 & J. Herbst & Edna & Toni P. & perhaps the Baptistown garageman, & Covici, Cowley, and Harrison as well. Rejection (A.Q.), sex, and withdrawal. "You can't trust D."—Rorschach & Eileen Berryman. How many have been disaffected by direct personal attacks: G.B., E.P., W.H.A., M.K., Wm. P., P.R., A.T.—R.P.B., indirectly through H.D.B.—J.L. (poem & Hutchins)—nervousness again—E.S.S. (But at Harvard it was sometimes pride, jealousy, or rivalry on the part of one or another.)

Jay's conduct has been the same kind of thing with others. Emily Sweetser [who had worked for New Directions]? Albert Erskine? Harry Levin, and Perry Miller [Harvard professor and author]? But then there are those who like me very much—despite destructive actions—Sherburn, Baker, Irving Howe, Margaret Marshall, Wm. Phillips, Saul Bellow, Oscar Handlin and [his wife] Mary—and those who accept them for a long time, only to become totally disaffected— as with W.B. & E.P. & possibly Gruenthal. One important difficulty which I almost always forget is that the weakness or viciousness, rivalry or jealousy or resentment or desperation of others may always be present, and when any of these tendencies become intensely active, my own way of reacting—direct attack—leads to temporary or lasting disaffection, e.g., Berryman's letter about my last book—the assumption or expectation is that others will be good & good to me— e.g., truthful, generous, noble—and when they fail to be—e.g., Saul —I become very angry.

"What a marvelous human being."

"He told me how very talented you are."

"Highly amusing."

"Ransom thinks that you're wonderful."

"Dr. G. thinks that you're a genius."

"I have known minds & minds—but . . ."

"Something very special"—R.P.B. to J.C.

"Polly Hanson is in awe of you." Mrs. Ames said, "Delmore is such a dear."

Philip Rahv: Delmore can't love anyone.

George Palmer's report of the comment on a student's praise: "No one can be that good." E.P.: "Better than Schapiro, better than T.S.E.!"

C. Aiken said the poem in *Art News* was "miraculous." J.H.: "Delmore has such a wonderful way of telling stories"; "Chiappe is a great admirer of yours"; "Wohlstetter a great admirer of yours." M. Greenberg's wife on how Goodman circle thought I was right in some ways. "Most wonderful human being I have ever known" & "Leslie thinks you're a genius. Jane admires you very much"; "Kenneth & Maurice have a special need for your approval." "The person who has thought more than anyone else," A.Q. & then Lynn Baker. Julie on exaggeration; Will's "I see [you] as you really are, as others see you." Will, the Agees, F.O.M., Saul on my being very cruel to women.

(The female student who said, "I never knew anyone who knows as much as he does about life.")

"You can't trust Delmore"—"One of your ruses"—"With Delmore, watch out."

Covici: One of the most gifted creative writers in America.

F.O.M.: He has so many ideas.

Gene Derwood [poet, painter, married to the poet and anthologist Oscar Williams]: Laughlin admires you very much & Oscar does, too.

The years in the country had the effect of intensifying the tendency to withdraw from others which had been strong before then and quite marked whenever I went somewhere—as at Kenyon & as in Chicago. It was this tendency that Bill Van K[euren] & Wallace Dickson perceived in Cambridge. "There are lots of people who would like to know you. It's something in you." Recurrent depressions were often the starting point, and then alcoholism continually made matters worse between 1941 & 1949.

November 18

Schedule for week of Nov. 18, 1957

Monday night—dinner with Dwight.

Send "A Colossal Fortune" to Ransom?

Write to Fulbright Commission.

Write to Donald Dike [the late Donald A. Dike was a professor of English at Syracuse University and the editor with David H. Zucker of the *Selected Essays of Delmore Schwartz* (the University of Chicago Press, 1970). Professor Dike was influential in Delmore's employment at Syracuse during the last years of his life and his retention despite sporadic breakdowns.]

Get top coat & haircut.

Call Potter and use car as pretext?

Pay some bills?

Get Jones's book at post office.

Try to write or rewrite Hedy Lamarr story for *Playboy*.

—Another change of address? Mayo?

. . .

Call Wm.?—try "A Colossal Fortune" on *PR* or get a book to review from them, from *The Hudson Review*—[editors] Morgan? Bennett?

Stop drinking every night, even if there are social occasions when I do drink.

Send light verse to Howard Moss at *The New Yorker*.

Call Chiappe—Columbia.

November 20

Yesterday was another poor day—except for a brief period early in the morning.

When did this blocked or depressed period begin?

Was it really at Mt. Sinai on the third or fourth day, or was it on the train to Boston? Or in South Sudbury, when nothing in Henry Miller's novels made the kind of pornographic sense which his writing had at other times? Perhaps this is a reactive depression which Dexedrine, liquor, and fury delayed. Certainly it was well under way on the Sunday when I returned to W. Twenty-third from W. Twelfth & stayed in the hotel.

February, March, April, and part of May 1955 / Two weeks in Sept. 1955, Oct. 1955, two weeks in Nov. 1955, and then, last fall, in Oct. 1956 & again during the last two weeks of Jan. 1956, and much of Feb. & March 1956.

November 21

Soon Mrs. Manning descended to the kitchen, where the children neglected the breakfast they would have otherwise been making. After expressing her displeasure that the breakfast was being forgotten, Mrs. Manning surrendered to the charm & the excitement of having a new child in the household.

The children had been born two years after each other, and until the birth of William Wordsworth Manning there had always been a baby in the family. It was William who alone failed to occupy this loved & familiar role for a long enough period. He had disappointed everyone save his mother when, after a tantrum, he was taken to the university psychological clinic, where the doctors soon discovered that he was a genius, first by talking to him and then by . . .

❁

Candida Manning—called Candy by all but her mother, seventeen, and the oldest of the Manning children—discovered the infant as she opened the black barred basement door and stooped to get four bottles of milk. The child had been set in a bassinet next to the milk, and Candy, lifting the child up and forgetting the milk, exclaimed in delight: "A baby! A baby!" She ran back into the house, bearing the child up the first stair and at the head of the stairs crying aloud to her brother Daniel and her sister Linda, both of whom had been getting dressed when Candy descended for the morning milk.

Soon all six children were stamping up & down the stairs in jubilant excitement over the advent of the new child.

"HI" ["Hartford Innocents"]. Candy's honeymoon in Bermuda / Jamaica / Negroes again.

[The following is a reference to the summer of 1951, when the faculty of the Indiana School of Letters was invited to meet and talk with Alfred Kinsey, noted sociologist and biologist, famous for his studies of human sexual behavior.]

Kinsey—looked like a famished otter / Old stoneface / Insomnia / lined wife, pres. (captain) Indiana hiking society / knitting needles. Caroline [Gordon] Tate's query, Kinsey's answer: Yes: if I don't say I'm against it.

End: Candy is interviewed five years after by a N.Y. writer—who fails to get a story out of her—sends in his abandoned work. ["The Hartford Innocents" was published in *Successful Love and Other Stories*, Corinth Books, New York, 1961; Persea Books, Inc., New York, 1985.]

November 25

Tragedy is not something heretofore unknown to others. Nor the downfalling, nor the melancholy—and again and again, I have come back, out of the pit and the catacomb / After the fear each time of final loss & the obsessed concern with the passage of time.

Debts & involvements / Now, not as before / Never so lacking in funds & friends / But—in the past—the tendency to drink far too much was a greater . . .

Undated

The motive of all dream is not, as Freud maintained for many years, "wish-fulfillment" or hallucinatory gratification. So many dreams are nightmares or, at any rate, so ridden by anxiety & dread that Freud himself, attempting to explain unpleasant dreams, interpreted [them] as governed by masochism, a desire for punishment, or . . .

November 27

What has been & is happening to me? Why have I become depressed to such an extent that it is difficult for me to find anything interesting for more than a few minutes at most? The conscious is tied down to one subject, and returns to it again & again. The psychological causes may or may not be sufficient to explain the depression as a block (fury & resentment, anger, rejection, guilt). But they did not operate in July & August as they have since about the middle of October (summons server). The block was in operation after I had been in Mt. Sinai for the first two days—throughout August I was very active, excited, and voluble.

November 29

Thurs., Nov. 28. Thanksgiving dinner at the Hanlons'. Mrs. Light & Arlene's sister, sixteen. Howard Hart high on marijuana. Only eight D.s [Dexedrine]. Robert Cass.

Weds. Nov. 27. Almost a whole pint of gin before dinner & the rest of it in the middle of the night & five or six s.t.s.

This has been going on since what day in October? It had begun on Halloween, when I went to dinner at the Schapiros'. It was probably under way long before that, at Mt. Sinai, during the third & fourth day that I was there, when the immediate excitement of getting out of Bellevue ended and I did not have any D[exedrine] to keep me charged up as I did when I left and went to the Cartaret the next morning. Where did I stay that Sunday night? Gray?

"I have nothing else," she said, after asking me if I liked the shoes she was wearing. They were pinched & looked like bathing shoes, and when I told her that I did not think they looked very well on her, she became very annoyed.

"If you feel talkative"—"I can't tell you not to go to Germany"—"Mrs. Ames says that you're such a dear" [Elizabeth Ames, director of Yaddo]. "The Fosters said you were wonderful at Syracuse"—"Polly Hanson [poet and executive secretary at Yaddo] says she is in awe of you, she admires your poems so much." I said: "I used to like to live in the country but I don't anymore." "A.Q. is very polite & absolutely hostile to me—her young man has good manners but nothing else."

"I don't think you talked too much at Mrs. Ames's." (Irish whiskey right after & just before dinner.) "Sicily & the painter (What is your social position?)."

"A.Q. has no idea of her own motives or the reactions of others. She does have a social manner."

"I did not choose my father."

Argument about coffee: after she had decided, she said she was very nervous. The first morning, perhaps because A.Q. had impressed her, she offered to get the coffee. She [Elizabeth] went swimming with lover boy & others—and then with him alone?—and then she called off a swimming date with lover boy [Leonard Wolf].

Discussion of American dollars:

July 6th: wanted Kenyon checks sent to Flemington immediately.

Did not offer to take me to Syracuse, or tell me not to go: and was not present when I returned at 7, right after dinner. [Delmore drove to Syracuse to give a lecture and was upset when he returned that Elizabeth had walked into Saratoga to buy cigarettes with the musician and composer Gordon Binkerd.]

Gordon Binkerd's Symphony: which excited her so much.

Did she speak to Cowley [Delmore's editor at Viking Press] of what she planned to do? Malcolm? Cowley? will help you.

"You have an admirer." "Is L[eonard] W[olf] a good poet?" This was when I had returned from Syracuse—or perhaps the second day. When I told her that he was not—that [his work] was characterized by an abstract sensuality like her stepfather's paintings, she looked distressed. Then asked me where I had seen his poems—another kind of look of distress when I answered *The Hudson Review*, and an affectation of dismissal when I said: "You seem to be quite interested in L.W."

She said L.W. was not intelligent, but jumped from topic to topic, and one of the days after S[yracuse], she denied that he was amorous!

Her face fell & she lost interest when I talked of the girl at S. who was unable to write because she wanted to write only of her relation to her mother.

Efficiency about departure, letter to Spender—new tire.

Tues., July 16 [probably day of Delmore's return from Syracuse]. Mrs. Ames thought she had seen E. go by—to play croquet—and sent [author] Leonard Ehrlich's young niece to get her. But she did not return until after 10.

She was eager to stop at Saul Bellow's and perhaps because it would then be easier to stay in New York (come to), or perhaps so that I would have some friend to call upon!

She had written to H[ilton] K[ramer] about getting a show to review & perhaps he was one of those she called. ("She left me a number to call.") Leslie [Katz] twice.

"Have you been taking a lot of Dexedrine?"

Visit to Gruenthal (Picasso show) in June: letters to Josie & father.

She wanted me to get my birth certificate before Yaddo— She expressed no desire to stop in Woodstock.

She argued against accepting the L.C. [Library of Congress] Lecture (on May 21). [Delmore's lecture "The Present State of Poetry" was delivered in February 1958 and was published in *American Poetry at Mid-century*, Washington, D.C.: Library of Congress, 1958.]

The world as will & as idea. Aesthetic attitude, contemplative attitude.

What is the difference between the sunset in the sky & the sunset in a painting? A living face & the same face in a photograph & in a portrait? The singing of a bird & the aria in an opera? Conflict in actual life & conflict in a novel or a play?

The work of art is bounded. It has a beginning, middle, and end. It can be repeatedly experienced (a lake, a view, etc. can also). In fiction we see more of what is happening than in actual experience, save when it is a memory, and not always then. In experiencing works of art we become the music, the poem, and the admired building, the comely statue and the vivid painting. Our sensations are sensations which have already been scrutinized and organized by another human being: i.e., our sensations have already been experienced, discriminated, selected. Our ordinary sensations come upon us diffusely and in disorder, or at a lower degree of order, or an order determined by practical need . . .

In ordinary experience, the attention of a human being is determined by practical activity and [a] practical goal—by unconscious motives & feelings. [Therefore] it is—which is equally important—involved in the activities of others, the passage of time, the continuum of space (in the city, in the street, in the country, or in the field, by the lake or upon the mountain): there are accidental encounters, unavoidable disorder: i.e., a good deal of what occurs is isolated, unrelated, and unconnected: motives, purposes, and states of mind are not immediately and directly present. In a w. of a. [work of art] nothing is isolated, unrelated, or unconnected . . .

Art as the conversion of experience into consciousness per se: ordinary experience, the state of being of reading a book, etc.

The object of art is more organized than ordinary experience . . . [It] is set apart . . . i.e., it is in a frame, performed upon a stage, printed upon a page, played by an orchestra. The o.a. [object of art] is rooted in conditions of its own which free it from the conditions of ordinary experience: it is not in itself subject to growth & decay, the successions & changes which occur from hour to hour during the waking day: the o.a. is an experience which has already been controlled, mastered: it has been made available to consciousness: it has been made consciousness.

(Sunset, early-morning light, lakes, countrysides, views, summer, snow / love & love poems / names & nicknames, photographs, souvenirs, tombstones, carved hearts, memorials.)

What are the necessary conditions—the assumptions about the nature of existence—which must be made so that the reader or beholder can give himself to a work of fiction?

S. T. C[oleridge]: Temporary suspension of disbelief (the sustained positive affirmation of belief)—identification & identifications —characters as types, symbols, and as possessing a typicality—

What is happening to the imaginary being might very well happen to (a) me, (b) those I know, (c) all human beings.

What has happened (is happening) is not so accidental that it may not happen again.

Fiction is more philosophical than philosophy—Kierkegaard.

The visions of the visual—the painter's realization through painting of a certain way of seeing.

Names, carved initials / ghosts, fairy tales, gods / inferno.

Expression, possession—description as possession / Daedalus, Castorp, Bloom, Swann, Prufrock, "A Lady," Anna Karenina, Pierre & Andrei.

Carved initials, names & nicknames are externalizations of inner feelings. By this means the inner feelings are made available (viable) to consciousness—become objects to which consciousness can return at will.

Undated

Behold how the dream
Meets the future's
      Guillotine

"Razumovsky Qu[artet]"
Brandenberg Concerto
Goldberg Variations

Behold how a child with a piece of chalk
Can inscribe upon the sidewalk
Meanings far more comprehensive
Than the Milky Way—for all its immensity

Max Jacob
"I saw the old rag man
      Whom I do not know
& I gave him a noble
      & famous name:
          Dostoevsky"

Love is destiny: or, as the poet wrote long ago: "Call us what you will, we are made such by love."

Most human beings think love is extremely interesting & important. I myself often, looking upon the lives of other human beings, said to myself, Love is Destiny, and called to mind sayings and sentences which had or seemed to bear the same meaning. Just as the proverb says that love makes the world go round, so the poet of Hell & Heaven speaks of the love which moves the sun & the other stars, describing the universe itself and his own experience. Another witness, in another century, said, or seemed to say, the same thing . . .

December 1–3

> Another day has gone away
> Gone to dusk a winter afternoon
> As cold as a lake shining
> In a looking glass—

Sun., Dec. 1. Luigi's, Broyard's speech.
Nov. 30. Copying all day. Beckett.
Tuesday, Dec. 3. Anatole Broyard on the telephone & Bob MacGregor in the Eighth St. Bookstore during midafternoon.
(On Sept. 20 I was still going along fairly well.)

December 5

Still another day of emptiness—as empty without effort as yesterday was, with effort—the effort of copying & then of rereading and trying to revise the draft I wrote so quickly in July 1955. / Obsession continues obsessive. But there are small changes which may be the beginning of a RADICAL CHANGE—since the desire which appeared in so many dreams for weeks is wholly undesirable when I think of it while awake.

It will be five months in a few weeks: which may be enough to be the beginning of getting to the point where what occurred last summer no longer takes up so much of my mind.

I tried to read *Time*. My eye jumps all over the page.

December 10

> The motion & the lineage of the river's riverhood
> Was hidden at a source & in a cause
> Neither the sun itself nor the moon itself
> Controlled or touched—

Shackleton: The study of an intense egotist in search of stability. The world has always contained astonishing founts (amounts) of physical energy.

> When mental & emotional energy
>   are bound
> (with equal explosive force)
> within one skin—
> When pride & ambition,
> Charm & truculence, poetry & rhetoric
> Call the discordant tune—that
> Trouble starts & continues
> [. . .]

December 12

> The heart of another human being
> Is like a dark heart: and the heart
> Of a young girl, above all
>
> Who can command
> Another's heart: who has ever
> Commanded another's heart?
>
> Here hearts are tried
> As gold in the fire
>
> Give all thy heart
>
> The very heart of loss

(Tyranny, irony, litany.)
Bluebloods are seldom full-blooded.
(Sallacci from *KC*! 6.7.55): Are we men or are we moose?
A great deal of love / Is lost in tennis.
Sitting Bull has been standing up / Next to an established cigar store for a long time.
Lux begat Thomas Alva Edison.
"God shave the King."
Nothing is lost / Nothing is ended.

> We are now
> In New Bedlam
> Full of radios!
> Broadcasts day & night
>
> The bondage of ambition
> Chained to hope & to hopes

Undated

Dostoevsky: Almost every reality, though it has its immutable laws, is incredible & improbable.

"A dark shadow seemed to have passed over his face."

"There's nothing like a mystery. A mystery! A mystery! And do you remember, Prince, who it was who proclaimed, 'There shall be time no longer'? It was proclaimed by the great & mighty angel in the Apocalypse."

December 17

When I try to remember what happened during 1931 and the five years after 1931, I often have the same feeling as when I think [of] the years before the twentieth century: the feeling that I did not live during that time. The reason for this feeling is fairly clear: so much which no one expected has occurred, so many radical changes have transformed life in America, that I must make a deliberate effort of imagination to regain the years when those I knew & I myself were in our first youth—still boys and girls, and still so young that most of us were sure that most of our hopes would be fulfilled—fairly soon . . .

Money is Life / Never despair / Accept your limitations & forgive yourself.

Each of us naturally thinks of himself & herself as an individual, as unique, and as separate & different from & apart from other human beings at least part of the time, when we are alone or in sleep's underworld. The reason that this sense of the self is universal to one or another degree is clear enough whenever we are in a public place, among strangers—in a great city, for example, in one of the hotels, or in railroad stations or in the coach of a train. The very nature of physical being is vivid evidence that each of us is an individual— separate from all the others of our kind. But this impression is profoundly deceptive and in the end essentially false. It is an illusion and it is a delusion. Each of us, at any moment whatever, exists as in the solitude of a railroad coach: there are other passengers seated behind us, next to us, or ahead of us, and in coaches ahead or behind the coach in which we think we sit in solitude: the others who travel with us at every moment are those we have known—not only our parents, brothers & sisters, but our friends, too, and, equally perhaps, those we have hated or who have hated us, injured us, excited sorrow or scorn in us.

December 18

Have we not paid
Death's blackmail
At duskfall & before
The Phoenix morning

Ambition and hope
Have been among us
Inhabited our houses
Not as guests, children,
      or ghosts
[. . .]

K[ilroy's] C[arnival]

Where will I be when this [is] over? What will have happened
to me? How many teeth will I have? How many Yankee dollars?

It is commonly thought, in certain circles, that all human beings
in America who are not Anglo-Saxons are unquestionably Negroes.

Will I ever again seem or be the kind of a writer I seemed to
others, sometimes (perhaps to some even now) (although I do not
know).

The fundaments of the Impressionists (Expressionists).

I need that like I need a hole in the head.

I need that like a mouse needs a hatrack.

December 21

Yesterday was
Another very poor day—
After I had walked to
8th St.—Fourth Ave. &
Then to 14th—in
A pouring rain—

Undated

I called you, decided to consult you first, when I had funds, so
that, if you do not want to handle the case, I can give the case to one
or another of the attorneys who have been recommended during the
past few months.

And then, too, in addition to saving valuable time for both of us,
this written account may make it much easier for you to question me
about what is most important legally when I see you.

To begin, then, with the background which may [not] be as
relevant as I think, I was given a *Kenyon Review* award in Jan. 1957.
The funds for the grant are provided by the Rockefeller Foundation,

and three writers are chosen each year. [These] grants . . . are explicitly intended to enable writers to devote an entire year to a particular project . . .

Shortly after, in Feb. 1957, I was offered a Fulbright Award to teach American Literature at the University of Berlin during the academic year of 1957–58. I did not want to accept this, since it would interfere with the specific purpose of the *Kenyon* award, but I did so on the advice of the psychiatrist whom my wife had been seeing for several [years] and who had repeatedly said to me that I ought to try to get my wife as far from her family as I could, for reasons that have to do with her relation to her family, particularly her stepfather, long before I knew her.

In January 1957, my wife also began to write reviews of new paintings for *Arts* magazine. Since we were then living in N.J., this involved her coming and staying in New York for three days each month. (In N.Y. my wife's behavior had been increasingly strange for some time.) When in May 1957 I was invited to give a lecture at the Library of Congress in Jan. 1958, my wife became violently (incomprehensibly) angry, but despite the fact that giving the lecture meant coming back to America and then returning to Berlin, I felt that I must accept the invitation because it was a considerable honor . . .

During the previous eight months, however, she had told others of her intentions—sometimes in writing, sometimes in conversation (to Gruenthal, to her mother, to her father). She had also withdrawn various large sums of money from our joint bank account. [The "large sums" were payments by check of overdue bills to the plumber, the fuel oil company, and such.] The money on deposit consisted of the sum given me by the *KR* as a fellowship to write during 1957, and of other sums I had earned by literary work.

Since the *Kenyon Review* award was given me specifically to devote an entire year to the writing of poetry, I did not want to accept the Fulbright Grant in 1957. It meant sacrificing part of 1957 to teaching and thus was contrary to the intention of the *Kenyon* award.

Undated

I have been told to write you [Elizabeth] what follows in the hope that you will consult a competent lawyer, show him this letter, and . . . Potter's advice & your own judgment have, at every point, made your legal position worse since last July. I have tried to delay taking any one of the several legal actions which your conduct since last Jan. . . . But I cannot do so much longer. I waited, thinking it was possible, though not very likely, that you would learn, be told to . . .

I would have been entitled even if you had not taken the steps you have . . . You and others would be liable according to law to one or another extent . . .

Professor [William] Rose [in *Heinrich Heine: Two Studies of His Thought and Feeling*] keeps to the middle way (deep appreciation, negative conclusions).

It is true, as he says, that Heine was extremely vague about the political significance & implications of the word "liberty." It was an emotional concept for him. And he once said that no one could grasp it who had not lost it, just as no one could conceive of spring who had not endured the rigors of winter. But however weak Heine may have been on the side of conservative political thought (and perhaps liberty is only a chimera) . . .

Nineteenth-century Liberalism / Iron Curtain / Hungary, Poland / the South, Civil Liberty.

. . . of mankind and the rights of man. The immediate result [of Napoleonic law] in the Rhineland had been the abolishment of the special status & Jewish disabilities which had restricted most Jews to the ghetto since the Middle Ages.

> Liberty is the new Religion
> The French are the chosen people
> The Rhine is the new Jordan
> Paris the new Jerusalem

> (Germans: Philistines)

> 1827:
> "The world is stupid,
>   Cold & full of
>   Dead violets"

Thérèse marries. Schenk[?] calls Heine "The Lost Nightingale."

> "Liberty! L.! Thou art but
>   A restless dream."

1958

Pegasus is a dark horse
Every time out
A thousand-to-one shot
The windfall, the jackpot

Lumber, cucumber, number, slumber / Raise the rate, berate, debate, pate, prate / Clean the slate, dissipate, masturbate.
Is sex coeducational? Let's make sex coeducational.

Delmore Schwartz
Gulled-pillaged
Pillaged. What was the
Use of all the feeling
Of being anxious
About the future?

It is either easy or impossible

Crackpot & Jackpot
Cat's pajamas—pig's valise

The blue blood flowed beneath
A well-bred enervation—fugitive
Seeds of sesame   opal
Moods / of / mascara—masquerade
                —The raided heart—
    (First blood: new bud)

[Summer Knowledge: New and Selected Poems, 1938–1958, was published by Doubleday in 1959; and a new edition by New Directions in 1967. Following is a tentative list of titles.]

Undated

Darkling Summer, Rumorous Dusk, Ominous Rain, Sarah, Jacob, Summer Knowledge, A Little Morning Music: (1) & (2), At a Solemn Musick, The Fulfillment, Vivaldi, [word?] Yorick, Swift: Presto, Gold Morning, Sweet Prince, Seurat, Oh, [Child] When You Go Down to Sleep & Sleep's Secession, The True-Blue American, The Would-be Hungarian, I Waken to a Calling, "I Am Cherry Alive," the Little Girl Sang, The First Morning of the Second World, The Brilliant Summer, Mounting & Ominous, The Conclusion, The Sequel, Hölderlin, Baudelaire.

Candlemas (Darkling) Summer,
Rumorous Dusk, Ominous Rain
I
A tattering of rain and then the reign
Of pour and pouring-down and down,
Where in the westward gathered the filming gown
Of gray and clouding weakness, and, in the mane
Of the light's glory and the day's splendor, gold and vain,
Vivid, more and more vivid, scarlet, lucid and more luminous:
Then came a splatter, a prattle, a blowing rain!
And soon the hour was musical and rumorous:
A softness of a dripping lipped the isolated houses,
A gaunt gray somber softness licked the glass of hours.

[These three lines are penciled between the two stanzas:]

The stone of autumn shone amid the summer's violen[ce]
Dusk we are to dusk returning
By candlelight we saw the heart of fall
II
Again, after a catbird squeaked in the special silence,
And clouding vagueness fogged the windowpane
And gathered blackness and overcast, the mane
Of light's story and light's glory surrendered and ended
—A pebble—a ring—a ringing on the pane,
A blowing and a blowing in: tides of the blue and cold
Moods of the great blue bay, and slates of gray
Came down upon the land's great sea, the body of this day
—Hardly an atom of silence amid the roar
Allowed the voice to form appeal—to call:
By kindled light we thought we saw the bronze of fall.

(London *Times Literary Supplement* with / *N.Y. Times* accepted 4.29.58 / + The Phoenix Summer).

[*This poem appears in* Selected Poems.]

May 15

Monday: a thrilled voice.

Sat., May 10. A.Q. I was extremely nervous and startled to be nervous: A.Q. looked more than the thirty-eight she is (+1), her nose sharpened, her face drawn, her hands rough & uncared for.

She looked sick & conflicted.

Questioned as to whether I was divorced (after: Are you living with Elizabeth?). "I like Elizabeth"—

Where did you find this specimen of my handwriting?

On my desk: that's why . . .

Affirmed lines 1 & 2: as hers & from Cambridge; denied line 3 & line 4.

(Will you call me? Said something quickly—"Of course I'll call you"; & then: "I won't be on Twelfth St.")

May 17

Kafka (copied): &

Everything is fantasy
Family, office, friends, street
Everything is fantasy
Whether far off or near
Woman is fantasy:
But the most immediate truth is this
That you are pushing / your head
        against the wall
    of a windowless & doorless cell.

The rigid delimitation
    Of human bodies
    Is terrifying.

The marvel,
The (insoluble) riddle
    Of not perishing
    Of silent guidance.

(Providence: provenance)

Sisyphus was a bachelor.

June 8

Week of June 1–8. Spoke to Schlomo Katz, [founding editor of] *Midstream*. Contract from Doubleday [for *New and Selected Poems*].

Sun., June 8, Sat. 7, Fri. 6, Thurs. 5—Weds. 4 Anne [K., a new close friend] in Providence / The White Horse [renowned West Village bar]: Marshall Allen: You are a screwball. Your problem is that you have no problem. Tues. 3. Lunch with Gene Lichtenstein, one of the fiction editors of *Esquire*. Mon. 2. Story accepted / Maxwell / Dwight / Dinner at Pappas.

Sun. At work all day on an explanation of "The Track Meet."

Sat. Quarrel with Anne. Irritated by Dexedrine & misplacing of letter.

June 15

Sunday. Awake at 6—at A.'s. Quarreling and quarrelsome: after complete numbness the night before and all of Saturday afternoon. "Discontinue the relationship, since so much hostility exists and is bound to grow." Bob Hartle came unexpectedly.

Saturday, 14. Dulled and dumbed all day long—

Friday, 13. Hung over.

Thursday. Awake too early, blocked, and everything far too difficult to do without forcing myself.

Ronnie [Bissell, a new friend who is referred to frequently]— Pleased by choice of restaurant—someone else—"But not really involved"—

Bank, shoes, haircut.

Too nervous to go uptown to see [William] Maxwell [of *The New Yorker*] about proofs of story.

["The Track Meet," was published in *The New Yorker*, February 28, 1959.]

Reginald Law's comment at the end of "TM" ["The Track Meet"] should, I think, at first surprise & perplex the reader in the same way as I the writer in writing it was perplexed & astonished, since . . .

When the reader comes [to] the paragraph in which the Englishman says to the narrator, "What [difference] does it make if it is a dream or not? —It is worse for you if it is only a dream," this should, I think, cause the reader genuine perplexity at first. But the perplexity ought to be curiosity, too.

The Track Meet (last week of May or first week of June).

Your attitude was the same when we discussed the news. You maintained that each item was a selection, and thus a distorted, one-sided version of experience. But each incident actually occurred and most of the incidents were more shocking than what occurred on the playing field. You dismissed the brutality of the news as an inaccurate, inadequate, or extremely one-sided account of experience, for the same reason that you discounted or dismissed the occurrences on the playing field, because it was extremely unpleasant and disturbing, but reality is sometimes more fearful than the most terrifying dream. You have used the superficial difference between what occurs in dreams and in actuality to sustain the soothing & pleasant version of reality.

Thursday, 12. "You're not really that successful"—"I wish I could ask you to stay." She had been to a cocktail party and returned in a taxi as I arrived.

I said that my first marriage had been spent at the movies and I had gotten married the second time in the way that, when a murder is committed, crackpots turn up at the police station to confess the crime.

She had not given up sex as her doctor told her [to]—and had kept the truth from her doctor, just as she had been silent about her dream, although she had spoken of meeting me at the White Horse & coming back here.

She did not want to speak of her age except to say that she was "not yet thirty."

I began to be depressed or blocked sometime in the last week of May or a little before then—the first time, probably, was when it was so difficult to write a letter to William Burford—or even before then, coming out or up erratically because of good news—as when *The New Yorker* took my story—I was going down on Thursday, May 22—when I went to Princeton & the farm & had so little to say—it was just on Tuesday & Wednesday that I wrote, with much difficulty, the addition to "The Track Meet"—and it was during the next three days that I tried to write a letter of explanation for Maxwell: so it has been three weeks at least, and perhaps more than a month— For the last day of genuine excitement occurred on Tuesday, May 20, when Howard Moss told me to call Maxwell—and after lunch with him, I met Meyer, Lillian, and Van den Haag. On Monday, May 19, I talked wildly and with passionate anger to Emily Scarlett [Elizabeth's mother]. No, it has not really been a full three weeks.

But I began to slow down before then, writing very little. (I had a hard time when [Elizabeth] Libby Reardon [a friend who worked for Delmore in selecting poems and preparing the manuscript of *Summer Knowledge*] was here and I tried to finish "The Pajamas Opera.")

The afternoon I had lunch with Alison—Sat., May 10th—was perhaps the beginning of depression or block. There was a loss of assurance during lunch itself and much nervousness and a feeling of horror that I had been so wrong: had I been so wrong? How did I happen to acquire the note? At any rate, a sense of rejection began on that day?

It was during the following week—or was it?—it must have been—
that I had dinner with Pat[ricia] Blake [translator and editor], and
she wanted to depart soon after dinner. It was on a Monday, the day I
saw Jason [Epstein] at Doubleday's. And it was some time during that
week or the week after—it was the week after, on Thursday, May 22
—that I had lunch with R.B.

June 26

Now the train is leaving New York, passing through the wornout
apartment slums of Harlem. Negro women are looking out of open
windows, leaning on their elbows, gazing at whatever passes in the
street.

The train slows, stops at 125th St., throbs.

A squeal: a lurch: creaking: the throbbing rises to a steady thud
of the wheels.

The Cardinal Hayes Hospital—a railroad bridge—billboards on
posters on apartment backs—

(A year ago today? & a year from now?)

He was going away from a bond which had become bondage. And
grown in guilt. He was going toward a region of excitement, where new
beings were & one girl pretty enough to—support pride?

July 21

Still in the dead depths—since the last week of May—May 22 or
May 23—perhaps, in another month?

Master, heaven does not concern itself with tedium.

There is a special kind of vain solicitude which merely weakens
what it would aid, all care and tenderness crippling the one protected
from the dangerous.

Possession, supercession, aggression, session, Hessian, question.

August 1–3

Friday. Howie Frisch [book dealer and a friend from the thirties]
—someone to talk to.

Saturday. Awake at 6—called at 9. The farm & the house. "Disturbing"—she was very upset: "How long were you married?" "It must
have been quite lonely for E. here." To the Clinton House. Tappan,
Nyack.

Then from 1 to 5 the gruelling search for a motel, a hotel, a place
to sleep, settling for Downing St. at last.

Sunday. 11. Friendly morning, love, shopping, breakfast, the park.
(Discussion of the night before.) The Tavern on the Green, two movies
—*The Adultress*, Zola's *Thérèse Raquin*—growing nervousness.

August 4

Now I feel lost again—as I did last November, and during the last two weeks of October, and during the first three weeks of January (until two days before I went to Washington)—the excitement of February, March, and April began to fade or subside when I saw A.Q. —on the 10th of May (it was a Saturday)— Everything began to be wrong right after that, but slowly, a little more each day.

Last week of June, Surowitz. Dennis, and then the Handlins in Cambridge and then the Hotel Astor (Fri. A[nne] K., July 4). Sunday, Provincetown.

Just one month ago tomorrow—on the Cape, Jack Cudahy, Catherine Holst, Mrs. & Mr. Lopez, Wm.'s friend Nate Bacon (colored & blind)—

At Dennis—the Cockney boy, the eighty-six-year-old landlady, Shirley Wood, the Tower, "*Attendez*," a "wrenched foot, limping: guilty about A."

At Syracuse: "Is it really true that James Jones got a million dollars from Hollywood for the rights to his new novel?" Dikes, Browns, Hoffmans.

August 7

Thurs. Called [William] Maxwell, who said that there had been no decision about the Ford grants—was amused to hear about Rita Hayworth's mustache (on a poster bill) & the views of the students of Creative Writing at Syracuse (that whoever drew the mustache above her upper lip, far from disliking Rita Hayworth, liked her far too much).

"I honestly can't help you," Maxwell said, and hoped that among my plans was another story for *The New Yorker*. He certainly did not sound as if I was going to get a Ford grant.

Called [Charles] Jacobs [lawyer], who thought that Surowitz [lawyer] might be ignorant not dishonest when he suggested that I borrow on my house—from N.J. bank—and made no mention of Oscar.

August 12

First visit to Yaddo, August 5—Sept. 1—Dec. 15, 1939.
Last visit to Yaddo, July 3—July 23, 1957.

August 15

Today, after the mail & after I had concluded that everything was over, Provincetown.

Thurs. Last night Vasiliki, Liz, Alan, Richard Nason [poet]. Too much to drink.

Weds. I called Dwight & Mike Liben [short story writer]: Mike's voice changed, I think, when I said I was the one who was calling. I walked away from Jay in Sheridan Square.

August 19

ACT ONE

Andromache: There will be no Trojan War, Cassandra!

Cassandra: I bet there will be, Andromache!

A.: The anger of the Greeks is justified! We will bundle their darling Helen and give her back.

C.: We will be rude, stubborn, intransigent. We will refuse to return Helen. And the Trojan War will certainly occur.

A.: You would be right if Hector were not here. But he is here, Cassandra. He has returned once again. I can hear the trumpets. Hector will certainly assert himself. When he departed three months ago, he promised that this would be the last war.

C.: It is the last. The next one has not yet begun.

A.: Don't you ever get tired of foreseeing, predicting & prophesying catastrophe?

C.: I foresee nothing, I predict nothing. All that I do . . .

[The above is from Giraudoux's *La Guerre de Troie n'aura pas lieu*.]

Zola's Camera

The creative artist who gains great popular fame may seem to contradict or complicate—this point: in fact, he does not, however intense his love of popularity, for unless each new work is a continuation—which is to say, an imitation & a repetition of his previous work—he risks his fame with each new work and sometimes, as with Shakespeare, Rembrandt, Melville, James, and Yeats, he loses.

Quote Yeats: *Responsibilities*: "Until my precious things / Are but a / Post which passing dogs defile / (Seeing that fame has long since vanished / Being but a part of ancient ceremony)." [This quotation from the "Closing Rhyme" in *Responsibilities* is inaccurate.]

Again the fallow periods in the careers of great popular writers & painters are inexplicable: if fame & success are taken to be primary motives, incentives & aims—

Zola demonstrates [that] the admiration of other human beings, although desirable & often desired, was not the artist's essential aim. Some, e.g., Stendhal, believed that posterity would confer posthumous fame upon them; others expected, or hoped, that the next generation would respond to their work—but the need which moved them cannot have been the impression which their work made upon other human beings—since more [often] than not the poems were unpublished, their paintings ignored, their novels unread.

(Melville & Rembrandt provide a contrast, since both lost their early fame. But one gradually ceased to work, while the other continued, like H. James.)

August 22

Today I went to see Charles Jacobs, the lawyer recommended by Oscar Handlin. He said very little & what he said was quite confusing. He spoke of Surowitz as perhaps changing his mind because of "later developments" & not wanting to continue the case for that reason. Lawyers, he said, are seldom bought off. The house would not, he thought, be mine merely through the publication of papers, since the title was joint. And yet, despite the infrequency of any lawyer being bought off, he spoke of Surowitz as being engaged in "legal blackmail." He thought I ought to allow S. a chance to continue—"See what he does in another two weeks."

I called S.'s office & his secretary said he was not yet back, would not be back until after Labor Day.

Everyone—Oscar, Mike, and Marshall Allen—were in favor of or recommended that I keep S. on the case.

Jacobs described the difference between withdrawal & being fired as having to do (1) with the sum he was paid; (2) his participation (unless he withdraws) in the continuance of the suit.

[The following draft of a letter contained many repetitions and false starts that have been omitted. Delmore had filed suit against Hilton Kramer, the editor of Arts, *for conspiracy and false arrest, as it was Mr. Kramer's complaint of intimidation and harassment that led to the police interviewing Delmore, who behaved so wildly that he was taken to Bellevue. The suit came to nothing, but legal briefs proliferated.]*

And various conversations since last March, on the phone or in your office, had the same meaning. At no time did you suggest that a legal move to secure title [to] my house would interfere with the suit for illegal imprisonment. And in fact you told me at one point that you had said to Gordon Potter that Elizabeth Pollet was in no position to contest a suit for the house since she had asked for a Reno decree. This should explain my impatience when I last spoke to you, early in July. Surely it was not entirely unreasonable to expect to get by July what I asked you to secure in March.

I can understand that the suit against Kramer may very well be prolonged . . .

H[artford] I[nnocents]

Candy: I'd rather have some man teach me than learn about sex by listening to the girls when they hold their bull sessions, after a hectic weekend.

Her mother had condemned her Yale beau, who came of [a] newly rich family in Minneapolis and who went to Yale, because he played "dirty hockey."

August 23

Hartford. R. Jarrell. See: *The Bennington Idea* by Barbara Jones. [Barbara Slatter Jones, *Bennington College: The Development of an Educational Idea*.] See: Women are here to stay (1938), twenty years ago.

Apple trees, a weeping willow, colonial houses of faculty, swimming pool & tennis courts. Play House or Assembly. Small classes, classrooms & conferences: individual conferences. President's office. The library, wooden benches, a shell bandstand (acoustics).

Lawns of the campus well manicured.

"On the table of the president's waiting room were copies of *Town & Country* & *Journal of the History of Ideas* and a little magazine that had no name." An umbrella stand (mahogany?) or hatrack, which looked like part of the *mise-en-scène* of an inexpensive restaurant thirty years ago.

Girls dressed in leotards, blue jeans, ballet slippers, skiing pants.

Nearby men's colleges: Lord Jeffrey, Williams, Amherst, Dartmouth. (Use Burford—Barbara.) One of the women says: "Are we men or are we moose?"

X: Had a black tongue (but a generous heart). "Thin-lipped & bloodless."

"Everything was blurred a little by attractiveness." Mary McCarthy: Mrs. Sorel.

She wore her black hair drawn tight as if it were a wig but it shone in glossy blackness, and looked alive as no wig ever did.

When she was amused or amusing, her smile was one in which her eyes contracted, almost closed tightly in a frown of delight and her wide mouth opened widely, showing the perfect whiteness of her teeth.

[Delight:] As one dazzled by sudden sunlight or as a young lady might look when she has been singled out among a throng of admirers and goosed by a matinee idol.

"Suffused in summer, blind in bliss."

President (Glennfrank) had a stuffed shirt & a canned mind.

Dogs: two French poodles. They understand French far more than most if not all of the teachers who conduct a guided tour of "great French literature."

In the evening, consciousness fills the emptiness it feels with fiction in one or another form: the fiction of Hollywood & of TV, the fiction of paperbacks, the pure fiction of music or the surrender, through choice spirits, to the suppressed, half-hidden fiction of the heart's infinite desire (for the Wild West, the South Seas, the Age of Chivalry, the Court of Louis XIV, or the absolute & immediate importance of Napoleon Bonaparte, Cleopatra, Genghis Khan, and Catherine de' Medici).

Lecture on Kandinsky & Non-Objective Art by the (Countess) Duchess Boulanger. Girls overwhelmed by references. How one must get to the fundament.

Defrocked history teacher: If you don't know the answer, say Asia Minor.

Ruel Wilson [son of Mary McCarthy and Edmund Wilson]: I am bored & Mother, too, is bored.

Emily S.: Some girl who walks & talks as if she were roller-skating, forever panting, forever careening toward & away from the others, and making with her presence the fresh sounds of steel upon asphalt.

She (who? the Baroness) lifted her head with slow majesty like a railroad opening & dividing—to permit the passage of a small tugboat which, for all its hooting, possesses a humility so immense & so absolute that the bridge, dividing, appears to be engaged in an overwhelming act of condescension.

Reactionary Instructor: I would like to answer as Lucky Luciano once did: "I was in New Jersey, shooting peasants."

"Had I been hatted, had I been gowned—"

Last night—Tambimutu [a poet from India and the editor of] *Poetry* N.Y.—wanted my address.

What prospect & what hope? I thought there was little enough or none until I came back from Washington last January 22 & had no sense of how I would be getting under way again. But the situation was different then & I had perhaps more claim on the sympathy of others than I do now, when I may appear to be flourishing because so many poems have appeared in print.

No word from Dwight—though I called him last week. Nor from Jason nor from Wm.

Thurs. White Horse. N[ancy] Shepherd snarled, "I can't hear you. We're waiting for someone—I'm sorry!"

The usual period of depression has been three months—last one began in the middle of October about a week after I came back from Boston with A.K. It had not really gotten under way until after the trip. But by the third week—on the night I visited the Schapiros it was really deep—and deepest of all from Thanksgiving Day until Xmas. I must have begun to get free, a little, while writing my lecture—and then, two days before going to Washington, I broke through, typing the little girl poem and "At a Solemn Musick." I was able to read a paperback on the train coming back from Washington—and once I had Marshall Allen's loan of $2,000, I was really out of the pit.

How I talked incessantly on the way to Boston & again, while there. It was a Thurs., the last game of the World Series had just been played—look up in *W. Almanac.* And Sputnik had been launched.

(Trip to Boston—still manic—Thurs., Oct. 10.)

Nov. 1, I moved from Hotel Carteret to 48 W. 12 St. It was a Monday—divorce decree arrived & Gordon Potter called. While I was at the Carteret, Meyer Schapiro called. During Nov. I had lunch with Dwight & found myself with nothing at all to say. A week after, I was too depressed to go to dinner at Dwight's.

I met Willie Poster [Greenwich Village writer] at Xmas, looking for a present for A.K. And again & again I walked into Anatole Broyard. Two social occasions: a party during Xmas week at Estelle Gehmann's & then, or before that party, the party at Wm.'s where guests were Hook, Anne Hook, Feitelson, Mrs. Leontiev, G. W. Arnold—and I was, Edna said, "so brilliant—"

It was sometime in the middle of January—as late as the third week—that Mrs. Scarlett's Xmas card arrived: and this was after I had said to Hanlon that I had received no Xmas card at all. During January, Oscar Williams & Anatole Broyard came calling, and there was another party at Wm.'s house—Sonya Rudikoff [writer and literary critic], Ralph Ellison were there, along with Norman Podhoretz & his wife, Midge, and H. J. Kaplan & Alfred & Anne [Birstein, novelist] Kazin, too.

I called Hook in Dec. about the N.Y.U. job & talked to Alfred about it in Jan. It was in January that I talked to Jay, who was very wary; MacGregor (whom I met on the street several times).

How I broke through when I met Jack Cudahy on the Cape: on May 23—it was a Thursday. I sank down in midafternoon, driving to the country & the house with the Hartles.

How long has it been since I last felt like eating dinner?

What prospect & hope for the immediate or near future?

1. Some legal change—either something done by Surowitz or by a new lawyer.

2. Ford grant.

3. Or getting sufficiently awakened to write something for *The New Yorker.*

4. A different attitude & a desire for final settlement on E.'s part: as soon as summer ends, then she may want to live in New York City & move about freely, see her friends & review art shows. But she may be working on a novel—or she may be in Europe, in San Francisco—or in some situation which frees her from any desire to get married again.

It was in late Jan. or early Feb. that I saw the Handlins and was so drunk by the time I had returned to 81 W. 12 St. that I fell down on the floor of the rooming house & found myself unable to get up. But it was joyous drunkenness—for I had been told about Cal's poem in *PR* by the Handlins.

Dr. Gruenthal: a visit & then at the party given by Norman Podhoretz.

"Are you surprised to see us?" Mrs. Gruenthal asked. I was so pleased I compared Gruenthal to Socrates. He had just said: "I don't know what genuine health is": & I said: "I've had many great teachers & the one who first said 'I don't know' was Socrates." Mrs. G. mocked her husband as Socrates by rubbing his forehead—he became annoyed and made her stop. It all occurred in conversation with Dwight & Dr. Gr. about *Life*'s Mayo Buckner. He had been in an insane asylum since five or six & Dwight, writing a letter to *Life*, praised his "noble silence" —or something of the sort.

S[herwood] Anderson was mentioned in Ph.'s letter. And it was full of meaningless coincidences which I had been seeing on all sides for weeks. One of them was Dwight's attack on Leonard Wolf, Yaddo's lover boy.

I forgot about the visit of Sandra Hochman [poet and novelist]— the girl who graduated from Bennington last year, writes poetry, and was on her way to Greece. It must have [been] the last Sunday of July —or the next to last—which would be right after I got back from Syracuse, July 20th or July 27th—much admiration of newly published poems—along with Jason, Mike Liben, Oscar Williams (?), Robert Hanlon, Bridget Murnaghan [poet] (who asked me, last night, why I was looking so unhappy), a sweet young thing who had met Josephine Herbst & been told by her how bright! I was & how I stayed up all of one night at her house, reading—she offered to get something for me, bring something for me, and she did go & get beer. She had left her number with her aunt, whom, after an hour, she went to meet downstairs for dinner.

I kept from consciousness while going back through the year the large amount of work I did in Feb., March, and April—and the help & difficulty I had with Libby Reardon. How I seemed to the Seville bartender, to be "one of those guys who ends up, if he keeps [on] like that, with a stone for a pillow."

And when I was already depressed, the luncheon with the young *Esquire* editor. The manic period stopped in the midst of an attempt to rewrite "The Pajamas Opera."

August 24

Yesterday dwindled into almost nothing by nightfall, although I did get some feeling of cheer and hope by writing a long summary— longer by far than any writing I have done for months—of the past three months & the past year, which might be evidence (like the handbook on divorce I looked at on Weds. & was able to read consecutively) that I am suffering from an emotional block more than anything else.

I succeeded in eating a real dinner, after the beers & only one martini—probably because I had eaten so little all day long.

August 26

"An Author's Brother-in-Law," "The Gift." Send out "Heights of Joy" to *Nugget* or get literary agent. Write to Ransom. Ask him for Indiana School of Letters job next summer—$1,500—minus.

Sell books? How?

August 29

"H[artford] I[nnocents]": A Choir of Innocence.

"This is priceless!" Ursula said joyously, clearly delighted. "It is perfectly priceless."

"What will President Goodknight do?" Catherine said gravely: for she was by nature serious & practical. "He must do something: And yet he has now been confronted—or surely he will soon be, your parents will certainly see to that—with a situation for which there is no precedent whatever—"

"And he has more trouble than he can handle in dealing with situations which are not without precedent," Caroline remarked, scorn and irony in her voice.

"Perhaps there is some precedent," Sarah [said].

"There is certainly no precedent for a student coming back to school with a Negro child," Ursula said, interrupting Sarah and speaking a little rudely.

August 31

9.1.57. Vasiliki Rosenfeld [widow of the writer Isaac Rosenfeld]: Don't tell anyone: I have two children & a job!

To Stanzioni [private detective]. How, except for Vasiliki, would it have been possible for him to have been briefed? On Saturday night (reason for banging on his door). Potter, Bellow, Kramer, Meyers. Call to MacGregor. Call to Vasiliki.

September 23

This morning alone & in bed
  Looking up at the dawn
I saw the falling year's ice sky, cold & gold
And thought and almost said
That I must die
The thought of death long since
  Lost the sovereign hold
It once possessed, the obsession & the dread.
  I thought of the dead.

October 6

"A Met[ropolitan] Gauntlet."

White Horse [tavern], dark horse, a hobby horse. "Chemical Mysticism." George Bernard, Rick Shaw. (As Hanlon carried Kathleen on his shoulders.)

October 9

> The pawnbrokers
>   Shall inherit the earth
> Or the undertakers & the electricians
> But not the disinterested
>   Peaceful loving
>   Musicians
> Who only bang the drum & hit the gong

October 18

Since Jan. 1, 1958:

1 book of poems / 28 poems, 29 +, 30, 31 poems, 32 poems (*Encounter* + 3. O. Williams).

1 new essay, 3 essays, 3 stories, 4 essays (Marilyn Monroe).

Accepted since Sept. 4: *Poetry* 4, *PR* 1, *NR* 2/3, *NY* 1 (1 p + 1 story), *M* 2. Since Jan.: 1 essay, 3 stories, *Com.* story, 11 poems + 2 *Com.*, 13 poems.

October 24

Suzy: Do you live around here?

Sloe eyes, brown hair, perfect angles, tall & sullen. Having the appearance of being slightly inattentive.

November 2

Neither R[onnie] nor A[nne] called today or yesterday.

What next? Who next?

When?

It is as if the month of December might be the beginning of marvels—hardly guessed—not yet dreamed. A falling off of work & spontaneity all week long—

November 3

Bank—455; + bills—310.

100—Synagogue, 110—*New Yorker*, 50—*PR*, 30—Brazil, 50–100— *Art News* = 340–390.

Doubleday certain 250, probable 250 +.

Poetry—100 +.

650–690.

November 5

Memoirs of L[iterary] C[ritic]

Thru the years I have had various adventures as a literary critic, bookworm, book reviewer—just plain worm. But few have been quite as astonishing & dumbfounding as what I came upon when I devoured paperbacks for about two years. At one point I consumed so many paperbacks that I had a hard time keeping myself a full supply from night to night. It's like other addictions—particularly cigarettes—one always dreads the poverty—however temporary—of running short, and one wonders how one managed to get along during the years before the addiction infected one [in] its insidious, malarial-like, hardly perceptible way. It has a stranglehold on consciousness long before consciousness has become aware of its growing helplessness, desperate need, and dependence. Indeed, a painful cure is necessary to get rid of the addiction to paperback fiction—and, as so often, the cure sometimes turns out to be worse than the disease. The Early Early & the Late Late Late Show on TV & a doubleheader on TV between the Giants & Dodgers can be just [as] all-devouring of time & all-enslaving of consciousness.

There are many interesting things in paperback fiction (sometimes the worse they are, the more interesting), though—it is almost needless to say—the interest does not precisely inhere in what the authors intend (working very hard but very fast) to be the genuine cause & substance of interest.

Undated

As the poet said—
I wonder by my troth
What thou [&] I did
Before we loved
　　　Drank & smoked
　　　Read paperbacks

He meant to return to nature
As a purely domestic animal

The rams' horns
Sound for silence
The standard of Zion is hoisted

"University of Life, Bad Art."

KC: The Chinese shall inherit the earth.

Hemlock, wedlock, wetlock, hammock, buttock, headlock, Yale lock.

KC: Guilty of free association: An hour has sixty minotaurs / Can't tell an owl from houris [?], a stripteaser from a nymphomaniac.

December 1

Boiling, sodden, sot, be sotten, sudden.

Gruenthal: She adored you. *Je l'adore.* Joe [Elizabeth's father's] letter: *Tu l'as trop aimé.*

No mail & no word, day after day.

Art News, Jewish Museum, *PR*—Wm., Surowitz, Ford.

Undated

I have been told to write you [Elizabeth] what follows, much of which you know, in one or another way; but which you may not know in relation to my intentions or in relation to the law.

When, as a result of an unmistakable frame-up, I was illegally arrested and detained at Bellevue, during the morning before this occurred, I wrote several letters and talked to several people, and, since there was no warrant for my arrest, allowed myself to be taken into custody only because David Bazelon, the only lawyer I could reach, told me to go. I was told that I was being taken to St. Vincent's, and when I was then [taken] instead to Bellevue, I sent word through Potter asking you to get me into an adequate hospital. Your answer, I was told, was that "Miss Pollet does not wish to do anything at present." The Bellevue Hospital records state that I was "oriented and cooperative" during the first three days, but on the fourth night I had a "seizure." It was not until March that I saw the records and found out that I had a heart attack & came close to dying. False information had been given about me at Bellevue, indicating that I might be epileptic and saying nothing of the fact that I had habitually taken sleeping tablets. The cause of the attack was the abrupt withdrawal of sedation; it would not otherwise have occurred, and it would not have been serious if I had not been put in a straitjacket.

The suddenness and brutality with which you abandoned [me] puzzled me, but hardly explained your sustained eagerness for months before then to get me to go to Germany. The laws of N.J. & N.Y. provide a legal separation for anyone who wishes to terminate a marriage. In a like way your unwillingness to give me title to the house combined with your obvious intensity about my going to Germany to make it quite clear that you [were not] simply interested in what the law provides, the termination of your marriage. Moreover, you had been warned by Dr. Gruenthal that I would not go to Germany, and that I would find out why you wanted me to go. And finally, the expense of getting a bogus divorce, which can be invalidated at any time, would have been sufficient in itself to indicate that you had a great deal to conceal.

I cannot [go] into much more detail without risking the prolongation of what is at best a slow process. What I can say, however, is that it is impossible for me to secure what, according to the law, are my rights except by taking a succession of legal actions.

Apart from avoiding all that may cause me to stop—it is possible to begin anywhere, with any person or incident—it is, I think, not only possible but in every way desirable, perhaps even necessary, if I might be exact & complete & make this record truly a history of love. The attempt not to stop, yet to reach precision and completeness & justice makes me think I ought to write . . .

The time when a four-letter word was the incantation, the open sesame to the heart of a woman prone to be chaste unto frigidity . . .

American loneliness (Violence & Desperation).

Only a Janitor's D[aughter] / But, boy, how she hauled ashes. (Rashes, cashes, mustaches.)

O ye Daughters of the Hudson & the Delaware.

Steamshipliner's D[aughter], Chimney Factor's Daughter / But, boy, was she well stacked!

Mood, crude, feud, lewd.

The People, sir, are a great beast.

Bang, bang yourself / Bong, throng, tong.

Drummer's Daughter / But, boy, how she could bang!

Huckster's / But, boy, how she could huck!

Cymbals, the "heavy emphasis on percussion" (concussion).

> From Mozart's Turkish March
> To the clangor of a Shriners' parade

Charade, masquerade, persuade, dissuade, dismayed.

Service, nervous, impervious / cat-tharsis, catastrophe, cat-elope, catkin / timbre—tone, color / September, ember, neck, nectar / curvaceous, orchidean, orchidaceous.

December 5

> *Cymbals*
> A majestic clash of cymbals
> & clang or banging rang out
> Used as the punctuation
> Of chants & alleluias

I Corinthians 13. "Though I speak with the tongues of men & of angels, yet have not charity. I am become as sounding brass / or a tinkling cymbal." But while cymbals ring, ting, ding, clang, bang, hiss, sizzle, and swish, they never do anything as measly as tinkle.

> Eve of snow
> The sky an intense gray
> The eve of snow sky
> An
> Intense egg white
> A boiling linen gray

December 6

Visit to Schapiros in the morning. $50 & promise of help—through Kaplan—"which you richly deserve." They have spoken to no one— they give their word that this is so.

At 2:30—R.B.—tears at reproach—invitation to dinner, quieted by poetry, beer, and reassurance that nothing is irrevocable.

White Horse at 6—until 8.

On Eleventh St.: Wm. wished to discuss Giant trade, and wanted to know what I was doing up so early & did not wish to hear about Blackmur.

On Weds., A.K. Wm. who, after giving his word that he knew nothing, said, "Maybe E. is working on *Arts*," and said also (telling not to tell anyone!) that Kramer had tried to get a job on *Commentary* during the early fall.

December 8

On July 22, 1957, Elizabeth Pollet Schwartz and I registered at the Hotel St. George in Brooklyn. At 8:30 the following morning she left the hotel ostensibly to secure my birth certificate from the B'klyn Board of Health. During the previous day she had insisted on coming to Brooklyn from Yaddo Estate, in Saratoga Springs, N.Y., although I was ill, to get the birth certificate so that I could apply for the passport I would need to go to Berlin on a Fulbright scholarship six weeks later.

She secured the birth certificate & sent it to me by special delivery with a brief letter announcing that she was not going to return to our home in New Jersey nor going with me to Germany. She gave as her only reason that . . .

My wife, however, said that she wanted me to accept [the Fulbright to go to Germany], giving as her only reason her desire to go abroad, which seemed quite strange & perplexing to me. But I did accept, since my wife was under a psychiatrist's treatment and he had said several times that my wife might benefit greatly if it were possible to live for a sustained period of time at a considerable distance from her family & friends.

How often does the termination of a marriage require that a husband go to Germany?

*[There is as much crossed out as remains in this very rough draft
for a poem.]*

> Let me / not
>   To the marriage
>   Of true minds
> When I remember how my years were / spent
> (Devoted to a promise)
> Ere half of manhood's summer had been passed
> Of how, because
>   I thought one's marriage vow surpassed,
> Or was the root . . . All other hopes
> When I remember the seven years which went
> Like a long dream believed to be entirely true
> And like a promise which if the intent
> persisted . . .

December 26

Gruenthal: I am sorry for everyone, including myself.

Sun. Packed—called Nancy—Howard [Moss] (nothing except to ask for some more poems).

Last night called Meyer about Kaplan: he seemed to fear that I would write him, asked me not to mention him, yet said on the other hand that he would probably be consulted by Kaplan.

Drunk by seven: called A.K.

K.C.: Paper Tigers write books.

If you don't have a dog, you can hide your bones & bonus: & write doggerel.

Those who live by the word / Will die listening.

Nothing succeeds like excess.

Those who are cagey live in a cage of fear & of dread—that others are equally treacherous.

Kilroy is trying to split the ego, experiments with peas & squares the circle for practice.

The ego is its own alter-Iago: Doppelgänger, that old Doppelgänger of mine.

Undated

Da! Nyet!

Pedestrian, equestrian / aviary & bestiary / amphibian / subterranean, Mediterranean / monastic, plastic, spastic, fantastic, elastic.

December 29

La Guerre de Troie / Sodom: In both plays Giraudoux's under-lying theme is the struggle with oncoming and certain catastrophe—the Trojan War and the destruction of the world.

Also in December (today), *Halfway Down the Stairs* by Charles Thompson.

The doom to one stratum—the lower middle class—of American society.

Undated

Tally since January 1958

Essays & Reviews, New or Reprinted: "Masterpieces as Cartoons," R[eprinted]; "T.S.E. as Int[ernational] Hero," R; "The Present State of Poetry," N[ew]; "Hardy," R; "The Nightmare of History," N; "Novels & the News," N; "Roethke," N; "The Fiction of Hemingway," R.

Stories: "An American Fairytale"; "The Track Meet"; "The Gift"; "Successful Love," R; *Kilroy's Carnival.*

Poems: *N.Y.*—(1) "The Dark & Falling Summer" (2) "Vivaldi" (3) "During December's Dusk" (4) "A Little Morning Music."

Com.—(1) "Jacob" (2) Poem (3) Sonnet (4) "Abraham" (5) "Sarah."

Poetry—(1) "The Kingdom of Poetry" (2) "Swift" (3) "The Brilliant Summer" (4) "Summer Knowledge" (5) "St. of Narcissus."

NYT—1, 2; *PR* 1 poem, 2, 3; *NR* 1, 2, 3, 4; *Mutiny* 1, 2; *Art News* 1, "Seurat"; *Prairie Schooner* 1, 2, 3; *Chicago Review* 1; *KR* 1, 2, 3, 4, 5, 6.

+ "Spiders," "To Robert Frost," "Poetry Recapitulates Ontology."

"Memoirs of a Metropolitan Childhood," "Love Stories," "The Bell," "The Hartford Innocents," "An Author's Brother-in-Law," "The Heights of Joy," "A Dish of Ice Cream," "The Fur Coat."

Unfinished: "An Encounter in Times Square," "A Piece of Wood," "Memoirs of an Editor" (1) (2).

Scenario and 20 pp. of *Kilroy's Carnival.*

Rewritten: last two pp. of "The Track Meet."

December 31

Alone—alone but free of all bondage to anyone but myself—on the last night of the year of 1958—save for the need of drugs only—having overcome many difficulties and the most difficult weaknesses & temptations—

Who knows—B U T G O D—what the future may hold—frustration, another foolish marriage. But both are less likely now that I have made so many mistakes—

(Thus A.K. & R.B.—both resisted.)

(Perhaps I ought to celebrate the New Year's beginning by taking—)

An untimely Death from not taking care of myself, working too hard and using too many drugs.

1959

January 3

Last night, at the White Horse, Bridget [Murnaghan] said she had sent me a telegram: "Did you get my wire?" But none has arrived. In the wire, she offered to serve the summons on E.

R.B. called; was having dinner with Sam; offered to come "tomorrow morning." "We both very well can't come," she said; the idea, I suppose, was to make me jealous.

Meyer [Schapiro] had no answer when I asked him how he separated Bellevue from what he called a conspiracy. He was silent & hostile, as he has been the last few times I've gone to see him.

This is the way he was each time I suggested an appeal to Kaplan. And it was only by going [over] his head that I succeeded—probably Meyer restricted the sum to $1,000.

Undated

Yesterday, when he [Meyer Schapiro] came to see me, he was full of questions about lawyers & what I would do if the suit against Kramer simply remained pending indefinitely. He offered to speak to S., just as, today, he offered to suggest a lawyer.

He is willing to admit—as Dwight was not—that Bellevue was a case of illegal arrest. But not that it was the result of any prior "conspiracy"—the cover-up of Laughlin & E. may be the result of threats, since M. was interested when I said Gr[uenthal] had been threatened by J. L. (I did not say: in 1953).

His & Lillian's [the Schapiros] willingness to suggest a lawyer.

How do you separate the two: Bellevue & conspiracy? Silence.

Standing up, cold & silent, at the end of an hour of conversation. As F. O. M[atthiessen] in Nov. 1939, when I came looking for a job at Harvard.

Lillian: It certainly looks like it. Two weeks ago: How did I find out about *Arts*? Friday: Who told you?

The Sunday before last Will refused to see me.

Now I must guard against renewed stalling: it is likely that it will be known that I have gotten $1,000 from [J.M.] Kaplan [Meyer Schapiro was instrumental in obtaining the grant, which was given through the New School]—Doubleday's advance may also be known—through Dwight at least—

("How do you find out about these things?")

Meyer's question about how I found out about *Arts* last week was repeated yesterday—which could mean (as several other questions suggest) a definite effort to help E. & J.L. Dr. Gr. may also be involved.

Meyer lied about (1) coming to see me before writing; (2) renewed efforts on his friends' part.

Another one of Meyer's peculiar questions yesterday: Had I gone to Jason [Epstein] & Random House about my novel?

Also his new interest in my lawyer.

Perhaps I am wrong to put off getting a new lawyer until after seeing Roger Straus on Wednesday. In any case, I must not underestimate S.'s capacity to delay & obstruct matters: the house has probably been . . .

Yes: must wait until after Roger—perhaps he will even question me about . . .

Yesterday—Weds.—at 11—Straus & Giroux both very friendly— and Giroux asked how much I would need for six months. Straus's doubts were based on my failure to finish a novel in the past—for Schocken, for example. And all might have gone well had I not asked S. after Giroux left, privately, to recommend a lawyer. "I'm chicken, Delmore," he said. "No, you're not," I said. Then, at the elevator, as I was about to depart, he said, "You may be right. Laughlin is / may be unpredictable." Although he had said continually, before then, that he could handle the matter. His switch troubled me as I left to come home —troubled me so much that I called R.S. at the Int. Bar. A meeting was going on—I waited there for him to return my call. When he did, after about half an hour, his "Delmore" was quite cordial—but when I said I would give him any assurance he wanted that an advance would not be used for legal expenses, he said: "Such a thought never entered my mind."

K.C.: Odysseus—Show me the way to go home.

Promiscuity is just around the corner / coroner.

Promiscuity is one of the most severe forms of at once frustration & optimism. Few human activities are influenced so much by the doctrine of the individual's uniqueness & the dogma of freedom in itself as happiness.

I visited Ronnie this morning in her new apartment. She had written scornfully and reproachfully of me in her journal as being very selfish & incapable of ever wholly understanding (or something like that) another human being. And [her psychiatrist] had said to her that I "was a marvelous artist but very independent" and someone who needed another person—a woman unlike her—to take care of him.

She seemed very cheerful—most cheerful of all in reporting Aaron Bell's [an old friend of Elizabeth's] comments—that all I said of E. was paranoidal fabrication, no money had been taken—there was no involvement with J.L. No matter what is or has been wrong about my behavior . . .

Gerty MacDowell, Cyclops. Paddy Dignam, Circe, Bella Cohen, Blazes Boylan, Buck Mulligan, the Englishman, Simon Daedalus, Eumaeus, the Sirens, the Bar Girls, the British Tommies, the Nymph, Zoe, the Accusing Women, the Priest.

1904–1914: ten years: Joyce is in exile. This is Joyce's return, like Ulysses, to his native city.

It is Thursday & it is much warmer after days of fearful cold & wind.

Anatole reported, last winter, that Tanya was in town & it is even possible that the announcement of an avant-garde film in which Jackie Matisse was appearing was intended to get me interested in another girl.

E.'s remark in March or April 1956—"I must tell Dr. Gr. that you said I would marry J. if I left you"—like his query: "She has never been interested in a rich young man, has she? She has never shown any interest in that direction?"—together with his: "What do you want [her] for, anyway?" and his careful lie about asking her if she had become involved with another young man ("I would not tell you if she were: but I did ask her & she said she would be afraid"). And, again, his insistence on California in May 195[?] (E.'s: Tell him that I am furious at him)—or possibly Cornell (as being out of reach) are further evidence, if any were necessary. Bellevue's cost: the cover-up by Phelps at Woodstock in Aug. 1947.

The same is true of J.L.'s buying *Arts* after Kramer had tried to get a job at *Commentary*.

Possibly—it is now Gillmor.

A job with *Newsweek*, as suggested by Meyer twice, may have its source in Gr.—

Surely, despite Roger Straus, who may [be] vulnerable in his social relationships, there must be someone who is beyond pressure & who will really help me—at least to get the house & then to wait it out.

If E. is involved with another man who has money, he is in jeopardy, too.

Last night I made a big hit, as we used to say on Wash. Hts., with George Hahn [business entrepreneur]. But a cot again. Annoyed Dick Bagley.

January 10

The death of others
Near to us & dear to us
Is death's terror
Is what terrifies us

The death of other human beings
Is far more important
Than one's own death
The experience of dying
Is—perhaps—the most revealing / clearest
Of all windows / views

Is this true? really true?

January 11

N. Y. T[imes], H. L. Matthews: A dictatorship is like a wild party in which a good time is had by the dictator & his cronies—and everybody else has the hangover.

F[innegans] W[ake]: The Authorized King James version of Anglo-Irish International Basic English.

April 3

Try Shawn—after Dwight's departure—in nine days—on the 24th. Ask Meyer to speak to Hess.

Write to Straus after D.'s departure.

TLS, 4.3.59: The changing of words by one another: "Metaphor is not simply the perception of similarity in dissimilar things but the changing of words by one another, and syntax is rich in methods of doing this."

April 4

Repeated: Has L. threatened the doctor?

Yesterday & Friday, Meyer's questions:

Have you gone with your novel to Jason Epstein at Random House? What will you do if your lawyer just does nothing? Why don't you get a job?

April 9

Straus / Lasky—Kaplan   quote / Proofs—page / Roseman / Mention Schapiro / Harrison / Relief / Lasky / Robert Lowell / Call Wm., ask for rent money until house is sold / *Art News* / George Palmer / Wallace Dickson.

April 13

Light & gas turned off. Finished correcting galleys. Wrote to Ginsberg.

Spoke to movers.

Visited Dwight—$150 (not $250) / Sid Kline & Louis Thompson —$10 + $1.

Cheered by "A Little Morning Music" in *The New Yorker*. "Rough copy" which Dwight let me take, but after taking a pack of cigarettes from me. "Seurat": [Tom] Hess [editor of *Art News*, which did first publish "Seurat's Sunday Afternoon Along the Seine"] no longer is sure that he likes the poem!

April 15

Bank, Con Ed.

Notebook. Dec.: The Present State of Poetry, *Kilroy's Carnival*, Vivaldi, During December's Death, The Mind Is an Ancient & Famous Capital.

Jan.: The Conclusion, *PR*. Essay in *Modern Literary Criticism*.

Feb. 2: The Fear & Dread of the Mind of the Others, *NR*.

Feb. 28: "The Track Meet," *NY*.

March: Abraham, Sarah, *Com[mentary]*, Sarah, *N.Y. H.T.*

April: The Nightmare of History, *NR*, Novels & the News, A Little Morning Music.

May: Four poems in *Poetry*, Roethke review, Seurat, Cupid's Chant, Gold Morning, Sweet Prince.

July: The Gift, *PR*.

August 22: *S[ummer] K[nowledge]*: New & Selected Poems, 1938–1958.

Nov.: An Am. F. Tale [An American Fairy Tale] *Com[mentary]*. Selected articles and stories.

Sept.: The Dark & Falling Summer.

July: Poem, *PR*; poem, *NYT*

May: Kingdom of Poetry

Thurs., 30. Broyard. Weds. 29, Tues. 28, Mon. 27.

Sun. 26—A[nne] K. Depressed, all over nervousness-making, worn out, told about R.B. by someone capable of "doing you a great deal of harm."

Sat. 25. Fri. 24. Dinner with Jeanne Adams [counselor at Institute of International Education].

Thurs. 23. A.K. Legal Aid Society. Won't lend you money. Weds. 22.

Weds. A.K. Quarrel, finished. Thurs. Fri. Jeanne Adams. Sat. A.K., Sun. A.K., Mon. A.K. / Anne Truxell's [painter] cocktail party, the Aikens, Claire MacAllister [actress and poet]. Café Renaissance: Beekman Towers. Virgin: does not excite me in the least, manager, home.

E. in acute poverty: Bosh, said Gloria Macdonald.

Thurs. Called Cal Lowell, spoke to Liz Hardwick. Wrote to Harrison & George Palmer.

Fri. $75 for *NR* review.

Sun. Take care of yourself. Be good to yourself. A.K., R.B.— nervousness, poor lovemaking, plus loneliness! cooped up, imprisoned.

Runaround from Ed Feingersh [photographer], Dick Bagley, Little, Brown & Co., Roger Straus, Helen Frankenthaler, Kyman (of Paul, Weiss, etc., "The Stevenson firm") (represents *Arts* & Leslie Katz & Jason Epstein), and from Rosenman, too, to a certain extent—as from Bridget Murnaghan, Marshall Allen.

Jane Lougée—Doubleday—Hess.

Call me, let me know what is happening: just worn out: someone who told me of Ronnie is capable of doing you tremendous harm: Hutchins?

Mary Aiken kissed me.

Selden Rodman [poet and editor] said that I looked more authoritative.

Undated

TLS: "Between the Dream and the Reality" [Between Reality and Dream," *TLS*, April 1959]: "I have been developing a few fundamental thoughts ever since I began to write—" [Miguel di] Unamuno.

KC?
How sweet it is to recall pain
      & unhappiness
In times of pleasure joy
      & fulfillment!

(Dante reversed q.v.)

[*The following comments refer to* Freedom and History, *the Semantics of Philosophical Controversies and Ideological Conflicts, by Richard Peter McKeon. McKeon was a Professor of Philosophy, History, and Greek at the University of Chicago.*]

The ideal possibility of a new understanding by the union of historical knowledge and philosophical fact is illustrated and demonstrated by the fullness and detail which McKeon gives to the concepts of love, truth, freedom, and imitation. These four key ideas have preoccupied Western society since Socrates: they have had a complicated and checkered career which is far from ended. As McKeon establishes each of these ideas in relation to important modern problems he shows that the need of philosophical activity is unending: it is a need which cannot be terminated or satisfied once and for all, but must recur like the necessity of being fed.

The virtues of Mr. McKeon's method—particularly his use of the history of ideas as the basis of philosophical analysis—cannot be overestimated, particularly when so much learning combines with so much sensitivity to difficult, urgent modern problems. But how popular can this new perspective become? Mr. McKeon himself wonders. And one must, faced with the denseness and close reasoning of his expository style. The adoption of this historical and philosophical point of view would mean a break with ancient deep-rooted modes of thinking which are natural, habitual, spontaneous, and above all convenient and useful. Human culture is now international and pan-historical, but there is little evidence that the human mind can take advantage of these resources to liberate itself from the labyrinth McKeon describes: To accept McKeon's perspective, the Surrealist painter would have to acknowledge that all painting need not be Surrealist. The existentialist thinker would have to admit that all other schools of thought are not verbalism and abstraction; the modern literary critic would have to recognize that his characteristic views are ancient recurrent fallacies. But if this desirable ideal is realized to any degree, it will be because of a book like this one; it will be because history and philosophy have been possessed, mastered, and united.

May 8

Thurs. 7, Edna $100, E. called her two weeks before. Weds. 6, Tues. 5 (label), Mon. 4—no again from Little, Brown. Sun. 3, Sat. 2, Fri. 1.

A reactive depression? to the way in which I can get nowhere with the lawsuit? and with the other sex?

Kaplan & A.K. / As it was last summer, probably, from the end of May until the 28th of Aug.—then there was some strong guilt about A.K. & R.B. & rage at Surowitz.

But the manic phase lasted so long this time—Sept., Oct., Nov., Dec., Jan., Feb., March & two or three weeks of April—roughly eight months.

David Slavitt [novelist] / money / Kermitt Lansner.

Partial concession by agreeing to sale of house?

May 14

Eight Dexedrine with a lift for an hour, during which I copied pages of Rilke. Then the bleakness and emptiness came back. I walked twice to the park, stopped, the second time, at the Riviera—Liz Cooper was there and her young shiftless friend Bill, and Wolfe O'Meara. And by 4 I had hurried to the White Horse, where I drank five, six, seven, or eight gin-and-tonics. Jeanne Adams came in and sat next to me and leaned against me. Later Zoe Broadwin—Harvard 1947—came in alone and greeted me as Delmore. But Jeanne kept me from talking to her, questioning me about why I was depressed. I argued with Dick Bagley [film maker] about Joyce—I was really arguing with some feeling he has about himself which he projects onto modern literature and art. Tom Clancy [folk singer, actor] defended Joyce, too, and then left me in the middle by praising O'Casey (whom I have not really read). I began to feel maudlin as Bagley left after buying me a drink and calling me "one of the major poets of the century"! And I threw up (as I had on Tuesday, in the morning) after taking two s.t.s.

May 15

And so it has gone again, all the dimness and all the grayness and all the numbness. Last year it lasted from the 22nd of May until the 28th of August, and in 1957 from the last week of October until the 19th of January. So many months of so many years in the pain of boredom, the disease of the silenced sensibility. Last December is unclear —probably a reactive depression. And this new depression may be more reactive than anything else: A.K. (April 17), the Legal Aid Society (April 24), J.M. Kaplan's second refusal, together with the cumulative effect of too many s.t.s & too much drinking. I pulled out of December very quickly when told I was going to get another $1,000 from J.M.K. And I wrote poems, letters, "The Bell," two good reviews. "Why do you want a pretty girl at your age?" Rutherford Goodwin asked me.

(Dec.: *Kilroy's C., S. of N. [Studies of Narcissus]*, "Vivaldi.")

May 17

Perhaps the worst is over—yesterday I thought I began to feel— as I walked to 47th St.—as I felt when I had a heart attack in April 1956, after being up much of the night and visiting Mrs. Kunitz [Elizabeth was living with Eleanor and her and Stanley Kunitz's small daughter Gretchen]. ("Jane & Leslie thought you had a heart attack," E. said—perhaps because Dr. G. had suggested this way of telling me of the dangers of too much Dexedrine & too little sleep.)

I had been awake since 6 and had taken eight Dexedrine tablets by 10 and had slept no more than five or six hours the night before.

This morning I woke at 7, but managed to drowse and half-sleep until 11, when I went out to breakfast.

A.K.'s reasons were perhaps the beginning of this depression— combined with anxiety & disappointment about the suit. I was very nervous on Fri., April 24, the day I went to the Legal Aid Society. "You're very nervous," said George Cummings, quite drunk, yesterday at 1, at the White Horse. I was unable to eat most of my meat-loaf sandwich.

I drank two whiskies at an Eighth Ave. bar & then took a sleeping tablet, came home, took another s.t., and drank a quart of beer.

Yesterday letter from Emily Scarlett, asking me to sell the house. [Elizabeth's mother had put up collateral to stop the bank foreclosing the mortgage.]

May 19

Friday, April 17 or April 10th, Sunday, April 19th. If it began then, then a month has ended, one-third is over—perhaps. For today is the 19th of May. It is a Tuesday—on Thursday I go to have lunch with David Slavitt at the Yale Club.

May 20

Washington Sq. Park
There is nothing in the park
The idle people
Sitting & gazing with unfocused eye
At nothing—save perhaps for the momentary ripple
When a girl's round hips waken forlorn surmise
[. . .]

May 24

Thurs. David Slavitt at the Yale Club: then Greenstein, and the document of sale signed. [Delmore signed an agreement giving Dwight Macdonald power of attorney to sell the house and stipulating the division of proceeds. Without this, no real-estate agent would proceed.]

This is the twenty-fourth day of May 1959. And the living death within me continues, untouched, finding no interest for very long in anything looked at or read. Nor in conversation. So it has been, again and again, after a manic rage & surge.

Yesterday & today I woke just before six o'clock. And slept yesterday afternoon between 3 & 6 with the help of beer & sleeping tablets. And after visiting Meyer in the morning. (At 6, I was very hungry and went out to breakfast and came back and dozed until 9.)

Every night between six & nine s.t.s—with cans of beer to get me to sleep & to get me back to sleep. And going to bed between 6 & 7 without dinner more often than not.

May 27

No appetite for lunch or for dinner almost every day. Loss of insight & loss of excitement—of almost every kind. The blear of boredom and unattractiveness over everything within and outside of me.

"Where is there an end of it?"

June 7

Jacob & Joseph

Joseph is in Egypt now: he is as I was in the pit of that accustomed depth & height of solitude, a stranger in a strange land—the monkeyland of Egypt—the land which is the gift of a river. And there again, just as before, the more he understands, the less he is understood & the less loved. This I saw, when I beheld the love which dogs & servants bore my brother Esau. This is what I saw once more that look upon his brothers' faces. He is no more a stranger in Egypt than he was passing among his brothers when he wore the coat of my most willing love—no more estranged than in the pit they chose, although he descends into the pits & forests of the dreams of others.

June 20

May 23–June 20: A biography of Kafka. O'Hara (Reddington, the Irish, guilt of the male, and Yale). Wolfe. Mark Twain's Letters. Henry James's *The Awkward Age*, 40 pp. A story by Somerset Maugham. A description of the Greenville trial by Rebecca West. *The Embezzler* by James M. Cain. Gauguin, Huxley, Kay Boyle, Babbitt—just turning the pages.

Thurs. night. Dwight in the afternoon: I can't.

A.'s return—the effect of the book upon her.

Fri. Coming up & out of the pit, if increasing nervousness is any sign: waiting all day long for the chest to arrive, in the sticky heat. A.'s outburst, in the morning, amid tears that she hated her father and what made it worse was that he loved her very much. To the Jai Alai for dinner—despite two martinis, I could not eat very much.

Sat. An argument at noon—"Can't make love on schedule," etc. Sweet Briar girl's story in the papers. Hilton Kramer on Waverly Place looking back three times, and looking, I thought, scared or troubled, at least, to see me. The intense feeling that the long depression was over as I discussed plans with A.

Noon. First time since June 16—almost complete failure.

Almost no sign of beginning of energy again. I think it was like this last August—the 23rd & then a drop until the 26th.

Whether we are at home—or far from home—we are divorced from the reality of the present moment—since it is a part of the unknown future which is gradually & slowly coming into existence.

The self continually secretly and hiddenly invents and augments that selfhood which . . .

Poetry is patient and immortal.

(Rich, niche, bitch, itch, kitch, ditch, switch.)

"As deaf as a yawn." "Happy tight."

Passionate friendships / Come & go.

> This is the day & the night
> The night & the day
> Of beginning once again
> Perhaps—

> *KC*
> Is it possible to be
>   destroyed by joy?
> (*Vive la France!*)
> Go away—deadness, deafness, emptiness

Dwight's letter, offer $9,000 [for the house].

The Quiet American. Last week Sunday night, *Dr. No*, Ian Fleming. *Judith* by Giraudoux—Sunday afternoon. Two paperbacks on Monday night; 15 pp. of *Antony & Cleopatra.*

July 6

It continues and continues, day after day—as it has since the middle of April: in two or three weeks, it will be three months of deafness & blindness and the loss of all the power of responsiveness & invention.

July 7

Today began as if perhaps I might be beginning to swing over but the feeling did not last very long—

And now, at 2:30, the same immense vacancy—after copying a page and a half of Rilke, painfully enough and after staring too much—fruitlessly.

July 8

Away! Away!
Let the day perish that I was born

To understand is not to forgive but to condemn.

July 14

A.K.: "Disgusting, weak"—no sunshine in your heart ("Do you think there is when you're not depressed?")—"gossip," "I may spend a few days with my family" (Answer: "By all means"). Smiled with pleasure—the pleasure of anticipation probably.

"We are not going to spend next winter here—I may. But not with you."

Vance Bourjaily, *The Violated*—bad in a pretentious way—save for two lines, a phone call in which a village girl says to a playboy (like Rubirosa): "Why does someone like you want to have dinner with someone like me?" and "The jackpot is always made up of bell-fruit."

July 23

Again, another dragging and empty day; in the morning I talked to Dwight on the phone and he told me that he had not heard from E.—a story at variance to Gloria [Macdonald]'s saying, last Friday, that D. was writing to E. He also said that he would talk to her & that the price did seem low. I read as much as I could of *TLS*: then I shaved, bathed, tidied up, went to the bank, got my other coat from the cleaner's, brought a jacket & a pair of pants to the cleaner's, bought *The New Yorker*. I succeeded in reading one story in it & one poem.

Yesterday afternoon A. called and said she would be coming in tonight—either before or after dinner.

At 6 I went to the White Horse, drank five gin-and-tonics, had an egg nog for dinner—two cans of beer were enough to put me to sleep. I decided to go to the WH only after looking for a paperback & finding none.

This is what is wrong and has always been wrong—and it is something which money could hardly do more than make a little less painful.

July 27

Mon. Called Dwight & got Gloria, told her that the agreement was for a minimal price of $12,000.

Awake on Sunday night while it was still dark—it was dark for at least two hours. Very lively all morning on Dexamyl. But Sunday was a long & dead day & today has been, too, since 12.

July 29

When I remember
   Splashing al fresco happiness

If you want to reform a man
   Begin with his grandmother

   We must endure
The journey on the train: wait and be bored
Beside the sparkling river: be sad and dull
Although the day is very beautiful
And brassy sunlight like a military band
Marches toward victory
   Triumphantly

Let's look at pictures, postures, and impostors.
Like an ostrich / curved in on himself.
How many heartbeats has infatuation dissipated?

"My stomach, my throat has been cut."
The world is in the mind: the world is in the heart.

We are the lyres of the gods
        Reality's extremes
The eagle and the dove
        The hawk & the canary
The chipmunk and the elephant
The hippopotamus [?] and the swan
            Nature's extremes
Describe & circumscribe Reality
This thought was like distant thunder's
                erratic
                    drums
Over the distant mountains: when the summer day
Swiftly darkened: and the air
Was suddenly cool
The depths of nature require
Awe and tenderness, a solemn attentive seriousness

Baudelaire: Sleep that sinister adventure.
"You're up before breakfast this morning."

July 30

Roberta's Apartment
The boys were extremely nice. And she had no choice, none whatever. After six months of looking for an apartment and finding one with Lola, she had found herself forced to look again when Lola suddenly married the young man she had been seeing for two years. So Roberta, faced with another exhausting round of apartment-hunting for months, had told Jack & Mark quite delicately that she [would] live with them . . . They were really unbelievable. They were marvelous housekeepers, devoted cooks, neat, precise, unobtrusive, capable of reticence, and aware with trigger-quick sensitivity of the times when silence or absence were immediately desirable.
"You'll be perfectly safe."
"We'll take good care of you."
What subjects do you discuss with them?
Oh, housework, curtains, wallpaper.
How to brew coffee well. How to bake a cake.

The smell of summer
        And the spell of death
The green wall of summer, & the
        tall falls of death

The green fires of summer, & the black wires
of death

The spilling fragrance of the bright air
Quivering in heat
Vibrant with heat

The hills and heights of summer
And the depth of death

The will of summer
And the wall of death

The soul of summer & the hidden hope [?] of
death.

KC: Oracle: Make a better mousetrap. Corner the world.
(Ambush-anguish-sandwich.) Lila Ambush, an international spy
—Gladys Tights, a burlesque beauty.

July 31

What wings are these, faint and far off
And high—oh, very high—and circling
Content to fly aloft having no thought
Of eventual descent

Yesterday I was U P—just as I was on Mon. & Sat.—but more
than on either day. And today I am down again—on Sun. night & on
Tues. night I awoke while it was still dark & did not take more than
four s.t.s— But last night six s.t.s, the new issue of *The New Yorker*
was full of meaning & I was lively, though very nervous, at the White
Horse. During the afternoon I found myself beginning a poem and
then a story almost in spite of myself.

August 1

The fading of the roses
And the forsythia
The blighted marigold
The faded rose

When all that was was very beautiful
When all that is begins to be
Quite beautiful, more & more radiantly
Beautiful. O then it is that we
Must call to mind the tunnel &
the pit

Poem: Scene

The heart cannot be commanded
See how we try, how one seeks
    To obey
The dictates which have descended
From the hearts of others
    Fathers, mothers,
      Teachers, and the most admired,
    The most loved—

However often the heart is persuaded
    Whether
It is only to that which in darkness
    Or in ignorance it waited
Only that which is wanted and feared—
    So much of failing
In finding that self-deceived
    It pretended
Was nothing very much, after all
    —Among all.

Destiny is a shore and the breakers
    And the rocks
And all of us stroll on the boardwalk
    above
The insatiable sea, as if we did not
    see
The fatal merciless ocean in motion
      below us
Destiny is the accident of accidents
For which the whole of life is a
    Brief penance
Since we have raised vibrant pennants
    And a variety of vivid flags
Upon the poles above the stadium
—And they are whipping in the wind in all pride

How shall we be protected
    Against
    The pleasure
    Of feeling
That we have set our wills
    In command
Upon the sea as on the land.

In all we dreamed
The part we dreaded

The sensational summer

The blue chips, the gilt-edged, the gold-plated
The straight flush, the grand slam
                    The jackpot

                    The nonesuch
                        The all-American
                            The all-star

The asterisks. A woman runs / A terrible asterisk!
Swinging over again?

                    KC
        Destiny seldom provides
                Very much traction
        Or a great deal of purchase
        Destiny often takes sides unfairly!
                Destiny presides & abides.
        History is the alibi of weaklings
        The rhetoric of demagogues—the last straw
        Of the exhausted.

KC: Heresy loves orthodoxy.

                                        August 2

                Old beaver was a monstrous beast
                He had two seasons, famine & feast
                But pussycat was very droll
                And satisfied merely to stroll

                He made it all up
                            As he went along
                He was looking & looking
                            For a certain red herring
                So big it made Moby Dick
                Merely by contrast . . .

                Rambler Roses! American Beauties!

                The form of the fern
                            Is feather-like

Holy Mackerel
& tuna! Chicken of the sea!

With a low roar
 Like coal going down a chute

We walked where we would
We talked as we should
Under the blue & the green & the gold
 And we do not once again stare
 Toward what was not yet there
The wind & the rain, the night & the cold

Coco rico, vertigo, indigo.

Locked in your hearts are the past & the future.

You are under contrast, and taxed by comparison, sentenced to one criterion: Eureka! Excelsior! Open Sesame!

August 3

Sunday I woke with a hangover at about 6:30, too much beer & too little to eat the day before: and I thought I was going to be riding along, as on Saturday—for Rilke and Joyce came alive for a while in between D.P.s. But by 2 or 3, this ceased to be true, I became very nervous (the right knee) & by 4:30 so unnerved that I took a Seconal. From then until Anne returned at 9, the same old dreariness was back —though I walked on Eighth St., visited the Marlboro, and ate dinner after one beer.

August 6

Another dreary day trying to force myself up. Dwight called again. $3,600 is the most I can get unless he is able to persuade E. (He may have been simply holding back.) But, at any rate, I will get the money, in cash, in three weeks' time.

August 13

Memory Book, 1931–32 (The Freshman Year: Memoirs of a Metropolitan Boyhood).

When, in the fall of 1931, I went to the University of Wisconsin, I regarded my departure from New York City as the beginning of manhood.

Zukofsky, the refectory, Blanche Berger, couple supposed to get married upon graduation. Dean Goodknight, rocking chair, Alexander Meiklejohn.

The first and second rooming-house scandals.

The boys from Chicago, Hubert the drunken reporter, Martha Champion (Coca-Cola bottle).

Hurrah for Ernest Hemingway—Have you ever read Hart Crane?

Bus trip—Jean Tate—bus driver's offer of a bound volume of the *Criterion*. Are you a medical student? Told to neck with her—

Date with Anne Sluss, whose mother lectured to women's clubs on D. H. Lawrence and who did not want to be a prostitute: how she became hysterical when I was an hour late—wrote her mother that she had been "stood up"—and how all the girls in her house broke into hysterical tears (because it was Saturday night and they had no dates).

August 14

["The Fulfillment" is the same as in Summer Knowledge. *This poem and "Vivaldi" on p. 646 (shorter in the notebook version) are included here to show that Delmore, in the midst of disintegration and desperation, was writing poems in a key of transcendence and exaltation.]*

The Fulfillment
(copied 8.14.59, still paralyzed)

"Is it a dream?" I asked. To which my fellow
Answered with a hoarse and dulled insistence
"Dream, is it a dream? What difference
Does it make or mean. If it is only a dream,
It is the dream which we are. Dream or the last resort
Of reality, it is the truth of our minds:
We are condemned because this is our consciousness."

Where we were, if we were there, serene and shining
Each being moved and sang with the sleekness of rivers,
United in a choir, many and one, as the spires of
     flames in fire,
Flowing and perfected, flourishing and fulfilled forever,
Rising and falling as the carousel and palace of
     festival and victory.

"I was told often enough," my fellow said—
"You were told too—and you as little believed—
Beware of all your desires. You are deceived
(As they are deceived and deceptive, urgent and passing!)
They will be wholly fulfilled. You will be dead.
They will be gratified. And you will be dead!"

In a fixed fascination, wonderstruck, we gazed,
Marveling at the fulfillment so long desired and praised.
There, effort was like dancing's its own pleasure
There, all things existed purely in the action of joy—
Like light, like all kinds of light, all in the
                          domination
     of celebration existed only as the structures of joy.

Then, as we gazed in an emotion more exhausting than
                          mountains
Then, when we knew at last where we had come,
It was then that we saw what was lost as we knew
           where we had been
(Or knew where we had been as we saw all that was lost!)
And knew for the first time the richness and poverty
Of what we had been before and were no more
The striving, the suffering, the dear dark hooded
                mortality
Which we had been and never known, which we had
      resisted, detested, feared, and denied, the
        rocks and the flowers
             and the faces
of the needs and the hopes which had given us our reality.

August 15

    Yesterday at 3 p.m.—after waking at 5 & trying to force myself to work until then—I cheered up at the idea of my book coming up and making a real impression. And went to get the available part of the *Times* and found a review by Babette Deutsch—tepid praise at the most—on p. 22—beginning by speaking of two influences—Shakespeare & the Depression—subtracting the Depression & the atomic age & blowing up Shakespeare. Referring to candor & courage & being personal & singling out "The Kingdom of Poetry," almost alone, for praise at one remove! & all called "Two Decades in Verse."

    Stevens's incomparable discoveries—S. has some fine things of his own to say—grace & honesty & courage—a good second-rate poet—

    Rejected her poems for *PR.*

    She reviewed my first book for *HT* unfavorably.

    Less favorable than Eberhart's review of *VFP [Vaudeville for a Princess].*

    Placed so far back, it will hardly be seen by many readers.

    Not likely to encourage or impress a publisher—or a prize committee.

    After two lead reviews & three Speaking of Books & all other reviews but one, in front.

Brown gave the reviewer too few words, chose an unimportant reviewer.

As last year he sent back essay on Novel, saying he was over-committed—and did not—like so many others—acknowledge my LC [Library of Congress] lecture (Maxwell, Chiappe, Kaplan, Moss, Kazin, etc., etc.).

It's time to cultivate resignation—seeing that "Fame has perished this long while."

I must think of—

The house on Ellery St., where I lived alone, drank until I was [a] problem drinker, fell in love foolishly & vainly, and wasted the years when I should have been at the height of my powers: during most of the Second World War & after.

August 18

The Three Fates
Language, music, ambition chained & bound
The heart and mind to the exile or poverty of art
But he knew his need and destiny
He was imprisoned—as a being apart—
Stigmatized by the necessity of solitude

Barred as an object in the sunlight's blaze
Is by the very light itself striped by dark shades

Until the very heights and palisades
(He gave all strength and hope to climb & mount)
Became the dungeon darkness of his days

Language and music were ambition's loam
And every hope became—in the end—a poem

August 20

Tally. 1949–1950. After rejections from Random House, Houghton Mifflin, and a literary agent, I give E.'s [Elizabeth Pollet] novel to J.L. [James Laughlin]—despite misgivings & a desire, for years, to get another publisher.

Fall 1950—E.'s novel is published.

Spring 1951 or 1952—J.L. refuses to pay me for work on pilot issue of *Perspectives USA* ($3,000 or $2,500).

Winter 1952—Paperback advance on new printing of E.'s novel is applied to advance for hardback edition.

Undated

1953—Job with ND. Job with *Perspectives*. Dec. 1952—Jan. 1953 —second job with *Perspectives*—mss. concealed from me by Hayden Carruth [on the staff of *Perspectives USA*]—fired by J.L. & then rehired by Hutchins.

Diogenes—Princeton—mirages.

J.L. suggests I take a teaching job elsewhere.

August 1953—fired from *Perspectives* by Ronald [Freelander].

1954–1955—Freelander / Faulkner, Hemingway / *Perspectives* suspended.

Jan.–Feb. 1956. Payment for *Perspectives* issue reduced by subtracting additional pay for essay on Hemingway (I had been paid too much by Eleanor Peters [assistant to the publisher]).

Nov. or Dec. 1955—fired by MacGregor from New Directions— $50 a month—

NR 1955 / Chicago 1954 / Princeton II, I / Kenyon / Indiana I, Indiana II.

August 27

Ugly, vain, and pompous as turkeys in early autumn.

Quiz Program

What is a square? A square is a crushed circle.

What is a pipsqueak? A pipsqueak is a defeated flute, a moribund.

What is a sourball? A sourball is an unrequited sweetheart.

How is my French accent? Wonderful: you sound like George Gershwin in Paris.

> Let us not forget
> That most kinds of hostility
> Are [a] form of intimacy

> He was astonished to hear
> That Americans in Paris they
> Had quarreled: astonished
> Because he had not thought
> They knew each [other] well enough
> To quarrel

He learned—alas!—that all / most kinds of hostility were merely an unfortunate form of intimacy.

Story of the Royalist Heart. Story of the Borrowed Car. Story of the Fur Coat—third writing. Story of Academic Comedy. Pajamas

Opera—third writing. Story of Sonny—second writing. Tessa, Nela—a Metropolitan Gauntlet—

Story of the first overnight trip to the summer camp in the Adirondacks, at Valley Forge—Uncle Joe, Uncle Louis, Louise the nurse.

The story of how Dean Buck became dean—Oliver College, Holmes University—of my promotion, of my divorce—of the Schorers' disbelief.

August 28

Summer & autumn of 1947. Julie I—Klonsky. Julie II—Pembroke. Anne Sterling. Jean Follette. Tessa, Nela, Helen, Rose Dickson, Catherine Dickson. E.P.: July 1947. Will Barrett, William Phillips, Philip Rahv.

Spring 1947. Elizabeth Hardwick, Jane Lougée. Mills.
Cyanide, suicide.
Tipple, nipple, triple, ripple / demented or (dis)contented.
Hostility is a form of intimacy.

September 29

KC or end of poem: A rolling stone gathers no remorse.
New Jersey studies porgies' habits.
KC: Why are lemons yellow? Because they are shy & self-effacing. In a like way, oranges are the cocks and orchids, the peacocks of the animal kingdom.

Undated

A hat is an attitude
A hat—is the top of a mountain
A hat is worn in certain holy places
To acknowledge the superior power
God is clever but not dishonest
Let God atone for *his* sins
Freud: God—you should have given me
A better mind

Names of hats, metaphorical equations.
Telescope, spy glass, opera glasses (wonder-curiosity-interest-voyeurism).

But: A spire is at once
    An attitude and an emotion
An emotion transformed to an attitude

Let none deceived by emotion marry
    "on the rebound"
        (sour grapes)

The attitude of the high hat
Feels as chill as the cold shoulders

The queen of spades has breasts as white and hard as billiard balls.
The Nature of the Universe.
The Ways of the Animals in Love & Creation.

October 1

[*A much longer poem,* "Gold Morning, Sweet Prince," *in* Selected Poems *includes some of the lines in the following verse.*]

KC: The Atomies of which a Beautiful Girl Consists

Sonatina Sonnet
Hast thou not heard
What the passionate player of Avon avowed
[. . .]
. . . Let the humble or the proud
Say what they will out of their intimate sense
Of what existence is & it must be allowed
The spasm generates a chasm of disgust
Which may arise from disappointed lust or trust
—A gentle king destroyed in innocent sleep
A girl by Pro-Consul Hypocrisy seduced
A child by Archduke Ambition crippled and killed
A loving loyal wife by a husband loving and brave
Falsely suspected, accused—of handkerchiefs
Ophelia lies in the river named Forever
Never never never never never
        Cordelia is out of breath and Lear
Knows at last & knows too late . . .

And yet all hearts all girls
    Are in the end betrayed
Beyond disgust
    In a treason without reason

Goliath, Leviathan, Behemoth, Golem—

    Once David struck Goliath down
    And there we have been living ever since
    Once Orpheus charmed the beasts of hell
    And there we have been living ever since

    Are all hearts & all girls
            In the [end] betrayed
    Beyond disgust

                              Undated

    The night my father got me
    His mind was not upon me

    Destiny is dynasty: the sins of the fathers
    Are the years of the sons—

          O Gertrude, Gertrude
When sorrows come, they come not single spies
But in battalions: first, her father slain:
[Next, your son gone, and he most violent author]
Of his own just remove; the people muddied,
Thick and unwholesome in their thoughts [and whispers]
For poor [good] Polonius' death, and we have done
                        but greenly
In hugger-mugger to inter him; poor Ophelia,
Divided from herself and her fair judgment,
Without the which we are pictures or mere beasts
[. . .]
                [Hamlet IV, v]

        Phoenix Lyric
    "L'automne,
       L'été, j' entends le vrai"
          (La Consolation du Voyageur)

    By summer I heard the truth
    I knew the truth when by the autumn
    I no longer had need to seek
    The truth—to discover it & also
            To confront it,
    To face it down like a howling
               dog

Defending his master, as if all were
   Strangers, enemies & antagonists
Bent on destroying what he as a dog defended—

Sufficient unto the
   day
Is the day thereof
The fear of death
Is the love of life
Suicide is hatred
     Vivaldi
    Allegro con molto
To part the unparted curtains, to bring the
      chandeliers
Into the saraband of courtiers who
    Have bowed & curtsied,
Turned somersaults in circuses, climbed
     masts & towers,
Or dived as from a glittering tower
     to a glistening lake
Springing, daring & assured, fearless & precise
To find in the darkness of the dark church
What music is: this is what music is
It has no meaning and is possessed by all meaning
For music says:
   Remorse, here is the scar of healing,
   Here is a window, O curiosity,
   And here, O sensuality, a sofa
   Behold, for ambition's purposeless energy
   Mountains rising beyond mountains
   More tense and steep than any known
     before

    II Adagio
Devout
The processional (having a solemn majesty,
Though childlike acrobats like flowers decorate
With flourishes and entrechats the passage
    to success,
As queens serene, crowned by poise, are slowly
Drawn in cars by dragons domesticated in
    the last of wars)
Is uttered again, freshly and fully, newly and
    uniquely
Uniquely and newly fully and freshly repeated once
    again

III

The iron petal of the flower possesses morning's
           intuition.
The cellist is as Gautama Buddha, curved like
                    an almond.
The first violinist is St. Francis of Assisi
          blessing the trees, the cats, the birds,
          calling to them and calling
          them his brothers and his sisters.
Noah conducts the ark of all the dark beauty.
The full orchestra responds to the virtuoso's
              cadenza
"Love is the dark secret of everything,
Love is the open secret of everything,
An open secret as useless as the blue."

Music is not water, but it moves like water
It is not fire but it soars as warm as the sun
It is not rock, it is not fountain,
But rock and fountain, clock and
                mountain
Abide within it, bound together
In radiance pulsing, vibrating, and reverberating,
Dominating the domination of the weather.

IV *Coda*

The music declares:
"Is this what you want? Is this the good
          News for which [you] come?
To be, to become and to participate in the
        sweet congress of serene attention?
Silent, attentive, motionless, waiting
(Having transformed impatience into anticipation)
Save for the heart clutching itself and the
             Hushed breathing.

V

The answered question is: Our being, our presence,
             Our surrender.
Consciousness has consented, is consumed, has
         Surrendered to hear only the players
           playing.
Consciousness has become purely and only
           listening.

This is the dark city of the innermost wish.
The vivid world has been barred,
The press of desire shut out.
This is the city of the innermost wish
The motion beyond emotion
This is the immortality of mortality, this is
The grasped reality of reality, moving forward
Now and forever.

[The following lines are from a final notebook found in the hotel room where Delmore died, July 11, 1966.]

The poisonous world flows into my mouth
Like water into a drowning man's.

INDEX